H•O•C•K•E•Y
HALL OF
FAME

THE OFFICIAL REGISTRY OF THE GAME'S HONOUR ROLL

H•O•C•K•E•Y
HALL OF
FAME

THE OFFICIAL REGISTRY OF THE GAME'S HONOUR ROLL

EDITED BY DAN DIAMOND

DOUBLEDAY CANADA LIMITED

Copyright © 1996   Hockey Hall of Fame and Dan Diamond and Associates, Inc.

Canadian Cataloguing in Publication Data

Diamond, Dan
        Hockey Hall of Fame : the official registry of the game's honour roll

First ed. has subtitle: the official history of the game and its greatest stars.

ISBN 0-385-25609-4

1. Hockey Hall of Fame.   2. Hockey - Canada - Biography.
3. Hockey - United States - Biography.   4. Hockey - Canada - History.
5. Hockey - United States - History.   I. Title.

GV848.5.A1D52 1996   796.962'092'2   C96-930609-4

Editor: Dan Diamond
Photo editor: Ralph Dinger
Statistics: Ernie Fitzsimmons
Statistical editing: James Duplacey
Additional Writing: Eric Zweig

For the Hockey Hall of Fame: Phil Pritchard, Craig Campbell

Scanning, colour correction, film output: Stafford Graphics, Toronto

Design: First Image, Holland Landing, Ontario

Printed and bound in Canada by Metropole Litho, Montreal and Drummondville

Project management: Dan Diamond and Associates, Inc. Toronto

Published in Canada by
Doubleday Canada Limited
105 Bond Street
Toronto, Ontario, Canada
M5B 1Y3

96 97 98 99 00 01   1   2   3   4   5

H•O•C•K•E•Y
HALL OF
FAME

THE OFFICIAL REGISTRY OF THE GAME'S HONOUR ROLL

C•O•N•T•E•N•T•S

HOCKEY HALL OF FAME

BOARD OF DIRECTORS

Ian Morrison, *Chairman*	Toronto, Ontario
Walter I. Bush, Jr., *Vice-Chairman*	Minnetonka, Minnesota
John Barnett	Toronto, Ontario
Murray Costello	Ottawa, Ontario
Gordon Craig	Toronto, Ontario
C. Dennis Flynn	Toronto, Ontario
L. Yves Fortier, C.C., Q.C.	Montreal, Quebec
Robert W. Goodenow	Toronto, Ontario
James M. Gregory	Toronto, Ontario
William C. Hay	Calgary, Alberta
Douglas Holyday	Etobicoke, Ontario
Leslie Kaplan	Philadelphia, Pennsylvania
Chris Korwin-Kuczynski	Toronto, Ontario
Lawrence G. Meyer	Washington, D.C.
Harry Sinden	Boston, Massachusetts
Stephen J. Solomon	New York, New York
Rt. Hon. John Turner	Toronto, Ontario

EXECUTIVE OFFICERS

Ian Morrison, *Chairman*	Toronto, Ontario
Walter I. Bush, Jr., *Vice-Chairman*	Minnetonka, Minnesota
John R. Dow	Toronto, Ontario
Secretary and General Counsel	
Jeffery D. Denomme	Toronto, Ontario
Vice-President, Finance and Operations/Treasurer	
Bryan F. Black	Aurora, Ontario
Vice-President, Marketing and Communications	
Philip Pritchard, *Curator*	Burlington, Ontario

SELECTION COMMITTEE

William C. Hay, *Chairman*	Calgary, Alberta
Keith Allen	Philadelphia, Pennsylvania
Kevin Allen	Ypsilanti, Michigan
Red Fisher	Montreal, Quebec
Cliff Fletcher	Toronto, Ontario
Emile Francis	West Palm Beach, Florida
James M. Gregory	Toronto, Ontario
George Gross	Toronto, Ontario
Dick Irvin	Montreal, Quebec
Frank Mathers	Hummelstown, Pennsylvania
Richard M. Patrick	Vienna, Virginia
Marty Pavelich	Big Sky, Montana
Jim Proudfoot	Toronto, Ontario
Bertrand Raymond	Montreal, Quebec
Serge Savard	Montreal, Quebec
Frank Selke	Islington, Ontario
Harry Sinden	Boston, Massachusetts
Frank Udvari	Kitchener, Ontario

STAFF

EXECUTIVE

Ian Morrison	Chairman
Bryan Black	Vice-President, Marketing and Communications
Jeff Denomme	Vice-President, Finance and Operations
Kelly Massé	Executive Assistant

RESOURCE CENTRE

Phil Pritchard	Manager, Resource Centre and Acquisitions
Craig Campbell	Assistant Manager, Resource Centre
Craig Baines	Special Projects Co-ordinator
Jefferson Davis	Archivist and Research Specialist
Doug MacLellan	Contract Photographer

EXHIBITS AND BUILDING SERVICES

Ray Paquet	Manager, Exhibit Development and Technology
Barry Eversley	Manager, Building Services

MARKETING AND GUEST SERVICES

Christine Simpson	Manager, Marketing
Christena Wilson	Associate Manager, Guest Services
Jeff Graham	Associate Manager, Guest Services
Karyn Knott	Group Sales Co-ordinator

SPIRIT OF HOCKEY STORE

Craig Beckim	Associate Manager, Merchandising
Tim McWilliams	Associate Manager, Retail Operations

SPECIAL EVENTS AND FACILITY SALES

Scott North	Manager, Special Events and Facility Sales
Jan McCabe	Special Event Co-ordinator
Jennifer Reid	Special Event Co-ordinator

ACCOUNTING AND OFFICE SERVICES

Sandra Buffone	Manager, Accounting and Office Services
Sylvia Lau	Accountant
Anita Goel	Accounting Data Entry
Marilyn Robbins	Office Services Co-ordinator
Pearl Rajwanth	Receptionist

Inquiries should be directed to:

Hockey Hall of Fame
BCE Place
30 Yonge Street
Toronto, Ontario Canada   M5E 1X8

Info Line (rates, hours, groups, etc.)	416 360-7765
Administration	416 360-7735
Resource Centre and Retail Store fax	416 360-1316
Administration fax	416 360-1501

Personnel current as of September 1, 1996

A Message From Scotty Morrison
Chairman, Hockey Hall of Fame

WELCOME TO THE HOCKEY HALL OF FAME and to this book, *Hockey Hall of Fame, the Official Registry of the Game's Honour Roll.*

The Hockey Hall of Fame was founded in 1943 to acknowledge those who have developed Canada's great winter sport. Our mandate is to preserve the history of the game of ice hockey and, in particular, to honour those whose outstanding accomplishments have contributed to the development of the game.

This book has a long history of its own as well. Its roots stretch back to the early 1960s when the first curator of the Hockey Hall of Fame, Bobby Hewitson, worked with journalist John Fitzgerald to prepare a collection of short biographies of honoured members that was published as *Hockey's Heritage.* M.H. (Lefty) Reid, the Hall's next curator, supplemented Hewitson's work into the 1980s. A version most recently appeared in 1988. The book you are holding builds on these efforts, adding new inductees, a complete statistical panel for every honoured player, unique photographs and an array of interesting sidebars that highlight the evolution of the game. It is like the Hockey Hall of Fame itself; both are packed with what makes the game special.

The Hockey Hall of Fame is now in its fourth year at BCE Place in downtown Toronto and continues to celebrate outstanding achievements and spectacular moments in hockey. While committed to preserving the game's storied past, the Hockey Hall of Fame is also "so much fun . . . you won't know what hit you!" From playing virtual goal or shooting pucks to stopping Gretzky and Messier in a simulated game, calling the play-by-play on hockey's greatest goals or simply marveling at the Stanley Cup and the spectacular collection of NHL trophies, the Hockey Hall of Fame has something for fans of all ages.

I hope that this book will serve not only as a valuable resource but—like the Hockey Hall of Fame—as an entertaining celebration of the best of hockey.

See you at the Hockey Hall of Fame!

Scotty

Scotty Morrison
Chairman

HOCKEY HALL OF FAME

ELIGIBILITY REQUIREMENTS FOR ELECTION

There shall be four classes of honoured membership in the Hockey Hall of Fame—players, veteran players, builders and referees/linesmen.

Candidates for election as Honoured Members in the player category or veteran player category shall be chosen on the basis of their playing ability, sportsmanship, character and their contribution to their team or teams and to the game of hockey in general. A maximum of three players shall be elected in any one year. In the veteran player category, if three or fewer candidates have been nominated, the maximum number of candidates to be elected shall not be more than one. If four or more candidates have been nominated, the maximum number of candidates to be elected shall not be more than two.

Candidates for election as Honoured Members in the builder category shall be chosen on the basis of their coaching, managerial or executive ability, sportsmanship, character and their contribution to their organization or organizations and to the game of hockey in general. In the builder category, if three or fewer candidates have been nominated, the maximum number of candidates to be elected shall not be more than one. If four or more candidates have been nominated, the maximum number of candidates to be elected shall not be more than two.

Candidates for election as Honoured Members in the referee or linesman category shall be chosen on the basis of their officiating ability, sportsmanship, character and their contribution to the game of hockey in general. A maximum of one referee or linesman shall be elected in any one year.

Player candidates must have concluded their careers as active players for a minimum of three playing seasons before their election except where, by outstanding pre-eminence and skill and upon request by the Selection Committee, the Board of Directors may reduce or eliminate such waiting period.

A candidate in the veteran player category must have concluded his career as an active player for a minimum of 25 seasons before his election.

A candidate in the builder category may be either active or inactive at the time of his election.

A candidate for election in the referee or linesman category must have concluded his career as an active referee or linesman for a minimum of three playing seasons before his election.

Members of the Hockey Hall of Fame Selection Committee shall be ineligible for election as an Honoured Member in any category for so long as they continue to be members of the Hockey Hall of Fame Selection Committee and for the balance of the calendar year in which they cease to be a member.

Any candidate whose nomination has been considered by the Hockey Hall of Fame Selection Committee on three separate occasions and has not been elected as an Honoured Member shall not be eligible for further consideration until the fourth annual meeting of the Hockey Hall of Fame Selection Committee following the last consideration.

NOMINATION OF CANDIDATES

All nominations must be presented by a member of the Hockey Hall of Fame Selection Committee. Each member of the Selection Committee may not make more than three nominations in the player category and one in each of the veteran player, builder and referee or linesman categories for each annual election proceeding.

Nominations shall contain the fullest possible data concerning the record and merits for each candidate

Individuals who are not members of the Selection Committee may provide support materials and recommend candidates for consideration as potential nominees, but only members of the Selection Committee are permitted to make official nominations.

All nominations must be made in writing and filed with the Chairman of the Hockey Hall of Fame's Board of Directors no later than midnight (Toronto time) on May 15th of each year.

The Chairman of the Selection Committee may request further investigation of any candidate nominated. Any additional information obtained will made known to the members of the Selection Committee before election proceedings take place.

ELECTION

The Hockey Hall of Fame Selection Committee is not required to elect a minimum number of candidates. To be elected, a duly nominated candidate must receive three-quarters of the votes cast by the members of the Selection Committee in attendance at the annual selection meeting.

PIONEER YEARS

1885-1926

R. PHILLIPS
SPARE

J. F. McGILLIVRAY
SECRETARY

J. LINK
TRAINER

F. A. HUDSON
MANAGER

J. HALL
SPARE

WM. NOTMAN & S
MONTREAL

R. BEAUDRO
R. WING

T. HOOPER
ROVER (VICE CAPT.)

T. PHILLIPS ✕
L. WING (CAPT.)

W. McGIMSIE
CENTRE

S. GRIFFIS
C. POINT

E. GIROUX
GOAL

A. ROSS ✕
POINT

KENORA THISTLES
WORLD'S CHAMPIONS

Six members of the Kenora Thistles are enshrined in the Hockey Hall of Fame. The Thistles' Stanley Cup win in 1907 makes Kenora, Ontario, the smallest town to win the trophy since Cup competition began in 1893.

SIR MONTAGU ALLAN
BUILDER

IN 1908, SIR H. MONTAGU ALLAN, Montreal sportsman and financier, donated the Allan Cup to be awarded annually to Canada's best senior amateur hockey team. When the Stanley Cup became a professional trophy, William Northey of Montreal prevailed upon Allan to donate the trophy. It was valued at between $300 and $500 at that time.

In its first year of competition, the Montreal Victorias accepted the trophy but the Ottawa Cliffsides won the league. Queen's University challenged the Cliffsides and defeated them to become the first Allan Cup champions. A board of Trustees governed all challenges for the trophy until 1928 when it was donated outright to the Canadian Amateur Hockey Association.

Allan was born in 1860 in Montreal and died in September, 1951.

Inducted 1945.

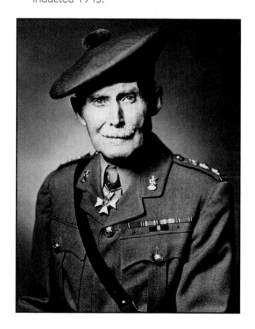

JACK ADAMS
CENTRE • TORONTO, VANCOUVER (PCHA), OTTAWA

JACK ADAMS was one of the most successful executives in the history of the NHL. He was an outstanding player before joining the Detroit organization in 1927 as manager-coach. Born June 14, 1895, in Fort William, Ontario, Adams played in the Northern Michigan Senior League at the age of 16. After amateur stints in Peterborough and Sarnia, Ontario, he turned pro in 1918 joining the Toronto Arenas, winners of the Stanley Cup in 1917-18.

Adams was 24 when he joined Vancouver and went on to lead the Pacific Coast Hockey Association with 26 goals in 1921-22. He later played for the Toronto St. Pats and for Ottawa's Stanley Cup winners of 1926-27 with King Clancy, George Boucher, Frank Nighbor, Cy Denneny, Frank Finnigan and Alex Connell.

As coach and manager of the Red Wings, Adams sold hockey in Detroit. He was an innovator, developing the hockey farm system and building winning teams. His Detroit clubs won 12 regular season championships including a string of seven straight, and seven Stanley Cups. Only seven times in 35 years under Adams did the Wings miss the playoffs. His greatest personal satisfaction came from the development of Gordie Howe.

Following his departure from the Wings in 1962 Adams was named president of the Central Pro League. He died on May 1, 1968.

Inducted 1959.

DAN BAIN
CENTRE • WINNIPEG (MHL)

DONALD H. (DAN) BAIN was an extraordinary sportsman who is often referred to as Manitoba's all-time greatest athlete.

Though born in Belleville, Ontario, on February 14, 1874, he moved with his family to Winnipeg at the age of six and spent the rest of his life there. He never played professional hockey but was a member of two Stanley Cup champions with the Winnipeg Victorias of 1895-96 and 1900-01. Bain was a great leader on the ice, played centre and captained the Victorias in four Stanley Cup challenge rounds. They defeated the Montreal Victorias for their initial Cup triumph and the Montreal Shamrocks for their second.

Dan Bain's talents as an athlete enabled him to win championship honours in various sports over a span of more than 35 years. He won the Manitoba three-mile roller skating title first, and at 17 was the champion gymnast of Winnipeg. He was the one-mile bicycle racing champion for three years, from 1894 to 1896. By 1903, when he had retired from active hockey competition, he turned to rifle shooting and captured the Canadian trap-shooting title. There seemed to be no sport that Dan Bain could not master. Over ensuing years, right up to 1930, he continued to add to his laurels, winning championships in speed-skating, roller skating, snowshoeing, lacrosse and golf.

Undoubtedly an outstanding athlete in any era, Dan Bain died at the age of 88 on August 15, 1962.

Inducted 1945.

HOBEY BAKER
ROVER • PRINCETON, ST. NICHOLAS

THE NAME OF HOBEY BAKER is a legend in United States college hockey history. He was born Hobart Amery Hare Baker — but everyone called him Hobey — in Wissahickon, Pennsylvania, on January 15, 1892. Somewhere, very early in life, Hobey learned the arts of effortless skating and stickhandling. He was a master craftsman with a stick; it was often said that once the puck touched his stick, he never had to look down again. He entered Princeton University in 1910, proficient not only in hockey but in football, golf, track, swimming and gymnastics.

In his senior year, he captained the football team and dropkicked a 43-yard field goal to tie a game with Yale. He also captained the hockey team in his final two years. A rover, he was a one-man team called "Baker and six other players."

After graduation in 1914, Hobey joined the St. Nicholas hockey team. After a series in which his team won the Ross Cup from the Montreal Stars, a Montreal newspaper reported: "Uncle Sam had the cheek to develop a first-class hockey player ... who wasn't born in Montreal ...." Baker joined the Lafayette Escadrille, a flying unit, during World War I and here, too, performed admirably. He survived the War but crashed while testing a new plane and was killed on December 21, 1918.

The Hobey Baker Award is presented annually to the outstanding player in U.S. college hockey.

Inducted 1945.

CLINT BENEDICT
GOALTENDER • OTTAWA (NHA), OTTAWA, MTL. MAROONS

CLINT BENEDICT spent 17 years in the NHL and is considered one of the great goaltenders of all time. Born in Ottawa on September 26, 1894, he played on four Stanley Cup-winning teams — three with the Ottawa Senators and one with the Montreal Maroons — as well as playing for Ottawa in the 1915 Cup final which was won by Vancouver.

He started playing hockey at the age of six and moved into senior ranks while still only 15. At the age of 37, he was forced into retirement after stopping two rifle-like shots off the stick of Howie Morenz. The first shot shattered his nose and, in a later game, the second injured his larynx. The first Morenz shot affected Benedict's vision and prompted him to become one of the first in pro hockey to try wearing a face mask, but he threw it away after a 2-0 loss to Chicago. "The nosepiece protruded too far and obscured my vision on low shots," he recalled.

Benedict also influenced a change in the rule that prohibited goaltenders stopping play by falling on the puck. Benedict stated that, "if you did it a bit sneaky and made it look accidental, you could fall on the puck without being penalized." Other netminders copied him and eventually it became part of the game. His final NHL season was 1929-30.

In Stanley Cup play, Benedict had 16 shutouts and an average of 2.16 goals-against per game. He died November 12, 1976, in Ottawa.

Inducted 1965.

BENEDICT'S MASK...

Nearly thirty years before Jacques Plante made it a standard piece of goaltending equipment, Clint Benedict of the Montreal Maroons had been the first netminder to try to protect his face with a mask.

On January 7, 1930, a blast off the stick of Howie Morenz struck Benedict between the eyes, cutting his forehead and breaking his nose. The goaltender was taken to the hospital for repairs. It would be six weeks before Benedict's injuries healed sufficiently to allow him to return to the nets.

When Benedict came back on February 20, he sported a leather facemask that left only his eyes exposed. The new innovation, however, did not offer the goaltender the protection he had hoped for. Soon after he began wearing the mask, Benedict was hurt again in a goalmouth scramble. He quickly abandoned his new piece of equipment and when his nose was broken a third time just before the end of the season, he promptly announced his retirement.

DICKIE BOON
DEFENCE • MTL. AAA (CAHL), MTL. WANDERERS (FAHL)

ONE OF THE IMMORTAL "Little Men of Iron," Richard (Dickie) Boon was born January 10, 1878, in Belleville, Ontario. Boon started his illustrious career with Montreal South in 1895 and played for the Montreal Monarch Hockey Club in 1897 before moving up to the Montreal AAA juniors. By the 1901-02 season, he was with the Montreal AAA's senior club which successfully challenged the Winnipeg Victorias for the Stanley Cup in 1902. The outstanding ability of this team won its players the collective nickname of the "Little Men of Iron" after their 2-1 victory.

In 1903, Dickie became manager of the Montreal Wanderers, a post which he held until the Westmount Arena was destroyed by fire in 1918. Boon finished his playing career with the Wanderers in the 1904 and 1905 seasons, after which he became their director and coach. During his time with the team they won three Stanley Cup challenges and moved from the Federal League, which they entered in 1904, to the National Hockey Association.

A fast, wiry defenceman, Boon weighed 120 pounds in his playing days and is considered to be the first man to use the poke-check to steal the puck from opposing players. Boon, who was an outstanding roller skater in his day, lived in Outremont, Quebec, until his death on May 3, 1961 at the age of 83.

Inducted 1952.

RUSSELL BOWIE
CENTRE/ROVER • MTL. VICTORIAS (CAHL, ECAHA)

BOTH A ROVER AND CENTRE, Russell (Dubbie) Bowie was an outstanding product of the seven-man era in hockey. Born in Montreal, on August 24, 1880, Bowie remained a rigid amateur throughout his playing days while rejecting several offers of professional contracts. This great stickhandler once turned down a grand piano offered to him by the Montreal Wanderers in return for his services on the ice.

Bowie, whose style was something like that of the great Nels Stewart, collected a total of 234 goals in 80 games over a 10-year period with the Montreal Victorias. A wizard with a stick, he played his entire career with this team from 1898 to 1908, when a broken collarbone brought his playing days to an end. A slim 112 pounds when he joined the Vics at age 17, he played on his first Stanley Cup championship team the same year. In the 1907 season, Bowie scored a total of 38 goals in 10 games and is one of the few players ever to score 10 goals in a single game. When Bowie retired from the game he had an average of nearly three goals per game.

Following his retirement he went on to become an outstanding referee. Russell Bowie died April 8, 1959, in Montreal, at the age of 79.

Inducted 1945.

"PUNCH" BROADBENT
RIGHT WING • OTTAWA (NHA), OTTAWA, MTL. MAROONS, NY AMERICANS

THE NHL RECORD for scoring in consecutive games belongs to Harry (Punch) Broadbent who scored in 16 straight games during the 1921-22 season. Punch Broadbent was an excellent right winger, an artist with the puck and with his elbows. He once led the NHL in both scoring and penalty minutes. "I had a hard time controlling those elbows of mine," he recalled, referring to the 1921-22 season when he led the league with 32 goals.

Born in Ottawa on July 13, 1892, Broadbent played most of his career in that city. He played amateur with New Edinburgh and the Ottawa Cliffsides and was called up to play pro hockey at the age of 16, although used sparingly. He joined Ottawa of the NHA in 1912-13 and scored 21 goals. Two seasons later, he scored 24 goals but left to serve with the Canadian armed forces in World War I where he was awarded the Military Medal. In 1919, he rejoined Ottawa and stayed six seasons with their NHL club until sold to the Montreal Maroons in an attempt by the NHL to balance the league.

He came back to Ottawa for the 1927-28 season, went to the New York Americans in 1928-29, and when the stock market crashed, wired Americans' owner Bill Dwyer that he was through. He quit hockey and joined the Royal Canadian Air Force. In 11 NHL seasons, Broadbent scored 122 goals. He was also on four Stanley Cup-winning teams, three at Ottawa and one with the Maroons. He died March 6, 1971.

Inducted 1962.

GEORGE BOUCHER

FORWARD / DEFENCE OTTAWA (NHA), OTTAWA, MTL. MAROONS, CHICAGO

AN OUTSTANDING DEFENCEMAN from a celebrated hockey family, George (Buck) Boucher played pro for 20 years, 15 in the NHL. Before turning to pro hockey, George played three years of football with the Ottawa Rough Riders and was considered a great halfback.

He was born in Ottawa on August 19, 1896, and his hockey began in the Ottawa City League. He moved up to the Senators in 1915 where he played with stars like Eddie Gerard, Horace Merrill, Sprague Cleghorn, Lionel Hitchman and King Clancy. This Ottawa Senators team won the Stanley Cup four times between 1920 and 1927. Midway through the 1928-29 season, George was sold to the Montreal Maroons. Two and a half years later he went to Chicago.

An active player until 1934, he also coached Chicago, Ottawa, Boston and St. Louis. He brought the Allan Cup to Ottawa while coaching the Senators in 1949 and also helped select and train the Ottawa RCAF team that won the Olympic championship in 1948. George also coached the Boston Bruins' farm club, the Bruin Cubs, in the Canadian-American League.

He had four other brothers who were outstanding players and all but one played major-league hockey. While George was with Ottawa, Frank played in Vancouver and New York and Billy and Bob played with the Canadiens. During his NHL career, George scored 122 goals, an outstanding total for a defenceman of that era. He died October 17, 1960, in Ottawa.

Inducted 1960.

GEORGE BROWN

BUILDER

GEORGE V. BROWN was a pioneer of hockey in the United States. In 1910, when the old Boston Arena was built, he organized the Boston Athletic Association hockey team, which initiated top amateur hockey competition in the Eastern U.S. in addition to playing international games with ranking Canadian colleges and club teams. When the Boston Arena was destroyed by fire in 1918, he formed the corporation which constructed a new arena, served as manager of the building and still operated the BAA team. Hockey flourished in the area and, although he was not associated with the introduction of pro hockey there, he soon became prominently involved. When the Bruins moved into the new Boston Garden in 1928, he helped form the Canadian-American Hockey League and entered a team. This was a forerunner of the American Hockey League.

Always in the foreground of international track and field, Brown assumed similar stature in Olympic hockey at the 1924 Games. He was also a founder of the Boston Marathon. Brown became general manager of both the Arena and Boston Garden in 1934, positions he held at the time of his death in 1937.

Inducted 1961.

FRANK CALDER

BUILDER

A STRONG SILENT SCOT, FRANK CALDER proved a perfect choice as president when the National Hockey League was formed in 1917. He had been secretary of the old National Hockey Association and he imbued confidence in those with whom he was associated.

Through the hectic formative days of the NHL, through many rule changes and disputes, Frank Calder sat at the head of the league an unruffled, calm, firm executive. It was his astute guidance that established for the NHL the stature that in now enjoys. A keen follower of many sports, Calder's knowledge of athletics equipped him to adjudicate player and team grievances.

To commemorate his years of service, the Calder Trophy, and later the Calder Memorial Trophy, were presented by the NHL to be awarded to each season's top rookie. In addition, the American Hockey League championship trophy is the Calder Cup.

He was born on November 17, 1877 and died February 4, 1943.

Inducted 1947.

HARRY CAMERON

DEFENCE • TORONTO (NHA), MTL. WANDERERS (NHA), TORONTO, OTTAWA, MONTREAL, SASKATOON (WCHL, WHL)

OVER A 14-YEAR SPAN in three major hockey leagues, Harry Cameron scored 171 goals in 312 games.

He was born February 6, 1890, in Pembroke, Ontario, and went on to play pro with Toronto and the Wanderers of the National Hockey Association; Toronto, Ottawa and the Canadiens of the NHL; and Saskatoon of the Western Canada League. He is best remembered for his ability to impart a curve to his shot. Cameron is believed to be one of the first to do this without modifying his stick.

Harry Cameron played on three Stanley Cup champions that were based in Toronto. He was a member of the Torontos of 1914, the Arenas of 1918 and the St. Patricks of 1922.

A 154-pound defenceman, Cameron almost invariably topped defence players in scoring, one year finishing in fourth place in the scoring race against such formidable opposition as Newsy Lalonde, Joe Malone, Frank Nighbor, Cy Denneny, Babe Dye and Punch Broadbent. In November, 1923, Cameron was sent to Saskatoon as part of a deal that saw Joe Matte go to Vancouver. He later played for Minneapolis and St. Louis, returning to Saskatoon in 1932-33 as coach of the Sheiks in the Prairie League. Harry Cameron died October 20, 1953, in Vancouver.

Inducted 1962.

SPRAGUE CLEGHORN

DEFENCE • RENFREW (NHA), MTL. WANDERERS (NHA), OTTAWA, TORONTO, MONTREAL, BOSTON

SPRAGUE CLEGHORN was one of the greatest but roughest defence players the game of hockey has ever known. Born in Montreal, in 1890, he played in either the National Hockey Association or the National Hockey League from 1911 to 1928.

He played with the New York Crescents in 1909-10 and moved to Renfrew of the NHA the following season. He went on to play six seasons with the Montreal Wanderers, two full seasons with Ottawa, a season split between Ottawa and Toronto, four with the Canadiens and three with Boston. He started out as a forward but was moved back to defence to play alongside Cyclone Taylor at Renfrew. He tried to emulate Taylor's great rushing style and for five years was the darling of the Wanderers' fans, once scoring five goals in one game. In 17 seasons — he missed 1917 because of a broken leg — Cleghorn scored 163 goals. He also played with two Stanley Cup championship teams, the Ottawa club of 1920 and the Canadiens of 1924.

Cleghorn had not been a popular player in Ottawa and, in 1921, when he joined the Canadiens, he appeared to have a vendetta against his former teammates. Many brawls broke out between these two teams, climaxing in the 1923 playoffs when Cleghorn assaulted Lionel Hitchman with a vicious cross-check. He drew a match penalty and suspension from the final game along with a $200 fine levied by his own manager. He died in Montreal on July 11, 1956.

Inducted 1958.

RUSTY CRAWFORD

LEFT WING/CENTRE • QUEBEC (NHA), OTTAWA, TORONTO, SASKATOON (WCHL), CALGARY (WCHL)

RUSTY CRAWFORD was born in Cardinal, Ontario, on November 7, 1885, and played hockey until he was 45 years of age. A fast-skating forward with a lefthanded shot, Crawford could play wing or centre with equal dexterity.

He enjoyed several seasons of amateur hockey before turning professional and playing for two Stanley Cup champions. His amateur career started with three seasons in Verdun, Quebec. In 1909, he moved to western Canada and played two seasons for Prince Albert and one for Saskatoon. His talent attracted the Quebec Bulldogs and he joined them for the 1912-13 season, helping them win the Stanley Cup despite losing two of three games to Victoria on the latter's ice. This was the first Cup challenge between East and West and the trustees refused to recognize Victoria as challengers.

Crawford remained with Quebec until 1917-18 when he went to Ottawa for four games before joining the Toronto Arenas. Toronto won the Stanley Cup that year, defeating Vancouver in a five-game series. Rusty stayed another season with Toronto, went to Saskatoon in 1920, to Calgary until 1925 and joined Vancouver in 1926. He ended his career with Minneapolis in 1929. He died December 19, 1971.

Inducted 1962.

JACK DARRAGH

RIGHT WING •
OTTAWA (NHA), OTTAWA

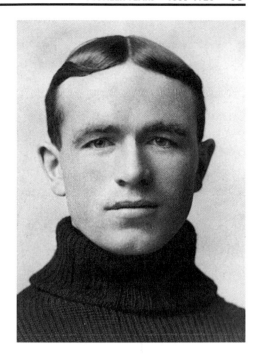

JACK DARRAGH was another product of Ottawa, a city that produced many great hockey players in the early 1900s. He was born in Canada's capital city on December 4, 1890, and became a master mechanic of the game. Darragh never played for any other city and at his peak was a member of a unit called the "Super Six." This club also had in its lineup such stalwarts as Clint Benedict, Sprague Cleghorn, Eddie Gerard, Buck Boucher, Frank Nighbor, Punch Broadbent and Cy Denneny.

Jack started playing hockey in Church League competition, with a team called Stewartons. He moved up to the famed Cliffsides seniors and made the jump to the professional ranks in 1911, immediately joining a Stanley Cup champion. He went on to play for three more teams that won hockey's top prize, in 1919-20, 1920-21 and 1922-23. He also played on the Ottawa team that was defeated by Vancouver in the 1914-15 playoffs. Although he was a lefthanded forward, he was usually employed on right wing and once played on a great line with Nighbor and Denneny. When Broadbent moved up to right wing, Darragh shifted over to left. One of Darragh's cleverest moves was an accurate backhand. He was also noted for clean play, slick stickhandling and an ability to turn on the speed when required.

Jack Darragh was also a fine scorer; he had 22 goals in the 22-game schedule of 1919-20. He died June 25, 1924, in Ottawa.

Inducted 1962.

"SCOTTY" DAVIDSON

FORWARD • TORONTO (NHA)

ALLAN "SCOTTY" DAVIDSON shot like a meteor from junior ranks and starred as a professional until his life was snuffed out while serving in Belgium during World War I. Davidson was born in Kingston, Ontario in 1890, and very early in life showed all the attributes of a great hockey player. He was a strong, powerful skater, played very cleanly, possessed an overpowering shot and was a tremendous back-checker. Although he played only two years as a pro before the War, he was and still is considered one of the great right wingers of all-time.

A rugged, powerful youth, Scotty learned his hockey under the coaching of James T. Sutherland who is often called the "Father of Hockey." Davidson was a standout with the Kingston Frontenac juniors of 1909-10 and 1910-11 when the club won the Ontario Hockey Association title. He led the team from a three-goal, first-game deficit to capture its second championship with a goal in the final minute of the deciding contest. It was that game that made Davidson one of the most talked-about players of his day.

He signed to play the 1912-13 season with Jack Marshall's Toronto team in the National Hockey Association, immediately starring at right wing. That team won the Stanley Cup in 1913-14. Davidson scored 19 goals in 20 games, his first season as a pro, and increased his output in the Cup-winning season. Davidson was serving with the First Canadian Contingent at the time of his death on June 6, 1915.

Inducted 1950.

• •

FORMATION OF THE NHA...

On November 25, 1909, delegates from the Eastern Canada Hockey Association (the top league in Canada at the time) held a meeting at the Windsor Hotel in Montreal. Among the minor bits of new legislation they introduced came a major announcement. The ECHA would be scrapped and in its place would be the new Canadian Hockey Association — a league that would not include the Montreal Wanderers, whom the rest of the owners wanted to exclude because they had moved into a smaller arena, thereby reducing their opponents' share of the gate.

Ambrose O'Brien was similarly denied an entry in the new Canadian Hockey Association for a team in his hometown of Renfrew, Ontario. O'Brien's millionaire father also owned teams in the northern Ontario towns of Cobalt and Haileybury and would soon be convinced to finance a new French-Canadian team in Montreal: *les Canadiens*.

Ambrose and Jimmy Gardner of the Wanderers joined forces and formed their own league — the National Hockey Association.

It quickly became apparent that the rival leagues could not co-exist, and when Gardner and O'Brien convinced the owners of the Ottawa Senators and Montreal Shamrocks to join them, the CHA disbanded. Though franchises would change, the NHA would remain the dominant league in hockey until its own internal conflicts forced it to be restructured as the National Hockey League in 1917.

• •

Cy Denneny

Left Wing • Tor. Shamrocks (NHA), Toronto (NHA), Ottawa (NHA), Ottawa, Boston

Although he was not a fast skater, Cy Denneny possessed an accurate shot that enabled this left winger to rank among the greats of professional hockey. He was born December 23, 1891, in Farran's Point, Ontario, a village since covered by the St. Lawrence seaway system. In 1897, his family moved to Cornwall where Denneny played his early hockey.

In 1912, he played for Russell, Ontario, in the Lower Ottawa Valley League and a year later joined the O'Brien Mine team in the Cobalt Mining League. Denneny's pro career began in 1914, with the Toronto Shamrocks of the National Hockey Association, and he played there for two seasons before joining the Ottawa Senators of the NHA in 1916. He stayed with the Senators through their transition into the NHL, leaving them after 1927-28 to become a player, coach and assistant manager of the Boston Bruins for one season. The Bruins won the Stanley Cup that year, making a total of five Cups for Denneny in his 14-year playing career. His best individual season was 1917-18 when he scored 36 goals in 22 games. During 12 NHL seasons, Cy scored a total of 246 goals.

Cy retired as a player after one year at Boston and became an NHL referee for a year. He coached junior and senior amateur teams in Ottawa during 1931-32, coached the Ottawa Senators in 1932-33 and retired for good when the team left the league after that season. He died in September, 1970.

Inducted 1959.

Graham Drinkwater

Defence/Forward • Mtl. Victorias (AHA, CAHL)

Long before hockey became a professional sport, one of the greatest stars of the game was Graham Drinkwater. Although he never played professionally, Drinkwater played for four teams that won the Stanley Cup.

When the Cup was first presented in 1893, he was still at McGill University, gaining fame as a hockey and football standout. His first championship came during the 1892-93 season while he was a member of the Montreal AAA junior team. The following autumn, Drinkwater played on the McGill junior football championship team and in 1894 was a member of the McGill intermediate hockey team that also won a title. He left McGill to join the Montreal Victorias in 1895 and his winning ways followed him. The Victorias won the Stanley Cup, lost it to the Winnipeg Victorias in 1895-96, and then came back to claim three Cup triumphs. Drinkwater was team captain in the 1898-99 victory.

Graham Drinkwater was born in Montreal on February 22, 1875. He died September 27, 1946, in Montreal.

Inducted 1950.

EARLY CUPS IN MONTREAL...

The Montreal Canadiens have won the Stanley Cup a record 24 times, but even before their first title back in 1916, the Stanley Cup was already an old habit in Montreal from its original days as a challenge trophy.

The Stanley Cup was first awarded in 1893 to the Montreal Amateur Athletic Association, who earned the honour by finishing in first place in the Amateur Hockey Association of Canada — the top senior league of its day. The AAA repeated as champions the following year before seeing their title pass to the rival Montreal Victorias.

In 1896, the Stanley Cup left Montreal for the first time, but only briefly. The Winnipeg Victorias beat their Montreal counterparts in a challenge in February, only to see the Cup return to Montreal in a subsequent challenge in December.

The Montreal Victorias remained Stanley Cup champions until 1899, when, like the AAA, they saw their title taken by another local team: the Montreal Shamrocks. The Shamrocks kept the Cup in Montreal until 1901, when again the Winnipeg Victorias managed to take it west. Once again, though, the Cup would not be gone for long. In 1902, the the Montreal AAA won it back again. As the first decade of Stanley Cup history came to a close, the prized trophy had been awarded 13 times. Ten times it had gone to a team from Montreal.

THOMAS DUNDERDALE

CENTRE • WINNIPEG (MHL), MTL. SHAMROCKS (NHA), QUEBEC (NHA), VICTORIA (PCHA), PORTLAND (PCHA), SASKATOON (WCHL), EDMONTON (WCHL)

ELECTED to the Hockey Hall of Fame in 1974, Thomas Dunderdale is the first Australian to achieve this honour. He was born May 6, 1887, in Benella, Australia. His parents, who had earlier moved from England, came to Canada and settled in Ottawa in 1904, moving to Winnipeg nine years later .

When the National Hockey Association formed in 1910, he returned east to play for the Shamrocks in Montreal, moving to Quebec to play for the Bulldogs in 1911. Lured to Victoria, British Columbia, in 1912, Dunderdale remained in the Pacific Coast Hockey Association through 1923 and wrapped up his playing career in 1924 with Saskatoon and Edmonton of the Western Canada Hockey League. While in the PCHA, he played four years with Victoria and three with Portland before returning for five more seasons in Victoria. Dunderdale played both centre and rover and, in both 1913 and 1914, led the league in scoring.

During his 12 seasons with the PCHA he scored more goals than any other player in the league. He scored in every one of Victoria's 15 games in 1914 and was named the league's all-star centre. His pro totals are 223 goals in 273 regular-season games, plus six goals in 11 playoff games. A righthanded shot, Dunderdale stood only five-foot-eight and weighed 148 pounds at the peak of his playing career. He was a deft stick-handler and fast skater. When he finished playing, he coached and managed teams in Los Angeles, Edmonton and Winnipeg and resided in the latter city at the time of his death on December 15, 1960.

Inducted 1974.

CHAUCER ELLIOTT

REFEREE

CHAUCER ELLIOTT succumbed to cancer on March 13, 1913 at the age of 34. But although his life was brief, he earned great respect as an outstanding athlete and sportsman.

Born in Kingston, Ontario, in 1879, he excelled in many sports including hockey, baseball and football. He played point and was captain of the Queen's University hockey team. He also captained the Granite football team, Canadian champions in 1899. In 1903, he joined the Toronto baseball team in the Eastern League and three years later coached the Toronto Argonauts football club. That same year, 1906, he coached the Hamilton Tigers who won the Canadian football championship. The following year, he joined the Montreal AAA as football coach.

Chaucer Elliott became a hockey referee in 1903 and for 10 years was regarded as one of the best in Canada. Wherever he went, Elliott made friends and held them with a magnetic personality. As a referee, he enjoyed the complete confidence of the players and as a result, was always in great demand. It was said of him: "The harder the task, the better he liked it and no gamer man ever stood in a pair of skates." Inducted 1961.

"BABE" DYE

RIGHT WING • TORONTO, HAMILTON, CHICAGO, NY AMERICANS

ALTHOUGH SMALL in stature — 5'8", 150 pounds — Cecil (Babe) Dye had a distinguished athletic career. Born May 13, 1898, in Hamilton, Ontario, he moved to Toronto before he was one year old. He was a left-footed punter in senior football and was offered $25,000 (a fabulous sum in those days) to play baseball for Connie Mack's Philadelphia Athletics.

His official hockey career began in 1917 with the Toronto Aura Lee, Ontario's junior champions. He joined the Toronto St. Pats for the 1919-20 season, where he found it difficult to break the starting lineup but still scored 11 goals in 21 games. In the next six seasons, using superb stickhandling and a phenomenally hard shot, he scored 163 goals in 149 games. He led the league in goal-scoring three times, twice scored in 11 consecutive games and twice scored five goals in a game. He went on to play for Chicago in the expanded NHL of 1926-27, but to all intents his career ended when he broke a leg in the 1927 training camp and missed most of the season. He played two more NHL seasons, but scored only one goal.

Babe played for one Stanley Cup winner, the St. Pats of 1921-22, and scored nine goals in the five-game final against Vancouver. He later coached the Chicago Shamrocks in the American Association and was a referee in the NHL for five years in the late 30s. Dye became a foreman with a Chicago paving contract firm and remained with them until his death on January 2, 1962.

Inducted 1970.

FRANK FOYSTON
CENTRE • TORONTO (NHA), SEATTLE (PCHA), VICTORIA (WCHL, WHL), DETROIT

FRANK FOYSTON was born February 2, 1891, in the small village of Minesing, Ontario, about 60 miles north of Toronto. He first played hockey in a small, covered rink in Minesing but moved into an organized league with the Barrie Dyments Colts at the age of 17. By the time he was 20, he was ready to step into senior hockey and played for Eaton's of Toronto in 1911-12 when they won the Ontario Hockey Association senior championship.

Later in 1912, Frank became a professional with Toronto of the National Hockey Association and played centre for that team when it won the Stanley Cup in 1913-14. By 1915-16 he was on his way to the Seattle Metropolitans and a season later was part of the first American team to win the Stanley Cup. He stayed with Seattle for nine years, shifting to Victoria for two seasons, and was once again on a Stanley Cup winner when the Cougars were victorious in 1924-25. When Detroit purchased the team, Foyston went east and stayed in the Motor City for four seasons, retiring as an NHL player after the 1927-28 campaign.

As well as playing for three Stanley Cup champions, Foyston reached the finals on three other occasions. He lived in Seattle, Washington, until his death on January 19, 1966.

Inducted 1958.

ART FARRELL
FORWARD •
MTL. SHAMROCKS (AHA, CAHL)

A FORWARD throughout his short but productive career with the Montreal Shamrocks, Arthur F. Farrell played on two first-place teams in the Canadian Amateur Hockey League as well as on two Stanley Cup champions. Farrell was a stylish player, along the lines of Syl Apps and Joe Primeau and is considered to be one of the men responsible for changing hockey. Farrell's play shifted hockey from an individual's game to one that favoured complete team effort.

Born of February 8, 1877, he joined the Montreal Shamrocks in 1897 and played with the club through the 1901 playoffs. He played on a line with Harry Trihey at centre and Fred Scanlan on the wing. During his four years with the team — he missed the 1898 season — Farrell scored a total of 29 goals in 26 regular-season games and added 13 more in eight play-off encounters. The Shamrocks captured the first of their two straight Stanley Cups in 1899, when they also finished in first place in the league. Farrell's best playoff came the next season when he scored 10 goals in five games. In this series, he scored four goals in each of two games against the Halifax Crescents.

On March 2, 1901, Farrell had the best game of his career as he scored five goals against the Quebec Bulldogs. The Shamrocks finished third that season and lost to the Winnipeg Victorias in the playoffs. He died February 7, 1909.

Inducted 1965

FRANK FREDRICKSON
CENTRE • VICTORIA (PCHA, WCHL, WHL), DETROIT, BOSTON, PITTSBURGH

FRANK FREDRICKSON was born in Winnipeg on June 11, 1895 and established himself as an amateur standout before becoming a professional in 1920. He went on to become a star in the Pacific Coast Hockey Association, Western Canada Hockey League and the NHL.

Fredrickson played his first senior hockey with the Winnipeg Falcons during the 1913-14 season. Two years later, he was captain of the University of Manitoba Bisons. He took time out from hockey to serve in the Canadian forces in World War I, but upon returning from overseas in 1919, joined the Falcons and captained them to both an Allan Cup triumph and the 1920 Olympic crown at Antwerp. Frank signed with Lester Patrick's Victoria Aristocrats (later renamed the Cougars) at Christmas of the same year and remained with that team until the WCHL was sold to eastern interests.

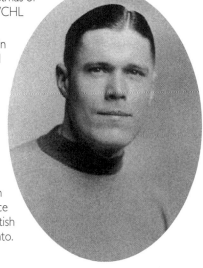

The Cougars defeated the Montreal Canadiens to win the 1925 Stanley Cup playoff but lost the next year's final to the Montreal Maroons. His career took him to Detroit for half a season, to Boston, and, in 1928-29, to Pittsburgh. He was coach, manager, and centre for Pittsburgh when a leg injury virtually ended his playing days. Fredrickson retired after the 1930-31 season when he played with Detroit.

In the PCHA and WCHL, Frank scored 131 goals and led the league in 1920 and 1923. He continued to coach in Winnipeg in 1931-32, at Princeton University in 1933-34 and 1934-35, for the Royal Canadian Air Force during World War II and at the University of British Columbia after the War. He died May 28, 1979, in Toronto.

Inducted 1958.

JIMMY GARDNER

LEFT WING • MONTREAL AAA (CAHL), MTL. WANDERERS (FAHL, ECHA, NHA), CALUMET (IHL), PITTSBURGH (IHL), MTL. SHAMROCKS (ECAHA), NEW WESTMINSTER (PCHA), MONTREAL (NHA)

Jimmy Gardner was born in Montreal on May 21, 1881, and learned his hockey with another great player of that time, Dickie Boon. They played on the sidewalks and in an area known as Boon's Lane. Gardner was to enjoy more than a decade as an outstanding player and was associated with two great teams, the Montreal Hockey Club's "Little Men of Iron," and the Montreal Wanderers. Those "Little Men of Iron" won the Stanley Cup in 1901-02 after a stubborn stand against Winnipeg. The Wanderers won in 1909-10.

A talented leftwinger, Gardner played for several different clubs. After one season with the Montreal HC and another with the Wanderers, he went to Calumet, Michigan, where he played two seasons. In 1907, he moved on to Pittsburgh and after one season there, returned to Montreal and played with the Shamrocks. He rejoined the Wanderers just in time to be on his second Stanley Cup winner. The year 1911 saw him go to New Westminster of the Pacific Coast Hockey Association, but after two seasons he again returned to Montreal. Jimmy played for the Canadiens for two seasons, then retired to a coaching role with that club for another two years.

Gardner shifted to officiating in the 1917-18 season, refereeing in the minors and then the Western Canada Hockey League in 1923-24. He took another fling at coaching with the Hamilton Tigers of 1924-25 but that team withdrew from the league in a celebrated salary dispute. He died in Montreal, on November 7, 1940.

Inducted 1962.

EDDIE GERARD

FORWARD, DEFENSE • OTT. VICTORIAS (FAHL), OTTAWA (NHA), OTTAWA, TORONTO

A star participant in football, paddling, cricket, tennis, lacrosse and hockey, Eddie Gerard was born in Ottawa on February 22, 1890.

Eddie turned professional with the Ottawa Senators in the 1913-14 season and became their captain in the 1920-21 campaign. During his 10 years with the team he was on four Stanley Cup winners, although one championship was won while he was on loan to the Toronto St. Pats.

Gerard's first victory in the Stanley Cup came in 1919-20 with a triumph over the Seattle Metropolitans. This was followed by victories over the Vancouver Millionaires in 1920-21 and both Vancouver and the Edmonton Eskimos in 1922-23. In the 1921-22 playoffs he was loaned to Toronto St. Pats to replace the injured Harry Cameron. The St. Pats played and defeated the Vancouver Millionaires and Gerard is credited with being the deciding factor in this win.

Known as a gentleman on and off the ice, he played his defense position well and cleanly. Gerard retired in 1924 because of asthma and coached the Montreal Maroons to a Stanley Cup victory in 1925-26. He remained with the Maroons until 1930, then joined the New York Americans as manager. He went back to the Maroons after the 1932 season and joined the St. Louis Eagles in 1934-35 but was forced to quit halfway through the year. Gerard died in Ottawa at the age of 47 on December 7, 1937.

Inducted 1945.

THE WINNIPEG FALCONS...

Hockey actually made its Olympic debut at the Summer Games in 1920, four years before the creation of the first Winter Olympics. The Winnipeg Falcons beat the University of Toronto to win the Allan Cup that year. The team was drawn from the large Icelandic community in Winnipeg and had faced much prejudice in a city that prided itself on its British heritage. Now, they were boarding a boat for Belgium to play for their country.

It was apparent to all that Canada and the U.S. were the the top teams among the six entrants at the Olympics in Antwerp, and while the Americans humiliated Switzerland 29-0 in their opening game the Falcons did not wish to embarrass their opponents. "We tried to limit ourselves to 14 or 15 goals a game against the European teams," captain Frank Fredrickson explained. "Believe me, it was difficult."

The luck of the draw put the Canadians up against the U.S. in the second game, and the Falcons outplayed them more than the 2-0 score indicated. Against Sweden in the gold medal game, the Canadians posted an easy 12-1 victory. "I guess it's safe to confess that we gave it to them," Fredrickson later said of the lone goal his team surrendered at the Olympics. "The Swedes went wild. They were yelling and cheering, shaking hands with themselves and with us. It was great."

JACK GIBSON

BUILDER

JACK GIBSON is recognized as organizer of the first pro hockey league in the world — the International League of 1904-08. This league consisted of teams from three Michigan centres — Houghton, Calumet and Sault Ste. Marie — plus Pittsburgh and the Canadian Soo.

Born September 10, 1880, in Berlin, Ontario, he graduated from Detroit Medical School and set up a dental practice at Houghton. A fine player and member of Ontario's Intermediate champions in 1897, he organized the Portage Lake team in 1902-03 and soon became captain as well as leading scorer. The 1903-04 team played 26 games, winning 24 times while scoring 273 goals and allowing only 48 against. Opponents included teams from Pittsburgh, St. Paul, St. Louis and also the famous Montreal Wanderers whom they defeated twice, 8-4 and 9-2, before 5,000 fans in the Amphidrome at Houghton.

Such greats as Riley Hern, Hod and Bruce Stuart and Cyclone Taylor played in the league and all but Hod Stuart were teammates of Gibson. That Portage Lake team is considered by many oldtimers as one of the greatest ever assembled. Portage Lake, in the spring of 1905, challenged Ottawa's famous Silver Seven to a championship series and in 1906 a similar challenge was issued to Montreal. Both were refused. It was at this time that Canadian teams offered handsome contracts to the great Portage Lake players and Gibson returned to Canada. He eventually set up practice in Calgary where he resided until his death on October 7, 1955.

Inducted 1976.

BILLY GILMOUR

FORWARD •
OTTAWA (CAHL, FAHL, ECAHA, NHA), MTL. VICTORIAS (ECAHA)

A TALENTED right winger for the Ottawa Hockey Club, Billy Gilmour was born in Ottawa on March 21, 1885. Gilmour joined the Ottawa Silver Seven in the 1902-03 season from McGill University and stayed with the club for three consecutive Stanley Cup victories. His best season was 1902-03 when he collected 10 goals in seven games. He also scored five goals in four games in the playoffs. The Silver Seven repeated as winners of the Stanley Cup in 1903-04 and 1904-05 but lost their hold on the Cup in 1905-06. It was at the end of this season that Billy retired for a year.

He returned to hockey in 1907-08 with the Montreal Victorias of the Eastern Canada Amateur Hockey Association. The following season he played for the Ottawa Senators in the ECAHA. The Senators won the Stanley Cup in 1908-09 and Gilmour finished the season with 9 goals in 11 games. He hung up his skates for the next six years before attempting a comeback that lasted only two games in 1915-16. He scored one goal against Georges Vezina of the Montreal Canadiens on January 15, 1916. Following this season he retired officially as a player. He was 73 when he died in Mount Royal, Quebec, on March 13, 1959.

Inducted 1962.

OTTAWA AND THE STANLEY CUP...

According to legend, Lord Stanley of Preston had expected his beloved Ottawa hockey club to win the trophy he donated in 1893. But ten years would pass before the name of Ottawa was inscribed on the Stanley Cup. Though the Cup was a long time in coming to the city, it soon appeared that it might never leave. No team in the challenge era of Stanley Cup history ever put the trophy on the line as often as the Ottawa "Silver Seven." And no team was ever as successful.

Ottawa won its first Stanley Cup in 1903, beating the Montreal Victorias in a two-game playoff to determine the championship. The deciding game was an 8-0 rout. High scores, and highly aggressive play, would typify the reign of the Silver Seven, who defeated nine more challengers over the next three years before finally seeing their trophy pass to the Montreal Wanderers.

The most famous challenge during Ottawa's Stanley Cup streak came from a team in Dawson City. Travelling 4,000 miles by dogsled, boat and train, the Yukon squad was beaten 9-2 and 23-2 in the two-game set. The second game saw Frank McGee score 14 goals — a Stanley Cup record not likely to be surpassed!

"MOOSE" GOHEEN

DEFENCE / FORWARD •
ST. PAUL ATHLETIC CLUB

IT WAS SAID of Francis Xavier (Moose) Goheen that he was "the only individual three-man rush in hockey." Goheen was born in White Bear, Minnesota, on February 9, 1894, and was one of the truly great hockey players produced in the United States.

He was an outstanding athlete in football, baseball and hockey, but it was the latter sport that brought him international acclaim. In the season of 1915-16, Goheen was a member of the St. Paul Athletic Club team that won the McNaughton Trophy as U.S. amateur champions. St. Paul won again the following season before Goheen joined the U.S. Army and served overseas in World War I. By 1920, he was back with St. Paul for another successful bid for the McNaughton Trophy. He was selected to the U.S. Olympic team that year, competing in Antwerp, but declined an offer to play for the 1924 Olympic team because of business reasons. When St. Paul became a professional club in 1925-26, Goheen was drafted by the Boston Bruins but refused to report, being reluctant to leave his job with the Northern States Power Company.

Moose Goheen was one of the first hockey players to wear protective headgear. Although primarily a defenceman, he was a prolific scorer and was noted for rink-length rushes. He died November 13, 1979, in St. Louis, Missouri.

Inducted 1952.

"SHORTY" GREEN

RIGHT WING •
HAMILTON, NY AMERICANS

OFTEN REMEMBERED as captain of the Hamilton Tigers who staged the first player strike in the history of the NHL, Wilfred (Shorty) Green had many other claims to fame. Green was born in Sudbury, Ontario, on July 17, 1896, and showed such good early form that he never played junior hockey.

He played two seasons with the Sudbury Intermediates, then moved up in 1914-15 to play with the Sudbury Seniors who won the Northern Ontario Hockey Association title. Green played with the Sudbury Wolves until early 1916 when he enlisted in the Canadian Army. He was gassed at Passchendale in 1917 and returned home the following year. Green joined the Hamilton Tigers and helped them win the Allan Cup in 1919, then returned to Sudbury and played there until the autumn of 1923 when he turned professional with the Hamilton Tigers in the NHL. The Tigers won league honours in 1925 and Shorty, as captain, was spokesman for the players who refused to participate in a playoff game unless the club paid a $200-per-player compensation. The owners refused to give in and Toronto and the Canadiens played a series to decide the title.

The Hamilton franchise was shifted to New York and Green scored the first goal in Madison Square Garden as the newly-formed New York Americans bowed 3-1 to the Canadiens on December 19, 1925. He continued with the Americans until a serious injury sidelined him in 1927. He coached until retiring in 1933. Shorty Green died April 19, 1960.

Inducted 1962.

MIKE GRANT

DEFENCE • MTL. VICTORIAS (AHA, CAHL), MTL. SHAMROCKS (CAHL)

ALTHOUGH BEST KNOWN for his ability and leadership in hockey, Mike Grant was also an outstanding speedskater. Born in January of 1874, Grant won titles in three different age groups when he was 11. The titles he held were for under-12, under-14 and under-16 age classifications. Following these victories, he was asked to try out for the Montreal Crystals junior hockey club and subsequently made the team. Grant became the team's captain and led them to the junior championship. A short time later he became the captain of the Crystals intermediate club which won the championship on two other occasions.

In 1894, Grant joined the Montreal Victorias and soon was elected captain. He led them to a Stanley Cup victory in 1895 but the club lost the Cup the following season to Winnipeg. Montreal recaptured the Cup in December 1896 and retained it in through 1898. During his career, Mike Grant played with three Montreal teams — the Crystals, Shamrocks and Victorias — and was the captain of each. When his career came to a close he had been captain on four Stanley Cup victors.

When he was not playing, Grant often refereed games in the same league. He became one of the first Canadian hockey ambassadors after he retired, demonstrating and organizing hockey exhibitions in the U.S. He died August 19, 1955. Inducted 1950.

SI GRIFFIS

ROVER/DEFENCE •
RAT PORTAGE (MHL SR.),
KENORA (MHL SR.), VANCOUVER (PCHA)

SI GRIFFIS brought a combination of dazzling speed and intelligence to hockey, first coming to prominence with the great Kenora, Ontario, team that successfully challenged for the Stanley Cup in 1906-07.

Born September 22, 1893 in Onaga, Kansas, he was a big man of 195 pounds but became known as the fastest man in the game. Griffis started as a rover in the seven-man game of that era but later moved back to play cover point (defence). In addition to the Stanley Cup triumph at Kenora, Griffis was captain of the Vancouver Millionaires that won in 1914-15, although he did not play in the Cup series due to a broken leg. Griffis was given a purse of gold by the citizens of Kenora and offered a fine home but moved to Vancouver after the Cup-winning season. He retired from hockey until 1911 when the Patricks started the Pacific Coast Hockey Association. On his opening night with the Millionaires he played the full 60 minutes, scoring three goals and assisting on two others. He remained with the team until 1918 when he retired permanently.

Si Griffis, also nicknamed Sox, was outstanding in several other sports. He won many events as an oarsman and, in 1905, successfully stroked the Junior Four at the Canadian Henley Regatta in St. Catharines, Ontario. Si was a champion lefthanded golfer and in later life became a great 10-pin bowler. He died on July 9, 1950, at the age of 67. Inducted 1950.

JOE HALL

FORWARD/DEFENCE • WINNIPEG (MHL SR.),
PORTAGE LAKES (IHL), QUEBEC (ECAHA, NHA),
BRANDON (MHL SR.), MTL. AAA (ECAHA),
MTL. SHAMROCKS (ECAHA, NHA),
MTL. WANDERERS (ECHA), MONTREAL

ONE OF THE TRUE slam-bang defencemen in the game past or present, "Bad" Joe Hall was a professional hockey player for 14 years until tragedy claimed him on April 5, 1919.

He was born May 3, 1882, in Staffordshire, England, but his family moved to Canada and settled in Winnipeg when he was two years old. They moved to Brandon, Manitoba, in 1900 and Hall, who had started playing hockey in 1897, joined the Winnipeg Rowing Club and Brandon teams until turning pro in 1905 season with Portage Lakes. He played for Brandon in 1906-07. Kenora took him east for the Cup series against the Montreal Wanderers, although he did not play.

Hall moved east to play for Montreal teams from 1908 to 1910. He played for the Quebec Bulldogs from 1910-11 through 1916-17, winning Stanley Cups in 1912 and 1913. He finished his career with the Montreal Canadiens. The Canadiens won the NHL title in 1918-19 and went west to play for the Stanley Cup in Seattle.

The series with Seattle, winners of the Pacific Coast Hockey Association title, was deadlocked after five games with each team having two wins and a tie when the local Department of Health cancelled further play because of an influenza epidemic. Joe Hall was the most seriously stricken of several players, dying from influenza on April 5, 1919.

Inducted 1961.

GEORGE HAY

LEFT WING • REGINA (WCHL),
PORTLAND (WHL), CHICAGO, DETROIT

MANY EXPERTS called George Hay the greatest stickhandler in hockey when he played in the NHL during the 1920s. He was one of the so-called little men — he weighed around 156 pounds — who thrived on professional competition. Although born in Listowel, Ontario, in January 10, 1898, George's early hockey was played in Winnipeg.

A gangling youngster, he became an excellent stickhandler with the Winnipeg Monarchs juniors of 1915 and 1916. Also playing on the Monarchs was Dick Irvin, who went on to become a good player and great coach. George played the 1920 and 1921 seasons with the Regina Vics before turning professional with the Regina Caps, again teaming with Irvin. During four years in the Saskatchewan capital, Hay scored 85 goals.

He moved on to the Portland Rosebuds where he scored 19 goals and, when the team was sold to Chicago, both Hay and Irvin moved into the NHL. Hay had a poor season with Chicago, playing much of it with torn ligaments in his left shoulder, and was dealt to Detroit prior to the 1927-28 season. With the Cougars (later the Red Wings), Hay led the club with 22 goals and 13 assists. The NHL's 10 coaches selected an all-star team that year and Hay was named to the forward unit with centre Howie Morenz and right winger Bill Cook. King Clancy and Eddie Shore were the defencemen and Roy Worters the goalie. In his five NHL seasons, Hay scored 74 goals and collected 60 assists. He died July 13, 1975, in Stratford.

Inducted 1958.

RILEY HERN

GOALTENDER • PORTAGE LAKES (IHL), MTL. WANDERERS (ECAHA, ECHA, NHA)

RILEY HERN played on seven championship teams in his first nine years in hockey.

He was born in St. Mary's, Ontario, on December 5, 1880, and started playing hockey with the local Ontario Hockey Association junior team as a goaltender. He moved up through intermediate and senior ranks and for a time played forward with a team in London, Ontario. Riley went to Houghton, Michigan, in 1904 as goaltender for the Portage Lakes team. The Montreal Wanderers signed him as a goalie in 1906 and he made that city his permanent home. Hern received much credit for the Wanderers winning the Stanley Cup that season. During the next five years he was one of the outstanding players on the team as the Wanderers won the Stanley Cup again in 1907-08 and 1909-10.

The pressures of business finally forced him out of athletics after the 1910-11 season but he remained in constant touch with the game as a referee and goal judge. Riley Hern's interests extended into many phases of Montreal life in both sports and business. He was champion of Rossmere Golf Club, president of the St. Rose Boating Club and a member of several other sports organizations. He also served as president or as a director of many business organizations. Hern died in Montreal on June 24, 1929.

Inducted 1962.

W.A. HEWITT

BUILDER

CHRISTENED WILLIAM ABRAHAM at birth on May 15, 1875, in Cobourg, Ontario, he was seldom referred to as anything but W.A. in more than 60 years' association with hockey. He moved to Toronto in 1879, later joined the Toronto *News* as a sportswriter and spent 41 years in the newspaper business, 32 as sports editor of the Toronto *Star*.

As well as being head of one of Canadian sports' most famous families — son Foster is also a Hockey Hall of Fame member — he was secretary of the Ontario Hockey Association from 1903 to 1961, registrar and treasurer of the CAHA for 39 years and manager of three Olympic champion Canadian hockey teams. W.A. also helped form the Big Four football league in 1907, served terms as president and secretary of the Canadian Rugby Union, acted as patrol judge at Woodbine racetrack as early as 1905 and was presiding steward at Ontario racetracks for 14 seasons.

He was responsible for an important hockey innovation: tired of disputes over whether a puck had gone between the goal posts, he came up with the idea of draping a fish net over them, so shots would be caught. It was the first set of goal nets. He was also the first attractions' manager of Maple Leaf Gardens when it opened in 1931. He died September 8, 1966.

Inducted 1947.

1900s

• 1900: The new century starts as the old one ended, with the Montreal Shamrocks as Stanley Cup champions. • The use of hockey gloves is now quite common. • 1901: The Intercollegiate Hockey League is formed in the United States. Members include Columbia, Dartmouth, Harvard, Princeton and Yale. • 1902: The Canadian Amateur Hockey League declares any club defaulting a game shall pay the other team $100. • 1903: Ottawa "Silver Seven" win the Stanley Cup. • Montreal Shamrocks finish the CAHL season 0-8. • 1904-05: Jack Gibson, a hockey-playing dentist from Berlin (now Kitchener), Ontario, who has been paying Canadian players to join his team in Houghton, Michigan, obtains the backing to form the game's first professional league, the International Hockey League. • Teams are based in Michigan, as well as Pittsburgh and Sault Ste. Marie, Ontario. • 1906: The Montreal Wanderers end Ottawa's Stanley Cup reign. Lester Patrick rallies his troops for a 12-10 win in the two-game series after nearly allowing a nine-goal lead to slip away. • 1907: Owen McCourt of Cornwall in the Federal Amateur Hockey League dies as the result of head injuries suffered in a stick-swinging incident. Charles Masson is charged with manslaughter, but later acquitted. • 1908: The Ontario Professional Hockey League is Canada's first outright professional circuit. Teams are based in Toronto, Brantford, Guelph and Berlin. • Future NHL star Newsy Lalonde leads the OPHL with 29 goals in nine games. • 1909-10: The National Hockey Association emerges as the game's dominant new league.

BOBBY HEWITSON
REFEREE

BOBBY HEWITSON was one of many great sports personalities who emerged from the Jesse Ketchum School of Toronto. Although small in stature he achieved outstanding success in both lacrosse and football, and later he became a highly respected hockey official.

Hewitson was born January 23, 1892 in Toronto. He was a member of two championship teams in 1913, the Maitlands lacrosse club which won the Ontario junior championship, and the Capitals which he quarterbacked to the Canadian junior football title. He started a career in sportswriting around this same time, working first for the Toronto *Globe* and later for the Toronto *Telegram*, from which he retired as sports editor in 1957.

Bobby Hewitson became a referee prior to 1920, handling games not only in hockey but in lacrosse and football as well. He went on to officiate 10 years in the NHL. He was also active in many other areas of sport. He was secretary of the Canadian Rugby Union for almost 25 years, was closely associated with horse racing and was an original member of the Hot Stove League on hockey broadcasts. He became the first curator of both the Hockey Hall of Fame and Canada's Sports Hall of Fame, retiring in 1967. He died January 9, 1969.

Inducted 1963.

"HAP" HOLMES
GOALTENDER • TORONTO (NHA), SEATTLE (PCHA), TORONTO, VICTORIA (WCHL, WHL), DETROIT

IF THERE HAD BEEN a trophy for the leading netminder during the period that Harry (Hap) Holmes played, he would have won it eight times. This outstanding goalie starred in five professional hockey leagues: the National Hockey Association, Pacific Coast Hockey Association, Western Canada Hockey League, Western Hockey League and the NHL.

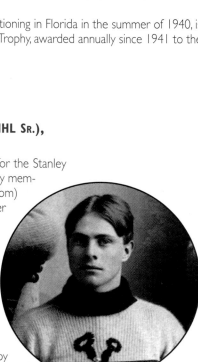

Born in Aurora, Ontario, in 1889, Holmes turned pro with the new Toronto franchise in the NHA in 1912-13. His career spanned 16 years with teams in Toronto, Seattle, Victoria and Detroit. He played on seven championship teams and four Stanley Cup winners.

Holmes had a goals-against average of 2.90 in 405 league games. His Cup teams included Toronto in 1913-14 and 1917-18, Seattle in 1916-17 and Victoria in 1924-25. Holmes registered 41 league shutouts and another four in playoff competition.

After three seasons and one Stanley Cup in Toronto, Holmes moved to Seattle where he was a standout for the first team to take the Stanley Cup to a U.S. city. The Cup seemed to follow Holmes around as he returned to Toronto and helped the Arenas win it in 1917-18. He then returned to the west and for eight seasons was a standout in the PCHA, WCHL & WHL. He was the league's leading goalie in six seasons against such outstanding rivals as Hugh Lehman and George Hainsworth.

He was Seattle's goalie in the 1918-19 Cup series that finished without a winner due to an influenza epidemic that forced the suspension of play. With the windup of the WHL in 1926, players went en masse to the expanded NHL and Holmes shifted to Detroit, where he played two years before retiring.

The memory of this great goalie, who died while vacationing in Florida in the summer of 1940, is perpetuated through the Harry "Hap" Holmes Memorial Trophy, awarded annually since 1941 to the leading goalie in the American Hockey League.

Inducted 1972.

TOM HOOPER
FORWARD • RAT PORTAGE (MNSHL), KENORA (MHL SR.), MTL. WANDERERS (ECAHA), MTL. AAA (ECAHA)

THE TEAM from Kenora, Ontario, challenged three times for the Stanley Cup before finally winning in January, 1907. One of the key members of that Cup-winning team was Charles Thomas (Tom) Hooper, a hometown boy who was to play on one other world championship team, the Montreal Wanderers of 1907-08.

Hooper was born in the town of Rat Portage (later renamed Kenora) on November 24, 1883. He played his first organized hockey in 1900 on his high school team. That team was so good that it defeated the town's senior team in an exhibition contest. In 1901, Hooper and Tommy Phillips moved up to the senior club and helped it win the Manitoba and Northwestern League championship. That team was known as the Thistles and by 1903 it challenged Ottawa for the Stanley Cup, losing a two-game series.

Kenora again challenged for the Cup in 1905. This time the Thistles won the first game but lost the next two in Ottawa. They challenged again in 1906, but because of the lateness of the season, the playoff was delayed until January of 1907. The Thistles' persistence paid off in a Cup victory. Two months later, however, the Thistles and Wanderers met again in Winnipeg and the Cup returned to Montreal. Hooper switched to the Wanderers in 1907-08 after his team folded, retiring at the end of the season. He died on March 20, 1960.

Inducted 1962.

"BOUSE" HUTTON
GOALTENDER • OTTAWA (CAHL)

ALTHOUGH HE IS CHIEFLY REMEMBERED and honoured as a hockey goaltender, John Bower (Bouse) Hutton was a great performer in many sports. Born October 24, 1877, he was a goalie in both hockey and lacrosse, and a fine fullback in football. He had the unique distinction of being the only man to play on a Stanley Cup winner, and on Canadian lacrosse and football championship teams in the same year.

In 1904, the Ottawa Capitals won the Minto Cup and were rewarded with a trip to England. The Minto Cup had been presented that season for the team winning the junior lacrosse title in Canada. The Ottawa Rough Riders, for whom Hutton played, also won a national football title and the Silver Seven, with Hutton in goal, won the Stanley Cup.

Hutton played goal for the Ottawa team that won the Canadian Amateur Hockey Association intermediate title in 1898-99 and also moved up to play two games with the Silver Seven that same year. He stayed with that club for six seasons, averaging 2.90 goals-against in a recorded 36 games. He earned his only two shutouts of regular-season play in 1901-02. Hutton also played in 12 games in Stanley Cup competition, allowing 28 goals. Bouse Hutton was in goal when Ottawa won the Stanley Cup in 1902-03 and 1903-04. He retired from active competition but continued to coach junior and senior teams in Ottawa for several years. He died on October 27, 1962. Inducted 1962.

HARRY HYLAND
RIGHT WING • MTL. SHAMROCKS (ECHA), MTL. WANDERERS (NHA), NEW WESTMINSTER (PCHA), MTL. WANDERERS, OTTAWA

VERY FEW ATHLETES can boast that they have played on two national championship teams in the same year. Harry Hyland, a very versatile performer, played on the 1909-10 Montreal Wanderers team that won the Stanley Cup. The same year, he was also a member of the Salmonbellies team that won the Minto Cup, symbolic of Canadian professional lacrosse supremacy.

Harry was born in Montreal on January 2, 1889, and played his early hockey in that city with Galics, St. Ann's, Chatelle and Excelsiors (1905) and the Shamrocks. He turned professional with the Shamrocks for the 1908-09 season although still within junior age limits. In his first game, he scored two goals in a 9-8 win over Quebec. He shifted to the Wanderers in time to play on their Stanley Cup-winning team but was lured to the Pacific Coast Hockey Association for the 1911-12 season. He joined New Westminster and this team went on to win the league championship with Hyland scoring 26 goals in 15 games. Hyland rejoined his former Montreal team in 1913 and on January 27 of that year scored eight goals in the Wanderers' 10-6 victory over Quebec. The Wanderers finished second to Quebec that season with Hyland scoring a total of 27 goals. He remained with the Wanderers until 1918 when he joined Ottawa, where he finished his active career.

A prominent writer once said: "Hyland was one of the greatest right wingers of his day, and teamed with Dr. Gordon Roberts to form one of the best scoring combinations in the game." He died August 8, 1969, in Montreal.

Inducted 1962.

THE KENORA THISTLES...

The early history of the Stanley Cup is filled with colourful tales of small-town teams competing with larger cities for the Stanley Cup. Teams from New Glasgow, Nova Scotia, Smiths Falls, Ontario, Brandon, Manitoba, and Dawson City, Yukon, to name but a few, all had their shot at the Cup in the days when the prized mug was still a challenge trophy. But only the 1907 Kenora Thistles were ever able to claim hockey's top prize.

After losing challenge matches to the Ottawa Silver Seven in 1903 and 1905 (when the town was still known as Rat Portage), the Thistles finally won the Stanley Cup with 4-2 and 8-6 victories over the Montreal Wanderers in January of 1907. Their championship reign would prove to be short-lived, as the Wanderers recaptured the trophy in a Stanley Cup rematch that March.

DICK IRVIN
CENTRE • PORTLAND (PCHA, WHL), REGINA (WCHL), CHICAGO

DICK IRVIN was an outstanding player and coach. He was born on July 19, 1892, in Limestone Ridge, near Hamilton, Ontario. His family moved to Winnipeg in 1899 and it was there he embarked on a hockey career.

Dick was a standout through church league and junior hockey with the Strathconas. He moved up to the senior Monarchs in 1912, as an emergency replacement, and scored six goals in two games of the Allan Cup final although his team lost to the Winnipeg Victorias. The Monarchs played an exhibition series in 1914 against the Toronto Rugby and Athletic Association and in one of those games Irvin scored all nine goals in a 9-1 victory. He remained with the Monarchs for the 1914-15 season when they won the Allan Cup.

He turned pro with the Portland Rosebuds the next season and finished third in the league scoring race. Irvin joined the Canadian Army and went overseas in World War I. He returned to pro hockey in 1921 and played four seasons with the Regina Caps before returning to Portland, where he scored 31 goals in 30 games. Irvin moved to Chicago for the 1926-27 season. He was the first captain of the Hawks and collected 18 goals and 18 assists, finishing second to Bill Cook in the league scoring race. He fractured his skull in the 12th game of 1927-28 campaign and played one more season before ending his playing career.

After coaching Chicago, he moved to Toronto in 1931 for a Stanley Cup-winning season. He also coached the Montreal Canadiens from 1940-55, winning the Stanley Cup three times. He died March 16, 1957.

Inducted 1958.

"MOOSE" JOHNSON
LEFT WING, DEFENCE • MTL. AAA (CAHL), MTL. WANDERERS (ECAHA, ECHA, NHA), NEW WESTMINSTER (PCHA), PORTLAND (PCHA), VICTORIA (PCHA)

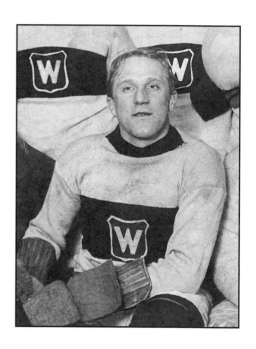

ERNEST (MOOSE) JOHNSON was born in Montreal on February 26, 1886 and, as his name implies, grew to be a big man. He possessed great hockey ability and started playing as a junior around 1900 . By 1903-04, Ernie was playing for the Montreal Amateur Athletic Association.

"As a beginner, I once played junior Friday night, intermediate Saturday afternoon and senior Saturday night," Johnson recalled in later days. Johnson turned professional with the Montreal Wanderers and played with them on four Stanley Cup championship winners — 1905-06, 1906-07, 1907-08 and 1909-10. He joined the New Westminster Royals of the Pacific Coast League in 1912. This team moved to Portland at the beginning of World War I. The club, led by Johnson, won its league title in 1915-16. He later played with Victoria and several other minor league teams. He finished his pro career in 1931.

He earned the nickname Moose from the Victoria hockey club, and also became known as the player with the longest reach in hockey history. Moose had the longest stick in the game and his reach, fully extended, was 99 inches. "The year I quit they buried my stick," he said. "It was the longest stick ever used. In those days, there were no size regulations and they couldn't take it away from me because it was my means of livelihood." He died in White Rock, British Columbia, on March 25, 1963.

Inducted 1952.

"DUKE" KEATS
CENTRE • TORONTO (NHA), EDMONTON (WCHL, WHL), BOSTON, DETROIT, CHICAGO

IT IS DOUBTFUL that any great hockey player ever bounced around through more teams in more leagues than Gordon (Duke) Keats.

Duke was born in Montreal on March 1, 1895, but his family moved to North Bay, Ontario, where he started his itinerant hockey career. At the age of 14 he was paid $75 a month to play in the Cobalt area. He went on to North Bay and, at 17, jumped to the National Hockey Association with Toronto. It was the coaching of Eddie Livingstone at Toronto that Keats credits with making him a great centre. Subsequently, he returned to amateur play with Peterborough, Ontario, went back to Toronto and then into the Canadian Army to serve overseas in World War I.

Following the war, he went to Edmonton and played for a first-class amateur team. Keats stayed with Edmonton when the team turned pro in 1919-20, leading the Western Canada Hockey League in scoring in 1922-23. The WCHL was sold by the Patricks in 1926 so Keats joined Boston of the NHL and transferred to Detroit part way through the season. The next season, he was with Chicago but after an argument with the owner, Major Frederic McLaughlin, moved to the American Association. Tulsa paid $5,000 for his transfer which proved to be money well-spent as Keats won the scoring title. Keats remained in hockey in various capacities across western Canada for many years. He died January 16, 1972.

Inducted 1958.

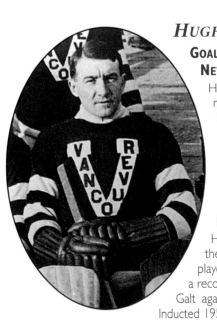

JACK LAVIOLETTE

DEFENCE/LEFT WING • MTL. NATIONALS (FAHL), U.S. SOO (IHL), MTL. SHAMROCKS (ECHA), MONTREAL (NHA), MONTREAL

THE CANADIAN HOCKEY ASSOCIATION and the National Hockey Association were fighting for control of the sport of hockey in the autumn of 1909. When the ice chips settled, only the NHA survived. One club involved in this struggle between the two leagues was the Canadiens of Montreal. The Canadiens had been formed by Jack Laviolette who secured financial backing from T.C. Hare and J. Ambrose O'Brien.

Laviolette is one of only three athletes named to both the Hockey Hall of Fame and Canada's Sports Hall of Fame prior to 1970. He was named to the latter as a lacrosse player. Born in Belleville, Ontario, on July 27, 1879, he moved to Valleyfield, Quebec, at an early age and played with the Overlands and Canadian Pacific Telegraphs in amateur hockey. He joined a team at Sault Ste. Marie, Michigan, and was selected as an International League all-star.

When he formed the Canadiens, Laviolette played point (defence) but later moved up to play on a line with Didier Pitre and Newsy Lalonde. Jack had great speed and earned the nickname "Speed Merchant." He played on a Stanley Cup winner in 1915-16 and retired at the end of the 1917-18 season. Laviolette lost a foot in an accident in the summer of 1918 but, amazingly, came back to do some refereeing. He died January 10, 1960, in Montreal. Inducted 1962.

"NEWSY" LALONDE

ROVER/CENTRE • CORNWALL (FAHL), CDN. SOO (IHL), PORTAGE (MHL SR.), TORONTO (OPHL), MONTREAL (NHA), RENFREW (NHA), VANCOUVER (PCHA), MONTREAL, SASKATOON (WCHL, WHL), NY AMERICANS

EDOUARD (NEWSY) LALONDE was born in Cornwall, Ontario, on October 31, 1887, and as a youth worked in a newsprint plant. That's where he acquired the nickname Newsy — and it stuck with him through an outstanding athletic career.

Lalonde's hometown produced many outstanding athletes in both lacrosse and hockey but, in the opinion of many experts, he was the premier performer in both sports. In 1950, Lalonde was named Canada's outstanding lacrosse player of the half-century. Lalonde began a somewhat riotous professional hockey career in Cornwall in 1905, and he was to be a dominant figure for almost 30 seasons. His hockey travels took him to play in Toronto, Woodstock, Sault Ste. Marie and Renfrew in Ontario, as well as in Vancouver and Saskatoon in western Canada, the New York Americans and, of course, the Montreal Canadiens in the NHL. He completed his active connection with the game as coach of the Canadiens.

He was a brilliant goal-scorer but also was known as one of the roughest players of his day. Feuds between Lalonde and Joe Hall, when the latter played with Quebec Bulldogs, helped fill Montreal's old Westmount Arena. Newsy scored 441 goals in 365 games and was a scoring champion five different times while playing in the National Hockey Association, Pacific Coast Hockey Association, the Western Canada Hockey League and the NHL. He once scored 38 goals in an 11-game schedule and, while with Vancouver, scored 27 goals in 15 games. He died November 21, 1971, in Montreal. Inducted 1950.

HUGHIE LEHMAN

GOALTENDER • CDN. SOO (IHL), BERLIN (OPHL), GALT (OPHL), NEW WESTMINSTER (PCHA), VANCOUVER (PCHA, WCHL, WHL), CHICAGO

HUGHIE LEHMAN was born in Pembroke, Ontario, on October 27, 1885, and became one of the outstanding netminders of his era. Lehman played goal for 23 years, 21 as a professional, and earned the nickname "Old Eagle Eyes."

He broke into hockey with Pembroke and was a member of the club that won the Citizen Shield in 1905-06. The next season, he played with Sault Ste. Marie, in the International Professional League. In 1907-08, he returned to Pembroke to play semi-pro hockey but played the following three seasons with Berlin (now Kitchener) in the Ontario Professional Hockey League. When the Pacific Coast Hockey Association was formed in 1911-12, Lehman joined the New Westminster Royals and stayed with them for three seasons. He joined the Vancouver Millionaires in 1914-15 and played with that team until the league was sold by the Patricks after the 1925-26 season.

Hughie returned east with most of the Western league players and spent the 1926-27 season with Chicago of the NHL. He retired after the 1927-28 season when he was co-coach of Chicago with Barney Stanley. Lehman played on eight Stanley Cup challengers but was successful only once, with Vancouver in 1914-15. He also shares a record with Percy LeSueur of having played for two different challenging teams within two months. He played for Galt against Ottawa and for Berlin against the Wanderers in 1909-10. Lehman died April 8, 1961, in Toronto. Inducted 1958.

Percy LeSueur

Goaltender • Smiths Falls (FAHL), Ottawa (ECAHA, ECHA, NHA), Tor. Shamrocks (NHA), Toronto (NHA)

The hockey career of Percy LeSueur spanned 50 years, but he gained his fame as the goaltender of the Ottawa Senators from 1906 to 1914.

LeSueur was born in Quebec City on November 18, 1881, and died in Hamilton, Ontario, on January 27, 1962. He acted in many capacities connected with hockey: player, coach, manager, referee, inventor, arena manager, broadcaster and columnist. Peerless Percy, as he was nicknamed, played on Stanley Cup winners in 1908-09 and 1910-11. He joined the Senators in March, 1906, after playing intermediate hockey at home and senior hockey in Smiths Falls, Ontario, where he switched from right wing to goal. He replaced Billy Hague in the nets after Ottawa lost the first game of a Stanley Cup series, 9-1, to the Montreal Wanderers. Ottawa fought back to tie the round at 10-10 but two shots by Lester Patrick eluded LeSueur and Montreal won the Cup.

He was captain of the Senators for three years and manager and coach for part of the 1913-14 season. He was traded to Toronto in 1914, joined the 48th Highlanders in 1916 and did not return to play after World War I. He became a referee, then coached in Ontario. He was the first manager of the Detroit Olympia. LeSueur is credited with inventing the gauntlet-type glove for goalies and the net used by the National Hockey Association and the NHL from 1912 to 1925. LeSueur was also an original member of radio's Hot Stove League.

Inducted 1961.

"Mickey" MacKay

Rover/Centre • Vancouver (PCHA, WCHL, WHL), Chicago, Pittsburgh, Boston

He was often called "The Wee Scot," but Duncan McMillan (Mickey) MacKay was a big star of professional hockey in its formative years. In the words of Frank Patrick, for whom MacKay played for several seasons: "MacKay was a crowd-pleaser, clean, splendidly courageous, a happy player with a stylish way of going. He was sensational in quick breakaways, a sure shot in alone with a goalie, and could stick-handle. He was outstanding in every way."

MacKay was born in Chesley, Ontario, on May 21, 1894, and played with the Chesley Colts until Barney Stanley lured him to western Canada. Still a junior, he played senior hockey at Edmonton and at Grand Forks, British Columbia, until Patrick hired him to play for the Vancouver Millionaires of the Pacific Coast Hockey Association. In his rookie season there, MacKay scored 33 goals, 10 more than Cyclone Taylor, and missed the scoring title by one point. He played with Vancouver through the 1925-26 season, won the goal-scoring title three times and scored 202 goals in 258 games. The Millionaires won one Stanley Cup, during the 1914-15 season.

Mickey moved to Chicago for the 1926-27 season and was the team's leading scorer in 1927-28. In 1928-29, he played half a season with Pittsburgh, but joined Boston in time to help them win the Stanley Cup. He retired after the end of the next season, while with Boston as business manager. On May 21, 1940, Mickey suffered a heart attack while driving a car near Nelson, British Columbia. The car was involved in an accident and he died. Inducted 1952.

"Steamer" Maxwell

Rover • Wpg. Monarchs (MHL Sr.), Wpg. Falcons (MHL Sr.)

Although he had several offers to turn pro, Fred Maxwell remained an amateur throughout his career. He picked up the nickname "Steamer" because of his tremendous ability to skate.

He was born in Winnipeg on May 19, 1890, and played rover in the seven-man game then in vogue. Maxwell joined the Winnipeg Monarchs in 1914-15. This team went on to win the Allan Cup, defeating Melville, Saskatchewan, in the final series. Steamer stayed with the Monarchs through the following season when he retired to become the team's coach for two seasons.

He shifted over to coach the Winnipeg Falcons in 1918-19 and took that team to an Allan Cup triumph in 1920. The Falcons also won the first Olympic hockey tournament that year. He stayed with the Falcons through 1924-25. In 1925-26, he coached the Winnipeg Rangers to the Manitoba championship. He next coached the Winnipeg Maroons of the American Professional Hockey League, staying with the club until the league terminated in 1927-28.

Maxwell returned to coaching amateur teams, both junior and senior, and, in 1929-30, coached the Elmwood Millionaires to both the junior and senior Manitoba championships. He coached another World championship club in 1934-35 when the Winnipeg Monarchs won the title at Davos, Switzerland. Maxwell also officiated many games between 1910 and 1940, in both pro and amateur ranks. He died September 11, 1975.

Inducted 1962.

JOE MALONE

**CENTRE • QUEBEC (ECHA, CHA, NHA),
WATERLOO (OPHL), MONTREAL,
QUEBEC, HAMILTON**

JOE MALONE was a remarkable marksman who performed scoring miracles in both the National Hockey Association and the NHL. The late Charles L. Coleman, author of *The Trail of the Stanley Cup*, credits Malone with 379 goals between his first professional game in Quebec in 1908-09 and his retirement in 1923-24.

In his eight biggest seasons — five with Quebec, two with Hamilton and one with the Montreal Canadiens — he scored 280 goals in 172 games. Malone led the NHA in scoring in 1912-13, and tied Frank Nighbor in 1916-17 with 41 goals in 19 games. Malone topped the NHL in its first season, 1917-18, with the phenomenal total of 44 goals in 20 games. Some of his outstanding single-game performances include: nine goals against the Sydney Millionaires in a 1913 Stanley Cup playoff game; eight against the Montreal Wanderers in 1917; and seven against Toronto in 1920, a mark that still stands as an NHL single-game record.

Joe Malone was born in Quebec City on February 28, 1890. He played his first organized hockey with the junior Crescents in 1907. In 1908-09, he played with the Quebec seniors and for Waterloo, Ontario in 1909-10. He went on to play seven seasons with the Quebec Bulldogs, two with the Montreal Canadiens, one more with Quebec two with Hamilton and two more with Montreal. He retired in 1923-24 after playing a few home games for the Canadiens. He died May 15, 1969.

Inducted 1950.

JACK MARSHALL

**WINNIPEG (MHL SR.) MTL. AAA (CAHL),
CDN. SOO (IHL),
MTL. WANDERERS (FAHL, ECAHA, NHA),
MTL. MONTAGNARDS (FAHL),
MTL. SHAMROCKS (ECAHA, ECHA),
TORONTO (NHA)**

JACK MARSHALL was associated with five Stanley Cup winners and two other teams that challenged for the Cup during his 17-year hockey career. He is first noted in hockey record books as having played with the Winnipeg Victorias when they won the Cup in 1900-01. He was born in St. Vallier, Quebec, on March 14, 1877.

An outstanding centre, he played the next two seasons with the Montreal AAA. He moved to the Montreal Wanderers for two seasons but, by 1906-07, was playing for the Montreal Montagnards. Jack was back with the Wanderers in 1907, switched to the Montreal Shamrocks for the following two seasons and then returned once again to the Wanderers, where he stayed through 1912. By that time, he had shifted to defence.

Shortly after Toronto entered the National Hockey Association in 1913, Marshall was hired as playing manager, winning the Stanley Cup in 1914. It was Marshall's fifth and last Cup although he played another year in Toronto and two with the Wanderers before retiring.

Marshall was also an outstanding soccer player, having played for the Point St. Charles team that won the Caledonia Cup three times in the 1890s. In football, he played for the championship Britannia club in 1897. He died in Montreal on August 7, 1965.

Inducted 1965.

1910s

• 1910: Cyclone Taylor is reportedly paid $5,250 to play for Renfrew in the National Hockey Association. • The game is changed from two thirty-minutes halves to three twenty-minute periods • 1911-12: Frank and Lester Patrick form the Pacific Coast Hockey Association. • The NHA introduces six-man hockey with the elimination of the rover. • 1913-14: The NHA and PCHA agree that their league champions will compete for the Stanley Cup. • 1915: Vancouver becomes the first PCHA team to win the Cup. • 1916: Montreal Canadiens win their first Stanley Cup title. • 1917: Seattle becomes the first American team to win Lord Stanley's mug. • 1917-18: In an effort to rid themselves of Toronto's Eddie Livingston, the rest of the NHA owners re-form their circuit as the National Hockey League. • 1919: The Stanley Cup series between Seattle and Montreal is postponed due to a world-wide epidemic of Spanish Influenza • Joe Hall of the Canadiens loses his life to the virus.

FRANK McGEE
CENTRE/ROVER •
OTTAWA (CAHL, FAHL, ECAHA)

THE NAME OF FRANK McGEE was written into the hockey record book in 1905 with one spectacular scoring splurge. On January 16, 1905, McGee scored 14 goals in a Stanley Cup game as Ottawa trounced a weary Dawson City, Yukon, team, 23-2. Of McGee's 14 goals, eight were scored consecutively in a span of eight minutes and 20 seconds. Three of these were scored in 90 seconds and the fourth came just 50 seconds later, Cup records for three-goal and four-goal individual performances.

Born in 1880, Frank McGee played centre and rover for the famous Ottawa Silver Seven between 1903 and 1906 and although he had lost the sight of one eye prior to joining the club, became one of the best forwards in the game. He combined exciting speed with extraordinary stickhandling ability to average almost three goals per game. McGee finished his career with 71 goals in 23 games and had another 63 goals in 22 playoff encounters. He scored five goals in a game seven times during his career.

Ottawa won the Stanley Cup in McGee's first season with the club, but he didn't play a prominent role until 1903-04 when he scored 21 goals in eight Cup games. His scoring spree against Dawson City came the following season. McGee was a lieutenant in the Canadian Army when he was killed in action on September 16, 1916, in Courcelette, France.

Inducted 1945.

BILLY McGIMSIE
FORWARD • RAT PORTAGE (MNSHL, MHL SR.), KENORA (MHL SR.)

MANY OF HOCKEY'S great players achieved their fame as members of several teams, but Billy McGimsie was an exception. He played all of his major league hockey with one team, the Kenora (Rat Portage) Thistles.

Born in Woodsville, Ontario, on June 7, 1880, Billy moved to Rat Portage (later Kenora) with his family when he was one year old. He played up through minor ranks in church, school and mercantile hockey before joining the Thistles, a team he starred with for 10 years as a centre-ice performer. The Thistles challenged Ottawa for the Stanley Cup in 1903 but lost a two-game series. Two years later, they challenged Ottawa again with the same result. Undaunted they came back a third time in 1906 but because of the lateness of the season, the series was delayed until January of 1907. A two-game series was played in Montreal against the Wanderers and Kenora won both, the first by a score of 4-2 and the second, 8-6. This achievement put Kenora into the record book as the smallest town to ever win the Cup. Two months later, in March, 1907, the Thistles and Wanderers played a challenge series in Winnipeg and the Wanderers triumphed to take the Stanley Cup back to Montreal.

With McGimsie on the Cup-winning team were Eddie Giroux, Art Ross, Si Griffis, Tom Hooper, Tom Phillips and Roxy Beaudro. McGimsie's career ended when he dislocated his shoulder in an exhibition game in Ottawa. He died in Calgary on October 28, 1968.

Inducted 1962.

HOCKEY GOES TO WAR...

The First World War saw the suspension of play in many amateur leagues across Canada, and while action continued in the two major professional circuits of the day — the NHA/NHL and the Pacific Coast Hockey Association — many past, present, and future stars had gone overseas to take part in the much bigger contest being played on the fields of France and Belgium. Some would give their lives to the struggle.

Many hockey players who went overseas found themselves serving in Britain's Royal Flying Corps. In the primitive days of aerial warfare, good balance and an ability to withstand the cold were thought to be important attributes in a pilot. Good skaters were considered ideal.

Harry Watson was among the most successful hockey pilots, as he was credited with bringing down eight enemy aircraft. Frank Fredrickson never saw combat (though his troop ship was torpedoed in the Mediterranean), but was considered such a skilled flyer he was used instead to train other pilots in flight schools.

GEORGE MCNAMARA,

DEFENCE • CDN. SOO (IHL)
MTL. SHAMROCKS (ECAHA, ECHA),
HALIFAX (MPHL),
WATERLOO (OPHL),
TOR. TECUMSEHS (NHA),
TOR. ONTARIOS (NHA),
TOR. BLUESHIRTS (NHA),
TOR. SHAMROCKS (NHA),
TOR. ARENAS (NHA),
TOR. 228TH BATTALION (NHA)

GEORGE MCNAMARA was a big and rugged Irishman who, along and his equally strong brother Howard, formed a powerful defence unit that became known throughout Ontario as "The Dynamite Twins."

Born in Penetanguishene, Ontario, on August 26, 1886, George moved to Sault Ste. Marie, Ontario, at an early age. He grew up in a hockey atmosphere for the sport was booming on both sides of the border at that time. He made his first appearance as a pro in 1906 and played with a several different clubs before he joined the Toronto Tecumsehs of the NHA for the 1912-13 season.

George remained in Toronto and joined the Canadian Army for World War I. He was a member of the 228th Sportsmen's Battalion and briefly played for that team in the NHA until it ceased operation on February 10, 1917, to proceed overseas. After the war, he returned to the Canadian Soo and coached the Sault Ste. Marie Greyhounds to the Allan Cup in 1924.

George McNamara died March 10, 1952. Inducted 1958.

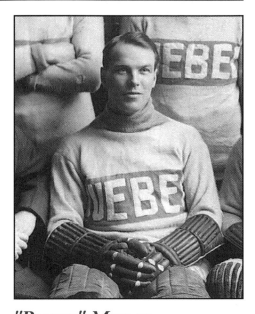

"PADDY" MORAN

GOALTENDER •
QUEBEC (CAHL, ECAHA, ECHA, NHA),
ALL-MONTREAL (CHA),
HAILEYBURY (NHA)

PATRICK JOSEPH (PADDY) MORAN played top-level hockey for 16 seasons. He was a member of the Quebec Bulldogs for 15 of these years and, although he retired a year before the NHL was formed, is regarded as one of the greatest standup goaltenders in the game.

Paddy was born in Quebec City, on March 11, 1877, and played his first organized hockey at the age of 15 with Sarsfield, a city juvenile team. He moved on to the Quebec Dominion juniors for two seasons and by 1895-96 moved up to the Crescent intermediate team. He stayed with this club through it Canadian intermediate championship season of 1900-01.

Moran began his career with the Quebec Bulldogs in 1901-02 and except for a one-season fling with All-Montreal and Haileybury, Ontario, in 1909-10, he remained with that team. Although Paddy never had an outstanding goals-against average, his ability was held in high esteem by knowledgeable hockey men of that era. His standup style earned him a reputation as a stick-stopping goalie good enough to help the Bulldogs win two consecutive Stanley Cups, in 1911-12 and 1912-13.

Moran died in Quebec, on January 14, 1966. Inducted 1958.

FRANCIS NELSON

BUILDER

FRANCIS NELSON was versed in practically all sports. Though best-known for his interests in thoroughbreds, he became an important member of the OHA in its struggling years.

When John Robertson became president of the OHA in its 10th year of existence, he realized that he needed capable men around him to make the organization a success. He called upon Nelson, sports editor of the Toronto *Globe*, for assistance. Nelson served as a OHA vice-president from 1903 to 1905, retiring with Robertson after the 1905 season.

The following season he was named OHA Governor to the Amateur Athletic Union of Canada and was later elected a life member. He died in April, 1932. Inducted 1947.

REG NOBLE

LEFT WING/CENTRE/DEFENCE • TORONTO (NHA), MONTREAL (NHA), TORONTO, MTL. MAROONS, DETROIT

REG NOBLE was born in Collingwood, Ontario, on June 23, 1895, and went on to become one of the finest left wingers in hockey. Championships seemed to follow him wherever he went. His career began with Collingwood Business College and he moved up to the town's junior team and helped it win the OHA Group title in 1914-15 before losing to Berlin in the provincial semi-finals. The following season, he played for the Toronto Riversides, winning OHA senior honours.

Noble moved into professional hockey with Toronto in 1916-17 but the club disbanded partway through the season. He was sent to the Montreal Canadiens but the league ruled that he had arrived too late in the season to play in the Stanley Cup finals which the Canadiens lost to Seattle. The NHL was organized the follow

ing year and Reg played for the Toronto Arenas who won the Stanley Cup. He scored 28 goals in 20 games that season.

The Arenas became the St. Patrick's in 1919-20 and Noble played for this team when it defeated Vancouver in the Cup final of 1921-22. He was traded to the Montreal Maroons in 1924 and came out a winner again when the Maroons won the Cup in 1925-26.

A trade took him to the Detroit Cougars where he played five years as a defenceman, returning to the Maroons early in the 1932-33 season to finish out his NHL playing career with a total of 167 goals. Noble played one more season with Cleveland of the International League. He refereed in the NHL for two seasons.

He died in Alliston, Ontario, on January 19, 1962. Inducted 1962.

FRANK NIGHBOR

LEFT WING/CENTRE • TORONTO (NHA), VANCOUVER (PCHA), OTTAWA (NHA), OTTAWA, TORONTO

HE WAS OFTEN called the Flying Dutchman or the Pembroke Peach, but by whatever name he was known, Frank Nighbor was a slick 160-pound package of stickhandling ability.

He was a 60-minute centre with the Ottawa Senators from 1915 to 1929, and was one of the game's great exponents of the poke-check. He was shifty and always ready with a lightning thrust of his oversize stick that was a constant menace to the opposing team's best players.

Nighbor was born in, Pembroke, Ontario, on Jan. 26 1893, and played his early hockey there. He played the 1910-11 season in Port Arthur, Ontario, and turned professional with Toronto in 1912. His first Stanley Cup triumph came with the Vancouver Millionaires when they defeated Ottawa in the 1914-15 final. The next season, he returned to Ottawa and remained with the Senators until the last half of 1929-30, his final season as a player, when he played for Toronto

While with the Senators, Nighbor played on four more Stanley Cup champions: 1919-20, 1920-21, 1922-23, and 1926-27. He was also the initial winner of two of the league's great trophies, the Hart and the Lady Byng. Nighbor won the Hart, awarded to the MVP to his team, in 1923-24, and the Lady Byng in 1924-25 and 1925-26.

Frank Nighbor died at his home in Pembroke on April 13, 1966. Inducted 1947.

WILLIAM NORTHEY

BUILDER

WILLIAM NORTHEY was president of the Montreal AAA during some of the club's greatest years and was named a life member of the Canadian Amateur Hockey Association. He also helped supervise construction of the original Montreal Forum and was for many years managing director of the building.

Northey's main interest was amateur hockey and, in 1908 when the Stanley Cup was taken over by professional interests, it was he who prevailed upon Sir Montagu Allan to present the Allan Cup. He also became the first trustee of this Cup which represents Canadian senior amateur hockey supremacy. He was born in Leeds, Quebec, on April 29, 1872, and died April 9, 1963. Inducted 1947.

AMBROSE O'BRIEN

BUILDER

AMBROSE O'BRIEN was actively connected with hockey from his earliest years, playing in his hometown of Renfrew, Ontario. He later played with the University of Toronto Varsity Blues.

In 1909, when the Eastern Canada Hockey Association was the only professional league in that part of the country and Renfrew's application for admission was rejected, O'Brien almost single-handedly organized the rival National Hockey Association. To do this, his father, M.J. O'Brien, financed four clubs, but his main interest was in bringing the Stanley Cup to Renfrew. For the soon-to-be-famous Creamery Kings team, O'Brien signed such stars as Lester and Frank Patrick, Fred Whitcoft and Cyclone Taylor. He helped launch one of the most famous teams in NHL history at the same time — the Montreal Canadiens. Other teams in the NHA were the Montreal Wanderers, Cobalt, Haileybury, Montreal Shamrocks and Ottawa.

It was decided that the O'Brien Cup, a silver trophy given by M. J. O'Brien, would be awarded to the champion of the NHA. This trophy was later adopted by the NHL. It is no longer

awarded and rests in the Hockey Hall of Fame. J. Ambrose O'Brien was born May 27, 1885, and died April 25, 1968, in Ottawa.

Inducted 1962.

FRANK PATRICK

BUILDER

THE NATIONAL HOCKEY LEAGUE rule book carries 22 pieces of legislation which were introduced by Frank Patrick, one of the most important of which was the origination of the blue line. Frank was born in Ottawa on December 21, 1885, and learned his hockey in Montreal where he was a star player with McGill University.

At 18, he refereed in the Montreal Senior League and at 20 refereed his first Stanley Cup game. He and his brother Lester played with the famous Renfrew team where he starred as a brilliant stickhandler and fast-breaking defenceman. Frank visualized artificial ice arenas and the operation of a pro league on the Pacific Coast. The Patricks built the first artificial rinks in Canada — Vancouver's cost $350,000, seated 10,000 and was the largest building in the country. He became president of the Pacific Coast League when it was formed in 1911, owned, managed and coached the Vancouver club and also played defence. This team won a Stanley Cup in 1915. In 1926, he engineered the biggest deal in hockey to that time, selling the entire league to eastern interests. He later served as managing-director of the NHL, as a coach with Boston and manager with the Canadiens. Frank Patrick died June 29, 1960.

Inducted 1958.

THE PACIFIC COAST HOCKEY ASSOCIATION...

They had both been amateur stars in the east. Both also played in the most important new pro league of its day (the National Hockey Association). But when they established a league of their own in the west, brothers Frank and Lester changed the way hockey was played forever.

There were many obstacles to overcome in creating the Pacific Coast Hockey Association, not the least of which was the mild West Coast climate. Too warm to rely on natural ice, as was done in the east, the Patricks built Canada's first artificial ice rinks in Vancouver and Victoria. Frank owned, coached, managed and played for the team in Vancouver, while Lester performed the same duties in Victoria. A third, non-Patrick team, was placed in New Westminster for the inaugural 1911-12 season.

The pace of innovation in the Pacific Coast Hockey Association was fast and furious. The Patricks were the first to put numbers on players' backs for identification. They were the first to tabulate assists and the first to allow goalies to flop to the ice to make saves. They painted the first bluelines on the ice, allowed forward passing and introduced penalty shots and a playoff system.

The PCHA was also the first Canadian league to expand into the United States. In 1915, a franchise was placed in Portland, Oregon. A year later, the Rosebuds (Portland is the "Rose City") were playing for the Stanley Cup. That same season, Seattle had joined the PCHA and in 1917, the Metropolitans became the first American franchise to win hockey's top prize.

Despite its progressive nature, the West Coast's small population base eventually made it impossible for PCHA teams to compete with those in the east. Big-league pro hockey in the west collapsed in 1926, but the game was much improved for having been there.

LESTER PATRICK

DEFENCE/ROVER • BRANDON (NWHL), WESTMOUNT (CAHL), MTL. WANDERERS (ECAHA), NELSON (SR.), EDMONTON (SR.), RENFREW (NHA), VICTORIA (PCHA, WHL), SPOKANE (PCHA), SEATTLE (PCHA), NY RANGERS

IT IS IMPOSSIBLE to describe the many contributions Lester Patrick made to the game of hockey throughout his lifetime as a player, coach, manager, owner and NHL governor. He was one of hockey's immortals and is identified with many of the major developments in style of play, organization and expansion of the game.

He was one of the first rushing defencemen in hockey. As a coach and executive, he inaugurated hockey's first major farm system. With his brother Frank, he devised the profitable playoff system still in use today and was responsible for many rule improvements. He introduced pro hockey to British Columbia and was a guiding force behind its rise in the northeastern United States.

Lester Patrick was born in Drummondville, Quebec, on December 31, 1883, where he developed into a tremendous skater and stickhandler. He broke into pro hockey as a defenceman with Brandon, Manitoba, in 1903, and joined the Montreal Wanderers in 1905-06 where he played on two successive Stanley Cup winners before moving to Canada's west coast.

Lester and Frank both played for Renfrew, Ontario, and then built arenas in Vancouver and Victoria, British Columbia, where they formed the Pacific Coast Hockey Association. Lester captained and managed the Victoria Aristocrats in 1912-13 when they defeated Quebec for the world title, although the Stanley Cup was not at stake.

After he and Frank sold the WHL in 1926, Lester became manager of the New York Rangers. The Rangers won three Stanley Cups under his guidance, in 1927-28, 1932-33, and 1939-40. He died in Victoria, British Columbia, on June 1, 1960. Inducted 1947.

TOMMY PHILLIPS

LEFT/RIGHT WING • MTL. AAA (CAHL), TOR. MARLBOROS (OHA), RAT PORTAGE (MHL SR.), KENORA (MHL SR.), OTTAWA (ECAHA), EDMONTON (SR.), VANCOUVER (PCHA)

HOCKEY OLDTIMERS who could recall the game as it was played in the early 1900s agreed that Thomas Neil Phillips was perhaps the greatest hockey player they had ever seen.

Tommy was born in Kenora, Ontario, on May 22, 1883. He played hockey as a schoolboy in Kenora before going east to attend McGill University. He played for both McGill and the Montreal AAA, signing with the latter in 1902-03. Tommy, or "Nibs" as he was often called, attended college in Toronto in 1904 and helped the Marlboros win the Ontario Hockey Association senior championship.

By 1905, Phillips was back in Kenora and was captain of the Thistles when that team that made two strong challenges for the Stanley Cup. They lost their first bid, despite Phillips' best efforts. Invading Ottawa, they scored a sensational 9-3 upset in the first game. Ottawa came

back to take the second 4-2 and the third 5-4 to retain the Cup. In 1907, Kenora travelled to Montreal to play the Wanderers and Phillips scored all the goals in a first-game 4-2 triumph. Kenora also won the second game, 8-6, and the Stanley Cup was theirs. Two months later, the Wanderers challenged the Thistles again and regained the trophy.

Phillips played right wing for Ottawa in 1907-08, having been converted to the position because captain Alf Smith refused to relinquish Phillips' customary spot on the left side. As a right winger, he scored 26 goals in 10 games. Phillips had everything a good player should have — whirlwind speed, a bullet-like shot and stickhandling wizardry — and he was regarded as being without peer as a backchecker. He died in Toronto on November 30, 1923.

Inducted 1945.

DIDIER PITRE

DEFENCE/FORWARD •
MTL. NATIONALS (FAHL, CAHL),
U.S. SOO (IHL),
MTL. SHAMROCKS (ECAHA),
EDMONTON (SR.), MONTREAL (NHA),
VANCOUVER (PCHA), MONTREAL

DIDIER PITRE was the idol of French-Canadian hockey followers in the early, rough-and-ready days of the game. He weighed about 200 pounds, had a shot "like a cannonball," and could skate with tremendous speed for a big man.

He was born September 1, 1883, in Valleyfield, Quebec, and entered big-league hockey of the day as a defenceman with the Montreal Nationals of the Federal Amateur Hockey League. Pitre played in the International Pro League with Jack Laviolette, returning with him to Canada to play on the Montreal Shamrocks' defence in 1908. He was added to the Edmonton squad that challenged for the Stanley Cup prior to the 1908-09 season.

When Laviolette formed the Canadiens in 1909, Pitre was the first player he signed. He remained with the team until his retirement in 1923, except for the 1913-14 season when he played for Vancouver. The high-speed skating style of both Laviolette and Pitre led sportswriters to designate the team as the "Flying Frenchmen." After two seasons, Pitre's goal production jumped as he was moved up to right wing to better utilize his speed. His biggest scoring year was 1914-15 when he registered 30 goals, about half the team's total. Laviolette moved up to left wing on a line with Pitre and Newsy Lalonde and the trio led the Canadiens to the Stanley Cup in 1915-16.

He died July 29, 1934.

Inducted 1962.

FRANK RANKIN

ROVER • EATON'S (EAA), ST. MICHAEL'S (OHA)

IN THE EARLY DAYS of organized hockey, long before Howie Morenz came on the scene, Stratford, Ontario, was a stronghold of the sport. And one of the best known names in the area was Rankin: Charlie, Gordon, Ramsay and Frank were hockey standouts.

Frank was born April 1, 1889, and right from the start was destined to play for championship teams. He was a rover in the era of seven-man hockey and played a very prominent role in the Stratford juniors' winning of the Ontario Hockey Association in three consecutive seasons — 1906-07, 1907-08 and 1908-09. When department-store owner John C. Eaton (later Sir John) formed the Eaton Athletic Association in Toronto in 1910, Frank Rankin played rover and captained the Eaton's hockey team to the Ontario title in both 1910-11 and 1911-12. Each year they advanced to the Allan Cup final, only to lose to the Winnipeg Victorias.

Rankin joined Toronto St. Michael's and played in three consecutive OHA finals from 1912-13 to 1914-15. He later went on to become a successful coach and, in 1924, directed the Toronto Granites to an Olympic championship, winning the world amateur title in a series played at Chamonix, France. He died July 23, 1932.

Inducted 1961.

HARVEY PULFORD

DEFENCE •
OTTAWA (AHA, CAHL, FAHL, ECAHA)

FEW MEN in Canadian sport can equal the great all-round record of athletic achievement set by Harvey Pulford. He was outstanding in many sports: hockey, football, lacrosse, boxing, paddling, rowing and squash.

Although he was born in Toronto, in 1875, he spent most of his life in Ottawa where he won championships in virtually every sport in which he participated. He was a defence star of the Ottawa Hockey Club from 1893 to 1908 and played on Stanley Cup winners in 1902-03, 1903-04, and 1904-05.

He started in the championship field when he was 13, earning the title of all-round sports champion at Ottawa's Model School. Pulford didn't stop until he was almost 50, winning the Ottawa squash championship in 1923-24. In between, his record is almost unbelievable. He played for the Ottawa Rough Riders who won Canadian football titles in 1898, 1899, 1900 and 1902. He played for the Capitals who ruled Canadian lacrosse from 1897 to 1900. He was light-heavy and heavyweight boxing champion of eastern Canada from 1896 to 1898. He was eastern Canadian double and single-blade champion in paddling in 1898 and his list of rowing achievements at national and international levels is too long to include.

Pulford is best remembered in hockey as a clean but hard-hitting defenceman who contributed to Ottawa's Stanley Cup victories over Kenora and Dawson City.

He died in Ottawa, Ontario, on October 31, 1940. Inducted 1945.

GEORGE RICHARDSON

FORWARD • 14TH REGIMENT (OHA), QUEEN'S U. (CAHA)

THE RICHARDSON name was well-known in Kingston, Ontario, around the turn of the century where George Richardson added further laurels in a brief but sensational amateur hockey career.

He was born in Kingston in 1887, and gained early fame as a member of the Queen's University team that won the Canadian Amateur Hockey Association senior championship in 1909. Most of his senior hockey was played with the 14th Regiment of Kingston. The Regiment team was either a champion or a strong contender throughout Richardson's years with the club. This team lost the Ontario Hockey Association final series to Stratford in 1906-07 but came right back the following season to win the OHA senior title. In the 1908-09 Allan Cup final, Queen's University, representing the OHA, added Richardson to its roster and won the Cup.

Richardson entered the army during World War I. He went overseas as a company commanding officer of the Canadian Expeditionary Force and was killed in action on the night of February 9, 1916. Queen's University in Kingston named its football stadium after Richardson to commemorate his achievements. Inducted 1950.

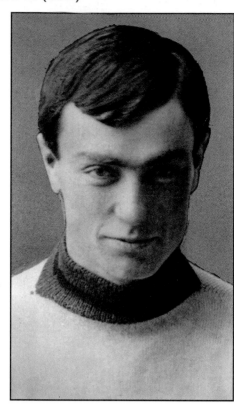

JOHN ROSS ROBERTSON

BUILDER

THERE ARE THREE great monuments to the memory of John Ross Robertson: The Ontario Hockey Association, the now defunct Toronto *Telegram* newspaper and Toronto's Hospital for Sick Children. Though never a player, Robertson looked upon hockey as a worthy sport and in 1898 began a six-year term as president of the OHA. The same year, he donated three trophies for annual competition, designating one each to be awarded to the champions in the senior, intermediate and junior divisions. Supporting his benevolence, in his first speech to the OHA, Robertson stated: "A manly nation is always fond of manly sports. We want our boys to be strong, vigorous and self-reliant and must encourage athletics. Sport should be pursued for its own sake."

A Member of Parliament, Robertson was offered a knighthood but declined. He was born December 28, 1841 and died May 31, 1918.

Inducted 1947.

GORDON ROBERTS

LEFT WING • OTTAWA (CHA, NHA), MTL. WANDERERS (NHA), VANCOUVER (PCHA), SEATTLE (PCHA)

GORDON ROBERTS was a great left winger who played professional hockey while acquiring a medical degree at McGill University in Montreal. Despite being a great goal-scorer throughout his career, Roberts never played for a championship team. He joined Ottawa in 1910, and helped them defend the Stanley Cup against Edmonton. His line was outstanding that season, but the team lost the Cup to the Montreal Wanderers.

He entered McGill in 1911, and played six seasons with the Wanderers, reaching the playoffs only once. Roberts was at his best in 1914 and 1915, playing on a line with Harry Hyland and Odie Cleghorn. A strong and tireless player, he had a tremendous shot that Clint Benedict, the Ottawa goalie, claimed would curve as a result of Roberts powerful wrist action.

On graduation from McGill in 1916, he left for the west coast, where he practiced medicine and continued to play hockey. Roberts signed with Vancouver and was sensational with the Millionaires. In 1916-17, he scored 43 goals in 23 games, an all-time scoring record for the Pacific Coast Hockey Association. His hospital duties took him to Seattle the next year and he joined the Metropolitans where he again starred. He didn't play in 1918-19 but returned to play for Vancouver in 1919-20 and wound up his playing career that year on a team with Jack Adams and Cyclone Taylor. Born September 5, 1891, Roberts died September 2, 1966.

Inducted 1971.

ART ROSS

DEFENCE • MTL. WESTMOUNT (CAHL), BRANDON (MHL SR.), KENORA (MHL SR.), MTL. WANDERERS (ECAHA, ECHA, NHA), HAILEYBURY (NHA), OTTAWA (NHA), MTL. WANDERERS

ART ROSS was many things to the game of hockey. He was a pioneer, innovator, strategist, promoter, coach, manager and outstanding player. His name is indelibly etched into the history of the sport.

Art Ross was born in Naughton, Ontario on January 13, 1886, and was a defenceman during a 14-year playing career that started with Westmount of the Canadian Amateur Hockey League in 1905. He played for Brandon, Manitoba, and Kenora, Ontario, in 1907, and led the latter club to a Stanley Cup victory. His only other Stanley Cup as a player came the next year with the Montreal Wanderers. Ross subsequently played for Haileybury (Ontario), the Wanderers again, Ottawa, and then once more with the Wanderers where he finished his playing career in 1918.

Ross refined many aspects of the sport. He improved the design of both the puck and goal net used in the NHL and left his mark on the game in many other ways. The Art Ross Trophy is awarded annually to the scoring champion of the NHL. Ross died in Boston on August 5, 1964.

Inducted 1945.

CLAUDE ROBINSON

BUILDER

CLAUDE ROBINSON was born December 17, 1881, in Harrison, Ontario, but at an early age moved to Winnipeg where he became an important member of the Winnipeg Victorias hockey club, first as a player and later as an executive. The Vics brought both the Allan Cup and the Stanley Cup to Winnipeg while Robinson was part of the organization. It was Robinson who first suggested the formation of a national association to stage amateur hockey championships and he became the first secretary when the Canadian Amateur Hockey Association was formed in 1914.

Robinson managed the Canadian team at the 1932 Winter Olympic Games, which were played in the town of Lake Placid, New York. He was later named a life member of the CAHA. He died June 27, 1976, in Vancouver.

Inducted 1947.

THE FIRST LABOR DISPUTE...

The owners were crying poor. The players said they only wanted what was fair. The owners said they needed a salary cap. The players said they wouldn't accept it. It looked like a winter without hockey. The year was 1911 and the pro game faced its first labor dispute.

The 1910 season had seen great upheaval in the game. By offering huge salaries, the new National Hockey Association had won its war with the rival Canadian Hockey Association, but emerging as the game's dominant power had exacted a price. The owners looked to recoup their financial losses in 1911 by imposing a salary cap of $5,000 per team. Bruce Stuart, captain of the Ottawa Senators, said the players would never accept a cap and threatened to organize his own league. Art Ross said that he'd help him.

The owners did not take the players' threat seriously until they stopped agreeing to contracts. "We are all suffering from the writers' cramp," quipped Stuart, "and cannot sign up."

But the players revolt was short-lived. When Stuart was not able to get the arena owners to back him over the NHA, the new league was abandoned. Players began signing contracts with their old teams. The dispute had lasted about a month and while no regular-season games were lost, training camp had been disrupted.

While there is evidence many owners eventually ignored the salary cap, or found ways around it, Bruce Stuart could get no more than a $650 offer from Ottawa. He played just four games and retired. Art Ross played on and agitated for players' rights again in 1914 and 1915, when his actions almost got him barred from hockey. Ironically, he would go on to a long career in management with the NHL's Boston Bruins.

PHILIP D. ROSS

BUILDER

WHEN LORD STANLEY of Preston donated a challenge cup for Canadian hockey supremacy in 1893 he named Philip Dansken Ross of Ottawa as one of its trustees. No man had more to do with important decisions concerning the Cup and the development of hockey in its early days than Ross who remained a trustee for 56 years.

Born in Montreal on January 1, 1858, his association and concern stemmed from his playing career. Ross was a teammate of the Hon. Edward Stanley on the Rebels, a team that did much to introduce and popularize hockey in Ontario and also provoked the interest of Edward's father, the Governor-General. Lord Stanley donated the world's most famous hockey trophy.

As an athlete, Ross' record was impressive: captain of the McGill University football team that played Harvard in 1876; member of several Canadian rowing championship crews; a fine lacrosse player and also founder of several golf clubs. He was also trustee of the Minto Cup (Canadian lacrosse championship).

After retirement as a player he continued to referee, and to extend financial support to sports associations. As a trustee of the Stanley Cup he was vigilant about abuses in competition which would injure the trophy's reputation. Ross died July 7, 1949, but not before delegating to the NHL "full authority to determine and amend ... conditions of competition for the Stanley Cup ... providing always that the winners ... shall be acknowledged 'World's Professional Hockey Champions.'"

Inducted 1976.

BLAIR RUSSEL

RIGHT WING/CENTRE • MTL. VICTORIAS (CAHL, ECAHA)

AN EXCELLENT two-way player throughout his career as an amateur with the Montreal Victorias, Blair Russel was often overshadowed by the great Russell Bowie. Russel played centre when Bowie was at his usual position of rover, but he shifted to right wing when Bowie moved up. This pair made up the most potent scoring threat in hockey at that time.

When the ECAHA became a fully professional league in 1909, Russel refused offers to play for the Montreal Wanderers and retired. He coached the Montreal Victorias in 1910.

Russel was born in Montreal on September 17, 1880, and played all his major hockey with the Victorias. He scored 110 goals in 67 games and once registered seven in a game against the Shamrocks in 1904. He also had a six-goal game and a five-goal game. Like many of the good players of his time, he was a very clean player who was equally adept at scoring and checking. In a vote conducted by daily newspapers of Toronto and Montreal at that time, Russel was named to an all-star team along with such greats as Bowie, Harvey Pulford, Frank McGee, Alf Smith and Billy Gilmour. All of these players are members of the Hockey Hall of Fame.

Following his retirement as a player, Blair Russel settled into a successful business career in Montreal. He died in Montreal on December 7, 1961.

Inducted 1965.

ERNIE RUSSELL

ROVER/CENTRE • MTL. AAA (CAHL), MTL. WANDERERS (ECAHA, ECHA, NHA)

ERNIE RUSSELL was a fast skater and an accomplished stickhandler, equally at home playing centre or rover. Although he weighed only 140 pounds, he proved to be a very proficient scoring machine. He is remembered in Montreal, where he was born October 21, 1883, for his feat of scoring three goals in five successive games.

In the Eastern Canada Amateur Hockey Association schedule of 1907, Ernie scored 42 goals in nine games. Russell was captain of the Sterling Juniors in 1903 when they won the junior championship of Canada. That same year, he also captained the Montreal Amateur Athletic Association football team which won a Canadian junior title.

Ernie first appeared in senior hockey with the Winged Wheelers in 1905, but the remainder of his playing career was spent with the Montreal Wanderers. This team won the Stanley Cup four times with Russell in the lineup — 1905-06, 1906-07, 1907-08 and 1909-10. Although he played for the Wanderers, Ernie maintained membership in the MAAA for other sports. This didn't suit the Wanderers who expelled him from their membership. Because of this he didn't play hockey in 1908-09. When he returned in 1909-10, Russell and Newsy Lalonde engaged in a furious struggle for the scoring championship, which Lalonde won by scoring nine goals in the last game of the season. Russell won a scoring title of his own in 1906-07 with 42 goals. He scored at least one goal in 10 consecutive games in 1911-12. He died in Montreal on February 23, 1963.

Inducted 1965.

JACK RUTTAN

**DEFENCE • ST. JOHN'S COLLEGE (MUHL),
MANITOBA VARSITY (WSHL),
WINNIPEG HC (WSHL)**

JACK RUTTAN enjoyed a long and illustrious career in hockey, both as a player and coach in the amateur ranks. His stature in Winnipeg, where he was born April 5, 1889, was such that he became an example for younger players.

Ruttan's playing career began with the Armstrong's Point team which won the juvenile championship of Winnipeg in 1905-06. He switched to the Rustler club the following season and played on another city juvenile winner. By 1907-08, Jack was playing for the St. John's College team, winners of the Manitoba University Hockey League. Rattan joined the Manitoba Varsity team which won the 1909-10 championship of the Winnipeg Senior Hockey League. He stayed with the Varsity through two more seasons and then played for the Winnipeg Hockey Club. This team was exceedingly successful, winning everything from the Winnipeg League championship to the Allan Cup national senior title.

Ruttan remained in hockey for many years. In 1919-20, he coached senior hockey and officiated in the Winnipeg Senior League from 1920 through 1922. He coached the University of Manitoba Bisons in 1923. He died January 7, 1973.

Inducted 1962.

FRED SCANLAN

**FORWARD •
MTL. SHAMROCKS (AHA, CAHL),
WPG. VICTORIAS (MHL SR.)**

ONE OF THE GREAT forward lines in the early days of hockey played for the Montreal Shamrocks. Each member of this line — Harry Trihey, Art Farrell and Fred Scanlan — went on to be elected to the Hockey Hall of Fame.

Scanlan joined the club in 1898 and quickly became part of the forward foursome, which also included rover Jack Brannen. The Shamrocks, a team that began play in 1893 at St. Mary's College, won consecutive Stanley Cup victories in 1899 and 1900 after finishing in first place in their league in both seasons. Scanlan remained with the Shamrocks through 1901, and then shifted to the Winnipeg Victorias, with whom he remained until he decided to retire in 1903. At the close of his career, he was credited with having scored 16 goals in 31 games. He also scored six goals in 17 playoff contests.

Fred Scanlan played in the era when forward passing was not allowed. Under these rules, the puck was advanced up the ice by a forward whose linemates were strung out abreast of the puck-carrier. The rover trailed the play. Goals were scarce and a premium was placed on stickhandling excellence. The late Frank J. Selke, himself a member of the Hockey Hall of Fame, described Scanlan as, "the workhorse of the great Shamrock forward line, always ready for his share of the new-style combination attacks, combining heady play with an accurate shot."

Inducted 1965.

THE MONTREAL WANDERERS...

The Montreal Wanderers had a brief but controversial existence. Formed by James Strachan in 1903, the team consisted mostly of disgruntled players lured away from the 1902 Stanley Cup champion Montreal Amateur Athletic Association. Excluded from joining the Canadian Amateur Hockey League, they banded together with three other teams to form the rival Federal League. In 1906, they abandoned that circuit to join the new Eastern Canada Amateur Hockey Association.

The ECAHA brought the Wanderers their first Stanley Cup success in a thrilling series with the Ottawa Silver Seven. Having taken the first game of the two-game, total-goal series 9-1,

the Wanderers let their huge lead slip away before two late goals by Lester Patrick salvaged a 12-10 victory on aggregate. The Wanderers were champions again in 1907 and 1908. Another Stanley Cup title came in 1910, a year that had seen the club play a key role in the formation of yet another new league, the National Hockey Association.

In 1917, the Wanderers were one of the charter members when the NHA was re-formed as the National Hockey League. This time, their luck ran out. Six games into the season, the Montreal Arena burned down. The Wanderers folded, and a colourful part of hockey history was over.

Oliver Seibert

FORWARD • BERLIN (WOHA), CANADIAN SOO (IHL), LONDON (OPHL), GUELPH (OPHL)

SKATING AND HOCKEY were traditions of the Seibert family of Berlin, Ontario. Berlin was later renamed Kitchener, but the Seibert name has remained over the years as one of the greatest in the area. Oliver was a very speedy and versatile player. He started as a goaltender for Berlin, but switched to forward and starred for many years.

He was born in Berlin, on March 18, 1881, and at one time played on a team composed entirely of members of his family. Oliver was a leader in many respects. He was one of the first Canadians to play on artificial ice when he took part in an exhibition game in St. Louis. He also fashioned his own pair of skates made by cutting blades out of a piece of solid steel and fastening them to his shoes with screws. He was also the first Berlin player to turn pro when he joined the Canadian Soo club of the IHL.

Oldtimers like to recall the time Oliver skated against a trotter. The horse had a one-mile record of 2:13, but Oliver, wearing his old rocker skates, won a match race of one mile over a course laid on the ice of the Grand River. It was claimed he could skate as fast backward as forward.

Oliver was the father of Earl Seibert, another Hall of Fame member.

Oliver Seibert died May 15, 1944.

Inducted 1961.

"BULLET JOE" SIMPSON

DEFENCE • EDMONTON (WCHL), NY AMERICANS

JOE SIMPSON was a man who proved himself on the ice and on the battlefield where he won the Military Medal. He was born Harold Joseph Simpson in Selkirk, Manitoba, on August 13, 1893, and became an outstanding defenceman in both amateur and professional hockey.

In his prime, Simpson was described by Newsy Lalonde as "the greatest living hockey player." Simpson was not an exceptionally big player for a defenceman, but had speed to burn, earning him the nickname "Bullet Joe." He played amateur hockey in 1914-15 with the Winnipeg Victorias before joining the Winnipeg 61st Battalion hockey club which went on to win the Allan Cup.

The Battalion went overseas in 1916 and Joe served with the 43rd Cameron Highlanders and rose to the rank of lieutenant. He was wounded twice in battles at the Somme and Amiens, where he won the Military Medal. Returning to hockey following World War I, Simpson played two seasons with the Selkirk Fishermen. He later joined the Edmonton Eskimos and played four professional seasons with that club. Twice during his tenure with the Eskimos, the team won the Western Canada Hockey League championship with Simpson a major contributor to the team's success.

Joe joined the New York Americans of the NHL in 1925-26. Edmonton had received many offers for his services from both the Vancouver Maroons and the Ottawa Senators before finally selling him to New York. He remained with that team as a player until 1931, managed the Americans from 1932 until 1935, and then managed New Haven and Minneapolis before retiring from the game. He died in December, 1973.

Inducted 1962.

THE WESTERN CANADA HOCKEY LEAGUE...

Professional hockey was growing in popularity as domestic life returned to normal after World War I. The game's two dominant leagues—the NHL and the Pacific Coast Hockey Association — were soon joined by a third: the Western Canada Hockey League.

The WCHL began operating in Edmonton, Calgary, Regina, and Saskatoon for the 1921-22 season. It's life would prove short, but during its brief run it showcased such stars at Dick Irvin, "Duke" Keats, and "Bullet Joe" Simpson, to name just a few. The Edmonton Eskimos and Calgary Tigers would even play for the Stanley Cup.

In its second season, the WCHL began playing an interlocking schedule with the PCHA, and by 1924 the two leagues had merged. In 1925, the Victoria Cougars gave the WCHL its first Stanley Cup champion.

The following season, the Regina Caps moved to Portland, Oregon and the league was renamed the Western Hockey League. Unfortunately, 1926 would prove to be the west's last hurrah. Unable to compete with the larger centres of the east, the WHL folded and many of its players' contracts were sold to new NHL clubs in New York, Detroit and Chicago.

COOPER SMEATON

REFEREE

ALTHOUGH HE HAD more than one offer to become a professional hockey player, Cooper Smeaton instead became an outstanding official, refereeing for more than a quarter of a century. Smeaton refereed amateur hockey games before Emmett Quinn appointed him in 1913 to the staff of the National Hockey Association. In that capacity, he handled many Allan and Stanley Cup games.

He managed the Philadelphia Quakers of the NHL in the season of 1930-31, but returned to refereeing the following year when Philadelphia withdrew from the league. Smeaton was appointed head referee of the NHL and continued until 1937 when he retired to devote his time to business.

Born July 22, 1890, in Carleton Place, Ontario, Smeaton moved to Montreal as a child. He played baseball, football, basketball and hockey for the Westmount AAA, went overseas in the First World War and won the Military Medal. In 1946, Smeaton was appointed a trustee of the Stanley Cup by P.D. Ross of Ottawa, a position he held until his death on October 3, 1978, in Montreal.

Inducted 1961.

FRANK SMITH

BUILDER

THE METROPOLITAN TORONTO HOCKEY LEAGUE, a wide-spread organization of minor amateur teams and probably the biggest minor hockey league in the world, had a very humble beginning. Four days after Christmas, 1911, a group of men met in the living room of a Toronto home to form a hockey league. The home belonged to Frank Smith and he became secretary of the league, known as the Beaches Hockey League, which eventually grew into the MTHL.

Smith was a good organizer, and a good secretary; so good that he held the position for more than 50 years, resigning in 1962. His efforts over the years were first recognized when he was named an MTHL Life Member. Then, in 1947, he received the Ontario Hockey Association Gold Stick Award. The Canadian Amateur Hockey Association also bestowed its top award on Smith and, in 1961, he received the City of Toronto Award of Merit.

Frank D. Smith was born June 1, 1894, and died June 11, 1964.

Inducted 1962.

ALF SMITH

RIGHT WING • OTTAWA (AHA, CAHL, FAHL, ECAHA), KENORA (MHL SR.)

ALF SMITH was the oldest of seven brothers, most of whom had a tryout with Ottawa in the 1890's. Only three were able to stick with this first-class hockey club, and of the three, two have been inducted into the Hockey Hall of Fame. Alf was elected in 1962; Tommy in 1973.

Alf Smith was born in Ottawa, Ontario, on June 3, 1873, and played his first hockey with the Ottawa Electrics. He then played for the Ottawa Capitals and moved on to Pittsburgh. He returned to Ottawa in 1895 and showed an early penchant for rough play. After three seasons, Smith dropped out of hockey but returned, at the age of 30, after Ottawa won the Stanley Cup in 1902-03. He helped the team win the league championship and the Stanley

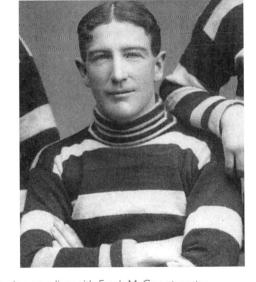

Cup in the succeeding two seasons, playing right wing on a line with Frank McGee at centre.

Ottawa lost the Cup to the Wanderers in 1905-06. He and Harry Westwick joined Kenora in that team's unsuccessful bid to defend the Stanley Cup against the Wanderers in March, 1907. Smith played the 1907-08 season with Ottawa, then returned the following season to Pittsburgh to play in a pro City League. That was his final year as a player, but he remained in the game as a coach, with Renfrew, Ottawa, the New York Americans, Moncton (New Brunswick), and North Bay (Ontario).

Inducted 1962.

TOMMY SMITH

LEFT WING/CENTRE • OTT. VICTORIAS (FAHL), OTTAWA (ECAHA), PITTSBURGH (IHL), BRANTFORD (OPHL), COBALT (NHA), GALT (OPHL), MONCTON (MPHL), QUEBEC (NHA), TOR. ONTARIOS (NHA), MONTREAL (NHA), QUEBEC

TOMMY SMITH was born September 27, 1885, in Ottawa, one of 13 children. Five of the eight boys in his family became proficient hockey players. His brother Alf was inducted into the Hockey Hall of Fame in 1962. Tommy was known as a little bulldog of a player at five-foot-four and 150 pounds.

Smith played school and junior hockey in Ottawa and moved up to senior with the Ottawa Vics of the Federal Amateur Hockey League in 1906. He led the league in scoring and added six goals playing with the Senators in three games at the end of the season. In 1907, he joined Pittsburgh in the International League, led the team with 31 goals in 23 games and, in 1909, led all scorers in the Ontario Professional Hockey League, playing rover for Brantford. Typhoid fever kept him idle in 1910, but he again led the scoring race in 1911, playing centre for Galt, which won the league title but lost to Ottawa in a challenge for the Stanley Cup.

In 1912, he moved to Moncton, New Brunswick, of the Maritime Pro League. Again, Smith's team won the league title but lost in another Cup challenge to the NHA champion Quebec Bulldogs. Smith played for Quebec the next season, finally being part of a Stanley Cup triumph. He was a linemate of Joe Malone and Jack Marks, finishing just four goals behind Malone, who had 43 to win the scoring crown.

Smith was dealt to the Canadiens in 1917, retiring from hockey when the NHA dissolved the next year. Smith came back to play 10 games with Quebec in 1919-20, but was scoreless and retired as a player at age 35.

He was leading scorer in his league numerous times and scored in 14 consecutive games in 1912-13. He scored nine goals in a game twice, in 1909 and 1914, and scored eight in a game in 1906. His nine-goal effort with Quebec in 1914 was a record in the NHA, matching the total posted by Newsy Lalonde four seasons earlier.

Tommy Smith died August 1, 1966.

Inducted 1973.

LORD STANLEY OF PRESTON

BUILDER

FREDERICK ARTHUR, Lord Stanley of Preston was Governor-General of Canada from 1888 to 1893. During his final year in office, he donated a trophy to be awarded to the championship hockey club of Canada. This was the Dominion Hockey Challenge Cup originally costing 10 guineas (equivalent to $50 at the time), a bowl that has become known as the Stanley Cup and has been augmented and altered into the trophy that today is awarded to the NHL's playoff champion. It is the oldest trophy for which professional athletes compete in North America and now stands almost three feet in height.

Until 1906, only amateur clubs played for the Stanley Cup but since 1910, the trophy has become symbolic of professional hockey supremacy. It travelled east and west for several years, but when the Western Canada Hockey League disbanded in 1926, the NHL took control of the Cup. Only NHL teams have competed for it since that date.

Inducted 1945.

GOVERNOR GENERAL'S TROPHIES...

Like a great many British aristocrats of the day, the men who served Canada as Governor General around the turn of the century considered themselves to be sportsmen. Often they would express a great love for the games they found in the country they served. Three such men would leave a lasting mark on Canada.

Lord Stanley was shy in public. Imagine his surprise at the excitement his name generates more than a century after he returned to Britain. Lord Minto, if he is remembered at all, is not recalled for his efforts to foster closer ties between English- and French-Canadians, but for the Minto Cup, awarded to the top junior box lacrosse team in Canada each year. Lord Grey oversaw a difficult transition period as Canada began moving from British colony to nationhood. Fans of Canadian football don't give that much thought come late November.

BARNEY STANLEY

**FORWARD/DEFENCE •
VANCOUVER (PCHA), CALGARY (WCHL),
REGINA (WCHL), EDMONTON (WCHL, WHL),
CHICAGO**

IN A 15-YEAR professional hockey career, Russell (Barney) Stanley played every position on the ice except goaltender. Despite his long and successful tenure in the game, his only Stanley Cup win came in his first year as a pro.

Barney came up through the amateur ranks, playing for Paisley, Ontario, and three Edmonton clubs between 1909 and 1915. He turned pro and joined the Vancouver Millionaires on February 15, 1915, and this club went on to win the Cup.

Stanley remained with the Millionaires through 1918-19 and then spent a season as playing coach of the amateur Edmonton Eskimos. In 1920-21, he returned to pro ranks as player and coach of the Calgary Tigers. He stayed with Calgary for two seasons before assuming similar duties with the Regina Capitals through 1923-24. In the next two seasons, he played with the Edmonton Eskimos before spending the 1926-27 season as player and coach of the Winnipeg Maroons. Barney coached and managed the Chicago Black Hawks in 1927-28, playing the following season with the Minneapolis Millers. He returned to coaching with the Edmonton Pooler juniors for three years.

He played all three forward positions during the first half of his career, shifting to defence in later years. An outstanding goal-scorer, he twice scored five goals in a game. Stanley was born in Paisley, Ontario, on June 1, 1893, and died May 16, 1971, in Edmonton. Inducted 1962.

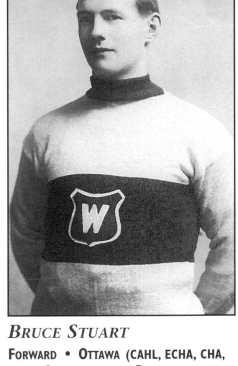

BRUCE STUART

FORWARD • OTTAWA (CAHL, ECHA, CHA, NHA), QUEBEC (CAHL), PITTSBURGH (IHL), PORTAGE LAKES (IHL), MTL. WANDERERS (ECAHA)

BRUCE STUART played on three Stanley Cup champions. He played for the Montreal Wanderers when they won the Cup in 1907-08, and with the Ottawa Senators for two Cup triumphs, in 1908-09 and 1910-11.

Born in Ottawa in 1882, Bruce developed into an all-round forward, capable of playing any frontline position, although he excelled as a rover in seven-man hockey. He joined the Senators in 1898-99 and played with them for two seasons before joining the Quebec Bulldogs. During his two years with Ottawa, he scored 12 goals in six games. After a season in Quebec, he rejoined the Senators in before moving to the International Pro League with Pittsburgh and Portage Lakes.

Bruce moved to the Montreal Wanderers in 1907-08 and helped them win a Stanley Cup. In 1908-09, he became captain of the Ottawa Senators and led that team to another Stanley Cup triumph. After losing out the following year, Stuart and the Senators came back to win the Cup again in 1910-11. In his three Cup victories, Stuart scored 17 goals in seven games. In regular-season play, he once scored six goals in a game against Quebec. He also had two five-goal games.

Stuart died in Ottawa, on October 28, 1961. Inducted 1961.

HOD STUART

DEFENCE • OTTAWA (CAHL), QUEBEC (CAHL), PORTAGE LAKES (IHL), CALUMET (IHL), PITTSBURGH (IHL), MTL. WANDERERS (ECAHA)

A TRAGIC DIVING ACCIDENT on June 23, 1907, in Belleville, Ontario, ended the life and hockey career of Hod Stuart, one of hockey's first great defencemen.

Rated one of the best of his or any other time, Hod Stuart was born in Ottawa in 1879 and rose up through the minor ranks in that city. With his brother, Bruce, he broke into big-time hockey with the Ottawa Senators in 1898-99. They moved together to the Quebec Bulldogs in 1900-01 and while Bruce returned to Ottawa after a season, Hod remained in Quebec.

Both brothers soon opted for pro careers in the United States. The Montreal Wanderers negotiated for Hod's services in December of 1906 but he turned them down, stating that he had signed a contract to captain and play for Pittsburgh that winter. On December 27, 1906, he was scheduled to play a game against the Michigan Soo but refused to go on the ice because of a disagreement with the referee. He packed his bags and joined the Wanderers for what was to be his final season.

The Wanderers won the Stanley Cup in March, 1907, defeating the Kenora Thistles. Kenora had won the Cup only two months previously. During his playing career, Hod scored a total of 16 goals in 33 games in Canadian leagues. His U.S. totals are much higher.

Inducted 1945.

CAPT. JAMES SUTHERLAND
BUILDER

OFTEN REFERRED TO as the Father of Hockey, Captain James T. Sutherland was an ardent supporter of the game who worked diligently on its behalf. Born October 10, 1870, he made his hometown of Kingston, Ontario, a famous hockey centre during the years prior to World War I.

As a coach of the Kingston Frontenac Juniors, Sutherland guided several championship teams and fanned the hockey flame throughout Eastern Ontario. He first became connected with the Ontario Hockey Association as district representative and his drive and keen interest enabled him to rise through the organization's ranks until he became president in 1915. He served two years in that office and later, after returning from overseas service in World War I, moved on to become president of the Canadian Amateur Hockey Association in 1919.

Captain Sutherland was honoured as a life member of both the OHA and CAHA. He died in Kingston on September 30, 1955.

Inducted 1947.

"CYCLONE" TAYLOR,
DEFENCE / FORWARD •
PORTAGE LA PRAIRIE (MHL SR.),
PORTAGE LAKES (IHL), OTTAWA (ECAHA, ECHA),
RENFREW (NHA), VANCOUVER (PCHA)

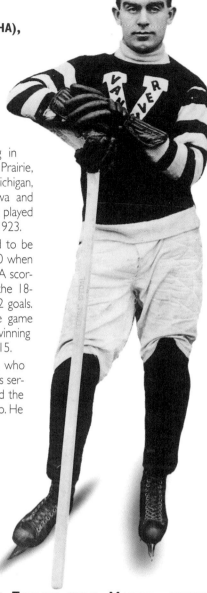

FRED "CYCLONE" TAYLOR was a brilliant hockey player in every phase of the game and starred at defence, centre and rover. When he played defence for Ottawa and Renfrew, his furious rushes earned him his famous nickname.

Taylor was born in Tara, Ontario, on June 24, 1883, but first attracted attention while playing in Listowel, Ontario. He later played in Portage la Prairie, Manitoba, before turning pro with Portage Lakes, Michigan, in 1906. He spent two-year hitches with Ottawa and Renfrew and then joined Vancouver in 1912-13. He played in Vancouver until the end of his playing career in 1923.

Cyclone's scoring feats are legend. He seemed to be like old wine — he improved with age. He was 30 when he joined Vancouver and went on to win five PCHA scoring titles while playing as a rover and centre. In the 18-game schedule of 1917-18, Taylor rapped home 32 goals. The previous season, he scored six goals in one game against Victoria. Taylor played on two Stanley Cup-winning teams, Ottawa in 1908-09 and Vancouver in 1914-15.

Fred Taylor was honoured by King George VI, who awarded him the Order of the British Empire for his services during World War II. In 1960, Cyclone turned the sod for the Hockey Hall of Fame building in Toronto. He died June 9, 1979, in Vancouver.

Inducted 1947.

JACK WALKER
ROVER/LEFT WING • PORT ARTHUR (NOHL), TORONTO (NHA), MONCTON (MPHL),
SEATTLE (PCHA), VICTORIA (WCHL, WHL), DETROIT

JACK WALKER played only two seasons in the NHL, but he enjoyed 30 years of close association with the game and won many honours as a centre and rover.

He was born in Silver Mountain, Ontario, on November 29, 1888, and learned the game in nearby Port Arthur. Starting in 1906, he played on four consecutive city championship teams. He played for Moncton of the Maritime League in 1912-13 and for the Toronto Blueshirts who won the Stanley Cup in 1913-14. After two seasons in Toronto, he went west to Seattle and, in 1916-17, again contributed to a Stanley Cup victory. Walker's third Stanley Cup came with the 1924-25 Victoria Cougars. Detroit purchased his contract before the 1926-27 season. He played two seasons with them before returning west to join Seattle. In 1931-32, Walker went on to play and manage in California with teams in Hollywood and Oakland. He retired after that season to manage, coach and referee in the Pacific Coast League.

Jack Walker is known as the man who originated the hook-check, but his other contributions to the game were noted wherever he played. He was voted MVP with Seattle in 1920, with Detroit in 1927 and 1928, and with Seattle again in 1930. He also spent many hours with young players, coaching and teaching them his hook-checking techniques. He died in Seattle, on February 16, 1950.

Inducted 1960.

Taylor's Backwards Goal...

FEBRUARY 12, 1910, was a date circled on the calendars of many hockey fans in the town of Renfrew, Ontario. For years, the hockey powers in Ottawa had prevented Renfrew teams from competing for the Stanley Cup. Now, their local heroes, the Renfrew Creamery Kings (already better known as the Renfrew Millionaires) would battle the defending Cup champion Ottawa Senators in a key meeting in the inaugural campaign of the National Hockey Association.

The game was eagerly anticipated in Ottawa, too. It would be the first chance for the fans there to show their anger at Cyclone Taylor, the star player of their 1909 Stanley Cup team who had bolted for the big bucks being offered by Renfrew's wealthy owners.

Taylor tried to make light of the situation. A few days before the game, he casually joked to Senators goalie Percy LeSueur that he would score on him after beating his former teammates while skating backwards. Word got out—and out of context—and soon the game had yet another angle. Much to the delight of the Ottawa fans, Taylor was shut out as the Senators scored an 8-5 victory. But Renfrew fans would get their revenge.

On March 8, the Senators paid a return visit to their neighbors in the Ottawa Valley. Both teams were no longer in contention for the Stanley Cup, but a victory over the hated Senators would be almost as sweet. The Renfrew players pulled out all the stops in an astonishing 17-2 victory. There are fans who attended the game that night who went to their graves insisting Taylor had scored his backwards goal. Others maintain he merely turned his back on LeSueur at the last moment before hoisting the puck past him. Taylor, who lived nearly 96 years, would never say for sure just what he had done!

HARRY TRIHEY
CENTRE • MTL. SHAMROCKS (AHA, CAHL)

HARRY TRIHEY was prominent both in sports and as a militiaman. He organized the 55th Regiment, out of which emerged the 199th Battalion, Duchess of Connaught's Own Irish Canadian Rangers. He became Lieutenant-Colonel and Commanding Officer of the 199th.

Born December 25, 1877, Trihey starred in hockey, lacrosse and football. A powerful man, he was a smart stickhandler and was the first to utilize a three-man line, leaving the rover free to roam. He also encouraged defencemen to carry the puck. On February 4, 1899, he scored 10 goals when the Shamrocks downed Quebec 13-4, a record never duplicated in regular season play. He was rover and captain of the Shamrocks when they won the Cup in 1898-99 and 1899-1900, and had earlier starred at McGill University. Although not noted for his speed, he had a deadly shot and was a clever skater.

After retiring as a player, Trihey became secretary-treasurer of the Canadian Amateur Hockey League and, later, the league president. He led the league through its disputes with the Federal League in 1904-05 and eventually became an advisor to the Montreal Wanderers, remaining associated with that club for many years. He refereed many league and Stanley Cup games. Trihey died in Montreal on December 9, 1942.

Inducted 1950.

GEORGES VEZINA
GOALTENDER • MONTREAL (NHA), MONTREAL

GEORGES VEZINA is one of the most renowned goaltenders in the history of the NHL. His name is perpetuated by the trophy presented annually to the top goaltender in the NHL as selected by the league's general managers.

He was born in Chicoutimi, Quebec, on January 7, 1888, and was so cool under pressure that he came to be known as the "Chicoutimi Cucumber." Vezina was the nearest thing to the perfect athlete, never missing a game from the time he broke into the NHL until he retired 15 years later. He was a strong competitor on the ice, and always a gentleman, seldom becoming excited in the heat of sustained goal-mouth action.

Vezina first played goal in his hometown and turned pro with the Montreal Canadiens in 1910-11. He played a total of 328 consecutive league games and 39 more in the playoffs, allowing 1,267 goals-against. He was very adroit and was able to muffle a drive and clear it while seldom allowing a rebound. Until 1922, goalies were not allowed to drop to their knees to stop the puck, making his 3.45 goals-against per game average even more remarkable. Georges played on five championship teams and on Stanley Cup winners in 1915-16 and 1923-24. His final game was played November 28, 1925, when he started against Pittsburgh despite severe chest pains. He had to retire after one period. This was the first indication of tuberculosis, which claimed him on March 26, 1926.
Inducted 1945.

MARTY WALSH
CENTRE • QUEEN'S U. (OHA), CANADIAN SOO (IHL), OTTAWA (ECAHA, ECHA, NHA)

MARTY WALSH was born in Kingston, Ontario, on October 16, 1884 and gained his first hockey notoriety with Queen's University club of the Ontario Hockey Association, that challenged Ottawa's Silver Seven in 1906. Ottawa's great centre, Frank McGee, found himself playing against Walsh. Queen's lost, but Walsh made such a fine impression that Ottawa tried to sign him after McGee retired.

Walsh didn't immediately accept the Ottawa offer. Instead, he joined the International Pro League where he broke a leg. When his leg mended, he joined Ottawa in 1908.

Walsh was a very nimble and tricky skater with a knack for always being in the right position for a shot. He was a dangerous goal scorer who played on Stanley Cup winners in 1908-09 and 1910-11. Other players on that first Cup winner included Percy LeSueur, Fred Lake, Cyclone Taylor, Bill Gilmour, Albert (Dubbie) Kerr and Bruce Stuart. Walsh had many games in which he scored a large number of goals, including: 10 against Port Arthur on March 16, 1911; seven against Montreal on March 7, 1908; six against Galt on January 5, 1910; and six against Renfrew on January 24, 1911. He was the leading scorer in the National Hockey Association for three seasons.

Marty Walsh died in Gravenhurst, Ontario, in 1915.

Inducted 1962.

HARRY E. WATSON
CENTRE • TOR. DENTALS (OHA), TOR. GRANITES (OHL), TOR. NATIONAL SEA FLEAS (OHA)

HARRY E. (MOOSE) WATSON is considered one of the greatest all-round forwards in the history of hockey. He was born in St. John's, Newfoundland, on July 14, 1898, and travelled extensively before moving to Toronto in 1915. In between, he attended school in England and moved to Winnipeg with his family in 1908. When he went to Toronto, Watson played for the St. Andrew's College and Aura Lee junior clubs. He moved from Aura Lee into senior hockey but played only a few games before joining the Canadian army in World War I.

Watson played for the Toronto Dentals in 1919, moving over to the Toronto Granites the following year. The Granites won the Allan Cup in 1921-22 and 1922-23, adding the Olympic championship in 1924. Watson was an outstanding player for Canada in the Olympics, scoring 13 of 30 goals in one game against Czechoslovakia. A fast man for his huge size, Watson was offered a $30,000 contract to play the 1925-26 season with the Montreal Maroons. He was regarded as the best amateur centre in Canada at the time. Harry had previously declined the offer of a pro contract from the Toronto St. Pats.

Only a part-time player in his later years, Watson was with the Toronto National Sea Fleas, as both player and coach in 1931 when that team went on to win the Allan Cup. He died in Toronto, on September 11, 1957.

Inducted 1962.

THE TORONTO GRANITES...

When Olympic organizers announced that there would be an International Winter Sports Week held in Chamonix, France in January of 1924, there was little trouble deciding who would represent Canada at what would become the first Winter Olympics. The country would send its top amateur team, the Toronto Granites.

When the Granites arrived in France, they found a huge outdoor ice surface had been prepared with six-inch boards used to enclose a section that measured 185-by-90 feet. If the rink seemed strange, at least the rules would be familiar. The games would be played to Canadian standards, with one exception.

At the insistence of the Americans, goaltenders would be required to remain standing at all times.

Although they never got a full practice on the unusual French ice, Canada crushed Czechoslovakia 30-0 in their opening game, beat Sweden 22-0, and then destroyed Switzerland 33-0. On a hot day with slow, slushy ice, the Granites beat Britain 19-2 in the semifinals and advanced to face the Americans for the gold medal.

The U.S. had run up equally impressive scoring statistics in reaching the finals, but the Granites defeated them 6-1 in a hard-fought game to bring the gold medal home to Canada.

FRED WAGHORNE
REFEREE

IN 50 YEARS of officiating more than 2,000 hockey games and 1,500 lacrosse games, Fred C. Waghorne was responsible for several innovations and rule changes.

He is credited with initiating the system of dropping the puck on faceoffs. Previously the puck was placed on the ice between the stick blades of the players. He also implemented the use of a whistle rather than a handbell to stop play.

Another unusual rule change came about because of a decision Waghorne had to make in the course of a game. Hockey pucks in this era were made in two pieces that were glued together. When a split puck ended up half in the net and half on the ice, Waghorne ruled no goal, reasoning that a puck conforming in size to the league rules had not passed between the goal posts.

Fred C. Waghorne was one of the pioneers of the Toronto Hockey League which was organized as the Beaches Hockey League in 1911. Born in Tunbridge Wells, England, in 1866, he died in 1956 at the age of 90.

Inducted 1961.

HARRY WESTWICK
ROVER • OTTAWA (AHA, CAHL, FAHL, ECAHA), KENORA (MHL SR.)

AN ELUSIVE style for a man of comparatively small physique earned Harry Westwick the nickname "Rat" during his early days as a member of the Ottawa Senators.

Westwick was born in Ottawa, Ontario, on April 23, 1876, and started his hockey career as a goaltender. He was also a fine lacrosse player, starring with the famous Ottawa Capitals for several seasons. In hockey, he played goal for the Ottawa Seconds but was soon converted to play rover and went on to become one of the game's outstanding competitors at this position. He played for the Aberdeens of the Ottawa City League and graduated to the Senators in 1895. He played for that team when it won three consecutive Stanley Cups, starting in 1902-03.

Westwick had his most productive season and playoffs in 1904-05, scoring a total of 24 goals in 13 games, as the Senators, who were also known as the Silver Seven, won their third consecutive Stanley Cup.

Westwick retired before another Cup came to Ottawa in 1908-09. Following his retirement as a player, he retained a close connection with the sport, refereeing briefly in the National Hockey Association. He died in Ottawa on April 3, 1957.

Inducted 1962.

CHANGES THROUGHOUT THE ERA...

THE LATTER DAYS of the nineteenth century and early years of the twentieth were a period of great change. Telephones, telegraphs and radio kept the world better informed than ever before. Bicycles and automobiles gave people a freedom of movement they had never known. Airplanes promised an even more amazing future.

Hockey, too, witnessed great change. Everything from the equipment players wore to the rinks they played in, and the cities in which those rinks were built was evolving. A game that had begun outdoors on frozen ponds had moved indoors, first to drafty wooden buildings that had to stay cold in order to maintain their natural ice, and then to large brick palaces that offered comfortable temperatures and artificial ice. Tube skates allowed players to move much faster than they ever could on their old, flat blades, and better stick-making techniques meant that pucks were flying faster. As a result, equipment had to be changed to give better protection.

Once a strictly amateur game, the best players were now being paid to perform as the professional game had spread from its roots in eastern Canada right across the west and into the United States. And as the game evolved, so too did its most prestigious trophy. Originally presented in 1893 as a challenge trophy to be held by the amateur champion of the Dominion of Canada, the Stanley Cup soon became the exclusive property of the top professional leagues of the day, first the NHA and the PCHA and then the National Hockey League. As early as 1917, it had crossed the border into America when the Seattle Metropolitans defeated the Montreal Canadiens. Like the rest of the world, hockey was changing. There would be no looking back.

FRED WHITCROFT
ROVER • KENORA (MHL SR.), EDMONTON (SR.), RENFREW (NHA)

FREDERICK WHITCROFT was a rover in the days of seven-man hockey. A large man, he was extremely fast and possessed great stickhandling ability which enabled him to become a prolific scorer.

Although he was born in Port Perry, Ontario in 1883, Fred first drew attention to his playing ability in the Peterborough, Ontario, area. He played for the Peterborough Colts in 1901 when they won the Ontario Hockey Association junior championship, defeating a good Stratford team in the final series. He played the 1905 season with Midland, Ontario, but returned to Peterborough to captain the intermediate club which won the OHA championship the following season. He shifted his services to western Canada for a season and came back to Ontario to play for the Kenora Thistles when they won the Stanley Cup in January, 1907.

At the end of the 1907 season, Whitcroft moved to Edmonton, scoring 49 goals as captain of a senior club that unsuccessfully challenged Ottawa for the Stanley Cup.

After retiring as a player, Whitcroft moved to Vancouver. He travelled considerably in the ensuing years, visiting many far-flung parts of the world. He died in Vancouver in 1931.

Inducted 1962.

"PHAT" WILSON
DEFENCE • PORT ARTHUR WAR VET'S (NOHA), IROQUOIS FALLS (NOHA), PORT ARTHUR BEARCATS (MHL SR., TBHL)

ALTHOUGH HE ENTERTAINED numerous offers to become a professional hockey player, Gordon Allan (Phat) Wilson remained an amateur throughout a lengthy career as a player and coach. Wilson was born in Port Arthur, Ontario, on December 29, 1895, and developed into one of the finest defencemen of his era.

His first senior team was the Port Arthur War Veterans. He joined the club in 1918 and remained with it until 1920. The following season he played with Iroquois Falls of the Northern Ontario Hockey Association, defeating the Soo Greyhounds for the league title. He returned to the Port Arthur Bearcats and was a member of the team that won the Allan Cup in 1925, 1926 and 1929. In 1930, Wilson played with the same team, winning the western Canada title.

A flashy type of defenceman, Wilson starred with the Port Arthur club for many seasons. He was with the team when it toured western Canada in 1926 and 1928. He retired as a player in 1933 at the age of 37, remaining as coach of the club. He coached the Bearcats in two other seasons, 1938 and 1940.

As a youth, Phat had also been a standout baseball player. He retired from the Port Arthur Public Utilities Commission at the age of 65 and resided in that city (since renamed Thunder Bay) until his death in August, 1970.

Inducted 1962.

THE ALLAN CUP...

WITH THE STANLEY CUP quickly becoming a professional trophy after the turn of the century, the Allan Cup was donated in 1908 to be awarded annually to the top senior amateur hockey team in Canada. For many years, it rivalled the Stanley Cup as the game's most prestigious trophy.

While professional teams were limited to Canada's bigger cities, virtually every community in the country boasted at least one good senior amateur squad. Local loyalties were also cemented by the fact that, unlike professional teams, most amateur players had grown up in the towns they represented. Amateur hockey was perceived as wholesome community entertainment; the pro game still was seen as being faintly unsavory. Even in Toronto and Montreal, local amateur clubs would often outdraw the professional teams.

Like the Stanley Cup, the Allan Cup was a challenge trophy in its earliest days. Interest mounted so quickly, and there were soon so many challenges, that a series of regional playoffs had to be established. The east-west rivalry these tournaments sparked further fueled the country's passions. By the 1920s, Allan Cup champions were winning for Canada at the Olympic Games, and teams like the Whitby Dunlops, Penticton Vees and Trail Smoke Eaters continued to represent Canada abroad into the 1960s.

HOCKEY'S FIRST GOLDEN ERA

1926-1943

The NHL's All-Stars played the Toronto Maple Leafs in a benefit for injured Toronto star Ace Bailey on Valentine's Day, 1934. Despite the presence of a dozen future Hall of Fame inductees in this photo, the Leafs defeated the All-Stars 7-3. The Morenz family is well represented. Howie is in the front row, third from right. Howie Jr. is the mascot sitting on the ice

CHARLES ADAMS

BUILDER

IT WAS CHARLES FRANCIS ADAMS who made hockey and the Adams name synonymous in Boston. Always an ardent fan, he saw the Stanley Cup finals of 1924 in Montreal and immediately set out to get an NHL franchise for Boston. With Art Ross, he formed the Bruins and they played the first NHL game in the United States on December 1st of the same year.

Born October 18, 1876, in Newport, Vermont, he worked his way from grocery store boy to head of a major U.S. chain, but his main love remained hockey. In 1926, he purchased the entire Western Canada Hockey League from the Patrick brothers for $300,000. Secured for the Bruins were such stars as Eddie Shore, Harry Oliver, Mickey MacKay and Duke Keats while numerous other fine players were made available to Detroit, Chicago and New York. As a result of this player-wealth, the NHL blossomed into a big-time operation.

In 1927, he guaranteed the sum of $500,000 over a five-year span, for the 24 home games the Bruins would play in each NHL season's schedule. This financial guarantee resulted in the construction of Boston Garden, where Adams saw his team win three Stanley Cups before his death in 1947.

Inducted 1960.

WESTON ADAMS SR.

BUILDER

FROM NOVEMBER 1, 1924, when his father, the late Charles F. Adams was awarded an NHL franchise, until his death on March 19, 1973, Weston W. Adams, Sr. was continuously and intimately associated with the Boston Bruins. After graduation from Harvard where he played goal, he became a director of the Bruins and, in 1932, president of the Boston Tigers, a Bruins' farm team. He succeeded his father as Bruins' president in 1936 but, when the U.S. entered World War II, served actively in the Pacific with the navy, retiring at war's end with the rank of Commander. At this time the club's corporate structure was changed as a merger was effected with the Boston Garden Arena Corporation. Weston Adams, Sr. relinquished his club presidency although remaining a majority stockholder at the Garden.

When the Bruins' fortunes flagged he set about an intensive recruiting program and personally scouted all over North America. He became chairman of the board of the Boston Garden in 1956 and two years later was elected chairman of the hockey club as well. By 1964 he was club president again, remaining in office until 1969 when he retired in favour of his son, Weston, Jr. He was club president during two Bruins' Stanley Cup victories — 1939 and 1941 — and assembled the executive, associates and coaching staff which produced two more — 1970 and 1972. He is also responsible for the now-common practice of removing the goaltender for an extra attacker on a delayed penalty call. These were the crowning awards for a man who made an enormous contribution to the game of hockey.

Inducted 1972.

FRANK AHEARN

BUILDER

FRANK AHEARN was the pride, the power and the passion behind Ottawa's great NHL days of the 1920s. Numerous stars of that era played for him, and all held him in high esteem. Previously active in promoting both junior and senior amateur hockey, he turned to the pro sport in the early 1920s for two reasons: he had an aversion to the phony amateurism of the day and also wanted to see a new arena built. Ahearn bought out Tommy Gorman in 1924, became sole owner of the Ottawa Senators and assembled a playing lineup with such stars as Hooley Smith, Alex Connell, Allan Shields, Alex Smith, Jack Adams, Frank Finnigan, Hec Kilrea, George Boucher, Frank Nighbor and Syd Howe. His team won the Stanley Cup in 1926-27.

The Depression halted his benevolence and he reluctantly was obliged to sell off his star attractions in a series of outstanding deals. He eventually disposed of his rink holdings but despite his shrewd player sales, his hockey losses were estimated at $200,000. Ahearn was born May 10, 1886, in Ottawa and died November 17, 1962.

Inducted 1962.

"ACE" BAILEY
LEFT WING • TORONTO

IRVIN (ACE) BAILEY'S NHL career was relatively brief, due to a disastrous incident on December 12, 1933, when a collision with Eddie Shore resulted in a fractured skull that terminated his playing days. But in the 7-1/2 seasons as an outstanding winger with the Toronto Maple Leafs, Bailey established himself as both a scorer and a defensive star.

Born July 3, 1903, in Bracebridge, Ontario, he played both hockey and lacrosse. He played junior hockey with Toronto St. Mary's and senior with Peterborough where he was known as an adept scorer and checker.

He signed with the Toronto St. Patricks and when they became the Maple Leafs, he, along with Hap Day and Babe Dye, were the cornerstones of the new club. Bailey was the club's top scorer until Charlie Conacher hit his stride, leading the NHL in both scoring and points in 1928-29. He also played on the Stanley Cup-winning team of 1931-32.

When the Kid Line (Conacher-Jackson-Primeau) stole the scoring glory with the Leafs, Bailey combined with Baldy Cotton as one of the finest penalty-killing duos in the league. Bailey's puck-ragging efficiency was renowned and it was while he was performing this specialty that his near-fatal accident occurred in Boston. After several weeks near death he came around and effected a complete recovery.

Ace later coached, then joined the staff of minor officials at Maple Leaf Gardens where he remained for many years. In 313 NHL games, Ace scored 111 goals and had 82 assists. He died April 7, 1992.

Inducted 1975.

MARTY BARRY
CENTRE • NY AMERICANS, BOSTON, DETROIT, MONTREAL

THE RECORD BOOKS show that Marty Barry was almost 24 years old before he made it into the NHL to stay. Once there, however, he achieved great success.

Marty was born December 8, 1905, in St. Gabriel, Quebec, a place best known as Valcartier Camp to men who served in World War I. He was a product of Montreal amateur hockey, playing in the Mount Royal Intermediate League with Gurney Foundry in the 1922-23 season. He played a season with St. Michael's, then two with St. Anthony.

Newsy Lalonde signed him to play for the New York Americans in the spring of 1927, but he played only nine games. He went to the Philadelphia Arrows and then to the New Haven Eagles in 1928-29 where he won the league scoring title. He finally made the NHL to stay with the Boston Bruins in the 1929-30 season and remained with them until 1935 when he was traded to Detroit.

It was with the Red Wings that he played on a line with Herbie Lewis and Larry Aurie that was of the most effective combinations in the league. The Wings won the Stanley Cup in 1935-36 and 1936-37, Barry won the Lady Byng Trophy and was named to the First All-Star Team in 1936-37. Barry completed his NHL career with the Montreal Canadiens in 1939-40 then turned to coaching. He died August 20, 1969, at his home in Halifax, Nova Scotia.

Inducted 1965.

ACE BAILEY INCIDENT...

Because of the long-running feud between Maple Leafs boss Conn Smythe and Art Ross of the Bruins, matches between Toronto and Boston were always hard-fought. The game on December 12, 1933 was even rougher than most.

During the second period, Boston's Eddie Shore was checked hard by King Clancy at the end of one of the Bruins defenceman's patented rushes. As Clancy scooped up the loose puck and headed for the Boston end, Toronto's Ace Bailey dropped back toward his own blueline. An angry Shore blindsided Bailey, whose head struck the ice when he fell. As Bailey lay motionless, Red Horner attacked

Shore and cut him badly. Bailey had suffered a broken skull. A series of delicate operations managed to save his life, but his hockey career was over. Shore recovered from his injuries and was back playing by the end of January after serving a 16-game suspension.

On February 14, 1933, the first All-Star Game in NHL history was held as a benefit for Ace Bailey. Prior to the game, he met Shore at centre ice and the two shook hands amid a thunderous ovation from the fans at Maple Leaf Gardens.

FRANK BOUCHER
CENTRE • OTTAWA, VANCOUVER (PCHA, WCHL, WHL), NY RANGERS

FRANK BOUCHER devoted more than a half-century to hockey and, above all else, was a gentleman. Considered one of game's great playmakers, he won the Lady Byng Trophy seven times in eight seasons and was finally given permanent possession of the original trophy.

Born October 7, 1901, in Ottawa, he was a member of a hockey-playing family. At one time, four Bouchers were playing major league hockey — George with Ottawa, Billy and Bob with the Canadiens and Frank with Vancouver.

Tommy Gorman offered him $1,200 a year to play for Ottawa and he leapt at the chance. Ottawa was a powerhouse team featuring stars Frank Nighbor, Clint Benedict, Eddie Gerard, Cy Denneny, Punch Broadbent and brother George Boucher — all members of the Hockey Hall of Fame. At first Frank rode the bench with another fellow named King Clancy. He played the next four years with the Vancouver Maroons, but when the western leagues broke up, he went to New York and wound up centring Bill and Bun Cook on one of the great lines of the era.

Frank stayed with the Rangers' organization from 1926 until 1944, playing on two Stanley Cup winners and was three times named to the first all-star team and once to the second. Although retired as a player, he coached the Rangers to another Stanley Cup win in 1939-40. He died December 12, 1977, in Kemptville, Ontario.

Inducted 1958.

FRANK BRIMSEK
GOALTENDER • BOSTON, CHICAGO

FRANK BRIMSEK was a star virtually from the day he stepped into the NHL. He was also one of the first players born in the United States who rose to stardom in the sport. A goaltender, he was such a fierce competitor that he didn't even like to have goals scored on him in practice.

Born September 26, 1915, in Eveleth, Minnesota, he replaced the great Cecil (Tiny) Thompson in the Boston nets early in the 1938-39 season and went on to win both the Vezina Trophy as the league's top goalie and the Calder Trophy as the outstanding rookie. He was almost immediately tabbed "Mr. Zero" because he twice registered shutout strings of three games in a row. Brimsek played in the NHL through the 1949-50 season, finishing his career with a one year stint in Chicago. He missed two seasons during World War II while he served in the U.S. Coast Guard, aboard a patrol boat in the South Pacific.

It would be difficult to exceed that success of his first season, but Brimsek remained a star, playing on another Stanley Cup winner in 1940-41 and winning another Vezina Trophy in 1941-42. He was also voted twice to the Second All-Star Team. In the 1940s, the Vezina and All-Star berths were hotly contested by Brimsek, Bill Durnan and Turk Broda, the top goaltenders of the era.

Inducted 1966.

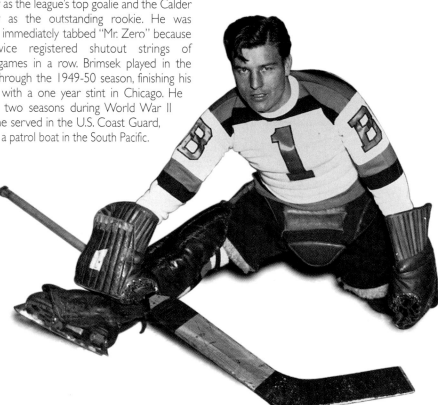

WALTER BROWN
BUILDER

WALTER BROWN left a rich legacy to the sports world. At the time of his death in 1964, he was president of Boston Garden, chairman of the Basketball Hall of Fame Corporation, member of the Hockey Hall of Fame Governing Committee and past president of the IIHF. He was also co-owner and president of the Boston Bruins and the Boston Celtics.

Born February 10, 1905, he followed in the footsteps of his father, George V. Brown, as a strong promoter of hockey in schools and colleges. He succeeded his father as general manager of Boston Garden in 1937. For several years he took amateur teams globetrotting to Europe. He coached the Boston Olympics between 1930 and 1940 when this team won five U.S. national amateur championships and one world title. He was a genial man, often outspoken, but a man who devoted his life to sport in general and hockey in particular.

He died September 7, 1964. Inducted 1962.

J.P. BICKELL
BUILDER

BORN SPETEMBER 26, 1884, JOHN PARIS BICKELL had a brilliant career as an industrialist, mining executive, financier and public servant whose hockey involvement came in a roundabout manner. Through a business association with Charlie Querrie, managing director of the Toronto St. Pats hockey club, Bickell became a silent partner with $25,000 invested. When the St. Pats were purchased by the newly formed Maple Leaf hockey club in 1927, Conn Smythe convinced Bickell to transfer his interests, both financial and personal, to the Leafs. Bickell supported Smythe's view that a new arena was needed and provided financial knowledge and support so that Maple Leaf Gardens stock was sold and the building erected in five months during the worst economic depression of the 20th century.

He became the first president, and chairman of the board of Maple Leaf Gardens, serving until his death on August 22, 1951. He also set the Gardens on a solid financial basis by appointing a bank colleague, George Cottrelle, as financial overseer. His memory is perpetuated by the Bickell Memorial Cup, awarded at the discretion of Maple Leaf Gardens' directors to a member of the Leafs' team who performs with a very high standard of excellence.

Inducted 1978.

BILLY BURCH
CENTRE • HAMILTON, NY AMERICANS, BOSTON, CHICAGO

BILLY BURCH was born in Yonkers, New York, on November 20, 1900, but came to Canada as a boy and learned his hockey around Toronto. He turned pro with the Hamilton Tigers in 1923 and centred a line of the Green brothers, Redvers (Red) and Wilfred (Shorty), which carried the team to first place in the NHL in 1924-25. Burch was awarded the Hart Trophy that season as the most valuable player to his team.

The Hamilton team was shifted to the U.S. where it became the New York Americans in 1925 and Burch, an excellent playmaker and stickhandler, was made captain. In 1926-27, he was winner of the Lady Byng Trophy, but missed part of the 1927-28 season because of a knee injury. Billy remained with the Americans until 1932, when he was sold to Boston, who in turn let him go to Chicago. This was his last active year as, near the end of the season, he broke a leg and decided to retire.

Billy Burch led his teams in scoring in the seasons of 1923, 1924, 1925, 1926 and 1928. His record shows that in 390 regular season games, he scored 137 goals and earned 53 assists. A strike and lockout of Hamilton players over playoff bonus money in 1925 cost Burch his best chance to be on a Stanley Cup winner. The Tigers had finished first but were dropped from the playoffs when they could not come to terms with management regarding payment for the series. He died in December, 1950.

Inducted 1974.

NHL IN AMERICA...

In 1914, the Pacific Coast Hockey Association became the first Canadian league to expand into the United States when a team was placed in Portland, Oregon. It would be another ten years before the NHL made a similar move south. Once it began, though, U.S. expansion progressed rapidly.

The Boston Bruins were the first American team in the NHL, joining the league with the Montreal Maroons in 1924. A year later, the Hamilton Tigers relocated and became the New York Americans. The Pittsburgh Pirates also joined the league. In 1926, the New York Rangers, Chicago Black Hawks and Detroit Cougars (later the Falcons, then Red Wings) joined the NHL.

A mere three seasons after the NHL entered the U.S., American franchises outnumbered Canadian ones six to four. For the next 12 years the NHL operated with Canadian and American divisions.

Angus Campbell

Builder

ANGUS CAMPBELL was an athlete who combined ability with intellect. He was born March 19, 1884, in Stayner, Ontario, and received his early education there. He graduated from the University of Toronto in 1911 with a B.A.Sc. degree in mining engineering.

Campbell played hockey and lacrosse while at the U. of T. and was on championship teams in both sports. During the 1909-10 season he was in Cobalt, Ontario, where he held a student mine position, and played on a team with such greats as Walter Smaill, Art Ross, Herb Clarke and Tommy Smith. He returned to Cobalt after graduation and played hockey there until 1914.

After his hockey career, Campbell played an important part in the development of amateur hockey in Northern Ontario. He was first president of the Northern Ontario association when the NOHA was formed in 1919. He later became an executive on the Ontario Hockey Association. He died in 1976, in Toronto.

Inducted 1964.

Tex's Rangers...

In 1920, boxing promoter G.L. "Tex" Rickard formed a group to build a new Madison Square Garden in New York. Almost as an afterthought, an ice-making plant was installed. In 1925, the facility was leased to the New York Americans. When they proved a box-office success, Rickard decided the arena should have a hockey team of its own. The first group of players assembled were dubbed "Tex's Rangers" by sportswriters in a playful reference to the famed Texas lawmen. That name stuck, and the New York Rangers were born.

Neil Colville

Centre • NY Rangers

NEIL COLVILLE played his entire pro career with one organization — the New York Rangers. He is best remembered as a member of New York's famous "Bread Line" with his brother Mac and Alex Shibicky. Born August 4, 1914, in Edmonton, he played three seasons of junior hockey in and around Edmonton before moving into the Rangers' organization. Early in 1934, he joined the New York Crescents, a Rangers' farm team in the Eastern Amateur League. That season, the Crescents won the league title. He advanced to the Philadelphia Ramblers for the 1935-36 season. The Ramblers were league champions as well and Colville was leading scorer until about six weeks from the end of the schedule when he was sidelined by an injury.

Colville moved up to the Rangers in 1936 and played on the Bread Line for six years. During these years, the Rangers won the Stanley Cup in 1940 and the NHL championship in 1942. Neil captained the team for six seasons and was named to an all-star team three times. From 1942 to 1945, he was with the Canadian armed forces, stationed in Ottawa where he captained the 1942-43 Allan Cup-winning Ottawa Commandos. He served as a navigator with the Royal Canadian Air Force until 1945, when he was discharged, returning to the Rangers where he played four more seasons on defence. He died December 26, 1987.

Inducted 1967.

Joseph Cattarinich

Builder

HE WAS OFTEN called "The Quiet One". Born November 13, 1881 in Levis, Quebec, Cattarinich was a man of few words whose word was his bond. He was a selfless athlete who excelled at lacrosse and was also a good hockey player.

As a goaltender, he was playing against Chicoutimi and could not help but notice the sensational play of the opposing netminder. He prevailed upon his manager to sign the Chicoutimi goalie unselfishly giving up his position to someone he felt was better. That other goalie was Georges Vezina who became a legend for the Montreal Canadiens.

Cattarinich played an important role in the development of the National Hockey League, in a manner which usually went unnoticed because he wanted it that way. On November 3, 1921, Cattarinich, Leo Dandurand and Louis Letourneau purchased the Montreal Canadiens for $11,000 and built the club into the "Flying Frenchmen" with many of the great stars of the era such as Newsy Lalonde, Howie Morenz, Joe Malone, Aurel Joliat, Vezina and others.

Under this management the club enjoyed glorious years, winning the NHL title and the Stanley Cup on three occasions. Letourneau retired in 1931, but the other two kept the Canadiens until 1935 when they sold the team for $165,000. Cattarinich would like to have retained the club but Depression-era economics time made it impossible.

On December 7, 1938, while recovering from an eye operation, he suffered a heart attack and died in New Orleans. Inducted 1977.

"KING" CLANCY

DEFENCE • OTTAWA, TORONTO

THE IRISH OF OTTAWA produced many fine athletes, but none more outstanding than Francis (King) Clancy. He was one of the most refreshing athletes ever to compete in the NHL. Clancy was born February 25, 1903, and acquired the name King through inheritance from an equally outstanding father.

He played amateur hockey with St. Brigid's, but signed to play professionally at the age of 18 with the Ottawa Senators. King became a regular with that club after the retirement of Eddie Gerard and quickly established himself as an outstanding player. In 1930, Clancy was the key figure in what has since been called "the best deal in hockey." Conn Smythe, manager of the Toronto Maple Leafs, paid the then-unheard-of sum of $35,000 and two players to acquire Clancy from Ottawa. Smythe obviously saw the leadership qualities he desired in Clancy and the King repaid him by leading the Leafs to their first Stanley Cup victory in 1931-32.

He was twice named to each of the First and Second NHL All-Star Teams and remained an outstanding rushing defenceman until he retired early in the 1936-37 season. Clancy coached the Montreal Maroons for the first half of the 1937-38 season and then became a referee. He returned to coach the Leafs from 1950 to 1953 before moving up to become assistant manager. "The time to quit is when it's no longer fun," King once said, and hockey remained fun for him throughout his life. He died November 8, 1986, in Toronto.

Inducted 1958.

"DIT" CLAPPER

RIGHT WING/DEFENCE • BOSTON

FEW PLAYERS have accomplished as much in their hockey careers as Aubrey (Dit) Clapper, who was the first NHLer to play in the league for 20 years. His steady genius graced NHL arenas from 1927 to 1947.

He was only 13 when he played junior at Oshawa, Ontario and was just 19 when he became a regular with the Boston Bruins. In between, he played for the Toronto Parkdale Canoe Club. Through his 20 seasons with Boston, Clapper played nine seasons at right wing and 11 on defence and was regarded as "an athlete's athlete." He was a big player, over six feet and 200 pounds, but most often used his heft to stop fights.

Dit scored his 200th goal in Toronto in 1941, giving his Bruins a 1-0 victory over the Maple Leafs. He finished with 228 goals and 246 assists in the regular season along with 13 goals and 17 assists in the playoffs. His highest single-season scoring mark was 41 goals in the 44-game schedule of 1929-30. Clapper played on three Stanley Cup championship teams with Boston: 1928-29, 1938-39, and 1940-41. He was also named three times to each of the first and second NHL All-Star Teams.

On February 12, 1947, Dit Clapper officially retired from playing hockey. The Boston Bruins retired his number 5 sweater and he was elected to the Hockey Hall of Fame. He coached the Bruins for two years and returned to hockey from business life to coach the Buffalo Bisons of the American Hockey League for one season in 1960. Born February 9, 1907 in Newmarket, Ontario, he died January 21, 1978, in Peterborough, Ontario.

Inducted 1947.

1920s DEVELOPMENTS

• 1924-25: Hamilton Tigers players are suspended after striking for more pay. 1925-26: Hamilton franchise transferred to New York City where the team was called the Americans. Pittsburgh granted new franchise. Odie Cleghorn is named playing coach of the hockey Pirates and is first to change players "on the fly." • Goalie pads not to exceed 12 inches in width. • Team aggregate payroll not to exceed $35,000. 1926-27: Western Hockey League folds. Players are sold to NHL clubs, including three new franchises: New York Rangers, Detroit Cougars and Chicago Black Hawks. • Blue line now 60 feet from the goal line. Formerly, blue lines were 20 feet from centre ice. Forward passing is only allowed in this now-enlarged neutral zone. • Not enough offence: 84 out of 224 games end in shutouts. 1927-28: Toronto St. Pats sold to Toronto Maple Leafs Hockey Club. • Detroit Olympia opens. • Limit on player salaries removed • Frank Boucher wins the first of seven Lady Byng trophies. 1928-29: Back passes into a team's defensive zone now considered delay of game.

CHARLIE CONACHER
RIGHT WING • TORONTO, DETROIT, NY AMERICANS

HE WAS BIG and strong, and with a heavy shot that was the nemesis of every goaltender in the NHL. That was Charlie Conacher, member of a famous athletic family, who played 12 seasons in the league before retiring.

Considered one of the greatest right wingers of any era, Conacher was born December 10, 1909, in Toronto. He was as neat and shifty around the net as he was adept at blasting through with a bullet-like shot. He made the jump into the NHL directly from junior hockey. He last played amateur for the Toronto Marlboros in the 1928-29 season, joining the Maple Leafs after the Marlboros had won the Memorial Cup. Conacher played nine seasons with Toronto before being traded to Detroit where he played for a year.

From 1939 until 1941, he was with the New York Americans, retiring at the end of that season. During his NHL career, Conacher scored 225 goals and won the scoring title in 1933-34 and 1934-35. In all, he was the league's top goal scorer on five occasions, sharing the lead with Bill Cook in 1931-32 and Bill Thoms in 1935-36. He was a first all-star three times and second all-star on two occasions.

Charlie turned to coaching junior hockey after leaving the NHL, winning the Memorial Cup with Oshawa in 1944. He returned to the NHL in 1947 to coach the Chicago Black Hawks. He left Chicago after the 1949-50 season and retired into the business world.

He died December 30, 1967, in Toronto.

Inducted 1961.

LIONEL CONACHER
DEFENCE • PITTSBURGH, NY AMERICANS, MTL. MAROONS, CHICAGO

LIONEL CONACHER was an imposing presence on the ice and a fine defensive tactician. "The Big Train" stood 6'1" and 195 pounds and primarily played left defence.

Born in Toronto May 29, 1900, he first skated when he was 16. He was on the ice when the first amateur hockey game play-by-play was broadcast on the radio on February 8, 1923. By this time he had turned down contract overtures by both the Toronto St. Patricks and Montreal Canadiens. An athletic scholarship to Bellefonte Academy in Pittsburgh gave reason for Conacher to head south. He captained the Pittsburgh Yellow Jackets to the U.S. amateur title in 1924 and 25.

Conacher turn pro on November 11, 1925 when he retooled the champion Yellow Jackets into the newly named Pirates of the NHL. He scored the first goal in franchise history. The following season he was dealt to the New York Americans where played four seasons. In 1929-30, he served as the club's playing-coach but gave up that role when the Montreal Maroons traded for his services prior to the 1930-31 season. He joined Chicago in 1933 and helped the Black Hawks win their first Stanley Cup. The following year, he returned to the Montreal Maroons where he would play his final three NHL campaigns. He added another championship when the Maroons won the Stanley Cup in 1935. He finally retired from the NHL after the 1937 playoffs.

Conacher was the Hart Trophy runner-up on two occasions, in 1934 and again in 1937. He played in the historic Ace Bailey Benefit Game in 1934., the forerunner to the NHL All-Star game.

Lionel Conacher's hockey career was often over shadowed by his excellence in other sports, particularly football and lacrosse. He was named Canada's male athlete and football player of the half-century in 1950.

He was elected to the Ontario Legislature in 1937 and the federal House of Commons in 1949, serving until his death on May 26, 1954. He is a charter member of the Canadian Sports Hall of Fame (1955), Canadian Football Hall of Fame and Museum (June 19, 1963) and Canadian Lacrosse Hall of Fame and Museum (January 19, 1966).

Inducted 1994.

RULE CHANGES OF 1929-30...

OFFENSIVE PRODUCTION in hockey had declined dramatically during the 1920s. Double-digit numbers in shutouts had become the norm for NHL goalies and, in 1928-29, George Hainsworth reached an all-time high with 22 shutouts in just 44 games. The average number of goals scored by both teams combined that season was three!

In 1929-30, the NHL made several moves to increase offensive production. The most important new rule allowed forward passing inside the attacking zone. (Previously, passing had only been allowed in the defensive end and neutral zone). The results were extreme. Little more than a month into the season, goal-scoring had jumped to seven per game. Changes would again have to be made.

A new rule for the rest of the 1929-30 season decreed that no offensive player would be allowed to precede the puck into their opponent's zone. Hockey's modern offside rule had been born.

ALEX CONNELL

GOALTENDER • OTTAWA, DETROIT, NY AMERICANS, MTL. MAROONS

ALEX CONNELL set a goaltending record during the 1927-28 season that has stood the test of time. He registered six consecutive shutouts and was not scored upon for 446 minutes and nine seconds, a record that still holds firm almost 70 years later. He was known as the "Ottawa Fireman," partly because of his position as secretary of the Ottawa Fire Department and partly because he often put out the fire of opposition marksmen.

Born in Ottawa February 8, 1901, Connell was also a standout baseball and lacrosse player. He was a catcher in the Interprovincial League and played on Ottawa's Eastern Canada lacrosse champions of the 1920s. Connell entered hockey almost by accident, being talked into playing goal while serving in the army at Kingston in World War I. Returning to civilian life, he played for St. Brigid's and for the Cliffsides where his trademark became the small black cap he wore while tending goal.

He turned pro with the Ottawa Senators in 1924 when the team's regular goalie, Clint Benedict, went to the Montreal Maroons. With Connell in goal, Ottawa won the Stanley Cup in 1926-27. The following year he set his fabulous shutout streak. That year he allowed only 57 goals in 44 games. Alex retired in 1933 but soon made a comeback and helped the Montreal Maroons win the Stanley Cup in 1935. He continued to coach junior teams until 1949, spending several seasons with the St. Patricks College juniors. He died in Ottawa on May 10, 1958.

Inducted 1958.

BILL COOK

RIGHT WING • SASKATOON (WCHL, WHL), NY RANGERS

DURING HIS 12-YEAR STAY in the NHL, Bill Cook scored 228 goals and added 140 assists. He was a member of one of the all-time great lines, with brother Bun Cook and playmaking centre Frank Boucher. A strong sharpshooter, he played on two Cup champions with the Rangers in 1927-28 and 1932-33.

Born October 8, 1895, in Brantford, Ontario, Bill played junior, intermediate and senior hockey in Kingston and Sault Ste. Marie before turning professional in 1922 with the Saskatoon Sheiks. Cook became a star during four years in the Western Canada Hockey League, winning the scoring championship on three occasions. In 1924-25, he scored 31 goals in 30 games.

The New York Rangers entered the NHL in 1926, coinciding with the demise of the WHL, and the Rangers purchased the contracts of both Cook brothers, later adding Boucher to form their great scoring unit. Bill Cook added the NHL scoring crown to his laurels in that first season, scoring 33 goals in 44 games. He tied Charlie Conacher with 34 goals to lead the league in 1931-32 and won the honours outright the following season with 28 goals. He retired from the NHL in 1937 after being named to the first all-star team three times and to the second team on one occasion. His WCHL record was 88 goals and 53 assists. He died April 6, 1986, in Kingston, Ontario.

Inducted 1952.

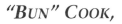

"BUN" COOK,

LEFT WING • SASKATOON (WCHL, WHL), NY RANGERS, BOSTON

FRED (BUN) COOK enjoyed immense success as an amateur and a professional. He registered 302 point in an 11-year NHL career and was recognized as an innovator and credited with being the first to perfect the drop pass.

Born September 18, 1903, Cook played minor hockey in his hometown of Kingston, Ontario before helping Sault Ste. Marie to the Allan Cup championship in 1924. The following season, he travelled west to Saskatoon to make his pro debut.

Cook and his brother Bill joined the newly established New York Rangers in 1926. Both contributed to the club's Stanley Cup win in 1928. Bun and Bill Cook combined with Frank Boucher to form one of hockey's most creative forward combinations. This trio led New York to its second Cup in 1933.

After a memorable decade in New York, Cook joined the Boston Bruins for the 1936-37 season, retiring at its conclusion with 158 goals and 144 assists for 302 points. He was an NHL Second Team All-Star in 1931 and a perennial favourite with fans at Madison Square Garden.

A student of hockey, Cook went on to a successful coaching career, taking over behind the bench for the Providence Reds of the AHL in 1937. His club won the Calder Cup in 1938 and 1940. He then moved on to the AHL Cleveland Barons and dominated the league, winning five playoff championships between 1945 and 1954. He coached two additional season in the Eastern Professional league before retiring in 1958. He died March 19, 1988.

Inducted 1995.

ART COULTER
DEFENCE • CHICAGO, NY RANGERS

ART COULTER was born in Winnipeg on May 31, 1909, and started his hockey career with the Pilgrim Athletic Club in that city in 1924. He became a pro in 1929 in Philadelphia and entered the NHL with the Chicago Black Hawks in 1931-32.

An athlete of exceptional physical strength and endurance, he had a fierce, aggressive devotion to the principles of team play. A defenceman, he partnered Taffy Abel as a strong unit when Chicago won the Stanley Cup in 1933-34. He made the second NHL all-star team in 1934-35, but in mid-season of the following year was traded to the Rangers for Earl Seibert in a deal that was to prove beneficial to both clubs. A prototype of the solid defensive defenceman, Coulter succeeded Bill Cook as the Rangers' captain in 1935-36 and was chosen to the second all-star team three more times — 1937-38, 1938-39 and 1939-40 — against such formidable opposition as Eddie Shore and Dit Clapper of the Bruins, Ebbie Goodfellow of Detroit, Earl Seibert of Chicago and Babe Siebert of the Canadiens. He played on another Stanley Cup winner with the Rangers in 1940 and, after two more seasons, entered the Canadian Armed Forces during World War II, ending his pro career. During his 11 NHL seasons, Art Coulter had a record of 30 goals and 82 assists. This appears not too impressive by modern standards, but Coulter's value is measured by his leadership qualities and concentration on defensive responsibilities.

Inducted 1974.

BILL COWLEY
CENTRE • ST. LOUIS, BOSTON

IN A 13-YEAR NHL career, Bill Cowley established a reputation as a remarkable playmaker able to pass the puck "on a dime" to his wingmen. Cowley turned professional with the St. Louis Eagles for the 1934-35 season. One year later, he was purchased by the Boston Bruins and remained with them until retiring after the 1946-47 season.

He played on championship teams in 1938-39, 1939-40 and 1940-41, and on Stanley Cup winners the first and third year of that skein. Bill Cowley was twice voted winner of the Hart Trophy as the MVP to his team — 1941 and 1943 — and was selected to the First All-Star Team four times and to the Second Team once. His lifetime regular-season record in the NHL is 195 goals and 353 assists, plus 12 goals and 34 assists in playoff competition. Indicative of his great playmaking, he won the NHL scoring title in 1940-41 with 62 points — 17 goals and 45 assists — in 46 games. In the 1943-44 season he amassed 72 points in 36 games, only to lose the scoring title when injury sidelined him for the last six weeks of the schedule.

Born in Bristol, Quebec, on June 12, 1912, Cowley moved to Ottawa in 1920. After retiring as a player, he coached teams at Renfrew (Ontario) and Vancouver, before opening and operating hotels in Smiths Falls, Ontario, and in Ottawa. He died December 31, 1993.

Inducted 1968.

LEO DANDURAND
BUILDER

THE NAME OF LEO DANDURAND was synonymous with the promotion, development and progress of major sports, not only in Quebec but across North America. Born July 9, 1889, in Bourbonnais, Illinois, he came to Canada in 1905.

Leo was interested in all sports and had a golden touch, born of extraordinary executive ability and a geniality that made him liked by all. He became associated with Joseph Cattarinich, and later with Louis Letourneau to become known as the Three Musketeers of Sport. This trio bought the Montreal Canadiens on November 3, 1921, for $11,000 and built the club into the "Flying Frenchmen" featuring many or the top players of the day. Sixteen years later, the club was sold for $165,000.

Dandurand was also a director of Montreal Royals baseball club and a key figure in the rejuvenation of pro football in Montreal. He was also very active in horse racing. In earlier years, he had been a referee in the National Hockey Association. He died June 26, 1964.

Inducted 1963

"HAP" DAY
LEFT WING/DEFENCE •
TORONTO, NY AMERICANS

CLARENCE DAY was an exemplary young man with a provocative sense of humour, earning him the nickname Happy, or Hap. He was born in Owen Sound, Ontario, on June 1, 1901. In his amateur career, Day played junior with Midland Juniors and senior with the Hamilton Tigers before joining the University of Toronto while he studied pharmacy. Charlie Querrie talked him into playing professionally with the Toronto St. Patricks on Dec. 13, 1924. He went on to enjoy 33 years of association with pro hockey, as a player, coach, referee and general manager.

Day became an outstanding defenceman and paired with King Clancy to form one of the great units of all time. He was captain of the first Toronto Maple Leafs team to win the Stanley Cup, in 1931-32, scoring three goals in that year's playoffs. During his playing career, Day scored a total of 86 goals and assisted on another 116. He played his final season, 1937-38, with the New York Americans, became a referee for two seasons, then returned to the Leafs and became a highly successful coach. Day-coached teams won five Stanley Cups including three in a row from 1947 to 1949. The most memorable of his victories came in 1942 against Detroit when the Red Wings won the first three games of the final before the Leafs rebounded to win the final four games and the Cup.

Day became the Leafs' manager in 1950 and retired in 1957 to enter business life. As a coach, he also guided the West Toronto Nationals to a Memorial Cup in 1936.

He died Feb. 17, 1990.

Inducted 1961.

GORDIE DRILLON
LEFT WING • TORONTO, MONTREAL

GORDIE DRILLON played only seven seasons in the NHL — six with Toronto and one with the Canadiens — but in that time scored 155 goals for an average of more than 22 a season. This was in an era when a 20-goal season was outstanding. Drillon led the league in both goals and points in 1937-38 and was a member of the 1941-42 Cup-winning Leafs.

Born October 23, 1914, in Moncton, New Brunswick, he broke into the Leafs' lineup in 1936-37 as a temporary replacement for the ailing Charlie Conacher. Drillon stood six feet tall and weighed 185, and although not as aggressive as Conacher, proved to be a great goal-scorer. His knack of being in position for a shot on goal was similar to that of Nels Stewart. He was a standout in the next two seasons, winning the Lady Byng in 1937-38, and was selected to the NHL's First All-Star Team in both 1937-38 and 1938-39.

The Leafs won the league championship in 1937-38, sparked by the line of Drillon, Syl Apps and Bob Davidson. In 1940-41 he led the team in scoring for the third straight season and in his final season with the Leafs, earned a berth on the Second All-Star Team playing on a line with Apps and Nick Metz. He was sold to Montreal and played one more season, finishing his NHL career with a 50-point effort from 28 goals and 22 assists. He died September 22, 1986.

Inducted 1975.

JIMMY DUNN
BUILDER

AT THE TIME of his induction into the Hockey Hall of Fame in 1968, Jimmy Dunn had completed 50 years of service to hockey.

His involvement in the game began immediately after World War I, where he served with distinction, winning the Military Medal for bravery. Jimmy served as league secretary, convener and timekeeper when his leagues became part of the Manitoba Amateur Hockey Association in 1927. In 1942 he became MAHA vice-president and three years later began a six-year tenure as president. Later, he served as the Canadian Amateur Hockey Association's vice-president and president.

He retained an active interest in Manitoba hockey affairs, acting as convener of international tournaments in 1967 and 1968 and secretary-treasurer of the Manitoba Hockey Players Federation, Inc.

Jimmie Dunn held offices in a variety of other sports: baseball, softball, football, lacrosse, speed skating, basketball, boxing and track and field. And through it all, he always retained the respect and admiration of others for his dedication and resolution.

Born March 24, 1898, he resided in Winnipeg until his death January 7, 1979.

Inducted 1968.

"Red" Dutton
Defence • Calgary (WCHL, WHL), Mtl. Maroons, NY Americans

In his playing days, Mervyn (Red) Dutton was one of the most penalized players in hockey. Opposing forwards had plenty of respect for this crashing defenceman. He later served as NHL president in 1943-44 and 1944-45, continuing to earn great respect both for himself and for the NHL.

Red was born July 23, 1898, in Russell, Manitoba, but for most of his life made Calgary his home. His hockey career almost ended before it began. He stopped a shrapnel blast at Vimy in World War I and barely avoided amputation of his leg. Miraculously, he recovered and diligently practiced seven hours a day to strengthen the leg so he could play hockey. This hard work paid off as Dutton played professionally with Calgary from 1921 through 1926.

When the Patricks sold the Western Hockey League to eastern interests, Dutton signed with Eddie Gerard and the Montreal Maroons. Dutton stayed with the Maroons until 1930 when he shifted to the New York Americans. In 1936, he took over coaching and managing the club and remained with the Amerks until 1942 when the team ceased operations.

When Frank Calder, the NHL president, died in 1943, Dutton was asked to fill the post and remained as head of the league until Clarence S. Campbell assumed the position in 1946. Although a rugged, fiery player, Dutton was a model of decorum as president. His executive abilities carried on into his business life where he was equally successful.

He died March 15, 1987. Inducted 1958.

Charlie Gardiner
Goaltender • Chicago

Charlie Gardiner was at the height of his career when tragedy struck. Rated by many as the outstanding goaltender of his generation, he died of a brain tumor at the age of 29, at his home in Winnipeg. Gardiner was born in Edinburgh, Scotland, on December 31, 1904, and became one of the few U.K.-born players to win a steady job in the NHL. The curly-headed Scot came to Canada with his family in 1911 and because he was a poor skater, took up goaltending. He was so good at this, however, that he played competitive intermediate hockey at the age of 14. By 1925 he was playing senior hockey in Selkirk, Manitoba, seniors and moved up to the pro ranks with the Winnipeg Maroons the following year.

He joined the Chicago Black Hawks in the autumn of 1927, as an understudy to the great Hughie Lehman. In a seven-year career with the Hawks, Gardiner played in 316 games, allowed only 664 goals for an average of 2.02 goals-against, and registered 42 shutouts. He also played in 21 Stanley Cup contests, posting five shutouts and giving up only 35 goals for a phenomenal 1.37 goals-against average. Gardiner won the Vezina Trophy twice, in 1931-32 and 1933-34. He was selected to the First All-Star Team on three occasions and to the Second All-Star Team once.

Gardiner was an intelligent player, providing leadership and valuable assistance to the players in front of him. He played a daring game, never hesitating to dive into a pack of players for the puck or to skate far out of his net to break up a play. Elected 1945.

Black Hawks Coaches...

In the earliest days of the Chicago Black Hawks, club president Fred McLaughlin changed coaches at a rapid rate.

Pete Muldoon was the first to go, getting fired after leading the club into the playoffs in 1926-27, its inaugural season. Legend has it that Muldoon then cursed the team by saying they would never finish first without him. It would be 40 years before Chicago ever posted the best record in the NHL!

Meanwhile, Muldoon's successors were bounced from behind the Black Hawks bench even more quickly than he was. Ten different men coached the team in its first seven years. Even a Stanley Cup was no guarantee of success.

After leading Chicago to its first title in 1933-34, Tommy Gorman found himself out of work. Hired by the Montreal Maroons, he promptly led them to a Stanley Cup—beating out the Black Hawks in the very first playoff round!

EBBIE GOODFELLOW
CENTRE • DETROIT

ONE OF THE MANY players who came out of Ottawa to star in the NHL, Ebbie Goodfellow was born in Canada's capital city on April 9, 1906. Ebbie's amateur hockey was played with the Montagnards where, in 1927-28, he was an all-star centre and leading scorer as the team won the City Championship. He was spotted by Detroit who assigned him to the Olympics of the Canadian Professional League in 1928-29. Here he again achieved all-star status and led the league in scoring. He moved up to the NHL club in 1929-30 and scored 17 goals. The next season, Goodfellow led the American Division of the league with 25 goals.

Ebbie moved to defence in the 1934-35 season and continued to star. He was named to the NHL's Second All-Star Team in 1935-36 and the First Team in 1936-37 and 1939-40. Goodfellow also won the Hart Trophy as NHL MVP in 1939-40. He played on three Stanley Cup winners: 1935-36, 1936-37 and 1942-43.

He was captain of the Red Wings for five seasons, turning that post over to Sid Abel after the 1942-43 when he retired. In all, Ebbie played 557 games with Detroit and scored 134 goals. Combined with 190 assists, he had a total of 324 career points. Goodfellow retired to Florida and was a member of the Hockey Hall of Fame Selection Committee. He died September 9, 1985.

Inducted 1963.

TOMMY GORMAN
BUILDER

HOCKEY, lacrosse, horse racing (flat and harness), baseball and figure skating — those are some of the sports with which Tommy Gorman was associated during his long career. For many years he was sports editor of the Ottawa Citizen, so it can be said that this Ottawa Irishman — born there on June 9, 1886 — was surrounded by sports activity all his life.

He played lacrosse well and was a member of the Canadian Olympic team in 1908. In 1917, he joined the Ottawa hockey club and participated in the foundation of the NHL that same year. He managed or coached seven Stanley Cup teams (three in Ottawa, two for the Canadiens and one each with Chicago and the Montreal Maroons). Tommy helped to hold the old NHA together when he picked up the Ottawa franchise during World War I. He died May 15, 1961.

Inducted 1963.

HERB GARDINER
DEFENCE • CALGARY (WCHL, WHL), MONTREAL, CHICAGO

THE TRUE HOCKEY potential of Herb Gardiner will never be known. He didn't arrive in the NHL until he was 35 when he quickly established his credentials by winning the Hart Trophy as the most valuable player to his team.

Herb was born May 8, 1891, in Winnipeg, and began his hockey career in 1908 with the Winnipeg Victorias. In 1909 and 1910 he played for the Northern Crown Bank in the Bankers' League but was out of hockey for the next eight years. From 1910 to 1914 he was on a survey party for the Canadian Pacific Railway and spent the next four years in the Canadian Army. He served overseas from 1915 to 1918 and won his commission in the field before being invalided home. He went back to surveying in the summer but played for the Calgary Tigers of the Western Canada Hockey League.

In 1924, his team unsuccessfully challenged the Montreal Canadiens for the Stanley Cup. Herb so impressed his opponents that he was asked to join the Canadiens for the 1926-27 season when he won the Hart Trophy. He stayed with the Canadiens until, during the 1929 season, he was loaned to Chicago where he acted as manager. Montreal recalled him for the playoffs but later sold him to Boston, which in turn, sold him to the Philadelphia Arrows of the Canadian-American League. He was manager and coach of the Arrows, staying in Philadelphia until 1949, later coaching the Ramblers and Falcons. He died January 11, 1972.

Inducted 1958.

GEORGE HAINSWORTH

GOALTENDER • SASKATOON (WCHL, WHL), MONTREAL, TORONTO

GOALTENDER GEORGE HAINSWORTH established two brilliant records during 11 seasons in the NHL. Both came during the 1928-29 season. Hainsworth allowed only 43 goals in 44 games and recorded a remarkable total of 22 shutouts.

Born in Toronto on June 26, 1895, Hainsworth moved as a youth to Kitchener, Ontario, and made his debut in both hockey and baseball in that city. His composure under fire and his unquestionable skill brought him to the attention of the Kitchener Juniors in 1912. He quickly moved up through intermediate and senior teams, winning championships at every level including an Allan Cup in 1918.

Hainsworth turned professional with Saskatoon in 1923-24 and remained with that team until shifting to the Canadiens in 1926-27. He was an immediate sensation in Montreal, winning the Vezina Trophy in his first three seasons with the team.

The Canadiens ran into difficulties in the early 1930s and Hainsworth was traded to Toronto for Lorne Chabot. He remained with the Maple Leafs until his retirement midway through the 1936-37 season. He came back to appear in a few games for the Canadiens before retiring permanently.

He died October 9, 1950. Inducted 1961.

JIM HENDY

BUILDER

JIM HENDY was hockey's first great statistician. Born in the Barbados on May 6, 1905, he emigrated to Van-couver at the age of six and first learned about hockey as a rink rat in the arena built by the Patrick brothers.

As a young man, Hendy left home several times, trying his hand as a rancher, and sailor. He worked as a telegrapher and writer, all the while sustaining his hockey interest by compiling players' performances and personal statistics. Hendy published the first edition of "The Hockey Guide" in 1933 and continued to produce the book annually through 1951 when the pressure of other work forced him to give it up. He turned over his records and rights to the NHL, asking only that they continue his work.

He was at one time publicist for the New York Rangers, president of the U.S. Hockey League, and general manager of a highly successful AHL franchise at Cleveland, where he resided at the time of his death on January 14, 1961.

Inducted 1968.

FOSTER HEWITT

BUILDER

ON MARCH 22, 1923, FOSTER WILLIAM HEWITT aired one of hockey's first radio broadcasts, from Toronto's Mutual Street Arena. Beginning that night he became the eyes and ears of radio listeners and, later, television viewers across Canada. Foster described thousands of hockey games, including national, world and Olympic championships in Canada, the United States and in Europe. He also described for Canadian listeners and many faithful followers in the northern U.S., important contests in almost all major sports. His length of service exceeded that of any sportscaster anywhere in the world and his contribution to the growth and development of hockey was so impressive that his name and fame became known around the world.

Son of William A. Hewitt, Foster was born November 21, 1902, in Toronto. He was intercollegiate boxing champion while attending the University of Toronto. Foster went on to become a success in the business world where he owned and operated his own radio station until he retired in 1981. He died April 21, 1985. Inducted 1965.

BRYAN HEXTALL
RIGHT WING • NY RANGERS

ON AND OFF THE ICE, BRYAN ALDWYN HEXTALL was a credit to the game of hockey. In the words of Hockey Hall of Fame member James Dunn: "He is a very clean-living individual and an excellent ambassador for professional hockey." Hextall was born July 31, 1913, in Grenfell, Saskatchewan, but played his minor hockey in Poplar Point, Manitoba.

He played on the Manitoba juvenile championship team of 1929-30, graduating to play junior for the Winnipeg Monarchs and Portage La Prairie before turning professional with the Vancouver Lions of the Western Hockey League in 1934. The Lions won the WHL championship in 1935-36. Hextall transferred to Philadelphia the next season and moved up to the New York Rangers of the NHL in 1936-37. He played with the Rangers through 1947-48 and during that span played in 449 league games, recording 187 goals and 175 assists.

He led the NHL in points in 1941-42 with 56 on 24 goals and 32 assists and was selected to the First All-Star Team three times and to the Second Team twice. He scored 20 or more goals in seven of his 11 NHL seasons and scored the overtime winner in the 1940 Stanley Cup-winning game against Toronto.

Bryan Hextall was a businessman in Poplar Point but devoted considerable time to coaching and assisting minor hockey. Two of his sons and one of his grandsons (Ron) played in the NHL. He died July 25, 1984. Inducted 1969.

"RED" HORNER
DEFENCE • TORONTO

REGINALD (RED) HORNER is one of the few members of the Hockey Hall of Fame who was known as one of the NHL "badmen" during his playing days. For the 12 seasons of his NHL career with the Toronto Maple Leafs, Horner was the undisputed badman of the league.

An aggressive six-foot-one, 200-pounder, Horner led the NHL in penalties for eight successive seasons — 1932-33 through 1939-40. He set a league record for penalties in a single season, spending 167 minutes in the box in 43 games in 1935-36, a mark that stood for 20 years.

Born May 28, 1909, in Lynden, Ontario, Horner moved up to the Leafs directly from the Marlboro juniors in the 1928-29 season. He became the Leafs' captain in 1937-38, an honour he considers the highest of his playing career. Red scored 42 goals and added 110 assists but, more important, his play provided an inspirational force behind the colourful Toronto teams of the 1930s. Horner was not a graceful skater, but he could break as fast as anyone except King Clancy and Howie Morenz. He was also a fine playmaker. His former manager, the late Conn Smythe, said: "Horner was the policeman for the club. Because of his courage and colour, he was one of the best drawing cards in the league. Truly he helped establish the NHL as a popular attraction."

Inducted 1965.

THE 1940 NEW YORK RANGERS ...

Success came almost instantly for the New York Rangers. In their very first season in the NHL (1926-27), they finished comfortably atop the new American Division with the third-best record in the league. In just their second season, the Rangers were Stanley Cup champions. Twice in the next four years they reached the Finals again before capturing their second Stanley Cup in 1933. When they were Stanley Cup champions again in 1940, their three titles in 13 years gave them more than anyone else in the NHL over the same span.

Madison Square Garden had become the place to be and be seen in New York City. The "dinner jacket" crowd the Rangers attracted often included other national sports celebrities, Broadway entertainers, local politicians and New York's society elite. No one at the time would have guessed another 54 years would pass before the Stanley Cup would make its fourth trip to the Garden.

The beginning of the end for the Rangers' success came during World War II when military service badly depleted a star-studded roster. In the 25 years from 1942 until NHL expansion in 1967, the Rangers missed the playoffs 18 times — more than anybody else in the "Original Six" NHL.

SYD HOWE
CENTRE • OTTAWA, PHILADELPHIA, TORONTO, ST. LOUIS, DETROIT

THE INTANGIBLE but vital assets of a great hockey player are identified with the career of Syd Howe, an unselfish player who played centre, wing and defence during 17 seasons in the NHL.

Howe was born September 28, 1911, in Ottawa and died May 20, 1976, in the same city. He started skating on double runners at age three, graduating to single-bladed skates two years later. Living next to a school, he spent many hours on the school's rink. He starred at both public and high school levels in Ottawa and was a member of the first Ottawa team to play in the Memorial Cup finals, losing to Regina in 1928. Howe played senior the following season with the Rideaus and, in 1930, turned pro with the Ottawa Senators of the NHL. He followed a nomadic career for some time, being loaned to the Philadelphia Quakers and then the Toronto Maple Leafs before returning to Ottawa at the start of the 1932-33 season.

Syd was with the Senators when they transferred to St. Louis in 1934. Jack Adams then purchased him for the Detroit Red Wings. The late Jim Norris credited Howe as being the man who started the upsurge in attendance at Detroit. Howe set a modern record on February 3, 1944, when he scored six goals in one game against the Rangers in Detroit. He was also on the ice when Mud Bruneteau scored the goal that ended the longest game in Stanley Cup history. During his NHL career, Howe scored 237 goals and had 291 assists.

Inducted 1965.

MICKEY ION
REFEREE

MICKEY ION became a hockey referee in 1913, handling his first professional game in New Westminster, British Columbia. "There's nothing but ice-water running through his veins," said King Clancy about Ion, an obvious reference to his cool and detached manner of officiating. Clancy, who became a premier referee himself, learned the art from Ion.

Mickey Ion was born February 25, 1886, in Paris, Ontario, and grew into a fine baseball and lacrosse player. The latter sport was his first love, and he progressed into professional ranks with teams in Toronto, Vancouver, and New Westminster.

He began to referee amateur hockey games on Canada's west coast where he caught the eye of Frank Patrick, who gave him the opportunity to work professional matches. Mickey became a top official of the Pacific Coast Hockey Association, but when it became inactive he moved east and joined the NHL staff. He refereed the memorable Howie Morenz memorial game, played in the Montreal Forum on November 2, 1937, and continued as an NHL official until 1941. He died October 26, 1964, in Seattle, Washington.

Inducted 1961.

THE PIRATES AND THE QUAKERS...

The city of Pittsburgh has a long association with hockey dating back before the 1900s. Not surprisingly, when the NHL began moving into American cities in the 1920s, one of the first places they went was the Steel City.

The Pittsburgh Yellow Jackets had won the United States Amateur Hockey Association title in 1924 and 1925 and when the NHL granted a franchise to the city for the 1925-26 season, the club was given the opportunity to turn pro. Lionel Conacher and his teammates jumped at the chance.

Odie Cleghorn was brought in to coach the club, which was renamed the Pittsburgh Pirates. He compensated for the team's lack of star power by employing a three-line system and mastering the art of changing on the fly. The Pirates earned a playoff spot in their first season, but this success would not last.

By their fourth year, the Pirates had tumble into the NHL basement. In 1929-30, their record plunged to 5-36-3. No longer drawing crowds in Pittsburgh, the team moved to Philadelphia. The change in location did nothing to change the team's fortunes. The Philadelphia Quakers were a dreadful 4-36-4 in 1930-31 before disappearing from the NHL. The NHL would not return to Pittsburgh or Philadelphia until 1967.

"BUSHER" JACKSON
LEFT WING • TORONTO, NY AMERICANS, BOSTON

AN EXCELLENT LEFT WINGER, Harvey (Busher) Jackson collected 241 goals and 234 assists in 633 NHL games. In playoff competition he had 18 goals and 12 assists in 71 games.

Born in Toronto on January 19, 1911, Jackson signed with the Toronto Maple Leafs in 1929. He combined with Charlie Conacher and Joe Primeau to form the brilliant "Kid Line." He was on three league champions and one Cup winner (1931-32) in Toronto. He led the league in scoring with 28 goals and 25 assists in 1931-32 and was named to NHL All-Star teams on five occasions. He was a First Team selection in 1931-32, 1933-34, 1934-35 and 1936-37, and a Second Team member in 1932-33.

When Conacher suffered injuries and Primeau retired in 1936, Busher played on a unit with his brother Art and Pep Kelly. The following year he was teamed on a potent line with Syl Apps and Gordie Drillon. He injured his shoulder in the 1938-39 season finals against Boston in what proved to be his last appearance with Toronto. He was dealt with three other players to the New York Americans for Sweeney Schriner. In 1942 he went to the Bruins, closing out his playing career in 1943-44. Jackson died June 25, 1966, in Toronto.

Inducted 1971.

"CHING" JOHNSON
DEFENCE • NY RANGERS, NY AMERICANS

FROM THE FALL of 1926 until the spring of 1938, Ivan (Ching) Johnson stood out as one of the most colourful defencemen in the NHL. He spent 11 years with the New York Rangers and was named to the First All-Star Team three times and the Second Team twice.

Johnson's NHL career ended with the New York Americans in 1937-38. He played in 436 games and acquired 808 minutes in penalties. Ching, who picked up his nickname as a boy, was born in Winnipeg, Manitoba, on December 7, 1897. After returning from military service in 1919, he played with the Winnipeg Monarchs. Shortly after, he moved to Eveleth, Minnesota, and played three years with the Eveleth Miners. Johnson then moved to Minneapolis and played three more years with the Millers before moving his talents to the NHL. Although he was already a 28-year-old veteran, the Rangers purchased his contract when the New York franchise was formed in 1926, starting Johnson on his colourful pro career.

He played defence with a zest for hard-hitting that led to several injuries, such as a broken leg, broken collar bone and broken jaw. He retired from the NHL at the age of 41 but continued to play until he was 46 for teams in Minneapolis; Marquette, Michigan; Washington, D.C. and Hollywood, California. In his final season he was player-coach of the Hollywood Wolves. He died June 16, 1979, in Takoma Park, Maryland. Inducted 1958.

COLOURFUL LINES...

As the demands of the game saw schedules and rosters expand, hockey in the 1930s became less focused on the talents of its individual stars. Unlike today, when coaches shuffle their rosters endlessly, most of the attention then was given to the combined talents of great forward lines.

One of the NHL's first great forward lines featured Frank Boucher and brothers Bill and Bun Cook. This threesome was formed when the New York Rangers were born in 1926 and played together for 10 years. In 1929-30, the Boston Bruins combo of Cooney Weiland, Dutch Gainor, and Dit Clapper rewrote the NHL record book and was dubbed "the Dynamite Line." That same season saw the Toronto Maple Leafs promote young wingers Busher Jackson and Charlie Conacher. When Joe Primeau was assigned to centre them, the "Kid Line" was born. Soon, Boston had "the Kraut Line" of Milt Schmidt, Woody Dumart, and Bobby Bauer — so named for their German heritage.

In 1939-40, Schmidt, Dumart, and Bauer became the first forward line to finish 1-2-3 in the NHL scoring race. That feat would be duplicated only by Montreal's "Punch Line" of Lach, Richard, and Blake (1944-45) and Detroit's "Production Line" of Lindsay, Abel, and Howe (1949-50).

AUREL JOLIAT
LEFT WING • MONTREAL

HE WAS CALLED the Mighty Atom or the Little Giant, this man named Aurel Joliat who spent 16 seasons as a member of the Montreal Canadiens in the NHL. Born in Ottawa on August 29, 1901, Joliat was a star kicking fullback with the Ottawa Rough Riders and Regina Wascana Boat Club before a broken leg led him to concentrate on hockey.

His early ice experience came with the Ottawa New Edinburghs and Iroquois Falls Eskimos. He went west on a harvest excursion train and stayed to play with the Saskatoon Sheiks but the Canadiens dealt off the great Newsy Lalonde for this "unknown kid, Joliat."

In 1923-24, his second season in Montreal, Joliat was teamed with Howie Morenz and Billy Boucher. He went on to become one of the greatest left wingers in NHL history. He weighed 160 pounds when he first joined the Canadiens but by 1925, had dropped to 125 and seldom weighed more than 135 in subsequent years.

Despite six shoulder separations, three broken ribs, and a nose broken on five occasions, Joliat went on to score 270 goals, tying Morenz on the all-time list. He was also noted as an outstanding checker, capable of stopping an opponent, wheeling on a dime and starting a rush of his own. Joliat played on three Stanley Cup-winning teams — 1923-24, 1929-30 and 1930-31 — and won the Hart Trophy in the 1933-34 season. He was also selected to four NHL All-Star Teams. He died June 2, 1986, in Ottawa.

Inducted 1947.

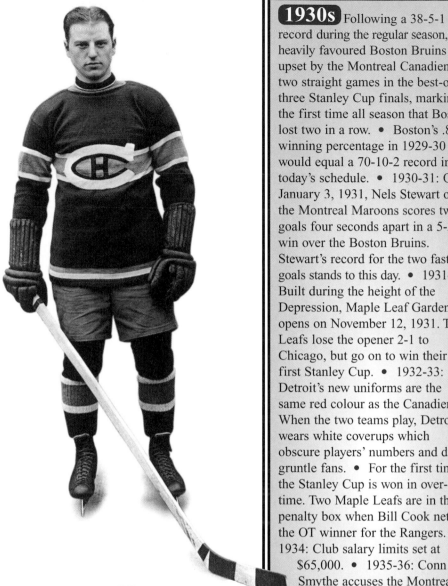

GENERAL JOHN KILPATRICK
BUILDER

GENERAL JOHN REED KILPATRICK always made the proud boast that he was New York's number one hockey fan. Although an outstanding athlete in many sports, as a young man he readily admitted that the National Hockey League provided his favourite spectator sport.

Born June 15, 1889, Kilpatrick emblazoned his name into the records of both track and football while attending Yale University. He captained Yale's 1911 track team and its 1910 football team which was unscored upon throughout the season. He was twice voted All-American end by football selectors and is credited with being the first to throw an overhand forward pass, against Princeton in 1907. He was voted into the National Football Hall of Fame in 1955. The General served in both World War I and World War II and received several decorations.

As president of Madison Square Garden and the New York Rangers for 22 years, he became not only a keen hockey fan but an astute executive. He was an original director of the NHL Players' Pension Society which was established in 1946 and remained on the Board until his death on May 7, 1960. He was elected an NHL Governor in 1936 and during his years with the Rangers twice watched them win the Stanley Cup. Inducted 1960.

1930s Following a 38-5-1 record during the regular season, the heavily favoured Boston Bruins are upset by the Montreal Canadiens in two straight games in the best-of-three Stanley Cup finals, marking the first time all season that Boston lost two in a row. • Boston's .875 winning percentage in 1929-30 would equal a 70-10-2 record in today's schedule. • 1930-31: On January 3, 1931, Nels Stewart of the Montreal Maroons scores two goals four seconds apart in a 5-3 win over the Boston Bruins. Stewart's record for the two fastest goals stands to this day. • 1931-32: Built during the height of the Depression, Maple Leaf Gardens opens on November 12, 1931. The Leafs lose the opener 2-1 to Chicago, but go on to win their first Stanley Cup. • 1932-33: Detroit's new uniforms are the same red colour as the Canadiens. When the two teams play, Detroit wears white coverups which obscure players' numbers and disgruntle fans. • For the first time, the Stanley Cup is won in overtime. Two Maple Leafs are in the penalty box when Bill Cook nets the OT winner for the Rangers. • 1934: Club salary limits set at $65,000. • 1935-36: Conn Smythe accuses the Montreal Maroons of spreading sand on the floor of the Maple Leafs dressing room to slow up his forwards by blunting their skates. • 1937: Over 10,000 fans view a service held at the Montreal Forum where Howie Morenz' body lay in state following his death on March 8, 1937. Thousands more line the route of the funeral cortege. • For the final five games of the season, Chicago experiments with a line-up featuring five American-born players; Ike Klingbeil, Butch Schaeffer, Milton Brink, Al Suomi and Bun LaPrairie. • 1938-39: With the Depression claiming three of the NHL's 10 franchises, the league reverts back to a single-division format. Six of seven NHL teams qualify for the playoffs.

HERBIE LEWIS
LEFT WING • DETROIT

CALGARY, ALBERTA was the birthplace of Herbie Lewis, "The Duke of Duluth", April 17, 1905. The royal nickname was a result of his four unforgettable years with the Duluth Hornets. He was the undisputed chief drawing card in the American Hockey Association, as well as being both the highest paid, and most sought after man in the loop.

Lewis began his 11-year tenure in the NHL after being drafted in 1928 by the Detroit Cougars (later known as the Red Wings). He was a fast skater, an accurate playmaker, and a great sportsman. In 1933, Hack Adams named the productive left winger to the Red Wings captaincy, while Toronto's Conn Smythe, Detroit's most formidable foe, acknowledged the line of Lewis, Cooney Weiland and Larry Aurie as "the best Line in hockey, coming and going".

Herbie Lewis skated in the starting lineup in the first-ever NHL All-Star Game, held for the benefit of Ace Bailey in 1934. He was with the Wings in 1935-36 when they won their first Stanley Cup and figured prominently the following year when he netted four goals and three assists in the playoff finals for back-to-back Detroit Stanley Cup wins.

Lewis played NHL hockey during a time of growth and change. In his tenure with the Detroit Club, he wore the emblems of the Cougars, the Falcons and the Red Wings. In the Motor City he is still hailed as one of the favourite stars of Olympic Stadium. He died January 20, 1991.

Inducted 1989.

THOMAS LOCKHART
BUILDER

THOMAS F. LOCKHART had a long and illustrious connection with amateur hockey in the United States. He was born March 21, 1892 and although his early interests were mainly cycling and track and field, he became involved with hockey in 1932 when he organized and promoted amateur hockey at Madison Square Garden in New York.

The following year, he organized the Eastern Amateur Hockey League and in 1935 became its president. In 1937, Lockhart organized the Amateur Hockey Association of the United States and served as its first president. Between 1932 and 1952, he supervised the Metropolitan Amateur League, and at intervals, coached and managed the New York Rovers. For the final six years of that span he was business manager of Rangers.

Lockhart was also a member of the U.S. Olympic Committee and delegate to the International Ice Hockey Federation. Tommy, as he was known to his many friends, was also active in the U.S. Amateur Athletic Union, serving as vice-president of the Metropolitan Association and vice-chairman of its boxing committee. He died May 18, 1979, in New York. Inducted 1965.

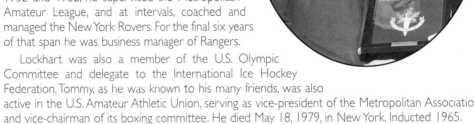

PAUL LOICQ
BUILDER

PAUL LOICQ was born in Brussels in 1890, graduated from university as a lawyer and served with distinction as a colonel in the Belgian Army during World War I, being cited for bravery. He started skating in 1906 and three years later was selected as a member of Belgium's national hockey team, playing continuously for his country until retirement after the 1924 Olympic Games at Chamonix, France.

Loicq was elected president of the International Ice Hockey Federation in 1927 and served with honour and distinction for 20 years, not only as an executive, but as a referee of international stature. During his term as IIHF president international hockey made great strides. Not only did the game's popularity increase rapidly across Europe, largely through his efforts, but it was his influence that resulted in hockey being accepted as an Olympic sport.

Loicq was posthumously elected to the Hockey Hall of Fame in 1961 and the Hall's official crest was presented to his widow on December 4, 1961, by the president of the Belgian Olympic Committee.

Inducted 1961.

1930 WORLD CHAMPIONS...

In the winter of 1929-30, a team of amateur players from the Toronto area sponsored by the sporting goods company CCM toured Europe to promote and teach hockey. During their tour, the IIHF staged a European Championship that was won by Germany. When the team, simply called the "Canadas of Toronto" beat the Germans 6-1, they were declared hockey's first World Champion.

SYLVIO MANTHA
DEFENCE • MONTREAL, BOSTON

SYLVIO MANTHA enjoyed 14 seasons in the NHL as a hard-rock defenceman. During that span he played for nine first-place teams and three Stanley Cup winners. Unlike many NHL players, he didn't have to wait long for his taste of champagne from the Stanley Cup.

He joined the Montreal Canadiens in 1923-24, the first year they won the Cup as an NHL team. Montreal won twice more with Mantha in the lineup, in 1929-30 and 1930-31.

Sylvio was born in Montreal on April 14, 1903, and learned his hockey there. His first important team was the Notre Dame de Grace juniors in 1918-19, and he moved up through intermediate and senior ranks, finally playing for the Nationals in the Quebec Senior League before turning professional.

Although he played as a forward in amateur ranks, Mantha was moved back to defence after part of his first season with the Canadiens, remaining there for the balance of his career. He became a player-coach with Montreal in 1935-36 and then moved to the Boston Bruins where he finished his playing days in 1936-37. For the next two years, Mantha acted as a linesman in the NHL and a referee in the American Hockey League. He remained in Montreal and continued to coach junior and senior teams for many years. Mantha scored 63 goals and earned 72 assists in the NHL. He was named to the league's Second All-Star Team in 1930-31 and 1931-32. He died August 7, 1974.

Inducted 1960.

HOWIE MORENZ
CENTRE • MONTREAL, CHICAGO, NY RANGERS

THEY SAID THAT he had colour in his every motion, that his brilliance stood out in an era of colourful and brilliant hockey players. They were talking of course, about Howie Morenz who was a runaway leader in a 1950 Canadian Press poll to select the outstanding hockey player of the half-century.

Morenz was born in Mitchell, Ontario, on September 21, 1902, and began his hockey career at nearby Stratford. He was signed to a pro contract by Leo Dandurand of the Montreal Canadiens and joined that club for the 1923-24 season. Morenz was an immediate million-dollar box office attraction. He had reckless speed and his headlong rushes set turnstiles clicking wherever the Canadiens played. He was nicknamed "the Babe Ruth of Hockey" by sportswriters in the United States.

Morenz performed in the NHL for 14 seasons, earning a variety of nicknames like "the Canadien Comet," the "Hurtling Habitant," the "Mitchell Meteor," and the "Stratford Streak." He had great stickhandling ability and a snapping shot. Morenz played with the Canadiens for 11 seasons, before being traded to Chicago. He went to the New York Rangers midway through 1935-36 and came back to the Canadiens for the 1936-37 season. He broke his leg in a game on January 28, 1937, leading to his death on March 8, 1937.

During his career, Morenz scored 270 goals and won the Hart Trophy three times — 1927-28, 1930-31 and 1931-32. In 1929-30, he scored 40 goals in 44 games and in 1924-25 scored 27 goals in 30 games. He was twice named to the First All-Star Team and once to the Second. Inducted 1945.

MAJOR FREDERIC McLAUGHLIN
BUILDER

MAJOR FREDERIC McLAUGHLIN pioneered the development of hockey in Chicago. In 1926, when Lester and Frank Patrick oversaw the dispersal of Western Hockey League players to NHL clubs in eastern Canada and the U.S., McLaughlin was involved in the negotiations. The Chicago Black Hawks were formed, named after the famous Black Hawk regiment which he commanded during World War I, and McLaughlin became the first president of the organization.

Public acceptance was poor, at first, when games were played in the Chicago Coliseum and eventually the Major purchased controlling interest in the club, moving into the new Chicago Stadium in December, 1929. Soon, league attendance records were set.

Under McLaughlin's ownership, the Black Hawks captured the Stanley Cup in 1934 and 1938.

Major McLaughlin was born in Chicago on June 27, 1877, and died there on December 17, 1944.

Inducted 1963.

JAMES NORRIS, SR.
BUILDER

JAMES NORRIS was born December 10, 1879, in St. Catharines, Ontario, and spent his early years in Montreal. He became a wealthy grain broker, establishing head offices in Chicago.

He was a champion squash player and a good tennis player in Montreal, but developed a strong enthusiasm for hockey when he played for the Victorias of that city. Hockey remained his favourite sport. Norris purchased the Chicago Shamrocks of the American Hockey Association in 1930 and three years later, with his son James D., bought Detroit's Olympia and its NHL franchise. They changed the team name from the Falcons to the Red Wings, patterning their new logo after the "winged wheel" of the Montreal Athletic Association, and immediately set out in pursuit of the Stanley Cup. Two years later, the Red Wings won, repeating in the following season of 1936-37 and again in 1942-43 under the Norris banner.

James Norris was a firm believer in the maintenance of a strong farm system for his Red Wings, which kept the team competitive throughout the Norris years. At one time, Norris and his three children also owned Chicago Stadium and a majority interest in the Madison Square Garden Corporation, which owned the New York Rangers. James Norris died December 4, 1952.

Inducted 1958.

JAMES D. NORRIS
BUILDER

JAMES D. NORRIS inherited two great things from his father — great wealth and great interest in sports. The father-son combination acquired the Detroit Red Wings and the Olympia in 1933. In the next 10 years Detroit won three Stanley Cups: 1935-36, 1936-37 and 1942-43. During this span, James D. either signed or helped develop many stars of the NHL including Hockey Hall of Fame members Sid Abel, Ted Lindsay, Jack Stewart, Red Kelly, and Gordie Howe.

In 1946, James D. and partner Arthur Wirtz assumed ownership of the Chicago Black Hawks. This was a team that had finished last three straight seasons, but together they built a valuable franchise, following the same guidelines that had been successful in Detroit. It paid off in a Stanley Cup victory in 1961.

A well-spoken man, Norris had many interests, both in sports and in business. He was president of the International Boxing Club for nine years, promoted numerous championship bouts, owned a racing stable and had other extensive personal holdings. He was born Nobvember 6, 1906 and died February 25, 1966.

Inducted 1962.

WINGS WIN TWO...

Of the four American teams that joined the NHL in the 1920s and went on to be part of the "Original Six," Detroit was the last to win the Stanley Cup. But the Red Wings made up for lost time by recording a significant first.

Detroit's Stanley Cup run in 1936 began with a 1-0 victory over the Montreal Maroons in the first game of the playoffs. The winning goal was scored by Mud Bruneteau after 116:30 of overtime in what is still the longest game in NHL history. The Red Wings went on to sweep the best-of-five series in three games before beating Toronto in four for their first championship.

No American team had ever won back-to-back Stanley Cups, but the Red Wings appeared up for the task. Despite losing defencemen Doug Young and Orville Roulston to broken legs during the season, Detroit still ran up the league's best record. However, when the Wings opened the playoffs, they would also be without star scorer Larry Aurie, who also broke his leg just before the end of the regular schedule. To make matters worse, goalie Normie Smith suffered a serious elbow injury in a first-round playoff victory over the Montreal Canadiens.

With the New York Rangers leading the 1937 Stanley Cup Final two games to one, replacement goalie Earl Robertson took over centre stage. The rookie recorded a shutout in a 1-0 victory in game four, then blanked the Rangers again for a 2-0 win in the fifth and deciding game. The Red Wings had their back-to-back Cups. No U.S. team would win more than two Stanley Cups in a row until the New York Islanders won four straight from 1980 to 1983.

● ● ● ● ● ● ● ● ● ● ● ● ● ● ● ● ● ● ● ●

MONTREAL MAROONS...

The Montreal Maroons entered the NHL during the first true expansion of the league in 1924. Following a trail blazed by the Montreal Wanderers, the Maroons would become the favourite team of the city's English population while the Canadiens remained the darlings of the Quebecois. The two rivals would soon share the Montreal Forum, which was, in fact, built for the Maroons.

The Maroons were a woeful 9-19-2 in their first NHL season, but made significant changes for 1925-26. They decided to dump many of their veteran castoffs and go with promising youngsters like Nels Stewart and Babe Siebert. Stewart promptly led the NHL in scoring and captured the Hart Trophy in his rookie season while leading the Maroons to a Stanley Cup title in just their second year.

Stewart and Siebert were soon teamed with Hooley Smith, and the powerful "S-Line" kept the Maroons competitive into the 1930s. Only Smith, though, was still with the squad when it won its second Stanley Cup in 1935. Soon afterwards, the lingering Depression and the rumblings of war in Europe would scare off many of the Maroons' financial backers. The team was forced to fold after the 1937-38 season.

● ● ● ● ● ● ● ● ● ● ● ● ● ● ● ● ● ● ● ●

LYNN PATRICK
LEFT WING • NY RANGERS

LYNN PATRICK was a member of "Hockey's Royal Family," but he never took undue advantage of his nobility. His father, Lester, was named to the Hockey Hall of Fame in 1947 and his uncle, Frank, in 1958; others of the Patrick family have been associated with hockey for almost a century.

Born February 3, 1912, in Victoria, British Columbia, Lynn's youth was spent in a non-hockey environment. He didn't play organized hockey until he joined a senior Montreal club. He was a member of Victoria's Canadian championship basketball team and played football with the Montreal Winged Wheelers and the Winnipeg Blue Bombers. His father, who was coach and manager of the New York Rangers, fearing charges of nepotism, wouldn't give Lynn a chance with the club until warned by another manager, "either put him on your list, or I'll put him on ours."

Lynn's NHL debut was modest, but he progressed to twice lead the Rangers in scoring. He played for the Rangers' Stanley Cup-winning team of 1940 and was named a First All-Star in 1941-42 and a Second All-Star in 1942-43. His NHL record includes 145 goals and 190 assists in 455 games, plus 10 goals in 44 playoff games.

In 1943 he joined the U.S. Army as a private and was discharged after World War II as a lieutenant, rejoining the Rangers briefly before moving on to New Haven of the American Hockey League as coach.

He coached five seasons in Boston, his Bruins never missing the playoffs, and then spent the next 10 years in the front office. In 1966 he became general manager of the St. Louis Blues and spent three brief stints as coach before retiring as a senior vice-president in 1977. He died January 26, 1980, of a heart attack after attending a hockey game. Inducted 1980.

HARRY OLIVER
CENTRE/RIGHT WING • CALGARY (WCHL, WHL), BOSTON, NY AMERICANS

HARRY OLIVER was born October 26, 1898, in Selkirk, Manitoba, and started his hockey career on the ponds of his home town. He went on to greatness with the Boston Bruins and the New York Americans in an NHL career that spanned 11 seasons.

Oliver was considered the ideal type of athlete of his day. Although he weighed only 155 pounds, he moved with the speed and grace of a thoroughbred and was called "smooth as silk" by the late Harry Scott, sports editor of the Calgary Albertan, who had previously performed with the Montreal Canadiens himself. Oliver's appearance and deportment were exemplary, both on and off the ice. In his entire career, Oliver never spent more than 24 minutes in the penalty box in the course of a season.

He played with the Selkirk juniors in 1917 and 1918, moving up to the town's western Canadian champion senior club in his second year. He moved to Calgary in 1920 to play in the Western League, remaining there until 1926 when he was sold to the Boston Bruins. He played on a Stanley Cup winner in 1928-29, and was traded to the Americans in 1934, where he remained three more years.

During his pro career, Oliver scored 217 goals and had 133 assists — 90 and 48 with the Calgary Tigers of the WHL and 127 and 85 in the NHL. He died June 16, 1985, in Winnipeg.

Inducted 1967.

ALLAN PICKARD
BUILDER

ALTHOUGH he was born in Exeter, Ontario, on January 2, 1895, and spent his early years there, Allan W. Pickard spent many years as a hockey executive in western Canada. He was an organizer and administrator of the Regina YMCA League in the mid-1920s and from this league grew the Regina Parks League, one of the largest and best-organized in the country.

During the late 1920s he served as a coach, executive and president of the Regina Aces, a senior team. At that time he became an executive member of the Saskatchewan Amateur Hockey Association. Al Pickard became SAHA president in 1941 and served two terms. He was also president of the Saskatchewan Senior League during the period it produced such outstanding stars as Hockey Hall of Fame members Elmer Lach and Max and Doug Bentley. Pickard was also president of the Western Canada Senior League, governor of Saskatchewan's Junior League and of the Western Canada Junior League, and president of the Canadian Amateur Hockey Association for three years — 1947-48 through 1949-50. A life member of both the SAHA and CAHA, Pickard died April 7, 1975.

Inducted 1958.

JOE PRIMEAU
CENTRE • TORONTO

JOE PRIMEAU was both a great hockey player and a great coach. He was the only man to coach teams which won the Memorial Cup, Allan Cup and Stanley Cup at junior, senior and NHL levels of competition.

Joe was born in Lindsay, Ontario, on January 29, 1906, but didn't don skates until he was 12 years old. He first attracted attention as a centre for St. Michael's College juniors. Conn Smythe signed Primeau to a professional contract in 1927 with the Toronto Maple Leafs, but he played much of the season with Ravinas and won the scoring title in the Canadian Pro League. Joe moved up to the Leafs in 1928 but finished the season with London and didn't arrive in the NHL to stay until 1929-30.

He became the centre on Toronto's famous Kid Line with Charlie Conacher and Busher Jackson on the wings, and although his linemates were more dazzling, Joe was the smooth passer who made their exploits possible. He was a tenacious checker and an extremely clean player, often referred to as "Gentleman Joe." He was also a strong penalty-killer.

Primeau was fifth in the NHL scoring race in 1929-30, and second in 1931-32 and 1933-34. He was selected to the NHL's Second All-Star Team in 1933-34 as well. He won the Lady Byng Trophy in 1931-32. He retired as a player to go into business in 1937, but continued as a great coach for the next 23 years. He died May 14, 1989.

Inducted 1963.

SENATOR DONAT RAYMOND
BUILDER

FOR 40 YEARS, Senator Donat Raymond was the spark behind professional hockey in Montreal. Although a keen hockey follower for several years, his first official connection with the game came in 1923 with the formation of the Canadian Arena Company. This is the firm that built the Montreal Forum and acquired the Canadiens in 1937.

Born January 3, 1880, Raymond's interest stemmed from the days he held box seats at Westmount Arena. When it burned in 1918, he realized Montreal needed an adequate replacement and so became president of the company that built the Forum and formed the Maroons to play in the NHL. The Canadiens played in Mount Royal Arena at the time, but became Forum tenants in 1925, precipitating a rivalry with the Maroons that packed the arena with fans whenever the two teams played.

The Depression of the 1930s forced the Maroons to fold. The Canadiens might have suffered a similar fate but for the faith and financial support of Sen. Raymond who absorbed the losses until fortunes took a turn for the better. He remained president of the company until 1955 when he became chairman of the board. He held this office until his death on June 5, 1963.

Inducted 1958.

MIKE RODDEN
REFEREE

BY HIS OWN COUNT, MIKE RODDEN refereed 2864 hockey games, 1187 of which were in the NHL. Rodden was born April 24, 1891 in Mattawa, Ontario, and had an illustrious record in Canadian sport.

Although he was inducted into the Hockey Hall of Fame as a referee, he also was a fine player, coach and sportswriter. In hockey, he played for Queen's University, Haileybury and the Toronto St. Patricks. He coached at Toronto's De La Salle College, St. Mary's, St. Patricks and the University of Toronto.

It was perhaps in football that Mike Rodden gained his greatest coaching glories. He was the guiding hand behind 27 championship teams in that game, including five in the Inter-Provincial Union, two in the Ontario Rugby Football Union and two winners of the Grey Cup.

As a youth, Mike had played hockey, baseball and lacrosse before entering the University of Ottawa where he took up football. He moved to Queen's University and in 1918 became assistant sports editor of the Toronto *Globe*. He was promoted to sports editor in 1928, remaining until 1936. In 1944, Mike became sports editor of the Kingston *Whig-Standard*, retaining that position until retiring in 1959. He died January 11, 1978, in Kingston, Ontario.

Inducted 1962.

"SWEENEY" SCHRINER
LEFT WING • NY AMERICANS, TORONTO

DAVID (SWEENEY) SCHRINER was a celebrated hockey player who divided his NHL career between two teams, the New York Americans and the Toronto Maple Leafs.

Schriner was born in Saratov, Russia, on November 30, 1911. He was raised in Calgary and played all of his amateur hockey in that western Canadian city. He played in public school before moving on to the North Hill midgets, the Tigers juvenile team and the Canadians junior club. When he moved up to senior, he played with the Calgary Bronks, then coached by Rosie Helmer who later coached Schriner when he played with the Americans.

An outstanding left winger, Schriner turned pro in 1933-34 with Syracuse. The following season, he moved up to New York and was so proficient that he won the Calder Trophy as the league's outstanding rookie, scoring 18 goals. He remained with the Americans until the end of the 1938-39 season when he was traded to Toronto in return for five players.

Schriner stayed in Toronto for the balance of his NHL career, scoring 201 goals in 11 NHL campaigns. While with the Americans, he was twice scoring champion of the league, winning in 1935-36 with 45 points and 1936-37 with 46. As a member of the Maple Leafs, Schriner played on two Stanley Cup winners, scoring six goals in the Leafs' Cup win in 1941-42 and three in their victory of 1944-45. Sweeney was also named to the league's First All-Star Team in 1935-36 and the Second Team in 1936-37. He died July 4, 1990.

Inducted 1962.

EARL SEIBERT
DEFENCE • NY RANGERS, CHICAGO, DETROIT

EARL SEIBERT played 15 seasons in the NHL, and established himself as one of the game's all-time great defencemen. Earl was voted to NHL All-Star Teams in ten consecutive seasons, making the First Team in 1935, 1942, 1943 and 1944. He was noted for his rushing ability and accounted for 89 goals and a total of 273 points in scheduled league games, adding another nine goals and eight assists in playoff competition.

Born in Kitchener, Ontario, on December 7, 1911, Earl began skating at an early age and was a consistent winner in the annual skating carnival in Kitchener. His speed and strong body-checking as a junior player caught the eye of several pro clubs and he eventually turned pro in 1929 with the Springfield Indians, a farm club for the New York Rangers. He moved up to the Rangers in the 1931-32 season and almost immediately became a standout on defence. The Rangers traded him to Chicago in 1935-36 for Art Coulter, and nine years later, he was traded to Detroit in exchange for three players.

Seibert was a shot-blocker, willingly dropping to the ice to stop shots before they reached the goal. Off the ice, Earl was a cheerful individual with an amazing fund of good humor. Earl's father, Oliver, was previously elected to the Hockey Hall of Fame, making them the first father-son player combination so honoured. He died in May of 1990.

Inducted 1963.

EDDIE SHORE

DEFENCE • REGINA (WCHL), EDMONTON (WHL), BOSTON, NY AMERICANS

IN THE DAYS when the NHL was filled with colourful players, Eddie Shore took a back seat to no one. He had an explosive temper and hockey ability to match.

Eddie Shore was born in Ft. Qu'Appelle, Saskatchewan, on November 25, 1902, and moved up through amateur ranks to the Melville Millionaires in the season of 1923-24. From there, he graduated to the pros with the Regina Caps of the Western Canada Hockey League. The following season, he played with Edmonton.

Shore broke into the NHL in 1926-27 with the Boston Bruins and in subsequent seasons was to personify the most vigorous aspects of a hard, rough and fast game. His great talent was to take over the offense and set up plays, literally knocking down any opponent in his way. This, of course, brought him an abundance of penalties and he became involved in many hard-fought battles.

Eddie Shore is the only defenceman to win the Hart Trophy four times — 1932-33, 1934-35, 1935-36, and 1937-38. He was also voted to the NHL All-Star Team on eight occasions. He played on two Stanley Cup winners in 1928-29 and 1938-39. Shore scored 105 goals and added 179 assists. He wound up his NHL career with the New York Americans in the 1939-40 season. Shore's contribution to hockey was a dynamic one. His records stand, and will continue to stand the test of time. He died March 16, 1985.

Inducted 1947.

"BABE" SIEBERT

LEFT WING • MTL. MAROONS, NY RANGERS, BOSTON, MONTREAL

A GREAT HOCKEY PLAYER, with a heart as big as his massive body, Albert (Babe) Siebert was a broad-shouldered who played with complete confidence.

The Babe was born in Plattsville, Ontario, on January 14, 1904, and played his minor hockey in Zurich, Ontario. He played for Kitchener in the Ontario Hockey Association junior league in 1922-23. Although still a junior, he moved up to play for the Niagara Falls seniors in 1924-25 and made the jump to the NHL the following season with the Montreal Maroons.

Siebert was an outstanding left winger, and combined with Nels Stewart and Hooley Smith to form the highly-rated S-line which played effectively for five seasons. This combination was broken with dramatic suddenness in 1932 with two trades; Stewart went to Boston and Siebert to the New York Rangers. Siebert was later traded to Boston himself and then returned to Montreal this time to play for the Canadiens in 1936-37.

At this stage in his career, Siebert's speed had gone, but he had developed into a defenceman so proficient that he was voted the Hart Trophy that season. Babe excelled at blocking out the opposition, using his weight, strength and balance to skate attackers off to the side. He was named to the First All-Star Team on defence in three consecutive seasons, beginning in 1935-36.

He died in a drowning accident on August 25, 1939, in St. Joseph, Ontario, and the third NHL All-Star Game was played to benefit his family.

Inducted 1964.

NEW YORK AMERICANS...

Joining the league for the 1925-26 season, the New York Americans introduced NHL hockey to Manhattan a year before the New York Rangers. Unfortunately, the "Amerks," in their star-spangled red, white, and blue uniforms, proved to be more colourful than talented.

The Americans were owned by bootlegger "Big Bill" Dwyer, who paid $75,000 for the Hamilton Tigers franchise after the team was suspended for going on strike during the 1925 playoffs. Because of the team's Hamilton connection, the Americans would actually spend much of their existence in the NHL's Canadian Division.

Over the years, the team would boast some of the biggest names in hockey. Too bad for their fans most of those players arrived in New York long past their prime! One of the team's truly great stars was Roy "Shrimp" Worters who, in 1929, became the first goalie to win the Hart Trophy.

During the 1930s, the Americans were clearly losing the battle for New York City's hockey fans. An attempt to forge a separate identity from the Rangers saw the team called the Brooklyn Americans in 1941-42. When the switch failed to attract additional support, the franchise folded.

"Hooley" Smith
Right Wing • Ottawa, Mtl. Maroons, Boston, NY Americans

Born January 7, 1903, in Toronto, Reginald (Hooley) Smith played his amateur hockey in that city and was a standout member of the Granites, winners of the Olympic hockey championship for Canada in 1924.

He turned professional the following year with Ottawa of the NHL, playing right wing, and it was here that he developed a sweeping hook-check that made him a formidable two-way player. The Senators won the Stanley Cup in 1926-27, but Smith encountered personal problems in the final against Boston. Always a fiery player, he attacked Harry Oliver, earning a one-month suspension, effective at the start of the next season. Ottawa dealt the five-foot-ten, 160-pounder to the Montreal Maroons before that next season and once again, his team was in the Cup final, losing to the Rangers.

With the Maroons, Smith combined with Nels Stewart and Babe Siebert to form the great "S-Line," combining scoring power with aggressive play. Later, Smith captained the Maroons team that won the Stanley Cup in 1935 and was selected First Team All-Star centre the next season. His only previous All-Star recognition came in 1931-32, when he was voted to the Second Team.

Smith was traded to Boston in 1936-37 and after one season joined the New York Americans where he completed his career with his 200th goal in 1940-41. His best individual scoring seasons were 1929-30 when he had 21 goals and 1932-33 when he had 20. In his final year in the NHL, Smith spent some time playing defence.

He died August 24, 1963, in Montreal. Inducted 1972.

Ottawa Senators...

The 1920s were glory days for the Ottawa Senators as four Stanley Cup wins established the team as an NHL powerhouse. But with a population of only 150,000, Ottawa was the NHL's smallest city and by 1928, the financial strain was showing. The Senators were always a big draw on the road, but when the league turned down the club's request for a larger percentage of visiting gate receipts, Ottawa was forced to sell off its talent.

The fire sale began when Hooley Smith was purchased by the Montreal Maroons. Soon, Cy Denneny, George Boucher and Frank Nighbor were all moved, and King Clancy was sold to Toronto for a record $35,000.

With its stars gone, support for the team diminished further. The Senators actually withdrew from the league in 1931, but were back for the 1932-33 season. By 1934, though, the team was dead. After a season as the St. Louis Eagles in 1934-35, this once-proud franchise disappeared from the NHL.

Conn Smythe
Builder

Conn Smythe was a fearless leader, both on the battlefield where he served overseas with distinction both World Wars, and on the ice where he fielded many battling hockey teams.

Born in Toronto on February 1, 1895, he is best remembered as the man who brought respectability to professional hockey. Smythe first gained hockey prominence as captain of the University of Toronto Varsity team that won the Ontario championship in 1915. He coached the Varsity seniors to the 1927 Allan Cup and, playing as the Varsity Grads, to the 1928 Olympic title as well.

He was hired by the newly established New York Rangers, but was released after assembling the team that won the 1928 Stanley Cup. He then purchased the Toronto St. Pats and changed the club's name to the Maple Leafs.

By November, 1931, thanks to the bulldogging perseverance of Smythe, Maple Leaf Gardens was constructed and became the team's home. He became managing director and later president of the Gardens, retiring in 1961 after his teams had won seven Stanley Cups. Smythe had other successful interests — a horse-racing stable (winning the Queen's Plate in 1953 and 1967) and a sand and gravel business — but two things close to his heart were his long association with the Ontario Society for Crippled Children and personal supervision of the construction of the old Hockey Hall of Fame. He died November 18, 1980, in Toronto.

Inducted 1958.

NELS STEWART
CENTRE • MTL. MAROONS, BOSTON, NY AMERICANS

WHEN NELS STEWART, Babe Siebert and Hooley Smith played as the famed "S-Line" of the Montreal Maroons, they were considered to be the most feared trio in hockey. Centering this great line was Nels Stewart who was born December 29, 1900, in Montreal.

Stewart was the top marksman of the three and his deadly accurate shot earned him the nickname "Old Poison" from goalies around the NHL. He scored 134 goals and added 56 assists during the five years the "S-Line" played as a unit.

A burly 200-pounder, he skated with short, toddling steps and used a stick with so flat a lie that he had to play the puck almost between his skates. But he was truly "Old Poison," collecting a total of 324 goals and 191 assists in 650 league games. He was the first player to score more than 300 goals in the NHL, and was the league's all-time goal-scoring leader for many years until surpassed by Maurice Richard.

Stewart learned his hockey in Toronto, where his family had moved when he was a boy. He grew up in the city's Balmy Beach district where he became friends with his future linemate, Hooley Smith. He joined the Maroons for the 1925-26 season, scoring 34 goals in his rookie season. He topped that mark only once when he scored 39 in 1929-30. He was traded to Boston in 1932 and played three seasons with the Bruins before moving to the New York Americans. He remained with them until retiring in 1939-40, except for 1936-37 when he played part of the season in Boston.

Stewart won the Hart Trophy in 1925-26 and 1929-30 and played for a Stanley Cup winner in 1925-26. He died August 21, 1957, at his summer home near Toronto. Inducted 1962.

"TINY" THOMPSON
GOALTENDER • BOSTON, DETROIT

IN AN ERA when great goaltenders were an important part of every NHL team, Cecil (Tiny) Thompson was one of the most consistent performers in the game. The tag of "Tiny" was something of a misnomer: he stood five-foot-ten and weighed around 170 pounds. Other NHL goaltenders at that time included stars such as George Hainsworth, Roy Worters, Charlie Gardiner and Lorne Chabot, but Thompson still won the Vezina Trophy on four occasions: 1929-30, 1932-33, 1935-36 and 1937-38.

Thompson was born in Sandon, British Columbia, on May 31, 1903, and played his early hockey there. He also played amateur hockey for the Calgary Monarch Juniors, the Pacific Grain Seniors, the Bellevue Bulldogs and for Duluth. He signed with Minneapolis in 1925, playing two years as an amateur and another two years with the same club when it turned professional.

The Boston Bruins purchased the contracts of Thompson and Cooney Weiland before the 1928-29 season, with Thompson taking over as the first-string goaltender from Hal Winkler. He remained with the Bruins for 10 seasons. He played his final two NHL seasons with Detroit. His lifetime goals-against per game average in regular-season competition was 2.08; his playoff average was a remarkable 1.88 goals-against per game. In addition to his Vezina Trophy triumphs, Thompson was selected to NHL All-Star Teams on four occasions.

His most memorable game was a marathon overtime session against Toronto in 1933. The game went into 104 minutes and 46 seconds of overtime before Toronto won, 1-0. Thompson died February 9, 1981. Inducted 1959.

LLOYD TURNER
BUILDER

LLOYD TURNER was Mr. Hockey to fans in Calgary and most of western Canada. He built teams, leagues and arenas in a lifetime career.

Turner was born in Elmvale, Ontario, August 9, 1884 and lived in Sault Ste. Marie and Fort William before arriving in Calgary in 1909. At the Soo, he played with the famous McNamaras and in Fort William he coached, played and managed. In Calgary, Turner had ice installed in an old roller-skating rink, organizing both a team and a league to play in this new facility. This new league produced the Calgary Tigers, Stanley Cup challengers in 1924. Hockey Hall of Fame greats Red Dutton and Herb Gardiner played for the Tigers.

Turner moved to Minneapolis and Seattle, but came back to Calgary in 1931 and reorganized the Western Canada Hockey League. He contributed to the revival of Allan Cup competition during the early 1930s. Perhaps most rewarding was his organization of Alberta's Native tribes into tournament competition. He died April 7, 1976, in Calgary. Inducted 1958.

"Cooney" Weiland
Centre • Boston, Ottawa, Detroit

Born in Egmondville, Ontario, on November 5, 1904, Ralph Weiland acquired the nickname "Cooney" as a child. He played 11 seasons in the NHL with Boston, Detroit and the old Ottawa Senators and was a member of two Stanley Cup champions with the Bruins of 1928-29 and 1938-39, his first and last seasons in the NHL.

In 11 seasons, he totalled 188 goals and 170 assists in 557 regular-season games and 14 goals and 12 assists in the playoffs. His best season saw him score 43 goals in 44 games in 1929-30. He was voted to the NHL's Second All-Star Team in 1934-35.

A very slick stickhandler, Weiland came to the Bruins from Minneapolis. In Boston, he became part of the "Dynamite Line" with Dit Clapper and Dutch Gainor. Cooney was sold to Ottawa for the 1932-33 season and then went to Detroit, but returned to Boston in 1935-36 in a trade for Marty Barry. He remained with Boston until his retirement as a player. He coached the Bruins beginning in 1939-40. They won their third Stanley Cup — and last until 1969-70 — under his guidance in 1940-41.

Weiland played his minor hockey at Seaforth, Ontario, and went to Owen Sound, Ontario, to play junior in 1923. Owen Sound won the Memorial Cup in 1924. From 1925 through 1928 he played in Minneapolis. After leaving the Bruins, he coached at Hershey and New Haven in the American Hockey League. He was later named coach of the Harvard University Crimson, a position he held until his retirement in 1971. He died July 3, 1985.

Inducted 1971.

Arthur Wirtz
Builder

Arthur Wirtz was a Chicago native born January 23, 1901 who joined forces in the 1930s with James Norris. They formed a company to acquire Detroit's NHL franchise and the Olympia Stadium, both of which were in receivership. It was from this beginning that Wirtz expanded into hockey and substantially contributed not only to the growth of hockey in the United States but, literally, to its survival.

In 1933, along with James Norris and James D. Norris, Wirtz acquired control of the Chicago Stadium Corporation, taking it out of receivership as well. A tenant of the building was the Chicago Black Hawks hockey team, then owned by Major Frederic McLaughlin. The Norrises and Wirtz later acquired control of Madison Square Garden, the St. Louis Arena and other facilities.

In 1954, two years after James Norris' death, Wirtz and James D. Norris bought the Chicago team from McLaughlin's estate. This purchase compelled them to divest themselves of their hockey interests in Detroit. Both lost approximately $2½ million rebuilding the Hawks while attendance was at an all-time low but the franchise soon became one of the most successful in the NHL, winning the Stanley Cup in 1961. In 1966, with the death of James D. Norris, Wirtz was primarily responsible for persuading the NHL to include St. Louis in its expansion plan. Wirtz sold the St. Louis Arena to the Salomon family, owners of the new St. Louis Blues. Arthur Wirtz died July 21, 1983.

Inducted 1971.

Roy Worters
Goaltender • Pittsburgh, NY Americans, Montreal

One of the smallest goalies ever to play in the NHL, Roy Worters was the first netminder to win the Hart Trophy as the NHL player most valuable to his team. Worters was only 5'3" and seldom weighed more than 130 pounds, but he starred for 12 seasons, often with teams that gave him a minimum amount of protection.

He won the Hart Trophy in 1928-29 and added the Vezina Trophy in 1930-31. He was also named to the league's Second All-Star Team on two occasions. Known as "The Shrimp" by his teammates, Roy first played in the NHL for the Pittsburgh Pirates. He joined the New York Americans in 1928-29 and, except for one game in the 1929-30 season when he played for the Montreal Canadiens, completed his pro career with that team. Worters averaged 2.27 goals-against in 484 league games. In 1931, he demanded and received a three-year contract that called for a salary of $8,500 per season — an unheard-of sum for goalies in those days.

He is credited with being the first goalie to use the back of his hands to divert shots to the corners. A gritty player, he played his last seven games in 1936-37 with a severe hernia, defying anyone to take him out of the lineup.

Worters' interest in hockey continued long after he retired as a player. He was active in the NHL Oldtimers Association and also worked on behalf of crippled children. Born in Toronto October 19, 1900, he died November 7, 1957, in Toronto. Inducted 1969.

When Dynasties Ruled the Ice

1943–1967

Dave Keon and Terry Sawchuk would later find themselves as teammates with the Toronto Maple Leafs, sharing a Stanley Cup championship in 1967.

SID ABEL
CENTRE • DETROIT, CHICAGO

THERE IS LITTLE in hockey that Sid Abel has not done — and done well. He began his NHL career in 1938 with the Detroit Red Wings and spent nine full seasons and parts of three others in a Detroit uniform. He was an All-Star at two different positions, a Hart Trophy winner, and captain of the Wings at 24, establishing himself as one of the league's great centres on Detroit's famed "Production Line" between Gordie Howe and Ted Lindsay.

Abel scored 189 goals in the NHL, including a personal high of 34 in the 1949-50 season and a league-leading 28 in 1948-49. Abel left Detroit in 1952 to become playing coach of the Chicago Black Hawks, leading that team to its first playoff berth in nine seasons.

Sid left Chicago after two seasons to become a commentator on Red Wings' television broadcasts. He returned to coaching midway through the 1957-58 season as Wings' coach when Jimmy Skinner was forced to resign due to illness. He became general manager in 1962, succeeding Jack Adams. In his 10-1/2 years behind the Wings' bench, Abel was a "player's coach" — one who liked to be close to his team. During that time his teams won a league championship and made the Stanley Cup playoffs seven times.

Abel was born February 22, 1918, in Melville, Saskatchewan. Inducted 1969.

• •

WAR YEARS...

After the outbreak of World War II, the NHL attempted to carry on as normally as possible, but by the 1942-43 season, it looked as though hockey would be forced to shut down. Only recognition by the U.S. and Canadian governments of the importance of the game to public morale convinced the NHL to continue operations.

More than 80 players had joined the armed forces by 1943, a huge percentage of the rosters in the six-team NHL. Boston had seen its entire high-scoring "Kraut Line" drafted. Toronto was without captain Syl Apps. The Rangers lost brothers Lynn and Muzz Patrick. Many more of the game's top stars were gone as well. Some hockey experts argued that with the league weakened, any records set during the war years should not be counted, but their suggestions were never acted upon.

War-time hockey prolonged the careers of many veterans and gave first opportunities to unproven youngsters. Future stars like Butch Bouchard, Ted Kennedy, Elmer Lach, Ted Lindsay, and Rocket Richard all got their start during the war.

• •

SYL APPS
CENTRE • TORONTO

ALTHOUGH a modest, quiet type, Syl Apps was a great inspirational leader of the Toronto Maple Leafs. His entire professional career was spent with Toronto, most of it as team captain. He joined the Leafs in 1936 and became the first winner of the Calder Trophy, awarded at that time by NHL president Frank Calder to the outstanding rookie in the league.

Apps played seven more seasons before becoming a member of the Canadian Armed Forces during World War II. In that time he played on one Stanley Cup winner, was voted to the First All-Star Team at centre twice and to the Second Team three times, and won the Lady Byng Trophy in 1941-42.

Returning to the Leafs for the 1945-46 season, Apps continued his fine play and in the next three seasons scored 24, 25 and 26 goals to bring his career total to 201 — an average of 20 per season. He also led the Leafs to two more Stanley Cup triumphs before retiring after the 1947-48 season.

Syl Apps was born January 18, 1915, in Paris, Ontario, and was an exceptionally fine athlete, even as a youngster. He played both hockey and football for McMaster University in Hamilton, excelling at both sports. In his final junior year, he played amateur hockey with the Hamilton Tigers. He was also a great pole-vaulter, winning the Canadian and British Empire championship in 1934 and the Canadian again in 1935. He finished sixth in the 1936 Olympic Games to earn a point for Canada. Inducted 1961.

JOHN ASHLEY
REFEREE

WHEN HE RETIRED following the 1971-72 season, John Ashley was regarded as the top official in the NHL. "I never hesitated putting him into any key game under any situation," said former NHL referee-in-chief Scotty Morrison. "He was the wheelhorse of our officiating staff, who performed his duties with great credit to himself and to the League," said former NHL President Clarence Campbell.

Born March 5, 1930, in Galt, Ontario, Ashley lived in Preston, Ontario, until age 21 when he moved to Kitchener. A former player, he graduated from junior ranks (Galt, Toronto Marlboros, Stratford and Guelph) to play with Pittsburgh and Syracuse of the American Hockey League. He later played senior hockey at Stratford. His officiating career began in Kitchener minor hockey. After one season, he moved into the Ontario Hockey Association and signed an NHL contract in 1959, working his first season in the AHL and Eastern Pro Hockey League with spot assignments in the NHL.

During the next 12 seasons, he handled 17 games as a linesman and 605 games as a referee in regular-season play as well as working 59 Stanley Cup playoff matches. In 1971, he became the first man to referee the seventh game in each of three Stanley Cup playoff series that required that number of games. Following retirement as a referee, he was employed by the NHL, scouting young officials. Inducted 1981.

GEORGE ARMSTRONG
RIGHT WING • TORONTO

GEORGE ARMSTRONG was born in Skead, Ontario, on July 6, 1930, and grew up in the Sudbury area. He was the son of a Scotsman and his Native wife — a background that entitled him to claim aboriginal ancestry, which he has always done proudly.

Sent to the Toronto Maple Leafs' organization by scout Bob Wilson, he was a standout junior at Stratford and with the Toronto Marlboros. He played for the Marlboro senior team which won the Allan Cup in 1950. It was while at the national senior finals in Alberta that an Indian tribe officially dubbed him "Big Chief Shoot-the-puck," and he has been known as "The Chief" ever since. It was a suitable nickname for the man who was team captain for 13 of his 21 years in the NHL.

Armstrong did not possess great speed or maneuverability but was a diligent, positional player who became one of the Leafs' best men, not only on the ice but in the dressing room where his leadership qualities enabled him to bring out the best in everyone with whom he associated. In 1187 regular-season NHL games George scored 296 goals, added 417 assists and was team captain when the Leafs won the Stanley Cup in 1962, 1963, 1964 and 1967. En route to these four championships, the Leafs played a total of 45 playoff games in which Armstrong recorded 18 goals and 21 assists — establishing himself as a money player.

Inducted 1975.

"BUNNY" AHEARNE
BUILDER

JOHN FRANCIS (BUNNY) AHEARNE was born in Ireland November 19, 1900, but lived most of his life in England. Opening a travel agency in London in 1928, his base broadened into hockey and for more than 40 years he played a prominent, often dominant role on the international scene.

Ahearne became secretary of the British Ice Hockey Association in 1933 and retained that position for 40 years. As BIHA delegate to the International Ice Hockey Federation from 1934 until the outbreak of World War II in 1939, he also managed the British Nationals, a team that won the 1936 Olympic gold medal. He became an IIHF executive member and, in 1947, played a key role in negotiating the return of Canada and the U.S. to active membership. Elected an IIHF vice-president in 1955, he became president two years later and served in one of these two positions until retiring in 1975. His influence was unquestionable.

During the Ahearne years, the IIHF championship became a leading international sports event. International hockey had grown to 26 nations competing in three divisions by 1977, the year of his election to the Hall of Fame. He saw the importance of television and negotiated lucrative broadcast rights sales, providing security for the organization. He popularized "dasher-board advertising" decades before its first appearance in North American rinks, and insisted that a good share of the proceeds be used to help finance lesser IIHF competitions.

For more than two decades Bunny Ahearne ruled European, Olympic and other international ice hockey events. His personal contribution is difficult to underestimate. He died April 11, 1985.

Inducted 1977.

HAROLD BALLARD
BUILDER

HAROLD BALLARD was born July 30, 1903, in Toronto, and from a very tender age was associated with his father in the manufacturing of ice skates that bore the family name. It was a short step to participation in all aspects of amateur hockey and, ultimately, to national recognition as coach and manager of the 1932 Allan Cup-winning Toronto Nationals. Transferring allegiance to the Marlboro organization, he became its principal executive and financial backer in both senior and junior hockey, as well as in lacrosse. His Marlboro juniors won the Memorial Cup seven times and the seniors also won the Allan Cup in 1950.

In 1961, he became one of three principal owners and chief executive of Maple Leaf Gardens. Always deeply conscious of the game's overall welfare, he was a vigorous sponsor of amateur hockey at all levels and an active and respected participant in the affairs of the National Hockey League. He was a prime supporter of the first series with the Soviets and provided Maple Leaf Gardens without charge as a training camp for Team Canada in 1972. With no fanfare, he also wholeheartedly supported the handicapped and disadvantaged, supplying facilities without cost and often aiding with ideas and financing. He has been honoured by the Ontario Hockey Association, the City of Toronto and the Canadian Rehabilitation Council for the Disabled, among others, for outstanding service.

Flamboyant, often misunderstood by those who did not know him but respected by those who did, Harold Ballard gave a half-century of dedicated support to hockey. He died April 11, 1990.

Inducted 1977.

ANDY BATHGATE
RIGHT WING • NY RANGERS, TORONTO, DETROIT, PITTSBURGH, VANCOUVER (WHA)

ANDY BATHGATE was a player of rare skill. He had an awesome shot but delighted in setting up goals for his linemates, as shown in his 624 assists in 1069 NHL regular-season games. He also scored 349 regular-season goals, plus 21 goals and 14 assists in 54 play-off contests.

He was a marvelous skater and deft puck-handler but just making it to the NHL was a tribute to his fortitude. Born August 28, 1932, in Winnipeg, he played his minor hockey in suburban West Kildonan. He signed with the Guelph Juniors in 1951 and on his first shift on the ice took a check that damaged his left knee. Surgery in 1952 implanted a steel plate beneath his kneecap that plagued Bathgate throughout his career. Despite this, he missed only five games in nine seasons with the Rangers.

Bathgate enjoyed his greatest season in 1958-59 when he scored 40 goals, had 88 points and won the Hart Trophy as the league's MVP. In 1961-62 he tied Bobby Hull for most points in the season, but Hull was awarded the Ross Trophy on the basis of most goals scored. Andy was traded to Toronto in 1963-64, the principal man in a seven-player deal, and played on his only Stanley Cup winner. He was later acquired by Detroit and then by Pittsburgh in the 1967 expansion draft. After one season with the Penguins and two more with Vancouver of the Western League, he completed his NHL career, returning to Pittsburgh in 1970-71. He later played in Switzerland and the WHA. Bathgate was named twice to each of the NHL's First and Second All-Star Teams against stiff competition from three other great right wingers: Gordie Howe, Maurice Richard and Bernie Geoffrion.

Inducted 1978.

FATHER DAVID BAUER
BUILDER

BORN NOVEMBER 2, 1924, DAVID BAUER was a member of a large and athletic family from Kitchener-Waterloo, Ontario. A highly skilled left winger, he played on the Oshawa Generals team that won the Memorial Cup in 1944. While teammates like Bill Ezinicki, Ted Lindsay, and Gus Morton went on to pursue professional hockey careers, Bauer felt a different calling, and went on to become a Basilian priest.

Following his ordination in 1953, he joined the teaching staff of St. Michaels College, and guided the school's Junior A team to a Memorial Cup win in 1961.

Father Bauer had a dream that Canadian boys could play elite amateur hockey without forgoing higher education. In 1961, under the auspices of the Canadian Amateur Hockey Association, he began building a Canadian National Team comprised of University of British Columbia students who would represent their country at the 1964 Olympics. Under his leadership, the "Nats" became a close-knit squad that exemplified the ideals of sportsmanship. They did not bring home a medal from the Olympics, but their determination was a source of pride to Canada. Although Bauer's "dream team" never returned with anything better than a bronze medal in international competition, he nevertheless legitimized the notion of a national amateur team.

Father David Bauer died November 9, 1988, in Goderich, Ontario.

Inducted 1989.

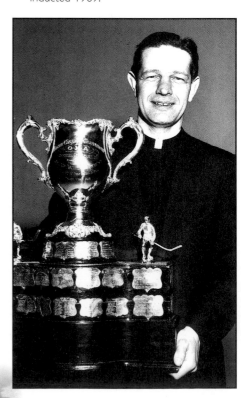

Jean Beliveau
Centre • Montreal

"Rarely has the career of an athlete been so exemplary. By his courage, his sense of discipline and honour, his lively intelligence and finesse, his magnificent team spirit, Beliveau has given new prestige to hockey," said Pierre Trudeau, Prime Minister of Canada, at Jean Beliveau Night, March 24, 1971, in the Montreal Forum.

"... it is hard, but I will play no more. I only hope I have made a contribution to a great game," Jean Beliveau stated as he announced his retirement from the NHL on June 9, 1971. Born August 31, 1931, in Trois Rivieres, Quebec, Jean Beliveau was to become a living legend. "Le Gros Bill," as he became known because of his six-foot-three, 205-pound frame, scored 507 goals during his 18 full seasons in the NHL. But he was of a character that would have made him great and won him respect anywhere, even if he had scored but half that number. When he retired, Jean was named to an executive position with the Montreal Canadiens and designated official spokesman of the organization. This was just an acknowledgement of the capacity he had been filling for a number of years, if not by words, then by actions.

He joined the Canadiens as a pro in the 1953-54 season, having played five NHL games as an amateur up from the Quebec Aces in two previous seasons — and from the first was a team leader, although he didn't officially become team captain until 1961. His highest single goal-scoring season was 1955-56 when he not only won the Art Ross Trophy as scoring champion with 47 goals and 41 assists, but also won the Hart Trophy as the NHL's most valuable player. Three seasons later, he had a 45-goal effort. In 1963-64, Jean was again voted winner of the Hart Trophy and the following year won the first Conn Smythe Trophy as the most valuable player in the Stanley Cup playoffs. In his final season, 1970-71, Jean collected 16 playoff assists and ended his playing career on a winning note as the Canadiens were upset winners of the Cup.

When Beliveau signed with the Canadiens, he received a five-year $100,000 contract, plus bonuses — a fantastic figure for that era, and became the game's most publicized rookie to that time. Statistically, in addition to his 507 regular-season goals, Beliveau added 712 assists as well as recording 79 goals and 97 assists in 162 playoff games. He played on 10 Stanley Cup championship teams.

Including playoffs, Jean played 1287 NHL games. He was named six times to the NHL's First All-Star Team and four times to the Second. Jean also scored 25 or more goals in 13 seasons, had 80 game-winning goals, three four-goal games and 18 three-goal games during his brilliant career. The Jean Beliveau Trophy is awarded annually to the top scorer in the Quebec Major Junior Hockey League.

Inducted 1972.

Doug Bentley
Left Wing • Chicago, NY Rangers

Douglas Bentley had all the attributes of a great hockey player. He had speed, scoring power, stamina, showmanship and was a fine back-checking left winger. All he lacked was size — his playing weight was 145 pounds — but his ability more than offset that.

He showed such outstanding early ability that at only 16, he played senior hockey for Delisle, the Saskatchewan town where he was born September 3, 1916. In 1938-39, he played on a team with four of his brothers in Drumheller, Alberta.

In 1939 he began a 12-year stint with the Chicago Black Hawks of the NHL. For several seasons he was united with his brother Max and Bill Mosienko on one of the NHL's best forward units, the "Pony Line." All three scored more than 200 goals during their NHL careers, Doug getting 219 and winning a scoring title in 1942-43. He was also named to the First All-Star Team three times: in 1942-43, 1943-44 and 1946-47.

A singular honour was bestowed on him in 1950 when a Chicago newspaper voted him the Half-Century Award as Chicago's best player up to that year.

The one honour that eluded Doug Bentley throughout his career was that he never played on a Stanley Cup winner. Although he retired from the NHL in 1951, Doug remained in the game as a player, coach and scout. He also made a brief NHL comeback with the New York Rangers in 1953-54. He died in Saskatoon on November 24, 1972.

Inducted 1964.

MAX BENTLEY
CENTRE • CHICAGO, TORONTO, NY RANGERS

MAX BENTLEY was so frail-looking that he tried out with three NHL teams before getting a chance to stick. At 145 pounds, he was passed over by Boston, and when he tried out in Montreal, the doctor told him he had a bad heart and shouldn't play hockey. But Chicago finally took a chance on him and Max became known as "The Dipsy-Doodle Dandy of Delisle," going on to become a great playmaking and puck-handling centres.

He was born March 1, 1920, in Delisle, Saskatchewan, a member of a family of 13 children that became known as the outstanding hockey family in the West. At the height of his Chicago stardom, Max was the key figure in an amazing NHL trade. Toronto gave up five high-quality players for Bentley and an amateur player. With the Hawks, he had been a member of the famous Pony Line with brother Doug and Bill Mosienko, both of whom are Hockey Hall of Fame members. With Toronto, Max continued his sparkling play and was a part of three Stanley Cup championship teams.

Max Bentley won the Hart Trophy in 1945-46, the Lady Byng Trophy in 1942-43 and the Art Ross Trophy in 1944-45 and 1945-46. He also was voted to the First All-Star team in 1945-46. In 646 NHL games, Max scored 245 goals and had 299 assists for a total of 544 points. He scored 18 goals in 51 playoff games. He died January 19, 1984.

Inducted 1966.

"TOE" BLAKE
LEFT WING • MTL. MAROONS, MONTREAL

HECTOR (TOE) BLAKE was tabbed very early in life as a coming superstar of hockey. Ensuing events bore this out for he succeeded not only in becoming a great player, but an outstanding coach, too. Born August 21, 1912, in Victoria Mines, Ontario, Blake played his first organized hockey in the Sudbury-Nickel Belt League in 1929-30.

For the next year and a half, Blake played senior hockey but returned to play junior for the latter part of 1931-32 when he was a member of the team that won the Memorial Cup. Blake played for the Hamilton Tigers, then a senior team, for most of the next three seasons until joining the Montreal Maroons in February of 1934.

The Maroons won the Stanley Cup in 1934-35, but Blake sat on the bench. He started the next season with Providence but joined the Canadiens in February when the Maroons traded him and Bill Miller for goalie Lorne Chabot. The rest is NHL history as Blake starred with the Canadiens until retiring on January 11, 1948, when he broke his leg.

Blake won the NHL scoring title in 1938-39 and the Lady Byng Trophy in 1945-46. For several seasons he was part of one of the NHL's greatest forward lines with Elmer Lach and Maurice ("The Rocket") Richard. He scored 235 goals in 578 league games, played on two Stanley Cup winners and won the Hart Trophy in 1938-39. He was named to the NHL First All-Star team three times and to the Second Team on two occasions.

He returned to the Canadiens as coach in 1955-56. His teams won eight more Stanley Cups before he retired following the 1967-68 season. He died May 17, 1993. Inducted 1966.

LEO BOIVIN
DEFENCE • TORONTO, BOSTON, DETROIT, PITTSBURGH, MINNESOTA

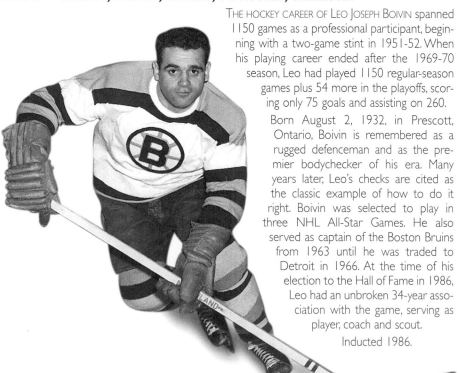

THE HOCKEY CAREER OF LEO JOSEPH BOIVIN spanned 1150 games as a professional participant, beginning with a two-game stint in 1951-52. When his playing career ended after the 1969-70 season, Leo had played 1150 regular-season games plus 54 more in the playoffs, scoring only 75 goals and assisting on 260.

Born August 2, 1932, in Prescott, Ontario, Boivin is remembered as a rugged defenceman and as the premier bodychecker of his era. Many years later, Leo's checks are cited as the classic example of how to do it right. Boivin was selected to play in three NHL All-Star Games. He also served as captain of the Boston Bruins from 1963 until he was traded to Detroit in 1966. At the time of his election to the Hall of Fame in 1986, Leo had an unbroken 34-year association with the game, serving as player, coach and scout.

Inducted 1986.

JOHNNY BOWER
GOALTENDER • NY RANGERS, TORONTO

"WHEN THE COMPETITION got stiffer, I worked three times as hard. Competition drove me," said Johnny Bower, a remarkable hockey player and a remarkable man.

Johnny Bower was born November 8, 1924, in Prince Albert, Saskatchewan, the only boy in a family of nine. Always a goalie, he started without pads or skates until someone gave them to him. He played minor hockey until 1940, when he enlisted in the Canadian Army. After four years, two of them overseas, he was discharged and was still young enough to play junior. Johnny actually had two outstanding hockey careers: one in the minor pro leagues and one in the NHL. Drafted in 1945 by Cleveland, he bounced around the minors for 14 years, except for 1953-54 when he played for the New York Rangers. He won both the Les Cunningham Trophy as the American Hockey League's most valuable player and the Harry Holmes Trophy as the league leading goaltender on three occasions. He was the Western League's top goalie in his one season with Vancouver.

Drafted by Toronto Maple Leafs, he began his second career of 11 full NHL seasons in 1958-59. "He was an inspiration to us," said former Leaf captain George Armstrong. "He shamed others into hard work. John gave everything he could in workouts, and we weren't going to let that old guy show us up." During his tenure with the Leafs the team won four Stanley Cups, he was named once to the NHL's First All-Star Team and he played in five All-Star games. He shared the Vezina Trophy in 1964-65 with Terry Sawchuk and had a 2.52 career goals-against average. He had 37 regular-season shutouts and five more in 74 playoff games, to go with his 2.54 playoff average.

Inducted 1976.

"BUTCH" BOUCHARD
DEFENCE • MONTREAL

WHEN EMILE (BUTCH) BOUCHARD first reported to the Montreal Canadiens' training camp, he was young, eager, and rough around the edges. But, at 185 pounds, he was one of the heaviest men in camp. He was so keen, he rode a bicycle 50 miles to get to training camp and then proceeded to throw his weight around, much to the chagrin of some of the veterans.

But Bouchard made the team that first season, 1941-42, and for 15 years was an outstanding defenceman in the NHL. In this era of many great rearguards Bouchard was voted to the First All-Star Team three times and to the Second twice. Although he had great size and extraordinary strength, Bouchard never took advantage of his physical power to bully an opponent. He was robust but not unfair, feared but respected by his rivals.

He scored 49 goals and had 144 assists as a playmaking defenceman. He was captain of the Canadiens from 1948-49 to 1955-56 and played a big role in establishing Montreal as one of hockey's outstanding dynasties.

Born September 11, 1920 in Montreal, Bouchard's contribution to the game goes far beyond his activity as a player. After his retirement from the NHL, he has served as coach and president of junior teams. The Emile "Butch" Bouchard Trophy is awarded annually to the top defenceman in the Quebec Major Junior Hockey League.

Bouchard's son Pierre also played defence and was a crowd favourite with the Canadiens.

Inducted 1966.

THE THIRD BENTLEY...

From the six Sutters of Viking, Alberta to Hod and Bruce Stuart at the turn of the century, hockey has long been a family affair. One of the all-time great brother acts was Max and Doug Bentley. Much less known is their older brother, Reg.

Born May 3, 1914, Reg Bentley joined Max and Doug with the Chicago Black Hawks on New Year's Day 1943, playing right wing on a line with his already well-established siblings. While his brothers wound up in the Hall of Fame, Reg's NHL career lasted just 11 games. He scored one goal and collected two assists.

"TURK" BRODA
GOALTENDER • TORONTO

JACK ADAMS, former manager and coach of Detroit Red Wings, once said about Walter (Turk) Broda: "He hasn't a nerve in his body. He could tend goal in a tornado and never blink an eye." This statement, made before Broda became renowned in the NHL, proved prophetic. His hockey trail is heavily dotted with championships and he went on to become known as one of the greatest "money goalies" of all time.

Born May 15, 1914, in Brandon, Manitoba, Broda starred in amateur hockey with Brandon juvenile and junior teams, playing his last junior year with the Winnipeg Monarchs in 1933-34. He played for the International League champion Detroit Olympics in 1935-36 and shortly after was sold to the Toronto Maple Leafs for a then-record price of $8,000.

His pro career, all with the Leafs, spanned 16 seasons with two years lost to duty in the Canadian armed forces during World War II. He won the Vezina Trophy in 1940-41 and 1947-48 and shared it with Al Rollins in 1950-51 when Rollins played 39 games and Broda 31.

It was in playoff competition that Broda really excelled. He earned 13 shutouts in 102 playoff games, posting a phenomenal 1.98 goals-against record. Broda also played on five Stanley Cup winners. He died in Toronto on October 17, 1972.

Inducted 1967.

JOHN BUCYK
LEFT WING • DETROIT, BOSTON

JOHN BUCYK brings outstanding credentials to the Hockey Hall of Fame. When he retired as a player after the 1977-78 season, he left behind a record of 1540 games, 556 goals and 813 assists for a total of 1369 points in a career that spanned 23 years in the NHL. At that time he trailed only Gordie Howe, Phil Esposito and Stan Mikita on the list of all-time point scorers.

He also is remembered as a winner of the Lady Byng Trophy in 1971 and 1974, a member of Stanly Cup-winning teams in Boston in 1970 and 1972, and as a First All-Star in 1970-71 and Second All-Star in 1967-68. He scored 51 goals during the 1970-71 season.

Born May 12, 1935 in Edmonton, he became a stocky left winger with a reputation for hanging tough in close action around the opposition's nets. "I never knew anyone who could hit harder, especially with a hip check," said former teammate Bobby Orr. Johnny stood six feet tall and weighed 215 pounds in his playing days. Bucyk played two pro seasons with Edmonton of the Western Hockey League where he set records as a rookie, then graduated to the Detroit Red Wings for another two years before moving on to the Boston Bruins in a trade for Terry Sawchuk prior to the 1957-58 season. He stayed and starred in Boston for another 21 years.

For a number of seasons he played with unproductive Boston teams, but was an integral part of the Bruins' revitalization in the 1970s.

Inducted 1981.

BRODA'S WEIGHT...

In late November of 1949, with his Maple Leafs slumping and the Grey Cup game capturing most of the headlines for Canadian football, Conn Smythe hatched a plan to shake up his team and win back the sports pages. After a 6-3 loss to Chicago on November 27, Smythe announced that his roly-poly goalie Turk Broda would ride the bench until he lost a significant amount of weight.

With newspaper photographers snapping shots, Broda and Smythe signed a contract whereby the goalie would bring down his playing weight or look for another line of work. "The Turk is still fighting the Battle of the Bulge," Smythe declared. "He'll play goal for us if he keeps down to the weight I stipulated. If he doesn't, he'll be hurt where it hurts most—in the pocketbook." The amiable Broda posed for pictures sitting on a weigh scale and around the family dinner table. Daily reports were issued on his weight reduction.

A week later, after missing one game (which the Leafs lost to Detroit 2-0), a slimmed-down Broda returned to the Leafs' net ten pounds lighter. A crowd of 13,359 at Maple Leaf Gardens cheered every one of his 22 saves that night as Turk blanked the Rangers 2-0.

JACK BUTTERFIELD
BUILDER

JACK BUTTERFIELD has been described as an administrator with a surgeon's touch.

Born August 1, 1919, in Regina, Saskatchewan, Butterfield was a dynamic and effective administrator of the game. Perhaps more than any other individual, he helped keep minor pro hockey alive during the years of National Hockey League expansion and competition for players from the World Hockey Association. These two factors came close to killing minor pro hockey, but Butterfield provided the strong hand to lead it through its most trying period.

As president of the American Hockey League, a league which provided hundred of players to the NHL, Butterfield spearheaded indemnification negotiations, twice rewrote the AHL constitution and bylaws, and several times revised player contract forms to stay abreast of a constantly changing hockey world. Jack came well prepared to assume the AHL presidency in 1966.

His days as a player were cut short by an injury and he became a public relations man and trainer for the AHL New Haven Eagles, working for his uncle, Eddie Shore. He later served as team business manager at Fort Worth of the U.S. Hockey League and Oakland of the Western Hockey League before returning to Springfield of the AHL to work as rink manager, concessions manager, trainer, coach and finally general manager. His proven dedication and achievement make him a worthy inductee to the Hockey Hall of Fame. A trophy named in his honour is awarded annually to the AHL's playoff MVP.

Inducted 1980.

FRANK BUCKLAND
BUILDER

FRANK BUCKLAND was born May 23, 1902, in Gravenhurst, Ontario. His first involvement with hockey at the amateur level was in Toronto while he was a coach, then manager, then president of a junior club. Upon graduation from university he took a position in Peterborough, Ontario, where he coached junior and senior teams from 1932 to 1940.

Buckland was elected to the Ontario Hockey Association executive and continued working in amateur hockey, becoming president of the OHA for a two-year term in 1955. In 1961, he was elected treasurer of that organization, still serving with distinction in that office at the time of his election to the Hockey Hall of Fame in 1975.

The Canadian Amateur Hockey Association recognized his outstanding service in 1965 when it presented him with the CAHA Meritorious Award. The same year, the OHA presented Buckland with its Gold Stick Award and, in 1973, he was named a Life Member of the OHA. In 1974, the Province of Ontario presented him with its Sports Achievement Award. Buckland made amateur hockey his life's work.

Inducted 1975.

CLARENCE CAMPBELL
BUILDER

CLARENCE S. CAMPBELL was a Rhodes Scholar who chose to make hockey his career. It was a fortunate choice for the game because he rose to the game's highest office as President of the National Hockey League.

Born July 9, 1905, in Fleming, Saskatchewan, Campbell was raised in western Canada. He graduated from the University of Alberta, then from Oxford University in England. Prior to succeeding Mervyn (Red) Dutton as NHL President in 1946, Campbell distinguished himself as a lawyer, then as a Canadian Army officer in World War II. He commanded the 4th Canadian Armed Division headquarters throughout operations in Europe and joined the Canadian War Crimes Unit in 1945. An average athlete, he made his name as an administrator although he refereed lacrosse and NHL hockey prior to World War II. He was also a curler and a golfer.

Two of his outstanding achievements as President of the NHL were the establishment in 1946 of the NHL Pension Society and the successful guidance of the league's expansion from six to 12 teams in 1967-68. In 1977 he retired after 31 years as NHL President. He died June 24, 1984.

Inducted 1966.

BILL CHADWICK
REFEREE

IT DIDN'T TAKE BILL CHADWICK long to make his mark as an official in the NHL. The likeable American spent one year as linesman in the NHL in 1940, then moved up to referee hundreds of regular-season and Stanley Cup contests until he retired in 1955.

Chadwick's career was built on a love for hockey, a determination to succeed — and the failure of someone else to show up. Born October 10, 1915, in New York City, his playing days were launched with the Stock Exchange team in the Metropolitan League. He won promotion to the New York Rovers of the Eastern Amateur League where, while sitting out a game with injuries, he was asked to substitute for a referee who had failed to appear. He took an immediate liking to this aspect of the sport.

As a referee, he found that he didn't know what to do with his hands, so he decided to use them to denote the reason for penalties. For a holding penalty, Chadwick grabbed his wrist and for a tripping penalty he slapped his shin. At first, observers thought he was showboating, but it quickly became apparent that he had added a new and desirable asset to the game, making it more understandable to players and fans alike.

Inducted 1964.

ALEX DELVECCHIO
CENTRE • DETROIT

ALEX DELVECCHIO played a total of 22 full seasons and parts of two other with the Detroit Red Wings before retiring on November 9, 1973. He is only the second player in NHL history to play more than 20 seasons with one club. Teammate Gordie Howe is the first.

In 13 seasons he scored 20 or more goals and had a career total of 456 goals and 825 assists, plus 35 goals and 69 assists in the playoffs. An exceptionally clean player, Alex was a three-time winner of the Lady Byng Trophy for combining gentlemanly conduct with a high standard of play. He was also named to two positions on all-star teams: centre in 1952-53 and left wing in 1958-59, both on the Second Team. Except for the 1956-57 season when an ankle injury caused him to miss 22 games, he missed only 21 other games in his career. He competed in 1549 regular-season games, plus 121 in the playoffs. He collected a total of only 383 penalty minutes, never receiving more than 37 minutes in a season.

In his lengthy career, Alex was a member of many outstanding Detroit teams: Stanley Cup winners in 1951-52, 1953-54 and 1954-55 and Prince of Wales Trophy winners on six occasions when the trophy went to the team finishing first in NHL regular-season play. At the time of his retirement, Delvecchio ranked second to Gordie Howe in NHL records for games played, seasons played, most assists and most points. An affable, cigar-smoking player, Alex earned the nickname "Fats" early in his career, not because of obesity but for his round, pleasant face and warm, friendly smile.

He was born December 4, 1931, in Fort William, Ontario, and graduated to the NHL from the junior Oshawa Generals. Inducted 1977.

FRANK DILIO
BUILDER

SINCERITY WAS FRANK DILIO'S most valued asset. During his many years of service with Quebec amateur and junior hockey, he maintained a broad outlook, realizing that amateur hockey's role was to provide boys with good, fair competition. Hockey Hall of Fame members Rocket Richard and Emile Bouchard, along with many other stars, emerged from these leagues while he was associated with them.

Born April 12, 1912, in Montreal, Frank Dilio established an early interest in sports at St. Ann's Boys' School, under the direction of the Christian Brothers. He was secretary of their juvenile club in 1931, later joining the Quebec Amateur Hockey Association as secretary and moving up to become president by 1939. In 1943, he became registrar of the QAHA and added the duties of secretary in 1952. He held both positions until resigning in 1962.

In 1963, he received the Canadian Amateur Hockey Association's Meritorious Award. Inducted 1964.

"WOODY" DUMART
LEFT WING • BOSTON

WOODROW (WOODY) DUMART was born on Dec. 23, 1916 in Kitchener, Ontario. Dumart played his junior hockey in his home town before being called up to the Boston Bruins in 1936. Dumart spent his entire professional career in Boston before retiring at the conclusion of the 1954 season.

Woody Dumart, along with his lifetime friends and teammates Milt Schmidt and Bobby Bauer, became members of the "Kitchener Line" (also known as the "Kraut Line") with the Bruins. With the famed trio leading the attack during the 1930's and 40's, the Boston Bruins captured two Stanley Cups, their first in 1938-39, and again two years later. During the 1939-40 season, Schmidt, Dumart, and Bauer finished first, second, and third respectively in the NHL scoring race.

In 1941, all three teammates enlisted in the Royal Canadian Air Force during World War II. The trio spent three years serving their country before returning to the Bruins' lineup for the 1945-46 seasons.

Known as one of the best two-way players of his time, Dumart was often called upon to cover some of the games greatest players. He maintained a good scoring punch, reaching the 20-goal plateau in five different seasons, and was named to the All-Star team on three occasions.

Dumart went on to play 16 seasons with the Bruins, recording 211 goals and 218 assists for a total of 429 points. He also added 27 points in post season play to go along with two Stanley Cups.

Inducted 1992.

GEORGE DUDLEY
BUILDER

GEORGE DUDLEY was active in amateur hockey for more than 50 years. He was born in Midland, Ontario, April 19, 1894, and played hockey in his home town, but served as an executive after obtaining his law degree in 1917.

At the time of his on death May 8, 1960, he was treasurer of the Ontario Hockey Association, president of the International Ice Hockey Federation and head of the hockey section of the 1960 Olympic Games. Dudley was first elected to the Canadian Amateur Hockey association executive in 1925, served as its president from 1940 to 1942, became secretary in 1945 and later served as secretary-manager. He travelled throughout the world on behalf of both the CAHA and IIHF and was instrumental in arranging some of the first visits to Canada by hockey teams from Russia.

Inducted 1958.

BILL DURNAN
GOALTENDER • MONTREAL

BEFORE HE REACHED the NHL at the age of 27, Bill Durnan had won more glory than many people gain in a lifetime. Born in Toronto on January 22, 1915, Bill first achieved recognition as goalie for the Sudbury juniors in the 1933-34 Ontario Hockey Association finals. He played for contending teams in the Northern OHA for three seasons before connecting with an Allan Cup champion as goalie for the Kirkland Lake Blue Devils in 1939-40.

His ambidextrous brilliance caught the eye of people in Montreal and they persuaded him to join the senior Montreal Royals. From there, it was only a short jump to the Canadiens where he was an instant sensation, winning the Vezina Trophy in 1943-44, his first season as a pro. Durnan played seven seasons with the Canadiens and although his pro career was comparatively brief, he clearly established himself as one of the game's top goaltenders.

Bill won the Vezina Trophy six out of seven times, missing only in 1947-48 when Turk Broda of Toronto won the award. He was a six-time NHL First Team All-Star, played on four league championship teams and two Stanley Cup winners. In 1948-49, he established the modern NHL record for consecutive shutouts with four, playing 309 minutes and 21 seconds of shutout hockey. He played 383 scheduled games, allowing 901 goals for an average of 2.36 goals-against per game, with 34 shutouts. He died in Toronto on October 31, 1972.

Inducted 1963.

FERN FLAMAN
DEFENCE • BOSTON, TORONTO

FERN FLAMAN played 17 seasons with the Boston Bruins and Toronto Maple Leafs from 1944-45 to 1960-61. During his career he scored 34 goals and 174 assists in 910 games. A standout defenceman, he played on the 1951 Stanley Cup champion Maple Leafs appeared in six All-Star Games. He was a classic stay-at-home defenceman who was recognized for his devastating bodychecks.

Flaman was born on Jan. 25, 1927 in Dysart, Saskatchewan. He spent 46 years as an ambassador for the game of hockey as a player, coach, general manager, player representative and scout. Flaman skated on championship teams with the Boston Olympics and Hershey Bears, and he earned a Stanley Cup ring with the 1951 Toronto Maple Leafs. He spent 14 seasons with the Boston Bruins where he was selected to six All-Star teams. Flaman also served as captain of the Bruins for four seasons. In 1963-64, he wore all three hats for the Rhode Island Reds as that team's coach and general manager, and as a player as well. He was inducted into the Rhode Island Hockey Hall of Fame in 1965. He went on to win league titles in the AHL, WHL and CHL. From 1970 until his retirement in 1989, Flaman was coach of the Northwestern University Huskies, leading the ECHA club to numerous championship titles, including four "Beanpot" trophies and the Hockey East title in 1989. He was selected as the U.S. College Coach-of-the-Year in 1982 and has over 250 career collegiate victories.

Inducted 1990.

BILL GADSBY
DEFENCE • CHICAGO, NY RANGERS, DETROIT

TOUGH SITUATIONS were almost commonplace to Bill Gadsby. Both on and off the ice, he faced them all the same way — head on.

Born August 8, 1927, in Calgary, Alberta, he spent 20 seasons in the NHL and proved himself to be a defenceman of outstanding ability. A left-handed shot, he stood six feet and weighed 185 pounds. When only 12, he and his mother were aboard the ship Athenia, returning from England at the outbreak of World War II. The ship was torpedoed and they spent five hours in the Atlantic before being rescued. Then, in 1952, he was captain of the Chicago Black Hawks when struck by polio but beat this crippling disease and went on to become one of the few players to endure 20 seasons in the NHL.

Gadsby graduated from Edmonton junior hockey, signed to play pro with the Chicago Black Hawks and was sent to Kansas City for seasoning. He moved up to the Hawks early in 1946-47 and remained with them through 18 games of the 1954-55 campaign when he was traded to New York. Another trade took him to Detroit for the 1961-62 season and he played his last five seasons with the Wings. He returned to coach the Wings in 1968-69 and for two games of the 1969-70 schedule, when he was suddenly dismissed. Gadsby was named to the NHL's First All-Star Team three times and to the Second Team four times, but never played on a Stanley Cup winner.

Inducted 1970.

1945-55

• **1945**: A well-behaved crowd of 7,687 waits patiently inside the Detroit Olympia for almost three hours for a game with the Rangers on January 18th. The New York team was delayed by bad weather. The game finally starts at 11:13 and ends at 12:56 am. The Red Wings win 7-3.

• **1946-47**: Approval is given to award $1,000 to the winners of the Hart, Vezina, Calder, and Lady Byng trophies. Similar money would be awarded to players named to the NHL's First and Second All-Star Teams as well.

• **1947-48**: Elmer Lach wins the first Art Ross Trophy, as the NHL's scoring leader.

• **1949-50**: The NHL's schedule is expanded to 70 games, where it will remain until 1967.

• Goaltending great Bill Durnan announces he is not happy with the Montreal fans and will retire at season's end.

• **1951**: Attendance in Chicago reaches an all-time low when just 4,400 fans witness a 7-3 loss to the Rangers on February 18.

• **1952-53**: Fourteen new players join the New York Rangers, including Gump Worsley, Harry Howell, and Andy Bathgate who all go on to Hall of Fame careers.

• **1954-55**: The Norris Trophy is officially accepted as a yearly honour. • Detroit tops the NHL standings for seventh consecutive year, and wins its seventh Stanley Cup.

BERNIE GEOFFRION
RIGHT WING •
MONTREAL, NY RANGERS

BERNARD (BOOM BOOM) GEOFFRION was born February 16, 1931, and moved from junior to the Canadiens in 1951, scoring eight goals in 18 games. The 5'11", 185-pounder went on to register 393 NHL goals before retiring after the 1967-68 season. This total ranked him fifth on the all-time NHL scoring list at the time.

Although named to All-Star Teams only three times, Geoffrion blazed his name into the record book on several occasions. He won the Art Ross Trophy as scoring champion twice (1955 and 1961), the Hart Trophy as the most valuable player to his team (1961) and the Calder Trophy as top rookie during his first full season (1951-52). His career coincided with that of two of the game's greatest right wingers, Gordie Howe and Maurice "The Rocket" Richard. He joined Richard as the second player to reach the 50-goal plateau in one season (1960-61), the year he achieved a personal high of 95 points. Other highlights of his career include a five-goal game on February 19, 1955, against New York.

Geoffrion retired as a player after the 1963-64 season, but came back after missing two seasons to score 17 goals with New York. Physical infirmities ended his playing career in 1967-68. He turned to coaching, first with the Quebec Aces and then in the NHL with the Rangers, the Atlanta Flames and the Canadiens.

Inducted 1972.

GLENN HALL
GOALTENDER • DETROIT,
CHICAGO, ST. LOUIS

ONE OF THE MAGICAL NAMES in hockey is Glenn Hall, the veteran goalie who played 18 seasons in the NHL, four with Detroit, 10 with Chicago and four with St. Louis. He was consistently one of the league's outstanding goaltenders and an All-Star selection 11 times, finishing with a career goals-against average of 2.51.

Born October 3, 1931, in Humboldt, Saskatchewan, "Mr. Goalie" led the NHL in shutouts in six seasons, including his rookie campaign when he won the Calder Trophy. In all he had 84 regular-season shutouts. He holds the NHL record for most consecutive complete games by a goaltender (502) and appeared in 906 league games. At the time of his retirement he held playoff goaltending records for most games (115) and most minutes played (6889). His playoff goals-against average was 2.79. His name appears on the Vezina Trophy three times and in the NHL's expansion season of 1967-68, he was awarded the Conn Smythe Trophy for his superior goaltending on behalf of the St. Louis Blues.

Hall was the first player selected by the Blues in the 1967 Expansion Draft and posted goals-against averages of 2.48, 2.17, 2.91 and 2.41 with St. Louis. He recorded 16 shutouts with the Blues and helped lead them to the Stanley Cup finals in three consecutive seasons. Until 1968-69, Hall played without a mask.

Inducted 1975.

1961: THE RACE TO 50...

Hockey hadn't seen a 50-goal scorer since Rocket Richard recorded 50 goals in 50 games in 1944-45. Gordie Howe and Jean Beliveau came close during the 1950s, but, as the 1960-61 season progressed, two new snipers were taking aim.

In the early going, Frank Mahovlich seemed to have the best chance to reach 50. Scoring at nearly a goal-a-game rate, the Big M had 36 goals in 41 games by early January. At about the same time, Bernie Geoffrion missed six games with injuries. Boom Boom scored two goals in his first game back in February, but his total of 28 was far behind Mahovlich, who now had 41. Nagging injuries, though, slowed the Leafs winger. His production began to decline just as Geoffrion's heated up.

By March 8, a Geoffrion hat-trick gave him 16 goals in 10 games and 46 for the season. He was now just one behind Mahovlich. In his next game, Boom Boom tallied two more to pass the Big M. His sixth goal in three games then gave him 49.

Geoffrion scored his 50th goal of the 1960-61 season with two games left on the 70-game schedule. He'd tied the Rocket, but couldn't pass him. Mahovlich wound up two goals short.

BILL HANLEY
BUILDER

AT THE AGE OF 32, BILL HANLEY gave up the security of his family's business and cast his lot with the game of hockey. He went on to spend 27 years with the Ontario Hockey Association.

Born in Ireland of Canadian parents on February 28, 1915, Hanley grew up in Toronto and, after service in the Royal Canadian Navy, helped as a timekeeper for junior games at Maple Leaf Gardens in his spare time. Soon he was timekeeper for Leafs games as well. He was asked to assist George Panter, business manager of the OHA and, although the money wasn't good, Hanley wanted to work in hockey on a full-time basis. He learned from three of the best: Panter, George Dudley and W.A. (Billy) Hewitt. He stayed on as secretary-manger of the OHA until retirement in 1974. During that tenure, Bill Hanley saw and was part of many changes in the game.

He regarded Bobby Orr as the greatest player to come out of the OHA during his time, and rates teams from St. Michael's College and the Junior Canadiens among the very best. His greatest pride in working with the OHA for so many years was that, no matter who the people were, no one ever left his office feeling that they had obtained anything less than a fair hearing. He died September 17, 1990. Inducted 1986.

HOCKEY AND BASEBALL...

While many hockey stars have been great amateur baseball or softball players, only one man has managed to combine the two into successful pro careers. From 1921 to 1926, Babe Dye spent his winters on the rinks of the NHL and his springs and summers playing minor-league baseball in the International League. He gave the credit for his two-sport success to his mother, whom he claimed was a better athlete than he ever was. His father had died while he was an infant.

A broken leg in training camp with the Chicago Black Hawks in 1927 hampered the rest of Babe's hockey days and prematurely ended his baseball career. No one has ever duplicated Dye's unique two-sport feat, but Doug Harvey came close. He spent two seasons playing ball in the Ottawa Border Baseball League and later turned down a pro offer from the old Boston Braves.

DOUG HARVEY
DEFENCE • MONTREAL, NY RANGERS, DETROIT, ST. LOUIS

DOUG HARVEY was a superior athlete who excelled in many sports. Born December 19, 1924, in Montreal, he played baseball, football and hockey — all of them well.

Doug played 22 seasons of professional hockey, 14 of them with the Montreal Canadiens where he played on six Stanley Cup championship teams. He won the Norris Trophy as top NHL defenceman seven times, virtually monopolizing this award from the 1954-55 season through 1961-62.

A left-handed shot, he stood five-foot-eleven and weighed 180 pounds. Harvey was an excellent blocker, had uncanny puck control and could set the pace of a game. He could skate with the best in the game, making passes that were both timely and accurate, and was rarely off-target in his shooting. Such was the calibre of this great defenceman that he was selected to NHL All-Star Teams on 11 occasions.

Although not a prolific goal scorer — 88 goals in regular-season play and eight in the playoffs — several of Harvey's goals came at crucial times for his team. Twice in key playoff games, an opposing forward stole the puck from him to score tying goals; minutes later, in each instance, he scored the winner. His passing ability is demonstrated by the 452 assists he recorded in regular-season play. He seemed to be able to play as well as the game situation required.

Doug Harvey is always mentioned when the greatest defencemen of all time are being compared. He seldom took himself seriously and often relieved dressing room tension by a well-timed funny remark. He was traded to the New York Rangers in 1961-62 to become a playing-coach but did not at that time relish coaching responsibility and was eventually signed as a free agent by Detroit. He was signed by St. Louis where he finished his playing career. He died December 26, 1989. Inducted 1973.

GEORGE HAYES
LINESMAN

GEORGE HAYES served the NHL with distinction for 20 seasons, becoming the first NHL official to work more than 1,000 games, serving all but two seasons as a linesman — a position where he was totally at ease.

Born June 21, 1914, in Montreal, he moved to Ingersoll, Ontario at an early age and except when he was officiating, spent the balance of his life there.

He began officiating in minor and high school hockey 1936-37 and moved up to the OHA in 1941-42, the American Hockey League in 1943-33, and on to the NHL in April, 1946. Hayes went on to work 1,544 regular-season games, 149 more in the playoffs and 11 NHL All-Star Games.

Hall of Fame referee Frank Udvari said of Hayes, "when I had a difficult game to referee, I wanted George on the ice. He was the best linesman that I have ever been associated with." Another honoured referee, Red Storey, praised Hayes as the best and most colourful linesman ever to work in the NHL.

At 6'3" and 220 pounds, Hayes commanded respect, both for his size and for his ability to maintain control. His officiating career ended in 1964 after a disagreement with the league over the need for an eye test. He died November 19, 1987, in Ingersoll. Inducted 1988.

TIM HORTON
DEFENCE • TORONTO, NY RANGERS, PITTSBURGH, BUFFALO

TIM HORTON was born January 12, 1930, in Cochrane, Ontario, and from the time he moved to Toronto to accept a hockey scholarship at St. Michael's College, was recognized as a potential star.

After graduating from junior ranks and playing three seasons with Pittsburgh of the American Hockey League, he became a NHL player to stay in 1952-53 when he joined the Toronto Maple Leafs. A defenceman who shot righthanded, he stood five-ten, weighed 180 pounds and had strength few chose to challenge. He was to play almost 18 full seasons with Toronto, one each with the New York Rangers and Pittsburgh and then two with Buffalo before a tragic accident ended his life on February 21, 1974.

Horton was an excellent skater, noted for his rushing ability and powerful slapshot from the point as well as for the great strength he employed with intelligence and remarkable self-restraint. He had a reputation as a peacemaker, flinging bodies out of piles during altercations and deterring over-eager opposing battlers with a grasp known as the "Horton Bear Hug."

Away from the ice he was unassuming, usually quiet, and devoted to his family of four daughters. Tim played on four Stanley Cup winners with Toronto in the 1960s and was named six times to All-Star Teams: to the First Team in 1963-64, 1967-68 and 1968-69, and to the Second Team in 1953-54, 1962-63 and 1966-67. He played 1,446 scheduled games with 115 goals, 403 assists and 1,611 penalty minutes. In 126 playoff games, Horton had 11 goals and 39 assists while drawing 183 minutes in penalties. "Playing with him was a wonderful experience," recalled former defence-mate Allan Stanley. "He was the finest man I ever knew, on or off the ice, a great leader without a mean streak in him."

Inducted 1977.

. . . .

THE LEAFS OF THE 1960S ...

They may not have had the most talent, but few teams ever gave more of what they did have than Punch Imlach's Toronto Maple Leafs. After 11 years without winning the Stanley Cup, the Leafs finally emerged victorious again in 1962. "Bert Olmstead was so tired that he couldn't get off the bench," Imlach recalled of that victory. But the Leafs blend of a few young pups with Punch's "old pappies" proved that they possessed the stuff of champions again in 1963 and 1964. Never did the combination prove more successful than in 1967, when the Leafs upset the Montreal Canadiens to win their most recent Stanley Cup title.

. . . .

GORDIE HOWE
RIGHT WING • DETROIT, HOUSTON (WHA), NEW ENGLAND (WHA), HARTFORD

"BOTH ON AND OFF THE ICE, GORDIE HOWE's conduct ... has demonstrated a high quality of sportsmanship and competence which is an example to us all. He has earned the title: Mr. Hockey." Lester B. Pearson, former Prime Minister of Canada.

"Never in history ... has there been such an obvious and dramatic loss by a single sport. There's no way hockey can ever repay you its debt of gratitude." Clarence Campbell, President of the NHL.

When Gordie Howe first retired from the NHL in 1971 after 25 glorious seasons, he said: "Say 'retired,' not 'quit.' I don't like the word quit." And that's one thing he never did during his brilliant career with the Detroit Red Wings, Houston Aeros and New England and Hartford Whalers. In all, he played 32 demanding big-league seasons in five different decades, establishing himself as one of the sport's greatest-ever talents.

Gordie was born May 31, 1928, in Floral, Saskatchewan and played his last amateur game with the Saskatoon Lions juveniles. He played one year of minor pro with Omaha of the U.S. Hockey League before joining Detroit for the 1946-47 season. He had an effortless skating style and deceptive speed that, combined with his tremendous strength and ability to shoot with equal dexterity from either side, made him a difficult man to stop. At six-feet, and 205 pounds, he was tough, but not in a bullying way.

Howe also earned numerous nicknames, such as "Mr. Elbows" from his opponents and "Power" from his teammates. He could also have been called "The Most" as he established more records than any other NHL player. Remaining are: most NHL seasons (26), games (1767). He also holds the record for most selections to NHL All-Star Teams with 21 of which 12 were First Team selections.

He retired after the 1970-71 season, but came back to play seven more seasons beginning in 1973-74 when he joined with his sons Mark and Marty to form an all-Howe family forward line for the WHA's Houston Aeros. In the WHA, Howe was an all-star, posting seasons of 96, 99, 100 and 102 points. When Hartford joined the NHL in 1979-80, Howe, then 51, played one last season in the NHL, appearing in the 1980 All-Star Game.

Gordie is a great ambassador for hockey off the ice, attending banquets, signing thousands of autographs and doing much little-publicized charity and community work. For excellence and durability, his career will probably never be matched.

Inducted 1972.

GORDIE AND THE RANGERS...

When Gordie Howe was 15 years old, he was invited to his first NHL training camp—with the New York Rangers! Howe attended the team's workouts in Winnipeg, but the young boy was lonesome and homesick. The Rangers offered him a scholarship to Notre Dame College in his home province of Saskatchewan, but Howe only wanted to go home. A year later, travelling to Windsor with a trainload of his hockey-playing pals, Howe attended his first training camp with the Detroit Red Wings. The rest is hockey history.

HARRY HOWELL
DEFENCE • NY RANGERS, OAKLAND, CALIFORNIA, LOS ANGELES, NY/NEW JERSEY (WHA), SAN DIEGO (WHA), CALGARY (WHA)

HARRY HOWELL appeared in more games than any defenceman in the history of major league hockey. He played 1,581 games, 1,411 in the NHL and 170 in the WHA. He turned pro in 1952 with the Rangers and retired as a player in 1976.

Born December 28, 1932, in Hamilton, Ontario, his durability was such that he missed only 17 games in his first 16 years in New York, and his 1,160 games and 17 seasons were a team record for the Rangers. Harry stood six-foot-one, weighed 200 pounds and was a left-handed shot. His main regret was that he never played on a Stanley Cup winner. However, he was named to the NHL's First All-Star Team in 1966-67 and won the Norris Memorial Trophy as the league's top defenceman that same year.

He was sold to Oakland (later California) in 1969 and then to Los Angeles in 1971. He later played and coached WHA teams in New York, New Jersey, San Diego and Calgary. In his 24-year playing career, Howell scored 101 goals and assisted on 360 others. He moved on to an administrative post in 1976 when he joined the NHL's Cleveland Barons as assistant general manager. Harry later became general manager and was serving in that capacity when the Barons merged with Minnesota in 1978.

Inducted 1979.

BOBBY HULL

LEFT WING • CHICAGO, WINNIPEG (WHA), WINNIPEG, HARTFORD

AS EARLY AS AGE 10, BOBBY HULL was tagged as a sure-fire NHL player — and he didn't disappoint the experts. Born January 3, 1939, in Pointe Anne, Ontario, Hull progressed rapidly through minor hockey ranks and joined the Chicago Black Hawks to stay in the 1957-58 season.

Although he didn't invent the slapshot, Bobby's booming blaster made many goalies cower. He led the NHL in goals scored in seven separate seasons. He had blurring speed on the ice and unerring accuracy with a slapshot that many tried to emulate. In 16 NHL seasons, Hull scored 610 goals and added 560 assists in regular-season play, and added 62 goals and 67 assists in Stanley Cup competition. His other NHL achievements were

many: first to score more than 50 goals in a season (54 in 1965-66); winner of the Art Ross Trophy three times, the Lady Byng Trophy once, the Hart Trophy twice, and the Lester Patrick Trophy for contribution to hockey in the U.S. once. Bobby also dominated All-Star selections, being named to the NHL First All-Star Team 10 times and to the Second Team twice.

Hull was in the vanguard of players who helped launch the World Hockey Association. His signing by the Winnipeg Jets in 1972 gave the new league much-needed credibility. With Winnipeg, he added another 303 goals and 335 assists in 411 games, including 77 goals in 1974-75.

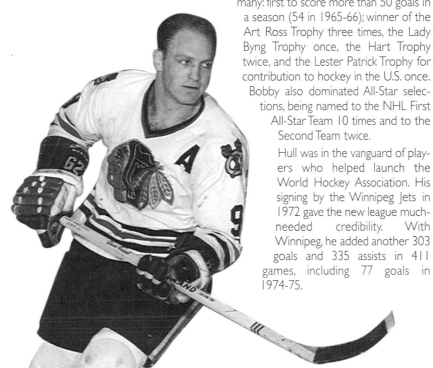

He was a two-time WHA scoring leader.

His blond good looks earned him the designation of the "Golden Jet" very early in his career and he was always a favourite with young fans because of his patience in response to requests for autographs.

Inducted 1983.

FRED HUME

BUILDER

A MIXTURE OF SPORTS and politics dominated the life of Fred Hume. Amateur hockey was one of his keen interests, although he later devoted himself to the professional game. He helped in the formation of the Western Hockey League and the development of the New Westminster Royals Hockey Club.

Hume was born May 2, 1892, in New Westminster, British Columbia. He served as mayor of that city and later moved to Vancouver where he also was elected mayor. He was a player and, later, president of the famed New Westminster Salmonbellies lacrosse team, president of the New Westminster Royals soccer club which won three Canadian titles, and at one time owned the Vancouver Hockey Club franchise. Under Hume's leadership, professional baseball came to Vancouver in 1955. Earlier, he had been a dominant force in bringing Vancouver its first Grey Cup Canadian Football League championship game as well as the British Empire Games in 1954. He died February 17, 1967.

Inducted 1962.

1955-60 HOW THE GAME LOOKED

- Straight sticks • Charlie Burns was the only player to wear a helmet. Burns was also the only U.S.-born player.
- Jacques Plante first wore a mask in a regular-season game on November 1, 1959 after being hit in the face by a shot from Andy Bathgate.
- All NHL rinks were flooded and scraped using Zambonis by 1955-56
- Beginning in January of 1956, teams wore dark jerseys at home; white on the road. Referees wore black-and-white stripes.

1955-60 ON THE ICE

- The Canadiens became the first team to score 250 goals in a season in 1957-58 • Rosters ranged from 16 to 18 skaters plus goaltenders • Montreal won 40 of 49 playoff games en route to five Cup championships
- Beliveau, Harvey and Plante made the NHL All-Star Team in each season. • Goals scored increased every season. A total of 1064 were scored in 1955-56; 1238 in 1959-60 • Bill Gadsby of the Rangers was the only defenceman to finish in the top-ten scorers in 1956.

TOMMY IVAN
BUILDER

TOMMY IVAN never played professional hockey — injuries cut short a promising career — but his list of achievements as a coach and manager is lengthy.

Born January 31, 1911, in Toronto, he first attracted attention as a coach of the Brantford, Ontario, junior team. Jack Adams brought him into the Detroit Red Wings' organization as a scout, then as a coach at Omaha and Indianapolis before moving into the NHL with the Wings in the 1947-48 season. At Detroit, Ivan coached six straight NHL championship teams and three Stanley Cups winners. He left Detroit in 1954-55 to join the Chicago Black Hawks as general manager. After coach Dick Irvin succumbed to illness, Ivan also coached in Chicago for a season and a half.

He is credited with much of the success in rebuilding the Hawks, who were losers both on the ice and at the gate, into an organization among the most successful in the league. He helped rebuild a fine farm system and under his tenure as general manager, the Hawks won their first Stanley Cup title in 23 years, in 1960-61, and their first regular season title in 1966-67.

Among the many highlights of his career, Tommy Ivan remembers coaching Gordie Howe in his first pro season; his Stanley Cup triumph of 1952 when the Wings swept the playoffs in eight straight games; and the six years he coached teams in All-Star Games, all victories.

Inducted 1974.

"PUNCH" IMLACH
BUILDER

GEORGE (PUNCH) IMLACH was born March 15, 1918, and raised in Toronto. He played on good army hockey teams at Cornwall and Camp Borden during World War II. A broken wrist pushed him into coaching. He never reached the NHL as a player, but it was as a coach and manager that he left his mark on the game.

Offered a position in Quebec, he joined the Quebec Senior League's Quebec Aces and played four seasons, two as playing coach. At age 31, he reluctantly quit as a player and took on the job of general manager, later becoming a co-owner. He moved into the NHL in 1958 as an assistant general manager of the Toronto Maple Leafs and took over as coach as well as general manager part way through 1958-59.

In his 11 seasons with Toronto, his teams made the playoffs 10 times and won four Stanley Cups. Out of hockey for a season (but occupied as a syndicated hockey columnist), he was named general manager and coach of the expansion Buffalo Sabres in May, 1970. He got Buffalo into the playoffs in their third season and to the Stanley Cup finals in 1975. He left Buffalo in December, 1978, and rejoined Toronto in July 1979, as both manager and coach. Continuing heart problems led to the termination of his Toronto contract after the 1981-82 season.

A determined, sometimes obstinate man, Imlach demanded loyalty and dedication from his players. Goalie Johnny Bower probably summed it up best when he said: "All a player has to do is try, give it his best shot, and Imlach will be in his corner." He died Dec. 1, 1987.

Inducted 1984.

BILL JENNINGS
BUILDER

BILL JENNINGS began his association with hockey in 1959 as counsel for the Graham-Paige Corporation when it acquired controlling interest in Madison Square Garden Corporation, which in turn owned the New York Rangers hockey club. He took an active role in the direction of the club from the outset and became president of the Rangers and its governor in the National Hockey League in 1962.

He was still holding both offices at the time of his election to the Hockey Hall of Fame in 1975. Throughout Jennings' association with the league, he was an ardent advocate of expansion and was one of its principal architects. Apart from his successful leadership of the Rangers, Bill Jennings took an active part in the recognition of U.S. participation in hockey and in 1966 was the originator of the Lester Patrick Award for persons who have rendered "outstanding service to hockey in the United States." For his own distinguished services, Jennings was himself recipient of this award in 1971.

He was also instrumental in the founding and successful operation of the Metropolitan Junior Hockey Association in the New York area, starting in 1966. Jennings was born December 14, 1920. He died August 17, 1981, in New York. The NHL's William M. Jennings Trophy, awarded annually to the goaltenders(s) for the team allowing the fewest goals-against, is named in his honour.

Inducted 1975.

THE LEAFS' RUN TO THE PLAYOFFS...

After missing post-season play two years in a row, the Toronto Maple Leafs started 1958-59 looking just as bad. On November 21, 1958, Punch Imlach was hired as general manager. Eight days later, he fired coach Billy Reay and took over behind the bench himself. Still, at the halfway mark of the season, Toronto was in last place.

Finally, in March, the Leafs began to catch fire. Unfortunately, it appeared there wasn't time to make a run at the playoffs. As late as March 14th, with just eight days left in the NHL season, Toronto sat seven points back of the fourth-place New York Rangers. The Rangers would be in Toronto that night for the first of a home-and-home weekend encounter. A win on Saturday would eliminate Toronto from the playoff hunt, but the Leafs scored a 5-0 victory and then kept their slim playoff hopes alive with a 6-5 win in New York on Sunday.

Two more Toronto wins and another Rangers loss left the Maple Leafs one point behind New York on the final night of the season. The Rangers were at home to Montreal, but were beaten 4-2 by the Canadiens. The Leafs rallied from a 3-0 deficit for a 6-4 win in Detroit. Toronto was in the playoffs.

The Leafs remained hot, beating Boston in seven games in the semifinals before losing the Stanley Cup to Montreal in five. Meanwhile, in New York, they were looking for scapegoats. Goalie Gump Worsley took much of the heat for the slump down the stretch. Some, though, looked back to the beginning of February when Rangers' tough guy Lou Fontinato was pummeled in a fight with Gordie Howe. The team, they said, was never the same again.

TOM JOHNSON
DEFENCE • MONTREAL, BOSTON

TOM JOHNSON was born in the small town of Baldur, Manitoba, on February 18, 1928. He didn't play hockey in a covered arena until he was 18, when he joined the junior Winnipeg Monarchs. Claimed by Montreal, he saw limited action the next year with the senior Royals and was sent to Buffalo for the 1948-49 season. His drive and enthusiasm made him an instant favourite and he was called up to stay with Montreal in the fall of 1950.

Under the guidance of coach Dick Irvin he became an outstanding defenceman. Johnson played 15 full seasons in the NHL. In 978 games he had 51 goals and 213 assists. His best season was 1958-59 when he won the Norris Trophy as the NHL's premier defenceman. Because of teammate Doug Harvey's great skill, Johnson never figured in Montreal's power play, but he was a leader when the team was short-handed. He had speed and skill in the corners, could wheel and lay a perfect pass, and didn't take foolish penalties. He frequently played centre when his team needed a goal late in a game.

He had the misfortune to suffer eye injuries twice, both accidentally inflicted by teammates. The second cut facial and eye muscles and threatened his sight. Because of his doubtful status as a player, he was left unprotected and claimed by the Boston Bruins. Shortly after, he was injured again when a skate severed nerves in his leg, forcing him to retire. Johnson played on six Stanley Cup winners and, in 1972, coached the Bruins to a championship.

Inducted 1970.

GORDON JUCKES
BUILDER

A MAN WHO ENJOYED success in three different careers, Gordon Juckes will be best remembered for his many outstanding contributions to hockey.

Born at Watrous, Saskatchewan, on June 20, 1914, Juckes became a newspaperman early in life in Melville, Saskatchewan. He enlisted in the Royal Canadian Artillery during the first few months of World War II and rose to the rank of major. His hockey background began as a player in minor hockey at Melville. He became president of the local club, then of the Saskatchewan Senior League. He was elected president of the Saskatchewan Amateur Hockey Association in 1953-54. Six years later he assumed the presidency of the Canadian Amateur Hockey Association. Appointed CAHA secretary-manager in 1960 (later changed to executive director), he served the CAHA well until retirement in 1978.

Juckes' contributions to hockey have been recognized in many ways: the U.S. Amateur Hockey Association diploma in 1962; diploma of honour of the International Ice Hockey Federation in 1967; CAHA Meritorious Award in 1976; plus life membership in the SAHA. At the time of his election to the Hockey Hall of Fame, he was also serving as a life member of the IIHF, and sat on the boards of Hockey Canada and the Canadian Olympic Association. He died October 5, 1994. Inducted 1979.

"RED" KELLY
DEFENCE/CENTRE • DETROIT, TORONTO

LEONARD (RED) KELLY is the antithesis of that old saying "nice guys finish last." The friendly redhead flashed across NHL headlines for 20 seasons, winning much acclaim and countless friends.

Born in Simcoe, Ontario, on July 9, 1927, he graduated to the NHL at the age of 19 from the Toronto St. Michael's Majors, an Ontario Junior A team. He played with the Detroit Red Wings for 12-1/2 seasons where he was a standout defenceman who was occasionally used as a forward. He was traded to the Toronto Maple Leafs where he completed his playing career as a centre. During that span Kelly was a four-time winner of the Lady Byng Trophy and the first winner of the Norris Trophy. In Detroit and Toronto, he played on eight Stanley Cup-winning teams. Kelly was named to the NHL's First All-Star Team six times and to the Second Team twice. He played for nine Prince of Wales Trophy-winning clubs. He also competed in 19 years of Stanley Cup playoff competition and 1,316 regular-season games.

With expansion of the NHL from six to 12 teams in 1967, Kelly retired as a player and accepted a coaching post with the Los Angeles Kings, guiding the team into the playoffs in the ensuing two seasons despite being hampered by what critics considered to be poor draft choices. He became coach of Pittsburgh in 1969 and Toronto in 1973.

Off the ice, Kelly was a Member of Parliament for three years from 1962 until 1965 when he decided he could no longer combine hockey and politics satisfactorily. Inducted 1969.

"TEEDER" KENNEDY
CENTRE • TORONTO

IF EVER THERE WAS a player who made it into the Hockey Hall of Fame on sheer hard work, it was Ted (Teeder) Kennedy. Never a free skater, Kennedy made up for this deficiency with a bull-dog tenacity and competitive spirit that made him one of the outstanding centres and leaders in the game's history. He sparked the Toronto Maple Leafs to five Stanley Cup triumphs during 13 full seasons in the NHL and, in 1954-55, was awarded the Hart Trophy as the MVP to his team in the NHL.

Kennedy was born in Humberstone, Ontario, on December 12, 1925, and was originally slated to play for the Montreal Canadiens. He attended their training camp when he was 16 but was so homesick that he packed up and left. The next year, Leafs traded the rights to Frank Eddolls, then in the Royal Canadian Air Force, for Kennedy and he broke into the NHL at the age of 18. His first Stanley Cup team was the 1944-45 Leafs and he became a dogged leader of the club in its first triple triumph — 1946-47 through 1948-49. He succeeded Syl Apps as team captain in 1948 and led the team to another cup triumph in 1950-51. He came out of retirement in January, 1957, to help the injury-riddled Leafs but retired to stay at the end of the season.

Kennedy is still remembered as one of the greatest face-off men in the game's history. In 696 league games, he scored 231 goals and collected 329 assists.

Inducted 1966.

HOCKEY POLITICIANS...

The early 1960s were a busy time for Red Kelly. He had to adjust to a new team, and a new position, when he was traded from Detroit to Toronto in 1961. By 1965, he'd won three Stanley Cups with the Maple Leafs, witnessed the birth of two children, and twice been elected as a Member of Parliament in Canada's federal government.

Legendary Liberal party organizer Senator Keith Davey first approached Kelly with the idea of running for office while still playing in the NHL. The Leaf centre declined, but later changed his mind and was elected in 1962. A snap election saw him go before the voters again in 1963. This time he defeated Conservative candidate Allan Eagleson.

Combining pucks with politics kept Kelly on the go. When in Ottawa, he rented ice in nearby Hull and practiced every day by himself. Game nights sometimes found him flying into cities just in time to play. By 1965, Kelly had had enough, and bowed out of the political arena.

Another Leaf star, Howie Meeker, also combined the dual roles of hockey player and politician, serving in Opposition with the Conservatives from 1951 to 1953. The Liberal Prime Minister of the day was Louis St. Laurent, a big Canadiens fan who enjoyed teasing Meeker about the rivalry.

Both Kelly and Meeker agree it would be much too difficult to combine their two careers today. Other players who served in the House of Commons— Lionel Conacher and Bucko MacDonald—did so after their playing days.

HOCKEY HALL OF FAME • SUPERSTAR GALLERY
PART ONE • THE SIX-TEAM ERA

TOE BLAKE

ACQUIRED BY THE CANADIENS IN FEBRUARY 1936, HECTOR "TOE" BLAKE WENT ON
LEAD MONTREAL TO A TOTAL OF TEN STANLEY CUP CHAMPIONSHIPS,
TWO AS A PLAYER AND EIGHT AS A COACH.

MILT SCHMIDT

THE PIVOT MAN ON THE FAMED "KRAUT LINE" AND THE HART TROPHY WINNER IN 1950-51,
MILT SCHMIDT SPENT 28 YEARS WITH THE BOSTON BRUINS
AS A PLAYER, COACH AND GENERAL MANAGER.

HARRY LUMLEY

THE YOUNGEST GOALTENDER TO EVER PLAY IN THE NHL, HARRY LUMLEY SAW ACTION WITH
FIVE NHL CLUBS DURING AN OUTSTANDING 16-YEAR CAREER THAT SAW HIM RECORD
A CAREER-HIGH 13 SHUTOUTS WITH TORONTO IN THE 1953-54 SEASON.

BILL GADSBY

BILL GADSBY, WHO OVERCAME ILLNESS AND INJURY TO PLAY 20 SEASONS IN THE NHL WITH
CHICAGO, THE NEW YORK RANGERS AND DETROIT, WAS ONE OF ONLY TWO DEFENCEMEN
TO FINISH AMONG THE NHL'S TOP TEN SCORERS IN A SINGLE SEASON DURING THE 1950S.

TERRY SAWCHUK

THE FIRST PLAYER IN HOCKEY HISTORY TO WIN ROOKIE-OF-THE-YEAR HONOURS IN
THREE DIFFERENT LEAGUES, TERRY SAWCHUK STILL HOLDS THE NHL'S GOALTENDING RECORDS
FOR WINS (447), GAMES PLAYED (971) AND SHUTOUTS (103).

GUMP WORSLEY

THE LAST HALL-OF-FAME GOALTENDER TO PLAY WITHOUT A MASK, GUMP WORSLEY WAS
REVITALIZED BY A TRADE FROM THE RANGERS TO THE CANADIENS THAT SAW HIM WIN THE
VEZINA TROPHY TWICE AND THE STANLEY CUP CHAMPIONSHIP FOUR TIMES IN FIVE YEARS.

JOHNNY BOWER

NICKNAMED "CHINA WALL" BECAUSE OF HIS AGE AND HIS GOALTENDING ABILITY, JOHNNY BOWER
LED THE NHL IN GOALS-AGAINST AVERAGE FOUR TIMES IN THE 1960S AND HELPED BACKSTOP
THE TORONTO MAPLE LEAFS TO A QUARTET OF STANLEY CUP TITLES.

MAURICE RICHARD

MAURICE "ROCKET" RICHARD OVERCAME THREE SERIOUS INJURIES EARLY IN HIS CAREER TO
BECOME THE NHL'S FIRST 50-GOAL SCORER AND THE GAME'S GREATEST PLAYOFF COMPETITOR.
RICHARD STILL HOLDS THE NHL RECORD FOR OVERTIME GOALS IN THE PLAYOFFS WITH SIX.

JOHN BUCYK

JOHN "CHIEF" BUCYK, WHO BECAME THE OLDEST PLAYER IN LEAGUE HISTORY TO RECORD
A 50-GOAL SEASON IN 1970-71, IS THE BOSTON BRUINS' ALL-TIME LEADER IN
SEASONS (21), GAMES (1436), GOALS (545) AND POINTS (1339).

PIERRE PILOTE

A THREE-TIME WINNER OF THE NORRIS TROPHY, PIERRE PILOTE
WAS NAMED TO THE NHL'S FIRST OR SECOND ALL-STAR TEAM IN
EIGHT CONSECUTIVE SEASONS FROM 1959-60 TO 1966-67.

TIM HORTON

OFTEN CONSIDERED TO BE THE STRONGEST MAN TO EVER PLAY THE GAME, DEFENCEMAN

TIM HORTON PLAYED ON FOUR STANLEY CUP-WINNING TEAMS IN TORONTO AND EARNED

SIX ALL-STAR BERTHS IN HIS 24-YEAR CAREER WITH THE LEAFS, RANGERS, PENGUINS AND SABRES.

FRANK MAHOVLICH

A NINE-TIME ALL-STAR AND ONE OF ONLY FOUR PLAYERS TO WIN TWO OR MORE STANLEY CUPS
WITH DIFFERENT TEAMS, FRANK MAHOVLICH WON FOUR CHAMPIONSHIPS WITH TORONTO
AND TWO WITH THE MONTREAL CANADIENS.

DAVE KEON

In addition to being a relentless forechecker and a creative playmaker, Dave Keon scored at least 20 goals in 11 of his 15 seasons with Toronto before moving on to play with three teams in the WHA and with Hartford in the NHL.

JEAN BÉLIVEAU

ONE OF HOCKEY'S MOST RESPECTED AND ADMIRED INDIVIDUALS, JEAN BÉLIVEAU
BROUGHT DISCIPLINE AND DEDICATION TO THE GAME FOR MORE THAN 40 YEARS
AS A PLAYER AND AS AN EXECUTIVE WITH THE MONTREAL CANADIENS.

GLENN HALL

KNOWN AS "MR. GOALIE" DURING HIS 18-YEAR HALL-OF-FAME CAREER IN DETROIT,
CHICAGO AND ST. LOUIS, GLENN HALL'S REMARKABLE RECORD OF STARTING AND FINISHING
502 CONSECUTIVE GAMES FROM 1955 TO 1962 WILL NEVER BE MATCHED.

EDDIE GIACOMIN

A DURABLE GOALTENDER WHOSE ACROBATIC STYLE MADE HIM A FAN FAVOURITE IN
MADISON SQUARE GARDEN, ED GIACOMIN SPENT 13 SEASONS IN THE NHL WITH
THE RANGERS AND RED WINGS, RECORDING 54 SHUTOUTS AND 289 VICTORIES.

GERRY CHEEVERS

ONE OF THE NHL'S GREAT "MONEY" GOALTENDERS, GERRY CHEEVERS SET AN NHL RECORD
WITH A 32-GAME UNBEATEN STREAK DURING THE 1971-72 SEASON AS HE GUIDED THE
BOSTON BRUINS TO THEIR SECOND STANLEY CUP TITLE IN THREE YEARS.

Rod Gilbert

Rod Gilbert overcame two serious back operations to play 18 seasons
in the NHL and is still the New York Rangers' all-time leader
in goals (406), assists (615) and points (1021).

GORDIE HOWE

MR. HOCKEY WAS NAMED TO THE FIRST OR SECOND ALL-STAR TEAM IN 21 OF 26
NHL SEASONS AND WAS THE GAME'S CAREER POINT-SCORING LEADER FROM JANUARY 16, 1960
TO OCTOBER 15, 1989, THE LONGEST REIGN IN LEAGUE HISTORY.

HENRI RICHARD

DIMINUTIVE IN SIZE BUT UNMATCHED IN WILL TO WIN, HENRI RICHARD — SHOWN HERE BATTLING
CHICAGO'S PIERRE PILOTE — PLAYED 20 SEASONS IN THE NHL AND WAS A MEMBER OF A RECORD
11 STANLEY CUP-WINNING TEAMS WITH THE MONTREAL CANADIENS FROM 1955 TO 1975.

FIVE HALL OF FAMERS

PHOTOGRAPHED DURING A MID-1960S ENCOUNTER BETWEEN THE MAPLE LEAFS AND
RED WINGS, ALEX DELVECCHIO (10, WHITE), NORM ULLMAN (7), ALLAN STANLEY (26), GEORGE ARMSTRONG
(10, BLUE) AND DAVE KEON (14) ARE ALL HONOURED MEMBERS OF THE HOCKEY HALL OF FAME.

BOBBY HULL

DUBBED THE "GOLDEN JET" BECAUSE OF HIS SPEED, SLAPSHOT AND BLOND HAIR, BOBBY HULL WAS
THE NHL'S DOMINANT LEFT WINGER IN THE 1960S AND ADDED GREATLY TO THE CREDIBILITY OF THE
UPSTART WORLD HOCKEY ASSOCIATION WHEN HE LEFT CHICAGO TO JOIN THE WINNIPEG JETS IN 1972.

STAN MIKITA

THE ONLY PLAYER TO WIN THREE INDIVIDUAL NHL REGULAR-SEASON AWARDS
(THE ART ROSS TROPHY, HART TROPHY AND LADY BYNG TROPHY) IN BACK-TO-BACK SEASONS,
STAN MIKITA WAS THE LAST FORWARD TO PLAY MORE THAN 20 SEASONS IN THE LEAGUE.

YVAN COURNOYER

YVAN "THE ROADRUNNER" COURNOYER EPITOMIZED THE TRADITION OF THE
"FLYING FRENCHMEN" IN MONTREAL, USING HIS SPEED, STYLE AND HOCKEY SENSE TO LEAD
THE CANADIENS TO 10 STANLEY CUP TITLES IN HIS 16 SEASONS WITH THE *BLEU BLANC ET ROUGE*.

ELMER LACH
CENTRE • MONTREAL

ELMER LACH brought great skills to the NHL. He had an unusual gift for playmaking, blinding speed, a high degree of courage, an intelligent approach to the game, and a spirit of dogged determination.

Lach was born in Nokomis, Saskatchewan, on January 22, 1918, and. as an amateur, played junior with the Regina Abbotts and senior with the Weyburn Beavers and Moose Jaw Millers. He turned professional in 1940-41 with the Montreal Canadiens and in the ensuing 14 seasons, posted an enviable record.

He played in 664 regular-season and 76 playoff games. In league play he amassed 215 goals and 408 assists, adding 19 goals and 45 assists in the playoffs. Elmer was selected to five All-Star Teams, making the First Team in 1944-45 with a total of 80 points — 26 goals and 54 assists in a 50-game schedule. Lach was also voted winner of the Hart Trophy that season. In 1947-48 he again led the league in scoring. Lach centred the Canadiens' great Punch Line between Rocket Richard and Toe Blake and, although he was a great offensive player, his coach, Dick Irvin, cited him for remarkable defensive play. Inducted 1966.

DAVE KEON
CENTRE • TORONTO, MINNESOTA (WHA), INDIANAPOLIS (WHA), NEW ENGLAND (WHA), HARTFORD

DAVE KEON was an amazing athlete who spent 22 seasons in pro hockey — 18 in the NHL and four in the WHA. He played a total of 1,296 regular-season games in the NHL, 301 in the WHA, and an additional 131 in the playoffs, picked up a total of only 151 penalty minutes.

Born March 22, 1940, in Noranda, Quebec, Keon became one of the best checking centres in the history of the game. He graduated from St. Mike's juniors to the Toronto Maple Leafs for the 1960-61 season and won the Calder Trophy as the NHL's best rookie. In ensuing years, he also won the Lady Byng Trophy twice (in 1962 and 1963) and the Conn Smythe Trophy as most valuable playoff performer in 1967.

Keon was a member of four Stanley Cup championship teams, including three in a row starting in 1962. He also earned a Second All-Star Team berth in 1971, competing against top centres like Jean Beliveau, Stan Mikita, Phil Esposito, Norm Ullman and Henri Richard.

After 15 seasons with Toronto of the NHL, Keon shifted to the World Hockey Association in 1975 and played for Minnesota, Indianapolis and New England over the next four seasons before returning to the NHL with the Hartford Whalers. He stayed with the Whalers through the 1981-82 season before retiring.

Inducted 1986.

EDGAR LAPRADE
CENTRE • NY RANGERS

EDGAR LAPRADE was a smooth-skating centre, a prolific penalty killer and a master of the "poke check."

Born October 10, 1919 in Mine Centre, Ontario, he played minor, junior and senior hockey in Port Arthur, Ontario, earning the Thunder Bay Senior Hockey League's MVP award in 1939 and 1941.

He joined the Canadian Army and played service hockey for the duration of World War II. Laprade was finally lured into pro hockey thanks to a five thousand dollar bonus from the New York Rangers for his mortgage on a house in Port Arthur. He joined the "Blueshirts" in 1945-46, winning the Calder Trophy as the NHL's top rookie. He was awarded the Lady Byng Trophy as the NHL's most gentlemanly player in 1950. Nicknamed "Beaver" by his teammates due to his work ethic and constant hustle, he shared the NY Rangers team MVP award in 1949 and won it outright in 1950. That year he led the Rangers in team scoring with 22 goals and 44 points. He was respected by opponents in the other five NHL cities. His skill and efforts on the ice was recognized as he was elected to play in the first four NHL All-Star Games from 1947 to 1950. He played with the Rangers until 1954-55, scoring 108 goals and 172 assists for 280 points in 501 regular-season games.

Inducted 1993.

AL LEADER
BUILDER

AL LEADER devoted his life to hockey in a manner that merited recognition. After 25 years of continuous service, Al Leader stepped down from the job of president of the Western Hockey League in 1969. During those years the league experienced periods of great financial and internal strain, but he prevailed to bring the league to a position of prestige and affluence.

Born December 4, 1903, in Barnsley, Manitoba, Al's hockey career began at age 16 as a player around Watson, Saskatchewan. His first administrative post was as secretary of the Seattle City League in 1933 and in the ensuing seven years he played, coached and managed teams, as well as officiating. In 1940, he organized a Defence Hockey League and from this he established contacts with pro hockey that in 1944 led to his election as secretary-manager of the Pacific Coast Hockey League. By 1948, the league had turned pro, and he became its first president. Leader, a former vice-president of Amateur Hockey Association of the United States, became a naturalized American citizen in 1933. He died May 8, 1982.

Inducted 1969.

ROBERT LEBEL
BUILDER

ROBERT LEBEL is a man who has devoted many years to hockey, initially as a player but mainly as an organizer and administrator.

Born September 21, 1905, in Quebec City, he came up through minor ranks to play in the Cote de Beaupre Junior League, then in the Quebec City Senior League and in New York State. He was founder and first president of the Interprovincial Senior League, serving from 1944 to 1947. Mr. LeBel became president of the Quebec Amateur Hockey League (1955-57), then the Canadian Amateur Hockey Association (1957-59), and finally the International Ice Hockey Federation (1960-62). He was the first French-Canadian to hold the latter two offices.

In 1964, he was named a life member of both the QAHA and the CAHA. He represented the latter body on the Governing Committee of the Hockey Hall of Fame. Mr. LeBel was president of the Quebec Junior A League and was trustee of both the George T. Richardson Memorial Trophy (Eastern Canada Junior championship) and the W.G. Hardy Trophy (Canadian Intermediate championship). He is a former mayor of the city of Chambly, Quebec, where he now resides.

Inducted 1970.

TED LINDSAY
LEFT WING • DETROIT, CHICAGO

TED LINDSAY was a remarkable hockey player and although he will always be known as "Terrible Ted," he will also be remembered as one of the greatest left wingers of all-time. Christened Robert Blake Theodore Lindsay, he was born in Renfrew, Ontario, on July 29, 1925, but gained his early hockey prominence in Kirkland Lake, Ontario.

He was a member of Toronto St. Michael's when they lost the Ontario junior final to Oshawa, but the latter club added him to their lineup in a successful bid to win the Memorial Cup in 1944. He joined Detroit later that year and quickly established himself as a leader, both on and off the ice. Lindsay played on the great "Production Line" with Sid Abel and Gordie Howe. That line played a major role in the phenomenal success of the Wings between 1948-49 and 1954-55 when they won seven consecutive league titles and the Stanley Cup four times.

Ted played 13 seasons with Detroit before being traded to Chicago prior to the 1957-58 season. He retired after the 1959-60 campaign but made a remarkable comeback with Detroit in 1964-65 and was an inspiration in their winning the Prince of Wales Trophy. He retired again, this time to stay, with 379 goals in his 17 NHL seasons. Lindsay was named to the First All-Star Team eight times and to the Second Team once.

Inducted 1966.

BERT LINDSAY...

Though his teammate Gordie Howe is much better known for his family connections, Ted Lindsay is also part of a hockey-playing father-son combo. Lindsay's father Bert was a goaltender in the early days of professional hockey. He first gained prominence with the famed Renfrew Millionaires, before spending four seasons with Victoria in the Pacific Coast Hockey Association. Bert Lindsay spent just one year in the NHL, tending goal for the Toronto Arenas during the 1918-19 season.

HARRY LUMLEY

GOALTENDER • DETROIT, NY RANGERS, CHICAGO, TORONTO, BOSTON

HARRY LUMLEY was an outstanding netminder who spent 16 seasons in professional hockey. He was the Vezina Trophy winner in 1953-54; a First Team All-Star in 1953-54 and 1954-55; and backstopped a Stanley Cup winner in 1950.

Born November 11, 1926, in Owen Sound, Ontario, the easy-going youngster showed such talent with the junior Barrie Colts that he was signed by the Detroit Red Wings at the age of 16. Within a couple of years he was with the Wings to stay and played six full seasons with Detroit before being replaced by another phenomenon named Terry Sawchuk. After two seasons with Chicago, he was traded to Toronto where he was simply outstanding.

In 1953-54 with the Leafs, Lumley had 13 shutouts, a modern-era NHL record that held up until Tony Esposito recorded 15 in 1969-70. In all, Lumley played 15 full seasons in the NHL. In 804 regular-season games he posted a very fine total of 71 shutouts — plus seven more in 76 playoff encounters. His goals-against record of 2.76 in regular-season action and 2.50 in the playoffs ranks with the best of any era.

Lumley completed his NHL career with the Boston Bruins, wrapping up a three-year stint in 1959-60. He retired to become a successful businessman in his home town. He didn't retire from competitive sport, however, and was active in standardbred racing, even taking his place behind the reins on occasion. Harry always had a full face and ruddy complexion, earning him the nickname "Apple Cheeks," which followed him throughout his career. Inducted 1980.

FRANK MAHOVLICH

LEFT WING • TORONTO, DETROIT, MONTREAL, BIRMINGHAM (WHA), TORONTO (WHA)

WHEN A SUPERSTAR retires there is usually a great deal of publicity. But when Frank Mahovlich retired as a hockey player in November, 1978, he did it in much the same way as he had tried to live his life — quietly and privately.

Hailed as a superstar while still an amateur, Frank was an enigma to hockey fans. He won the Calder Trophy as top NHL rookie in the 1957-58 season and did just about everything a player should be expected to do — but there were fans and hockey experts alike who felt he could have been even greater. "The Big M," as he became known, played on six Stanley Cup winners, four with Toronto and two with Montreal. He was selected to the NHL First All-Star Team three times and to the Second Team on six occasions.

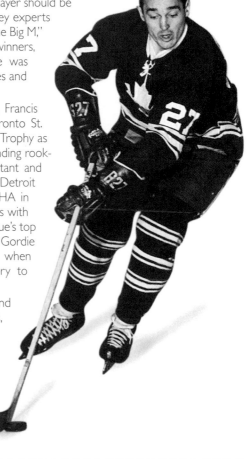

Born January 10, 1938, in Timmins, Ontario, Francis William Mahovlich played junior hockey with Toronto St. Michael's where he won the Red Tilson Memorial Trophy as the OHA Junior A MVP. Beginning with his outstanding rookie season in the NHL, Mahovlich was an important and productive player for three NHL teams: Toronto, Detroit and Montreal. He played four seasons in the WHA in Toronto and Birmingham. During his three seasons with the Detroit Red Wings he was part of one of league's top forward combinations with Alex Delvecchio and Gordie Howe. He was Howe's linemate in 1968-69 when Gordie became the third player in NHL history to record more than 100 points in a single season.

His swooping style earned him 533 goals and 1,103 total points in 1,181 regular-season games, and his NHL playoff record included 51 goals and 118 points in 137 games. He was a member of Team Canada '72, playing in six of the eight contests against the Soviet nationals. Throughout his career, Mahovlich's conduct on and off the ice was always of the highest standard. Inducted 1981.

• •

THE MAHOVLICH MILLION...

On Saturday morning, October 6, 1962, sports fans across North America were stunned to read newspaper stories claiming Toronto Maple Leafs star Frank Mahovlich had been sold to the Chicago Black Hawks for one million dollars.

The transaction had apparently taken place in the wee hours following the annual NHL All-Star Game dinner on Friday night. Maple Leafs owner Harold Ballard had reportedly been discussing his team's trouble negotiating a new deal with the "Big M" when James Norris declared he would pay any amount of money to land the Leaf's top goal scorer. After some haggling, the two agreed on one million dollars.

The deal was described in newspaper accounts as a game of "highball roulette," and no doubt the influence of alcohol had affected the decision. Nonetheless, a Norris cheque for one million dollars in Canadian funds found its way to the Maple Leafs' front office. At that point, Stafford Smythe announced the Toronto club would not complete the sale. As the Leafs were run by committee at the time, it was never made clear who might have had the authority to accept such an offer. Mahovlich was still a Leaf and would remain so until his trade to Detroit in 1968.

• •

John Mariucci
Builder

John Mariucci was born on May 8, 1916 in Eveleth, Minnesota, often called the birthplace of hockey in the United States. He became a standout in hockey and football, attending the University of Minnesota on a non-scholarship basis.

Mariucci was named All-American on the 1940 varsity hockey team and played on a national football championship team. As a professional, John played five seasons with the Chicago Black Hawks and was a solid defenceman. In 1952, he began a career that earned him the title "Godfather of Minnesota hockey." He encouraged high school hockey programs and recruited U.S. players for the U. of M. Previously, it had been stocked mainly with Canadian players. The Minnesota high school program increased from a handful of teams in 1952 to more than 150 by 1980, playing in covered rinks. Mariucci produced a dozen All-Americans as coach at Minnesota and coached the U.S. Olympic club to a silver medal at Cortina in 1956. He was associated as either coach or assistant coach with many U.S. international teams.

In 1967, he returned to the NHL as assistant to the general manager of the Minnesota North Stars, a position he still held at the time of his election to the Hall of Fame. He was a charter member of the U.S. Hockey Hall of Fame and winner of the Lester Patrick Trophy for contribution to hockey in the United States.

Mariucci's philosophy that American boys could participate at all levels of hockey was, in its day, avant-garde, but his unselfish contribution over several decades proved him correct and helped earn him a place in the Hockey Hall of Fame. He died March 23, 1987.

Inducted 1985.

Stan Mikita
Centre • Chicago

Born May 20, 1940, Stan Mikita arrived in Canada from Czechoslovakia in 1948, accompanied by his aunt and uncle. Enrolled in public school in St. Catharines, Ontario, at first he had a difficult time adapting to both a new country and a new language. Perhaps his dogged perseverance laid the framework for his entry into the NHL with the Chicago Black Hawks in 1958-59.

His determination in hockey led to impressive totals in both scoring and penalties minutes in Stan's early years. He played 20 full seasons in the NHL, plus parts of two others, and blazed an impressive trail. Stan's heady play made him a respected leader, and an integral part of the Chicago team which won the Stanley Cup in 1960-61, Chicago's only Cup win since 1937-38. Mikita was on NHL All-Star Teams on eight occasions, being picked to the First Team six times.

As he gained more experience in the league, his penalty totals dropped to the extent that Mikita became the the first player to win the Art Ross, Hart, and Lady Byng trophies as top scorer, MVP, and most gentlemanly player in the same season. He carried off this impressive triple win in two consecutive years — 1966-67 and 1967-68. He also won the scoring title in 1963-64 and 1964-65 and the Lester Patrick Trophy for outstanding contributions to hockey in the U.S. in 1976.

When Stan retired in 1979-80, he had played in 1,394 regular-season games, scored 541 goals and recorded 926 assists. In 155 playoff games he added 59 goals and 91 assists.

Mikita founded the American Impaired Hearing Association in 1972-73, for hard of hearing youngsters. He stages an annual tournament involving several teams of hearing-impaired hockey players in Chicago. Inducted 1983.

Hon. Hartland Molson
Builder

The Hon. Hartland Molson was born in Montreal on May 29, 1907. He was the son of Colonel Herbert Molson, one of the founders of the Canadian Arena Company, and had a lifelong interest in sports. He played for the Kingston Hockey Club in the 1926 Memorial Cup finals and was part of the Royal Military College football team that won the 1926 Dominion intermediate title.

Senator Molson was president and, following that, chairman of the Canadian Arena Company and Les Canadiens Hockey Club from 1957-68. As a member of the NHL finance committee, he played a vital role in strengthening owner-player relations and was one of six club owners who agreed to finance construction of the Hockey Hall of Fame building.

Before retiring from the Canadiens, Sen. Molson modernized the Forum, making it the largest arena in the NHL with excellent sight lines throughout. During World War II, he served with the Royal Canadian Air Force and was shot down during the Battle of Britain in 1940. He had risen to the rank of Group Captain and was awarded the Order of the British Empire when discharged in 1945. Appointed to the Canadian Senate in 1955, he has long been identified with philanthropic and charitable projects. Inducted 1973.

DICKIE MOORE
RIGHT WING • MONTREAL, TORONTO, ST. LOUIS

IN HIS EARLY STAGES OF HOCKEY, DICKIE MOORE was a tough competitor. Born January 6, 1931, in Montreal, he was tagged "Digging Dickie" at an early age and to his final game, his aggressive play merited praise from all who saw him in action.

Moore played significant roles in Memorial Cup triumphs by two Montreal junior teams, the Royals and the Canadiens. He joined the Royals of the Quebec Senior League in 1951-52. Halfway through that season, he was called up to the pro Canadiens and played with them until retiring after the 1962-63 season.

Dickie came out of retirement twice, playing 38 games with Toronto in 1964-65 and 27 games with St. Louis in 1967-68.

Although plagued with injuries throughout his career — bad knees, shoulder separations, broken hands and wrists — he twice led the NHL in scoring. His first title, in 1957-58, was achieved despite a broken left wrist incurred with three months left in the schedule. At his own request, a cast was placed on the wrist which enabled him to grip his stick and he never missed a game, topping the league with 36 goals and 48 assists. The following year, he scored 96 points, breaking the existing record of 95 set by Gordie Howe in 1952-53.

Moore was named left winger on the NHL First All-Star Team in 1957-58 and 1958-59 and was selected to the Second Team in 1960-61. In playoff competition he recorded 46 goals and 64 assists in 135 games. In 719 NHL regular-season games, Dickie scored 261 goals and added 347 assists for 608 points. His most important assets were spirit and competitive fire, which helped the Canadiens win six Stanley Cups during his 12 seasons with that team. Inducted 1974.

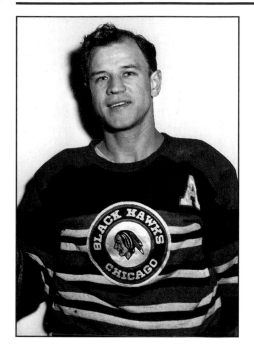

BILL MOSIENKO,
RIGHT WING • CHICAGO

THE CHICAGO BLACK HAWKS had a great forward unit known as the "Pony Line" during the 1940s. It was composed of the Bentley brothers, Max and Doug, and right winger Bill Mosienko. During a 14-year stay in the NHL, Mosienko was a very productive scorer, accounting for 258 goals and 540 points in 710 games. He spent a total of 20 years in professional hockey, playing in 1,030 games, and in that time accumulated only 129 minutes in penalties.

He was born in Winnipeg, Manitoba, on November 2, 1921, and played amateur hockey with the Tobans and Sherburns in that city. After two years with the Winnipeg Monarchs, a junior team, he turned pro at the age of 18 with the Hawks' organization. Bill played his first pro season with Providence and Kansas City, but late in 1941-42 joined the parent club and remained with them until retiring after the 1954-55 season. Mosienko won the Lady Byng Trophy in 1944-45 and was twice named to the NHL's Second All-Star Team — in 1944-45 and 1945-46. He also set an NHL record by scoring three goals in 21 seconds against the New York Rangers in New York on March 23, 1952.

After retiring as an NHL player, Mosienko and Alf Pike helped launch pro hockey in Winnipeg. Their team, the Warriors, won the Edinburgh Trophy in its first season, 1955-56. He continued to play with the Warriors through 1958-59 and coached the team in 1959-60.

He died July 9, 1994.

Inducted 1965.

FASTEST HAT-TRICK...

March 23, 1952 marked the final night of the 1951-52 NHL season. Already eliminated from the playoffs and settled into fifth and sixth place, the New York Rangers met Chicago in what would seem the definition of a meaningless game. It turned out to be anything but.

The Rangers held a comfortable 6-2 lead early in the third period when Chicago sent out the line of Gus Bodnar, George Gee and Bill Mosienko. At 6:09 of the third, Mosienko took a Bodnar pass, cut around the Rangers defence and narrowed the gap to 6-3. It took just 11 seconds for Bodnar to win the ensuing faceoff, spring Mosienko with a perfect pass, and watch him pot his second goal. At 6:30, Mosienko completed his hat-trick when he redirected Gee's pass into the net. In just 21 seconds, the Black Hawks were right back in a game they would go on to win 7-6.

Mosienko's 21-second spree came at the expense of Rangers rookie goaltender Lorne Anderson, who never played another game in the NHL. The three goals knocked more than a minute-and-a-half off Carl Liscombe's previous record for the fastest hat-trick. Only Jean Beliveau's three goals in 44 seconds, all with a two-man advantage in 1955, have ever approached Mosienko's mark.

"Buddy" O'Connor
Montreal, NY Rangers

Herbert (Buddy) O'Connor was a Montreal native, born June 21, 1916. Although he was not large as professional hockey players go (he stood 5-foot-7 and weighed 145 pounds), his smooth skating style and deft stickhandling made him one of the top performers of his era.

Like most youngsters of his time, Buddy O'Connor developed his hockey skills at assorted levels of amateur hockey, right up to the Montreal Royals' senior team which he joined while still retaining two years of junior eligibility. At the time, the Royals and other senior teams outdrew the Canadiens in fan support.

O'Connor was the kingpin of a noted trio called "the Razzle Dazzle Line," centering wingers Pete Morin and Gerry Heffernan, a unit which moved up to the Canadiens in the 1941-42 season. The Canadiens won the Stanley Cup in 1944 with Rocket Richard leading the way, but with Buddy O'Connor's playmaking skills playing a strong role.

O'Connor was traded to the New York Rangers at the beginning of the 1947-48 season, and had a career year with 24 goals and 36 assists for 60 points in 60 games. That season he earned the Lady Byng Memorial Trophy, and Hart Memorial Trophy as most Valuable player. In fact, it is remarkable that Buddy O'Connor collected a mere 34 penalty minutes in an NHL career that spanned 509 games.

O'Connor played his career as a centre, registering 140 goals in a 10-season career at a time when a 20-goal season was considered outstanding. He added 257 assists for 397 points in the NHL. His playoff record was 15 goals, 21 assists for 36 points in 53 games.

Buddy O'Connor died in Montreal, Aug. 24, 1977.

Inducted 1988.

Bruce Norris
Builder

Bruce Norris was born February 19, 1924 in Chicago, and 31 years later became one of the youngest owners in pro sport when he was named president of the Detroit Red Wings and the Olympia arena. A former collegiate player at Yale, Norris succeeded his sister, Marguerite Norris Riker, as Detroit's club president. The Norris family's ownership of the team had begun in 1933 when his father, James Norris, Sr., purchased the club and changed the name from the Falcons to the Red Wings.

Bruce Norris carried out an expansion program costing more than $2.5 million to make the Olympia one of the finest arenas in the NHL. Every seat in the building was padded. Although hockey was his favourite sport and enterprise, Bruce Norris had many other business interests. He was president of the vast Norris Grain Company and an avid cattle rancher, raising purebred Herefords at his permanent home, the 500-acre Daybreak Farm at Libertyville, Illinois. He died January 1, 1986.

Inducted 1969.

The 1950 Rangers...

In the 25 years of the Original Six era, the New York Rangers missed the playoffs 18 times and were knocked out in the first round on six occasions. Only the 1949-50 season stands as an oasis in this desert of despair.

The Rangers hero that year was goaltender Chuck Rayner. Though his goals-against average of 2.62 was only fourth-best in the league, his stellar work in the nets earned him the Hart Trophy, making him just the second goalie in NHL history to be named most valuable to his team. Rayner's goaltending led New York into the playoffs despite having the worst offense in the league.

The 1949-50 season had not looked promising when it began. After a victory on opening night, a seven-game winless streak quickly had the Rangers in last place. By the end of November, though, they had vacated the cellar. Christmas found them in second place. A rash of injuries looked to hurt their playoff chances but, while they fell to fourth place by season's end, the Rangers reached the post-season. With aging veteran Buddy O'Connor showing flashes of brilliance, New York beat Montreal in five games in the semifinals and advanced to play for the Stanley Cup for the first time since 1940.

Though the circus forced them out of Madison Square Garden and they had to play their "home" games in Toronto, the dream season appeared headed for the perfect finish, but Detroit wouldn't let it happen. The Rangers let game six slip away to the Red Wings, then blew 2-0 and then 3-2 leads in the seventh before they were beaten by Pete Babando at 8:31 of double overtime. The next Rangers' Stanley Cup was another 44 years away.

BERT OLMSTEAD
LEFT WING • CHICAGO, MONTREAL, TORONTO

BERT OLMSTEAD broke into the NHL with the Chicago Black Hawks during the 1948-49 season when he played nine games. He went on to play 13 full seasons in the NHL, establishing a reputation as one of the game's hard-nosed players. It was said that he couldn't skate, and his scoring records are not among the leaders, but he was a supreme motivator and knew how to bring out the best from his teammates. He was a winner.

Born September 4, 1926, in Scepter, Saskatchewan, he played junior hockey with Moose Jaw before turning pro with Kansas City of the U.S. Hockey League. After a full 1949-50 season at Chicago, he was traded to Detroit and then on to Montreal in 1950-51 where he became and integral cog in the Canadiens' machine that was to win the Stanley Cup in 1953, 1956, 1957 and 1958.

The Toronto Maple Leafs claimed him in the 1958 draft and Bert played a major role in the Leafs' rebuilding process. He was with the Leafs' Stanley Cup team in 1962, retiring after that season when claimed by the New York Rangers in the draft. Olmstead was voted to the NHL Second All-Star Team in 1953 and 1956 in an era when Ted Lindsay had a virtual lock on the First Team berth. He also led the NHL in assists with 48 in 1955 and a league-record 56 in 1956.

In 848 regularly-scheduled games, Olmstead scored 181 goals, assisted on 421 and collected 884 penalty minutes. His playoff record was 16 goals and 43 assists in 115 games. Former linemates Bernie Geoffrion and Jean Beliveau, both Hall of Famers, credit Olmstead as the leader on that line. "He didn't stand for any nonsense from us," Beliveau said, "and made me do smarter things than I would have done by myself."

Bert later tried his hand at coaching — he was the first coach at Oakland after the 1967 NHL expansion — but later retired from hockey and resides in Calgary.

Induced 1985.

PIERRE PILOTE
DEFENCE • CHICAGO, TORONTO

PIERRE PILOTE left the NHL at the end of the 1968-69 season having played in 976 games including playoffs. In that span, he recorded 559 points and 1,353 penalty minutes. He had also played on one Stanley Cup championship team, the Chicago Black Hawks of 1960-61, and in eight All-Star Games.

A premier rushing defenceman, Pilote stood five-ten and weighed 178 pounds. He broke into the NHL with Chicago in 1955-56 after serving his pro apprenticeship in Buffalo and soon established himself as a regular. During his first five full seasons with Chicago, he never missed a game but was finally forced out in 1962 with a shoulder separation.

Born at Kenogami, Quebec, on December 11, 1931, Pierre began skating shortly after learning to walk but didn't play organized hockey until he was 16, two years after his family had moved to Fort Erie, Ontario. The following year he played Junior B at Niagara Falls, progressing to two seasons of Junior A with the St. Catharines Teepees.

Pilote was voted to NHL All-Star Teams in eight consecutive years including Second Team berths in 1960, 1961 and 1962, and First Team selections in each of the next five seasons. He was also rated the NHL's outstanding defenceman and winner of the Norris Trophy in 1963, 1964 and 1965. Few defencemen in that era could match his scoring record of 80 goals and 418 assists in regular-season play. He was the Black Hawks' team captain from 1963 to 1968. Pilote played his final NHL season with the Maple Leafs in 1968-69. Inducted 1975.

HAWKS FINALLY WIN...

The seasons between 1946-47 and 1957-58 were lean years for the Chicago Black Hawks. The team missed the playoffs 12 out of 13 times and, with fan support dwindling, home games were sometimes moved to different cities. The franchise was in danger of collapse.

Bobby Hull's emergence as a super-star finally brought the crowds back to the Chicago Stadium in the late 1950s and a Stanley Cup victory in 1961 marked the Hawks' first title since 1938. Chicago would go on to rewrite the record book in the 1960s and — though no more Cups have followed — the Hawks have remained a solid NHL contender.

RUDY PILOUS

BUILDER

BORN IN WINNIPEG, August 11, 1914, Rudy Pilous played junior or minor pro hockey in Manitoba, British Columbia and England as well as with the New York Rovers, a farm club for the Rangers.

In 1941-42, he decided to set up a junior club in St. Catharines, Ontario. In their first season, his Falcons won their division but lost to Oshawa in the playoffs. His club made the playoffs the next two seasons, establishing St. Catharines on the hockey map. In 1946, he moved to Buffalo to act as a scout and promotions assistant. The next season, he was sent to Houston to help a faltering Huskies club win the U.S. Hockey League title. Buffalo sent him to the San Diego Skyhawks, who ultimately won the Pacific Coast championship in 1948-49. Pilous' reputation was established, both as a troubleshooter and as a promoter.

He won numerous laurels during his career: manager and coach of Memorial Cup winners at St. Catharines in 1954 and 1969; coach of the Stanley Cup winning Chicago Black Hawks in 1961; manager and coach of the Western Hockey League champion Denver Invaders in 1964; and manager of the World Hockey Association's Avco Cup-champion Winnipeg Jets in 1976 and 1978. Pilous later scouted for Detroit and Los Angeles of the NHL and was general manager of Toronto's NHL farm club at St. Catharines. He died December 11, 1994.

Inducted 1985.

JACQUES PLANTE

GOALTENDER • MONTREAL, NY RANGERS, ST. LOUIS, TORONTO, BOSTON, EDMONTON (WHA)

BORN IN SHAWINIGAN FALLS, QUEBEC, January 17, 1929, Jacques Plante was a remarkable athlete, a goaltender who played with total dedication. His contributions as a player and innovator are substantial.

A product of the Montreal system, he made two brief but spectacular appearances with the Canadiens before becoming a regular in 1954-55. In 20 games he allowed 31 goals and had five shutouts; he also played in 12 playoff contests, allowing just 22 goals while recording three more shutouts. Plante played through the 1962-63 season with Montreal before being traded to the New York Rangers.

He retired after two seasons in New York but, in 1968-69, was lured back into the NHL by an offer from the second-year expansion St. Louis Blues. Despite three seasons of inactivity and being 40 years of age, Plante combined with Glenn Hall to win the Vezina Trophy in St. Louis. It was his record seventh Vezina. After another season he was dealt to Toronto and continued to play strongly. The Leafs traded him to Boston near the end of the 1972-73 season, his last as an NHL player.

An extrovert, Jacques played his position with enthusiasm. His roving style excited fans everywhere. Throughout his career he was plagued with recurring asthma and after missing 13 games due to a sinusitis operation, he began using a mask in practice. Although not the first to wear one, he was the first to adopt it permanently and it has become a standard part of every goaltender's equipment. Management opposed the mask but following a face injury during a game, Plante refused to return without it. His subsequent brilliant play softened management's attitude and the rest is history.

An All-Star seven times — three First Team selections and four Second — he also won the Hart Trophy as MVP to his team in 1961-62. In 837 scheduled games he earned 82 shutouts and posted a goals-against average of 2.38. He also played for six Stanley Cup winners with 14 shutouts in 112 playoff games. He died February 27, 1986, at his home in Switzerland.

The Jacques Plante Trophy is awarded annually to the top goaltender in the Quebec Major Junior Hockey League. Inducted 1978.

PLANTE'S MASK...

In the first period of game at Madison Square Garden on November 1, 1959, Jacques Plante of the Montreal Canadiens took a backhander from Andy Bathgate flush in the face. The goaltender slumped to the ice with blood gushing from an open wound.

Prior to that night's game, Plante had begun wearing a plastic facemask during practice despite the objections of Canadiens coach Toe Blake, who argued that the mask would make his goalie less effective during games. Now, with his cut quickly stitched, Plante informed his coach he would not return to the ice unless he was permitted to wear his mask. Reluctantly, Blake agreed. Plante played brilliantly the rest of the night as the Canadiens went on to a 3-1 victory.

Blake hoped Plante would discard his protective shield, but he insisted on wearing it again when the Rangers visited Montreal four nights later. The result was an 8-2 victory. After a 2-2 tie with Chicago, he next blanked Toronto 3-0. Plante was clearly playing with a great deal of confidence, but Blake and manager Frank Selke still weren't convinced. Finally, after reeling off ten games without a defeat, Plante was permitted to wear his mask permanently.

"BABE" PRATT
DEFENCE • NY RANGERS, TORONTO, BOSTON

BABE PRATT POSSESSED three basic qualities of greatness: ability, leadership, and the rare knack of inspiring all those who played with him to a special effort.

Throughout his career it appears that when he joined a team, that team quickly became a championship club. In a 26-year hockey career from juvenile teams to Stanley Cup winners, Pratt played on 15 champions.

Born in Stoney Mountain, Manitoba, on January 7, 1916, he played on the first Winnipeg playground championship team. By 1931-32, he was a member of the Elmwood Maple Leafs and led them to the Manitoba midget title. The following year, Elmwood won the juvenile crown. A Manitoba junior title with Kenora followed in 1933-34, but before he moved to Kenora, Pratt played on five league championship teams — in one year.

Pratt turned pro with Philadelphia, the Ranger's farm club, and moved up to New York in January, 1936. He played on a Stanley Cup winner with the Rangers in 1939-40 and with the league championship team of 1941-42. In that Cup-winning season, Pratt teamed on defence with Ott Heller. They allowed only 17 goals-against over a 48-game schedule. He was traded to Toronto in November, 1942, and while with the Leafs, won the Hart Trophy in 1943-44 and was named to the First and Second NHL All-Star Teams.

In 1947, Pratt played with Hershey and, later, with New Westminster and Tacoma of the PCHL before retiring as a player. He died December 16, 1988.

Inducted 1966.

BOB PULFORD
LEFT WING • TORONTO, LOS ANGELES

BORN MARCH 31, 1936 in Newton Robinson, Ontario, Bob Pulford was a mainstay with the Toronto Maple Leafs for 14 seasons beginning in 1956-57. He joined the Leafs directly from the Toronto Marlboros after two Memorial Cup championships. His career spanned 1079 games. In that time he scored 281 goals and assisted on 362 others for 643 points.

He was a hard-working, two-way player who could score a key goal as well as shut down the opposing team's top line. In 1959 he was co-winner of the Leafs team MVP award. He was also a member of Toronto's four Stanley Cup winning teams in the 1960s. In 1964 he assisted on Bob Baun's memorable broken leg goal to defeat Detroit in overtime of the sixth game of the finals. In 1967, he scored the winning goal in the key third game in double overtime against the Canadiens.

He finished his career in Los Angeles spending two seasons as captain of the Kings. He hold the distinction of being the first president of the NHL Players' Association.

Since his retirement as a player, Pulford has coached in Los Angeles and Chicago. He became the general manager of the Blackhawks in 1982. Inducted 1991.

MARCEL PRONOVOST
DEFENCE • DETROIT, TORONTO

MARCEL PRONOVOST PLAYED 21 seasons in the NHL, 16 with Detroit and five with Toronto. He was on seven championship teams and four Stanley Cup winners in Detroit, adding another Stanley Cup triumph with the Maple Leafs in 1967. He was voted to the NHL First and Second All-Star Teams two times each.

But statistics tell only part of the story. A very competitive athlete, Marcel was a solid blueliner who combined stickhandling and graceful skating with natural incentive to give his best effort. He played a prominent role as a clubhouse leader with astute counselling to younger players. His dedication was inspiring to all who played with him.

Pronovost joined Detroit for the 1950 NHL playoffs after a fine season with Omaha of the U.S. Hockey League, and was immediately on a Cup-winner. He began the following season with Indianapolis of the AHL after suffering a broken cheekbone but finished with the Wings. The respect he gained around the NHL was demonstrated before a Detroit-Montreal game in 1960 at the Montreal Forum when admiring fans presented him with an automobile and his teammates gave him a diamond ring.

Traded to Toronto after the 1964-65 season, he was a key man in an eight-player deal that helped bring the Leafs a Stanley Cup in the final year before expansion. He stayed with Toronto three more seasons, became a coach at Tulsa, Oklahoma, of the Central Hockey League and retired from playing after 1969-70.

Born at Lac la Tortue, Quebec, on June 15, 1930, Pronovost played two seasons with the Windsor Spitfires of the OHA Junior League before turning pro with Omaha. In the NHL he played 1206 games, scoring 88 goals and assisting on 257. In NHL playoff action he had eight goals and 23 assists.

Inducted 1978.

BILL QUACKENBUSH
DEFENCE • DETROIT, BOSTON

BILL QUACKENBUSH WAS an excellent checker and one of the most effective rushing defencemen in the game. Not a thumping hitter, his main attribute was an ability to break up a rush without pounding an opponent into the boards.

Bill's record bears this out. He was named to five NHL All-Star Teams In 774 NHL games he collected a mere 95 minutes in penalties. His highest single-season total was 26 in 1946-47. He won the Lady Byng Trophy in 1948-49, playing the entire schedule without a penalty, and went a total of 131 games before incurring an infraction.

Born March 2, 1922, in Toronto, Quackenbush played junior at Brantford under Tommy Ivan who also coached him later as a pro at Detroit. Signed by the Wings, he was sent to Indianapolis for seasoning in 1942 and after being called up, played only 10 games before breaking his wrist. This prevented his playing on a Stanley Cup winner and also reduced his shooting power but he became a puck-control artist and amassed 222 assists to go with his 62 goals. In 80 playoff games he scored twice, drawing 19 assists and eight penalty minutes.

Bill played 14 NHL seasons, seven with Detroit and seven with Boston where he was a defensive stalwart. His average of 0.12 penalty minutes per game is a record not approached by any defenceman before or since.

Inducted 1976.

"CHUCK" RAYNER
GOALTENDER • NY AMERICANS, NY RANGERS

BORN AUGUST 11, 1920, in Sutherland, Saskatchewan, this great goaltender was christened Claude Earl Rayner, but early in his hockey career he picked up the nickname Chuck — and it stuck.

Rayner played his early hockey in his home town but, at the age of 15, went to Saskatoon to play in junior competition with the Wesleys team that reached the western Canada finals in 1935-36. He moved on to Kenora, Ontario, and for the next three seasons tended goal with the Thistles. In his final season with that team, 1938-39, his club advanced to the Memorial Cup finals, losing to the Oshawa Generals.

Rayner signed a professional contract with the Springfield Indians at the beginning of the 1940-41 season. After only a few games, he was sold to the New York Americans of the NHL, where he played 12 games that season. The following year, the New York club became the Brooklyn Americans, and Rayner played 36 games before joining the Royal Canadian Navy, serving until the end of World War II. By this time, the Americans franchise had folded and he had become the property of the New York Rangers. He played with the Rangers until the end of 1952-53 when he retired from the NHL.

Rayner was a very agile goalie. His goals-against average for 10 seasons in the NHL was 3.05, a very respectable figure when measured against the fact that the Rangers made the playoffs only twice.

In the 1949-50 season, Rayner won the Hart Trophy, awarded annually to the player judged most valuable to his team, and was named to the league's Second All-Star Team in 1948-49, 1949-50 and 1950-51. In three All-Star Games, he allowed only three goals in 4-1/2 periods of hockey, for an excellent 0.67 goals-against average. His goals-against average in 18 playoff games was 2.43. He recorded 25 shutouts in 425 league games.

Rayner retired to Kenora, Ontario.

Inducted 1973.

GOALIES SCORING...

Long before Billy Smith was ever credited with a goal, or Ron Hextall and Chris Osgood ever managed to bulge the twine, there was Chuck Rayner. Having scored once in an exhibition encounter, the New York goaltender was keen on becoming the first NHL netminder to score a goal in a league game.

Twice during the 1946-47 season, Rayner fired shots at the opposing goal without success. He made a third attempt on February 19, 1950. With Turk Broda pulled for an extra attacker, Rayner blocked a Toronto drive, rushed from his net and banked a long shot off the boards. The puck barely missed the yawning Toronto cage.

Amazingly, almost 45 years before Rayner's near miss, hockey witnessed its first goal by a goaltender. On February 18, 1905, Fred Brophy of the Westmount team in Montreal rushed the length of the ice and put a shot past future Hall-of-Famer Paddy Moran in the Quebec goal. A little more than a year later, on March 7, 1906, Brophy proved his first goal was no fluke when he rushed the length of the ice to score on Montreal Victorias netminder Nathan Frye.

KEN REARDON
DEFENCE • MONTREAL

KENNY REARDON HAD A HEADLONG, fearless style of play which accounted for many injuries during his NHL career, but his dashing disregard for personal safety made him a favourite of the fans around the league.

He was not a free-skater, but this did not impair his effectiveness. He would barge down the ice in the most direct line to either the opponent's net or the man he was checking. He loved the body-contact game.

Reardon came to the Montreal Canadiens as a green 19-year-old, determined to succeed, and his fine record shows that he did. He was born in Winnipeg, Manitoba, on April 1, 1921, and played for the city's championship under-12 team. When his parents died, he lived with a guardian uncle in British Columbia who sent him to a try-out with a junior team in Edmonton. Reardon made the team and played there two years before being signed by the Canadiens. World War II interrupted his pro career, but Kenny played with the Ottawa Commandos, the Army team that won the Allan Cup in 1942-43. He also played in Britain and Belgium, and, while serving in Europe, received Field Marshall Montgomery's Certificate of Merit.

Reardon rejoined the Canadiens for the 1945-46 season and for the next five seasons, was named to either the First or Second All-Star Team in the NHL. He played on a Stanley Cup winner in 1945-46.

He retired after the 1949-50 season and became a successful executive in the Montreal organization. Inducted 1966.

HENRI RICHARD
CENTRE • MONTREAL

ALTHOUGH RELATIVELY SMALL in stature, Henri Richard achieved great success during an NHL career that spanned 20 years. In 19 of those 20 seasons he played more than 50 games, despite predictions of a short stay in the league by many who thought he was too small.

Born February 29, 1936, in Montreal, Henri followed in the footsteps of his older brother, the illustrious Maurice (The Rocket) Richard. Stamina and toughness became trademarks of this extremely clever centre who stood only five-seven and weighed 160 pounds. Playing most of his career at a time when the NHL had an abundance of great centres, he was named an All-Star four times.

Henri broke into the NHL in 1955-56 with Montreal and in 1256 regular-season games, scored 358 goals. But it was as a playmaker that he excelled, collecting 688 assists, and twice leading the league in that category. He was an unselfish player, preferring to pass to a teammate rather than taking the shot on goal himself. Richard was also recognized for his sportsmanship. He won the Masterton Trophy in 1974, awarded annually to the player best exemplifying perseverance, sportsmanship and dedication to hockey.

A fast, smooth skater, his acceleration often baffled opponents; his style was both artistic and delightful. He was a member of a record 11 Stanley Cup teams and in 180 playoff games scored 49 goals and earned 80 assists. Henri was a credit to hockey, both on and off the ice.

Inducted 1979.

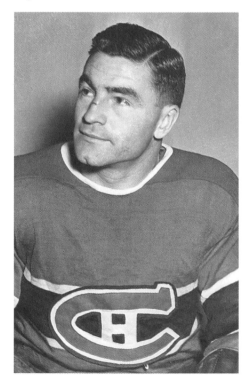

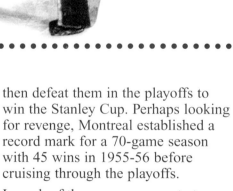

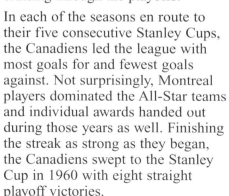

HABS DYNASTY...

Their roster read like a Who's Who of hockey. Names like Richard, Harvey, Plante, and Beliveau, Geoffrion, Moore, and Blake, were not only the greatest of their day, they remain among the greats of all time. From 1951 to 1960, they reached the Stanley Cup finals an unprecedented ten years in a row. In each of the last five years of that streak, the Montreal Canadiens were Stanley Cup champions.

The success of the Montreal dynasty of 1956 to 1960 may well have been born of the disappointment of 1954-55, when the suspension of Rocket Richard allowed the Detroit Red Wings to first pass the Canadiens for top spot in the regular season and then defeat them in the playoffs to win the Stanley Cup. Perhaps looking for revenge, Montreal established a record mark for a 70-game season with 45 wins in 1955-56 before cruising through the playoffs.

In each of the seasons en route to their five consecutive Stanley Cups, the Canadiens led the league with most goals for and fewest goals against. Not surprisingly, Montreal players dominated the All-Star teams and individual awards handed out during those years as well. Finishing the streak as strong as they began, the Canadiens swept to the Stanley Cup in 1960 with eight straight playoff victories.

"ROCKET" RICHARD
RIGHT WING • MONTREAL

WHENEVER THE NAME of Maurice Richard is mentioned, it immediately conjures up a vision of flashing skates and brilliant goal-scoring. He was know as "The Rocket" throughout an 18-year NHL career that saw him score 544 goals in 978 league games.

Maurice was born in Montreal on August 4, 1921, and played for the Verdun juniors and the Canadiens seniors before joining the NHL Canadiens in 1942-43. He scored five goals in his first 16 games, but a broken ankle sidelined him for the rest of the season. Although he was to miss only 12 games in the next six years, injuries followed The Rocket to the end of his playing days.

Richard was the first NHLer to score 50 goals in a season, reaching this total in 50 games in 1944-45. He also scored important goals, including 83 game-winners and 28 game-tying goals. In 133 playoff games he had 82 goals and 44 assists. On December 28, 1944, he spent the day moving into a new home, then went out and notched eight points with five goals and three assists. He was named to the NHL's First All-Star Team eight times and to the Second Team on six occasions.

A fiery-tempered player, Richard was once suspended from the playoffs for striking an official. This caused a riot that began in the Montreal Forum and spilled out into downtown Montreal, resulting in thousands of dollars of damage on the streets surrounding the arena. The game between the Canadiens and Red Wings was forfeited to Detroit. But despite his fury, Richard was dedicated to playing well. NHL President Clarence Campbell said of Richard: "We all have a lesson to learn from this man ...(it is) what this man has accomplished through complete and utter dedication to his work. Never ... have I met a man with such singleness of purpose and so completely devoted to his profession." Inducted 1961.

THE RICHARD RIOT...

During the third period of a March 13, 1955, game between Montreal and Boston, Maurice Richard attacked Hal Laycoe after the Bruins defenceman cut him with a high-stick to the head. In the ensuing fight and stick-swinging battle, linesman Cliff Thompson tried to restrain the Rocket but Richard twisted free and twice punched him in the face.

Three days later, NHL president Clarence Campbell suspended Richard for the remaining three games of the regular season and all of the playoffs. The next night, March 17, the Canadiens hosted the Detroit Red Wings at the Forum. Campbell attended the game and

Montreal fans pelted him with garbage. A fan hit him with a program after the first period. Then a tear gas canister exploded.

Thousands of fans rushed for the exits. Outside the Forum, a full-fledged riot erupted on Ste. Catherine Street. Seven hours of violence saw a half-million dollars in damage.

Richard's suspension cost him a chance at the NHL scoring title which he would never win in his remarkable career. It also cost Montreal first place in the standings. In the playoffs, the Richard-less Habs were beaten by Detroit in the Stanley Cup finals.

TERRY SAWCHUK
GOALTENDER • DETROIT, BOSTON, TORONTO, LOS ANGELES, NY RANGERS

TERRY SAWCHUK WAS one of the greatest goaltenders in hockey history — he played more seasons and more games, recording more shutouts than any other goalie in the history of the NHL. He played the position like a gymnast, peering out to spot the puck and dropping at lightning-speed into a butterfly crouch that closed off the lower corners of the net.

Sawchuk appeared in 971 regular-season games during 21 seasons in the NHL — 734 with Detroit, 102 with Boston, 91 with Toronto, 36 with Los Angeles and eight with New York. In regular-season action, he played in 953 complete games and had 2401 goals-against, for an average of 2.52. He registered 103 shutouts. Terry was the first player to win the rookie award in three professional leagues — the old U.S. Hockey League in 1947-48, the American Hockey League in 1948-49 and the NHL in 1950-51.

Some of his greatest moments came in the 1952 Stanley Cup playoffs when he led Detroit to the Stanley Cup in the minimum eight games, collecting four shutouts and allowing only five goals-against. He appeared in 106 Stanley Cup games, allowing 267 goals-against for a 2.54 average while earning 12 shutouts. Terry played for three Stanley Cup championship teams in Detroit and another with Toronto. He was a member of five NHL championship teams, all with the Red Wings. He won the Vezina Trophy three times with Detroit and shared the award with Johnny Bower in Toronto in 1964-65.

Sawchuk was named to the NHL's First All-Star Team three times — 1950-51, 1951-52 and 1952-53 — and to the Second Team on four occasions. Born December 28, 1929, in Winnipeg, Sawchuk died May 31, 1970, in New York City.

Inducted 1971.

MILT SCHMIDT
CENTRE • BOSTON

MILT SCHMIDT PLAYED centre on one of the most potent forward units in the history of the NHL. This line, which combined Schmidt with Woody Dumart and Bobby Bauer, was dubbed the "Kraut Line" by Albert "Battleship" Leduc, who played in the NHL in the 1920s and 1930s.

Schmidt was born in Kitchener, Ontario, on March 5, 1918. With the exception of three years spent in the Royal Canadian Air Force in World War II, he played for Boston from 1936-37 until midway through the 1954-55 season when he gave up playing to coach the Bruins. After seven seasons of coaching, Schmidt became the club's general manager.

As a player, Schmidt was a powerful, hard-hitting centre who never gave up the puck without a fight. He stood 5'11" tall and weighed 180 pounds. During his NHL career, he scored 229 goals and a total of 575 points. He won the league scoring title in 1939-40 and the Hart Trophy as the MVP to his team in 1950-51. He played for Stanley Cup-winning teams in 1938-39 and 1940-41. He was voted to the league's First All-Star Team in 1939-40, 1946-47 and 1950-51, and to the Second Team in 1951-52.

Schmidt played his early hockey in the Kitchener area. His last amateur team was the Kitchener-Waterloo Greenshirts. The first half of his rookie season as a professional was spent in Providence, but by the end of 1936-37, he had moved up to the Bruins to stay. During his years in the RCAF, Schmidt played for the Allan Cup-winning Ottawa Hurricanes. A strong, hard skater, Schmidt was also a clever stickhandler and always dangerous around the net. He never stopped trying. Inducted 1961.

FRANK SELKE
BUILDER

DEVOTION, DEDICATION AND DETERMINATION were key factors in the great success of Frank J. Selke, a man who served hockey as a coach, manager and executive for more than 60 years.

He was born May 7, 1893, in Kitchener, Ontario and although he started work at the age of 13 in a furniture factory and later became an electrician and union executive, almost all of his casual hours were spent in sports activities. He was 14 years old when he became manager of the Iroquois Bantams in his hometown. By 1918, employment brought him to Toronto where he became associated with Conn Smythe, and a friendship grew between the two men that flourished through the trying, early years of the Toronto Maple Leafs.

He left Toronto in 1946 after being assistant general manager to Smythe for three Stanley Cup teams, went to Montreal and managed six more Cup champions, retiring after 18 years as general manager of the Canadiens. Although he figured prominently in the construction of Maple Leaf Gardens, Cincinnati Gardens, Rochester War Memorial and numerous other arenas, he probably derived the most satisfaction from the part he played in establishing the Hockey Hall of Fame. He died July 3, 1985, in Rigaud, Quebec. Two Selke trophies are awarded annually to the NHL's top defensive forward and to the Quebec Major Junior Hockey League's most gentlemanly player. Inducted 1960.

CLINT SMITH
CENTRE • NY RANGERS, CHICAGO

FOR 10 SEASONS, Clint Smith symbolized the successful combination of skill and sportsmanship. He totalled a mere 24 penalty minutes to go along with 397 career points. He was a two-time winner and three-time runner-up in the Lady Byng trophy voting and the first player to win this award with two different teams. He was part of the New York Rangers' Stanley Cup winning side of 1939-40.

A native of Assiniboia, Saskatchewan, born December 12, 1913, Smith enjoyed a successful amateur career. He turned professional with the Rangers organization at the age of 18 and played his first full NHL season with in 1937-38. He was a Lady Byng runner-up in his first year in the league. The following season he won the award and duplicated this feat in 1943-44. He played three penalty-free seasons.

Prior to the 1943-44 campaign, Smith was sold to the Chicago Black Hawks. Smith's first season with the Hawks was very productive as he set an NHL record with 49 assists in a 50-game season. During this same year he and his Chicago linemates, Bill Mosienko and Doug Bentley, set a NHL record for a line with 219 total points.

Smith played four seasons with Chicago before retiring from the NHL after the 1946-47 season to become the playing coach of the Tulsa Oilers of the United States Hockey League. His first season with that club brought Smith a league MVP award and a berth in the USHL semi-finals. The following season Smith coached the USHL champion St. Paul Saints, the New York Rangers' farm club in that league.

After his retirement from hockey, Smith moved to Vancouver, where his involvement with the sport has continued. Prior to the NHL setting up a fund for "needy" players and families, Smith helped found the British Columbia Benevolent Hockey Association and served as its president for six years. In addition, he maintains a strong interest in the junior and juvenile hockey. Inducted 1991.

ALLAN STANLEY
DEFENCE • NY RANGERS, CHICAGO, BOSTON, TORONTO, PHILADELPHIA

ALLAN STANLEY WAS frequently described as the player who always seemed to be in somebody's shadow. In his rookie NHL season, although coach Frank Boucher openly campaigned for Stanley as the rookie of the year, teammate Pentti Lund won the Calder Trophy. During his 21-year NHL career as a defenceman, Stanley's play was often eclipsed by that of some of the game's all-time greats including Doug Harvey, Red Kelly, Tim Horton and Harry Howell. Yet he was one of the most durable of players, taking part in 1244 regular-season games and 109 playoff encounters.

Despite outstanding competition, Stanley was selected to the league's Second All-Star Team in 1960, 1961 and 1966. He also had the satisfaction of playing on four Stanley Cup winners with the Toronto Maple Leafs.

Born March 1, 1926, in Timmins, Ontario, Stanley played three seasons with Providence of the American Hockey League before breaking into the NHL with the New York Rangers as part of a deal in which the Rangers gave up two NHL-roster players, four minor leaguers and a sizeable amount of cash. He later played for the Chicago Black Hawks, Boston Bruins, and Toronto Maple Leafs before concluding his noteworthy career with the Philadelphia Flyers in 1968-69.

Stanley was never noted for his skating speed, but his exceptional anticipation of the unfolding play enabled him to remain in the NHL for more than two decades.

Inducted 1981.

"RED" STOREY
REFEREE

BORN IN BARRIE, ONTARIO, on March 5, 1918, Roy Alvin (Red) Storey first burst onto the sports scene in football, where he was a standout until injuries curtailed his career. But it was as an NHL referee from 1951 to 1959 that he made his greatest contribution. Storey was among the NHL's most colourful officials.

Storey played junior hockey for Barrie and one senior season with the Montreal Royals. Red's first claim to sports immortality came in 1938 as a member of the Toronto Argonauts football team. He came off the bench to score three touchdowns in the final 13 minutes of the Grey Cup game, one of them on a 102-yard run, to lead the Argos to a 30-7 victory over the Winnipeg Blue Bombers. A knee injury in 1940 prematurely ended his football career. He continued as a football official from 1946 to 1957 and also officiated lacrosse for 10 years. A standout in lacrosse as a player, he once scored 12 goals in a game for Ville St. Pierre, setting a Quebec record. Red was also a proficient baseball player.

Storey refereed more than 2000 hockey games at all levels. Looking back, he says his biggest thrill was "just being involved with a great bunch of guys."

Inducted 1967.

JACK STEWART
DEFENCE • DETROIT, CHICAGO

JOHN "BLACK JACK" STEWART probably earned his nickname because of his dark, handsome features, but many who played against him in the NHL might suggest that this outstanding defenceman's name was a tribute to his abilities as a punishing bodychecker.

He was born in Pilot Mound, Manitoba, on May 6, 1917, and played his early hockey there. Stewart played junior hockey in Portage La Prairie, Manitoba, for two seasons before signing a pro contract in 1938 with the Detroit Red Wings. The Wings sent him to Pittsburgh but recalled him for 33 games in the 1938-39 season and he quickly established himself as a great defenceman.

Stewart was a regular with Detroit through 1949-50. The Wings dealt him to Chicago where he finished his NHL career at the end of the 1951-52 season. Stewart played on Stanley Cup-winning teams in 1942-43 and 1949-50, and was named to five NHL All-Star Teams. He was a First Team selection in 1942-43, 1947-48 and 1948-49, and a Second Team pick in 1945-46 and 1946-47. He was also voted Detroit's most valuable player in the 1942-43 season.

After leaving the professional game, Stewart coached and managed the Chatham Maroons of the OHA senior league. He later coached teams in Windsor and Kitchener, Ontario, and in Pittsburgh of the American Hockey League. He retired from hockey in 1963.

Jack Stewart played in 565 NHL games, recording 115 scoring points. He died May 25, 1983, at his home near Detroit.

Inducted 1964.

ANATOLI TARASOV
BUILDER

BORN IN MOSCOW, December 10, 1919, Anatoli Vladimirovitch Tarasov is generally regarded as the architect of hockey power in the Soviet Union. A product of Soviet hockey himself, Tarasov coached his country's national team to nine straight world amateur championships and three consecutive Olympic titles before he retired after winning the gold medal at Sapporo, Japan, in 1972.

In the late 1940s and early 1950s he played for Soviet teams that progressed rapidly to become challengers for the world amateur championship. After retiring as a player, he became assistant to head coach Arkadi Cherneshev, and then became head coach himself. Under his coaching the Soviet national team soon was capable of beating Canada's senior amateur champions.

A keen student of the Canadian game, Tarasov converted many facets of that hockey to his own use. He was a strong believer in conditioning. He wrote many books on hockey and also supervised the Soviet Golden Puck tournament for boys in which more than one million youngsters were registered. In 1987 he served as a coaching consultant to the NHL's Vancouver Canucks.

He died June 23, 1995.

Inducted 1974.

WILLIAM THAYER TUTT
BUILDER

WILLIAM THAYER TUTT was born March 2, 1912, in Coronado, California, but his identification with hockey is integrally linked with Colorado Springs, Colorado.

He became active in the Amateur Hockey Association of the U.S. through his acquaintance with Walter Brown of Boston. When the National Collegiate Athletic Association sought a site for its first national championship hockey tournament, Tutt offered his family-owned Broadmoor Arena at Colorado Springs. He underwrote the costs of the tournament for its first 10 years until the event was able to pay its own way. He helped organize U.S. national ice hockey teams, negotiating and financing the first series in the U.S. against visiting Soviet teams in 1959. He hosted the 1962 International Ice Hockey Federation world championships, served as IIHF president from 1966 to 1969, and later as an IIHF vice-president and council member.

In 1972, Tutt succeeded Tommy Lockhart as president of AHAUS. The following year he was inducted into the U.S. Hockey Hall of Fame. In March, 1978, he was named a recipient of the Lester Patrick Trophy for outstanding service to hockey in the United States.

He died March 24, 1989.

Inducted 1978.

SOVIETS IN '54...

From 1920 to 1952, Canada earned gold medals in six of seven Olympic hockey tournaments. During a similar period, Canada also dominated the World Championships, winning 16 of 19 titles. But on March 7, 1954, a new era in international hockey began.

The 1954 World Hockey Championships were played in Stockholm, and Canadian officials had a difficult time finding an amateur club available to make the trip. Finally, they found a team in suburban Toronto: The East York Lyndhursts.

While perhaps not the strongest team Canada had ever sent overseas, the Lyndhursts had little trouble. They outscored their opposition 57-5 in winning the first six games of the round-robin tournament. The seventh and deciding game would be played against Moscow Dynamo.

The Moscow entry marked the first time the Soviet Union had ever sent a team to the World Championships. They had been more than ready to compete, running up a 5-0-1 record through their first six games. A crowd of 17,000 witnessed the first meeting between Canada and the Soviet Union on March 7. The Moscow squad built up a 4-0 first-period lead and upped its advantage to 7-1 through two. When it was over, the Soviets had upset Canada 7-2 to win the tournament.

The Soviets had used strong skating skills and a short passing game to claim their first World Championship in 1954. It was a combination that would become all too familiar to their opponents in the decades to come.

FRANK UDVARI

REFEREE

DESPITE THE MANY PHYSICAL RISKS of his business, Frank missed only two officiating assignments in 15 years. He refereed 718 regular-season and 70 playoff games in the NHL, 229 in the American Hockey League, seven in the Western League, 15 in the Eastern League and seven in the Central League, as well as serving as AHL referee-in-chief for many years.

Born in Yugoslavia on January 2, 1924, he moved to Canada at the age of seven, growing up in Kitchener. Only three years after refereeing his first minor league game, Frank officiated his first games in the NHL, handling 12 matches in the 1951-52 season. He remained in the NHL as a referee through 1965-66, recognized as the best man on staff for a number of seasons. He was appointed supervisor of NHL officials in 1966. In this capacity, he conducted officiating schools in Canada the United States and in Germany for the Canadian Army.

Carl Voss, the referee-in-chief who brought him into the NHL, said that he had never known a person who has set higher standards for himself. Co-workers considered him an unquestioned leader and he was influential in helping many junior members of the NHL officiating staff to success on the ice.

Off-ice, he was successful in business in the Kitchener-Waterloo area. He remained an active participant in youth programs of his community. Inducted 1973.

NORM ULLMAN

CENTRE • DETROIT, TORONTO, EDMONTON (WHA)

NORM ULLMAN — Norm to his friends — was born December 26, 1935, in Provost, Alberta. Twenty years later, he broke into the NHL with Detroit and spent the next 20 years plying his craft at centre ice for the Red Wings and Toronto Maple Leafs.

A quiet man who shunned the limelight, Ullman was often underrated, but his natural talent ultimately gained him recognition as one of the NHL's premier centres. In his 20 NHL seasons, Norm scored 490 goals and assisted on another 739. He was voted to two All-Star Team berths despite formidable opposition. In 16 of his 20 seasons, he scored 20 or more goals and led the league with 42 goals in 1964-65.

George "Punch" Imlach who coached Ullman in Toronto called him, "The best centre who ever played for me."

"Ullman is a bull terrier," said King Clancy, "he never quits on his forechecking patrol." Imlach acquired Ullman for the Leafs in 1967-68 as part of a "bombshell" trade with Detroit. Paul Henderson and Floyd Smith came with Ullman for Frank Mahovlich, Pete Stemkowski, Garry Unger and the rights to Carl Brewer.

Following his years in the NHL, Norm moved to the WHA for a final two seasons in which he added another 47 goals and 83 assists before retiring in 1977. An excellent stickhandler, he was also a strong skater noted for durability and consistency. When he retired, Ullman ranked in the top ten in both goals and assists among NHL all-time scoring leaders.

Inducted 1982.

1960-67 • The curved blade is introduced. Stan Mikita is often given credit for the innovation after noticing how the puck would dip and slice while shooting with a stick he had broken in practice. • Despite the increased use of curved sticks, overall team scoring in the league actually declines over the next three seasons. • 1962: All teams now have uniform numbers on the sleeves of their jerseys. • Bobby Hull becomes the first player to score more than 50 goals in a season when he finished the 1962-63 campaign with 54. • 1963-64: Gordie Howe becomes hockey all-time leading goal scorer with his 545th on November 10, 1963. • Terry Sawchuk sets a new NHL shutout record with the 95th of his career on January 18, 1964. • The NHL announces plans for a new trophy. The Conn Smythe Trophy will be awarded the the MVP of the playoffs. • 1965: Despite a high fever, Ed Johnston is forced to play goal against Toronto on January 30th when his replacement, Jack Norris, has his equipment stolen from the lobby of the Royal York Hotel. • 1966-67: On December 28, 1966, Alan Eagleson meets with Boston players to begin discussing a Players' Association. • The average age of an NHL player is 29, average weight is 183 lbs., average height is 5'11". • Stan Mikita becomes the first player to win three individual awards when he receives the Hart, Art Ross and Lady Byng trophies. • Toronto Maple Leafs win the last Stanley Cup of the "Original Six" era.

HARRY WATSON

LEFT WING • BROOKLYN, DETROIT, TORONTO, CHICAGO

HARRY WATSON patrolled the left wing with a quiet efficiency. He was known for his offensive ability complimented by deceptive speed, physical strength and capable defensive skills.

Born May 6, 1923, in Saskatoon, Watson was a junior star in his hometown. The husky winger joined the Brooklyn (New York) Americans for the 1941-42 NHL season. He scored 10 goals as an 18-year old NHLer. Following the demise of the Americans in 1942, Watson was claimed by the Red Wings where he helped Detroit to a Stanley Cup championship.

He joined the Royal Canadian Air Force in 1943 and played two years of service hockey. He rejoined the Red Wings for 1945-46 and was traded to the Leafs in 1947. In Toronto, he scored a career high 26 goals in 1948-49 and helped the Leafs win four Stanley Cups, frequently checking the opposition's top scorers.

Watson scored the eventual Stanley Cup-winning goal in 1948 and assisted on Bill Barilko's historic overtime Cup-winner in 1951. He joined the Black Hawks in 1954, providing leadership and experience.

In 809 regular season NHL games, Harry Watson scored 236 goals and 207 assists for 443 points. Following his last NHL season in 1956-57, Watson's career goals total left him behind only Gordie Howe, Maurice Richard and Ted Lindsay among active players. He was the Lady Byng Trophy runner-up in 1949 when he went through the entire season without a single penalty. He played in seven All-Star Games including the first three with the Toronto Maple Leafs.

He went on to coach minor-pro, junior and senior hockey and served as co-chairman of Toronto's Timmy Tyke minor hockey tournament in support of handicapped children. He was inducted into the Saskatoon and Saskatchewan Sports Halls of Fame in 1987.

Inducted 1994.

THE LAST AMERICAN...

For much of its existence, the New York Americans functioned as a last respite before the retirement home for a number of over-the-hill NHL veterans, but the team also managed to launch a few great careers too. Sweeny Schriner and Chuck Rayner were perhaps the best.

The Americans last season was 1941-42, when they adopted the name of Brooklyn in a last-ditch effort to increase fan support. Though the team died anyway, two teenagers who broke in that season kept the legacy of the club alive as both went on to lengthy careers.

Kenny Mosdell came straight out of juniors to join the Americans in 1941. When the club folded, he joined the army before resuming his NHL career with the Canadiens in 1945. He went on to win four Stanley Cups. Harry Watson was drafted by Detroit and promptly moved from the outhouse to the penthouse when the Red Wings won the Cup in 1943. A trade to Toronto in 1947 would see Watson bring his Stanley Cup collection to five.

Both Mosdell and Watson were NHL regulars until 1957, but Kenny earned the distinction of being the last of the Americans when he was called on to replace an injured Jean Beliveau for the Canadiens in the 1959 playoffs.

CARL VOSS

BUILDER

CARL VOSS will be remembered for his enormous contribution to the creation and development of referees and linesmen. Born January 6, 1907, in Chelsea, Massachusetts, he was a member of the Memorial Cup finalist Kingston Frontenacs of 1926 and had already played on two Grey Cup-winning football teams as a half-back with Queen's University.

In 1927 he became the first Toronto Maple Leaf, signing a contract the day Conn Smythe purchased the Toronto St. Pats and changed the club's name. Voss later played with the New York Rangers, and Americans, the Montreal Maroons and for Detroit, Ottawa, St. Louis, and Chicago. He was rookie-of-the year with Detroit in 1932-33, the first year this selection was made in the NHL. In 1937-38 he was Chicago's leading scorer and also scored the Stanley Cup-winning goal.

Carl Voss later became president of the U.S. Hockey League and in 1950 was named the first referee-in-chief of the NHL. As hockey developed he also became referee-in-chief of other minor pro leagues which used officials provided by the NHL. His travels took him up to 60,000 miles per season as he assessed the work of officials in as many as 125 games each year. He conducted hundreds of officiating schools and was one of hockey's most effective and enthusiastic ambassadors. He died September 13, 1973.

Inducted 1974.

"Gump" Worsley

Goaltender • NY Rangers, Montreal, Minnesota

Lorne (Gump) Worsley played goal for three NHL teams — the New York Rangers, Montreal Canadiens and Minnesota North Stars — and in a professional career that spanned 25 seasons, established an enviable record. Because of a physical resemblance to a popular comic strip personality, Worsley was nicknamed "Gump" early in his career, and it stuck.

His long career took him to teams in New Haven, St. Paul, Saskatoon, Vancouver, Providence, Springfield and Quebec in the minor leagues. At St. Paul, he won the Charles Gardiner Memorial Trophy as outstanding rookie of the U.S. League. In 1952-53, he won the Calder Trophy as the NHL's top rookie. Despite this, he spent the next season at Vancouver in the Western League where he was named most valuable player and outstanding goaltender.

In the NHL, in addition to the Calder, Worsley was twice a Vezina Trophy winner — in 1965-66 with Charlie Hodge and 1967-68 with Rogatien Vachon. He also played for four Stanley Cup championship teams with Montreal in 1965, 1966, 1968 and 1969. His NHL goals-against per game average was 2.91 for 860 regular-season matches, including 43 shutouts. In 70 playoff games, his goals-against average was 2.82 per game.

His finest season was 1967-68 when he played 40 games, had six shutouts and a remarkable 1.98 goals-against average. It wasn't until his final year of action with the Minnesota North Stars that he finally consented to wear a mask. He was born May 14, 1929, in Montreal.

Inducted 1980.

Masked Marvels...

Glenn Hall was one of the greatest netminders in hockey history, but Mr. Goalie would never be confused with the Chicoutimi Cucumber — the nickname Georges Vezina earned for his ability to remain calm. Perhaps Hall was extra nervous on November 13, 1968, when he wore a mask for the first time in an NHL game.

Things got off to a bad start for the St. Louis goalie when he flubbed a 60-foot shot from Vic Hadfield just 1:16 into the game. The Rangers were pressing for another goal moments later when Blues defenceman Noel Picard froze the puck to relieve the pressure. Referee Vern Buffey penalized Picard and Hall was incensed. Just 10 seconds into the New York power play, he flicked his glove at Buffey and connected with the referee's shoulder, earning himself a game misconduct.

With fellow goalie Jacques Plante out with a groin pull, the Blues had summoned Robbie Irons from the minors to serve as a backup. Coach Scotty Bowman, though, was less than confident in Irons' ability. He instructed the rookie to stall for time while Plante came down from the stands to suit up. After facing a few warmup shots, one of the straps on Irons' pads "suddenly" came loose and he went to the bench for repairs. Buffey wasn't buying it. He instructed the Blues to get the game going or face another delay of game penalty. Plante wasn't ready, so Bowman reluctantly sent Irons back onto the ice.

By 5:01 of the first period, Plante was dressed. Irons had seen only three minutes of action (and no shots on goal) when Plante replaced him. The young goalie was returned to the minors. Irons played with Fort Wayne of the IHL until the early 1980s, but never got another shot at the NHL.

New States of Play

1967 to Date

Soviet National Team goaltender Vladislav Tretiak thwarts Stan Mikita of Team Canada during game two of the "Summit Series" in September 1972. This eight-game tournament was the first on-ice meeting between the Soviets and the NHL's best. An aesthetic success and a narrow win for Team Canada, it laid the foundation for the Canada Cup and the World Cup of Hockey.

KEITH ALLEN

BUILDER

KEITH ALLEN contributed greatly to the building of the Philadelphia Flyers. Born in Saskatoon August 21, 1923, he spent parts of two seasons as a player with the Red Wings, and enjoyed nine outstanding years as coach of Detroit's farm team in Seattle of the WHL. In 1966 Allen accepted the position of coaching the expansion Philadelphia Flyers.

Allen played a major role in the selection of players like Bernie Parent, Gary Dornhoefer and Joe Watson during the Expansion Draft. He guided the Flyers to a first-place finish in 1967-68. In 1970 he was named general manager.

His shrewd trading and drafting enabled Philadelphia to win the Stanley Cup in 1974, becoming the first expansion team to do so. The Flyers won the Cup again in 1975 and reached the finals in 1976, 1980 1985 and 1987.

Allen stepped down as general manager following the 1982-83 season to serve as the Flyers' executive vice-president. He has devoted thirty years to the Philadelphia Flyers in a number of capacities while earning the reputation as one of the NHL's top administrators.

Inducted 1992.

NEIL ARMSTRONG

LINESMAN

NEIL ARMSTRONG became a certified official of the Ontario Hockey Association in the early 1950s and progressed rapidly up to the major leagues.

Armstrong first donned the striped jersey of an NHL official in 1957-58, as a part-time linesman, officiating 11 games that year. The league's officiating staff knew they had a quality official in Armstrong, and over the next 20 seasons he went on to work another 1733 regular-season games, 208 Stanley Cup playoff games and 10 All-Star Games.

Known as the "Ironman" of the officiating staff, Armstrong never missed an assignment in 16 seasons.

Of the 208 Stanley Cup playoff games in which Armstrong officiated, 48 games were in the Stanley Cup finals. Former NHL Referee-in-Chief and President of the Hockey Hall of Fame, Ian "Scotty" Morrison, once said of Armstrong's ability: "Neil's dedication to his profession and pride in his personal performances has always been outstanding."

Born in Plympton Township, Ontario, December 29, 1932, Armstrong went on to serve as a scout for the Montreal Canadiens after retiring from officiating, employing the same desire and dedication in that capacity he showed as a linesman.

Inducted 1991.

BILL BARBER

LEFT WING • PHILADELPHIA

BILL BARBER was a star player with the Philadelphia Flyers from 1973 until 1984. He scored 420 goals and 463 assists for 883 points in 903 career regular-season games for the Flyers. In 129 playoff games he notched 53 goals and 55 assists. He was an integral part of Philadelphia's Stanley Cup winning teams in 1974 and 1975.

Born in Callander, Ontario, July 11, 1952, Barber came out of the Ontario Hockey Association where he was a member of the Kitchener Rangers. In two seasons he averaged more than 100 points. In 1973, Barber was selected as Philadelphia's first choice, seventh over-all in the NHL Amateur Draft. He started his professional career with a Flyers farm team in 1973. After 11 games he was called up to the NHL as an injury replacement, and never left. In junior Barber had been a centreman but with the Flyers, coach Fred Shero used him as a left winger alongside Hall of Famer Bobby Clarke. In his rookie campaign, he recorded 30 goals and 34 assists.

One of his most memorable goals sent the final game of the 1976 Canada Cup into overtime. Barber was forced to end his career in April of 1984 after undergoing knee surgery. Since retiring as a player, he has remained in the Flyers organization. In 1996 he was named head coach of the Flyers' new farm club, the Philadelphia Phantoms of the American Hockey League.

Inducted 1990.

MIKE BOSSY
RIGHT WING • NY ISLANDERS

THE NAME MIKE BOSSY is synonymous with goal scoring. For ten seasons, he was one of the games' greatest right wingers and a key ingredient in the success of the New York Islanders.

Born January 22, 1957 in Montreal, Bossy was drafted 15th overall by the Islanders in 1977. His 53 goals as a rookie earned him the Calder Trophy. He went on to score 50 goals in 50 games 1980-81, matching Maurice Richard's feat in 1944-45.

In a career that spanned a decade, "Boss" fired 573 goals along with 553 assists for 1126 points. Bossy scored 50-or-more goals in his first nine seasons, including five 60-goal campaigns. He scored the Cup-winning goal in both the 1982 and 1983 finals and was the recipient of the Conn Smythe Trophy in 1982. In playoff action, Bossy tallied 85 goals and 160 points in 129 games.

He played for Team Canada in the 1981 and 1984 Canada Cup tournaments, scoring in overtime in 1984 to eliminate the Soviets.

He was a three-time Lady Byng Trophy winner and an eight-time NHL All-Star. He was the first Islander to hit career scoring marks of 500 goals and 1000 points.

A chronic back ailment forced him to retire.

Inducted 1991.

SCOTTY BOWMAN
BUILDER

SCOTTY BOWMAN has won more games that any other coach in NHL history and has won six Cup championships. He has also done an admirable job as a TV analyst, scout, and club executive.

Born September 18, 1933 in Montreal, Bowman was a protege of Sam Pollock, the general manager of the Montreal Canadiens. He learned well, guiding junior teams within the Canadiens organization to several winning seasons.

In 1967-68, he accepted a position with the newly formed St. Louis Blues as coach and general manager. In four seasons he led the Blues to the Stanley Cup finals three times. Pollock persuaded Bowman to return to the Habs as coach in 1971. Eight years in Montreal brought five Stanley Cup rings, as well as a Canada Cup victory in 1976.

In 1979 he became general manager, coach and director of hockey operations for the Buffalo Sabres, a position he held until 1987. The following season he was hired by Hockey Night in Canada as a hockey analyst, but following the 1990 season, became the Director of Player Development and, later coach of the Pittsburgh Penguins and Detroit Red Wings. He won the Stanley Cup with Pittsburgh in 1992, and reached the finals with Detroit in 1995.

Bowman won the Jack Adams Trophy as the NHL's top coach in 1977 and 1996.

Inducted 1991.

50 GOALS IN 50 GAMES...

In the NHL's first season of 1917-18, Joe Malone of the Montreal Canadiens led the league in scoring with the remarkable total of 44 goals in just 20 games. Over the years, as the rules and style of hockey changed, Malone's record total was rarely threatened. Finally, during the 1944-45 season, Malone was matched. In the 40th game of the schedule, Maurice "Rocket" Richard netted his 44th goal of the year. By season's end, he had totalled 50 goals in 50 games.

Even with the ever-increasing length of the NHL schedule, it would be 16 years before hockey saw its second 50-goal scorer. With expansion, it would take only 10 seasons after that until the record for goals was pushed to 76, and yet no one else was ever able to score 50 goals in 50 games until Mike Bossy did so in 1980-81.

Bossy scored his 50th goal against Ron Grahame of the Quebec Nordiques in the dying moments of the New York Islanders' 50th game of the season. But Bossy would not have long to cherish his remarkable achievement. The very next year, Wayne Gretzky obliterated his mark with his 50th goal in just 39 games en route to an NHL-record 92 goals that season.

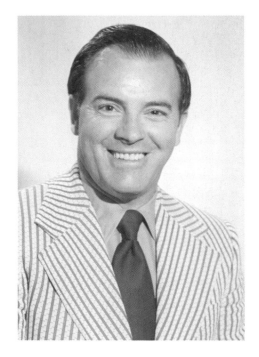

GERRY CHEEVERS
GOALTENDER • TORONTO, BOSTON, CLEVELAND (WHA)

GERRY CHEEVERS' sole objective was winning games. He played goal well enough for the Bruins to win the two Stanley Cup in 1970 and 1972 and reach the finals in 1977 and 1978.

Born December 7, 1940 in St. Catharines, Ontario, Cheevers was drafted out of the Toronto system in 1965 by Boston, and Joe Crozier, who had coached Cheevers at Rochester, told Boston people, "Cheevers is the most exciting goalie you'll ever see. He'll have your fans on the edge of their seats all night." He was a prophet, for Cheevers became one of the most popular Bruins of all time. Not only was he exciting in the way he'd handle the puck, pass to his defencemen, and challenge opposing shooters, but he was also capable of making brilliant saves at the right times. He was the ultimate clutch goalie of the 1960s and 1970s. He scrambled, he played the man and he was the leader of the handful of goalies who revolutionized the art of keeping the puck out of the net. He was the first goalie recognized by opponents as "a third defenceman."

His 13-season goals-against average was 2.89 in 418 games and 2.69 in 88 playoff games. In the midst of his fine career with Boston, he left the club to play 3½ seasons with Cleveland in the WHA. He returned to Boston in 1976, retiring as an active player at the end of the 1979-80 season because his knees had worn out. He was named coach of the Bruins in July of 1980 and compiled a record of 204-126-46 in his 4½ seasons as coach.

Inducted 1985.

BOBBY CLARKE
CENTRE • PHILADELPHIA

NO HOCKEY PLAYER worked harder than Bobby Clarke, the tenacious centreman who played 15 seasons with the Philadelphia Flyers. Beginning in 1969-70, his first season in the NHL, Clarke gave his coaches, teammates and fans full value, playing his regular shift, killing penalties and working the power-play.

Despite a life-long love of the sport, a hockey career must have seemed only a remote possibility to Bobby Clarke when, as a 15-year-old, he learned he had diabetes. Born in Flin Flon, Manitoba, on August 13, 1949, he played junior hockey in his hometown, leading the Western Canada Junior Hockey League in assists and points in his final two seasons. The Flyers drafted him 17th overall and he immediately excelled in the NHL.

His point totals steadily climbed until 1972-73, his fourth campaign in the NHL, when he became the first expansion-team player to record a 100-point season. Though just 23, his team leadership was recognized as coach Fred Shero named him team captain that same year. He won his first of three Hart Trophies as MVP to his team that season.

He was the workhorse and sparkplug of the Flyers' two Stanley Cup championship teams in 1973-74 and 1974-75. He was one of the NHL's best face-off men and, according to Fred Shero, was "the greatest player in the game for helping his team." The trophy awarded to the Western Hockey League's top scorer is named in his honour.

Inducted 1987.

THE BROAD STREET BULLIES...

They could beat you with muscle or with talent, but when it came right down to it, the Philadelphia Flyers could just plain beat you. Their willingness to do whatever it took to win, even if it meant stretching the rules, led fans to dub them "the Broad Street Bullies."

The Flyers of the mid-1970s were well coached by Fred Shero and guided on the ice by their inspirational captain, Bobby Clarke. After becoming the first expansion team to record 100 points in a season in 1973-74, Philadelphia knocked off the Atlanta Flames and New York Rangers in the playoffs to set up a final against the Boston Bruins for the Stanley Cup. Using their physical style to shut down the high-scoring Bruins, the Flyers built up a 3-2 lead through five games. In the sixth, Rick MacLeish tipped in a "Moose" Dupont drive in the first period and Bernie Parent made it stand up for a 1-0 victory. The Flyers became the first expansion team to capture the Stanley Cup.

Philadelphia repeated as Stanley Cup champions with a win over the Buffalo Sabres in 1975 and remained an NHL power well into the next decade.

YVAN COURNOYER
RIGHT WING • MONTREAL

FOR 15 NHL SEASONS "The Roadrunner" terrorized opposition defences with blazing speed and superb puck-handling skills. Although small of stature at only 5'7" and 178 pounds, Cournoyer broke into the NHL to stay with the Montreal Canadiens in 1964-65.

He was used sparingly at first, but in time proved he could hold his own against much bigger players. Before a recurring back injury ended his career in 1979, he scored 428 goals in 968 regular-season games. He also added 64 more in 147 playoff contests, en route to 10 Stanley Cup triumphs.

The speedy right winger was born in Drummondville, Quebec, on November 22, 1943, and graduated to the NHL Canadiens from the Junior Canadiens, spending only seven games in the minors with Quebec of the AHL. Used mainly on power plays in his career's early stages, Cournoyer established a reputation for durability and was named to the League's Second All-Star Team on four occasions. In 12 consecutive seasons he scored 24 or more goals and in the 1973 Stanley Cup playoffs was named winner of the Conn Smythe Trophy. His final tally of 863 points included 435 assists, and at the time of his retirement he shared the record for most points in a Stanley Cup final series (six goals, six assists) with Gordie Howe and Jacques Lemaire.

A truly clean player, Cournoyer was penalized a total of only 255 minutes throughout his career, an average of only 17 minutes per season. Inducted 1982.

MARCEL DIONNE
CENTRE • DETROIT,
LOS ANGELES, NY RANGERS

MARCEL DIONNE enjoyed 19 outstanding seasons in the NHL, with the Detroit Red Wings, Los Angeles Kings, and New York Rangers.

Born August 3, 1951 in Drummondville, Quebec, Dionne's three-year junior totasl including playoffs, were an amazing 507 points. He was selected second overall in the 1971 NHL Amateur Draft by the Detroit Red Wings. His excellent playmaking ability and clean style of play earned him the Lady Byng Trophy as the league's most gentlemanly player during 1974-75, his last season as a Red Wing.

Dionne spent the next 12 seasons as a member of the Los Angeles Kings before moving to the New York Rangers in 1986. As a member of the Kings, he centered the Triple Crown Line along with teammates Dave Taylor and Charlie Simmer. During that time Dionne won another Lady Byng Trophy and the Art Ross Trophy as the NHL's leading scorer in 1979-80. He was named to the All-Star Team on four occasions.

Dionne retired in 1989 with 1771 points, on 731 goals and 1040 points, placing him near the top of the NHL all-time scoring list.

Inducted 1992.

JOHN D'AMICO
LINESMAN

JOHN D'AMICO was the final survivor of the NHL's "Original Six" era. Born September 21, 1937, in Toronto, he worked his first regular-season assignment at Boston Garden on October 12, 1964. He began as a linesman, but worked briefly as a referee before returning to the lines.

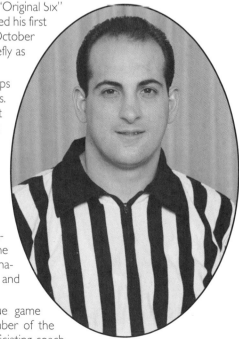

He was called the rock of the officiating corps and went on to work more than 1700 NHL games. In 1982 he stopped a puck and injured his arm but continued on. X-rays after the game revealed that the arm was broken.

D'Amico was a regular at Stanley Cup time, appearing in over 20 Stanley Cup finals. He also handled the lines at seven NHL All-Star games including 1971, 1973, 1976, 1978, 1980, 1984, and 1986.

His talents were recognized further in international hockey competition as he officiated at the 1976, 1981, 1984 and 1987 Canada Cup tournaments, as well as the 1979 Challenge Cup '79 and Rendez-Vous '87.

He worked his last National Hockey League game March 5, 1988. He went on to work as a member of the NHL's Officiating Supervisory Staff acting as an officiating coach.

Inducted 1993.

KEN DRYDEN

GOALTENDER • MONTREAL

KEN DRYDEN was a big man — six-foot-four and 210 pounds — so he covered a lot of the net during his days as a goalie with the Montreal Canadiens. "He's a damn octopus," is the way Phil Esposito described this native of Hamilton, Ontario, born August 8, 1947. But Ken had other attributes: he was an articulate scholar-athlete who starred as a student at Cornell University, then worked his way through law school with his earnings as an All-Star with the Canadiens.

He made his debut in the NHL at the end of the 1970-71 season, sparking the Canadiens to an upset Stanley Cup victory while winning the Conn Smythe Trophy as MVP in the play-offs. He won the Calder Trophy as NHL rookie of the year in 1971-72. In his seven-plus seasons with the Canadiens he had 46 shutouts and a 2.24 goals-against average, and played every game in helping Montreal win six Stanley Cups including four in succession from 1976 to 1979. Ken was named to five NHL All-Star Teams and won or shared the Vezina Trophy on five occasions. His forte was his consistency.

Dryden retired in 1979 at the age of 31 at a time when he was at the peak of his career and earning $200,000 annually. "It was a decision I had to make," he said calmly....."it seemed the time to do it." It was expected that he would enter law or politics following his retirement, but instead he took his wife and two children to England, settled down in a brownstone house in Cambridge and wrote a book based on his hockey experiences. He returned to Toronto in 1982 and later served as Commissioner of Youth for the Province of Ontario.

Inducted 1983.

ALAN EAGLESON

BUILDER

ALAN EAGLESON was born April 29, 1933 in St. Catharines, Ontario. A lawyer, his negotiating skills made him one of hockey's most influential men in the 1970s and 1980s.

In the early 1960s, Eagleson began a relationship with a budding hockey star named Bobby Orr, serving as his lawyer and agent. Eagleson landed a substantial rookie contract for Orr and he soon had many more NHL players as clients. Though he may have cast an unwelcome shadow in the boardrooms of team owners, he became a folk hero to the players who supported him as Executive Director of the fledgling NHL Players' Association, a post he held for a number of years. Eagleson was instrumental in increasing NHL players' salaries and in creating a stable relationship between players and management.

Eagleson's most visible contribution to the game was in the international arena. In the late 1960s, after Canada had withdrawn from international competition, he began a campaign to have Canada's best players meet their counterparts from the Soviet Union. By eliciting the cooperation of an army of businessmen, bureaucrats and government leaders, Eagleson helped Charles Hay to arrange the famous eight-game exhibition series in 1972 between Canadian NHL pros and the Soviet National team.

The astounding success of this match-up enabled Eagleson to assume a leadership role in the development of the Canada Cup tournament, staged four times between 1976 and 1991.

Inducted 1989.

TEAM CANADA 1972...

For years, the best amateur teams in Canada were easily able to win World Championships and Olympic gold medals, but by the 1960s this was no longer true. With the Soviet Union dominating international hockey, Canadian fans longed to see a series that would pit the best Canadian professionals against the best the Soviets had to offer. In September of 1972, they got their wish.

Most Canadians expected the 1972 Canada-Russia series to be a one-sided win for the NHL's best players. When the Soviets posted a 7-3 victory in the opening game in Montreal, the nation was stunned. Fans booed Team Canada in Vancouver as the Soviet victory there gave them a 2-1-1 lead through four games. Phil Esposito made an emotional plea for support on national television and the 3,000 fans who followed the team to Moscow did not let him down.

Though Team Canada dropped its first game in Russia, they stormed back to win games six and seven to even the series. Rallying again in the eighth and final game, Paul Henderson scored with just 34 seconds left in the series to give Canada a thrilling 6-5 victory. An entire nation rejoiced.

PHIL ESPOSITO

CENTRE • CHICAGO, BOSTON, NY RANGERS

IN 1968-69, PHIL ESPOSITO became the first NHL player to crack the 100-point barrier. He totalled at least 55 goals in five consecutive seasons; upon his retirement in 1981, only Wayne Gretzky had surpassed his single-season mark of 76 goals, set in 1970-71. He totalled 1590 points (717 goals and 873 assists) in 1282 games over an 18-season span.

Born in Sault Ste. Marie, Ontario, February 20, 1942. Phil spent two years in the minors before making it to the NHL with Chicago in 1963-64. Chicago traded him to Boston in a six-player deal in 1967. Shortly after joining the Bruins, Boston ended its 29-year drought with Stanley Cup victories in 1970 and 1972. Espo played 625 regular-season games for the Bruins, winning five NHL scoring titles and finishing second twice. He was also named to the NHL's First All-Star Team six times and to the Second Team twice. He won the Hart Trophy as the league's MVP twice, and, in 1978, was recipient of the Lester Patrick Trophy for contribution to hockey in the U.S.

He was traded to the New York Rangers in 1975-76 and finished his career in Madison Square Garden, retiring just before his 39th birthday. Esposito was also the individual leader and top point-scorer for Team Canada (7 goals, 6 assists) in 1972's remarkable Super Series against the Soviet Nationals.

Since retiring, he has served as general manager and coach with the New York Rangers and the Tampa Bay Lightning.

Inducted 1984.

TONY ESPOSITO

GOALTENDER • MONTREAL, CHICAGO

WHEN TONY ESPOSITO broke into the NHL with the Canadiens, he was often referred to as Phil's kid brother. Tony's abilities as a goaltender eventually earned him his own place in NHL history.

Born in Sault Ste. Marie, Ontario, April 23, 1943. Tony played college hockey scholarship at Michigan Tech University. He broke into the NHL during the 1968-69 season with the Canadiens, playing 13 games, and was claimed by Chicago in 1969. He won the starting job in Chicago and was superb until his retirement after the 1983-84 season.

He played a total of 886 games in the NHL, winning 423. He recorded 76 shutouts and posted a very fine 2.92 goals-against average. In 99 playoff games, Tony won 45, lost 53 and had a 3.07 average.

The younger of the Esposito brothers collected a fair share of silverware along the way. He won the Calder Trophy as the NHL's outstanding rookie in 1969-70, recording an incredible 15 shutouts that season, and twice shared the Vezina Trophy. He was also named to the NHL's First All-Star Team in 1970, 1972 and 1980.

One of Esposito's most prized memories remains the sharing of goaltending duties with Ken Dryden in 1972 when Team Canada played the Soviet Nationals.

Inducted 1988.

EMILE FRANCIS

BUILDER

EMILE FRANCIS was known as "The Cat" during his 14 years of playing pro hockey, including parts of six seasons spent with Chicago and the New York Rangers of the NHL, but it is his work as a coach, manager and executive which made him one of the most respected individuals in the game.

Born September 13, 1926, in North Battleford, Saskatchewan, he played for 12 pro teams before retiring at the end of the 1959-60 season to coach the Rangers-sponsored junior team at Guelph, Ontario. Two seasons later, he became assistant general manager of the Rangers, and was soon appointed general manager. Throughout the next 10 seasons he served three terms as coach while retaining the general manager's post.

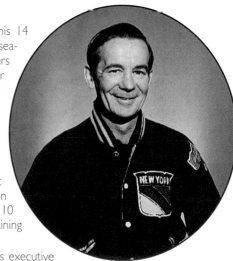

He joined the St. Louis Blues in April, 1976, as executive vice-president, general manager and coach, and it seemed "The Cat" needed his nine lives to handle it all. He did well in St. Louis, earning Hockey News Executive of the Year honours and, in 1982, the Lester Patrick Award for contribution to hockey in the United States. He was named president and general manager of the Hartford Whalers in May of 1983.

Francis is a strong supporter of youth hockey programs. He was a founder of the New York Junior League, supporter of the St. Louis Metro Jr. B League, and developed support for the Amateur Hockey Association of the U.S.

Inducted 1982.

BOB GAINEY

LEFT WING • MONTREAL

BOB GAINEY was one of the best two-way players to ever perform in the NHL. He retired in 1989 after 16 years with the Montreal Canadiens. He was a member of five Stanley Cup championship teams, and served as the Habs' captain from 1981 to 1989.

Born on Dec. 13, 1953, in Peterborough, Ontario, Gainey was chosen by Montreal eighth overall in the 1973 amateur draft. During the mid-1970's he developed into an outstanding checking left winger. In 1978 the Frank J. Selke Trophy was introduced to honour the league's top defensive forward, and Gainey was the recipient of this award the first four years it was presented.

In May, 1979, Gainey was awarded the Conn Smythe Trophy as the most valuable performer in post-season play after he led the Montreal Canadiens to their fourth consecutive Stanley Cup.

He was a key performer for Team Canada during the 1976 and 1981 Canada Cup tournaments. He also impressed during exhibition games between Montreal and touring Soviet clubs. Red Army and Soviet National Team coach Viktor Tikhonov described him as technically the world's best player.

On retiring from the NHL in 1989, Gainey served as a playing coach in France. He returned in 1990-91 as the coach of the Minnesota North Stars, leading the team to the Stanley Cup finals in his first year.

Although he was known more for his defensive prowess, Gainey registered career totals of 239 goals and 501 points in 1160 games. He was the Montreal captain for eight seasons and conducted himself with a great deal of class both on and off the ice.

Inducted 1992.

EDDIE GIACOMIN

GOALTENDER • NY RANGERS, DETROIT

EDDIE GIACOMIN'S SUCCESS as an NHL goaltender was a tribute to his dedication to hockey. He was born June 6, 1939, in Sudbury, Ontario, and when he was 15, tried out for a Junior A team and was cut. At 18, he attended a Detroit Red Wings' tryout camp and was again told that he wasn't good enough. He returned home to Sudbury and played in a midnight industrial league for two seasons before he got a chance to play for the Washington (D.C.) Presidents of the Eastern Hockey League.

Giacomin did so well in the EHL that he won a job with the Providence Reds of the profession-

al American Hockey League. He soon established himself as one of the AHL's best, but didn't get a chance to play in the NHL until he had spent seven years in the minors.

He joined the New York Rangers in 1965-66 when that franchise was rebuilding. In his second NHL season, he lead the Rangers into the playoffs, earned a First Team All-Star selection and posted nine shutouts. He went on to become one of the NHL's best and most durable goaltenders, playing in almost every game. He became a fan favourite in Madison Square Garden, making acrobatic saves and leaving the crease to retrieve the puck and pass it up to his forwards. The Rangers of this era were surprisingly strong in the playoffs, upsetting Boston in 1973 and Montreal in 1972 and 1974.

From 1965 to 1978, Giacomin won 289 games, had 54 shutouts and was a five-time All-Star. He was traded to Detroit in 1975-76 and played for the Red Wings until he retired in 1978. In 13 NHL seasons, Giacomin recorded a 2.82 goals-against per game average.

Inducted 1987.

ROD GILBERT

RIGHT WING • NY RANGERS

ROD GILBERT is an outstanding example of a person who overcame almost insurmountable odds to become successful in his chosen profession — as one of the top right wingers in the NHL.

Born July 1, 1941, in Montreal, he progressed through minor hockey to star as a junior in Guelph, Ontario. It was during a junior game that he skated over a piece of debris on the ice and suffered a broken back. He almost lost his left leg during two operations to correct the damage.

Although he was only five-foot-nine and weighed 175 pounds, Gilbert was an excellent skater and puck-handler who played almost 16 full seasons with the New York Rangers. In that time he set or equalled 20 team scoring records and, when he retired in 1977, Rod trailed only one other right winger (Gordie Howe) in total points. He had 406 goals and 615 assists in 1065 regular-season NHL games, plus 34 goals and 33 assists in 79 playoff encounters. Playing on a line with Jean Ratelle and Vic Hadfield in 1971-72, he scored 43 goals and 97 points, earning him First All-Star Team honours. He was voted to the Second Team in 1967-68 and played in eight All-Star Games during his career. In 1976, he was awarded the Masterton Trophy as the player "who best exemplified the qualities of perseverance, sportsmanship and dedication to hockey." This, too, was a tribute to Gilbert's courage in coming back from his original surgery and two spinal fusion operations to play in the NHL with fairness and dedication. Inducted 1982.

FRANK GRIFFITHS

BUILDER

FRANK GRIFFITHS founded and developed Northwest Sports Enterprises Limited in 1974 and under this company's auspices purchased the Vancouver Canucks Hockey Club on May 2 of that year. The franchise had previously been owned by the Medical Investments Corporation (Medicor) of Minneapolis, Minnesota since its inception on May 22, 1970. Since that time, Griffiths fostered relations with the Vancouver-based club and the province of British Columbia. In 1982, the team made it to the Stanley Cup finals.

A member of the NHL Board of Governors since 1974, Griffiths was appointed Vice-Chairman of the National Hockey League and named as a member of the National Hockey League Audit Committee in 1979. In this latter capacity, he made a significant contribution to the NHL by assisting a number of franchises in solidifying their finances to ensure their ongoing viability and success. He served in all capacities until 1987.

Frank A. Griffiths was born on December 17, 1916 in Burnaby, British Columbia, Canada. Although active during obligations with the NHL, Griffiths never sought the public eye. Committed to success and dedicated to the community, the Vancouver Canucks continue to be a strong member of the NHL. He died April 7, 1994.

Inducted 1993.

CHARLES HAY

BUILDER

CHARLES HAY will be remembered in sports history as the man who finally brought the best teams of Canada and the Soviet Union together in hockey's first international "Super Series." The retired oil company executive was instrumental in the negotiations which culminated in the Canada-Soviet series of September, 1972.

In December, 1968, he attended a meeting with representatives of the NHL, Canadian Amateur Hockey Association, Canadian business and government to organize a body that became known as Hockey Canada. He later became president of this organization which had been set up to operate a national hockey team to represent Canada in international competition. Hay worked diligently to co-ordinate efforts of amateurs and pros, bringing into being a strong national team. He overcame seemingly insurmountable obstacles to bring about the 1972 "Super Series" which many consider the greatest sports event in Canadian history.

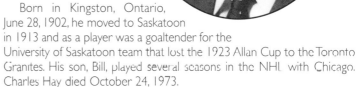

Born in Kingston, Ontario, June 28, 1902, he moved to Saskatoon in 1913 and as a player was a goaltender for the University of Saskatoon team that lost the 1923 Allan Cup to the Toronto Granites. His son, Bill, played several seasons in the NHL with Chicago. Charles Hay died October 24, 1973.

Inducted 1974.

BOB JOHNSON

BUILDER

BOB JOHNSON lived for hockey. Born in Minneapolis, March 4, 1931, Johnson began skating when he was four, and at the age of 13 won a city championship as a first-year coach.

Bob Johnson played amateur hockey in the City Park Board League and was captain of Minneapolis Central High School in his senior year. He played college hockey with North Dakota and Minnesota where he was the team's top scorer.

In 1956 he became the head coach of Warroad High School in Minnesota. After one season, Johnson moved to Roosevelt High School and won four city championships in six seasons. In 1963, he took the post at Colorado College and after three years moved on to the University of Wisconsin. Johnson guided the Badgers for 15 seasons, and captured three national titles. In 1977 he was named the NCAA coach of the year.

Bob Johnson joined the Calgary Flames organization in 1982, and guided the team for five seasons, reaching the Stanley Cup finals in 1986. After three seasons as executive director of USA Hockey, Johnson joined the Pittsburgh Penguins for the 1990-91 NHL season, becoming only the second U.S.-born coach to win a Stanley Cup championship.

Internationally, he coached the U.S. National Team from 1973 to 1975, and was responsible for Team USA at the 1976 Winter Olympics. Johnson also coached the U.S. squad during the 1981 and 1984 Canada Cup tournaments, and was named coach of the 1991 squad as well, but had to relinquish the job due to ill health.

Bob Johnson had a gift for inspiring his players and everyone who associated with him. He died November 26, 1991.

Inducted 1992.

SEYMOUR H. KNOX III

BUILDER

SEYMOUR H. KNOX III was committed to obtaining an NHL franchise for Buffalo and western New York state.

Born in Buffalo on March 9, 1926, Seymour Knox III, along with brother Northrup brought NHL hockey to Buffalo in 1970-71. Their efforts to obtain a franchise began with an application officially presented on October 19, 1965. Though Buffalo was not part of the NHL's six-team expansion of 1967, the Knoxes continued to argue for Buffalo's inclusion.

On December 2, 1969 their efforts were rewarded when it was announced that the NHL was expanding to Buffalo and Vancouver. Knox immediately assembled a first-rate hockey organization under the guidance of coach and general manager George "Punch" Imlach. The team qualified for the post-season in only its third season and reached the 1975 Stanley Cup finals.

A longtime member of the NHL's Board of Governors, Knox also was appointed a director of the United States Hockey Hall of Fame in Eveleth, Minnesota in 1972.

Seymour H. Knox III was a visible contributor to many worthwhile activities and causes throughout the Greater Buffalo area. The founding of the Buffalo Sabres in not all Knox has done to put Buffalo on the sporting map. He was a driving force behind the establishment of the Buffalo Bandits of the Major Indoor Lacrosse League and the Buffalo Blizzard of the National Professional Soccer League.

He died May 22, 1996

Inducted 1993.

GUY LAFLEUR

RIGHT WING • MONTREAL, NY RANGERS, QUEBEC

AFTER AN OUTSTANDING CAREER with the Quebec Remparts of the Quebec Junior League — one season saw him score 130 goals and add 79 assists for a record total of 209 points — Guy Lafleur embarked on a stellar career with the Montreal Canadiens in 1971.

Although his first-year stats were excellent for a rookie, 29 goals and a total of 64 points in 73 games, they were certainly no real indication of the blazing talent that would ultimately burst forth.

Guy Lafleur was Sept. 20, 1951, at Thurso, Quebec, and developed into a great right wing and centre ice player. He stood six feet tall and weighed 185 pounds, and had a flair which brought hockey fans to their feet in appreciation of his talent.

Lafleur was the first player in hockey history to score 50 or more goals in six consecutive seasons. He won the Art Ross Trophy (scoring) three times, the Hart Memorial Trophy (MVP) twice, and once earned the Conn Smythe Trophy (MVP in playoffs).

Lafleur blazed a brilliant path across the NHL during his heyday, being named to the NHL First All-Star Team from 1975 through 1980. He was the youngest to score 400 career NHL goals and the youngest to achieve 1,000 points. In a Canadiens career which lasted only 13 1/4 seasons, Guy Lafleur established himself as one of the premier scorers in the illustrious history of the Montreal franchise — with 518 goals, 728 assists and 1,246 points.

Even though he had been retired for several years, Lafleur returned to professional hockey in 1988 to play for the New York Rangers and then the Quebec Nordiques in his beloved city of Quebec. He remained a favourite of the fans until his second retirement in 1991.

The Guy Lafleur Trophy is awarded annually to the Quebec Major Junior Hockey League's playoff MVP.

Inducted 1988.

THE 1976-77 CANADIENS...

From 1976 to 1979, the Montreal Canadiens won four consecutive Stanley Cups while enjoying some of the greatest regular-season results in NHL history. Their best season during this stretch was 1976-77, when Montreal went 60-8-12 for an NHL record 132 points. Dominant on offense, defence and in goal, Guy Lafleur won both the Art Ross and Hart trophies, Larry Robinson won the Norris, and Ken Dryden and Bunny Larocque shared the Vezina Trophy. Lafleur, Robinson, Dryden and teammate Steve Shutt were selected to the First All-Star Team that year. Guy Lapointe was named to the Second Team.

JACQUES LAPERRIERE

DEFENCE • MONTREAL

JACQUES LAPERRIERE continued the Montreal Canadiens' tradition of recruiting big, mobile and talented defencemen. Born November 22, 1941, in Rouyn, Quebec, Laperriere played with the Junior Canadiens before joining Montreal's farm club in the Eastern Professional Hockey League. After a four-year apprenticeship in the EPHL, he joined the NHL Canadiens to stay in 1963-64 and proved he was ready for the big leagues by winning the Calder Trophy as the NHL's top rookie. He also earned his first of four NHL all-star team selections.

The Canadiens won the Stanley Cup in 1964-65, Laperriere's second full season, and went on to win it three times in the next four seasons. Laperriere was awarded the Norris Trophy as the NHL's top defenceman in 1965-66 and distinguished himself as a cool-headed player adept at controlling the pace of the game.

He played his entire NHL career in Montreal where he was part of six Stanley Cup winners. A serious knee injury forced him into retirement after the 1973-74 campaign.

He remained involved in hockey with the Canadiens and is still an assistant coach with the team.

Inducted 1987.

GUY LAPOINTE

DEFENCE • MONTREAL, ST. LOUIS, BOSTON

GUY LAPOINTE established himself as one of the game's top defencemen during a solid career highlighted with six Stanley Cup championships in the 1970s. Born in Montreal on March 18, 1948, Lapointe joined the Montreal Junior Canadiens in 1967-68. He turned pro at 19 and played his first NHL games in 1968-69. He became an NHL regular in 1970-71 and scored 15 goals as a rookie. By the mid-'70s, he was a member of Montreal's famed "Big Three" defensive corps featuring Serge Savard and Larry Robinson.

Lapointe bodychecked the opposition with authority. He often joined offensive rushes with the forwards and played the point on the powerplay. He was a fixture in the Montreal line-up for 12 seasons, recording personal bests with 28 goals and 1974-75 and 76 points in 1976-77. He was named to the NHL's First All-Star Team in 1973.

He was dealt to the St. Louis Blues late in the 1981-82 season where he spent the following year before finishing his career in Boston in 1983-84. Lapointe was a member of Team Canada in the 1972 Summit Series against the Soviet Nationals, as well as the Canadian squad that won the 1976 Canada Cup.

Following his playing career, Lapointe has coached and scouted in the NHL and the Quebec Major Junior Hockey League.

Inducted 1993.

JACQUES LEMAIRE

CENTRE • MONTREAL

JACQUES LEMAIRE was a remarkable player. Because he was a centre and matched against several all-time greats in the voting, he never achieved all-star recognition; yet his ability to deliver at the highest level of competition was outstanding. Jacques played 12 brilliant seasons with the Montreal Canadiens and was considered by teammates, management and opponents as a very underrated competitor.

The definition of a two-way hockey player, Lemaire was an integral part of eight Stanley Cup championships. In a total of 145 Stanley Cup games, he scored 61 goals and earned 78 assists for 139 points. He is one of only five players to twice score the Cup-winning goal.

Born September 7, 1945, in LaSalle, Quebec, Lemaire joined the Canadiens in 1967-68 and played his entire NHL career with Montreal, retiring after the 1978-79 season. In 853 regular season games, Lemaire scored 366 goals and added 469 assists for 835 points. His penalty total was a meagre 217 minutes.

Only when he went to Switzerland as a playing coach did his contribution to the Canadiens become apparent. Montreal's dominance of the NHL and Stanley Cup play waned after he retired. He returned to the Canadiens in 1983-84 as a member of the coaching staff, taking over as head coach midway through the schedule. He coached the New Jersey Devils to a Stanley Cup championship in 1995.

Said Danny Gallivan, veteran Hockey Night in Canada broadcaster: "Jacques was an exceptionally intelligent player and exemplary not only as a player, but as an individual."

Inducted 1984.

FRANK MATHERS
BUILDER

DURING MORE THAN FOUR DECADES as a player, coach and executive, Frank Mathers helped shape and strengthen the American Hockey League.

Born March 29, 1924 in Winnipeg, Mathers played professional football and hockey. After three years in the Toronto Maple Leafs organization, Mathers moved to the Hershey Bears of the AHL in the early 1950s. There, he became one of the league's all-time great defencemen.

While playing for Hershey, Mathers also took on the role of coach. Within two years, the Bears captured the first of three Calder Cups under his guidance. In 1962, Mathers retired as an active player to coach the Bears full-time. He became president and general manager of the club in 1973. The Bears went on to capture three more Calder Cup AHL championships.

After a 43-year career in Pennsylvania, he retired from the game of hockey following the 1990-91 season, and was honoured by the Hershey Bears with a Frank Mathers night. He was also awarded the Lester Patrick Trophy in 1987 for his outstanding service to hockey in the United States.

Inducted 1992.

JAKE MILFORD
BUILDER

JAKE MILFORD was an itinerant hockey player of superior talent who didn't make it into the NHL until mid-life, and then not as a player but as a manager.

Born July 29, 1914, in Charlottetown, Prince Edward Island, Jake was an excellent player in junior ranks, turning down pro offers with both Detroit and New York to play three years in England and, later, with Cleveland of the American Hockey League. He was a bombardier with the famed RCAF Lion Squadron during World War II, then bounced around minor pro leagues after the war, combining hockey with investments in the construction industry to become financially independent. Jake once made hockey history: Eddie Shore traded him from Springfield to Buffalo of the AHL — for two sets of used Art Ross goal nets.

Milford was in the Rangers' system for 14 years, grooming future stars and winning championships. A tribute to him was the Central Hockey League Coach of the Year Trophy, named in his honour. He became general manager of the Los Angeles Kings in late 1973 and guided that club to three strong second-place finishes behind the Montreal Canadiens. Milford became general manager of the Vancouver Canucks of the NHL in 1977, and made moves which strengthened the club sufficiently to reach the Stanley Cup finals in 1982.

Long noted as a shrewd judge of talent and an astute dealer at the trading table, Jake Milford developed many fine players, coaches and managers and could be totally objective in assessments. He died December 24, 1984, in Vancouver.

Inducted 1984.

LANNY McDONALD,
RIGHT WING • TORONTO, COLORADO, CALGARY

THE TORONTO MAPLE LEAFS selected Lanny McDonald fourth overall at the 1973 Amateur Draft. He was born February 16, 1953, in Hannah, Alberta. After an outstanding junior career in his home province, he jumped directly to the NHL with the Leafs in 1973-74. In Toronto, he is still remembered for his heroic overtime goal to eliminate the New York Islanders in the 1978 quarter-finals. In what attests to his character and grit, McDonald scored the goal nursing a broken bone in his wrist and a broken nose.

After six outstanding years with the Leafs, Lanny was dealt to the Colorado Rockies midway through the 1979-80 season. In 1980 he was named team captain, a post he would maintain until he was acquired by the Calgary Flames during the 1981-82 campaign.

He capped off a great career as he captained the Calgary Flames' first Stanley Cup championship in 1989. He appeared in four All-Star Games and represented his country at the 1981 IIHF World Championships.

McDonald was the recipient of the Bill Masterton Trophy in 1983 and named the NHL's Man of The Year in 1989. He was the first-ever recipient of the King Clancy Memorial Trophy in 1988 for dedication and service to hockey. He recorded a milestone 500 goals and 1006 points in 1111 NHL games.

His number "9" is the first number to be retired by the Calgary organization.

Inducted 1992.

BRIAN O'NEILL,

BUILDER

BRIAN O'NEILL was born January 25, 1929 and played minor, Junior "B" and collegiate hockey in his hometown of Montreal. He was hired as the NHL's Director of Administration in 1966.

He helped oversee the 1967 Expansion Draft and prepared regular-season schedules. He was appointed Executive Director in 1971 and Executive Vice-President in 1977. Upon the retirement of NHL President Clarence Campbell, O'Neill took over responsibility for player discipline. He administered the NHL Montreal office and supervised NHL Security.

O'Neill represented the league in negotiating agreements with European federations and with the Canadian Hockey League. He directed proceedings at the annual Entry Draft and served on many NHL committees.

Brian O'Neill stepped down from the position of NHL Executive Vice-President in 1992. He presently consults to the NHL, administering the Emergency Assistance Fund and acting as a league liaison with the NHL Physicians' Association.

In 1980, he was named to the Hockey Hall of Fame's Board of Governors and, in 1990, he was officially appointed Chairman of the Board. He held this position until he stepped down in 1992. He was appointed as a Trustee of the Stanley Cup in 1988.

Inducted 1994.

BOBBY ORR,

DEFENCE • BOSTON, CHICAGO

BOBBY ORR played only nine full seasons in the NHL but his achievements rank alongside those of the greatest superstars in the game. The outstanding NHL rookie in 1966-67, despite a knee injury that plagued him throughout his career, he was also named to the league's second All-Star Team.

Bobby held a monopoly on the Norris Memorial Trophy as the premier defenceman in the league and rated First All-Star team honours each of the next eight seasons. Orr also won the League's MVP honours three times, and — unheard of for a defenceman — twice won the scoring championship. He was the outstanding player in the playoffs in 1970 and 1972. He also won the Lou Marsh Trophy as Canada's top male athlete, and the Lester Patrick Trophy for contribution to hockey in the United States.

Born March 20, 1948, in Parry Sound, Ontario, he was marked for stardom long before his junior days at Oshawa. At 18, he broke into the NHL with Boston and became the keystone of a rebuilding program that saw Boston win two Stanley Cups with Orr on defence. He was the dominant player in the NHL, controlling the pace of every game in which he played. His knees were badly damaged, however and repeated surgery reduced his playing time and, eventually, his effectiveness.

In 1976 he became a free agent and signed with Chicago. In that year he also played for Canada in the inaugural Canada Cup series and was voted the outstanding player of the event. That was his last great performance on the ice. After a sixth knee operation and sitting out all of the 1977-1978 season, Orr attempted a comeback in 1978-79. His knees were not up to the task and after six games he retired as a player on November 8, 1978.

In 657 scheduled games Orr scored 270 goals and collected 645 assists. He changed the nature of the defenceman's role in modern hockey, making the position a glamorous one and moving the rearguard up into offensive play. Inducted 1979.

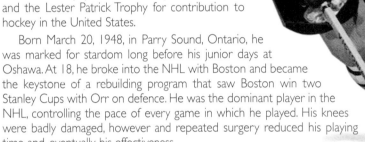

RUSHING DEFENCEMEN...

While Bobby Orr is hockey's greatest rushing defenceman, he was far from the first. Lester Patrick, perhaps inspired by Mike Grant of the old Montreal Victorias (whom he'd watched as a boy), began rushing the puck from his point position with Brandon in 1904. Patrick was criticized, but the move quickly gained favour with his childhood friend Art Ross. Soon, Fred Taylor would be dubbed "Cyclone" in honour of his own furious rushes from the defence. In the 1920s and 1930s, defencemen like Sprague Cleghorn, King Clancy and Eddie Shore would not only join, but lead, the offensive rush. In the 1940s, there was Flash Hollett. Later, Doug Harvey would set the standard for puck-carrying rearguards that Orr would one day surpass.

FRED PAGE

BUILDER

FRED PAGE has spent a lifetime fostering the growth of hockey both in Canada and internationally. Born in Port Arthur, Ontario, September 29, 1915, he was active as a player, referee, coach and administrator in Thunder Bay from the 1930s to the 1960s. He became an executive member with the Canadian Amateur Hockey Association in 1958. He served as Second Vice-President from 1962 to 1964 and First Vice-President from 1964 to 1966. He helped lead European visits by the Port Arthur Bearcats in 1961-62 and the Lacombe Alberta Rockets in 1963-64. From 1964 to 1967 he was a member of the Canadian National Team Committee.

Page was appointed CAHA president from 1966 to 1968. He helped negotiate a five-year agreement between the CAHA, the Amateur Hockey Association of the United States and the NHL.

In 1966, Page represented Canada at the International Ice Hockey Federation. From 1969 to 1972 he was the First Vice-President of the IIHF and Chairman, Hockey Directorate for the 1972 Winter Olympics.

In 1973, Page helped form the Pacific Coast Junior Hockey League assuming the position of Executive Director. He served as PCJHL president from 1975 to 1979 when the league amalgamated with the British Columbia Junior Hockey League. In 1981, Fred Page was appointed Executive Director. The following year he served as President and, since 1983, has been the league's Chairman of the Board.

Inducted 1993.

BERNIE PARENT

GOALTENDER • BOSTON, PHILADELPHIA, TORONTO, PHILADELPHIA (WHA)

BERNIE PARENT allowed 20 goals in his first game in the nets — mind you, he was only 11 — but, as frustrated playing opponents were to find out, he quickly honed his skills and became one of the best in the NHL until an eye injury prematurely ended his playing career in 1979.

Bernie was born April 3, 1945, in Montreal. He honed his craft, partly by watching the great Jacques Plante on televised games, and teamed with Doug Favell to backstop Niagara Falls to the Memorial Cup in 1965. Turning pro in 1965, he played 57 NHL games with Boston before being

claimed by Philadelphia in the 1967 expansion draft. He left the Flyers to play 65 games with Toronto of the NHL and 63 with Philadelphia of the WHA, coming back to the Spectrum to stay in 1972.

The Philadelphia franchise was building a defensive powerhouse and Parent backstopped the Flyers to two Stanley Cup triumphs in 1974 and 1975; the first by an expansion team.

Parent won the Conn Smythe Trophy as the outstanding player in the playoffs each of those two years; he also shared the Vezina Trophy with Tony Esposito in 1974 and won it outright in 1975. First Team All-Star honours the same two seasons came almost automatically. In 608 NHL regular-season games, Parent posted a fine 2.55 goals-against average, recording 55 shutouts. In 71 playoff games, he had six shutouts and an even better 2.43 goals-against mark.

Inducted 1984.

WORLD HOCKEY ASSOCIATION...

When the World Hockey Association began play in the fall of 1972, it marked the first time the NHL's dominance of professional hockey had been challenged since the collapse of the Western Hockey League in 1926.

Bernie Parent was the first NHL player to sign with the rival league, but it was Bobby Hull's defection to the Winnipeg Jets in June of 1972 that proved that the WHA meant business. Gerry Cheevers, Derek Sanderson, Ted Green, and J.C. Tremblay were among other NHL players to make the jump.

During its existence, more NHL stars, like Frank Mahovlich, Dave Keon, Jacques Plante, and Paul Henderson, would all see action in the WHA. Perhaps the league's biggest coup was convincing Gordie Howe to come out of retirement to play with sons Mark and Marty.

In addition to former NHL stars who prolonged their careers in the WHA, several future NHLers debuted in the rival league, including Wayne Gretzky. The WHA was also quicker than the NHL to tap into European talent. Still, after seven seasons and numerous failed franchises, the WHA ceased operation after the 1977-78 campaign. Four former WHA clubs—Edmonton, New England (Hartford), Quebec, and Winnipeg—were admitted to the NHL.

HOCKEY HALL OF FAME • SUPERSTAR GALLERY
PART TWO • MODERN CLASSICS

ANDY BATHGATE

ONE OF THE FIRST FORWARDS TO PERFECT A PINPOINT ACCURATE SLAPSHOT,
ANDY BATHGATE, SEEN HERE WEARING THE COLOURS OF THE PITTSBURGH PENGUINS,
WAS ALSO A GIFTED PLAYMAKER WHO LED THE NHL IN ASSISTS FOUR TIMES.

JACQUES PLANTE

A RESOURCEFUL INNOVATOR WHO FOREVER ALTERED GOALTENDING TECHNIQUE,
JACQUES PLANTE RETURNED TO THE NHL AFTER A BRIEF RETIREMENT AND WON
A RECORD SEVENTH VEZINA TROPHY WITH ST. LOUIS IN 1968-69 AT THE AGE OF 40.

BOBBY ORR

BOBBY ORR'S DAZZLING PUCK HANDLING AND STYLISH SKATING DRAMATICALLY REVAMPED
THE WAY DEFENCE WAS PLAYED AND LIFTED THE BRUINS FROM A SIXTH-PLACE FINISH IN 1967
TO THE STANLEY CUP CHAMPIONSHIP IN 1970 AND 1972.

KEN DRYDEN

KEN DRYDEN, WHO WON THE CONN SMYTHE TROPHY AS PLAYOFF MVP IN 1971
BEFORE WINNING ROOKIE-OF-THE-YEAR HONOURS IN 1972, LED THE NHL IN GOALS-AGAINST AVERAGE ON
FOUR OCCASIONS WHILE PLAYING ON SIX STANLEY CUP-WINNING TEAMS WITH MONTREAL.

BERNIE PARENT

THE ONLY GOALTENDER TO WIN THE CONN SMYTHE TROPHY IN BACK-TO-BACK PLAYOFF YEARS,
BERNIE PARENT RECORDED 55 SHUTOUTS AND 270 VICTORIES IN HIS
13-SEASON NHL CAREER WITH PHILADELPHIA, TORONTO AND BOSTON.

TONY ESPOSITO

KNOWN AS "TONY O" DURING HIS 16-YEAR NHL CAREER IN MONTREAL AND CHICAGO,
TONY ESPOSITO SET A MODERN ERA SHUTOUT RECORD WITH 15 FOR THE BLACK HAWKS IN
1969-70 EN ROUTE TO WINNING THE CALDER TROPHY AS THE NHL'S TOP ROOKIE.

DENIS POTVIN

THE FIRST DEFENCEMAN IN NHL HISTORY TO RECORD 1000 POINTS, DENIS POTVIN ANCHORED
THE NEW YORK ISLANDERS BLUELINE FOR 15 SEASONS AND HELPED LEAD THE CLUB TO
FOUR CONSECUTIVE STANLEY CUP TITLES FROM 1980 TO 1983.

BOBBY CLARKE AND GUY LAPOINTE

GUY LAPOINTE, RIGHT, IS THE ONLY MONTREAL DEFENCEMAN TO RECORD THREE CONSECUTIVE 20-GOAL SEASONS,
WHILE PHILADELPHIA'S BOBBY CLARKE WAS THE FIRST PLAYER FROM A EXPANSION TEAM TO WIN
THE HART TROPHY, CAPTURING THE AWARD IN 1973, 1975 AND 1976.

BRAD PARK

DEFENCE • NY RANGERS, BOSTON, DETROIT

BRILLIANT DEFENCEMAN Brad Park earned seven NHL All-Star Team selections in his 17-year NHL career, despite having undergone five major knee operations and four arthroscopic procedures.

Born July 6, 1948, in Toronto, he developed into a junior standout with the Toronto Marlboros before being drafted second overall by the Rangers in 1966. He played with the Rangers from 1969-70 to 1975-76 before being traded to Boston as part of the trade that brought Phil Esposito to New York. He played for the Boston Bruins through 1982-83 He played his final two years with Detroit.

A six-foot 200-pounder, Brad was always very effective on the powerplay and, despite numerous injuries, was able to play in 60-or-more games in all but four of his 17 NHL seasons. In a total of 1,113 NHL games, Park scored 213 goals, assisted on another 683 for 896 points, and accumulated 1,429 penalty minutes. He also earned 125 points (35 goals, 90 assists) in 161 playoff contests.

His First All-Star team nominations came in 1970, 1972, 1974, 1976 and 1978; Second Team honours came in 1971 and 1973. Park's dedication to the game was recognized in 1984 when he was awarded the Bill Masterton Trophy. Park was also part Team Canada in the 1972's eight-game series vs. the Soviet Nationals.

After retiring, he briefly coached the Red Wings in 1985 and later went on to do colour commentary on televised hockey games.

Inducted 1988.

MATT PAVELICH

LINESMAN

MATT PAVELICH is the first linesman to be inducted into the Hockey Hall of Fame. Born in Park Hill Gold Mines, Ontario, on March 12, 1934, he began officiating bantam and midget games in nearby Sault Ste. Marie at the age of 14. Five years later, after retiring as a player at the age of 19, he became referee-in-chief of the Northern Michigan Intermediate League and also officiated college games at Michigan Tech.

After impressing American Hockey League referee-in-chief Carl Voss with his performance in the AHL in 1955-56, Pavelich was ready for his NHL debut. On October 11, 1956, he worked his first NHL game in Boston Garden. He called his first Stanley Cup playoff game that same season.

He set an NHL record for officials when he worked his 148th Stanley Cup playoff game, surpassing George Hayes' mark of 147. This record was later broken by John D'Amico.

The brother of former Red Wing Marty Pavelich, Matt worked his 1,727th and final regular-season game on April 8, 1979. A member of the Sault Ste. Marie Hall of Fame, Pavelich also officiated in 11 NHL All-Star Games. Inducted 1987.

GILBERT PERREAULT

CENTRE • BUFFALO

FOR 17 SEASONS Gilbert Perreault's name was synonymous with that of the Buffalo Sabres. Known for his strong skating ability and the rare combination of power and finesse with the puck, he ranks high on the NHL's all-time scoring list with 512 goals and 814 assists, for 1326 points in 1,191 games.

Born in Victoriaville, Quebec, November 13, 1950, Perreault led the Montreal Junior Canadiens to two Memorial Cups in 1969 and 1970. He scored 51 goals and added 70 assists in only 54 games in 1969-70, winning the OHA's most valuable player award. Perreault was the first draft choice in Buffalo Sabres history when selected first overall in the 1970 NHL draft. In 1971 he captured the Calder Trophy as the NHL's top rookie.

In 1972 he was to play in the Summit Series between Canada and the Soviet Union. Perreault was used sparingly and left before the series was over to join the Sabres training camp. Although criticized for his departure, he went on to enjoy a superb season as centre of the "French Connection" line with Rick Martin and Rene Robert. That line set team records for goals, assists and points.

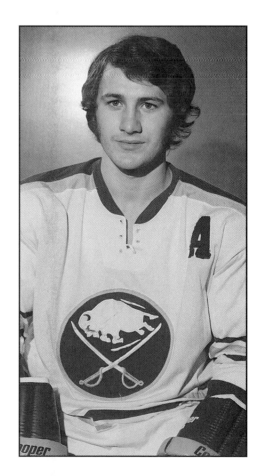

Perreault won the Lady Byng Trophy in 1973 and was named to the NHL Second All-Star Team in 1976 and 1977.

Inducted 1990.

"BUD" POILE

BUILDER

NORMAN (BUD) POILE was born February 10, 1924 in Fort William, Ontario. He signed his first professional contract with the Toronto Maple Leafs in 1942. In 1943, he led the Leafs in playoff scoring. After the war, Poile was member of the Leafs' Cup winning team of 1947. As a member of the Chicago Black Hawks the following year, he was selected to the NHL Second All-Star Team at right wing. His playing career would eventually take him to Toronto, Chicago, Detroit, New York and Boston. The only "original six" team he never played for was Montreal.

Poile has played an integral part in the development of the sport, both on the ice as a player and off the ice as an executive. After coaching champions in the minor leagues with Edmonton and San Francisco, he served as General Manager for Philadelphia and Vancouver in the NHL. He took over the Flyers for their inaugural year in the NHL and played a large part in building the Philadelphia championship teams of 1974 and 1975. He managed another new NHL franchise when he went to the Canucks from 1970 to 1973. From there, Poile moved to the World Hockey Association as executive vice-president.

He served as commissioner of the Central Hockey League from 1976 to 1984. During the 1983-84 season, International Hockey League commissioner Jack Riley stepped down, and Poile took on the top job for both leagues. That same year he was forced to suspend the operations of the CHL. He was commissioner of the IHL until 1989. That year he was awarded the Lester Patrick Trophy, recognizing the fine work he had done in establishing the IHL as a major development league for NHL talent. When he left, seven of the IHL's 10 teams were the top affiliates of NHL clubs. A trophy bearing his name is awarded to the playoff MVP in the IHL each year.

Inducted 1990.

SAM POLLOCK

BUILDER

DILIGENT, DEVOTED, DEDICATED — descriptive words applicable to Sam Pollock, but they tell only part of the reason why he was one of the most successful executives in the history of hockey. Sam's astuteness and single-mindedness of purpose made him unique among his contemporaries.

Born December 15, 1925, in Montreal, he became involved in hockey at an early age. He managed a softball team whose principal performers were Montreal Canadiens' hockey players, and also operated the Canadiens' midget hockey team. After six years in minor hockey, in 1947 he was officially employed by Club de Hockey Canadien, Inc. Three years later he became director of personnel, continuing in that capacity until 1964 when he was named a vice-president and general manager of the NHL club.

During the 30 years prior to his election to the Hockey Hall of Fame he was either coach and/or general manager of many championship teams. These included: Montreal Junior Canadiens, Memorial Cup, 1950; Hull-Ottawa Jr. Canadiens, Memorial Cup, 1958; Hull-Ottawa Canadiens, Eastern Pro League champs, 1961 and 1962; Omaha Knights, Central Pro League champs, 1964; and Club de Hockey Canadien, Stanley Cup champions nine times in 14 years. He also assembled Team Canada '76, winners of the Canada Cup.

Inducted 1978.

DENIS POTVIN

DEFENCE • NY ISLANDERS

THE ISLANDERS DRAFTED Denis Potvin first overall in 1973 to be the foundation for the development of their team. He became one of the all-time leading scorers among NHL defencemen, and the cornerstone of the Islanders dynasty teams. His offensive skills and rugged approach to the game made Potvin one of the game's most complete defencemen.

Born in Ottawa October 29, 1953, Potvin enjoyed an exceptional junior career with the Ontario Hockey Association's Ottawa 67's. During his last year in junior hockey, he set a single season record for points by a defenceman with 123, a record which stood until 1988-89.

He won the Calder Trophy as the NHL's top rookie with 54 points. in 1974. Following the 1975-76 season Potvin was awarded the James Norris Trophy as the top defencemen in the NHL, an award which he also won in 1978 and 1979. He experienced his most productive year in 1978-79 with 101 points. From 1980 to 1983, Potvin captained the Islanders to four consecutive Stanley Cup titles. He recorded 25 points in 18 playoff games in 1981.

Potvin retired in 1988 as a seven-time All-Star and the NHL's all time leader among defencemen in goals, assists and points.

JEAN RATELLE

CENTRE • NY RANGERS, BOSTON

JEAN RATELLE ended a 21-year NHL career in May, 1981, as the league's sixth-leading scorer with 1267 points on 491 goals and 776 assists.

In 1281 games, this classy centreman collected only 276 penalty minutes. In 123 playoff games, Ratelle has 32 goals and 66 assists for 98 points to go along with 24 minutes of penalties.

Ratelle spent 15 of his 21 seasons with the New York Rangers, many of them centering the very productive "G-A-G" or "Goal-A-Game Line" with Rod Gilbert and Vic Hadfield. Gilbert preceded him into the Hall of Fame in 1982. Ratelle and Gilbert were hockey playmates going back to their youth and over the course of approximately 30 years, Gilbert said he never saw Ratelle fight on or off the ice, and never heard him use profanity.

Jean Ratelle won the Lady Byng Trophy for gentlemanly play in 1972 and 1976, the Lester B. Pearson Award in 1972 as the most outstanding NHL player as selected by the players themselves, and the Bill Masterton Trophy in 1971 for exemplifying the qualities of perseverance, sportsmanship and dedication to hockey.

The words style, grace, dignity, elegance, skill, intelligence, instinct, and ambition have all been used in abundance to describe Ratelle by teammates and opponents alike. Like Montreal's great Jean Beliveau, Ratelle was a special player in the league and typified "class."

Jean Ratelle didn't make his mark in the NHL until he had almost five pro seasons under his belt. His early years saw him travel up and down from New York to Kitchener-Waterloo of the Eastern Pro League and Baltimore of the American Hockey League. He came up to the Rangers to stay in the 1964-65 season. He was born in Lac St. Jean, Quebec, October 3, 1940.

Inducted 1985.

LARRY ROBINSON

DEFENCE • MONTREAL, LOS ANGELES

LARRY ROBINSON combined with fellow Hall of Fame members Serge Savard and Guy Lapointe to form the Montreal Canadiens "Big Three" on defence in the 1970s.

Born in Winchester, Ontario on June 2, 1951, Robinson was drafted 20th overall by the Canadiens in 1971. He won a Stanley Cup in 1972-73, his rookie NHL campaign. He was a major contributors to Montreal's four consecutive Cup championships from 1976 to 1979 and won again in 1986.

His defensive prowess was complemented by his ability to move the puck. He won the Norris Trophy in 1977 and 1980 and earned six All-Star Team selections.

He established records for most playoff games (227) and most consecutive years in the playoffs (20.) He played in the NHL's annual All-Star Game on ten occasions and was part of the NHL squad that played the Soviet National Team in the three-game Challenge Cup of 1979. He was also a member of Team Canada in the 1976, 1981, and 1984 Canada Cup tournaments.

"The Big Bird" played three seasons in Los Angeles before retiring at the end of the 1991-92 season. He finished with 958 points in the regular season and 144 in the playoffs.

He was appointed an assistant coach with the New Jersey Devils in 1993 and was part of a Cup winner in 1995. He became the head coach of the Los Angeles Kings in 1995.

Inducted 1995.

GUNTHER SABETZKI

BUILDER

DR. GUNTHER SABETZKI did much to popularize hockey around the globe.

He was born in Dusseldorf, Germany on June 4, 1915 and played hockey until the age of 20. He turned to the administrative side of the game in 1952 when he was named manager of the hockey association of the German province of Nordheim-Westfalen. Sabetzki was a founding member of the German Hockey Association in 1963. He organized the European Cup in 1965 and was elected to the International Ice Hockey Federation Council in 1969. Six years later, he was named president, succeeding Bunny Ahearne. He stepped down from this position in 1994.

Sabetzki was a major player in the development of international hockey. In addition to the European Cup, he was involved in the planning of the eight-game series between Team Canada and the Soviet National Team in 1972, the Canada Cup tournament and various Olympic hockey competitions.

Inducted 1995.

SERGE SAVARD
DEFENCE • MONTREAL, WINNIPEG

DEDICATION TO THE TEAM concept was a trademark of Serge Savard throughout his hockey career. Born in Montreal, January 22, 1946, he played 15 seasons in the NHL with the Montreal Canadiens and two more with the Winnipeg Jets, totalling 1,040 regular-season games and 130 in the playoffs.

Serge was an integral part of a team with a mystique for winning. In 15 seasons with Montreal, including two as team captain, the Canadiens won the Stanley Cup eight times including four in succession from 1976 to 1979. He was a member of the 1972 Team Canada club which defeated the Soviet Nationals in the first series between the Soviets and the NHL's best. He was the only team member not to play in a losing game in the series.

Savard retired from the Canadiens in 1981 but was persuaded to join Winnipeg, a team which had failed to make the playoffs in its first two seasons in the NHL. With Savard in the lineup, the Jets earned 80 points in 1981-82, posting the largest single-season improvement in the league and qualifying for post-season play. These were remarkable achievements for a player whose career almost ended during his fourth and fifth seasons, when he twice suffered a badly broken leg.

After being voted top rookie with Houston of the Central Pro League in 1967, Savard joined the Canadiens, earning the Conn Smythe Trophy as MVP in the 1969 Stanley Cup playoffs. He is also a past winner of the Bill Masterton Trophy awarded to the player best exemplifying the qualities of perseverance, sportsmanship and dedication to hockey. He was a Second Team All-Star selection in 1979.

Savard served as managing director of the Canadiens from 1983 to 1995. Inducted 1986.

STEVE SHUTT
LEFT WING • MONTREAL, LOS ANGELES

STEVE SHUTT'S ABILITY to put the puck past opposing goaltenders enabled him to enjoy a solid 13-year career in the NHL including five Stanley Cup championships with the Montreal Canadiens.

Born in Toronto, July 1, 1952. Shutt starred for the Junior "A" Toronto Marlboros for three seasons, playing on a potent line with centre Dave Gardner and right winger Billy Harris. Shutt scored 70 goals in 1971 and led the league with 63 goals in 1972. The Montreal Canadiens selected him fourth overall at the 1972 Amateur Draft.

He played just six games in the AHL before being called up. He was used sparingly until 1974-75 when head coach Scotty Bowman teamed Shutt with Peter Mahovlich and Guy Lafleur. Shutt responded with 30 goals that year and 45 the next,

The following season, Shutt banged home 60 goals, setting an NHL record for left wingers that would stand until 1993. He scored his milestone 400th regular season NHL goal on December 20, 1983.

The L.A. Kings acquired Steve Shutt in 1984. He announced his retirement after the 1984-85 season. At that time he was ranked 20th on the all-time NHL scoring list. In playoff action, Shutt scored 50 goals points in 99 post-season games.

Following his playing days, Shutt worked as an assistant coach and broadcaster.

Inducted 1993.

HARRY SINDEN
BUILDER

HARRY SINDEN never played in the National Hockey League, but he stepped into the Boston Bruins organization with an impressive coaching record in minor pro hockey. Born September 14, 1932, in Collins Bay, Ontario, Harry was a fine senior amateur player. He captained the Whitby Dunlops to the Allan Cup senior amateur championship in 1957, winning the World Amateur title in 1958.

In 1965-66, as playing-coach of the Oklahoma City Blazers of the Central Pro Hockey League, he took the team to eight straight playoff wins and a championship. Under Sinden's guidance, the Boston Bruins in 1967-68 made the NHL playoffs for the first time in nine seasons. Two years later, the Bruins won their first Stanley Cup since 1940-41.

He went into private business the next season, but returned to the game in 1972 as coach of Team Canada for its memorable series against the Soviet Union. Harry molded a powerful unit of NHL stars that faltered, then came back to win the "Summit Series" four games to three, with one tie. He returned to the Boston organization early in the 1972-73 season and continues to serve as general manager of the Bruins. He is first NHL general manager to win 1000 games.

Inducted 1983.

POST EXPANSION DYNASTIES...

Since NHL expansion in 1967, the league has gone from six teams to 26. Yet for a long time, the Stanley Cup virtually remained the exclusive property of just three teams.

The Montreal Canadiens won eight Stanley Cups in the first 12 years after expansion, including a streak of four in a row from 1976 to 1979. When the Canadiens finally lost their grip on the Cup, the New York Islanders hoisted the trophy. They duplicated Montreal's feat of four in a row from 1980 to 1983 and almost made it five before losing to the Edmonton Oilers in the 1984 Stanley Cup finals. The Islanders won 19 consecutive playoff series during their streak.

The Oilers never managed to win more than two Cup titles in a row during their heyday, but their five titles between 1984 and 1990 certainly rank them with the Canadiens and Islanders as hockey's greatest post-expansion dynasties.

DARRYL SITTLER
CENTRE • TORONTO, PHILADELPHIA, DETROIT

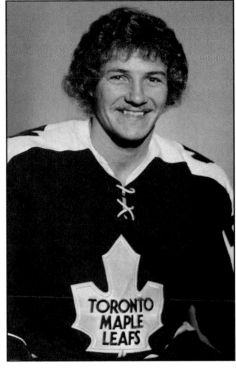

DARRYL SITTLER was born September 18, 1950 in Kitchener, Ontario. He rose to prominence in the National Hockey League early in his career with the Toronto Maple Leafs, and set a standard for excellence, hard work and fair play.

In 15 National Hockey League seasons, he scored 484 goals, and assisted on 637 more for a career point total of 1,121. At the time of his retirement in 1985, he stood 15th on the list of all-time scoring leaders.

Sittler is best remembered for his role as captain and leader with the Toronto Maple Leafs. He came to the Leafs from the London Knights for the 1970-71 season, and stayed with the club for 11 seasons. The legacy he left includes top spot on the Leafs all time career goals listing (389) and second place in the career assists column (527). He was the first Maple Leaf to score 100 points or more in a season, which he did in two different seasons — 1975-76 and 1977-78.

In many peoples minds, Sittler's greatest achievement came on the night of February 7, 1976, when in a game against Boston he scored six goals and assisted on four others, capturing a spot in the NHL record book. On the international front, Sittler became something of a Canadian national hero when he scored the overtime winner against Czechoslovakia in the 1976 Canada Cup series.

Sittler went on to play 2½ productive seasons with the Philadelphia Flyers, and finished his playing days with the Detroit Red Wings in 1985.

Throughout his career, Darryl Sittler displayed determination, strength of character, and leadership, both on and off the ice.

Inducted 1989.

BILL SMITH
GOALTENDER • LOS ANGELES, NY ISLANDERS

"BATTLIN' BILLY" SMITH was one of the top clutch goaltenders to play in the NHL, backstopping the New York Islanders to four consecutive Stanley Cup championships in the 1980s. He was equally well known for using his goal stick to punish opponents who tried to crowd the area directly in front of his net.

Born in Perth, Ontario, December 12, 1950, Smith was drafted by Los Angeles in 1970. He led the Kings' AHL farm club to the 1971 Calder Cup championship and played his first NHL games the following season before being claimed by the Islanders in the 1972 Expansion Draft.

By the mid-'70s, he was a part of one of the league's top netminding duos along with Glenn "Chico" Resch. In 1978, he earned MVP honours at the NHL All-Star Game. By 1979-80, he was the undisputed first-string goalie for the Islanders. He was a member of Team Canada at the 1981 Canada Cup. In 1981-82, he registered 32 wins, won the Vezina Trophy and was selected to the NHL's First All-Star Team. In 1982-83, he recorded the lowest goals-against average in the NHL. He later won the Conn Smythe Trophy as playoff MVP as the Islanders defeated Edmonton to win their fourth consecutive Stanley Cup.

He retired in 1989 with a career goals-against average of 3.17 and 305 wins. He twice posted 15 wins in one playoff year.

Following his retirement in 1989, he has worked as a goaltending coach with the Islanders and the Florida Panthers. He represented the NHL as an ambassador for hockey during the league's 75th anniversary season in 1991-92. The Islanders recognized his career by retiring his number "31" on February 20, 1993.

Inducted 1993.

ED SNIDER

BUILDER

BORN JAN. 6, 1933, IN WASHINGTON, D.C., Ed Snider's sports career actually began in football, and he first came to Philadelphia in 1964 as vice-president of the NFL Eagles. It was not long, however, before he conceived the idea of bringing major league hockey to town, and it was through his efforts that Philadelphia was awarded an NHL franchise in the league's 1967 expansion.

Since the club's inception, Snider has carefully guided its rise to prominence. In 1974, only seven seasons into the NHL, Snider's Flyers became the first expansion team to capture the Stanley Cup, repeating again the following season, and making four more appearances in the Cup finals, in 1976, 1980, 1985 and 1987.

In the club's first 20 seasons, it compiled a record of 816 wins, 496 losses and 266 ties for a .601 winning percentage, second only to the Montreal Canadiens in that time frame.

Snider's efforts were not confined to professional hockey. In 1976, he created Hockey Central, an organization whose sole purpose was to promote and develop youth hockey in the Delaware Valley. In 12 years, Hockey Central increased its membership from 300 to 900 amateur teams, and community investment from $20,000 to $250,000.

Snider's entrepreneurial talents helped pioneer the PRISM cable television network, one of the largest regional pay-TV operation in the USA, and he has launched numerous other business ventures related to sports and broadcasting.

In 1980, Ed Snider was awarded the Lester Patrick Trophy for his outstanding contribution to hockey in the U.S., and in the 1985 he was elected to the Pennsylvania Sports Hall of Fame.

Inducted 1988.

BILL TORREY

BUILDER

FEW HOCKEY EXECUTIVES have been able to formulate and implement a team's blueprint for success as well as Bill Torrey. As general manager of the New York Islanders he developed an expansion franchise into one of hockey's greatest Stanley Cup dynasties.

Born in Montreal June 23, 1934, Torrey's NHL tenure began by serving as executive vice-president of the expansion Oakland Seals in 1967. The team finished second in the NHL's West Division during 1968-69, its sophomore year. He accepted the general manager's job with the New York Islanders in 1972, becoming the new club's first employee.

Torrey drafted and traded wisely for the Islanders, enabling the club to quickly become competitive. He established the team's goaltending foundation by selecting Billy Smith and Glen Resch in the 1972 Expansion Draft. His first Amateur Draft with the Islanders brought Billy Harris, Lorne Henning, Bob Nystrom and Garry Howatt, all of whom went on to play important roles in the club's future success. The Isles reached the Stanley Cup semi-finals in their third year in the league and finished with 101 points in their fourth.

Torrey also drafted Denis Potvin in 1973, Clark Gillies and Bryan Trottier in 1974 and Mike Bossy and John Tonelli in 1977. By 1979-80, a dynasty was launched when the team won its first of four consecutive Stanley Cups.

The Florida Panthers hired Torrey in April, 1993, providing him with another opportunity to build another team from scratch. Working closely with Hall of Famer Bob Clarke, Torrey assembled a squad that enjoyed great success in its first year. The Panthers broke the expansion team record for wins (33), points (83) and winning percentage (.494). Torrey's stature as one of hockey's greatest team builders was assured when the Panthers reached the Stanley Cup finals in 1996, their third season in the league.

Inducted 1995.

VLADISLAV TRETIAK

GOALTENDER • CENTRAL RED ARMY (USSR), USSR NATIONAL (IIHF)

THE PLAY OF GOALTENDER Vladislav Tretiak was perhaps the greatest surprise of the the 1972 Super Series between the NHL's best and the Soviet National team

Born in Dmitrovo, USSR, April 25, 1952, Tretiak practiced with Moscow's Central Red Army senior club for the two years prior to his appointment to the roster at age 17. He was the Soviet League's first team all-star team goalie 14 consecutive times the from 1971-1984 and was a member of 13 league championship teams.

In North America, his performances were equally remarkable. Tretiak's play in 1972, was instrumental in changing North American perceptions of the strength of the Soviet game. In 1975, in what many regard as one of the finest hockey matches every played, Tretiak held the Montreal Canadiens to a 3-3 tie, in spite of being outshot 38-13. He was named MVP of the 1981 Canada Cup tournament and, in 1982, shutout the Canadiens 5-0, stopping 20 shots for the Soviet All-Stars.

On the International scene, Tretiak backstopped his national team to numerous world championships, Olympic gold medals and European titles. In 98 world championship games he registered a stunning 1.78 goals-against average. Throughout his 15-year career Tretiak dominated his part of the hockey world, winning the Gold Stick award as the outstanding play in Europe three consecutive times, from 1981 to 1983, before retiring in 1985.

One of the greatest ambassadors of Soviet hockey, Vladislav Tretiak remains a respected spokesman for the game around the world. He was the first Soviet-trained player to be elected to the Hockey Hall of Fame.

Inducted 1989.

JOHN ZIEGLER

BUILDER

JOHN A. ZIEGLER, JR. was born in Grosse Pointe, Michigan, on February 9, 1934. He grew up in St. Clair Shores, one of the hockey hotbeds in the state of Michigan. He was elected NHL President and Chief Executive Officer in September, 1977, the fourth person to hold this office since 1917. One of his first major accomplishments was to lead the league to an accommodation with the World Hockey Association. This resulted in the expansion of the NHL in 1979 with the addition of four former-WHA cities — Edmonton, Hartford, Quebec and Winnipeg.

During his tenure with the NHL, Ziegler forged a unique working relationship with the NHL Players' Association which is unparalleled in professional sport. Ziegler participated in owner-player negotiations since 1966 and served as co-chairman of the NHL owners' negotiating committee since 1977. During this period, the Collective Bargaining Agreement between the league and the players' association was renegotiated and significantly amended.

A graduate of the University of Michigan in 1957, Ziegler began to do legal work for Olympia Stadium, the Detroit Red Wings and Bruce Norris in 1959. In 1966, he joined the NHL Board of Governors as an Alternate Governor for the Red Wings.

An ardent sports fan, Ziegler played amateur hockey in the Detroit area from 1949 to 1969.

Inducted 1987.

BILL WIRTZ

BUILDER

BILL WIRTZ, born in Detroit on October 5, 1929, grew up in a hockey environment. His father, Arthur M. Wirtz, was a partner in the group that acquired the Detroit franchise in 1933 and converted it into a hockey dynasty. In this atmosphere Bill quickly identified with hockey and when his father and James D. Norris acquired the Chicago Black Hawks in 1952, he joined the organization.

A year later he became a vice-president and in 1966 joined the NHL Board of Governors. The Black Hawks enjoyed a resurgence and won the Stanley Cup in 1961. Bill became club president in 1966, the same season Chicago won its first league title. With league expansion in 1967, Chicago faltered but after finishing last in 1968-69, staged a remarkable reversal to win the East Division in 1969-70. Divisional realignment saw the Black Hawks play in the NHL's West Division beginning in 1970-71. Here the Hawks finished first on three consecutive occasions.

Beginning in the early 1970s, Bill's efforts to make expansion a success were recognized by his peers who on several occasions elected him to two-year terms as Chairman of the NHL Board of Governors. He contributed greatly to successfully negotiating collective bargaining agreements with the NHL Players' Association.

Inducted 1976.

HOCKEY HALL OF FAME HONOUR ROLL

YEAR OF INDUCTION IS LISTED AFTER EACH HONOURED MEMBER'S NAME.

PLAYERS

Abel, Sidney Gerald "Sid" 1969
* Adams, John James "Jack" 1959
Apps, Charles Joseph Sylvanus "Syl" 1961
Armstrong, George Edward 1975
* Bailey, Irvine Wallace "Ace" 1975
* Bain, Donald H. "Dan" 1945
* Baker, Hobart "Hobey" 1945
Barber, William Charles "Bill" 1990
* Barry, Martin J. "Marty" 1965
Bathgate, Andrew James "Andy" 1978
Béliveau, Jean Arthur 1972
* Benedict, Clinton S. 1965
* Bentley, Douglas Wagner 1964
* Bentley, Maxwell H. L. 1966
* Blake, Hector "Toe" 1966
Boivin, Leo Joseph 1986
* Boon, Richard R. "Dickie" 1952
Bossy, Michael 1991
Bouchard, Emile Joseph "Butch" 1966
* Boucher, Frank 1958
* Boucher, George "Buck" 1960
Bower, John William 1976
* Bowie, Russell 1945
Brimsek, Francis Charles 1966
* Broadbent, Harry L. "Punch" 1962
* Broda, Walter Edward "Turk" 1967
Bucyk, John Paul 1981
* Burch, Billy 1974
* Cameron, Harold Hugh "Harry" 1962
Cheevers, Gerald Michael "Gerry" 1985
* Clancy, Francis Michael "King" 1958
* Clapper, Aubrey "Dit" 1947
Clarke, Robert "Bobby" 1987
* Cleghorn, Sprague 1958
Colville, Neil MacNeil 1967
* Conacher, Charles W. "Charlie" 1961
* Conacher, Lionel Pretoria 1994
* Connell, Alex 1958
* Cook, Fred "Bun" 1995
* Cook, William Osser "Bill" 1952
Coulter, Arthur Edmund 1974
Cournoyer, Yvan Serge 1982
* Cowley, William Mailes "Bill" 1968
* Crawford, Samuel Russell "Rusty" 1962
* Darragh, John Proctor "Jack" 1962
* Davidson, Allan M. "Scotty" 1950
* Day, Clarence Henry "Hap" 1961
Delvecchio, Alex 1977
* Denneny, Cyril "Cy" 1959
Dionne, Marcel 1992
* Drillon, Gordon Arthur 1975
* Drinkwater, Charles Graham 1950
Dryden, Kenneth Wayne "Ken" 1983
Dumart, Woodrow "Woody" 1992
* Dunderdale, Thomas 1974
* Durnan, William Ronald "Bill" 1964
* Dutton, Mervyn A. "Red" 1958
* Dye, Cecil Henry "Babe" 1970

Esposito, Anthony James "Tony" 1988
Esposito, Philip Anthony "Phil" 1984
* Farrell, Arthur F. 1965
Flaman, Ferdinand Charles "Fern" 1990
* Foyston, Frank 1958
* Fredrickson, Frank 1958
Gadsby, William Alexander "Bill" 1970
Gainey, Bob 1992
* Gardiner, Charles Robert "Chuck" 1945
* Gardiner, Herbert Martin "Herb" 1958
* Gardner, James Henry "Jimmy" 1962
Geoffrion, Bernard "Boom Boom" 1972
* Gerard, Eddie 1945
Giacomin, Edward "Eddie" 1987
Gilbert, Rodrigue Gabriel "Rod" 1982
* Gilmour, Hamilton L. "Billy" 1962
* Goheen, Frank Xavier "Moose" 1952
* Goodfellow, Ebenezer R. "Ebbie" 1963
* Grant, Michael "Mike" 1950
* Green, Wilfred "Shorty" 1962
* Griffis, Silas Seth "Si" 1950
* Hainsworth, George 1961
Hall, Glenn Henry 1975
* Hall, Joseph Henry "Joe" 1961
* Harvey, Douglas Norman "Doug" 1973
* Hay, George 1958
* Hern, William Milton "Riley" 1962
Hextall, Bryan Aldwyn 1969
* Holmes, Harry "Hap" 1972
* Hooper, Charles Thomas "Tom" 1962
Horner, George Reginald "Red" 1965
* Horton, Miles Gilbert "Tim" 1977
Howe, Gordon "Gordy" 1972
* Howe, Sydney Harris "Syd" 1965
Howell, Henry Vernon "Harry" 1979
Hull, Robert Marvin "Bobby" 1983
* Hutton, John Bower "Bouse" 1962
* Hyland, Harry M. 1962
* Irvin, James Dickenson "Dick" 1958
* Jackson, Harvey "Busher" 1971
* Johnson, Ernest "Moose" 1952
* Johnson, Ivan "Ching" 1958
Johnson, Thomas Christian "Tom" 1970
* Joliat, Aurel 1947
* Keats, Gordon "Duke" 1958
Kelly, Leonard Patrick "Red" 1969
Kennedy, Theodore Samuel "Teeder" 1966
Keon, David Michael "Dave" 1986
Lach, Elmer James 1966
Lafleur, Guy Damien 1988
* Lalonde, Edouard Charles "Newsy" 1950
Laperriere, Jacques 1987
Lapointe, Guy 1993
Laprade, Edgar 1993
* Laviolette, Jean Baptiste "Jack" 1962
* Lehman, Hugh 1958
Lemaire, Jacques Gerard 1984
* LeSueur, Percy 1961
* Lewis, Herbert A. "Herbie" 1989

Lindsay, Robert B. Theodore "Ted" 1966
Lumley, Harry 1980
* MacKay, Duncan "Mickey" 1952
Mahovlich, Frank 1981
* Malone, Joseph "Joe" 1950
* Mantha, Sylvio 1960
* Marshall, John "Jack" 1965
* Maxwell, Fred G. "Steamer" 1962
McDonald, Lanny 1992
* McGee, Frank 1945
* McGimsie, William George "Billy" 1962
* McNamara, George 1958
Mikita, Stan 1983
Moore, Richard Winston "Dickie" 1974
* Moran, Patrick Joseph "Paddy" 1958
* Morenz, Howie 1945
* Mosienko, William "Billy" 1965
* Nighbor, Frank 1947
* Noble, Edward Reginald "Reg" 1962
* O'Connor, Herbert William "Buddy" 1988
* Oliver, Harry 1967
Olmstead, Murray Bert "Bert" 1985
Orr, Robert Gordon "Bobby" 1979
Parent, Bernard Marcel "Bernie" 1984
Park, Douglas Bradford "Brad" 1988
* Patrick, Joseph Lynn 1980
* Patrick, Lester 1947
Perreault, Gilbert 1990
* Phillips, Tommy 1945
Pilote, Joseph Albert Pierre Paul 1975
* Pitre, Didier "Pit" 1962
* Plante, Joseph Jacques Omer 1978
Potvin, Denis 1991
* Pratt, Walter "Babe" 1966
* Primeau, A. Joseph "Joe" 1963
Pronovost, Joseph René Marcel 1978
Pulford, Bob 1991
* Pulford, Harvey 1945
Quackenbush, Hubert George "Bill" 1976
* Rankin, Frank 1961
Ratelle, J.G.Y. Jean 1985
Rayner, Claude Earl "Chuck" 1973
Reardon, Kenneth Joseph "Ken" 1966
Richard, Joseph Henri 1979
Richard, J.H. Maurice "Rocket" 1961
* Richardson, George Taylor 1950
* Roberts, Gordon 1971
Robinson, Larry 1995
* Ross, Arthur Howie 1945
* Russel, Blair 1965
* Russell, Ernest 1965
* Ruttan, J.D. "Jack" 1962
Savard, Serge A. 1986
* Sawchuk, Terrance Gordon "Terry" 1971
Schmidt, Milton Conrad "Milt" 1961
* Schriner, David "Sweeney" 1962
* Seibert, Earl Walter 1963
* Seibert, Oliver Levi 1961

* Shore, Edward W. "Eddie" 1947
Shutt, Stephen "Steve" 1993
* Siebert, Albert C. "Babe" 1964
* Simpson, Harold E. "Bullet Joe" 1962
Sittler, Darryl Glen 1989
* Smith, Alfred E. 1962
Smith, Clint 1991
* Smith, Reginald "Hooley" 1972
* Smith, Thomas James "Tommy" 1973
Smith, William John "Billy" 1993
Stanley, Allan Herbert 1981
* Stanley, Russell "Barney" 1962
* Stewart, John Sherratt "Black Jack" 1964
* Stewart, Nelson "Nels" 1962
* Stuart, Bruce 1961
* Stuart, Hod 1945
* Taylor, Fred "Cyclone" (O.B.E.) 1947
* Thompson, Cecil R. "Tiny" 1959
Tretiak, Vladislav 1989
* Trihey, Col. Harry J. 1950
Ullman, Norman V. A. "Norm" 1982
* Vezina, Georges 1945
* Walker, John Phillip "Jack" 1960
* Walsh, Martin "Marty" 1962
* Watson, Harry E. 1962
Watson, Harry 1994
* Weiland, Ralph "Cooney" 1971
* Westwick, Harry 1962
* Whitcroft, Fred 1962
* Wilson, Gordon Allan "Phat" 1962
Worsley, Lorne John "Gump" 1980
* Worters, Roy 1969

*Deceased

BUILDERS

* Adams, Charles 1960
* Adams, Weston W. 1972
* Ahearn, Thomas Franklin "Frank" 1962
* Ahearne, John Francis "Bunny" 1977
* Allan, Sir Montagu (C.V.O.) 1945
  Allen, Keith 1992
* Ballard, Harold Edwin 1977
* Bauer, Father David 1989
* Bickell, John Paris 1978
  Bowman, Scott 1991
* Brown, George V. 1961
* Brown, Walter A. 1962
* Buckland, Frank 1975
  Butterfield, Jack Arlington 1980
* Calder, Frank 1947
* Campbell, Angus D. 1964
* Campbell, Clarence Sutherland 1966
* Cattarinich, Joseph 1977
* Dandurand, Joseph Viateur "Leo" 1963
  Dilio, Francis Paul 1964
* Dudley, George S. 1958
* Dunn, James A. 1968
  Eagleson, Robert Alan 1989
  Francis, Emile 1982
* Gibson, Dr. John L. "Jack" 1976
* Gorman, Thomas Patrick "Tommy" 1963
* Griffiths, Frank A. 1993
* Hanley, William "Bill" 1986
* Hay, Charles 1974
* Hendy, James C. 1968
* Hewitt, Foster 1965
* Hewitt, William Abraham 1947
* Hume, Fred J. 1962
* Imlach, George "Punch" 1984
  Ivan, Thomas N. 1974
* Jennings, William M. 1975
* Johnson, Bob 1992
* Juckes, Gordon W. 1979
* Kilpatrick, Gen. John Reed 1960
* Knox, Seymour H. III 1993
* Leader, George Alfred 1969
  LeBel, Robert 1970
* Lockhart, Thomas F. 1965
* Loicq, Paul 1961
* Mariucci, John 1985
  Mathers, Frank 1992
* McLaughlin, Major Frederic 1963
* Milford, John "Jake" 1984
  Molson, Hon. Hartland de M. 1973
* Nelson, Francis 1947
* Norris, Bruce A. 1969
* Norris, Sr., James 1958
* Norris, James Dougan 1962
* Northey, William M. 1947
* O'Brien, John Ambrose 1962
  O'Neill, Brian 1994
  Page, Fred 1993
* Patrick, Frank 1958

* Pickard, Allan W. 1958
* Pilous, Rudy 1985
  Poile, Norman "Bud" 1990
  Pollock, Samuel Patterson Smyth 1978
* Raymond, Sen. Donat 1958
* Robertson, John Ross 1947
* Robinson, Claude C. 1947
* Ross, Philip D. 1976
  Sabetzki, Dr. Gunther 1995
* Selke, Frank J. 1960
  Sinden, Harry James 1983
* Smith, Frank D. 1962
* Smythe, Conn 1958
  Snider, Edward M. 1988
* Stanley of Preston, Lord (G.C.B.) 1945
* Sutherland, Cap. James T. 1947
* Tarasov, Anatoli V. 1974
  Torrey, Bill 1995
* Turner, Lloyd 1958
* Tutt, William Thayer 1978
* Voss, Carl Potter 1974
* Waghorn, Fred C. 1961
* Wirtz, Arthur Michael 1971
  Wirtz, William W. "Bill" 1976
  Ziegler, John A. Jr. 1987

REFEREES/LINESMEN

  Armstrong, Neil 1991
  Ashley, John George 1981
  Chadwick, William L. 1964
  D'Amico, John 1993
* Elliott, Chaucer 1961
* Hayes, George William 1988
* Hewitson, Robert W. 1963
* Ion, Fred J. "Mickey" 1961
  Pavelich, Matt 1987
* Rodden, Michael J. "Mike" 1962
* Smeaton, J. Cooper 1961
  Storey, Roy Alvin "Red" 1967
  Udvari, Frank Joseph 1973

*Deceased

ELMER FERGUSON MEMORIAL AWARD WINNERS

In recognition of distinguished members of the newspaper profession
whose words have brought honour to journalism and to hockey.
Selected by the Professional Hockey Writers' Association.

* Barton, Charlie, Buffalo-Courier Express 1985
* Beauchamp, Jacques, Montreal Matin/Journal de Montréal 1984
* Brennan, Bill, Detroit News 1987
* Burchard, Jim, New York World Telegram 1984
* Burnett, Red, Toronto Star 1984
* Carroll, Dink, Montreal Gazette 1984
  Coleman, Jim, Southam Newspapers 1984
* Damata, Ted, Chicago Tribune 1984
  Delano, Hugh, New York Post 1991
  Desjardins, Marcel, Montréal La Presse 1984
  Dulmage, Jack, Windsor Star 1984
  Dunnell, Milt, Toronto Star 1984
* Ferguson, Elmer, Montreal Herald/Star 1984
  Fisher, Red, Montreal Star/Gazette 1985
* Fitzgerald, Tom, Boston Globe 1984
  Frayne, Trent, Toronto Telegram/Globe and Mail/Sun 1984
  Gatecliff, Jack, St. Catharines Standard 1995
  Gross, George, Toronto Telegram/Sun 1985
  Johnston, Dick, Buffalo News 1986
* Laney, Al, New York Herald-Tribune 1984
  Larochelle, Claude, Le Soleil 1989
  L'Esperance, Zotique, Journal de Montréal/le Petit Journal 1985
* Mayer, Charles, le Journal de Montréal/la Patrie 1985
  MacLeod, Rex, Toronto Globe and Mail/Star 1987
  Monahan, Leo, Boston Daily Record/Record-American/Herald American 1986
  Moriarty, Tim, UPI/Newsday 1986
* Nichols, Joe, New York Times 1984
* O'Brien, Andy, Weekend Magazine 1985
  Orr, Frank, Toronto Star 1989
  Olan, Ben, New York Associated Press 1987
* O'Meara, Basil, Montreal Star 1984
  Proudfoot, Jim, Toronto Star 1988
  Raymond, Bertrand, le Journal de Montréal 1990
  Rosa, Fran, Boston Globe 1987
  Strachan, Al, Globe and Mail/Toronto Sun 1993
* Vipond, Jim, Toronto Globe and Mail 1984
  Walter, Lewis, Detroit Times 1984
  Young, Scott, Toronto Globe and Mail/Telegram 1988

FOSTER HEWITT MEMORIAL AWARD WINNERS

In recognition of members of the radio and television industry
who made outstanding contributions to their profession and the game
during their career in hockey broadcasting. Selected by the NHL Broadcasters' Association.

  Cusick, Fred, Boston 1984
  Darling, Ted, Buffalo 1994
* Gallivan, Danny, Montreal 1984
* Hewitt, Foster, Toronto 1984
  Irvin, Dick, Montreal 1988
* Kelly, Dan, St. Louis 1989
  Lecavelier, René, Montreal 1984
  Lynch, Budd, Detroit 1985
  Martyn, Bruce, Detroit 1991
  McDonald, Jiggs, Los Angeles, Atlanta, NY Islanders 1990
  McFarlane, Brian, Hockey Night In Canada 1995
* McKnight, Wes, Toronto 1986
  Pettit, Lloyd, Chicago 1986
  Robson, Jim, Vancouver 1992
  Shaver, Al, Minnesota 1993
* Smith, Doug, Montreal 1985
  Wilson, Bob, Boston 1987

*Deceased

Player and Goaltender Statistics

NOTE: THE NUMBER THAT FOLLOWS "NHL TOTALS" INDICATES A PLAYER'S TOTAL NHL SEASONS.

SID ABEL

Centre. Shoots left. 5'11" 190 lbs., Born, Melville, Sask., February 22, 1918

			Regular Season					Playoffs				
Season	Club	League	GP	G	A	PTS	PIM	GP	G	A	PTS	PIM
1937-38	Flin Flon	SSHL	23	12	16	28	13	8	4	4	8	17
1938-39	Pittsburgh	AHL	41	21	24	45	27	...	...	...	...	...
	Detroit	NHL	15	1	1	2	0	6	1	1	2	2
1939-40	Indianapolis	AHL	21	7	11	18	10	...	...	...	...	...
	Detroit	NHL	24	1	5	6	4	5	0	3	3	21
1940-41	Detroit	NHL	47	11	22	33	29	9	2	2	4	2
1941-42	Detroit	NHL	48	18	31	49	45	12	4	2	6	6
1942-43	Detroit	NHL	49	18	24	42	33	10	5	8	13	4
1943-44			Military Servive									
1944-45			Military Service									
1945-46	Detroit	NHL	7	0	2	2	0	3	0	0	0	0
1946-47	Detroit	NHL	60	19	29	48	29	3	1	1	2	2
1947-48	Detroit	NHL	60	14	30	44	69	10	0	3	3	16
1948-49	Detroit	NHL	60	28	26	54	49	11	3	3	6	6
1949-50	Detroit	NHL	70	34	35	69	4	14	6	2	8	6
1950-51	Detroit	NHL	69	23	38	61	30	6	4	3	7	0
1951-52	Detroit	NHL	62	17	36	53	32	7	2	2	4	12
1952-53	Chicago	NHL	39	5	4	9	6	1	0	0	0	0
	NHL Totals	**14**	**612**		**283**	**472**	**376**	**97**	**28**	**30**	**58**	**79**

JACK ADAMS

Centre. Shoots right. 5'9", 175 lbs., Born, Fort William, Ont., June 14, 1895

			Regular Season					Playoffs				
Season	Club	League	GP	G	A	PTS	PIM	GP	G	A	PTS	PIM
1917-18	Toronto	NHL	8	0	0	0	15	2	2	0	2	3
1918-19	Toronto	NHL	17	3	3	6	17	...	...	...	...	...
1919-20	Vancouver	PCHA	22	9	6	15	18	2	0	0	0	0
1920-21	Vancouver	PCHA	24	17	12	29	60	2	3	0	3	0
1921-22	Vancouver	PCHA	24	26	4	30	24	7	7	1	8	25
1922-23	Toronto	NHL	23	19	9	28	42	...	...	...	...	...
1923-24	Toronto	NHL	22	13	3	16	49	...	...	...	...	...
1924-25	Toronto	NHL	27	21	8	29	66	2	1	0	1	7
1925-26	Toronto	NHL	36	21	5	26	52	...	...	...	...	...
1926-27	Ottawa	NHL	40	5	1	6	66	6	0	0	0	0
	NHL Totals	**7**	**173**	**82**	**29**	**111**	**307**	**10**	**3**	**0**	**3**	**12**

SYL APPS SR.

Centre. Shoots left. 6', 185 lbs., Born, Paris, Ont., January 18, 1915

			Regular Season					Playoffs				
Season	Club	League	GP	G	A	PTS	PIM	GP	G	A	PTS	PIM
1935-36	Hamilton	OHA Jr.	19	22	16	38	10	9	12	7	19	4
	Toronto	OHA Sr.	1	0	1	1	0	...	...	...	...	...
1936-37	Toronto	NHL	48	16	29	45	10	2	0	1	1	0
1937-38	Toronto	NHL	47	21	29	50	9	7	1	4	5	0
1838-39	Toronto	NHL	44	15	25	40	4	10	2	6	8	2
1939-40	Toronto	NHL	27	13	17	30	5	10	5	2	7	2
1940-41	Toronto	NHL	41	20	24	44	6	7	3	2	5	0
1941-42	Toronto	NHL	38	18	23	41	0	13	5	8	13	2
1942-43	Toronto	NHL	29	23	17	40	2	...	...	...	...	...
1943-44			Military Service									
1944-45			Military Service									
1945-46	Toronto	NHL	40	24	16	40	2	...	...	...	...	...
1946-47	Toronto	NHL	54	25	24	49	6	11	5	1	6	0
1947-48	Toronto	NHL	55	26	27	53	12	9	4	4	8	0
	NHL Totals	**10**	**423**	**201**	**231**	**432**	**56**	**69**	**25**	**29**	**54**	**8**

GEORGE ARMSTRONG

Right Wing. Shoots right. 6'1", 194 lbs., Born, Skead, Ont., July 6, 1930

			Regular Season					Playoffs				
Season	Club	League	GP	G	A	PTS	PIM	GP	G	A	PTS	PIM
1946-47	Coppercliff	NOHA	9	6	5	11	4	5	0	1	1	10
1947-48	Stratford	OHA Jr.	36	33	40	73	33	2	1	0	1	6
1948-49	Tor. Marlboros	OHA Sr.	3	0	0	0	2	...	...	...	...	...
	Tor. Marlboros	OHA Jr.	39	29	33	62	89	10	7	10	17	2
1949-50	Tor. Marlboros	OHA Jr.	45	64	51	115	...	...	...	...	...	...
1949-50	Tor. Marlboros	OHA Sr.	19	19	19	38	...	3	0	0	0	0
	Toronto	NHL	2	0	0	0	0	...	...	...	...	...
1950-51	Pittsburgh	AHL	71	15	33	48	49	13	4	9	13	6
1951-52	Pittsburgh	AHL	50	30	29	59	62	...	...	...	...	...
	Toronto	NHL	20	3	3	6	30	4	0	0	0	0
1952-53	Toronto	NHL	52	14	11	25	54	...	...	...	...	...
1953-54	Toronto	NHL	63	17	15	32	60	5	1	0	1	2
1954-55	Toronto	NHL	66	10	18	28	80	4	1	0	1	40
1955-56	Toronto	NHL	67	16	32	48	97	5	4	2	6	0
1956-57	Toronto	NHL	54	18	26	44	37	...	...	...	...	...
1957-58	Toronto	NHL	59	17	25	42	93	...	...	...	...	...
1958-59	Toronto	NHL	59	20	16	36	37	12	0	4	4	10
1959-60	Toronto	NHL	70	23	28	51	60	10	1	4	5	4
1960-61	Toronto	NHL	47	14	19	33	21	5	1	1	2	0
1961-62	Toronto	NHL	70	21	32	53	27	12	7	5	12	2
1962-63	Toronto	NHL	70	19	24	43	27	10	3	6	9	4
1963-64	Toronto	NHL	66	20	17	37	14	14	5	8	13	10
1964-65	Toronto	NHL	59	15	22	37	14	6	1	0	1	4
1965-66	Toronto	NHL	70	16	35	51	12	4	0	1	1	4
1966-67	Toronto	NHL	70	9	24	33	26	9	2	1	3	6
1967-68	Toronto	NHL	62	13	21	34	4	...	...	...	...	...
1968-69	Toronto	NHL	53	11	16	27	10	4	0	0	0	0
1969-70	Toronto	NHL	49	13	15	28	12	...	...	...	...	...
1970-71	Toronto	NHL	59	7	18	25	6	6	0	2	2	0
	NHL Totals	**21**	**1187**	**296**	**417**	**713**	**721**	**110**	**26**	**34**	**60**	**52**

IRVINE "ACE" BAILEY

Right wing. Shoots right. 5'10", 160 lbs., Born, Bracebridge, Ont., July 3, 1903

			Regular Season					Playoffs				
Season	Club	League	GP	G	A	PTS	PIM	GP	G	A	PTS	PIM
1922-23	Tor. St. Mary's	OHA Jr.	4	1	0	1	...	...	...	...	...	...
1923-24	Tor. St. Mary's	OHA Sr.	8	10	0	10	...	...	...	...	...	...
	Tor. Parkdale	OHA Jr.	9	5	0	5	...	...	...	...	...	...
	Tor. Parkdale	OHA Sr.	1	1	0	1	...	...	...	...	...	...
1924-25	Peterborough	OHA Sr.	8	5	0	5	2	...	3	0	3	2
1925-26	Peterborough	OHA Sr.	9	9	2	11	2	...	2	1	3	...
1926-27	Toronto	NHL	42	15	13	28	82	...	...	...	...	...
1927-28	Toronto	NHL	43	9	3	12	72	...	...	...	...	...
1928-29	Toronto	NHL	44	22	10	32	78	4	1	2	3	4
1929-30	Toronto	NHL	43	22	21	43	69	...	...	...	...	...
1930-31	Toronto	NHL	40	23	19	42	46	2	1	1	2	0
1931-32	Toronto	NHL	41	8	5	13	62	7	0	1	1	4
1932-33	Toronto	NHL	47	10	8	18	52	8	0	1	1	4
1933-34	Toronto	NHL	13	2	3	5	11	...	...	...	...	...
	NHL Totals	**8**	**313**	**111**	**82**	**193**	**472**	**21**	**3**	**4**	**7**	**12**

DAN BAIN

Centre. Born, Belleville, Ont., February 14, 1874

			Regular Season					Playoffs				
Season	Club	League	GP	G	A	PTS	PIM	GP	G	A	PTS	PIM
1895-96	Winnipeg Vics	MHL Sr.	...	...	...	...	...	2	3	0	3	...
1896-97	Winnipeg Vics	MHL Sr.		Not Available		...	...	...	...	...	...	...
1897-98	Winnipeg Vics	MHL Sr.		Not Available		...	...	...	...	...	...	...
1898-99	Winnipeg Vics	MHL Sr.	...	...	...	...	...	1	0	0	0	...
1899-1900	Winnipeg Vics	MHL Sr	...	...	...	...	...	3	4	0	4	...
1900-01	Winnipeg Vics	MHL Sr.	...	...	...	...	...	2	3	0	3	...
1901-02	Winnipeg Vics	MHL Sr.	...	...	...	...	...	3	0	0	0	...

HOBEY BAKER

Rover. Shoots right. 5'9", 160 lbs., Born, Wissachikon, PA, January 15, 1892

			Regular Season					Playoffs				
Season	Club	League	GP	G	A	PTS	PIM	GP	G	A	PTS	PIM
1906-07	St. Paul's	......		Not Available		...	...	...	...	...	...	...
1907-08	St. Paul's	......		Not Available		...	...	...	...	...	...	...
1908-09	St. Paul's	......		Not Available		...	...	...	...	...	...	...
1909-10	St. Paul's	......		Not Available		...	...	...	...	...	...	...
1910-11	Princeton	......		Not Available		...	...	...	...	...	...	...
1911-12	Princeton	......		Not Available		...	...	...	...	...	...	...
1912-13	Princeton	......		Not Available		...	...	...	...	...	...	...
1913-14	St. Nicholas	AHA Sr.		Not Available		...	...	...	...	...	...	...
1914-15	St. Nicholas	AHA Sr.	8	18	0	18	...	...	...	...	...	...
1915-16	St. Nicholas	AHA Sr.		Not Available		...	...	...	...	...	...	...

BILL BARBER

Left wing. Shoots left. 6', 195 lbs., Born, Callander, Ont., July 11, 1952

			Regular Season					Playoffs				
Season	Club	League	GP	G	A	PTS	PIM	GP	G	A	PTS	PIM
1969-70	Kitchener	OHA Jr.	54	37	49	86	42	...	...	...	...	...
1970-71	Kitchener	OHA Jr.	61	46	59	105	129	...	...	...	...	...
1971-72	Kitchener	OHA Jr.	62	44	63	107	89	...	...	...	...	...
1972-73	Richmond	AHL	11	9	5	14	4	...	...	...	...	...
	Philadelphia	NHL	69	30	34	64	46	11	3	2	5	22
1973-74	Philadelphia	NHL	75	34	35	69	54	17	3	6	9	18
1974-75	Philadelphia	NHL	79	34	37	71	66	17	6	9	15	8
1975-76	Philadelphia	NHL	80	50	62	112	104	16	6	7	13	18
1976-77	Philadelphia	NHL	73	20	35	55	62	10	1	4	5	2
1977-78	Philadelphia	NHL	80	41	31	72	17	12	6	3	9	2
1978-79	Philadelphia	NHL	79	34	46	80	22	8	3	4	7	10
1979-80	Philadelphia	NHL	79	40	32	72	17	19	12	9	21	23
1980-81	Philadelphia	NHL	80	43	42	85	69	12	11	5	16	0
1981-82	Philadelphia	NHL	80	45	44	89	85	4	1	5	6	4
1982-83	Philadelphia	NHL	66	27	33	60	28	3	1	1	2	2
1983-84	Philadelphia	NHL	63	22	32	54	36	...	...	...	...	...
	NHL Totals	**12**	**903**	**420**	**463**	**883**	**623**	**129**	**53**	**55**	**108**	**109**

MARTY BARRY

Centre. Shoots left. 5'11", 190 lbs., Born, St. Gabriel, Que., December 8, 1905

			Regular Season					Playoffs				
Season	Club	League	GP	G	A	PTS	PIM	GP	G	A	PTS	PIM
1927-28	Philadelphia	CAHL	33	11	3	14	70	...	...	...	...	...
	NY Americans	NHL	9	1	0	1	2	...	...	...	...	...
1928-29	New Haven	CAHL	35	19	10	29	54	2	0	1	1	2
1929-30	Boston	NHL	44	18	15	33	8	6	3	3	6	14
1930-31	Boston	NHL	44	20	11	31	26	5	1	1	2	4
1931-32	Boston	NHL	48	21	17	38	22	...	...	...	...	...
1932-33	Boston	NHL	47	24	13	37	40	5	2	2	4	6
1933-34	Boston	NHL	48	27	12	39	12	...	...	...	...	...
1934-35	Boston	NHL	48	20	20	40	33	4	0	0	0	0
1935-36	Detroit	NHL	48	21	19	40	16	7	2	4	6	6
1936-37	Detroit	NHL	47	17	27	44	6	10	4	7	11	2
1937-38	Detroit	NHL	48	9	20	29	34	...	...	...	...	...
1938-39	Detroit	NHL	48	13	28	41	4	6	3	1	4	0
1939-40	Montreal	NHL	30	4	10	14	2	...	...	...	...	...
	Pittsburgh	AHL	6	2	0	2	0	7	2	1	3	4
1940-41	Minneapolis	AHA	32	10	10	20	8	3	1	0	1	0
	NHL Totals	**12**	**509**	**195**	**192**	**387**	**231**	**43**	**15**	**18**	**33**	**34**

ANDY BATHGATE

Right wing. Shoots right. 6', 180 lbs., Born, Winnipeg, Man., August 28, 1932

			Regular Season					Playoffs				
Season	Club	League	GP	G	A	PTS	PIM	GP	G	A	PTS	PIM
1948-49	Winnipeg	MJHL	1	0	0	0	0	...	...	...	...	...
1949-50	Guelph	OHA Jr.	40	4	21	25	46	...	...	...	...	...
1950-51	Guelph	OHA Jr.	52	33	57	90	66	5	6	1	7	9
1951-52	Guelph	OHA Jr.	34	27	50	77	20	11	6	10	16	18
1952-53	Guelph	OHA Jr.	2	2	1	3	0	...	...	...	...	...
	NY Rangers	NHL	18	0	1	1	6	...	...	...	...	...
	Vancouver	WHL	37	13	13	26	29	9	11	4	15	2
1953-54	Vancouver	WHL	17	12	10	22	6	...	...	...	...	...
	NY Rangers	NHL	20	2	2	4	18	...	...	...	...	...
	Cleveland	AHL	36	13	19	32	44	9	3	5	8	8
1954-55	NY Rangers	NHL	70	20	20	40	37	...	...	...	...	...
1955-56	NY Rangers	NHL	70	19	47	66	59	5	1	2	3	2
1956-57	NY Rangers	NHL	70	27	50	77	60	5	2	0	2	27
1957-58	NY Rangers	NHL	65	30	48	78	42	6	5	3	8	6
1958-59	NY Rangers	NHL	70	40	48	88	48	...	...	...	...	...
1959-60	NY Rangers	NHL	70	26	48	74	28	...	...	...	...	...
1960-61	NY Rangers	NHL	70	29	48	77	22	...	...	...	...	...
1961-62	NY Rangers	NHL	70	28	56	84	44	6	1	2	3	4
1962-63	NY Rangers	NHL	70	35	46	81	54	...	...	...	...	...
1963-64	NY Rangers	NHL	56	16	43	59	26	...	...	...	...	...
	Toronto	NHL	15	3	15	18	8	14	5	4	9	25
1964-65	Toronto	NHL	55	16	29	45	34	6	1	0	1	6
1965-66	Detroit	NHL	70	15	32	47	25	12	6	3	9	6
1966-67	Detroit	NHL	60	8	23	31	24	...	...	...	...	...
	Pittsburgh	AHL	6	4	6	10	7	...	...	...	...	...
1967-68	Pittsburgh	NHL	74	20	39	59	55	...	...	...	...	...
1968-69	Vancouver	WHL	71	37	36	73	44	8	3	5	8	5
1969-70	Vancouver	WHL	72	40	68	108	66	16	7	5	12	8
1970-71	Pittsburgh	NHL	76	15	29	44	34	...	...	...	...	...
1971-1974				Did Not Play								
1974-75	Vancouver	WHA	11	1	6	7	2	...	...	...	...	...
	NHL Totals	**17**	**1069**	**349**	**624**	**973**	**624**	**54**	**21**	**14**	**35**	**76**

JEAN BÉLIVEAU

Centre. Shoots left. 6'3", 205 lbs., Born, Trois Rivieres, Que., August 31, 1931

			Regular Season					Playoffs				
Season	Club	League	GP	G	A	PTS	PIM	GP	G	A	PTS	PIM
1947-48	Victoriaville	Jr.	...	46	21	67	...	...	...	...	...	...
1948-49	Victoriaville	Jr.	...	48	27	75	54	...	...	...	...	...
1949-50	Quebec	QJHL	35	35	45	80	...	...	...	...	...	...
1950-51	Quebec	QJHL	46	61	63	124	...	12	12	13	25	...
	Quebec	QSHL	1	2	1	3	0	...	...	...	...	...
	Montreal	NHL	2	1	1	2	0	...	...	...	...	...
1951-52	Quebec	QSHL	59	45	38	83	88	15	14	10	24	14
1952-53	Quebec	QSHL	57	50	39	89	59	19	14	15	29	25
	Montreal	NHL	3	5	0	5	0	...	...	...	...	...
1953-54	Montreal	NHL	44	13	21	34	22	10	2	8	10	4
1954-55	Montreal	NHL	70	37	36	73	58	12	6	7	13	18
1955-56	Montreal	NHL	70	47	41	88	143	10	12	7	19	22
1956-57	Montreal	NHL	69	33	51	84	105	10	6	6	12	15
1957-58	Montreal	NHL	55	27	32	59	93	10	4	8	12	10
1958-59	Montreal	NHL	64	45	46	91	67	3	1	4	5	4
1959-60	Montreal	NHL	60	34	40	74	57	8	5	2	7	6
1960-61	Montreal	NHL	69	32	58	90	57	6	0	5	5	0
1961-62	Montreal	NHL	43	18	23	41	36	6	2	1	3	4
1962-63	Montreal	NHL	69	18	49	67	68	5	2	1	3	2
1963-64	Montreal	NHL	68	28	50	78	42	5	2	0	2	18
1964-65	Montreal	NHL	58	20	23	43	76	13	8	8	16	34
1965-66	Montreal	NHL	67	29	48	77	50	10	5	5	10	6
1966-67	Montreal	NHL	53	12	26	38	22	10	6	5	11	26
1967-68	Montreal	NHL	59	31	37	68	28	10	7	4	11	6
1968-69	Montreal	NHL	69	33	49	82	55	14	5	10	15	8
1969-70	Montreal	NHL	63	19	30	49	10	...	...	...	...	...
1970-71	Montreal	NHL	70	25	51	76	40	20	6	16	22	28
	NHL Totals	**20**	**1125**	**507**	**712**	**1219**	**1029**	**162**	**79**	**97**	**176**	**211**

CLINT BENEDICT

Goaltender. Catches right. Born, Ottawa, Ont., September 26, 1894.

			Regular Season								Playoffs							
Season	Club	League	GP	MIN	GA	SO	GAA	W	L	T	GP	MIN	GA	SO	GAA	W	L	T
1912-13	Ottawa	NHA	10	275	16	1	3.49	7	2	1	....	....	....	....	....	....	....	....
1913-14	Ottawa	NHA	9	474	29	0	3.67	5	3	0	....	....	....	....	....	....	....	....
1914-15	Ottawa	NHA	20	1243	65	0	3.14	14	6	0	2	120	1	1	0.50	1	1	...
1915-16	Ottawa	NHA	24	1447	72	1	2.99	13	11	0	....	....	....	....	....	....	....	....
1916-17	Ottawa	NHA	18	1103	50	1	2.72	14	4	0	2	120	7	0	3.50	1	1	....
1917-18	Ottawa	NHL	22	1337	114	1	5.12	9	13	0	....	....	....	....	....	....	....	....
1918-19	Ottawa	NHL	18	1113	53	2	2.86	12	6	0	5	300	26	0	5.20	1	4	....
1919-20	Ottawa	NHL	24	1443	64	5	2.66	19	5	0	5	300	11	1	2.20	3	2	....
1920-21	Ottawa	NHL	24	1457	75	2	3.09	14	10	0	7	420	12	2	1.71	5	2	....
1921-22	Ottawa	NHL	24	1508	84	2	3.34	14	8	2	2	120	5	1	2.50	0	1	1
1922-23	Ottawa	NHL	24	1486	54	4	2.18	14	9	1	8	482	10	3	1.24	6	2	....
1923-24	Ottawa	NHL	22	1356	45	3	1.99	16	6	0	2	120	5	0	2.50	0	2	....
1924-25	Mtl. Maroons	NHL	30	1843	65	2	2.12	9	19	2	....	....	....	....	....	....	....	....
1925-26	Mtl. Maroons	NHL	36	2286	73	6	1.91	20	11	5	8	480	8	4	1.25	5	1	2
1926-27	Mtl. Maroons	NHL	43	2748	65	13	1.42	20	19	4	2	132	2	0	0.91	0	1	1
1927-28	Mtl. Maroons	NHL	44	2690	77	7	1.72	24	14	6	9	555	8	4	0.87	5	3	1
1928-29	Mtl. Maroons	NHL	37	2300	57	11	1.49	14	16	7	....	....	....	....	....	....	....	....
1929-30	Mtl. Maroons	NHL	14	752	38	0	3.03	6	6	1	....	....	....	....	....	....	....	....
1930-31	Windsor	IHL	40	2400	94	1	2.35	....	....	....	....	....	....	....	....	....	....	....
	NHL Totals	**13**	**362**	**22319**	**864**	**57**	**2.32**	**191**	**142**	**28**	**48**	**2909**	**87**	**15**	**1.79**	**25**	**18**	**5**

DOUG BENTLEY

Left wing. Shoots left. 5'8", 145 lbs., Born, Delisle, Sask. September 3, 1916

			Regular Season					Playoffs				
Season	Club	League	GP	G	A	PTS	PIM	GP	G	A	PTS	PIM
1934-35	Regina Vics	SSHL	19	10	4	14	21	6	0	0	0	13
1935-36	Moose Jaw	SSHL	20	3	3	6	30	...	...	...	...	...
1936-37	Moose Jaw	SSHL	24	18	19	37	49	3	3	0	3	4
1937-38	Drumheller	SSHL	21	25	18	43	20	6	6	8	14	6
1938-39	Drumheller	SSHL	32	24	29	53	31	6	7	0	7	6
1939-40	Chicago	NHL	39	12	7	19	12	2	0	0	0	0
1940-41	Chicago	NHL	46	8	20	28	12	5	1	1	2	4
1941-42	Chicago	NHL	38	12	14	26	11	3	0	1	1	4
1942-43	Chicago	NHL	50	33	40	73	18	...	...	...	...	...
1943-44	Chicago	NHL	50	38	39	77	22	9	8	4	12	4
1944-45				Did Not Play								
1945-46	Chicago	NHL	36	19	21	40	16	4	0	2	2	0
1946-47	Chicago	NHL	52	21	34	55	18	...	...	...	...	...
1947-48	Chicago	NHL	60	20	37	57	16	...	...	...	...	...
1948-49	Chicago	NHL	58	23	43	66	38	...	...	...	...	...
1949-50	Chicago	NHL	64	20	33	53	28	...	...	...	...	...
1950-51	Chicago	NHL	44	9	23	32	20	...	...	...	...	...
1951-52	Chicago	NHL	8	2	3	5	4	...	...	...	...	...
	Saskatoon	PCHL	35	11	14	25	12	13	6	6	12	4
1952-53	Saskatoon	WHL	70	22	23	45	37	13	6	3	9	14
1953-54	Saskatoon	WHL	42	8	13	21	18	...	...	...	...	...
	NY Rangers	NHL	20	2	10	12	2	...	...	...	...	...
1954-55	Saskatoon	WHL	61	14	23	37	52	...	...	...	...	...
1955-56	Sask / Brandon	WHL	60	7	26	33	21	...	...	...	...	...
1956-57				Did Not Play								
1957-58	Saskatoon	WHL	19	11	16	27	0	...	...	...	...	...
1958-1961				Did Not Play								
1961-62	Los Angeles	WHL	8	0	2	2	2	...	...	...	...	...
	NHL Totals	**13**	**566**	**219**	**324**	**543**	**217**	**23**	**9**	**8**	**17**	**8**

MAX BENTLEY

Centre. Shoots left. 5'8", 158 lbs., Born, Delisle, Sask., March 1, 1920

			Regular Season					Playoffs				
Season	Club	League	GP	G	A	PTS	PIM	GP	G	A	PTS	PIM
1937-38	Drumheller	ASHL	26	28	15	43	10	5	7	1	8	2
1938-39	Drumheller	ASHL	32	29	24	53	16	6	5	3	8	6
1939-40	Saskatoon	ASHL	31	37	14	51	4	4	1	1	2	2
1940-41	Providence	AHL	9	4	2	6	0	...	...	...	...	...
	Kansas City	AHA	5	5	5	10	0	...	...	...	...	...
	Chicago	NHL	36	7	10	17	6	5	1	3	4	2
1941-42	Chicago	NHL	39	13	17	30	2	3	2	0	2	0
1942-43	Chicago	NHL	47	26	44	70	2	...	...	...	...	...
1943-44				Military Servive								
1944-45				Military Service								
1945-46	Chicago	NHL	47	31	30	61	6	4	1	0	1	4
1946-47	Chicago	NHL	60	29	43	72	12	...	...	...	...	...
1947-48	Chicago	NHL	6	3	3	6	0	...	...	...	...	...
	Toronto	NHL	53	23	25	48	14	9	4	7	11	0
1948-49	Toronto	NHL	60	19	22	41	18	9	4	3	7	2
1949-50	Toronto	NHL	69	23	18	41	14	7	3	3	6	0
1950-51	Toronto	NHL	67	21	41	62	34	11	2	11	13	4
1951-52	Toronto	NHL	69	24	17	41	40	4	1	0	1	2
1952-53	Toronto	NHL	36	12	11	23	16	...	...	...	...	...
1953-54	NY Rangers	NHL	57	14	18	32	15	...	...	...	...	...
1954-55	Saskatoon	WHL	40	24	17	41	23	...	...	...	...	...
1955-56	Saskatoon	WHL	10	2	2	4	20	...	...	...	...	...
1958-59	Saskatoon	WHL	26	6	12	18	2	...	...	...	...	...
	NHL Totals	**12**	**646**	**245**	**299**	**544**	**179**	**51**	**18**	**27**	**45**	**14**

HECTOR "TOE" BLAKE

Left wing. Shoots left. 5'10", 180 lbs., Born, Victoria Mines, Ont., August 21, 1912

			Regular Season					Playoffs				
Season	Club	League	GP	G	A	PTS	PIM	GP	G	A	PTS	PIM
1929-30	Cochrane	Int.	7	3	0	3	4	...	...	...	...	...
1930-31	Sudbury	NOHA	6	3	1	4	12	2	0	0	0	6
	Sudbury	NOHA	8	7	1	8	10	3	1	1	2	4
1931-32	Falconbridge	NOHA	10	8	1	9	18	2	1	0	1	2
	Sudbury	NOHA	3	5	0	5	4	...	...	...	...	...
1932-33	Hamilton	OHA Sr.	22	9	4	13	26	2	0	0	0	2
1933-34	Hamilton	OHA Sr.	23	19	14	33	28	4	3	4	7	4
1934-35	Hamilton	OHA Sr.	18	15	11	26	48	...	...	...	...	...
	Mtl. Maroons	NHL	8	0	0	0	0	1	0	0	0	0
1935-36	Providence	CAHL	33	12	11	23	65	7	2	3	5	2
	Montreal	NHL	13	1	2	3	28	...	...	...	...	...
1936-37	Montreal	NHL	43	10	12	22	12	5	1	0	1	0
1937-38	Montreal	NHL	43	17	16	33	33	3	3	1	4	2
1938-39	Montreal	NHL	48	24	23	47	10	3	1	1	2	2
1939-40	Montreal	NHL	48	17	19	36	48	...	...	...	...	...
1940-41	Montreal	NHL	48	12	20	32	49	3	0	3	3	5
1941-42	Montreal	NHL	47	17	28	45	19	3	0	3	3	2
1942-43	Montreal	NHL	48	23	36	59	16	5	4	3	7	0
1943-44	Montreal	NHL	41	26	33	59	10	9	7	11	18	2
1944-45	Montreal	NHL	49	29	38	67	35	6	0	2	2	5
1945-46	Montreal	NHL	50	29	21	50	2	9	7	6	13	5
1946-47	Montreal	NHL	60	21	29	50	6	11	2	7	9	0
1947-48	Montreal	NHL	32	9	15	24	4	...	...	...	...	...
1948-49	Buffalo	AHL	18	1	3	4	0	...	...	...	...	...
1949-50	Valleyfield	QSHL	43	12	15	27	15	3	0	1	1	0
	NHL Totals	**15**	**578**	**235**	**292**	**527**	**272**	**58**	**25**	**37**	**62**	**23**

LEO BOIVIN

Defence. Shoots left. 5'7", 190 lbs., Born, Prescott, Ont., August 2, 1932

			Regular Season					Playoffs				
Season	Club	League	GP	G	A	PTS	PIM	GP	G	A	PTS	PIM
1949-50	Port Arthur	TBJHL	18	4	4	8	32	5	0	3	3	10
1950-51	Port Arthur	TBJHL	20	16	11	27	37	6	2	3	5	10
1951-52	Pittsburgh	AHL	30	2	3	5	32	10	0	1	1	16
	Toronto	NHL	2	0	1	1	0	...	...	...	...	...
1952-53	Toronto	NHL	70	2	13	15	97	...	...	...	...	...
1953-54	Toronto	NHL	58	1	6	7	81	5	0	0	0	2
1954-55	Toronto	NHL	7	0	0	0	8	...	...	...	...	...
	Boston	NHL	59	6	11	17	105	5	0	1	1	4
1955-56	Boston	NHL	68	4	16	20	80	...	...	...	...	...
1956-57	Boston	NHL	55	2	8	10	55	10	2	3	5	12
1957-58	Boston	NHL	33	0	4	4	54	12	0	3	3	21
1958-59	Boston	NHL	70	5	16	21	94	7	1	2	3	4
1959-60	Boston	NHL	70	4	21	25	66	...	...	...	...	...
1960-61	Boston	NHL	57	6	17	23	50	...	...	...	...	...
1961-62	Boston	NHL	65	5	18	23	70	...	...	...	...	...
1962-63	Boston	NHL	62	2	24	26	48	...	...	...	...	...
1963-64	Boston	NHL	65	10	14	24	42	...	...	...	...	...
1964-65	Boston	NHL	67	3	10	13	68	...	...	...	...	...
1965-66	Boston	NHL	46	0	5	5	34	...	...	...	...	...
	Detroit	NHL	16	0	5	5	16	12	0	1	1	16
1966-67	Detroit	NHL	69	4	17	21	78	...	...	...	...	...
1967-68	Pittsburgh	NHL	73	9	13	22	74	...	...	...	...	...
1968-69	Pittsburgh	NHL	41	5	13	18	26	...	...	...	...	...
	Minnesota	NHL	28	1	6	7	16	...	...	...	...	...
1969-70	Minnesota	NHL	69	3	12	15	30	3	0	0	0	0
	NHL Totals	**19**	**1150**	**72**	**250**	**322**	**1192**	**54**	**3**	**10**	**13**	**59**

DICKIE BOON

Defence. 130 lbs., Born, Belleville, Ont., January 10, 1878

			Regular Season					Playoffs				
Season	Club	League	GP	G	A	PTS	PIM	GP	G	A	PTS	PIM
1899-1900	Montreal AAA	CAHL	8	2	0	2	...	...	...	...	...	...
1900-01	Montreal AAA	CAHL	7	3	0	3	...	...	...	...	...	...
1901-02	Montreal AAA	CAHL	8	2	0	2	...	3	0	0	0	3
1902-03	Montreal AAA	CAHL	7	3	0	3	...	4	0	0	0	...
1903-04	Mtl. Wanderers	FAHL	4	0	0	0	...	..	...	...	...	..
1904-05	Mtl. Wanderers	FAHL	8	0	0	0	...	...	...	...	...	...

MIKE BOSSY

Right Wing. Shoots right. 6', 185 lbs., Born, Montreal, Que. January 22, 1957

			Regular Season					Playoffs				
Season	Club	League	GP	G	A	PTS	PIM	GP	G	A	PTS	PIM
1972-73	Laval	QJHL	4	1	2	3	0	...	...	...	...	...
1973-74	Laval	QJHL	68	70	48	118	45	11	6	16	22	2
1974-75	Laval	QJHL	67	84	65	149	42	16	18	20	38	2
1975-76	Laval	QJHL	64	79	57	136	25	...	...	...	...	...
1976-77	Laval	QJHL	61	75	51	126	12	7	5	5	10	12
1977-78	NY Islanders	NHL	73	53	38	91	6	7	2	2	4	2
1978-79	NY Islanders	NHL	80	69	57	126	25	10	6	2	8	2
1979-80	NY Islanders	NHL	75	51	41	92	12	16	10	13	23	8
1980-81	NY Islanders	NHL	79	68	51	119	32	18	17	18	35	4
1981-82	NY Islanders	NHL	80	64	83	147	22	19	17	10	27	0
1982-83	NY Islanders	NHL	79	60	58	118	20	19	17	9	26	10
1983-84	NY Islanders	NHL	67	51	67	118	8	21	8	10	18	4
1984-85	NY Islanders	NHL	76	58	59	117	38	10	5	6	11	4
1985-86	NY Islanders	NHL	80	61	62	123	14	3	1	2	3	4
1986-87	NY Islanders	NHL	63	38	37	75	33	6	2	3	5	0
	NHL Totals	**10**	**752**	**573**	**553**	**1126**	**210**	**129**	**85**	**75**	**160**	**38**

EMILE "BUTCH" BOUCHARD

Defence. Shoots right. 6'2", 205 lbs., Born, Montreal, Que., September 11, 1920

			Regular Season					Playoffs				
Season	Club	League	GP	G	A	PTS	PIM	GP	G	A	PTS	PIM
1940-41	Montreal	QJHL	31	2	8	10	60	...	...	...	...	...
1941-42	Montreal	NHL	43	0	6	6	38	3	1	1	2	0
1942-43	Montreal	NHL	45	2	16	18	47	5	0	1	1	4
1943-44	Montreal	NHL	39	5	14	19	52	9	1	3	4	4
1944-45	Montreal	NHL	50	11	23	34	34	6	3	4	7	4
1945-46	Montreal	NHL	45	7	10	17	52	9	2	1	3	17
1946-47	Montreal	NHL	60	5	7	12	60	11	0	3	3	21
1947-48	Montreal	NHL	60	4	6	10	78	...	...	...	...	...
1948-49	Montreal	NHL	27	3	3	6	42	7	0	0	0	6
1949-50	Montreal	NHL	69	1	7	8	88	5	0	2	2	2
1950-51	Montreal	NHL	52	3	10	13	80	11	1	1	2	2
1951-52	Montreal	NHL	60	3	9	12	45	11	0	2	2	14
1952-53	Montreal	NHL	58	2	8	10	55	12	1	1	2	6
1953-54	Montreal	NHL	70	1	10	11	89	11	2	1	3	4
1954-55	Montreal	NHL	70	2	15	17	81	12	0	1	1	37
1955-56	Montreal	NHL	36	0	0	0	22	1	0	0	0	0
	NHL Totals	**15**	**785**	**49**	**144**	**193**	**863**	**113**	**11**	**21**	**32**	**121**

FRANK "RAFFLES" BOUCHER

Centre. Shoots left. 5'10", 170 lbs., Born, Ottawa, Ont., October 7, 1901

			Regular Season					Playoffs				
Season	Club	League	GP	G	A	PTS	PIM	GP	G	A	PTS	PIM
1921-22	Ottawa	NHL	24	9	1	10	4	2	0	0	0	0
1922-23	Vancouver	PCHA	29	11	9	20	2	6	2	1	3	4
1923-24	Vancouver	PCHA	28	15	5	20	10	7	3	1	4	2
1924-25	Vancouver	WCHL	27	16	12	28	6	...	...	...	...	...
1925-26	Vancouver	WHL	29	15	7	22	14	...	...	...	...	...
1926-27	NY Rangers	NHL	44	13	15	28	17	2	0	0	0	4
1927-28	NY Rangers	NHL	44	23	12	35	15	9	7	1	8	2
1928-29	NY Rangers	NHL	44	10	16	26	8	6	1	0	1	0
1929-30	NY Rangers	NHL	42	26	36	62	16	3	1	1	2	0
1930-31	NY Rangers	NHL	44	12	27	39	20	4	0	2	2	0
1931-32	NY Rangers	NHL	48	12	23	35	18	7	3	6	9	0
1932-33	NY Rangers	NHL	46	7	28	35	4	8	2	2	4	6
1933-34	NY Rangers	NHL	48	14	30	44	4	2	0	0	0	0
1934-35	NY Rangers	NHL	48	13	32	45	2	4	0	3	3	0
1935-36	NY Rangers	NHL	48	11	18	29	2	...	...	...	...	...
1936-37	NY Rangers	NHL	44	7	13	20	5	9	2	3	5	0
1937-38	NY Rangers	NHL	18	0	1	1	2	...	...	...	...	...
1943-44	NY Rangers	NHL	15	4	10	14	2	...	...	...	...	...
	NHL Totals	**14**	**557**	**161**	**262**	**423**	**119**	**56**	**16**	**18**	**34**	**12**

GEORGE BOUCHER

Defence. Shoots left. 5'9", 169 lbs., Born, Ottawa, Ont., August 19, 1896

			Regular Season					Playoffs				
Season	Club	League	GP	G	A	PTS	PIM	GP	G	A	PTS	PIM
1915-16	Ottawa	NHA	19	9	1	10	62	...	...	...	...	...
1916-17	Ottawa	NHA	18	10	3	13	27	...	2	1		3
1917-18	Ottawa	NHL	22	9	0	9	36	...	...	...	...	...
1918-19	Ottawa	NHL	17	5	2	7	21	5	2	1	3	9
1919-20	Ottawa	NHL	22	10	4	14	34	5	2	0	2	0
1920-21	Ottawa	NHL	23	12	5	17	43	7	5	0	5	18
1921-22	Ottawa	NHL	23	12	8	20	10	2	0	0	0	4
1922-23	Ottawa	NHL	23	15	9	24	44	8	2	1	3	8
1923-24	Ottawa	NHL	21	14	5	19	28	2	0	1	1	4
1924-25	Ottawa	NHL	28	15	4	19	80	...	...	...	...	...
1925-26	Ottawa	NHL	36	8	4	12	64	2	0	0	0	10
1926-27	Ottawa	NHL	44	8	3	11	115	6	0	0	0	28
1927-28	Ottawa	NHL	44	7	5	12	78	2	0	0	0	4
1928-29	Ottawa	NHL	29	3	1	4	60	...	...	...	...	...
	Mtl Maroons	NHL	12	1	1	2	10	...	...	...	...	...
1929-30	Mtl Maroons	NHL	39	2	6	8	50	3	0	0	0	2
1930-31	Mtl Maroons	NHL	31	0	0	0	25	...	...	...	...	...
1931-32	Chicago	NHL	43	1	5	6	50	2	0	1	1	0
1932-33	Boston	CAHL	9	0	0	0	8	...	...	...	...	...
	NHL Totals	**15**	**449**	**122**	**62**	**184**	**739**	**44**	**11**	**3**	**14**	**105**

JOHNNY BOWER

Goaltender. Catches left. 5'11", 189 lbs., Born, Prince Albert, Sask., November 8, 1924

			Regular Season								Playoffs							
Season	Club	League	GP	MIN	GA	SO	GAA	W	L	T	GP	MIN	GA	SO	GAA	W	L	T
1944-45	Prince Albert	SJHL	11	660	37	0	3.36	....	....	....	5	300	23	0	4.60	2	3	....
1945-46	Cleveland	AHL	42	2520	164	4	3.91	....	....	....	....	....	....	....	....	....	....	....
	Providence	AHL	1	60	4	0	4.00	....	....	....	....	....	....	....	....	....	....	....
1946-47	Cleveland	AHL	40	2400	124	3	3.10	....	....	....	....	....	....	....	....	....	....	....
1947-48	Cleveland	AHL	31	1860	83	1	2.68.	....	....	....	....	....	....	....	....	....	....	....
1948-49	Cleveland	AHL	37	2200	127	3	3.45	....	....	....	5	320	23	0	4.31	2	3	....
1949-50	Cleveland	AHL	61	3660	201	5	3.30	....	....	....	9	548	27	0	2.96	4	5	....
1950-51	Cleveland	AHL	70	4200	213	5	3.04	44	21	5	11	703	32	0	2.73	8	3	....
1951-52	Cleveland	AHL	68	4080	165	3	2.43	44	19	5	5	300	17	0	3.40	2	3	....
1952-53	Cleveland	AHL	61	3660	155	6	2.54	....	....	....	11	732	21	4	1.72	7	4	....
1953-54	NY Rangers	NHL	70	4200	182	5	2.60	29	31	10	....	....	....	....	....	....	....	....
1954-55	Vancouver	WHL	63	3780	171	7	2.71	....	....	....	5	300	16	0	3.20	1	4	....
	NY Rangers	NHL	5	300	13	0	2.60	2	2	1	....	....	....	....	....	....	....	....
1955-56	Providence	AHL	61	3660	174	3	2.85	....	....	....	9	540	23	0	2.56	7	2	....
1956-57	Providence	AHL	57	3420	138	4	2.42				5	300	15	0	3.00	1	4	....
	NY Rangers	NHL	2	120	7	0	3.50	0	2	0	....	....	....	....	....	....	....	....
1957-58	Cleveland	AHL	64	3840	140	8	2.19	....	....	....	....	....	....	....	....	....	....	....
1958-59	Toronto	NHL	39	2340	107	3	2.74	15	17	7	12	746	39	0	3.25	5	7	....
1959-60	Toronto	NHL	66	3960	180	5	2.73	34	24	8	10	645	31	0	3.10	4	6	....
1960-61	Toronto	NHL	58	3480	145	2	2.50	33	15	10	3	180	9	0	3.00	0	3	....
1961-62	Toronto	NHL	59	3540	152	2	2.58	32	17	10	10	579	22	0	2.20	6	3	....
1962-63	Toronto	NHL	42	2520	110	1	2.62	20	15	7	10	600	16	2	1.60	8	2	....
1963-64	Toronto	NHL	51	3009	106	5	2.11	24	16	11	14	850	30	2	2.14	8	6	....
1964-65	Toronto	NHL	34	2040	81	3	2.38	13	13	8	5	321	13	0	2.60	2	3	....
1965-66	Toronto	NHL	35	1998	75	3	2.25	18	12	5	2	120	8	0	4.00	0	2	....
1966-67	Toronto	NHL	24	1431	63	2	2.64	12	9	3	4	155	5	1	1.94	2	0	....
1967-68	Toronto	NHL	43	2239	84	4	2.25	14	18	7	....	....	....	....	....	....	....	....
1968-69	Toronto	NHL	20	779	37	2	2.85	5	4	3	4	154	11	0	4.28	0	2	....
1969-70	Toronto	NHL	1	60	5	0	5.00	0	1	0	....	....	....	....	....	....	....	....
	NHL Totals	**15**	**549**	**32077**	**1347**	**37**	**2.52**	**251**	**196**	**90**	**74**	**4350**	**184**	**5**	**2.54**	**34**	**35**	**....**

RUSSEL BOWIE

Centre / Rover. Born, Montreal, Que., August 24, 1880

			Regular Season					Playoffs				
Season	Club	League	GP	G	A	PTS	PIM	GP	G	A	PTS	PIM
1898-99	Mtl. Victorias	CAHL	7	11	...	11	...	2	1	0	1	...
1899-1900	Mtl. Victorias	CAHL	7	15	...	15	...	...	...	...	...	...
1900-01	Mtl. Victorias	CAHL	7	24	...	24	...	...	...	...	...	...
1901-02	Mtl. Victorias	CAHL	7	13	...	13	...	...	...	...	...	...
1902-03	Mtl. Victorias	CAHL	7	22	...	22	...	2	0	0	0	3
1903-04	Mtl. Victorias	CAHL	8	27	...	27	...	...	...	...	...	...
1904-05	Mtl. Victorias	ECAHA	8	26	...	26	...	...	...	...	...	...
1905-06	Mtl. Victorias	ECAHA	9	30	...	30	...	...	...	...	...	...
1906-07	Mtl. Victorias	ECAHA	10	38	...	38	...	...	...	...	...	...
1907-08	Mtl. Victorias	ECAHA	10	28	...	28	...	...	...	...	...	...

FRANK BRIMSEK

Goaltender. Catches left. 5'9", 170 lbs., Born, Eveleth, MN, September 26, 1915

			Regular Season								Playoffs							
Season	Club	League	GP	MIN	GA	SO	GAA	W	L	T	GP	MIN	GA	SO	GAA	W	L	T
1934-35	Pittsburgh	Sr.	16	460	39	1	2.44	...	....	....	....	....	....	....	....	....	....	....
	Eveleth	Jr.	Not Available				....	....	....	....	....	....	....	....	....	....	....	....
1935-36	Pittsburgh	EHL	38	74	8	....	1.95	20	16	2	8	480	19	2	2.36	4	3	1
1936-37	Pittsburgh	EHL	47	142	3	....	3.02	19	23	5	....	....	....	....	....	....	....	....
1937-38	New Haven	AHL	1	60	2	0	2.00	0	1	0	....	....	....	....	....	....	....	....
	Providence	IHL	48	86	5	....	1.79	25	16	7	7	420	16	0	2.29	5	2	....
1938-39	Providence	IHL	9	540	18	0	2.00	....	....	....	....	....	....	....	....	....	....	....
	Boston	NHL	43	2610	68	10	1.56	33	9	1	12	863	18	1	1.25	8	4	....
1939-40	Boston	NHL	48	2950	98	6	1.99	31	12	5	6	360	15	0	2.50	2	4	....
1940-41	Boston	NHL	48	3040	102	6	2.01	27	8	13	11	678	23	1	2.04	8	3	....
1941-42	Boston	NHL	47	2930	115	3	2.36	24	17	6	5	307	16	0	3.13	2	3	....
1942-43	Boston	NHL	50	3000	176	1	3.52	24	17	9	9	560	33	0	3.66	4	5	....
1943-44			Military Service															
1945-46	Boston	NHL	34	2040	111	2	3.27	16	14	4	10	641	29	0	2.90	5	5	....
1946-47	Boston	NHL	60	3600	175	3	2.92	26	23	11	5	323	16	0	3.20	1	4	....
1947-48	Boston	NHL	60	3600	168	3	2.80	23	24	13	5	317	20	0	4.00	1	4	....
1948-49	Boston	NHL	54	3240	147	1	2.72	26	20	8	5	316	16	0	3.20	1	4	....
1949-50	Chicago	NHL	70	4200	244	5	3.49	22	38	10	....	....	...	....	....	....	....	....
	NHL Totals	**10**	**514**	**31210**	**1407**	**40**	**2.70**	**252**	**182**	**80**	**68**	**4365**	**186**	**2**	**2.56**	**32**	**36**	....

HARRY "PUNCH" BROADBENT

Right wing. Shoots right. 5'7", 183 lbs., Born, Ottawa, Ont., July 13, 1892

			Regular Season					Playoffs				
Season	Club	League	GP	G	A	PTS	PIM	GP	G	A	PTS	PIM
1912-13	Ottawa	NHA	20	20	0	20	15	...	...	...	...	...
1913-14	Ottawa	NHA	17	6	7	13	61	...	...	...	...	...
1914-15	Ottawa	NHA	20	24	3	27	115	5	3	0	3	...
1915-16			Military Service									
1916-17			Military Service									
1917-18			Military Service									
1918-19	Ottawa	NHL	8	4	2	6	12	5	2	0	2	12
1919-20	Ottawa	NHL	20	19	4	23	39	4	0	0	0	0
1920-21	Ottawa	NHL	9	4	1	5	16	7	2	0	2	6
1921-22	Ottawa	NHL	24	32	14	46	24	2	0	0	0	6
1922-23	Ottawa	NHL	24	14	0	14	32	8	6	1	7	12
1923-24	Ottawa	NHL	22	9	4	13	44	2	0	0	0	2
1924-25	Mtl Maroons	NHL	30	15	4	19	75	...	...	...	...	...
1925-26	Mtl Maroons	NHL	36	12	5	17	112	8	3	0	3	36
1926-27	Mtl Maroons	NHL	42	9	5	14	88	2	0	0	0	0
1927-28	Ottawa	NHL	43	3	2	5	62	2	0	0	0	0
1928-29	NY Americans	NHL	44	1	4	5	59	2	0	0	0	2
	NHL Totals	**11**	**302**	**122**	**45**	**167**	**553**	**42**	**12**	**1**	**13**	**81**

WALTER "TURK" BRODA

Goaltender. Catches left. 5'9", 190 lbs., Born, Brandon, Man., May 15, 1914

			Regular Season								Playoffs							
Season	Club	League	GP	MIN	GA	SO	GAA	W	L	T	GP	MIN	GA	SO	GAA	W	L	T
1933-34	Wpg. Monarchs	MHL Jr.	12	720	51	0	4.25	....	....	....	3	180	12	0	4.00	1	2	....
	Wpg. Monarchs	MHL Sr.	1	60	0	1	0.00	....	....	....	....	....	....	....	....	....	....	....
1934-35	Detroit	OHA Sr.	2	120	4	0	2.00	....	....	....	....	....	....	....	....	....	....	....
1935-36	Detroit	IAHL	47	2820	101	6	2.15	26	18	3	6	360	8	1	1.33	6	0	....
1936-37	Toronto	NHL	45	2770	106	3	2.30	22	19	4	2	133	5	0	2.26	0	2	....
1937-38	Toronto	NHL	48	2980	127	6	2.56	24	15	9	7	452	13	1	1.73	3	4	....
1938-39	Toronto	NHL	48	2990	107	8	2.15	19	20	9	10	617	20	2	1.95	4	6	....
1939-40	Toronto	NHL	47	2900	108	4	2.24	25	17	5	10	657	19	1	1.74	6	4	....
1940-41	Toronto	NHL	48	2970	99	5	2.00	28	14	6	7	438	15	0	2.06	3	4	.....
1941-42	Toronto	NHL	48	2960	136	6	2.77	27	18	3	13	780	31	1	2.39	8	5	....
1942-43	Toronto	NHL	50	3000	159	1	3.18	22	19	9	6	439	20	0	2.73	2	4	....
1943-44			Military Service															
1944-45			Military Service															
1945-46	Toronto	NHL	15	900	53	0	3.53	6	6	3	....	....	....	....	....	....	....	....
1946-47	Toronto	NHL	60	3600	172	4	2.87	31	19	10	11	680	27	1	2.38	8	3	....
1947-48	Toronto	NHL	60	3600	143	5	2.38	32	15	13	9	557	20	1	2.15	8	1	....
1948-49	Toronto	NHL	60	3600	161	5	2.68	22	25	13	9	574	15	1	1.57	8	1	....
1949-50	Toronto	NHL	68	4040	167	9	2.48	30	25	12	7	450	10	3	1.33	3	4	....
1950-51	Toronto	NHL	31	1827	68	6	2.23	14	11	5	9	509	9	2	1.06	5	3	1
1951-52	Toronto	NHL	1	30	3	0	6.00	0	1	0	2	120	7	0	3.50	0	2	....
	NHL Totals	**14**	**629**	**38168**	**1609**	**62**	**2.53**	**302**	**224**	**101**	**102**	**6406**	**102**	**13**	**1.98**	**58**	**43**	**1**

JOHN BUCYK

Left wing. Shoots left. 6', 215 lbs., Born, Edmonton, Alta., May 12, 1935

			Regular Season					Playoffs				
Season	Club	League	GP	G	A	PTS	PIM	GP	G	A	PTS	PIM
1949-50	Edmonton	AJHL	3	1	4	6	...	...	...	...	...	...
1950-51	Edmonton	AJHL	Not Available			...	...	...	...	...	...	...
1951-52	Edmonton	WCJHL	...	...	...	...	...	1	0	0	0	0
1952-53	Edmonton	WCJHL	34	19	11	30	24	13	5	1	6	14
1953-54	Edmonton	WJCHL	33	29	38	67	38	9	13	9	22	22
	Edmonton	WHL	2	2	0	2	2	...	...	...	...	...
1954-55	Edmonton	WHL	70	30	58	88	57	9	1	6	7	7
1955-56	Detroit	NHL	38	1	8	9	20	10	1	1	2	8
	Edmonton	WHL	6	0	0	0	9	...	...	...	...	...
1956-57	Detroit	NHL	66	10	11	21	41	5	0	1	1	0
1957-58	Boston	NHL	68	21	31	52	57	12	0	4	4	16
1958-59	Boston	NHL	69	24	36	60	36	7	2	4	6	6
1959-60	Boston	NHL	56	16	36	52	26	...	...	...	...	...
1960-61	Boston	NHL	70	19	20	39	48	...	...	...	...	...
1961-62	Boston	NHL	67	20	40	60	32	...	...	...	...	...
1962-63	Boston	NHL	69	27	39	66	36	...	...	...	...	...
1963-64	Boston	NHL	62	18	36	54	36	...	...	...	...	...
1964-65	Boston	NHL	68	26	29	55	24	...	...	...	...	...
1965-66	Boston	NHL	63	27	30	57	12	...	...	...	...	...
1966-67	Boston	NHL	59	18	30	48	12	...	...	...	...	...
1967-68	Boston	NHL	72	30	39	69	8	3	0	2	2	0
1968-69	Boston	NHL	70	24	42	66	18	10	5	6	11	0
1969-70	Boston	NHL	76	31	38	69	13	14	11	8	19	2
1970-71	Boston	NHL	78	51	65	116	8	7	2	5	7	0
1971-72	Boston	NHL	78	32	51	83	4	15	9	11	20	6
1972-73	Boston	NHL	78	40	53	93	12	5	0	3	3	0
1973-74	Boston	NHL	76	31	44	75	8	16	8	10	18	4
1974-75	Boston	NHL	78	29	52	81	10	3	1	0	1	0
1975-76	Boston	NHL	77	36	47	83	20	12	2	7	9	0
1976-77	Boston	NHL	49	20	23	43	12	5	0	0	0	0
1977-78	Boston	NHL	53	5	13	18	4	...	...	...	...	...
	NHL Totals	**23**	**1540**	**556**	**813**	**1369**	**497**	**124**	**41**	**62**	**103**	**42**

BILLY BURCH

Centre / left wing. Shoots left. 6', 200 lbs., Born, Yonkers, NY, November 20, 1900

			Regular Season					Playoffs				
Season	Club	League	GP	G	A	PTS	PIM	GP	G	A	PTS	PIM
1920-21	Tor. Aura Lee	OHA Sr.	10	10	0	10	...	...	...	...	...	...
1921-22	Tor. Aura Lee	OHA Sr.	9	13	9	22	...	2	2	0	2	...
1922-23	New Haven	AHA	...	4	0	4	...	...	...	...	...	...
	Hamilton	NHL	10	6	2	8	2	...	...	...	...	...
1923-24	Hamilton	NHL	24	16	2	18	4	...	...	...	...	...
1924-25	Hamilton	NHL	27	20	4	24	10	...	...	...	...	...
1925-26	NY Americans	NHL	36	22	3	25	33	...	...	...	...	...
1926-27	NY Americans	NHL	43	19	8	27	40	...	...	...	...	...
1927-28	NY Americans	NHL	32	10	2	12	34	...	...	...	...	...
1928-29	NY Americans	NHL	44	11	5	16	45	2	0	0	0	0
1929-30	NY Americans	NHL	35	7	3	10	22	...	...	...	...	...
1930-31	NY Americans	NHL	44	14	8	22	35	...	...	...	...	...
1931-32	NY Americans	NHL	48	7	15	22	20	...	...	...	...	...
1932-33	Boston	NHL	23	3	1	4	4	...	...	...	...	...
	Chicago	NHL	24	2	0	2	2	...	...	...	...	...
	NHL Totals	**11**	**390**	**137**	**53**	**190**	**251**	**2**	**0**	**0**	**0**	**0**

HARRY CAMERON

Defence. Shoots right. 5'10", 155 lbs., Born, Pembroke, Ont.., February 6, 1890

			Regular Season					Playoffs				
Season	Club	League	GP	G	A	PTS	PIM	GP	G	A	PTS	PIM
1910-11	Pembroke	Sr.	6	8	1	9	...	2	4	0	4	...
1911-12	Port Arthur	NOHA	12	6	0	6	...	2	2	0	2	...
1912-13	Toronto	NHA	20	9	0	9	20	...	...	...	...	...
1913-14	Toronto	NHA	19	15	4	19	22	2	0	2	2	6
1914-15	Toronto	NHA	17	12	8	20	43	...	...	...	...	...
1915-16	Toronto	NHA	24	8	3	11	70	...	...	...	...	...
1916-17	Toronto	NHA	14	7	4	11	32	...	...	...	...	...
	Mtl. Wanderers	NHA	6	2	1	3	9	...	...	...	...	...
1917-18	Toronto	NHL	21	17	1	18	34	7	3	0	3	9
1918-19	Toronto	NHL	7	7	2	9	23	...	...	...	...	...
	Ottawa	NHL	7	4	1	5	12	5	4	0	4	6
1919-20	Toronto	NHL	7	3	1	4	0	...	...	...	...	...
	Montreal	NHL	16	8	5	13	11	...	...	...	...	...
1920-21	Toronto	NHL	24	18	9	27	35	2	0	0	0	0
1921-22	Toronto	NHL	24	19	8	27	18	7	0	0	0	27
1922-23	Toronto	NHL	22	9	6	15	21	...	...	...	...	...
1923-24	Saskatoon	WCHL	29	10	10	20	16	...	...	...	...	...
1924-25	Saskatoon	WCHL	28	13	7	20	21	2	1	0	1	0
1925-26	Saskatoon	WHL	30	9	3	12	12	2	0	0	0	0
1926-27	Saskatoon	PHL	31	26	19	45	20	4	1	0	1	4
1927-28	Minneapolis	AHA	19	2	3	5	32	...	...	...	...	...
1928-29	St. Louis	AHA	34	14	3	17	30	...	...	...	...	...
1929-30	St. Louis	AHA	46	14	6	20	34	...	...	...	...	...
1930-31	St. Louis	AHA	37	4	3	7	30	...	...	...	...	...
1931-32			Did Not Play									
1932-33	Saskatoon	NWHL	9	0	0	0	4	...	...	...	...	...
	NHL Totals	**6**	**127**	**85**	**32**	**117**	**137**	**21**	**7**	**0**	**7**	**36**

GERRY CHEEVERS

Goaltender. Catches left. 5'11", 185 lbs., Born, St. Catharines, Ont., December 7, 1940

			Regular Season								Playoffs							
Season	Club	League	GP	MIN	GA	SO	GAA	W	L	T	GP	MIN	GA	SO	GAA	W	L	T
1956-57	Tor. St. Mike's	OHA Jr.	1	60	4	0	4.00	....	....	....	....	....	....	....	....	....	....	....
1957-58	Tor. St. Mike's	OHA Jr.	1	60	3	0	3.00	....	....	....	....	....	....	....	....	....	....	....
1958-59	Tor. St. Mike's	OHA Jr.	6	360	28	0	4.67	....	....	....	....	....	....	....	....	....	....	....
1959-60	Tor. St. Mike's	OHA Jr.	36	2160	111	5	3.08	21	10	3	....	....	....	....	....	....	....	....
1960-61	Tor. St. Mike's	OHA Jr.	30	1775	94	2	3.18	12	20	5	....	....	....	....	....	....	....	....
1961-62	Toronto	NHL	2	120	7	0	3.50	1	1	0	....	....	....	....	....	....	....	.....
	S.S. Marie	EPHL	29	1740	103	1	3.55	....	....	....	....	....	....	....	....	....	....	....
	Pitt / Rochester	AHL	24	1440	84	1	3.50	....	....	....	2	120	8	0	4.00	1	1	....
1962-63	Rochester	AHL	19	1140	75	1	3.95	....	....	....	....	....	....	....	....	....	....	....
	Sudbury	EPHL	51	3060	212	4	4.15	....	....	....	8	480	29	1	3.62	4	4	....
1963-64	Rochester	AHL	66	3960	187	3	2.84	....	....	....	2	120	8	0	4.00	0	2	....
1964-65	Rochester	AHL	72	4320	195	5	2.68	....	....	....	10	615	24	0	2.34	8	2	....
1965-66	Boston	NHL	7	340	34	0	6.00	0	4	1	....	....	....	....	....	....	....	....
	Oklahoma City	CHL	30	1760	73	3	2.49	....	....	....	9	540	19	0	2.11	8	1	....
1966-67	Boston	NHL	22	1298	72	1	3.33	5	11	6	....	....	....	....	....	....	....	....
	Oklahoma City	CHL	26	1520	71	1	2.80	....	....	....	11	677	29	1	2.57	8	3	....
1967-68	Boston	NHL	47	2646	125	3	2.83	23	17	5	4	240	15	0	3.75	0	4	....
1968-69	Boston	NHL	52	3112	145	3	2.80	28	12	12	9	572	16	3	1.68	6	3	....
1969-70	Boston	NHL	41	2384	108	4	2.72	24	8	8	13	781	29	0	2.23	12	1	....
1970-71	Boston	NHL	40	2400	109	3	2.72	27	8	5	6	360	21	0	3.50	3	3	....
1971-72	Boston	NHL	41	2420	101	2	2.50	27	5	8	8	483	21	2	2.61	6	2	....
1972-73	Cleveland	WHA	52	3144	149	5	2.83	32	20	0	9	548	22	0	2.40	5	4	....
1973-74	Cleveland	WHA	59	3562	180	4	3.03	30	20	6	5	303	18	0	3.56	1	4	....
1974-75	Cleveland	WHA	52	3076	167	4	3.26	26	24	2	1	59	23	0	4.60	1	4	....
1975-76	Cleveland	WHA	28	1570	95	1	3.58	11	14	1	....	....	....	....	....	....	....	....
	Boston	NHL	15	900	41	1	2.73	8	2	5	6	392	14	1	2.14	2	4	....
1976-77	Boston	NHL	45	2700	137	3	3.04	30	10	5	14	858	44	1	3.08	8	5	....
1977-78	Boston	NHL	21	1086	48	1	2.65	10	5	2	12	731	35	1	2.87	8	4	....
1978-79	Boston	NHL	43	2509	132	1	3.16	23	10	10	6	360	15	0	2.50	4	2	....
1979-80	Boston	NHL	42	2479	116	4	2.81	24	11	7	10	619	32	0	3.10	4	6	....
	NHL Totals	**13**	**418**	**24394**	**1175**	**26**	**2.89**	**230**	**103**	**74**	**88**	**5396**	**242**	**8**	**2.69**	**47**	**35**	....

FRANK "KING" CLANCY

Defence. Shoots left. 5'7", 155 lbs., Born, Ottawa, Ont., February 25, 1903

			Regular Season					Playoffs				
Season	Club	League	GP	G	A	PTS	PIM	GP	G	A	PTS	PIM
1921-22	Ottawa	NHL	24	4	5	9	19	2	0	0	0	2
1922-23	Ottawa	NHL	24	3	1	4	20	8	1	0	1	4
1923-24	Ottawa	NHL	24	9	8	17	18	2	0	0	0	6
1924-25	Ottawa	NHL	29	14	5	20	61	...	...	...	...	...
1925-26	Ottawa	NHL	35	8	4	12	80	2	1	0	1	8
1926-27	Ottawa	NHL	43	9	10	19	78	6	1	1	2	14
1927-28	Ottawa	NHL	39	8	7	15	73	2	0	0	0	6
1928-29	Ottawa	NHL	44	13	2	15	89	...	...	...	...	...
1929-30	Ottawa	NHL	44	17	23	40	83	2	0	1	1	2
1930-31	Toronto	NHL	44	7	14	21	63	2	1	0	1	0
1931-32	Toronto	NHL	48	10	9	19	61	7	2	1	3	14
1932-33	Toronto	NHL	48	13	12	25	79	9	0	3	3	14
1933-34	Toronto	NHL	46	11	17	28	62	3	0	0	0	8
1934-35	Toronto	NHL	47	5	16	21	53	7	1	0	1	8
1935-36	Toronto	NHL	47	5	10	15	61	9	2	2	4	10
1936-37	Toronto	NHL	6	1	0	1	4	...	...	...	...	...
	NHL Totals	**16**	**593**	**137**	**143**	**280**	**904**	**61**	**9**	**8**	**17**	**92**

AUBREY "DIT" CLAPPER

Right wing / defence. Shoots right. 6" 2", 200 lbs., Born, Newmarket, Ont., February 9, 1907

			Regular Season					Playoffs				
Season	Club	League	GP	G	A	PTS	PIM	GP	G	A	PTS	PIM
1925-26	Tor. Parkdale	OHA Jr.	2	0	0	0	...	...	...	...	...	...
1926-27	Boston	CAHL	29	6	1	7	57	...	...	...	...	...
1927-28	Boston	NHL	40	4	1	5	20	2	0	0	0	2
1928-29	Boston	NHL	40	9	2	11	48	5	1	0	1	0
1929-30	Boston	NHL	44	41	20	61	48	6	4	0	4	0
1930-31	Boston	NHL	43	22	8	30	50	5	2	4	6	4
1931-32	Boston	NHL	48	17	22	39	21	...	...	...	...	...
1932-33	Boston	NHL	48	14	14	28	42	5	1	1	2	2
1933-34	Boston	NHL	48	10	12	22	6	...	...	...	...	...
1934-35	Boston	NHL	48	21	16	37	21	3	1	0	1	0
1935-36	Boston	NHL	44	12	13	25	14	2	0	1	1	0
1936-37	Boston	NHL	48	17	8	25	25	3	2	0	2	5
1937-38	Boston	NHL	46	6	9	15	24	3	0	0	0	12
1938-39	Boston	NHL	42	13	13	26	22	12	0	1	1	6
1939-40	Boston	NHL	44	10	18	28	25	5	0	2	2	2
1940-41	Boston	NHL	48	8	18	26	24	11	0	5	5	4
1941-42	Boston	NHL	32	3	12	15	11	5	0	0	0	0
1942-43	Boston	NHL	38	5	18	23	12	9	2	3	5	9
1943-44	Boston	NHL	50	6	25	31	13	...	...	...	...	...
1944-45	Boston	NHL	46	8	14	22	16	7	0	0	0	0
1945-46	Boston	NHL	30	2	3	5	0	4	0	0	0	0
1946-47	Boston	NHL	6	0	0	0	0	...	...	...	...	...
	NHL Totals	**20**	**833**	**228**	**246**	**474**	**462**	**82**	**13**	**17**	**30**	**50**

BOBBY CLARKE

Centre. Shoots left. 5'10", 185 lbs., Born, Flin Flon, Man., August 13, 1949

			Regular Season					Playoffs				
Season	Club	League	GP	G	A	PTS	PIM	GP	G	A	PTS	PIM
1965-66	Flin Flon	SJHL	4	4	3	7	0	...	...	...	...	...
1967-68	Flin Flon	WCHL	59	51	117	168	148	15	4	10	14	2
1968-69	Flin Flon	WCHL	58	51	86	137	123	18	9	16	25	0
1969-70	Philadelphia	NHL	76	15	31	46	68	...	...	...	...	...
1970-71	Philadelphia	NHL	77	27	36	63	78	4	0	0	0	2
1971-72	Philadelphia	NHL	78	35	46	81	87	...	...	...	...	...
1972-73	Philadelphia	NHL	78	37	67	104	80	11	2	6	8	6
1973-74	Philadelphia	NHL	77	35	52	87	113	17	5	11	16	42
1974-75	Philadelphia	NHL	80	27	89	116	125	17	4	12	16	16
1975-76	Philadelphia	NHL	76	30	89	119	136	16	2	14	16	28
1976-77	Philadelphia	NHL	80	27	63	90	71	10	5	5	10	8
1977-78	Philadelphia	NHL	71	21	68	89	83	12	4	7	11	8
1978-79	Philadelphia	NHL	80	16	57	73	68	8	2	4	6	8
1979-80	Philadelphia	NHL	76	12	57	69	65	19	8	12	20	16
1980-81	Philadelphia	NHL	80	19	46	65	140	12	3	3	6	6
1981-82	Philadelphia	NHL	62	17	46	63	154	4	4	2	6	4
1982-83	Philadelphia	NHL	80	23	62	85	115	3	1	0	1	2
1983-84	Philadelphia	NHL	73	17	43	60	70	3	2	1	3	6
	NHL Totals	**15**	**1144**	**358**	**852**	**1210**	**1433**	**136**	**42**	**77**	**119**	**152**

SPRAGUE CLEGHORN

Defence. Shoots left. 5'10", 190 lbs., Born, Montreal, Que., March 11,1890

			Regular Season					Playoffs				
Season	Club	League	GP	G	A	PTS	PIM	GP	G	A	PTS	PIM
1909-10	NY Wanderers	AHA Sr.	8	7	0	7	...	...	...	...	...	...
1910-11	Renfrew	NHA	12	5	0	5	27	...	...	...	...	...
1911-12	Mtl. Wanderers	NHA	18	9	0	9	40	...	...	...	...	...
1912-13	Mtl. Wanderers	NHA	19	12	0	12	46	...	...	...	...	...
1913-14	Mtl. Wanderers	NHA	20	12	8	20	17	...	...	...	...	...
1914-15	Mtl. Wanderers	NHA	19	21	12	33	51	2	0	0	0	17
1915-16	Mtl. Wanderers	NHA	8	9	4	13	22	...	...	...	...	...
1916-17	Mtl. Wanderers	NHA	19	16	3	19	53	...	...	...	...	...
1918-19	Ottawa	NHL	18	6	6	12	21	5	2	2	4	55
1919-20	Ottawa	NHL	21	16	5	21	62	5	0	1	1	9
1920-21	Toronto	NHL	13	3	4	7	26	6	1	2	3	21
1921-22	Montreal	NHL	24	17	7	24	63	...	...	...	...	...
1922-23	Montreal	NHL	24	9	4	13	34	1	0	0	0	7
1923-24	Montreal	NHL	23	8	3	11	39	6	2	1	3	2
1924-25	Montreal	NHL	27	8	1	9	82	6	1	2	3	4
1925-26	Boston	NHL	28	6	5	11	49	...	...	...	...	...
1926-27	Boston	NHL	42	7	1	8	84	8	1	0	1	8
1927-28	Boston	NHL	33	2	2	4	14	2	0	0	0	0
1928-29	Newark	CAHL	3	0	0	0	0	...	...	...	...	...
	NHL Totals	**10**	**262**	**84**	**39**	**123**	**489**	**39**	**7**	**8**	**15**	**48**

NEIL COLVILLE

Centre. Shoots right. 6', 175 lbs., Born, Edmonton, Alta., August 4, 1914

			Regular Season					Playoffs				
Season	Club	League	GP	G	A	PTS	PIM	GP	G	A	PTS	PIM
1929-30	Edmonton	Jr.	...	12	1	13	...	...	...	...	...	...
1931-32	Edmonton	Jr.	...	7	3	10	...	...	...	...	...	...
1932-33	Edmonton	Jr.	...	...	...	...	...	...	...	...	...	...
1933-34	Edmonton	Jr.	9	14	4	18	13	2	4	2	6	5
1934-35	NY Cresents	EHL	21	24	11	35	16	8	8	4	12	2
1935-36	NY Rangers	NHL	2	0	0	0	0	...	...	...	...	...
	Philadelphia	CAHL	35	15	16	31	8	4	0	2	2	0
1936-37	NY Rangers	NHL	45	10	18	28	33	9	3	3	6	0
1937-38	NY Rangers	NHL	45	17	19	36	11	2	0	1	1	0
1938-39	NY Rangers	NHL	47	18	19	37	12	7	0	2	2	2
1939-40	NY Rangers	NHL	48	19	19	38	22	12	2	7	9	18
1940-41	NY Rangers	NHL	48	14	28	42	28	3	1	1	2	0
1941-42	NY Rangers	NHL	48	8	25	33	37	6	0	5	5	6
1942-43				Military Service								
1943-44				Military Service								
1944-45	NY Rangers	NHL	4	0	1	1	2	...	...	...	...	...
	Winnipeg	Sr.	6	5	4	9	4	...	...	...	...	...
	Ottawa	QSHL	5	1	2	3	0	7	2	5	7	4
1945-46	NY Rangers	NHL	49	5	4	9	25	...	...	...	...	...
1946-47	NY Rangers	NHL	60	4	16	20	16	...	...	...	...	...
1947-48	NY Rangers	NHL	55	4	12	16	25	6	1	0	1	6
1948-49	NY Rangers	NHL	14	0	5	5	2	...	...	...	...	...
	New Haven	AHL	11	0	3	3	8	...	...	...	...	...
1949-50	New Haven	AHL	17	3	4	7	13	...	...	...	...	...
	NHL Totals	**12**	**464**	**99**	**166**	**265**	**213**	**46**	**7**	**19**	**26**	**32**

CHARLIE CONACHER

Right wing. Shoots right. 6'1", 200 lbs., Born, Toronto, Ont., December 10, 1909

			Regular Season					Playoffs				
Season	Club	League	GP	G	A	PTS	PIM	GP	G	A	PTS	PIM
1926-27	N. Toronto	OHA Jr.	9	9	1	10	...	1	0	0	0	...
	N. Toronto	OHA Sr.	2	1	0	1	2	...	...	...	...	...
1927-28	Tor. Marlboros	OHA Jr.	9	11	0	11	...	2	1	0	1	...
	Tor. Marlboros	OHA Sr.	1	2	0	2	0	...	...	...	...	...
1928-29	Tor. Marlboros	OHA Sr.	8	18	3	21	...	2	7	0	7	...
1929-30	Toronto	NHL	38	20	9	29	48	...	...	...	...	...
1930-31	Toronto	NHL	37	31	12	43	78	2	0	1	1	0
1931-32	Toronto	NHL	44	34	14	48	66	7	6	2	8	6
1932-33	Toronto	NHL	40	14	19	33	64	9	1	1	2	10
1933-34	Toronto	NHL	42	31	20	52	38	5	3	2	5	0
1934-35	Toronto	NHL	47	36	21	57	24	7	1	4	5	6
1935-36	Toronto	NHL	44	23	15	38	74	9	3	2	5	12
1936-37	Toronto	NHL	15	3	5	8	13	2	0	0	0	5
1937-38	Toronto	NHL	19	7	9	16	6	...	...	...	...	...
1938-39	Detroit	NHL	40	8	15	23	39	5	2	5	7	2
1939-40	NY Americans	NHL	47	10	18	28	41	3	1	1	2	8
1940-41	NY Americans	NHL	46	7	16	23	32	...	...	...	...	...
	NHL Totals	**12**	**459**	**225**	**173**	**398**	**523**	**49**	**17**	**18**	**35**	**0**

LIONEL CONACHER

Defence. Shoots left. 6'2", 205 lbs., Born, Toronto, Ont, May 24, 1900

Season	Club	League	Regular Season GP	G	A	PTS	PIM	Playoffs GP	G	A	PTS	PIM
1919-20			Not Available			...	...	...	...	...	...	...
1920-21	Tor. Aura Lee	OHA Sr.	10	2	1	3	...	...	...	...	...	...
1921-22	Tor. Aura Lee	OHA Sr.	9	7	1	8	...	2	2	0	2	...
1922-23			Not Available			...	...	...	...	...	...	...
1923-24	Pittsburgh	AHA	20	12	0	12	...	8	5	1	6	...
1924-25	Pittsburgh	AHA	40	14	0	14	...	4	2	0	2	...
1925-26	Pittsburgh	NHL	33	9	4	13	64	2	0	0	0	0
1926-27	Pittsburgh	NHL	9	0	0	0	12	...	...	...	...	...
	NY Americans	NHL	30	8	9	17	81	...	...	...	...	...
1927-28	NY Americans	NHL	36	11	6	17	82	...	...	...	...	...
1928-29	NY Americans	NHL	44	5	2	7	132	2	0	0	0	10
1929-30	NY Americans	NHL	39	4	6	10	73	...	...	...	...	...
1930-31	Mtl Maroons	NHL	35	4	3	7	57	2	0	0	0	2
1931-32	Mtl Maroons	NHL	46	7	9	16	60	4	0	0	0	2
1932-33	Mtl Maroons	NHL	47	7	21	28	61	2	0	1	1	0
1933-34	Chicago	NHL	48	10	13	23	87	8	2	0	2	4
1934-35	Mtl Maroons	NHL	40	2	6	8	44	7	0	0	0	14
1935-36	Mtl Maroons	NHL	47	7	7	14	65	3	0	0	0	0
1936-37	Mtl Maroons	NHL	45	6	19	25	64	5	0	1	1	2
	NHL Totals	**12**	**498**	**80**	**105**	**185**	**882**	**35**	**2**	**2**	**4**	**34**

ALEX CONNELL

Goaltender. Catches left. 5'9", 160 lbs., Born, Ottawa, Ont. February 8, 1901

Season	Club	League	Regular Season GP	MIN	GA	SO	GAA	W	L	T	Playoffs GP	MIN	GA	SO	GAA	W	L	T
1923-24	Ottawa	OHA Sr.	12	740	14	5	1.14	8	4	0	....	....	....	....	....	....	....	....
1924-25	Ottawa	NHL	30	1852	66	7	2.14	17	12	1	....	....	....	....	....	....	....	....
1925-26	Ottawa	NHL	36	2231	42	15	1.13	24	8	4	2	120	2	0	1.00	0	1	1
1926-27	Ottawa	NHL	44	2782	69	12	1.49	30	10	4	6	400	4	2	0.60	3	0	3
1927-28	Ottawa	NHL	44	2760	57	15	1.23	20	14	10	2	120	3	0	1.50	0	2	0
1928-29	Ottawa	NHL	44	2820	67	7	1.43	14	17	13	....	....	....	....	....	....	....	....
1929-30	Ottawa	NHL	44	2780	118	3	2.55	21	15	8	2	120	6	0	3.00	0	1	1
1930-31	Ottawa	NHL	36	2190	110	3	3.01	10	22	4	....	....	....	....	....	....	....	....
1931-32	Detroit	NHL	48	3050	108	6	2.13	24	19	5	2	120	3	0	1.50	0	1	1
1932-33	Ottawa	NHL	15	845	36	1	2.56	4	8	2	....	....	....	....	....	....	....	....
1933-34	NY Americans	NHL	1	40	2	0	3.00	1	0	0	....	....	....	....	....	....	....	....
1934-35	Mtl. Maroons	NHL	48	2970	92	9	1.86	24	19	5	7	429	8	2	1.12	6	0	1
1935-36			Did Not Play															
1936-37	Mtl. Maroons	NHL	27	1710	63	2	2.31	10	11	6	....	....	....	....	....	....	....	....
	NHL Totals	**12**	**417**	**26030**	**830**	**81**	**1.91**	**199**	**155**	**59**	**21**	**1309**	**26**	**4**	**1.19**	**9**	**5**	**5**

FRED "BUN" COOK

Left wing. Shoots left, 5'11", 180 lbs., Born, Kingston, Ont., Sept. 18, 1903

Season	Club	League	Regular Season GP	G	A	PTS	PIM	Playoffs GP	G	A	PTS	PIM
1924-25	Saskatoon	WCHL	28	17	4	21	44	2	0	0	0	0
1925-26	Saskatoon	WHL	30	8	4	12	22	2	0	0	0	12
1926-27	NY Rangers	NHL	44	14	9	23	42	2	0	0	0	6
1927-28	NY Rangers	NHL	44	14	14	28	28	9	2	1	3	10
1928-29	NY Rangers	NHL	43	13	5	18	70	6	1	0	1	8
1929-30	NY Rangers	NHL	43	24	18	42	55	4	2	0	2	4
1930-31	NY Rangers	NHL	44	18	17	35	72	4	0	0	0	0
1931-32	NY Rangers	NHL	45	14	20	34	43	7	6	2	8	12
1932-33	NY Rangers	NHL	48	22	15	37	35	8	2	0	2	4
1933-34	NY Rangers	NHL	26	4	5	9	12	2	0	0	0	2
1934-35	NY Rangers	NHL	40	4	5	9	8	4	2	0	2	0
	NHL Totals	**11**	**473**	**158**	**144**	**302**	**427**	**46**	**15**	**3**	**18**	**57**

BILL COOK

Right wing. Shoots right. 5'10", 170 lbs., Born, Brantford, Ont., October 8, 1895

Season	Club	League	Regular Season GP	G	A	PTS	PIM	Playoffs GP	G	A	PTS	PIM
1922-23	Saskatoon	WCHL	30	9	16	25	19	...	...	...	...	...
1923-24	Saskatoon	WCHL	30	26	14	40	20	...	...	...	...	...
1924-25	Saskatoon	WCHL	27	22	10	32	79	2	0	0	0	4
1925-26	Saskatoon	WHL	30	31	13	44	222	2	0	2	6	...
1926-27	NY Rangers	NHL	44	33	4	37	58	2	1	0	1	4
1927-28	NY Rangers	NHL	43	18	6	24	42	9	2	3	5	26
1928-29	NY Rangers	NHL	43	15	8	23	41	6	0	0	0	6
1929-30	NY Rangers	NHL	44	29	30	59	56	4	0	1	1	11
1930-31	NY Rangers	NHL	43	30	12	42	39	4	3	0	3	2
1931-32	NY Rangers	NHL	48	34	14	48	33	7	3	3	6	2
1932-33	NY Rangers	NHL	48	28	22	50	51	8	3	2	5	4
1933-34	NY Rangers	NHL	48	13	13	26	21	2	0	0	0	2
1934-35	NY Rangers	NHL	48	21	15	36	23	4	1	2	3	7
1935-36	NY Rangers	NHL	44	7	10	17	16	...	...	...	...	...
1936-37	NY Rangers	NHL	21	1	4	5	6	...	...	...	...	...
1937-38	Cleveland	AHL	5	0	0	0	5	1	0	0	0	0
	NHL Totals	**11**	**474**	**229**	**138**	**367**	**386**	**46**	**13**	**11**	**24**	**72**

ART COULTER

Defence. Shoots right. 5'11", 190 lbs., Born, Lillyfield, Man., May 31, 1909

Season	Club	League	Regular Season GP	G	A	PTS	PIM	Playoffs GP	G	A	PTS	PIM
1929-30	Philadelphia	CAHL	35	2	2	4	40	2	0	0	0	2
1930-31	Philadelphia	CAHL	40	4	8	12	109	...	...	...	...	...
1931-32	Philadelphia	CAHL	26	9	4	13	42	...	...	...	...	...
	Chicago	NHL	14	0	1	1	23	2	1	0	1	0
1932-33	Chicago	NHL	46	3	2	5	53	...	...	...	....	
1933-34	Chicago	NHL	41	5	2	7	39	8	1	0	1	10
1934-35	Chicago	NHL	48	4	8	12	68	2	0	0	0	5
1935-36	Chicago	NHL	23	0	2	2	18	...	...	...	...	...
	NY Rangers	NHL	23	1	5	6	26	...	...	...	...	...
1936-37	NY Rangers	NHL	46	1	5	6	27	9	0	3	3	15
1937-38	NY Rangers	NHL	43	5	10	15	80	...	...	...	...	...
1938-39	NY Rangers	NHL	43	4	8	12	58	7	1	1	2	6
1939-40	NY Rangers	NHL	48	1	9	10	68	12	1	0	1	21
1940-41	NY Rangers	NHL	36	5	14	19	42	3	0	0	0	4
1941-42	NY Rangers	NHL	47	1	16	17	31	6	0	1	1	4
	NHL Totals	**11**	**465**	**30**	**82**	**112**	**543**	**49**	**4**	**5**	**9**	**61**

YVAN COURNOYER

Right wing. Shoots left. 5'7", 178 lbs., Born, Drummondville, Que., November 22, 1943

Season	Club	League	Regular Season GP	G	A	PTS	PIM	Playoffs GP	G	A	PTS	PIM
1961-62	Montreal	OHA	35	15	16	31	8	6	4	4	8	0
1962-63	Montreal	OHA	36	37	27	64	24	10	3	4	7	6
1963-64	Montreal	OHA	53	63	48	111	30	17	19	8	27	15
	Montreal	NHL	5	4	0	4	0	...	...	....	...	...
1964-65	Quebec	AHL	7	2	1	3	0	...	...	...	...	...
	Montreal	NHL	55	7	10	17	10	12	3	1	4	0
1965-66	Montreal	NHL	65	18	11	29	8	10	2	3	5	2
1966-67	Montreal	NHL	69	25	15	40	14	10	2	3	5	6
1967-68	Montreal	NHL	64	28	32	60	23	13	6	8	14	4
1968-69	Montreal	NHL	76	43	44	87	31	14	4	7	11	5
1969-70	Montreal	NHL	72	27	36	63	23	...	...	...	...	...
1970-71	Montreal	NHL	65	37	36	73	21	20	10	12	22	6
1971-72	Montreal	NHL	73	47	36	83	15	6	2	1	3	2
1972-73	Montreal	NHL	67	40	39	79	18	17	15	10	25	2
1973-74	Montreal	NHL	67	40	33	73	18	6	5	2	7	2
1974-75	Montreal	NHL	76	29	45	74	32	11	5	6	11	4
1975-76	Montreal	NHL	71	32	36	68	20	13	3	6	9	4
1976-77	Montreal	NHL	60	25	28	53	8	...	...	...	...	...
1977-78	Montreal	NHL	68	24	29	53	12	15	7	4	11	10
1978-79	Montreal	NHL	15	2	5	7	2	...	...	...	...	....
	NHL Totals	**16**	**968**	**428**	**435**	**863**	**255**	**147**	**64**	**63**	**127**	**47**

BILL COWLEY

Centre. Shoots left. 5'10", 165 lbs., Born, Bristol, Que., June 12, 1912

Season	Club	League	Regular Season GP	G	A	PTS	PIM	Playoffs GP	G	A	PTS	PIM
1930-31	Ott. Primrose	OHA Jr.	14	10	2	12	16	4	1	5	8	...
1931-32	Ott. Shamrocks	OHA Jr.	2	2	1	3	1	...	4	4	8	4
	Ott. Shamrocks	Sr.	...	...	...	...	...	1	0	0	0	0
1932-33	Ott. Shamrocks	Sr.	14	7	6	13	24	4	1	0	1	4
1933-34	Halifax	MSHL	38	25	25	50	42	6	2	2	4	2
1934-35	Tulsa	AHA	1	0	0	0	5	...	...	....	....	....
	St. Louis	NHL	43	5	7	12	10	...	...	...	....	...
1935-36	Boston	NHL	48	11	10	21	17	2	2	1	3	2
1936-37	Boston	NHL	46	13	22	35	4	3	0	3	3	0
1937-38	Boston	NHL	48	17	22	39	8	3	2	0	2	0
1938-39	Boston	NHL	34	8	34	42	2	12	3	11	14	2
1939-40	Boston	NHL	48	13	27	40	24	6	0	1	1	7
1940-41	Boston	NHL	46	17	45	62	16	2	0	0	0	0
1941-42	Boston	NHL	28	4	23	27	6	5	0	3	3	5
1942-43	Boston	NHL	48	27	45	72	10	9	1	7	8	4
1943-44	Boston	NHL	36	30	41	71	12	...	...	...	...	...
1944-45	Boston	NHL	49	25	40	65	12	7	3	3	6	0
1945-46	Boston	NHL	26	12	12	24	6	10	1	3	4	2
1946-47	Boston	NHL	51	13	25	38	16	5	0	2	2	0
	NHL Totals	**13**	**549**	**195**	**353**	**548**	**143**	**64**	**12**	**34**	**46**	**22**

RUSTY CRAWFORD

Left wing. Shoots left. 5'11", 165 lbs., Born, Cardinal, Ont.., November 7, 1885

Season	Club	League	Regular Season GP	G	A	PTS	PIM	Playoffs GP	G	A	PTS	PIM
1910-11	Prince Albert	Sr.	...	...	...	...	...	2	0	0	0	18
1911-12	Saskatoon	Sr.	Not Available...			...	..	...	...	...	...	
1912-13	Quebec	NHA	19	4	0	4	29	1	0	0	0	0
1913-14	Quebec	NHA	19	15	10	25	14	...	...	...	...	...
1914-15	Quebec	NHA	20	18	8	26	30	...	...	...	...	...
1915-16	Quebec	NHA	22	18	5	23	54	...	...	...	...	...
1916-17	Quebec	NHA	19	11	6	17	62	...	...	...	...	...
1917-18	Ottawa	NHL	12	2	0	2	12	...	...	...	...	...
	Toronto	NHL	7	1	0	1	17	2	2	1	3	0
1918-19	Toronto	NHL	18	7	3	10	51	...	...	...	...	...
1919-20	Saskatoon	SSHL	12	3	3	6	14	...	...	...	...	...
1920-21	Saskatoon	SSHL	14	11	7	18	12	4	2	2	4	4
1921-22	Saskatoon	WCHL	24	8	8	16	29	...	...	...	...	...
1922-23	Saskatoon	WCHL	19	7	6	13	10	...	...	...	...	...
	Calgary	WCHL	11	3	1	4	7	...	...	...	...	...
1923-24	Calgary	WCHL	26	4	4	8	21	7	1	1	2	6
1924-25	Calgary	WCHL	27	12	2	14	27	2	0	0	0	4
1925-26	Vancouver	WHL	14	0	0	0	8	...	...	...	...	...
1926-27	Minneapolis	AHA	32	2	3	5	51	6	3	0	3	13
1927-28	Minneapolis	AHA	34	4	2	6	27	8	3	0	3	10
1928-29	Minneapolis	AHA	40	9	3	12	33	4	0	0	0	0
1929-30	Minneapolis	AHA	45	3	4	7	32	...	...	...	...	...
	NHL Totals	**2**	**38**	**10**	**3**	**13**	**84**	**2**	**2**	**1**	**3**	**0**

JACK DARRAGH

Right wing. Shoots left. 5'10", 168 lbs., Born, Cornwall, Ont., December 4, 1890

			Regular Season					Playoffs				
Season	Club	League	GP	G	A	PTS	PIM	GP	G	A	PTS	PIM
1910-11	Ottawa	NHA	16	18	0	18	36	2	0	0	0	6
1911-12	Ottawa	NHA	17	15	0	15	10	...	...	...	...	...
1912-13	Ottawa	NHA	20	15	0	15	16	...	...	...	...	...
1913-14	Ottawa	NHA	20	23	5	28	69	...	...	...	...	...
1914-15	Ottawa	NHA	18	11	2	13	32	5	3	0	3	...
1915-16	Ottawa	NHA	21	16	5	21	41	...	...	...	...	...
1916-17	Ottawa	NHA	20	26	5	31	25	2	2	0	2	3
1917-18	Ottawa	NHL	18	14	0	14	29	...	...	...	...	...
1918-19	Ottawa	NHL	14	12	1	13	27	5	3	0	3	0
1919-20	Ottawa	NHL	22	22	5	27	22	5	5	2	7	3
1920-21	Ottawa	NHL	24	11	8	19	20	7	5	0	5	6
1921-22				Did Not Play								
1922-23	Ottawa	NHL	24	7	7	14	13	2	1	0	1	2
1923-24	Ottawa	NHL	18	2	0	2	2	2	0	0	0	2
	NHL Totals	**6**	**120**	**68**	**21**	**89**	**87**	**21**	**14**	**2**	**16**	**13**

ALLAN "SCOTTY" DAVIDSON

Right wing / defence. Shoots right. 6'1", 195 lbs., Born, Kingston, Ont., March 6, 1890

			Regular Season					Playoffs				
Season	Club	League	GP	G	A	PTS	PIM	GP	G	A	PTS	PIM
1912-13	Toronto	NHA	20	19	0	19	69	...	...	...	...	...
	Tor. Tecumsehs	NHA	...	...	...	...	...	2	0	0	0	0
1913-14	Toronto	NHA	20	23	13	36	64	2	0	2	11	...

CLARENCE "HAP" DAY

Defence / centre. Shoots right. 5'11", 190 lbs., Born, Owen Sound, Ont., June1, 1901

			Regular Season					Playoffs				
Season	Club	League	GP	G	A	PTS	PIM	GP	G	A	PTS	PIM
1922-23	Hamilton	OHA Sr.	11	4	11	15	...	2	0	0	0	...
1923-24	Hamilton	OHA Sr.	10	6	11	17	...	2	1	1	2	...
1924-25	Toronto	NHL	36	10	12	22	27	2	0	0	0	0
1925-26	Toronto	NHL	36	14	2	16	26	...	...	...	...	...
1926-27	Toronto	NHL	44	11	5	16	50	...	...	...	...	...
1927-28	Toronto	NHL	22	9	8	17	48	...	...	...	...	...
1928-29	Toronto	AHL	44	6	6	12	85	4	1	0	1	4
1929-30	Toronto	NHL	43	7	14	21	77	...	...	...	...	...
1930-31	Toronto	NHL	44	1	13	14	56	2	0	3	3	7
1931-32	Toronto	NHL	47	7	8	15	33	7	3	3	6	6
1932-33	Toronto	NHL	47	6	14	20	46	9	0	1	1	21
1933-34	Toronto	NHL	48	9	10	19	35	5	0	0	0	6
1934-35	Toronto	NHL	45	2	4	6	38	7	0	0	0	4
1935-36	Toronto	NHL	44	1	13	14	41	9	0	0	0	8
1936-37	Toronto	NHL	48	3	4	7	20	2	0	0	0	0
1937-38	NY Americans	NHL	43	0	3	3	14	6	0	0	0	0
	NHL Totals	**14**	**581**	**86**	**116**	**202**	**601**	**53**	**4**	**7**	**11**	**56**

ALEX DELVECCHIO

Centre. Shoots left. 6', 195 lbs., Born, Fort William, Ont., December 4, 1931

			Regular Season					Playoffs				
Season	Club	League	GP	G	A	PTS	PIM	GP	G	A	PTS	PIM
1946-47	Fort William	TBJHL	1	0	0	0	0	...	...	...	...	...
1948-49	Fort William	TBJHL	12	16	8	24	53	1	2	0	2	0
1949-50	Fort William	TBJHL	18	16	20	36	36	5	4	4	8	15
1950-51	Oshawa	OHA Jr.	54	49	72	121	36	...	...	...	...	...
	Detroit	NHL	1	0	0	0	0	...	...	...	...	...
1951-52	Indianapolis	AHL	6	3	6	9	4	...	...	...	...	...
	Detroit	NHL	65	15	22	37	22	8	0	3	3	4
1952-53	Detroit	NHL	70	16	43	59	28	6	2	4	6	2
1953-54	Detroit	NHL	69	11	18	29	34	12	2	7	9	7
1954-55	Detroit	NHL	69	17	31	48	37	11	7	8	15	2
1955-56	Detroit	NHL	70	25	26	51	24	10	7	3	10	2
1956-57	Detroit	NHL	48	16	25	41	8	5	3	2	5	2
1957-58	Detroit	NHL	70	21	38	59	22	4	0	1	1	0
1958-59	Detroit	NHL	70	19	35	54	6	...	...	...	...	...
1959-60	Detroit	NHL	70	19	28	47	8	6	2	6	8	0
1960-61	Detroit	NHL	70	27	35	62	26	11	4	5	9	0
1961-62	Detroit	NHL	70	26	43	69	18	...	...	...	...	...
1962-63	Detroit	NHL	70	20	44	64	8	11	3	6	9	2
1963-64	Detroit	NHL	70	23	30	53	11	14	3	8	11	0
1964-65	Detroit	NHL	68	25	42	67	16	7	2	3	5	4
1965-66	Detroit	NHL	70	31	38	69	16	12	0	11	11	4
1966-67	Detroit	NHL	70	17	38	55	10	...	...	...	...	...
1967-68	Detroit	NHL	74	22	48	70	14	...	...	...	...	...
1968-69	Detroit	NHL	72	25	58	83	8	...	...	...	...	...
1969-70	Detroit	NHL	73	21	47	68	24	4	0	2	2	0
1970-71	Detroit	NHL	77	21	34	55	6	...	...	...	...	...
1971-72	Detroit	NHL	75	20	45	65	22	...	...	...	...	..
1972-73	Detroit	NHL	77	18	53	71	13	...	...	...	...	...
1973-74	Detroit	NHL	11	1	4	5	2	...	...	...	...	...
	NHL Totals	**24**	**1549**	**456**	**825**	**1281**	**383**	**121**	**35**	**69**	**104**	**29**

CY DENNENY

Left wing. Shoots left. 5'7", 168 lbs., Born, Farrans Point, Ont., December 23, 1891

			Regular Season					Playoffs				
Season	Club	League	GP	G	A	PTS	PIM	GP	G	A	PTS	PIM
1914-15	Tor. Shamrocks	NHA	8	6	0	6	43	...	...	...	...	...
1915-16	Toronto	NHA	24	24	4	28	57	...	...	...	...	...
1916-17	Ottawa	NHA	10	3	1	4	25	2	1	0	1	8
1917-18	Ottawa	NHL	22	36	2	38	45	...	...	...	...	....
1918-19	Ottawa	NHL	18	18	4	22	43	5	2	0	2	0
1919-20	Ottawa	NHL	22	16	2	18	21	5	0	0	0	3
1920-21	Ottawa	NHL	24	34	5	39	0	7	4	2	6	20
1921-22	Ottawa	NHL	22	27	12	39	18	2	2	0	2	4
1922-23	Ottawa	NHL	24	21	10	31	20	8	3	1	4	6
1923-24	Ottawa	NHL	21	22	1	23	10	2	2	0	2	2
1924-25	Ottawa	NHL	28	27	15	42	16	...	...	...	...	...
1925-26	Ottawa	NHL	36	24	12	36	18	2	0	0	0	4
1926-27	Ottawa	NHL	42	17	6	23	16	6	5	0	5	0
1927-28	Ottawa	NHL	44	3	0	3	12	2	0	0	0	0
1928-29	Boston	NHL	23	1	2	3	2	3	0	0	0	0
	NHL Totals	**12**	**326**	**246**	**69**	**315**	**210**	**41**	**18**	**3**	**21**	**31**

MARCEL DIONNE

Centre. Shoots right. 5'8, 190 lbs., Born, Drummondville, Que., August 3, 1951

			Regular Season					Playoffs				
Season	Club	League	GP	G	A	PTS	PIM	GP	G	A	PTS	PIM
1969-70	St. Catharines	OHA Jr.	54	55	77	132	46	...	...	...	...	...
1970-71	St. Catharines	OHA Jr.	46	62	81	143	20	...	...	...	...	...
1971-72	Detroit	NHL	78	28	49	77	14	...	...	...	...	...
1972-73	Detroit	NHL	77	40	50	90	21	...	...	...	...	...
1973-74	Detroit	NHL	74	24	54	78	10	...	...	...	...	...
1974-75	Detroit	NHL	80	47	74	121	14	...	...	...	...	...
1975-76	Los Angeles	NHL	80	40	54	94	38	9	6	1	7	0
1976-77	Los Angeles	NHL	80	53	69	122	12	9	5	9	14	2
1977-78	Los Angeles	NHL	70	36	43	79	37	2	0	0	0	0
1978-79	Los Angeles	NHL	80	59	71	130	30	2	0	1	1	0
1979-80	Los Angeles	NHL	80	53	84	137	32	4	0	3	3	4
1980-81	Los Angeles	NHL	80	58	77	135	70	4	1	3	4	7
1981-82	Los Angeles	NHL	78	50	67	117	50	10	7	4	11	0
1982-83	Los Angeles	NHL	80	56	51	107	22	...	...	...	...	...
1983-84	Los Angeles	NHL	66	39	53	92	28	...	...	...	...	...
1984-85	Los Angeles	NHL	80	46	80	126	46	3	1	2	3	2
1985-86	Los Angeles	NHL	80	36	58	94	42	...	...	...	...	...
1986-87	Los Angeles	NHL	67	24	50	74	54	...	...	...	...	...
	NY Rangers	NHL	14	4	6	10	6	6	1	1	2	2
1987-88	NY Rangers	NHL	67	31	34	65	54	...	...	...	...	...
1988-89	NY Rangers	NHL	37	7	16	23	20	...	...	...	...	...
	Denver	IHL	9	0	13	13	6	...	...	...	...	...
	NHL Totals	**18**	**1348**	**731**	**1040**	**1771**	**600**	**49**	**21**	**24**	**45**	**17**

GORDIE DRILLON

Right wing. Shoots right. 6', 185 lbs., Born, Moncton, N.B., October 23, 1914

			Regular Season					Playoffs				
Season	Club	League	GP	G	A	PTS	PIM	GP	G	A	PTS	PIM
1930-31	Moncton	MJHL	6	14	4	18	...	1	...	...	......	...
	Moncton	NBIHL	3	1	0	1	...	1	1	0	1	...
1931-32	Moncton	MJHL	6	6	4	10	...	3	5	1	6	5
1932-33	Moncton	MJHL	4	13	3	16	0	2	2	1	3	4
	Moncton	MIHL	7	11	3	14	...	6	13	4	17	...
1933-34	Tor. Rangers	OHA Jr.	11	20	13	33	4	2	5	3	8	4
1934-35	Tor. Lions	OHA Jr.	11	17	9	26	2	5	2	1	3	6
	Tor. Dominions	Sr.	11	12	6	18	2	3	2	1	3	4
1935-36	Pittsburgh	IAHL	40	22	12	34	4	8	3	2	5	0
1936-37	Syracuse	AHL	5	2	3	5	0	...	...	...	...	...
	Toronto	NHL	41	16	17	33	2	2	0	0	0	0
1937-38	Toronto	NHL	48	26	26	52	4	7	7	1	8	2
1938-39	Toronto	NHL	40	18	16	34	15	10	7	6	13	4
1939-40	Toronto	NHL	43	21	19	40	13	10	3	1	4	0
1940-41	Toronto	NHL	42	23	21	44	2	7	3	2	5	2
1941-42	Toronto	NHL	48	23	18	41	6	9	2	3	5	2
1942-43	Montreal	NHL	49	28	22	50	14	5	4	2	6	0
	NHL Totals	**7**	**311**	**155**	**139**	**294**	**56**	**50**	**26**	**15**	**41**	**10**

GRAHAM DRINKWATER

Rover. Shoots right. 5'11", 165 lbs., Born, Montreal, Que., February 22, 1875

			Regular Season					Playoffs				
Season	Club	League	GP	G	A	PTS	PIM	GP	G	A	PTS	PIM
1892-93	Mtl. Victorias	AHA	3	1	0	1	...	...	...	...	...	...
1893-94				Not Available		...	...	...	...	...	...	...
1894-95	Mtl. Victorias	AHA	8	9	0	9	...	...	...	...	...	...
1895-96	Mtl. Victorias	AHA	8	7	0	7	...	1	1	0	1	...
1896-97	Mtl. Victorias	AHA	4	3	0	3	...	1	0	0	0	...
1897-98	Mtl. Victorias	AHA	8	10	0	10	...	...	...	...	...	...
1899-1900	Mtl. Victorias	CAHL	6	0	0	0	...	2	1	0	1	...

KEN DRYDEN

Goaltender. Catches left. 6'4", 210 lbs., Born, Hamilton, Ont., August 8, 1947

			Regular Season								Playoffs							
Season	Club	League	GP	MIN	GA	SO	GAA	W	L	T	GP	MIN	GA	SO	GAA	W	L	T
1970-71	Montreal	AHL	33	1899	84	3	2.68	....	....	....	....	....	....	....	....	....	....	....
	Montreal	NHL	6	327	9	0	1.65	6	0	0	20	1221	61	0	3.00	12	8	....
1971-72	Montreal	NHL	64	3800	142	8	2.24	39	8	15	6	360	17	0	2.83	2	4	....
1972-73	Montreal	NHL	54	3165	119	6	2.25	33	7	13	17	1039	50	1	2.89	12	5	....
1973-74				Did Not Play														
1974-75	Montreal	NHL	56	3320	149	4	2.69	30	9	16	11	688	29	2	2.53	6	5	....
1975-76	Montreal	NHL	62	3580	121	8	2.03	42	10	8	13	780	25	1	1.92	12	1	....
1976-77	Montreal	NHL	56	3275	117	10	2.14	41	6	8	14	849	22	4	1.56	12	2	....
1977-78	Montreal	NHL	52	3071	105	5	2.05	37	7	7	15	919	29	2	1.89	12	3	....
1978-79	Montreal	NHL	47	2814	108	5	2.30	30	10	7	16	990	41	0	2.48	12	4	....
	NHL Totals	**8**	**397**	**23352**	**870**	**46**	**2.24**	**258**	**57**	**74**	**112**	**6846**	**274**	**10**	**2.40**	**80**	**32**	**....**

WOODY DUMART

Left wing. Shoots left. 6 1", 200 lbs., Born, Kitchener, Ont., December 23, 1916

			Regular Season					Playoffs				
Season	Club	League	GP	G	A	PTS	PIM	GP	G	A	PTS	PIM
1933-34	Kitch-Waterloo	OHA Jr.	12	8	3	11	12	3	1	3	4	0
1934-35	Kitch-Waterloo	OHA Jr.	17	17	11	28	10	3	3	1	4	2
1935-36	Boston	NHL	1	0	0	0	0	...	...	...	...	...
	Boston	CAHL	46	11	10	21	15	...	...	...	...	...
1936-37	Boston	NHL	17	4	4	8	2	3	0	0	0	0
	Providence	IAHL	32	4	7	11	10	...	...	...	...	...
1937-38	Boston	NHL	48	13	14	27	6	3	0	0	0	0
1938-39	Boston	NHL	46	14	15	29	2	12	1	3	4	6
1939-40	Boston	NHL	48	22	21	43	16	6	1	0	1	0
1940-41	Boston	NHL	40	18	15	33	2	11	1	3	4	9
1941-42	Boston	NHL	35	14	15	29	8	...	...	...	...	...
	Ottawa RCAF	Sr.	...	...	...	...	...	...	7	5	12	2
1942-43			Military Service									
1943-44			Military Service									
1944-45			Military Service									
1945-46	Boston	NHL	50	22	12	34	2	10	4	3	7	0
1946-47	Boston	NHL	60	24	28	52	12	5	1	1	2	8
1947-48	Boston	NHL	59	21	16	37	14	5	0	0	0	0
1948-49	Boston	NHL	59	11	12	23	6	5	3	0	3	0
1949-50	Boston	NHL	69	14	25	39	14	...	...	...	...	...
1950-51	Boston	NHL	70	20	21	41	7	6	1	2	3	0
1951-52	Boston	NHL	39	5	8	13	0	7	0	1	1	0
1952-53	Boston	NHL	62	5	9	14	2	11	0	2	2	0
1953-54	Boston	NHL	69	4	3	7	6	4	0	0	0	0
1954-55	Providence	AHL	15	2	2	4	0	...	...	...	...	...
	NHL Totals	**16**	**771**	**211**	**218**	**429**	**99**	**82**	**12**	**15**	**27**	**23**

TOMMY DUNDERDALE

Centre. Shoots right. 5'8", 160 lbs., Born, Benella, Australia, May 6, 1887

			Regular Season					Playoffs				
Season	Club	League	GP	G	A	PTS	PIM	GP	G	A	PTS	PIM
1906-07	Strathconas	MHL Sr.	10	8	0	8	...	...	...	...	...	...
1907-08	Maple Leafs	MHL Sr.	3	1	0	1	...	...	...	...	...	...
1908-09	Shamrocks	MHL Sr.	5	14	0	14	...	...	...	...	...	...
1909-10	Mtl. Shamrocks	CHA	3	7	0	7	5	...	...	...	...	...
	Mtl. Shamrocks	NHA	12	14	0	14	19	...	...	...	...	...
1910-11	Quebec	NHA	9	13	0	13	25	...	...	...	...	...
1911-12	Victoria	PCHA	16	24	0	24	25	...	...	...	...	...
1912-13	Victoria	PCHA	15	24	5	29	36	3	3	0	3	...
1913-14	Victoria	PCHA	16	24	4	28	34	3	2	0	2	...
1914-15	Victoria	PCHA	17	17	10	27	22	...	...	...	...	...
1915-16	Portland	PCHA	18	14	3	17	45	5	1	1	2	3
1916-17	Portland	PCHA	24	22	4	26	141	...	...	...	...	...
1917-18	Portland	PCHA	18	14	6	20	57	...	...	...	...	...
1918-19	Victoria	PCHA	20	5	4	9	28	...	...	...	...	...
1919-20	Victoria	PCHA	22	26	7	33	35	...	...	...	...	...
1920-21	Victoria	PCHA	24	9	11	20	18	...	...	...	...	...
1921-22	Victoria	PCHA	24	13	6	19	37	...	...	...	...	...
1922-23	Victoria	PCHA	27	2	0	2	16	...	...	...	...	...
1923-24	Saskatoon	WCHL	6	1	0	1	4	...	...	...	...	...
	Edmonton	WCHL	11	1	1	2	5	...	...	...	...	...

BILL DURNAN

Goaltender. Catches both. 6', 185 lbs., Born, Toronto, Ont., Born, January 22, 1915

			Regular Season								Playoffs							
Season	Club	League	GP	MIN	GA	SO	GAA	W	L	T	GP	MIN	GA	SO	GAA	W	L	T
1931-32	N. Toronto	Jr.	8	480	17	1	2.12	....	....	....	4	240	10	1	2.50	....	....	0
1932-33	Sudbury	NOHA	....	....	....	...	....	....	....	....	....	....	....	....	....	....	....	....
	Sudbury	NOHA	6	360	6	2	1.00	....	....	....	2	120	4	0	2.00	....	....	....
1933-34	Sudbury	NOHA	....	....	....	....	....	....	....	....	....	....	....	....	....	....	....	....
	Toronto	OHA Jr.	11	660	21	4	1.91	....	....	....	1	60	5	0	5.00	0	1	....
1934-35	Toronto	OHA Sr.	2	120	9	0	4.50	....	....	....	....	....	....	....	....	....	....	....
	Tor. McColl	Sr.	15	900	62	0	4.13	....	....	....	....	....	....	....	....	....	....	....
1935-36	Tor. Dominions	Sr.	1	60	6	0	6.00	....	....	....	....	....	....	....	....	....	....	....
1936-37	Lakeshore	NOHA	....	....	....	....	....	....	....	....	....	....	....	....	....	....	....	.....
1938-39	Lakeshore	NOHA	....	....	....	....	....	....	....	....	....	....	....	....	....	....	....	....
1939-40	Lakeshore	NOHA	....	....	....	....	....	....	....	....	....	....	....	....	....	....	....	....
1940-41	Montreal	QSHL	34	2000	100	1	3.00	....	....	....	8	480	24	1	3.00	....	....	....
1941-42	Montreal	QSHL	39	2340	143	0	3.67	....	....	....	....	....	....	....	....	....	....	....
1942-43	Montreal	QSHL	31	1860	130	0	4.19	....	....	....	4	240	11	0	2.75	....	....	....
1943-44	Montreal	NHL	50	3000	109	2	2.18	38	5	7	9	549	14	1	1.53	8	1	....
1944-45	Montreal	NHL	50	3000	121	1	2.42	38	8	4	6	373	15	0	2.41	2	4	....
1945-46	Montreal	NHL	40	2400	104	4	2.60	24	11	5	9	581	20	0	2.07	8	1	....
1946-47	Montreal	NHL	60	3600	138	4	2.30	34	16	10	11	700	23	1	1.97	6	5	....
1947-48	Montreal	NHL	59	3505	162	5	2.77	20	28	10	....	....	....	....	....	....		....
1948-49	Montreal	NHL	60	3600	126	10	2.10	28	23	9	7	468	17	0	2.18	3	4	....
1949-50	Montreal	NHL	64	3840	141	8	2.20	26	21	17	3	180	10	0	3.33	0	3	....
	NHL Totals	**7**	**383**	**22945**	**901**	**34**	**2.36**	**208**	**112**	**62**	**45**	**2851**	**99**	**2**	**2.08**	**27**	**18**	....

MERVYN "RED" DUTTON

Defence. Shoots right. 6', 185 lbs., Born, Russell, Man., July 23, 1898

			Regular Season					Playoffs				
Season	Club	League	GP	G	A	PTS	PIM	GP	G	A	PTS	PIM
1919-20	Winnipeg	MHL Sr.	8	6	7	13	10	2	0	0	0	6
1920-21	Calagry	Big 4	15	5	3	8	38	...	...	...	...	...
1921-22	Calagry	WCHL	22	16	5	21	73	2	0	0	0	0
1922-23	Calagry	WCHL	18	2	4	6	24	...	...	...	...	...
1923-24	Calagry	WCHL	30	6	7	13	54	7	1	1	2	7
1924-25	Calagry	WCHL	23	8	4	12	72	2	0	0	0	6
1925-26	Calagry	WHL	30	10	5	15	87	...	...	...	...	...
1926-27	Mtl Maroons	NHL	43	4	4	8	108	2	0	0	0	4
1927-28	Mtl Maroons	NHL	42	7	6	13	94	9	1	0	1	29
1928-29	Mtl Maroons	NHL	44	1	3	4	139	...	...	...	...	...
1929-30	Mtl Maroons	NHL	44	3	13	16	98	4	0	0	0	4
1930-31	NY Americans	NHL	44	1	11	12	71	...	...	...	...	...
1931-32	NY Americans	NHL	47	3	5	8	107	...	...	...	...	...
1932-33	NY Americans	NHL	42	0	2	2	74	...	...	...	...	...
1933-34	NY Americans	NHL	48	2	8	10	65	...	...	...	...	...
1934-35	NY Americans	NHL	48	3	7	10	46	...	...	...	...	...
1935-36	NY Americans	NHL	46	5	8	13	69	3	0	0	0	0
	NHL Totals	**10**	**449**	**29**	**67**	**96**	**871**	**18**	**1**	**0**	**1**	**33**

CECIL "BABE" DYE

Right wing. Shoots right. 5'8", 150 lbs., Born, Hamilton, Ont., May 13, 1898

			Regular Season					Playoffs				
Season	Club	League	GP	G	A	PTS	PIM	GP	G	A	PTS	PIM
1919-20	Toronto	NHL	21	12	3	15	10	...	...	...	...	...
1920-21	Hamilton	NHL	1	2	0	2	0	...	...	...	...	...
	Toronto	NHL	23	33	2	35	32	2	0	0	0	9
1921-22	Toronto	NHL	24	30	7	37	18	7	11	2	13	5
1922-23	Toronto	NHL	22	26	11	37	19	...	...	...	...	...
1923-24	Toronto	NHL	19	17	2	19	23	...	...	...	...	...
1924-25	Toronto	NHL	29	38	6	44	41	2	0	0	0	0
1925-26	Toronto	NHL	31	18	5	23	26	...	...	...	...	...
1926-27	Chicago	NHL	41	25	5	30	14	2	0	0	0	2
1927-28	Chicago	NHL	10	0	0	0	0	...	...	...	...	...
1928-29	NY Americans	NHL	42	1	0	1	17	1	0	0	0	0
1929-30	New Haven	CAHL	34	11	4	15	16	...	...	...	...	...
1930-31	Toronto	NHL	6	0	0	0	0	...	...	...	...	...
	NHL Totals	**11**	**269**	**202**	**41**	**243**	**200**	**15**	**11**	**2**	**13**	**18**

PHIL ESPOSITO

Centre. Shoots left. 6'1", 205 lbs., Born, Sault Saint Marie, Ont., February 20, 1942

			Regular Season					Playoffs				
Season	Club	League	GP	G	A	PTS	PIM	GP	G	A	PTS	PIM
1961-62	St. Catharines	OHA Jr.	49	32	39	71	54	6	1	4	5	9
	S. S. Marie	EPHL	6	0	3	3	2	...	...	...	...	...
1962-63	St. Louis	EPHL	71	36	54	90	51	...	...	...	...	...
1963-64	St. Louis	CHL	43	26	54	80	65	...	...	...	...	...
	Chicago	NHL	27	3	2	5	2	4	0	0	0	0
1964-65	Chicago	NHL	70	23	32	55	44	13	3	3	6	15
1965-66	Chicago	NHL	69	27	26	53	49	6	1	1	2	2
1966-67	Chicago	NHL	69	21	40	61	40	6	0	0	0	7
1967-68	Boston	NHL	74	35	49	84	21	4	0	3	3	0
1968-69	Boston	NHL	74	49	77	126	79	10	8	10	18	8
1969-70	Boston	NHL	76	43	56	99	50	14	13	14	27	16
1970-71	Boston	NHL	78	76	76	152	71	7	3	7	10	6
1971-72	Boston	NHL	76	66	67	133	76	15	9	15	24	24
1972-73	Boston	NHL	78	55	75	130	87	2	0	1	1	2
1973-74	Boston	NHL	78	68	77	145	58	16	9	5	14	25
1974-75	Boston	NHL	79	61	66	127	62	3	4	1	5	0
1975-76	Boston	NHL	12	6	10	16	8	...	...	...	...	...
	NY Rangers	NHL	62	29	38	67	28	...	...	...	...	...
1976-77	NY Rangers	NHL	80	34	46	80	52	...	...	...	...	...
1977-78	NY Rangers	NHL	79	38	43	81	53	3	0	1	1	5
1978-79	NY Rangers	NHL	80	42	36	78	37	18	8	12	20	20
1979-80	NY Rangers	NHL	80	34	44	78	73	9	3	3	6	8
1980-81	NY Rangers	NHL	41	7	13	20	20	...	...	...	...	...
	NHL Totals	**18**	**1282**	**717**	**873**	**1590**	**910**	**130**	**61**	**76**	**137**	**137**

TONY ESPOSITO

Goaltender. Catches right. 5'11", 185 lbs., Born, Sault Ste. Marie, Ont. Born, April 23, 1943

			Regular Season								Playoffs							
Season	Club	League	GP	MIN	GA	SO	GAA	W	L	T	GP	MIN	GA	SO	GAA	W	L	T
1964-65	Michigan Tech.	WCHA	17	1020	40	1	2.35	....	....	....	....	....	....	....	....	....	....	....
1965-66	Michigan Tech.	WCHA	19	1140	51	1	2.68	....	....	....	....	....	....	....	....	....	....	....
1966-67	Michigan Tech.	WCHA	15	900	39	0	2.60	....	....	....	....	....	....	....	....	....	....	....
1967-68	Vancouver	WHL	63	3734	199	4	3.20	....	....	....	....	....	....	....	....	....	....	....
1968-69	Montreal	NHL	13	746	34	2	2.73	5	4	4		....	....	....	....	....	....	...
	Houston	CHL	19	1139	46	1	2.42	....	....	....	1	59	3	0	3.00	0	1	....
1969-70	Chicago	NHL	63	3763	136	15	2.17	38	17	8	8	480	27	0	3.37	4	4	....
1970-71	Chicago	NHL	57	3325	126	6	2.27	35	14	7	18	1151	42	2	2.19	11	7	....
1971-72	Chicago	NHL	48	2780	82	9	1.76	31	10	6	5	300	16	0	3.20	2	3	....
1972-73	Chicago	NHL	56	3340	140	4	2.51	32	17	7	15	895	46	1	3.08	10	5	....
1973-74	Chicago	NHL	70	4143	141	10	2.04	34	14	21	10	584	28	2	2.88	6	4	....
1974-75	Chicago	NHL	71	4219	193	6	2.74	34	30	7	8	472	34	0	4.32	3	5	....
1975-76	Chicago	NHL	68	4003	198	4	2.97	30	23	13	4	240	13	0	3.25	0	4	....
1976-77	Chicago	NHL	69	4067	234	2	3.45	25	36	8	2	120	6	0	3.00	0	2	....
1977-78	Chicago	NHL	64	3840	168	5	2.63	28	22	14	4	252	19	0	4.52	0	4	....
1978-79	Chicago	NHL	63	3780	206	4	3.27	24	28	11	4	243	14	0	3.46	0	4	....
1979-80	Chicago	NHL	69	4140	205	6	2.97	31	22	16	6	373	14	0	2.25	3	3	....
1980-81	Chicago	NHL	66	3935	246	0	3.75	29	24	13	3	215	15	0	4.19	0	3	....
1981-82	Chicago	NHL	52	3069	231	1	4.52	19	25	8	7	381	16	1	2.52	3	3	....
1982-83	Chicago	NHL	39	2340	135	1	3.46	23	11	5	5	311	18	0	3.47	3	2	....
1983-84	Chicago	NHL	18	1095	88	1	4.82	5	10	3	....	....	....	....	....	....	....	....
	NHL Totals	**16**	**886**	**52585**	**2563**	**76**	**2.92**	**423**	**307**	**151**	**99**	**6017**	**308**	**6**	**3.07**	**45**	**53**	....

ART FARRELL

Forward. Born, Montreal, Que., February 8, 1877

			Regular Season					Playoffs				
Season	Club	League	GP	G	A	PTS	PIM	GP	G	A	PTS	PIM
1896-97	Mtl. Shamrocks	AHA	2	2	0	2	...	...	...	...	...	...
1898-99	Mtl. Shamrocks	CAHL	8	8	0	8	...	1	2	0	2	...
1899-1900	Mtl. Shamrocks	CAHL	8	9	0	9	...	5	10	0	10	...
1900-01	Mtl. Shamrocks	CAHL	8	10	0	10	...	2	1	0	1	...

FERNIE FLAMAN

Defence. Shoots right. 5'10", 190. Born, Dysart, Sask., January 25, 1927

			Regular Season					Playoffs				
Season	Club	League	GP	G	A	PTS	PIM	GP	G	A	PTS	PIM
1942-43	Regina Abbotts	MHL Jr.	1	0	0	0	0	...	...	...	...	...
1943-44	Boston	EHL	31	11	9	20	...	...	...	...	...	...
1944-45	Boston	EHL	Not Available			...	...	...	...	...	...	...
	Boston	NHL	1	0	0	0	0	...	...	...	...	...
1945-46	Boston	EHL	45	11	23	34	80	12	2	7	9	11
	Boston	NHL	1	0	0	0	0	...	...	...	...	...
1946-47	Hershey	AHL	38	4	8	12	64	...	...	...	...	...
	Boston	NHL	23	1	4	5	41	5	0	0	0	8
1947-48	Boston	NHL	56	4	6	10	69	5	0	0	0	12
1948-49	Boston	NHL	60	4	12	16	62	5	0	1	1	8
1949-50	Boston	NHL	69	2	5	7	122	...	...	...	...	...
1950-51	Boston	NHL	14	1	1	2	37	...	...	...	...	...
	Toronto	NHL	39	2	6	8	64	9	1	0	1	8
	Pittsburgh	AHL	11	1	6	7	24	...	...	...	...	...
1951-52	Toronto	NHL	61	0	7	7	110	4	0	2	2	18
1952-53	Toronto	NHL	66	2	6	8	110	...	...	...	...	...
1953-54	Toronto	NHL	62	0	8	8	84	2	0	0	0	0
1954-55	Boston	NHL	70	4	14	18	150	4	1	0	1	2
1955-56	Boston	NHL	62	4	17	21	70	...	...	...	...	...
1956-57	Boston	NHL	68	6	25	31	108	10	0	3	3	19
1957-58	Boston	NHL	66	0	15	15	71	12	2	2	4	10
1958-59	Boston	NHL	70	0	21	21	101	7	0	0	0	8
1959-60	Boston	NHL	60	2	18	20	112	...	...	...	...	...
1960-61	Boston	NHL	62	2	9	11	59	...	...	...	...	...
1961-62	Providence	AHL	65	3	33	36	95	3	0	1	1	6
1962-63	Providence	AHL	68	4	17	21	65	6	0	2	2	0
1963-64	Providence	AHL	22	1	5	6	21	3	0	1	1	4
	NHL Totals	**17**	**910**	**34**	**174**	**208**	**1370**	**63**	**4**	**8**	**12**	**93**

FRANK FOYSTON

Centre / right wing. Shoots left. 5'9", 158 lbs., Born, Minesing, Ont., February 2, 1893

			Regular Season					Playoffs				
Season	Club	League	GP	G	A	PTS	PIM	GP	G	A	PTS	PIM
1912-13	Toronto	NHA	16	8	0	8	8	...	...	...	...	...
1913-14	Toronto	NHA	19	16	2	18	8	2	1	0	1	0
1914-15	Toronto	NHA	20	13	9	22	11	...	...	...	...	...
1915-16	Toronto	NHA	1	0	0	0	0	...	...	...	...	...
	Seattle	PCHA	18	9	4	13	6	...	...	...	...	...
1916-17	Seattle	PCHA	24	36	12	48	51	4	7	2	9	3
1917-18	Seattle	PCHA	13	9	5	14	9	2	0	0	0	3
1918-19	Seattle	PCHA	18	15	4	19	0	7	12	1	13	0
1919-20	Seattle	PCHA	22	26	3	29	3	7	9	2	11	0
1920-21	Seattle	PCHA	23	26	4	30	10	2	1	0	1	0
1921-22	Seattle	PCHA	24	16	7	23	25	2	0	0	0	3
1922-23	Seattle	PCHA	30	20	8	28	21	...	...	...	...	...
1923-24	Seattle	WCHL	30	17	6	23	8	2	1	0	1	0
1924-25	Victoria	WCHL	27	6	5	11	6	8	2	1	3	2
1925-26	Victoria	WHL	12	6	3	9	8	8	3	0	3	8
1926-27	Detroit	NHL	42	10	5	15	16	...	...	...	...	...
1927-28	Detroit	NHL	24	7	2	9	16	...	...	...	...	...
	Detroit	CAHL	19	3	2	5	14	...	...	...	...	...
1928-29	Detroit	CAHL	42	18	6	24	20	7	0	0	0	9
1929-30	Detroit	IAHL	31	2	1	3	6	3	0	0	0	0
	NHL Totals	**2**	**64**	**17**	**7**	**24**	**32**	**....**	**....**	**....**	**....**	**....**

FRANK FREDRICKSON

Centre. Shoots left. 5'11", 180 lbs., Born, Winnipeg, Man., June 11, 1895

			Regular Season					Playoffs				
Season	Club	League	GP	G	A	PTS	PIM	GP	G	A	PTS	PIM
1913-14	Wpg. Falcons	MHL Sr.	11	13	...	13	...	...	...	...	...	...
1914-15	Wpg. Falcons	MHL Sr.	8	10	...	10	...	1	1	...	2	...
1915-16	Wpg. Falcons	MHL Sr.	6	13	3	16	14	...	...	...	...	...
1916-17	Wpg. Falcons	MHL Sr.	8	17	3	20	40	...	...	...	...	...
1919-20	Wpg. Falcons	MHL Sr.	9	22	5	27	12	2	11	1	12	0
1920-21	Victoria	PCHA	21	20	12	32	3	...	...	...	...	...
1921-22	Victoria	PCHA	24	15	10	25	23	...	...	...	...	...
1922-23	Victoria	PCHA	30	39	16	55	26	2	2	0	2	4
1923-24	Victoria	PCHA	30	19	8	27	28	...	...	...	...	...
1924-25	Victoria	WCHL	28	22	8	30	43	8	6	3	9	8
1925-26	Victoria	WHL	30	16	8	24	89	8	2	3	5	16
1926-27	Detroit	NHL	16	4	6	10	12	...	...	...	...	...
	Boston	NHL	28	14	7	21	33	8	2	4	6	20
1927-28	Boston	NHL	41	10	4	14	83	2	0	1	1	4
1928-29	Boston	NHL	12	3	1	4	24	...	...	...	...	...
	Pittsburgh	NHL	31	3	7	10	28	...	...	...	...	...
1929-30	Pittsburgh	NHL	9	4	7	11	20	...	...	...	...	...
1930-31	Detroit	NHL	24	1	2	3	6	...	...	...	...	...
	Detroit	IHL	6	0	1	1	2	...	...	...	...	...
	NHL Totals	**5**	**165**	**37**	**36**	**73**	**206**	**10**	**2**	**5**	**7**	**26**

BILL GADSBY

Defence. Shoots left. 6', 185 lbs., Born, Calgary, Alta., August 8, 1927

			Regular Season					Playoffs				
Season	Club	League	GP	G	A	PTS	PIM	GP	G	A	PTS	PIM
1943-44	Calgary	Int.	9	4	1	5	4	...	...	...	...	...
1944-45	Edmonton	Jr.	Not Available...			...	...	...	...	...	...	
1945-46	Edmonton	Jr.	...	14	12	26	...	...	...	...	...	...
1946-47	Kansas City	USHL	12	2	3	5	8	...	...	...	...	...
	Chicago	NHL	48	8	10	18	31	...	...	...	...	...
1947-48	Chicago	NHL	60	6	10	16	66	...	...	...	...	...
1948-49	Chicago	NHL	50	3	10	13	85	...	...	...	...	...
1949-50	Chicago	NHL	70	10	24	34	138	...	...	...	...	...
1950-51	Chicago	NHL	25	3	7	10	32	...	...	...	...	...
1951-52	Chicago	NHL	59	7	15	22	87	...	...	...	...	...
1952-53	Chicago	NHL	68	2	20	22	84	7	0	1	1	4
1953-54	Chicago	NHL	70	12	29	41	108	...	...	...	...	...
1954-55	Chicago	NHL	18	3	5	8	17	...	...	...	...	...
	NY Rangers	NHL	52	8	8	16	44	...	...	...	...	...
1955-56	NY Rangers	NHL	70	9	42	51	84	5	1	3	4	4
1956-57	NY Rangers	NHL	70	4	37	41	72	5	1	2	3	2
1957-58	NY Rangers	NHL	65	14	32	46	48	6	0	3	3	4
1958-59	NY Rangers	NHL	70	5	46	51	56	...	...	...	...	...
1959-60	NY Rangers	NHL	65	9	22	31	60	...	...	...	...	...
1960-61	NY Rangers	NHL	65	9	26	35	49	...	...	...	...	...
1961-62	Detroit	NHL	70	7	30	37	88	...	...	...	...	...
1962-63	Detroit	NHL	70	4	24	28	116	11	1	4	5	36
1963-64	Detroit	NHL	64	2	16	18	80	14	0	4	4	22
1964-65	Detroit	NHL	61	0	12	12	122	7	0	3	3	8
1965-66	Detroit	NHL	58	8	12	17	72	12	1	3	4	12
	NHL Totals	**20**	**1248**	**130**	**437**	**567**	**1539**	**67**	**4**	**23**	**27**	**92**

BOB GAINEY

Left wing. Shoots left. 6'2", 200 lbs., Born, Peterborough, Ont., December 13, 1953

			Regular Season					Playoffs				
Season	Club	League	GP	G	A	PTS	PIM	GP	G	A	PTS	PIM
1970-71	Peterborough	OHA Jr.	4	0	0	0	0	...	...	...	...	...
1971-72	Peterborough	OHA Jr.	4	2	1	3	33	...	...	...	...	...
1972-73	Peterborough	OHA Jr.	52	22	21	43	99	...	...	...	...	...
1973-74	Nova Scotia	AHL	6	2	5	7	4	...	...	...	...	...
	Montreal	NHL	66	3	7	10	34	6	0	0	0	6
1974-75	Montreal	NHL	80	17	20	37	49	11	2	4	6	4
1975-76	Montreal	NHL	78	15	13	28	57	13	1	3	4	20
1976-77	Montreal	NHL	80	14	19	33	41	14	4	1	5	25
1977-78	Montreal	NHL	66	15	16	31	57	15	2	7	9	14
1978-79	Montreal	NHL	79	20	18	38	44	16	6	10	16	10
1979-80	Montreal	NHL	64	14	19	33	32	10	1	1	2	4
1980-81	Montreal	NHL	78	23	24	47	36	3	0	0	0	2
1981-82	Montreal	NHL	79	21	24	45	24	5	0	1	1	8
1982-83	Montreal	NHL	80	12	18	30	43	3	0	0	0	4
1983-84	Montreal	NHL	77	17	22	39	41	15	1	5	6	9
1984-85	Montreal	NHL	79	19	13	32	40	12	1	3	4	13
1985-86	Montreal	NHL	80	20	23	43	20	20	5	5	10	12
1986-87	Montreal	NHL	47	8	8	16	19	17	1	3	4	6
1987-88	Montreal	NHL	78	11	11	22	14	6	0	1	1	6
1988-89	Montreal	NHL	49	10	7	17	34	16	1	4	5	8
	NHL Totals	**16**	**1160**	**239**	**262**	**501**	**585**	**182**	**25**	**48**	**73**	**151**

CHARLIE "CHUCK" GARDINER

Goaltender. 5'8", 175 lbs., Born, Edinburgh, Scotland, December 31, 1904

			Regular Season								Playoffs							
Season	Club	League	GP	MIN	GA	SO	GAA	W	L	T	GP	MIN	GA	SO	GAA	W	L	T
1923-24	Winnipeg	MHL Sr.	1	60	0	1	0.00	1	0	0	....	....	....	....	....	....	....	....
1924-25	Selkirk	MHL Sr.	18	1080	33	2	1.83	....	....	....	2	120	6	0	3.00	0	2	....
1925-26	Winnipeg	MHL Sr.	38	2280	82	6	2.16	....	....	....	5	300	10	1	2.00	....	....	....
1926-27	Winnipeg	AHA	36	2203	77	6	2.14	17	14	5	3	180	8	0	2.67	0	3	...
1927-28	Chicago	NHL	40	2420	114	3	2.83	6	32	2	....	....	....	....	....	....	....	....
1928-29	Chicago	NHL	44	2758	85	5	1.85	7	29	8	....	....	....	....	....	....	....	....
1929-30	Chicago	NHL	44	2750	111	3	2.42	21	18	5	2	172	3	0	1.04	0	1	1
1930-31	Chicago	NHL	44	2710	78	12	1.73	24	17	3	9	638	14	2	1.32	5	3	1
1931-32	Chicago	NHL	48	2989	92	4	1.85	18	19	11	2	120	6	1	3.00	....	....	0
1932-33	Chicago	NHL	48	3010	101	5	2.01	16	20	12	....	....	....	....	....	....	....	....
1933-34	Chicago	NHL	48	3050	83	10	1.63	20	17	11	8	602	12	2	1.20	6	1	1
	NHL Totals	**7**	**316**	**19687**	**664**	**42**	**2.02**	**112**	**152**	**52**	**21**	**1532**	**35**	**5**	**1.37**	**12**	**6**	**3**

HERB GARDINER

Defence. Shoots left. 5'10", 190 lbs., Born, Winnipeg, Man., May 8, 1891

			Regular Season					Playoffs				
Season	Club	League	GP	G	A	PTS	PIM	GP	G	A	PTS	PIM
1919-20	Calgary	Big 4	12	8	9	17	6	2	0	0	0	2
1920-21	Calgary	Big 4	13	3	7	10	6	...	...	...	...	...
1921-22	Calagry	WCHL	24	4	1	5	6	...	2	0	0	0
1922-23	Calagry	WCHL	29	9	3	12	9	...	...	...	...	...
1923-24	Calagry	WCHL	22	5	5	10	4	7	3	1	4	0
1924-25	Calagry	WCHL	28	12	8	20	18	20	0	0	0	0
1925-26	Calagry	WHL	27	3	1	4	10	...	...	...	...	...
1926-27	Montreal	NHL	44	6	6	12	26	4	0	0	0	6
1927-28	Montreal	NHL	44	4	3	7	26	2	0	1	1	4
1928-29	Montreal	NHL	5	0	0	0	0	...	...	...	...	...
	Chicago	NHL	8	0	0	0	0	3	0	0	0	0
1929-30	Philadelphia	CAHL	1	0	0	0	0	...	...	...	...	...
1931-32	Philadelphia	CAHL	1	0	0	0	0	...	...	...	...	...
1934-35	Philadelphia	CAHL	12	0	0	0	0	...	...	...	...	...
	NHL Totals	**3**	**101**	**10**	**9**	**19**	**52**	**7**	**0**	**1**	**1**	**14**

JIMMY GARDNER

Left wing. Shoots left. 5'9", 180 lbs., Born, Montreal, Que., May 21, 1881

			Regular Season					Playoffs				
Season	Club	League	GP	G	A	PTS	PIM	GP	G	A	PTS	PIM
1901-02	Montreal AAA	CAHL	8	1	...	1	...	3	0	0	0	...
1902-03	Montreal	CAHL	3	3	...	3	...	2	1	0	1	...
1903-04	Mtl. Wanderers	FAHL	6	5	...	5	...	1	1	0	1	...
1904-05	Calumet	IHL	23	16	0	16	33	...	...	...	...	...
1905-06	Calumet	IHL	19	3	0	3	30	...	...	...	...	...
1906-07	Pittsburgh	IHL	20	10	8	18	61	...	...	...	...	...
1907-08	Mtl. Shamrocks	ECAHA	10	7	...	7	...	...	...	...	...	...
1908-09	Mtl. Wanderers	ECHA	12	11	...	11	51	2	0	0	0	0
1909-10	Mtl. Wanderers	NHA	13	13	...	13	67	1	0	0	0	6
1910-11	Mtl. Wanderers	NHA	14	5	...	5	35	...	...	...	...	...
1911-12	N. Westminster	PCHA	15	8	...	8	50	...	...	...	...	...
1912-13	N. Westminster	PCHA	13	3	4	7	21	...	...	...	...	...
1913-14	Montreal	NHA	15	10	9	19	12	...	...	...	...	...
1914-15	Montreal	NHA	2	0	0	0	0	...	...	...	...	...

BERNIE "BOOM BOOM" GEOFFRION

Right wing. Shoots right. 5'11", 185 lbs., Born, Montreal, Que., February 16, 1931

			Regular Season					Playoffs				
Season	Club	League	GP	G	A	PTS	PIM	GP	G	A	PTS	PIM
1947-48	Mtl. Nationals	QJHL	...	20	15	35	50	...	...	...	...	...
1948-49	Laval	QJHL	...	41	35	76	90	...	...	...	...	...
	Mtl. Royals	QSHL	2	0	1	1	0	...	...	...	...	...
1949-50	Laval	QJHL	34	52	34	86	...	...	...	...	...	...
	Mtl. Royals	QSHL	1	0	0	0	0	...	...	...	...	...
1950-51	Laval	QJHL	44	54	55	99	...	...	...	...	...	
	Montreal	NHL	18	8	6	14	9	11	1	1	2	6
1951-52	Montreal	NHL	67	30	24	54	66	11	3	1	4	6
1952-53	Montreal	NHL	65	22	17	39	37	12	6	4	10	12
1953-54	Montreal	NHL	54	29	25	54	87	11	6	5	11	18
1954-55	Montreal	NHL	70	38	37	75	57	12	8	5	13	8
1955-56	Montreal	NHL	59	29	33	62	66	10	5	9	14	6
1956-57	Montreal	NHL	41	19	21	40	18	10	11	7	18	2
1957-58	Montreal	NHL	42	27	23	50	51	10	6	5	11	2
1958-59	Montreal	NHL	59	22	44	66	30	11	5	8	13	10
1959-60	Montreal	NHL	59	30	41	71	36	8	2	10	12	4
1960-61	Montreal	NHL	64	50	45	95	29	4	2	1	3	0
1961-62	Montreal	NHL	62	23	36	59	36	5	0	1	1	6
1962-63	Montreal	NHL	51	23	18	41	73	5	0	1	1	4
1963-64	Montreal	NHL	55	21	18	39	41	7	1	1	2	4
1964-65			Did Not Play									
1965-66			Did Not Play									
1966-67	NY Rangers	NHL	58	17	25	42	42	4	2	0	2	0
1967-68	NY Rangers	NHL	59	5	16	21	11	1	0	1	1	0
	NHL Totals	**16**	**883**	**393**	**429**	**822**	**689**	**132**	**58**	**60**	**118**	**88**

EDDIE GERARD

Defence. Shoots left. 5'9", 168 lbs., Born, Ottawa, Ont., February 22, 1890

			Regular Season					Playoffs				
Season	Club	League	GP	G	A	PTS	PIM	GP	G	A	PTS	PIM
1913-14	Ottawa	NHA	11	6	7	13	34	...	...	...	...	...
1914-15	Ottawa	NHA	20	9	10	19	39	5	1	0	1	6
1915-16	Ottawa	NHA	24	13	5	18	57	...	...	...	...	...
1916-17	Ottawa	NHA	19	17	9	26	37	2	1	0	1	3
1917-18	Ottawa	NHL	22	13	0	13	32	...	...	...	...	...
1918-19	Ottawa	NHL	18	4	6	10	17	5	3	0	3	2
1919-20	Ottawa	NHL	21	9	3	12	19	5	2	1	3	6
1920-21	Ottawa	NHL	24	11	4	15	18	7	1	0	1	33
1921-22	Ottawa	NHL	21	7	9	16	16	2	0	0	0	8
	Toronto	NHL	...	...	...	...	...	1	0	0	0	0
1922-23	Ottawa	NHL	23	6	8	14	24	7	1	0	1	2
	NHL Totals	**6**	**129**	**50**	**30**	**80**	**106**	**26**	**7**	**3**	**10**	**23**

ED GIACOMIN

Goaltender. Catches left. 5'11", 180 lbs., Born, Sudbury, Ont., June 6, 1939

			Regular Season								Playoffs							
Season	Club	League	GP	MIN	GA	SO	GAA	W	L	T	GP	MIN	GA	SO	GAA	W	L	T
1959-60	Wash. / Clinton	EHL	4	180	13	0	3.25	....	....	....	....	....	....	....	....	....	....	....
	Providence	AHL	1	60	4	0	4.00	....	....	....	....	....	....	....	....	....	....	....
1960-61	NY / Clinton	EHL	51	3060	206	3	4.04	....	....	....	....	....	....	....	....	....	....	....
	Providence	AHL	43	2580	183	0	4.26	....	....	....	....	....	....	....	....	....	....	....
1961-62	NY Rovers	EHL	12	720	54	0	4.50	....	....	....	....	....	....	....	....	....	....	....
	Providence	AHL	40	2400	144	2	3.60	....	....	....	....	....	....	....	....	....	....	....
1962-63	Providence	AHL	39	2340	102	4	2.62	....	....	....	6	360	31	0	5.17	2	4	....
1963-64	Providence	AHL	69	4140	232	6	3.37	....	....	....	3	120	12	0	4.00	1	2	....
1964-65	Providence	AHL	59	3520	226	0	3.84	....	....	....	....	....	....	....	....	....	....	....
1965-66	NY Rangers	NHL	36	2096	128	0	3.66	8	19	7	....	....	....	....	....	....	....	....
	Baltimore	AHL	7	420	21	0	3.00	....	....	....	....	....	....	....	....	....	....	....
1966-67	NY Rangers	NHL	68	3981	173	9	2.61	30	25	11	4	246	14	0	3.41	0	4	....
1967-68	NY Rangers	NHL	66	3940	160	8	2.44	36	20	10	6	360	18	0	3.00	2	4	....
1968-69	NY Rangers	NHL	70	4114	175	7	2.55	37	23	7	3	180	10	0	3.33	0	3	....
1969-70	NY Rangers	NHL	70	4148	163	6	2.36	35	21	14	5	276	19	0	4.13	2	3	....
1970-71	NY Rangers	NHL	45	2641	95	8	2.15	27	10	7	12	759	28	0	2.21	7	5	....
1971-72	NY Rangers	NHL	44	2551	115	1	2.70	24	10	9	10	600	27	0	2.70	6	4	....
1972-73	NY Rangers	NHL	43	2580	125	4	2.91	26	11	6	10	539	23	1	2.56	5	4	....
1973-74	NY Rangers	NHL	56	3286	168	5	3.07	30	15	10	13	788	37	0	2.82	7	6	....
1974-75	NY Rangers	NHL	37	2069	120	1	3.48	13	12	8	2	86	4	0	2.79	0	2	....
1975-76	NY Rangers	NHL	4	240	19	0	4.75	0	3	1	....	....	....	....	....	....	....	....
	Detroit	NHL	29	1740	100	2	3.45	12	14	3	....	....	....	....	....	....	....	....
1976-77	Detroit	NHL	33	1791	107	3	3.58	8	18	3	....	....	....	....	...	....	....	....
1977-78	Detroit	NHL	9	516	27	0	3.14	3	5	1	....	....	....	....	....	....	....	....
	NHL Totals	**13**	**610**	**35693**	**1675**	**54**	**2.82**	**289**	**206**	**97**	**65**	**3834**	**180**	**1**	**2.82**	**29**	**35**	....

ROD GILBERT

Right wing. Shoots right. 5'9", 175 lbs., Born, Montreal, Que., July 1, 1941

			Regular Season					Playoffs				
Season	Club	League	GP	G	A	PTS	PIM	GP	G	A	PTS	PIM
1957-58	Guelph	OHA Jr.	32	14	16	30	14	...	...	...	...	...
1958-59	Guelph	OHA Jr.	54	27	34	61	40	10	5	4	9	14
1959-60	Guelph	OHA Jr.	47	39	52	91	40	5	3	3	6	4
	Trois-Rivieres	EPHL	3	4	6	10	0	5	2	2	4	2
1960-61	Guelph	OHA Jr.	47	54	49	103	47	6	4	4	8	6
	NY Rangers	NHL	1	0	1	1	2	...	...	...	...	...
1961-62	Kitch-Waterloo	EPHL	21	12	11	23	0	4	0	0	0	4
	NY Rangers	NHL	1	0	0	0	0	4	2	3	5	4
1962-63	NY Rangers	NHL	70	11	20	31	20	...	...	...	...	...
1963-64	NY Rangers	NHL	70	24	40	64	62	...	...	...	...	...
1964-65	NY Rangers	NHL	70	25	36	61	52	...	...	...	...	...
1965-66	NY Rangers	NHL	34	10	15	25	20	...	...	...	...	...
1966-67	NY Rangers	NHL	64	28	18	46	12	4	2	2	4	6
1967-68	NY Rangers	NHL	73	29	48	77	12	6	5	0	5	4
1968-69	NY Rangers	NHL	66	28	49	77	22	4	1	0	1	2
1969-70	NY Rangers	NHL	72	16	37	53	22	6	4	5	9	0
1970-71	NY Rangers	NHL	78	30	31	61	65	13	4	6	10	8
1971-72	NY Rangers	NHL	73	43	54	97	64	16	7	8	15	11
1972-73	NY Rangers	NHL	76	25	59	84	25	10	5	1	6	2
1973-74	NY Rangers	NHL	75	36	41	77	20	13	3	5	8	4
1974-75	NY Rangers	NHL	76	36	61	97	22	3	1	3	4	2
1975-76	NY Rangers	NHL	70	36	50	86	32	...	...	...	...	...
1976-77	NY Rangers	NHL	77	27	48	75	50	...	...	...	...	...
1977-78	NY Rangers	NHL	19	2	7	9	6	...	...	...	...	...
	NHL Totals	**18**	**1065**	**406**	**615**	**1021**	**508**	**79**	**34**	**33**	**67**	**43**

BILLY GILMOUR

Right wing. Born, Ottawa, Ont., March 21,1885

			Regular Season					Playoffs				
Season	Club	League	GP	G	A	PTS	PIM	GP	G	A	PTS	PIM
1902-03	Ottawa	CAHL	7	10	0	10	...	4	5	0	5	...
1903-04	Ottawa	CAHL		...	...	...	...	3	1	0	1	...
	McGill U.	College	Not Available...			...	...	...	...	...	...	
1904-05	McGill U.	College	Not Available...			...	...	...	...	...	...	
	Ottawa	FAHL	1	0	0	0	...	...	2	1	0	1
1905-06	Ottawa	ECHA	1	0	0	0	...	...	...	...	...	...
	McGill U.	College	Not Available...			...	...	...	...	...	...	
1906-07	McGill U.	College	Not Available...			...	...	...	...	...	...	
1907-08	Mtl. Victorias	ECAHA	10	4	0	4	...	...	...	...	...	...
1908-09	Ottawa	ECHA	11	9	0	9	74	...	...	...	...	...
	Ottawa	Int.	2	3	0	3	3	...	...	...	...	...
1910-11	New Edinburgh	OHA Sr.	Not Available...			...	...	...	...	...	...	
1912-1915			Did Not Play									
1915-16	Ottawa	NHA	2	1	0	1	0	...	...	...	...	...

FRANK "MOOSE" GOHEEN

Left Wing. Shoots left. 6', 220 lbs., Born, White Bear Lake, MN, February 8, 1894

			Regular Season					Playoffs				
Season	Club	League	GP	G	A	PTS	PIM	GP	G	A	PTS	PIM
1922-23	St. Paul Saints	AHA	20	11	0	11	...	...	...	...	...	...
1923-24	St. Paul Saints	AHA	20	8	0	8	...	8	1	3	4	...
1924-25	St. Paul Saints	AHA	32	6	0	6	...	...	...	...	...	...
1925-26	St. Paul Saints	AHA	36	13	10	23	87	...	...	...	...	...
1926-27	St. Paul Saints	AHA	27	2	7	9	40	...	...	...	...	...
1927-28	St. Paul Saints	AHA	39	19	5	24	96	...	...	...	...	...
1928-29	St. Paul Saints	AHA	28	7	4	11	39	8	2	0	2	20
1929-30	St. Paul Saints	AHA	35	9	6	15	47	...	...	...	...	...
1930-31	Buffalo	AHA	2	0	0	0	0	...	...	...	...	...
1932-33	St. Paul Saints	CHL	20	2	7	9	17	...	...	...	...	...

EBBIE GOODFELLOW

Forward / defence. Shoots left. 5'11", 180 lbs., Born, Ottawa, Ont., April 9, 1906

			Regular Season					Playoffs				
Season	Club	League	GP	G	A	PTS	PIM	GP	G	A	PTS	PIM
1928-29	Detroit	CPHL	42	26	8	34	45	7	3	2	5	8
1929-30	Detroit	NHL	44	17	17	34	54	...	...	...	...	...
1930-31	Detroit	NHL	44	25	23	48	32	...	...	...	...	...
1931-32	Detroit	NHL	48	14	16	30	56	2	0	0	0	0
1932-33	Detroit	NHL	41	12	8	20	47	4	1	0	1	11
1933-34	Detroit	NHL	48	13	13	26	45	9	4	3	7	12
1934-35	Detroit	NHL	48	12	24	36	44	...	...	...	...	...
1935-36	Detroit	NHL	48	5	18	23	69	7	1	0	1	4
1936-37	Detroit	NHL	48	9	16	25	43	9	2	2	4	12
1937-38	Detroit	NHL	30	0	7	7	13	...	...	...	...	...
1938-39	Detroit	NHL	48	8	8	16	36	6	0	0	0	8
1939-40	Detroit	NHL	43	11	17	28	31	5	0	2	2	9
1940-41	Detroit	NHL	47	5	17	22	35	3	0	1	1	9
1941-42	Detroit	NHL	9	2	2	4	2	...	...	...	...	...
1942-43	Detroit	NHL	11	1	4	5	4	...	...	...	...	...
	NHL Totals	**14**	**557**	**134**	**190**	**324**	**511**	**45**	**8**	**8**	**16**	**65**

MIKE GRANT

Point. Born, Montreal, Que., January, 1874

			Regular Season					Playoffs				
Season	Club	League	GP	G	A	PTS	PIM	GP	G	A	PTS	PIM
1893-94	Mtl. Victorias	AHA	5	0	0	0	...	1	0	0	0	...
1894-95	Mtl. Victorias	AHA	8	1	0	1	...	...	...	...	...	...
1895-96	Mtl. Victorias	AHA	8	3	0	3	...	2	0	0	0	...
1896-97	Mtl. Victorias	AHA	8	3	0	3	...	1	0	0	0	...
1897-98	Mtl. Victorias	AHA	8	1	0	1	...	...	...	...	...	...
1898-99	Mtl. Victorias	CAHL	7	2	0	2	...	2	0	0	0	...
1899-1900	Mtl. Victorias	CAHL	2	0	0	0	...	...	...	...	...	...
1900-01	Mtl. Shamrocks	CAHL	2	0	0	0	...	2	0	0	0	...
1901-02	Mtl. Victorias	CAHL	7	0	0	0	...	...	...	...	...	...

WILF "SHORTY" GREEN

Right wing. Shoots right. 5'10", 152 lbs., Born, Sudbury, Ont., July 17, 1896

			Regular Season					Playoffs				
Season	Club	League	GP	G	A	PTS	PIM	GP	G	A	PTS	PIM
1923-24	Hamilton	NHL	22	7	2	9	19	...	...	...	...	...
1924-25	Hamilton	NHL	28	18	1	19	75	...	...	...	...	...
1925-26	NY Americans	NHL	33	6	4	10	40	...	...	...	...	...
1926-27	NY Americans	NHL	21	2	1	3	17	...	...	...	...	...
1929-30	Duluth	AHA	2	0	0	0	2	...	...	...	...	...
1930-31	Duluth	AHA	1	0	0	0	8	...	...	...	...	...
	NHL Totals	**4**	**103**	**33**	**8**	**41**	**151**	**....**	**....**	**....**	**....**	**....**

SI GRIFFIS

Point / rover. Shoots left. 6'1", 195 lbs., Born, Onega, KN, September 22, 1883

			Regular Season					Playoffs				
Season	Club	League	GP	G	A	PTS	PIM	GP	G	A	PTS	PIM
1902-03	Rat Portage	MHL Sr	...	...	...	...	...	2	0	0	0	...
1904-05	Rat Portage	MHL Sr.	8	14	0	14	3	3	3	0	3	...
1905-06	Kenora	MHL Sr.	9	9	0	9	...	...	...	...	...	...
1906-07	Kenora	MHL Sr.	6	5	0	5	4	4	1	0	1	...
1909-10	Nelson	Sr.	Not Available...			...	...	...	...	...	...	...
1911-12	Vancouver	PCHA	15	8	0	8	18	...	...	...	...	...
1912-13	Vancouver	PCHA	14	10	3	13	30	...	...	...	...	...
1913-14	Vancouver	PCHA	13	2	3	5	21	...	...	...	...	...
1914-15	Vancouver	PCHA	17	2	3	5	32	...	...	...	...	...
1915-16	Vancouver	PCHA	18	7	5	12	12	...	...	...	...	...
1916-17	Vancouver	PCHA	23	7	4	11	34	...	...	...	...	...
1917-18	Vancouver	PCHA	8	2	6	8	0	7	1	0	1	9
1918-19	Vancouver	PCHA	2	0	2	2	0	2	1	1	2	0

GEORGE HAINSWORTH

Goaltender. Catches left. 5'6", 150 lbs., Born, Toronto, Ont., June 26, 1895

			Regular Season								Playoffs							
Season	Club	League	GP	MIN	GA	SO	GAA	W	L	T	GP	MIN	GA	SO	GAA	W	L	T
1919-20	Kitchener	OHA Sr.	8	480	16	1	2.00	6	2	0	2	120	6	0	3.00	....	....	....
1920-21	Kitchener	OHA Sr.	10	600	22	3	2.20	7	3	0	1	60	6	0	6.00	....	....	....
1921-22	Kitchener	OHA Sr.	10	600	38	1	3.80	3	7	0	....	....	....	....	....	....	....	....
1922-23	Kitchene	OHA Sr.	12	720	32	1	2.67	8	4	0	....	....	....	....	....	....	....	....
1923-24	Saskatoon	WCHL	30	1870	73	4	2.34	15	12	3	....	....	....	....	....	....	....	....
1924-25	Saskatoon	WCHL	28	1700	75	2	2.65	16	11	1	2	120	6	0	3.00	0	1	1
1925-26	Saskatoon	WHL	30	1812	64	4	2.12	18	11	1	2	128	4	0	1.88	0	1	1
1926-27	Montreal	NHL	44	2732	67	14	1.47	28	14	2	4	252	6	1	1.43	1	1	2
1927-28	Montreal	NHL	44	2730	48	13	1.06	26	11	7	2	128	3	0	1.41	0	1	1
1928-29	Montreal	NHL	44	2800	43	22	0.92	22	7	15	3	180	5	0	1.67	0	3	0
1929-30	Montreal	NHL	42	3008	108	4	2.15	20	13	9	6	481	6	3	0.75	5	0	1
1930-31	Montreal	NHL	44	2740	89	8	1.95	26	10	8	10	722	21	2	1.75	6	4	0
1931-32	Montreal	NHL	48	2998	110	6	2.22	25	16	7	4	300	13	0	2.60	1	3	0
1932-33	Montreal	NHL	48	2980	115	8	2.32	18	25	5	2	120	8	0	4.00	0	1	1
1933-34	Toronto	NHL	48	3010	119	3	2.37	26	13	9	5	302	11	0	2.19	2	3	0
1934-35	Toronto	NHL	48	2957	111	8	2.25	30	14	4	7	460	12	2	1.57	3	4	0
1935-36	Toronto	NHL	48	3000	106	8	2.12	23	19	6	9	541	27	0	3.00	3	6	0
1936-37	Toronto	NHL	3	190	9	0	2.84	0	2	1	....	....	....	....	....	....	....	....
	Montreal	NHL	4	270	12	0	2.67	2	1	1	....	....	....	....	....	....	....	....
	NHL Totals	**11**	**465**	**29415**	**937**	**94**	**1.91**	**246**	**145**	**74**	**52**	**3486**	**112**	**8**	**1.93**	**21**	**26**	**5**

GLENN HALL

Goaltender. Catches left. 5'11" 180 lbs., Born, Humbolt, Sask., October 3, 1931

			Regular Season								Playoffs							
Season	Club	League	GP	MIN	GA	SO	GAA	W	L	T	GP	MIN	GA	SO	GAA	W	L	T
1947-48	Humboldt	SJHL	5	300	17	0	3.40	....	....	....	2	120	15	0	7.50	0	2	....
1948-49	Humboldt	SJHL	24	1440	99	1	4.13	....	....	....	7	420	36	0	5.14	3	4	....
1949-50	Windsor	OHA Jr.	45	2620	158	1	3.61	....	....	....	....	....	....	....	....	....	....	....
1950-51	Windsor	OHA Jr.	54	3240	167	6	3.09	32	18	4	8	480	30	0	3.75	....	....	....
1951-52	Indianapolis	AHL	68	4080	272	0	4.00	....	....	....	....	....	....	....	....	....	....	....
1952-53	Detroit	NHL	6	360	10	1	1.67	4	1	1	....	....	....	....	....	....	....	....
	Edmonton	WHL	63	3780	207	2	3.29	....	....	....	15	905	53	0	3.51	10	5	....
1953-54	Edmonton	WHL	70	4200	259	0	3.70	29	30	11	12	720	44	2	3.67	7	6	....
1954-55	Edmonton	WHL	66	3960	187	5	2.83	....	....	....	9	546	18	1	1.98	8	1	....
	Detroit	NHL	2	120	2	0	1.00	2	0	0	....	....	....	....	....	....	....	....
1955-56	Detroit	NHL	70	4200	148	12	2.11	30	24	16	10	604	28	0	2.80	5	5	....
1956-57	Detroit	NHL	70	4200	157	4	2.24	38	20	12	5	300	15	0	3.00	1	4	....
1957-58	Chicago	NHL	70	4200	202	7	2.88	24	39	7	....	....	....	....	....	....	....	....
1958-59	Chicago	NHL	70	4200	208	1	2.97	28	29	13	6	360	21	0	3.50	2	4	....
1959-60	Chicago	NHL	70	4200	180	6	2.57	28	29	13	4	249	14	0	3.37	0	4	....
1960-61	Chicago	NHL	70	4200	180	6	2.57	29	24	17	12	772	27	2	2.10	8	4	....
1961-62	Chicago	NHL	70	4200	186	9	2.65	31	26	13	12	720	31	2•	2.58	6	6	....
1962-63	Chicago	NHL	66	3910	166	5	2.55	30	20	15	6	360	25	0	4.17	2	4	....
1963-64	Chicago	NHL	65	3860	148	7	2.30	34	19	11	7	408	22	0	3.26	3	4	....
1964-65	Chicago	NHL	41	2440	99	4	2.43	18	18	5	13	760	28	1	2.21	7	6	....
1965-66	Chicago	NHL	64	3747	164	4	2.63	34	21	7	6	347	22	0	3.81	2	4	....
1966-67	Chicago	NHL	32	1664	66	2	2.38	19	5	5	3	176	8	0	2.73	1	2	....
1967-68	St. Louis	NHL	49	2858	118	5	2.48	19	21	9	18	111	45	1	2.43	8	10	....
1968-69	St. Louis	NHL	41	2354	85	8	2.17	19	12	8	3	131	5	0	2.29	0	2	....
1969-70	St. Louis	NHL	18	1010	49	1	2.91	7	8	3	7	421	21	0	2.99	4	3	....
1970-71	St. Louis	NHL	32	1761	71	2	2.41	13	11	8	3	180	9	0	3.00	0	3	....
	NHL Totals	**18**	**906**	**53484**	**2239**	**84**	**2.51**	**407**	**327**	**163**	**115**	**6889**	**321**	**6**	**2.79**	**49**	**65**	**....**

JOE HALL

Defence / forward. Shoots right. 5'10", 175 lbs., Born, Staffordshire, Eng., May 3, 1882

			Regular Season					Playoffs				
Season	Club	League	GP	G	A	PTS	PIM	GP	G	A	PTS	PIM
1903-04	Winnipeg	MHL Sr.	...	...	...	...	...	3	1	0	1	...
1904-05	Brandon	MHL Sr.	8	11	0	11	...	...	...	...	...	...
1905-06	Portage Lakes	IHL	20	33	0	33	98	...	...	...	...	...
	Quebec	ECAHA	3	1	0	1	...	...	...	...	...	...
1906-07	Brandon	MHL Sr.	9	14	0	14	...	2	5	0	5	...
1907-08	Winnipeg	MHL Sr.	...	...	...	...	...	...	...	...	...	...
1908-09	Mtl. Wanderers	ECHA	5	10	0	10	18	...	...	...	...	...
	Winnipeg	MHL Sr.	2	2	0	2	...	...	...	...	...	...
1909-10	Mtl. Shamrocks	NHA	10	8	0	8	47	...	...	...	...	...
	Mtl. Shamrocks	CHA	1	7	0	7	6	...	...	...	...	...
1910-11	Quebec	NHA	10	0	0	0	20	...	...	...	...	...
1911-12	Quebec	NHA	18	15	0	15	30	2	2	0	2	2
1912-13	Quebec	NHA	17	8	0	8	78	2	3	0	3	0
1913-14	Quebec	NHA	19	13	4	17	61	...	...	...	...	...
1914-15	Quebec	NHA	20	3	2	5	52	...	...	...	...	...
1915-16	Quebec	NHA	23	1	2	3	89	...	...	...	...	...
1916-17	Quebec	NHA	19	6	6	12	74	...	...	...	...	...
1917-18	Montreal	NHL	21	8	3	11	113	2	0	2	2	6
1918-19	Montreal	NHL	17	7	1	8	85	10	0	0	0	25
	NHL Totals	**2**	**37**	**15**	**1**	**16**	**145**	**12**	**0**	**2**	**2**	**31**

DOUG HARVEY

Defence. Shoots left. 5'11", 180 lbs., Born, Montreal, Que., December 19, 1924

			Regular Season					Playoffs				
Season	Club	League	GP	G	A	PTS	PIM	GP	G	A	PTS	PIM
1942-43	Mtl. Navy	Sr.	4	0	0	0	0	...	...	...	...	...
	Montreal	QJHL	21	4	6	10	17	6	3	4	7	10
	Montreal	QSHL	1	0	0	0	0	...	...	...	...	...
1943-44	Montreal	QSHL	1	1	1	2	2	...	...	...	...	...
	Montreal	QJHL	13	4	6	10	34	4	2	6	8	10
	Montreal	Sr.	1	0	2	2	7	...	...	...	...	...
	Mtl. Navy	Sr.	15	4	1	5	24	5	3	1	4	15
1944-45	Mtl. Navy	Sr.	3	0	2	2	2	6	3	1	4	6
1945-46	Montreal	QSHL	34	2	6	8	90	11	1	6	7	37
1946-47	Montreal	QSHL	40	2	26	28	171	11	2	4	6	62
1947-48	Montreal	NHL	35	4	4	8	32	...	...	...	...	...
	Buffalo	AHL	24	1	7	8	38	...	...	...	...	...
1948-49	Montreal	NHL	55	3	13	16	87	7	0	1	1	10
1949-50	Montreal	NHL	70	4	20	24	76	5	0	2	2	10
1950-51	Montreal	NHL	70	5	24	29	93	11	0	5	5	12
1951-52	Montreal	NHL	68	6	23	29	82	11	0	3	3	8
1952-53	Montreal	NHL	69	4	30	34	67	12	0	5	5	8
1953-54	Montreal	NHL	68	8	29	37	110	10	0	2	2	12
1954-55	Montreal	NHL	70	6	43	49	58	12	0	8	8	6
1955-56	Montreal	NHL	62	5	39	44	60	10	2	5	7	10
1956-57	Montreal	NHL	70	6	44	50	92	10	0	7	7	10
1957-58	Montreal	NHL	68	9	32	41	131	10	2	9	11	16
1958-59	Montreal	NHL	61	4	16	20	61	11	1	11	12	22
1959-60	Montreal	NHL	66	6	21	27	45	8	3	0	3	6
1960-61	Montreal	NHL	58	6	33	39	48	6	0	1	1	8
1961-62	NY Rangers	NHL	69	6	24	30	42	6	0	1	1	2
1962-63	NY Rangers	NHL	68	4	35	39	92	...	...	...	...	...
1963-64	NY Rangers	NHL	14	0	2	2	10	...	...	...	...	...
	Quebec	AHL	52	6	36	42	30	9	0	4	4	10
	St. Paul	CHL	5	2	2	4	6	...	...	...	...	...
1964-65	Quebec	AHL	64	1	36	37	72	4	1	1	2	9
1965-66	Baltimore	AHL	67	7	32	39	80	...	...	...	...	...
1966-67	Detroit	NHL	2	0	0	0	0	...	...	...	...	...
	Balt. / Pittsburgh	AHL	52	2	18	20	32	9	0	0	0	2
1967-68	Kansas City	CHL	59	4	16	20	12	7	0	6	6	6
	St. Louis	NHL	...	...	...	...	...	8	0	4	4	12
1968-69	St. Louis	NHL	70	2	20	22	30	...	...	...	...	...
	NHL Totals	**20**	**1113**	**88**	**452**	**540**	**1216**	**137**	**8**	**64**	**72**	**152**

GEORGE HAY

Left wing. Shoots left. 5'10", 155 lbs., Born, Listowel, Ont., January 10, 1898

			Regular Season					Playoffs				
Season	Club	League	GP	G	A	PTS	PIM	GP	G	A	PTS	PIM
1919-20	Regina	SSHL	12	8	3	11	5	2	1	0	1	0
1920-21	Regina	SSHL	16	9	4	13	7	4	5	2	7	2
1921-22	Regina	WCHL	25	21	11	32	9	4	0	0	0	5
1922-23	Regina	WCHL	30	28	8	36	12	2	1	0	1	0
1923-24	Regina	WCHL	25	20	11	31	8	3	1	1	2	0
1924-25	Regina	WCHL	20	16	6	22	6	...	...	...	...	...
1925-26	Portland	WHL	30	19	12	31	4	...	...	...	...	...
1926-27	Chicago	NHL	35	14	8	22	12	2	1	1	2	2
1927-28	Detroit	NHL	42	22	13	35	20	...	...	...	...	...
1928-29	Detroit	NHL	39	11	8	19	14	2	1	0	1	2
1929-30	Detroit	NHL	44	18	15	33	8	...	...	...	...	...
1930-31	Detroit	NHL	44	8	10	18	24	...	...	...	...	...
1931-32	Detroit	IAHL	48	10	9	19	26	6	0	0	0	2
1932-33	Detroit	NHL	35	1	6	7	6	4	0	1	1	0
	Detroit	IAHL	9	6	1	7	6	...	...	...	...	...
1933-34	Detroit	IAHL	4	0	0	0	5	...	...	...	...	...
	Detroit	NHL	1	0	0	0	0	...	...	...	...	...
	NHL Totals	**7**	**242**	**74**	**60**	**134**	**84**	**8**	**2**	**3**	**5**	**2**

WILLIAM "RILEY" HERN

Goaltender. Catches right. 5'9", 170 lbs., Born St. Mary's Ont., December 5, 1880

			Regular Season								Playoffs							
Season	Club	League	GP	MIN	GA	SO	GAA	W	L	T	GP	MIN	GA	SO	GAA	W	L	T
1903 04	Portage Lakes	IHL	14	840	21	4	1.50	13	1	0	9	540	22	0	2.44	8	1	0
1904-05	Portage Lakes	IHL	24	1374	81	2	3.54	15	7	2	....	....		....	....	....	....	....
1905 06	Portage Lakes	IHL	20	1215	70	1	3.46	15	5	0	....	....	....	....	....	....	....	....
1906-07	Mtl. Wanderers	ECAHA	10	610	39	0	3.84	10	0	0	6	360	25	0	4.17	3	3	0
1907-08	Mtl. Wanderers	CAHA	10	610	52	0	5.12	8	2	0	5	300	16	0	3.20	5	0	0
1908-09	Mtl. Wanderers	ECHA	12	728	61	0	5.03	9	3	....	2	120	10	0	5.00	1	1	0
1909-10	Mtl. Wanderers	NHA	12	720	41	1	3.42	11	1	....	1	....	3	0	3.00	1	0	0
	Mtl. Wanderers	CHA	1	60	6	0	6.00	1	0	0	...	....	....	....	....	....	....	....
1910-11	Mtl. Wanderers	NHA	16	973	88	0	5.43	7	9	0	....	....	....	....	....	....	....	....

BRYAN HEXTALL

Right wing. Shoots left. 5'10", 183 lbs., Born, Grenfell, Sask., July 31, 1913

			Regular Season					Playoffs				
Season	Club	League	GP	G	A	PTS	PIM	GP	G	A	PTS	PIM
1931-32	Wpg. Monarchs	Sr.	4	0	0	0	0	1	2	0	2	0
1932-33	Portage	MHL Jr.	12	10	8	18	6	2	0	0	0	4
1933-34	Portage	MHL Jr.	7	6	4	10	8	...	...	...	...	...
	Vancouver	NWHL	5	2	0	2	0	...	...	...	...	...
1934-35	Vancouver	NWHL	32	14	10	24	27	8	0	0	0	10
1935-36	Vancouver	NWHL	40	27	9	36	65	7	1	2	3	15
1936-37	Philadelphia	AHL	18	29	23	52	34	6	2	4	6	6
	NY Rangers	NHL	1	0	1	1	0	...	...	...	...	...
1937-38	NY Rangers	NHL	48	17	4	21	6	3	2	0	2	0
1938-39	NY Rangers	NHL	48	20	15	35	18	7	0	1	1	4
1939-40	NY Rangers	NHL	48	24	15	39	52	12	4	3	7	11
1940-41	NY Rangers	NHL	48	26	18	44	16	3	0	1	1	0
1941-42	NY Rangers	NHL	48	24	32	56	30	6	1	1	2	4
1942-43	NY Rangers	NHL	50	27	32	59	28	...	...	...	...	...
1943 44	NY Rangers	NHL	50	21	33	54	41	...	...	...	...	...
1944-45	St. Catharines	OHA Sr.	1	0	1	1	0	...	...	...	...	...
1945-46	NY Rangers	NHL	3	0	1	1	0	...	...	...	...	...
1946-47	NY Rangers	NHL	60	20	10	30	18	...	...	...	...	...
1947-48	NY Rangers	NHL	43	8	14	22	18	6	1	3	4	0
1948-49	Clev / Wash'ton	AHL	57	18	23	41	16	...	...	...	...	...
	NHL Totals	**11**	**449**	**187**	**175**	**362**	**227**	**37**	**8**	**9**	**17**	**19**

HAROLD "HAP" HOLMES

Goaltender. Catches left. 5'10", 170 lbs., Born; Aurora, Ont., February 21, 1889

			Regular Season								Playoffs							
Season	Club	League	GP	MIN	GA	SO	GAA	W	L	T	GP	MIN	GA	SO	GAA	W	L	T
1912-13	Toronto	NHA	15	779	58	1	4.47	6	7	0	....	....	....	....	....	....	....	....
1913-14	Toronto	NHA	20	1204	65	1	3.24	13	7	0	2	120	2	1	1.00	1	1	0
1914-15	Toronto	NHA	20	1218	84	0	4.18	8	12	0	....	....	....	....	....	....	....	....
1915-16	Toronto	NHA	1	60	6	0	6.00	0	1	0	....	....	....	....	....	....	....	....
	Seattle	PCHA	18	1080	66	0	3.67	9	9	0	....	....	....	....	....	....	....	....
1916-17	Seattle	PCHA	24	1465	77	2	3.28	16	8	0	4	240	11	0	2.75	3	1	0
1917-18	Toronto	NHL	16	965	76	0	4.73	10	6	0	7	420	28	0	4.00	4	3	0
1918-19	Toronto	NHL	2	120	9	0	4.50	0	2	0	....		....	....	....	....	....	....
	Seattle	PCHA	20	1225	46	0	2.25	11	9	0	2	120	5	0	2.50	1	1	0
1919-20	Seattle	PCHA	22	1340	55	4	2.46	12	10	0	2	120	3	1	1.50	1	1	0
1920 21	Seattle	PCHA	24	1551	68	0	2.63	12	11	1	2	120	13	0	6.50	0	2	0
1921-22	Seattle	PCHA	24	1479	64	4	2.60	12	11	1	2	120	2	0	1.00	0	2	0
1922-23	Seattle	PCHA	30	1843	106	3	3.45	15	15	0	....	....	....	....	....	....	....	....
1923-24	Seattle	PCHA	30	1823	99	2	3.26	14	16	0	2	134	4	0	1.79	0	1	1
1924-25	Victoria	WCHL	28	1682	63	3	2.25	16	12	0	4	240	5	1	1.25	2	0	2
1925-26	Victoria	WHL	30	1847	53	4	1.72	15	11	4	4	248	6	1	1.45	2	0	2
1926-27	Detroit	NHL	41	2685	100	6	2.24	12	27	4	....	....	....	....	....	....	....	....
1927-28	Detroit	NHL	44	2740	79	11	1.73	19	19	6	....	....	....	....	....	....	....	....
	NHL Totals	**4**	**103**	**6510**	**264**	**17**	**2.43**	**40**	**53**	**10**	**7**	**420**	**28**	**0**	**4.00**	**4**	**3**	**0**

TOM HOOPER

Rover. Shoots left. 5'10", 175 lbs., Born, Rat Portage, Ont.., November 24, 1883

			Regular Season					Playoffs				
Season	Club	League	GP	G	A	PTS	PIM	GP	G	A	PTS	PIM
1904-05	Rat Portage	MHL Sr.	8	3	0	3	...	...	...	...	...	...
1905-06	Kenora	MHL Sr.	9	4	0	4	...	1	0	0	0	...
1906-07	Kenora	MHL Sr.	3	4	0	4	...	2	0	0	0	...
1907-08	Mtl. Wanderers	ECAHA	2	1	0	1	...	...	...	...	...	...
	Montreal AAA	ECHA	7	9	0	9	...	...	...	...	...	...
	Pembroke	Sr.	1	0	0	0	...	...	...	...	...	...

REGINALD "RED" HORNER

Defence. Shoots right. 6'202 lbs., Born, Lynden, Ont., May 28, 1909

			Regular Season					Playoffs				
Season	Club	League	GP	G	A	PTS	PIM	GP	G	A	PTS	PIM
1926-27	Tor. Marlboros	OHA Jr.	9	5	1	6	2	...	...	...	...	...
1927-28	Tor. Marlboros	OHA Jr.	9	4	5	9	2	...	...	...	...	...
	Tor. Marlboros	OHA Sr.	1	0	0	0	0	...	...	...	...	...
1928-29	Tor. Marlboros	OHA Sr.	2	0	0	0	...	...	...	...	...	...
	Toronto	NHL	22	0	0	0	30	4	1	0	1	2
1929-30	Toronto	NHL	33	2	7	9	96	...	...	...	...	...
1930-31	Toronto	NHL	42	1	11	12	71	2	0	0	0	4
1931-32	Toronto	NHL	42	7	9	16	97	7	2	2	4	20
1932-33	Toronto	NHL	48	3	8	11	144	9	1	0	1	10
1933-34	Toronto	NHL	40	11	10	21	146	5	1	0	1	6
1934-35	Toronto	NHL	46	4	8	12	125	7	0	1	1	4
1935-36	Toronto	NHL	43	2	9	11	167	9	1	2	3	22
1936-37	Toronto	NHL	48	3	9	12	124	2	0	0	0	7
1937-38	Toronto	NHL	47	4	20	24	82	7	0	1	1	14
1938-39	Toronto	NHL	48	4	10	14	85	10	1	2	3	26
1939-40	Toronto	NHL	31	1	9	10	87	9	0	2	2	45
	NHL Totals	**12**	**489**	**42**	**110**	**152**	**1254**	**71**	**7**	**10**	**17**	**170**

TIM HORTON

Defence. Shoots right. 5'10", 180 lbs., Born, Cochrane, Ont., January 12, 1930

			Regular Season					Playoffs				
Season	Club	League	GP	G	A	PTS	PIM	GP	G	A	PTS	PIM
1946-47	Cooper Cliff	Sr.	9	0	0	0	14	5	0	1	1	0
1947-48	Tor. St. Mike's	OHA Jr.	32	6	7	13	137	...	...	...	...	...
1948-49	Tor. St. Mike's	OHA Jr.	32	9	18	27	95	...	...	...	...	...
1949-50	Pittsburgh	AHL	60	5	18	23	83	...	...	...	...	...
	Toronto	NHL	1	0	0	0	2	1	0	0	0	2
1950-51	Pittsburgh	AHL	68	8	26	34	129	13	0	9	9	16
1951-52	Pittsburgh	AHL	64	12	19	31	146	11	1	3	4	16
	Toronto	NHL	4	0	0	0	8	...	...	...	...	...
1952-53	Toronto	NHL	70	2	14	16	85	...	...	...	...	...
1953-54	Toronto	NHL	70	7	24	31	94	5	1	1	2	4
1954-55	Toronto	NHL	67	5	9	14	84	...	...	...	...	...
1955-56	Toronto	NHL	35	0	5	5	36	2	0	0	0	4
1956-57	Toronto	NHL	66	6	19	25	72	...	...	...	...	...
1957-58	Toronto	NHL	53	6	20	26	39	...	...	...	...	...
1958-59	Toronto	NHL	70	5	21	26	76	12	0	3	3	16
1959-60	Toronto	NHL	70	3	29	32	69	10	0	1	1	6
1960-61	Toronto	NHL	57	6	15	21	75	5	0	0	0	0
1961-62	Toronto	NHL	70	10	28	38	88	12	3	13	16	16
1962-63	Toronto	NHL	70	6	19	25	69	10	1	3	4	10
1963-64	Toronto	NHL	70	9	20	29	71	14	0	4	4	20
1964-65	Toronto	NHL	70	12	16	28	95	6	0	2	2	13
1965-66	Toronto	NHL	70	6	22	28	76	4	1	0	1	12
1966-67	Toronto	NHL	70	8	17	25	70	12	3	5	8	25
1967-68	Toronto	NHL	69	4	23	27	82	...	...	...	...	...
1968-69	Toronto	NHL	74	11	29	40	107	4	0	0	0	7
1969-70	Toronto	NHL	59	3	19	22	91	...	...	...	...	...
	NY Rangers	NHL	15	1	5	6	16	6	1	1	2	28
1970-71	NY Rangers	NHL	78	2	18	20	57	13	1	4	5	14
1971-72	Pittsburgh	NHL	44	2	9	11	40	4	0	1	1	2
1972-73	Buffalo	NHL	69	1	16	17	56	6	0	1	1	4
1973-74	Buffalo	NHL	55	0	6	6	53	...	...	...	...	...
	NHL Totals	**24**	**1446**	**115**	**403**	**518**	**1611**	**126**	**11**	**39**	**50**	**183**

GORDIE HOWE

Right wing. Shoots right 6', 205 lbs., Born, Floral, Sask., March 31, 1928

			Regular Season					Playoffs				
Season	Club	League	GP	G	A	PTS	PIM	GP	G	A	PTS	PIM
1943-44	Saskatoon	Jr.	5	6	5	11	4	2	0	0	0	6
1944-45	Galt	OHA Jr.	...	...	...	...	...	...	...	...	...	...
1945-46	Omaha	USHL	51	22	26	48	53	6	2	1	3	15
1946-47	Detroit	NHL	58	7	15	22	52	5	0	0	0	18
1947-48	Detroit	NHL	60	16	28	44	63	10	1	1	2	11
1948-49	Detroit	NHL	40	12	25	37	57	11	8	3	11	19
1949-50	Detroit	NHL	70	35	33	68	69	1	0	0	0	7
1950-51	Detroit	NHL	70	43	43	86	74	6	4	3	7	4
1951-52	Detroit	NHL	70	47	39	86	78	8	2	5	7	2
1952-53	Detroit	NHL	70	49	46	95	57	6	2	5	7	2
1953-54	Detroit	NHL	70	33	48	81	109	12	4	5	9	31
1954-55	Detroit	NHL	64	29	33	62	68	11	9	11	20	24
1955-56	Detroit	NHL	70	38	41	79	100	10	3	9	12	8
1956-57	Detroit	NHL	70	44	45	89	72	5	2	5	7	6
1957-58	Detroit	NHL	64	33	44	77	40	4	1	1	2	0
1958-59	Detroit	NHL	70	32	46	78	57	...	...	...	...	...
1959-60	Detroit	NHL	70	28	45	73	46	6	1	5	6	4
1960-61	Detroit	NHL	64	23	49	72	30	11	4	11	15	10
1961-62	Detroit	NHL	70	33	44	77	54	...	...	...	...	...
1962-63	Detroit	NHL	70	38	48	86	100	11	7	9	16	22
1963-64	Detroit	NHL	69	26	47	73	70	14	9	10	19	16
1964-65	Detroit	NHL	70	29	47	76	104	7	4	2	6	20
1965-66	Detroit	NHL	70	29	46	75	83	12	4	6	10	12
1966-67	Detroit	NHL	69	25	40	65	53	...	...	...	...	...
1967-68	Detroit	NHL	74	39	43	82	53	...	...	...	...	...
1968-69	Detroit	NHL	76	44	59	103	58	...	...	...	...	...
1969-70	Detroit	NHL	76	31	40	71	58	4	2	0	2	2
1970-71	Detroit	NHL	63	23	29	52	38	...	...	...	...	...
1971-72				Did Not Play								
1972-73				Did Not Play								
1973-74	Houston	WHA	70	31	69	100	46	13	3	14	17	34
1974-75	Houston	WHA	75	34	65	99	84	12	8	12	20	20
1975-76	Houston	WHA	78	32	70	102	76	17	4	8	12	31
1976-77	Houston	WHA	62	24	44	68	57	11	5	3	8	11
1977-78	New England	WHA	76	34	62	96	85	14	5	5	10	15
1978-79	New England	WHA	58	19	24	43	51	10	3	1	4	4
1979-80	Hartford	NHL	80	15	26	41	42	3	1	1	2	2
	NHL Totals	**26**	**1767**	**801**	**1049**	**1846**	**1675**	**157**	**68**	**92**	**160**	**220**

SYD HOWE

Left wing / centre. Shoots left. 5'9", 180 lbs., Born, Ottawa, Ont., September 18, 1911

			Regular Season					Playoffs				
Season	Club	League	GP	G	A	PTS	PIM	GP	G	A	PTS	PIM
1929-30	Ottawa	Sr.	11	8	1	9	9	...	...	...	...	...
	London	Sr.	5	1	0	1	0	...	...	...	...	...
	Ottawa	NHL	12	1	1	2	0	2	0	0	0	0
1930-31	Philadelphia	NHL	44	9	11	20	20	...	...	...	...	...
1931-32	Syracuse	IHL	45	9	12	21	44	...	...	...	...	...
	Toronto	NHL	3	0	0	0	0	...	...	...	...	...
1932-33	Ottawa	NHL	48	12	12	24	17	...	...	...	...	...
1933-34	Ottawa	NHL	42	13	7	20	18	...	...	...	...	...
1934-35	St. Louis	NHL	36	14	13	27	23	...	...	...	...	...
	Detroit	NHL	14	8	12	20	11	...	...	...	...	...
1935-36	Detroit	NHL	48	16	14	30	26	7	3	3	6	2
1936-37	Detroit	NHL	45	17	10	27	10	10	2	5	7	0
1937-38	Detroit	NHL	48	8	19	27	14	...	...	...	...	...
1938-39	Detroit	NHL	48	16	20	36	11	6	3	1	4	4
1939-40	Detroit	NHL	46	14	23	37	17	6	2	2	4	2
1940-41	Detroit	NHL	48	20	24	44	8	9	1	7	8	0
1941-42	Detroit	NHL	48	16	19	35	6	12	3	5	8	0
1942-43	Detroit	NHL	50	20	35	55	10	7	1	2	3	0
1943-44	Detroit	NHL	40	32	28	60	6	5	2	2	4	0
1944-45	Detroit	NHL	46	17	36	53	6	7	0	0	0	2
1945-46	Detroit	NHL	26	4	7	11	9	...	...	...	...	...
	Indianapolis	AHL	14	6	11	17	0	5	2	0	2	0
1946-47	Ottawa	QSHL	24	19	21	40	4	11	2	1	3	0
	Ottawa	Sr.	1	2	1	3	0	...	...	...	...	...
1948-49	Ottawa Army	Sr.	1	0	0	0	0	...	...	...	...	...
	NHL Totals	**17**	**698**	**237**	**291**	**528**	**212**	**70**	**17**	**27**	**44**	**10**

HARRY HOWELL

Defence. Shoots left. 6'1", 200 lbs., Born, Hamilton, Ont., December 28, 1932

			Regular Season					Playoffs				
Season	Club	League	GP	G	A	PTS	PIM	GP	G	A	PTS	PIM
1949-50	Guelph	OHA Jr.	3	0	1	1	...	...	...	...	...	...
1950-51	Guelph	OHA Jr.	50	6	16	22	77	5	1	0	1	6
1951-52	Guelph	OHA Jr.	51	17	20	37	79	11	2	4	6	12
	Cincinnati	AHL	1	0	0	0	0	...	...	...	...	...
1952-53	NY Rangers	NHL	67	3	8	11	46	...	...	...	...	...
1953-54	NY Rangers	NHL	67	7	9	16	58	...	...	...	...	...
1954-55	NY Rangers	NHL	70	2	14	16	87	...	...	...	...	...
1955-56	NY Rangers	NHL	70	3	15	18	77	5	0	1	1	4
1956-57	NY Rangers	NHL	65	2	10	12	70	5	1	0	1	6
1957-58	NY Rangers	NHL	70	4	7	11	62	6	1	0	1	8
1958-59	NY Rangers	NHL	70	4	10	14	101	...	...	...	...	...
1959-60	NY Rangers	NHL	67	7	6	13	58	...	...	...	...	...
1960-61	NY Rangers	NHL	70	7	10	17	62	...	...	...	...	...
1961-62	NY Rangers	NHL	66	6	15	21	89	6	0	1	1	8
1962-63	NY Rangers	NHL	70	5	20	25	55	...	...	...	...	...
1963-64	NY Rangers	NHL	70	5	31	36	75	...	...	...	...	...
1964-65	NY Rangers	NHL	68	2	20	22	63	...	...	...	...	...
1965-66	NY Rangers	NHL	70	4	29	33	92	...	...	...	...	...
1966-67	NY Rangers	NHL	70	12	28	40	54	4	0	0	0	4
1967-68	NY Rangers	NHL	74	5	24	29	62	6	1	0	1	0
1968-69	NY Rangers	NHL	56	4	7	11	36	2	0	0	0	0
1969-70	Oakland	NHL	55	4	16	20	52	4	0	1	1	2
1970-71	California	NHL	28	0	9	9	14	...	...	...	...	...
	Los Angeles	NHL	18	3	8	11	4	...	...	...	...	...
1971-72	Los Angeles	NHL	77	1	17	18	53	...	...	...	...	...
1972-73	Los Angeles	NHL	73	4	11	15	28	...	...	...	...	...
1973-74	NY New Jersey	WHA	65	3	23	26	24	...	...	...	...	...
1974-75	San Diego	WHA	74	4	10	14	28	5	1	0	1	10
1975-76	Calgary	WHA	31	0	3	3	6	2	0	0	0	2
	NHL Totals	**21**	**1411**	**94**	**324**	**418**	**1298**	**38**	**3**	**3**	**6**	**32**

BOBBY HULL

Left wing. Shoots left. 5'10", 195 lbs., Born, Point Anne, Ont., January 3, 1939

			Regular Season					Playoffs				
Season	Club	League	GP	G	A	PTS	PIM	GP	G	A	PTS	PIM
1955-56	St. Catharines	OHA Jr.	48	11	7	18	79	6	0	2	2	9
1956-57	St. Catharines	OHA Jr.	52	33	28	61	95	13	8	8	16	24
1957-58	Chicago	NHL	70	13	34	47	62	...	...	...	...	...
1958-59	Chicago	NHL	70	18	32	50	50	6	1	1	2	2
1959-60	Chicago	NHL	70	39	42	81	68	3	1	0	1	2
1960-61	Chicago	NHL	67	31	25	56	43	12	4	10	14	4
1961-62	Chicago	NHL	70	50	34	84	35	12	8	6	14	12
1962-63	Chicago	NHL	65	31	31	62	27	5	8	2	10	4
1963-64	Chicago	NHL	70	43	44	87	50	7	2	5	7	2
1964-65	Chicago	NHL	61	39	32	71	32	14	10	7	17	27
1965-66	Chicago	NHL	65	54	43	97	70	6	2	2	4	10
1966-67	Chicago	NHL	66	52	28	80	52	6	4	2	6	10
1967-68	Chicago	NHL	71	44	31	75	39	11	4	6	10	15
1968-69	Chicago	NHL	74	58	49	107	48	...	...	...	...	...
1969-70	Chicago	NHL	61	38	29	67	8	8	3	8	11	2
1970-71	Chicago	NHL	78	44	52	96	32	18	11	14	25	16
1971-72	Chicago	NHL	78	50	43	93	24	8	4	4	8	6
1972-73	Winnipeg	WHA	63	51	52	103	37	14	9	16	25	16
1973-74	Winnipeg	WHA	75	53	42	95	38	4	1	1	2	4
1974-75	Winnipeg	WHA	78	77	65	142	41	...	...	...	...	...
1975-76	Winnipeg	WHA	80	53	70	123	30	13	12	8	20	4
1976-77	Winnipeg	WHA	34	21	32	53	14	20	13	9	22	2
1977-78	Winnipeg	WHA	77	46	71	117	23	9	8	3	11	12
1978-79	Winnipeg	WHA	4	2	3	5	0	...	...	...	...	...
1979-80	Winnipeg	NHL	18	4	6	10	0	...	...	...	...	...
	Hartford	NHL	9	2	5	7	0	3	0	0	0	0
	NHL Totals	**16**	**1063**	**610**	**560**	**1170**	**640**	**119**	**62**	**67**	**129**	**102**

JOHN "BOUSE" HUTTON

Goaltender. Catches left. Born, Ottawa, Ont. Born, Ottawa, Ont., October, 24, 1877

			Regular Season								Playoffs							
Season	Club	League	GP	MIN	GA	SO	GAA	W	L	T	GP	MIN	GA	SO	GAA	W	L	T
1898-99	Ottawa	CAHL	2	120	11	0	5.50	....	....	....	....	....	....	....	....	....	....	....
1899-1900	Ottawa	CAHL	7	420	19	0	2.71	....	....	....	....	....	....	....	....	....	....	....
1900-01	Ottawa	CAHL	7	480	20	0	2.50	....	....	....	....	....	....	....	....	....	....	....
1901-02	Ottawa	CAHL	8	480	15	2	1.70	....	....	....	....	....	....	....	....	....	....	....
1902-03	Ottawa	CAHL	8	530	26	0	3.80	....	....	....	4	240	5	1	1.25	3	0	1
1903-04	Ottawa	CAHL	4	240	15	0	3.75	....	....	....	8	480	23	1	2.86	6	1	1

HARRY HYLAND

Right wing / centre. Shoots right. 5'6", 156 lbs., Born, Montreal, Que., January 2, 1889

			Regular Season					Playoffs				
Season	Club	League	GP	G	A	PTS	PIM	GP	G	A	PTS	PIM
1908-09	Mtl. Shamrocks	ECHA	11	19	...	19	36	...	...	...	...	...
1909-10	Mtl. Wanderers	NHA	11	24	...	24	23	1	3	0	3	3
1910-11	Mtl. Wanderers	NHA	15	14	...	14	43	...	...	...	...	...
1911-12	N. Westminster	PCHA	15	26	...	26	44	...	...	...	...	...
1912-13	Mtl. Wanderers	NHA	20	27	...	27	38	...	...	...	...	...
1913-14	Mtl. Wanderers	NHA	18	30	12	42	18	...	...	...	...	...
1914-15	Mtl. Wanderers	NHA	19	23	6	29	49	2	0	0	0	26
1915-16	Mtl. Wanderers	NHA	20	14	0	14	69	...	...	...	...	...
1916-17	Mtl. Wanderers	NHA	13	12	2	14	21	...	...	...	...	...
	Mtl. St. Ann's	Sr.	...	3	1	4	...	...	...	...	...	...
1917-18	Mtl. Wanderers	NHL	4	6	0	6	9	...	...	...	...	...
	Ottawa	NHL	12	8	0	8	58	...	...	...	...	...
	NHL Totals	**1**	**16**	**14**	**....**	**16**	**0**	**...**	**...**	**...**	**...**	**...**

DICK IRVIN

Centre. Shoots left. 5'9", 162 lbs., Born, Limestone Ridge, Ont., July 19, 1892

			Regular Season					Playoffs				
Season	Club	League	GP	G	A	PTS	PIM	GP	G	A	PTS	PIM
1912-13	Strathconas	Sr.	7	32	...	32	1	1	0	0	0	0
	Wpg. Monatchs	MSHL	2	5	...	5	...	...	...	...	...	...
1913-14	Wpg. Monarchs	MSHL.	7	23	1	24	...	...	...	...	...	...
	Strathconas	Sr.	3	11	...	11	...	...	...	...	...	...
1914-15	Wpg. Monarchs	MHL Sr.	6	23	3	26	26	2	10	0	10	2
1915-16	Wpg. Monarchs	MHL Sr.	8	17	4	21	38	2	7	1	8	2
1916-17	Portland	PCHA	24	35	10	45	24	...	...	...	...	...
1917-18	Wpg. Yrpes	MHL Sr.	19	29	8	37	26	...	...	...	...	...
1918-19	Regina Vics	SSHL	Not Available...			...	...	...	...	...	...	
1919-20	Regina Vics	SSHL	12	32	4	36	22	2	1	0	1	4
1920-21	Regina Vics	SSHL	11	19	5	24	12	4	8	0	8	4
1921-22	Regina Caps	WCHL	20	21	7	28	17	4	3	0	3	2
1922-23	Regina Caps	WCHL	25	9	4	13	12	2	1	0	1	0
1923-24	Regina Caps	WCHL	29	15	8	23	33	2	0	0	0	4
1924-25	Regina Caps	WCHL	28	13	5	18	38	...	...	...	...	...
1925-26	Portland	WHL	30	31	5	36	29	...	...	...	...	...
1926-27	Chicago	NHL	43	18	18	36	34	2	2	0	2	4
1927-28	Chicago	NHL	12	5	4	9	14	...	...	...	...	...
1928-29	Chicago	NHL	39	6	1	7	30	...	...	...	...	...
	NHL Totals	**3**	**94**	**29**	**23**	**52**	**78**	**2**	**2**	**0**	**2**	**4**

HARVEY "BUSHER" JACKSON

Left wing. Shoots left. 5'11", 195 lbs., Born, Toronto, Ont., January 19, 1911

			Regular Season					Playoffs				
Season	Club	League	GP	G	A	PTS	PIM	GP	G	A	PTS	PIM
1927-28	Tor. Marlboros	OHA Jr.	4	4	0	4	2	...	...	...	...	...
1928-29	Tor. Marlboros	OHA Jr.	9	10	4	14	3	...	7	2	9	...
1929-30	Toronto	NHL	31	12	6	18	29	...	...	...	...	...
1930-31	Toronto	NHL	43	18	13	31	81	2	0	0	0	2
1931-32	Toronto	NHL	48	28	25	53	63	7	5	2	7	13
1932-33	Toronto	NHL	48	27	17	44	43	9	3	1	4	2
1933-34	Toronto	NHL	38	20	18	38	38	5	1	0	1	8
1934-35	Toronto	NHL	42	22	22	44	27	7	3	2	5	2
1935-36	Toronto	NHL	47	11	11	22	19	9	3	2	5	4
1936-37	Toronto	NHL	46	21	19	40	12	2	1	0	1	2
1937-38	Toronto	NHL	48	17	17	34	18	6	1	0	1	8
1938-39	Toronto	NHL	41	10	17	27	12	8	0	1	1	2
1939-40	NY Americans	NHL	43	12	8	20	10	3	0	1	1	2
1940-41	NY Americans	NHL	46	8	18	26	4	...	...	...	...	...
1941-42	Boston	NHL	26	5	7	12	8	5	0	1	1	0
1942-43	Boston	NHL	44	19	15	34	38	9	1	2	3	10
1943-44	Boston	NHL	42	11	21	32	25	...	...	...	...	...
	NHL Totals	**15**	**633**	**241**	**234**	**475**	**437**	**71**	**18**	**12**	**30**	**53**

ERNIE "MOOSE" JOHNSON

Defence / left wing. 5'11", 185 lbs., Born, Montreal, Que., February 26, 1886

			Regular Season					Playoffs				
Season	Club	League	GP	G	A	PTS	PIM	GP	G	A	PTS	PIM
1903-04	Montreal AAA	CAHL	2	1	...	1	...	...	...	...	...	...
1904-05	Montreal AAA	CAHL	9	8	...	8	...	...	...	...	...	...
1905-06	Mtl. Wanderers	ECAHA	10	12	...	12	...	...	...	...	...	...
1906-07	Mtl. Wanderers	ECAHA	10	14	...	14	2	6	8	...	8	...
1907-08	Mtl. Wanderers	ECHA	10	8	...	8	6	5	11	...	11	
1908-09	Mtl. Wanderers	ECHA	10	10	...	10	34	2	1	...	1	...
1909-10	Mtl. Wanderers	NHA	12	7	...	7	41	1	0	...	0	9
	Mtl. Wanderers	NHA	1	0	...	0	6	...	...	...	...	...
1910-11	Mtl. Wanderers	NHA	16	6	...	6	60	...	...	...	...	...
1911-12	N. Westminster	PCHA	14	9	...	9	13	...	...	...	...	...
1912-13	N. Westminster	PCHA	13	7	3	10	15	...	...	...	...	...
1913-14	N. Westminster	PCHA	16	3	5	8	27	...	...	...	...	...
1914-15	Portland	PCHA	18	6	4	10	21	...	...	...	...	...
1915-16	Portland	PCHA	18	6	3	9	62	5	1	0	1	9
1916-17	Portland	PCHA	24	12	9	21	54	...	...	...	...	...
1917-18	Portland	PCHA	15	3	2	5	3	...	...	...	...	...
1918-19	Victoria	PCHA	15	3	3	6	0	...	...	...	...	...
1919-20	Victoria	PCHA	21	0	5	5	22	...	...	...	...	...
1920-21	Victoria	PCHA	24	5	2	7	26	...	...	...	...	...
1921-22	Victoria	PCHA	13	1	1	2	12	...	...	...	...	...
1922-1925			Did Not Play									
1925-26	La Palais	CalHL	...	...	...	...	...	...	...	...	...	...
1926-27	Minneapolis	AHA	30	1	2	3	43	5	0	0	0	12
1928-29	Portland	PCHL	28	1	0	1	27	1	0	0	0	0
1929-30	Hollywood	CalHL	...	1	2	3	...	...	...	...	...	...
1930-31	San Francisco	CalHL	...	10	6	16	...	...	...	...	...	...

IVAN "CHING" JOHNSON

Defence. Shoots left. 5'11", 210 lbs., Born, Winnipeg, Man., December 7, 1897

			Regular Season					Playoffs				
Season	Club	League	GP	G	A	PTS	PIM	GP	G	A	PTS	PIM
1919-20	Wpg. Monarchs	Sr.	7	6	3	9	10	...	...	...	...	...
1920-21	Eveleth	AHA	...	...	...	...	...	...	...	...	...	...
1921-22	Eveleth	AHA	...	...	...	...	...	...	...	...	...	...
1922-23	Eveleth	AHA	...	4	0	4	...	...	...	...	...	...
1923-24	Minneapolis	AHA	20	10	0	10	...	...	...	...	...	...
1924-25	Minneapolis	AHA	40	8	0	8	...	...	...	...	...	...
1925-26	Minneapolis	AHA	38	14	5	19	92	3	2	0	2	6
1926-27	NY Rangers	NHL	29	3	2	5	66	2	0	0	0	6
1927-28	NY Rangers	NHL	42	10	6	16	146	9	1	1	2	46
1928-29	NY Rangers	NHL	8	0	0	0	14	6	0	0	0	26
1929-30	NY Rangers	NHL	30	3	3	6	82	4	0	0	0	14
1930-31	NY Rangers	NHL	44	2	6	8	77	4	1	0	1	17
1931-32	NY Rangers	NHL	47	3	10	13	106	7	2	0	2	24
1932-33	NY Rangers	NHL	48	8	9	17	127	8	1	0	1	14
1933-34	NY Rangers	NHL	48	2	6	8	86	2	0	0	0	4
1934-35	NY Rangers	NHL	29	2	3	5	34	4	0	0	0	2
1935-36	NY Rangers	NHL	47	5	3	8	58	...	...	...	...	...
1936-37	NY Rangers	NHL	35	0	0	0	2	9	0	1	1	4
1937-38	NY Americans	NHL	31	0	0	0	10	6	0	0	0	2
1938-39	Minneapolis	AHA	47	2	9	11	60	4	0	2	2	0
1939-40	Minneapolis	AHA	48	0	4	4	26	3	0	0	0	2
	NHL Totals	**12**	**436**	**38**	**48**	**86**	**808**	**61**	**5**	**2**	**7**	**161**

TOM JOHNSON

Defence. Shoots left. 6', 180 lbs., Born, Baldur, Man., February 18, 1928

			Regular Season					Playoffs				
Season	Club	League	GP	G	A	PTS	PIM	GP	G	A	PTS	PIM
1946-47	Wpg. Monarchs	MJHL	14	10	4	14	12	7	3	1	4	19
1947-48	Montreal	QSHL	16	0	4	4	10	...	...	...	...	...
	Montreal	NHL	1	0	0	0	0	...	...	...	...	...
1948-49	Buffalo	AHL	68	4	18	22	70	...	...	...	...	...
1949-50	Buffalo	AHL	58	7	19	26	52	5	0	0	0	20
	Montreal	NHL	1	0	0	0	0	...	...	...	...	...
1950-51	Montreal	NHL	70	2	8	10	128	11	0	0	0	6
1951-52	Montreal	NHL	67	0	7	7	76	11	1	0	1	2
1952-53	Montreal	NHL	70	3	8	11	63	12	2	3	5	8
1953-54	Montreal	NHL	70	7	11	18	85	11	1	2	3	30
1954-55	Montreal	NHL	70	6	19	25	74	12	2	0	2	22
1955-56	Montreal	NHL	64	3	10	13	75	10	0	2	2	8
1956-57	Montreal	NHL	70	4	11	15	59	10	0	2	2	13
1957-58	Montreal	NHL	66	3	18	21	75	2	0	0	0	0
1958-59	Montreal	NHL	70	10	29	39	76	11	2	3	5	8
1959-60	Montreal	NHL	64	4	25	29	59	8	0	1	1	4
1960-61	Montreal	NHL	70	1	15	16	54	6	0	1	1	8
1961-62	Montreal	NHL	62	1	17	18	45	6	0	1	1	0
1962-63	Montreal	NHL	43	3	5	8	28	...	...	...	...	...
1963-64	Boston	NHL	70	4	21	25	33	...	...	...	...	...
1964-65	Boston	NHL	51	0	9	9	30	...	...	...	...	...
	NHL Totals	**17**	**978**	**51**	**213**	**264**	**960**	**111**	**8**	**15**	**23**	**109**

AUREL JOLIAT

Left wing. Shoots left. 5'6", 136 lbs., Born, Ottawa, Ont., August 29, 1901

			Regular Season					Playoffs				
Season	Club	League	GP	G	A	PTS	PIM	GP	G	A	PTS	PIM
1922-23	Montreal	NHL	24	13	9	22	31	2	1	1	2	8
1923-24	Montreal	NHL	24	15	5	20	19	6	4	4	8	10
1924-25	Montreal	NHL	25	29	11	40	85	5	2	2	4	21
1925-26	Montreal	NHL	35	17	9	26	52	...	...	...	...	...
1926-27	Montreal	NHL	43	14	4	18	79	4	1	0	1	12
1927-28	Montreal	NHL	44	28	11	39	105	2	0	0	0	4
1928-29	Montreal	NHL	42	12	5	17	59	3	1	1	2	10
1929-30	Montreal	NHL	42	19	12	31	40	6	0	2	2	6
1930-31	Montreal	NHL	43	13	22	35	73	10	0	4	4	12
1931-32	Montreal	NHL	48	15	24	39	46	4	2	0	2	4
1932-33	Montreal	NHL	48	18	21	39	53	2	2	1	3	2
1933-34	Montreal	NHL	48	22	15	37	27	2	0	1	1	0
1934-35	Montreal	NHL	48	17	12	29	18	2	1	0	1	0
1935-36	Montreal	NHL	48	15	8	23	16	...	...	...	...	...
1936-37	Montreal	NHL	47	17	15	32	30	5	0	3	3	2
1937-38	Montreal	NHL	44	6	7	13	24	...	...	...	...	...
	NHL Totals	**16**	**654**	**270**	**190**	**460**	**757**	**54**	**14**	**19**	**33**	**89**

GORDON "DUKE" KEATS

Centre. Shoots right. 5'11", 195 lbs., Born, Montreal, Que., March 22, 1895

			Regular Season					Playoffs				
Season	Club	League	GP	G	A	PTS	PIM	GP	G	A	PTS	PIM
1915-16	Toronto	NHA	24	22	7	29	112	...	...	...	...	...
1916-17	Toronto	NHA	13	15	2	17	65	...	...	...	...	...
1917-18			Military Service									
1918-19			Military Service									
1919-20	Edmonton	Big 4	12	18	14	32	41	2	2	2	4	2
1920-21	Edmonton	Big 4	15	23	6	29	36	...	...	...	...	...
1921-22	Edmonton	WCHL	25	31	24	55	47	2	0	0	0	0
1922-23	Edmonton	WCHL	25	24	13	37	72	4	2	2	4	4
1923-24	Edmonton	WCHL	29	19	12	31	41	...	...	...	...	...
1924-25	Edmonton	WCHL	28	23	9	32	63	...	...	...	...	...
1925-26	Edmonton	WHL	30	20	9	29	134	2	0	1	1	9
1926-27	Boston	NHL	17	4	7	11	20	...	...	...	...	...
	Detroit	NHL	25	12	1	13	32	...	...	...	...	...
1927-28	Detroit	NHL	5	0	2	2	6	...	...	...	...	...
	Chicago	NHL	33	14	8	22	54	...	...	...	...	...
1928-29	Chicago	NHL	3	0	1	1	0	...	...	...	...	...
	Tulsa	AHA	39	22	11	33	18	4	0	1	1	10
1929-30	Tulsa	AHA	3	2	2	4	2	...	...	...	...	...
1930-31	Tulsa	AHA	43	14	10	24	44	4	0	1	1	6
1932-33	Edmonton	NWHL	25	8	7	15	146	8	1	4	5	0
1933-34	Edmonton	NWHL	25	8	6	14	8	2	0	0	0	2
	NHL Totals	**3**	**80**	**30**	**19**	**49**	**113**	**....**	**....**	**....**	**....**	**....**

LEONARD "RED" KELLY

Defence / centre. Shoots left. 6', 195 lbs., Born, Simcoe, Ont., July 9, 1927

			Regular Season					Playoffs				
Season	Club	League	GP	G	A	PTS	PIM	GP	G	A	PTS	PIM
1944-45	Tor. St. Mike's	OHA Jr.	1	0	0	0	0	...	...	...	...	...
1945-46	Tor. St. Mike's	OHA Jr.	26	13	11	24	18	11	1	0	1	7
1946-47	Tor. St. Mike's	OHA Jr.	30	8	24	32	11	9	3	3	6	9
1947-48	Detroit	NHL	60	6	14	20	13	10	3	2	5	2
1948-49	Detroit	NHL	59	5	11	16	10	11	1	1	2	6
1949-50	Detroit	NHL	70	15	25	40	9	14	1	3	4	2
1950-51	Detroit	NHL	70	17	37	54	24	6	0	1	1	0
1951-52	Detroit	NHL	67	16	31	47	16	5	1	0	1	0
1952-53	Detroit	NHL	70	19	27	46	8	6	0	4	4	0
1953-54	Detroit	NHL	62	16	33	49	18	12	5	1	6	0
1954-55	Detroit	NHL	70	15	30	45	28	11	2	4	6	17
1955-56	Detroit	NHL	70	16	34	50	39	10	2	4	6	2
1956-57	Detroit	NHL	70	10	25	35	18	5	1	0	1	0
1957-58	Detroit	NHL	61	13	18	31	26	4	0	1	1	2
1958-59	Detroit	NHL	67	8	13	21	34	...	...	...	...	...
1959-60	Detroit	NHL	50	6	12	18	10	...	...	...	...	...
	Toronto	NHL	18	6	5	11	8	10	3	8	11	2
1960-61	Toronto	NHL	64	20	50	70	12	2	1	0	1	0
1961-62	Toronto	NHL	58	22	27	49	6	12	4	6	10	0
1962-63	Toronto	NHL	66	20	40	60	8	10	2	6	8	6
1963-64	Toronto	NHL	70	11	34	45	16	14	4	9	13	4
1964-65	Toronto	NHL	70	18	28	46	8	6	3	2	5	2
1965-66	Toronto	NHL	63	8	24	32	12	4	0	2	2	0
1966-67	Toronto	NHL	61	14	24	38	4	12	0	5	5	2
	NHL Totals	**20**	**1316**	**281**	**542**	**823**	**327**	**164**	**33**	**59**	**92**	**51**

TED KENNEDY

Centre. Shoots right. 5'11", 180 lbs., Born, Humberson, Ont., December 12, 1925

			Regular Season					Playoffs				
Season	Club	League	GP	G	A	PTS	PIM	GP	G	A	PTS	PIM
1942-43	Port Colborne	OHA Sr.	23	23	29	52	15	...	...	...	...	...
	Toronto	NHL	2	0	1	1	0	...	...	...	...	...
1943-44	Toronto	NHL	49	26	23	49	2	5	1	1	2	4
1944-45	Toronto	NHL	49	29	25	54	14	13	7	2	9	2
1945-46	Toronto	NHL	21	3	2	5	4	...	...	...	...	...
1946-47	Toronto	NHL	60	28	32	60	27	11	4	5	9	4
1947-48	Toronto	NHL	60	25	21	46	32	...	8	6	14	0
1948-49	Toronto	NHL	59	18	21	39	25	9	2	6	8	2
1949-50	Toronto	NHL	53	20	24	44	34	7	1	2	3	8
1950-51	Toronto	NHL	63	18	43	61	32	11	4	5	9	6
1951-52	Toronto	NHL	70	19	33	52	33	4	0	0	0	4
1952-53	Toronto	NHL	43	14	23	37	42	...	...	...	...	...
1953-54	Toronto	NHL	67	15	23	38	78	5	1	1	2	2
1954-55	Toronto	NHL	70	10	42	52	74	4	1	3	4	0
1955-56			Did Not Play									
1956-57	Toronto	NHL	30	6	16	22	35	...	...	...	...	...
	NHL Totals	**14**	**696**	**231**	**329**	**560**	**432**	**78**	**29**	**31**	**60**	**32**

DAVE KEON

Centre. Shoots left. 5'9", 163 lbs., Born, Noranda, Que., March 22, 1940

			Regular Season					Playoffs				
Season	Club	League	GP	G	A	PTS	PIM	GP	G	A	PTS	PIM
1956-57	Tor. St. Mike's	OHA Jr.	4	1	3	4	0	...	...	...	...	...
1957-58	Tor. St. Mike's	OHA Jr.	45	23	27	50	29	9	8	5	13	10
1958-59	Tor. St. Mike's	OHA Jr.	46	16	29	45	8	15	4	9	13	8
1959-60	Tor. St. Mike's	OHA Jr.	47	33	38	71	31	10	8	10	18	2
	Kitch-Waterloo	OHA Sr.	1	1	0	1	0	...	...	...	...	...
	Sudbury	EPHL	4	2	2	4	2	...	...	...	...	...
1960-61	Toronto	NHL	70	20	25	45	6	5	1	1	2	0
1961-62	Toronto	NHL	64	26	35	61	2	12	5	3	8	0
1962-63	Toronto	NHL	68	28	28	56	2	10	7	5	12	0
1963-64	Toronto	NHL	70	23	37	60	6	14	7	2	9	2
1964-65	Toronto	NHL	65	21	29	50	10	6	2	2	4	2
1965-66	Toronto	NHL	69	24	30	54	4	4	0	2	2	0
1966-67	Toronto	NHL	66	19	33	52	2	12	3	5	8	0
1967-68	Toronto	NHL	67	11	37	48	4	...	...	...	...	...
1968-69	Toronto	NHL	75	27	34	61	12	4	1	3	4	2
1969-70	Toronto	NHL	72	32	30	62	6	...	...	...	...	...
1970-71	Toronto	NHL	76	38	38	76	4	6	3	2	5	0
1971-72	Toronto	NHL	72	18	30	48	4	5	2	3	5	0
1972-73	Toronto	NHL	76	37	36	73	2	...	...	...	...	...
1973-74	Toronto	NHL	74	25	28	53	7	4	1	2	3	0
1974-75	Toronto	NHL	78	16	43	59	4	7	0	5	5	0
1975-76	Minnesota	WHA	57	26	38	64	4	...	...	...	...	...
	Indianapolis	WHA	12	3	7	10	2	7	2	2	4	2
1976-77	Minnesota	WHA	42	13	38	51	2	...	...	...	...	...
	New England	WHA	34	14	25	39	8	5	3	1	4	0
1977-78	New England	WHA	77	24	38	62	2	14	5	11	16	4
1978-79	New England	WHA	79	22	43	65	2	10	3	9	12	2
1979-80	Hartford	NHL	76	10	52	62	10	3	0	1	1	0
1980-81	Hartford	NHL	80	13	34	47	26	...	...	...	...	...
1981-82	Hartford	NHL	78	8	11	19	6	...	...	...	...	...
	NHL Totals	**18**	**1296**	**396**	**590**	**986**	**117**	**92**	**32**	**36**	**68**	**6**

ELMER LACH

Centre. Shoots left. 5'10", 170 lbs., Born, Nokomis, Sask., January 22, 1916

			Regular Season					Playoffs				
Season	Club	League	GP	G	A	PTS	PIM	GP	G	A	PTS	PIM
1935-36	Regina	SJHL	2	0	1	1	2	4	3	0	3	6
1936-37	Weyburn	SSHL	23	16	6	22	27	3	0	1	1	4
1937-38	Weyburn	SSHL	22	12	12	24	44	3	2	1	3	0
1938-39	Moose Jaw	SSHL	29	17	20	37	23	10	6	4	10	8
1939-40	Moose Jaw	SSHL	30	15	29	44	20	8	5	9	14	12
1940-41	Montreal	NHL	43	7	14	21	16	3	1	0	1	0
1941-42	Montreal	NHL	1	0	1	1	0	...	...	...	...	...
1942-43	Montreal	NHL	45	18	40	58	14	5	2	4	6	6
1943-44	Montreal	NHL	48	24	48	72	23	9	2	11	13	4
1944-45	Montreal	NHL	50	26	54	80	37	6	4	4	8	2
1945-46	Montreal	NHL	50	13	34	47	34	9	5	12	17	4
1946-47	Montreal	NHL	31	14	16	30	22	...	...	...	...	...
1947-48	Montreal	NHL	60	30	31	61	72	...	...	...	...	...
1948-49	Montreal	NHL	36	11	18	29	59	1	0	0	0	4
1949-50	Montreal	NHL	64	15	33	48	33	5	1	2	3	4
1950-51	Montreal	NHL	65	21	24	45	48	11	2	2	4	2
1951-52	Montreal	NHL	70	15	50	65	36	11	1	2	3	4
1952-53	Montreal	NHL	53	16	25	41	56	12	1	6	7	6
1953-54	Montreal	NHL	48	5	20	25	28	4	0	2	2	0
	NHL Totals	**14**	**664**	**215**	**408**	**623**	**478**	**76**	**19**	**45**	**64**	**36**

GUY LAFLEUR

Right wing. Shoots right. 6', 185 lbs., Born, Thurso, Que., September 20, 1951

			Regular Season					Playoffs				
Season	Club	League	GP	G	A	PTS	PIM	GP	G	A	PTS	PIM
1966-67	Quebec	QJHL	8	1	1	2	0	...	...	...	...	...
1967-68	Quebec	QJHL	43	30	19	49	...	...	...	...	...	...
1968-69	Quebec	QJHL	49	50	60	110	83	...	...	...	...	...
1969-70	Quebec	QJHL	56	103	67	170	105	15	25	18	43	34
1970-71	Quebec	QJHL	62	130	79	209	135	14	22	21	43	24
1971-72	Montreal	NHL	73	29	35	64	48	6	1	4	5	2
1972-73	Montreal	NHL	69	28	27	55	51	17	3	5	8	9
1973-74	Montreal	NHL	73	21	35	56	29	6	0	1	1	4
1974-75	Montreal	NHL	70	53	66	119	37	11	12	7	19	15
1975-76	Montreal	NHL	80	56	69	125	36	13	7	10	17	2
1976-77	Montreal	NHL	80	56	80	136	20	14	9	17	26	6
1977-78	Montreal	NHL	78	60	72	132	26	15	10	11	21	16
1978-79	Montreal	NHL	80	52	77	129	28	16	10	13	23	0
1979-80	Montreal	NHL	74	50	75	125	12	3	3	1	4	0
1980-81	Montreal	NHL	51	27	43	70	29	3	0	1	1	2
1981-82	Montreal	NHL	66	27	57	84	24	5	2	1	3	4
1982-83	Montreal	NHL	68	27	49	76	12	3	0	2	2	2
1983-84	Montreal	NHL	80	30	40	70	19	12	0	3	3	5
1984-85	Montreal	NHL	19	2	3	5	10	...	...	...	...	...
1985-1988				Did Not Play								
1988-89	NY Rangers	NHL	67	18	27	45	12	4	1	0	1	0
1989-90	Quebec	NHL	39	12	22	34	4	...	...	...	...	...
1990-91	Quebec	NHL	59	12	12	28	2	...	...	...	...	...
	NHL Totals	**17**	**1126**	**560**	**793**	**1353**	**399**	**128**	**58**	**76**	**134**	**67**

NEWSY LALONDE

Centre. Shoots right. 5'9", 168 lbs., Born, Cornwall, Ont., October 31, 1887

			Regular Season					Playoffs				
Season	Club	League	GP	G	A	PTS	PIM	GP	G	A	PTS	PIM
1904-05	Cornwall	FAHL	2	1	...	1	...	...	...	...	...	...
1905-06	Woodstock	Sr.		Not Available...		...	...	...	...	...	...	
1906-07	Canadian Soo	IHL	18	29	4	33	27	...	...	...	...	...
	Cobalt	Sr.		Not Available...		...	...	...	...	...	...	
1907-08	Portage	MHL Sr.	1	0	...	0	0	...	...	...	...	...
	Toronto	OPHL	11	29	...	29	...	1	2	0	2	...
1908-09	Toronto	OPHL	11	24	...	24	...	...	...	...	...	...
1909-10	Montreal	NHA	7	18	...	18	40	...	...	...	...	...
	Renfrew	NHA	5	22	...	22	16	...	...	...	...	...
1910-11	Montreal	NHA	16	19	...	19	63	...	...	...	...	...
1911-12	Vancouver	PCHA	15	27	...	27	51	...	...	...	...	...
1912-13	Montreal	NHA	18	25	...	25	61	...	...	...	...	...
1913-14	Montreal	NHA	14	22	5	27	23	2	0	0	0	2
1914-15	Montreal	NHA	7	4	3	7	17	...	...	...	...	...
1915-16	Montreal	NHA	24	28	6	34	78	4	3	0	3	41
1916-17	Montreal	NHA	18	27	5	32	53	6	2	0	2	...
1917-18	Montreal	NHL	14	23	1	24	38	2	5	0	5	11
1918-19	Montreal	NHL	17	23	9	32	40	10	17	1	18	8
1919-20	Montreal	NHL	23	36	6	42	33	...	...	...	...	...
1920-21	Montreal	NHL	24	33	8	41	36	...	...	...	...	...
1921-22	Montreal	NHL	20	9	4	13	11	...	...	...	...	...
1922-23	Saskatoon	WCHL	29	30	4	34	44	...	...	...	...	...
1923-24	Saskatoon	WCHL	21	10	10	20	24	...	...	...	...	...
1924-25	Saskatoon	WCHL	22	8	6	14	42	2	0	0	0	4
1925-26	Saskatoon	WHL	3	0	0	0	2	2	0	0	0	2
1926-27	NY Americans	NHL	1	0	0	0	2	...	...	...	...	...
1927-28	Quebec	CAHL	1	0	0	0	0	...	...	...	...	...
	NHL Totals	**6**	**99**	**124**	**27**	**151**	**122**	**12**	**22**	**1**	**23**	**19**

JACQUES LAPERRIERE

Defence. Shoots left. 6'2", 190 lbs., Born, Rouyn, Que., November 22, 1941

			Regular Season					Playoffs				
Season	Club	League	GP	G	A	PTS	PIM	GP	G	A	PTS	PIM
1958-59	Hull / Ottawa	EOHL	1	1	1	2	2	2	0	0	0	0
1959-60	Brockville	Jr.	...	...	...	...	...	...	...	...	...	...
	Hull / Ottawa	EPHL	5	0	2	2	0	...	...	...	...	...
1960-61	Hull / Ottawa	EPHL	5	0	0	0	2	3	0	2	2	4
1961-62	Montreal	OHA Jr.	48	20	37	57	98	6	0	1	1	11
	Hull / Ottawa	EPHL	1	0	0	0	4	7	1	4	5	6
1962-63	Hull / Ottawa	EPHL	40	8	19	27	51	2	0	0	0	0
	Montreal	NHL	6	0	2	2	2	5	0	1	1	4
1963-64	Montreal	NHL	65	2	28	30	102	7	1	1	2	8
1964-65	Montreal	NHL	67	5	22	27	92	6	1	1	2	16
1965-66	Montreal	NHL	57	6	25	31	85	...	...	...	...	...
1966-67	Montreal	NHL	61	0	20	20	48	9	0	1	1	9
1967-68	Montreal	NHL	72	4	21	25	84	13	1	3	4	20
1968-69	Montreal	NHL	69	5	26	31	45	14	1	3	4	28
1969-70	Montreal	NHL	73	6	31	37	98	...	...	...	...	...
1970-71	Montreal	NHL	49	0	16	16	20	20	4	9	13	12
1971-72	Montreal	NHL	73	3	25	28	50	4	0	0	0	2
1972-73	Montreal	NHL	57	7	16	23	34	10	1	3	4	2
1973-74	Montreal	NHL	42	2	10	12	14	...	...	...	...	...
	NHL Totals	**12**	**691**	**40**	**242**	**282**	**674**	**88**	**9**	**22**	**31**	**101**

GUY LAPOINTE

Defence. Shoots left. 6', 205 lbs., Born, Montreal, Que., March 18, 1948

			Regular Season					Playoffs				
Season	Club	League	GP	G	A	PTS	PIM	GP	G	A	PTS	PIM
1965-66	Verdun	QJHL	37	7	13	20	96	...	...	...	...	...
1966-67	Verdun	QJHL		Not Available...		...	...	...	...	...	...	...
1967-68	Montreal	OHA Jr.	51	11	27	38	147	11	1	6	7	40
1968-69	Montreal	NHL	1	0	0	0	2	...	...	...	...	...
	Houston	CHL	65	3	15	18	120	3	1	0	1	6
1969-70	Montreal	NHL	5	0	0	0	4	...	...	...	...	...
	Montreal	AHL	57	8	30	38	92	8	3	5	8	6
1970-71	Montreal	NHL	78	15	29	44	107	20	4	5	9	34
1971-72	Montreal	NHL	69	11	38	49	58	6	0	1	1	0
1972-73	Montreal	NHL	76	19	35	54	117	17	6	7	13	20
1973-74	Montreal	NHL	71	13	40	53	63	6	0	2	2	4
1974-75	Montreal	NHL	80	28	47	75	88	11	6	4	10	4
1975-76	Montreal	NHL	77	21	47	68	78	13	3	3	6	12
1976-77	Montreal	NHL	77	25	51	76	53	12	3	9	12	4
1977-78	Montreal	NHL	49	13	29	42	19	14	1	6	7	16
1978-79	Montreal	NHL	69	13	42	55	43	10	2	6	8	10
1979-80	Montreal	NHL	45	6	20	26	29	2	0	0	0	0
1980-81	Montreal	NHL	33	1	9	10	79	1	0	0	0	17
1981-82	Montreal	NHL	47	1	19	20	72	...	...	...	...	...
	St. Louis	NHL	8	0	6	6	4	7	1	0	1	8
1982-83	St. Louis	NHL	54	3	23	26	43	4	0	1	1	9
1983-84	Boston	NHL	45	2	16	18	34	...	...	...	...	...
	NHL Totals	**16**	**884**	**171**	**451**	**622**	**893**	**123**	**26**	**44**	**70**	**138**

EDGAR LAPRADE

Centre. Shoots right. 5'8", 157 lbs., Born, Mine Centre, Ont., October 10, 1919

			Regular Season					Playoffs				
Season	Club	League	GP	G	A	PTS	PIM	GP	G	A	PTS	PIM
1935-36	Port Arthur	TBHL Jr.	14	13	10	23	6	4	4	2	6	2
1936-37	Port Arthur	TBHL Jr.	18	19	14	33	2	3	6	3	9	5
1937-38	Port Arthur	TBHL Jr.	18	23	11	34	9	5	6	0	6	0
1938-39	Port Arthur	TBHL Sr.	10	11	2	13	...	...	...	...	...	...
	Port Arthur	MHL JR.	...	7	4	11	...	...	...	...	...	...
1939-40	Port Arthur	TBHL Sr.	22	20	15	35	8	3	5	1	6	2
1940-41	Port Arthur	TBHL Sr.	20	26	21	47	7	4	2	1	3	0
1941-42	Port Arthur	TBHL Sr.	15	18	23	41	4	...	...	...	...	...
1942-43	Port Arthur	TBHL Sr.	8	7	10	17	0	3	7	4	11	4
	Mtl. RCAF	Sr.	1	0	1	1	2	12	1	4	5	4
1943-44			Military Service									
1944-45	Barriefield	Sr.	19	28	47	2	4	...	5	8	13	0
1945-46	NY Rangers	NHL	49	15	19	34	0	...	...	...	...	...
1946-47	NY Rangers	NHL	58	15	25	40	9	...	...	...	...	...
1947-48	NY Rangers	NHL	59	13	34	47	7	6	1	4	5	0
1948-49	NY Rangers	NHL	56	18	12	30	12	...	...	...	...	...
1949-50	NY Rangers	NHL	60	22	22	44	2	12	3	5	8	4
1950-51	NY Rangers	NHL	42	10	13	23	0	...	...	...	...	...
1951-52	NY Rangers	NHL	70	9	29	38	8	...	...	...	...	...
1952-53	NY Rangers	NHL	11	2	1	3	2	...	...	...	...	...
1953-54	NY Rangers	NHL	35	1	6	7	2	...	...	...	...	...
1954-55	NY Rangers	NHL	60	3	11	14	0	...	...	...	...	...
	NHL Totals	**10**	**501**	**108**	**172**	**280**	**42**	**18**	**4**	**9**	**13**	**4**

JACK LAVIOLETTE

Defence / right wing. Shoots right. 5'11", 170 lbs., Born, Belleville, Ont., August 27, 1879

			Regular Season					Playoffs				
Season	Club	League	GP	G	A	PTS	PIM	GP	G	A	PTS	PIM
1903-04	Mtl. Nationals	FAHL	6	8	...	8	...	...	...	...	...	...
1904-05	Michigan Soo	IHL	4	15	0	15	24	...	...	...	...	...
1905-06	Michigan Soo	IHL	17	15	0	15	28	...	...	...	...	...
1906-07	Michigan Soo	IHL	19	10	7	17	34	...	...	...	...	...
1907-08	Mtl. Shamrocks	ECHA	6	1	...	1	...	...	...	...	...	...
1908-09	Mtl. Shamrocks	ECHA	9	1	...	1	36	...	...	...	...	...
1909-10	Montreal	NHA	11	3	...	3	26	...	...	...	...	...
	Montreal	NHA	1	1	...	1	15	...	...	...	...	...
1910-11	Montreal	NHA	16	0	...	0	24	...	...	...	...	...
1911-12	Montreal	NHA	17	7	...	7	10	...	...	...	...	...
1912-13	Montreal	NHA	20	8	...	8	77	...	...	...	...	...
1913-14	Montreal	NHA	20	7	9	16	30	2	0	1	1	0
1914-15	Montreal	NHA	18	6	3	9	35	...	...	...	...	...
1915-16	Montreal	NHA	18	8	3	11	62	4	0	0	0	6
1916-17	Montreal	NHA	18	7	3	10	21	6	1	0	1	0
1917-18	Montreal	NHL	19	2	1	3	9	2	0	0	0	0
	NHL Totals	**1**	**18**	**2**	**0**	**2**	**6**	**2**	**0**	**0**	**0**	**0**

HUGH LEHMAN

Goaltender. Catches left. 5'8", 168 lbs., Born, Pembroke, Ont., October 27, 1885

			Regular Season								Playoffs							
Season	Club	League	GP	MIN	GA	SO	GAA	W	L	T	GP	MIN	GA	SO	GAA	W	L	T
1903-04	Pembroke	Sr.	5	300	22	0	4.50	1	4	0	....	....	....	....	....	....	....	....
1904-05	Pembroke	Sr		....	....	....	....	....	....	....	....	....	....	....	....	....	....	....
1905-06	Pembroke	Sr.	8	480	13	1	1.67	8	0	0	1	60	0	1	0.00	1	0	0
1906-07	Canadian Soo	IHL	24	1440	123	0	5.13	13	11	0	....	....	....	....	....	....	....	....
1907-08	Pembroke	Sr.	Not Available			....	....	....	....	....	....	....	....	....	....	....	....	
1908-09	Berlin	OPHL	14	840	65	0	4.64	9	6	0	....	....	....	....	....	....	....	....
1909-10	Berlin	OPHL	17	1020	74	1	4.35	11	6	0	1	60	7	0	7.00	0	1	0
	Galt	OPHL	2	120	15	0	7.50	0	2	0	....	....	....	....	....	....	....	....
1910-11	Berlin	OPHL	15	900	87	0	5.80	7	8	0	....	....	....	....	....	....	....	....
1911-12	N. Westminster	PCHA	15	912	77	0	5.07	9	6	0	....	....	....	....	....	....	....	....
1912-13	N. Westminster	PCHA	12	739	51	0	4.14	4	8	0	....	....	....	....	....	....	....	....
1913-14	N. Westminster	PCHA	16	997	81	0	4.88	7	9	0	....	....	....	....	....	....	....	....
1914-15	Vancouver	PCHA	17	1043	71	1	4.08	14	3	0	....	....	....	....	....	....	....	....
1915-16	Vancouver	PCHA	18	1091	69	0	3.80	9	9	0	....	....	....	....	....	....	....	....
1916-17	Vancouver	PCHA	23	1404	124	0	5.30	14	9	0	....	....	....	....	....	....	....	....
1917-18	Vancouver	PCHA	18	1179	60	1	3.05	9	9	0	2	120	2	1	1.00	1	0	1
1918-19	Vancouver	PCHA	20	1277	55	1	2.58	12	8	0	2	120	7	0	3.50	0	2	0
1919-20	Vancouver	PCHA	22	1334	65	1	2.92	11	11	0	2	120	7	0	3.50	1	1	0
1920-21	Vancouver	PCHA	24	1449	79	3	3.27	13	11	1	2	120	2	1	1.00	2	0	0
1921-22	Vancouver	PCHA	22	1318	62	4	2.82	12	10	0	2	120	0	2	0.00	2	0	0
1922-23	Vancouver	PCHA	25	1568	61	4	2.33	16	8	1	2	120	3	1	1.50	1	1	0
1923-24	Vancouver	PCHA	30	1843	81	1	2.64	13	16	1	2	134	3	0	1.34	1	0	1
1924-25	Vancouver	WCHL	11	662	30	0	2.72	7	4	0	....	....	....	....	....	....	....	....
1925-26	Vancouver	WHL	30	1820	90	3	2.97	10	18	2	....	....	....	....	....	....	....	....
1926-27	Chicago	NHL	44	2797	116	5	2.49	19	22	3	2	120	10	0	5.00	0	1	1
1927-28	Chicago	NHL	4	250	20	1	4.80	1	1	1	....	....	....	....	....	....	....	....
	NHL Totals	**2**	**48**	**3047**	**136**	**6**	**2.68**	**20**	**24**	**4**	**2**	**120**	**10**	**0**	**5.00**	**0**	**1**	**1**

JACQUES LEMAIRE

Centre. Shoots left. 5'10", 180 lbs., Born, La Salle, Que., September 7, 1945

			Regular Season					Playoffs				
Season	Club	League	GP	G	A	PTS	PIM	GP	G	A	PTS	PIM
1962-63	Lachine	QHJL	42	41	63	104	...	...	...	...	...	...
1963-64	Montreal	OHA Jr.	42	25	30	55	17	17	10	6	16	4
1964-65	Montreal	OHA Jr.	56	25	47	72	52	7	1	5	6	0
	Quebec	AHL	1	0	0	0	0	...	...	...	...	...
1965-66	Montreal	OHA Jr.	48	41	52	93	69	10	11	2	13	14
1966-67	Houston	CHL	69	19	30	49	19	6	0	1	1	0
1967-68	Montreal	NHL	69	22	20	42	16	13	7	6	13	6
1968-69	Montreal	NHL	75	29	34	63	29	14	4	2	6	6
1969-70	Montreal	NHL	69	32	28	60	16	...	...	...	...	...
1970-71	Montreal	NHL	78	28	28	56	18	20	9	10	19	17
1971-72	Montreal	NHL	77	32	49	81	26	6	2	1	3	2
1972-73	Montreal	NHL	77	44	51	95	16	17	7	13	20	2
1973-74	Montreal	NHL	66	29	38	67	10	6	0	4	4	2
1974-75	Montreal	NHL	80	36	56	92	20	11	5	7	12	4
1975-76	Montreal	NHL	61	20	32	52	20	13	3	3	6	2
1976-77	Montreal	NHL	75	34	41	75	22	14	7	12	19	6
1977-78	Montreal	NHL	76	36	61	97	14	15	6	8	14	10
1978-79	Montreal	NHL	50	24	31	55	10	16	11	12	23	6
	NHL Totals	**12**	**853**	**366**	**469**	**835**	**217**	**145**	**61**	**78**	**139**	**63**

PERCY LESUEUR

Goaltender. Catches left. 5'7", 150 lbs., Born, Quebec City, Que., November 18, 1881

			Regular Season								Playoffs							
Season	Club	League	GP	MIN	GA	SO	GAA	W	L	T	GP	MIN	GA	SO	GAA	W	L	T
1905-06	Smiths Falls	FAHL	7	420	16	1	2.30	7	0	0	2	120	14	0	7.00	0	2	0
	Ottawa	ECAHA	1	60	3	0	3.00	1	0	0	....	....	....	....	....	....	....	....
1906-07	Ottawa	ECAHA	10	602	54	0	5.38	7	3	0	....	....	....	....	....	....	....	....
1907-08	Ottawa	ECAHA	10	602	51	0	5.08	7	3	0	....	....	....	....	....	....	....	....
1908-09	Ottawa	ECHA	12	728	63	0	5.19	10	2	0	....	....	....	....	....	....	....	....
1909-10	Ottawa	ECHA	2	120	9	0	4.50	2	0	0	....	....	....	....	....	....	....	....
	Ottawa	NHA	12	730	66	0	5.43	9	3	0	4	240	15	0	3.75	4	0	0
1910-11	Ottawa	NHA	16	990	69	1	4.18	13	3	0	2	120	8	0	4.00	2	0	0
1911-12	Ottawa	NHA	18	1126	91	0	4.85	9	9	0	....	....	....	....	....	....	....	....
1912-13	Ottawa	NHA	18	934	65	0	4.18	7	10	0	....	....	....	....	....	....	....	....
1913-14	Ottawa	NHA	13	773	42	1	3.26	6	6	0	....	....	....	....	....	....	....	....
1914-15	Tor. Shamrocks	NHA	19	1145	96	0	5.03	8	11	0	....	....	....	....	....	....	....	....
1915-16	Toronto	NHA	23	1416	92	1	3.90	9	13	0	....	....	....	....	....	....	....	....

HERBIE LEWIS

Left wing / centre. Shoots left. 5'9", 163 lbs., Born, Calgary, Alta., April 17, 1905

			Regular Season					Playoffs				
Season	Club	League	GP	G	A	PTS	PIM	GP	G	A	PTS	PIM
1922-23	Calgary	CJHL	12	17	7	24	...	...	...	...	...	...
1923-24	Calgary	CJHL	Not Available...			...	...	...	...	...	...	
1924-25	Duluth	AHA	40	9	0	9	...	...	...	...	...	...
1925-26	Duluth	AHA	39	17	11	28	52	8	3	1	4	8
1926-27	Duluth	AHA	37	18	6	24	52	3	1	0	1	2
1927-28	Duluth	AHA	40	14	5	19	56	5	0	0	0	8
1928-29	Detroit	NHL	36	9	5	14	33	...	...	...	...	...
1929-30	Detroit	NHL	44	20	11	31	36	...	...	...	...	...
1930-31	Detroit	NHL	43	15	6	21	38	...	...	...	...	...
1931-32	Detroit	NHL	48	5	14	19	21	2	0	0	0	0
1932-33	Detroit	NHL	48	20	14	34	20	4	1	0	1	0
1933-34	Detroit	NHL	43	16	15	31	15	9	5	2	7	2
1934-35	Detroit	NHL	47	16	27	43	26	...	...	...	...	...
1935-36	Detroit	NHL	45	14	23	37	25	7	2	3	5	0
1936-37	Detroit	NHL	45	14	18	32	14	10	4	3	7	4
1937-38	Detroit	NHL	43	13	18	31	12	...	...	...	...	...
1938-39	Detroit	NHL	42	6	10	16	8	6	1	2	3	0
1939-40	Indianapolis	AHL	26	1	6	7	6	3	1	2	3	0
1940-41	Indianapolis	AHL	2	1	0	1	0	...	...	...	...	...
	NHL Totals	**11**	**483**	**148**	**161**	**309**	**248**	**38**	**13**	**10**	**23**	**6**

TED LINDSAY

Left wing. Shoots left. 5'8", 160 lbs., Born, Renfrew, Ont., July 29, 1925

			Regular Season					Playoffs				
Season	Club	League	GP	G	A	PTS	PIM	GP	G	A	PTS	PIM
1943-44	Oshawa	OHA Jr.	...	...	...	...	...	...	...	...	...	...
	Tor. St. Mike's	OHA Jr.	22	22	7	29	24	12	13	6	19	16
1944-45	Detroit	NHL	45	17	6	23	43	14	2	0	2	6
1945-46	Detroit	NHL	47	7	10	17	14	5	0	1	1	0
1946-47	Detroit	NHL	59	27	15	42	57	5	2	2	4	10
1947-48	Detroit	NHL	60	33	19	52	95	10	3	1	4	6
1948-49	Detroit	NHL	50	26	28	54	97	11	2	6	8	31
1949-50	Detroit	NHL	69	23	55	78	141	13	4	4	8	16
1950-51	Detroit	NHL	67	24	35	59	110	6	0	1	1	8
1951-52	Detroit	NHL	70	30	39	69	123	8	5	2	7	8
1952-53	Detroit	NHL	70	32	39	71	111	6	4	4	8	6
1953-54	Detroit	NHL	70	26	36	62	110	12	4	4	8	14
1954-55	Detroit	NHL	49	19	19	38	85	11	7	12	19	12
1955-56	Detroit	NHL	67	27	23	50	161	10	6	3	9	22
1956-57	Detroit	NHL	70	30	55	85	103	5	2	4	6	8
1957-58	Chicago	NHL	68	15	24	39	110	...	...	...	...	...
1958-59	Chicago	NHL	70	22	36	58	184	6	2	4	6	13
1959-60	Chicago	NHL	68	7	19	26	91	4	1	1	2	0
1960-1964			Did Not Play									
1964-65	Detroit	NHL	69	14	14	28	173	7	3	0	3	34
	NHL Totals	**17**	**1068**	**379**	**472**	**851**	**1808**	**133**	**47**	**49**	**96**	**194**

HARRY LUMLEY

Goaltender. Catches left. 6'1", 200 lbs., Born, Owen Sound, Ont., November 11, 1926

			Regular Season								Playoffs							
Season	Club	League	GP	MIN	GA	SO	GAA	W	L	T	GP	MIN	GA	SO	GAA	W	L	T
1943-44	Indianapolis	AHL	52	3120	147	0	2.83	....	....	....	5	300	18	0	3.60	2	3	....
	NY Rangers	NHL	1	20	0	0	0.00	0	0	0	....	....	....	....	....	....	....	....
	Detroit	NHL	2	120	13	0	6.50	0	2	0	....	....	....	....	....	....	....	....
1944-45	Indianapolis	AHL	21	1260	46	2	2.19	....	....	....	....	....	....	....	....	....	....	....
	Detroit	NHL	37	2220	119	1	3.22	24	10	3	14	871	31	2	2.14	7	7	0
1945-46	Detroit	NHL	50	3000	159	2	3.18	20	20	10	5	310	16	1	3.10	1	4	....
1946-47	Detroit	NHL	52	3120	159	3	3.06	22	20	10	....	....	....	....	....	....	....	....
1947-48	Detroit	NHL	60	3592	147	7	2.46	30	18	12	10	600	30	0	3.00	4	6	....
1948-49	Detroit	NHL	60	3600	145	6	2.42	34	19	7	11	726	26	0	2.15	4	7	....
1949-50	Detroit	NHL	63	3780	148	7	2.35	33	16	14	14	910	28	3	1.85	8	6	....
1950-51	Chicago	NHL	64	3785	246	3	3.90	12	41	10	....	....	....	....	....	....	....	....
1951-52	Chicago	NHL	70	4180	241	2	3.46	17	44	9	....	....	....	....	....	....	....	....
1952-53	Toronto	NHL	70	4200	167	10	2.38	27	30	13	....	....	....	....	....	....	....	....
1953-54	Toronto	NHL	69	4140	128	13	1.85	32	24	13	5	321	15	0	2.80	1	4	....
1954-55	Toronto	NHL	69	4140	134	8	1.94	24	21	22	4	240	14	0	3.50	0	4	....
1955-56	Toronto	NHL	59	3520	159	3	2.71	21	28	10	5	304	14	1	2.76	1	4	....
1956-57	Buffalo	AHL	63	3780	264	0	4.19	....	....	....	....	....	....	....	....	....	....	....
1957-58	Buffalo	AHL	17	1020	63	1	3.71	....	....	....	....	....	....	....	....	....	....	....
	Boston	NHL	25	1500	71	3	2.84	11	10	4	1	60	5	0	5.00	0	1	....
1958-59	Providence	AHL	58	3480	208	4	3.59	....	....	....	....	....	....	....	....	....	....	....
	Boston	NHL	11	660	27	1	2.45	8	2	1	7	436	20	0	2.75	3	4	....
1959-60	Boston	NHL	42	2520	147	2	3.50	18	19	5		....	....	....	....	....	....	....
1960-61	Kingston	EPHL	2	120	7	0	3.50	....	....	....	....	....	....	....	....	....	....	....
	Winnipeg	WHL	61	3660	213	0	3.49	....	....	....	....	....	....	....	....	....	....	....
	NHL Totals	**16**	**804**	**48107**	**2210**	**71**	**2.76**	**333**	**326**	**143**	**76**	**4778**	**199**	**7**	**2.50**	**29**	**47**	**....**

MICKEY MACKAY

Centre. Shoots left. 5'9", 145 lbs., Born, Chesley, Ont., May 21, 1894

			Regular Season					Playoffs				
Season	Club	League	GP	G	A	PTS	PIM	GP	G	A	PTS	PIM
1914-15	Vancouver	PCHA	17	33	11	44	9	3	4	2	6	9
1915-16	Vancouver	PCHA	14	12	7	19	32	...	...	...	...	...
1916-17	Vancouver	PCHA	23	22	11	33	37	...	...	...	...	...
1917-18	Vancouver	PCHA	18	10	8	18	31	7	7	5	12	15
1918-19	Vancouver	PCHA	17	9	9	18	9	...	...	...	...	...
1919-20	Calgary	Big 4	11	4	6	10	14	...	...	...	...	...
1920-21	Vancouver	PCHA	21	10	8	18	15	2	0	3	3	0
1921-22	Vancouver	PCHA	24	14	12	26	20	9	1	0	1	6
1922-23	Vancouver	PCHA	30	28	12	40	38	6	3	0	3	16
1923-24	Vancouver	PCHA	28	21	4	25	2	7	3	0	3	2
1924-25	Vancouver	WCHL	28	27	6	33	17	...	...	...	...	...
1925-26	Vancouver	WHL	27	12	4	16	24	...	...	...	...	...
1926-27	Chicago	NHL	34	14	8	22	23	2	0	0	0	0
1927-28	Chicago	NHL	36	17	4	21	23	...	...	...	...	...
1928-29	Pittsburgh	NHL	10	1	0	1	2	...	...	...	...	...
	Boston	NHL	30	8	2	10	18	3	0	0	0	2
1929-30	Boston	NHL	37	4	5	9	13	6	0	0	0	4
	NHL Totals	**4**	**147**	**44**	**19**	**63**	**79**	**11**	**0**	**0**	**0**	**6**

FRANK MAHOVLICH

Left wing. Shoots left. 6', 205 lbs., Born, Timmins, Ont., January 10, 1938

			Regular Season					Playoffs				
Season	Club	League	GP	G	A	PTS	PIM	GP	G	A	PTS	PIM
1953-54	Tor. St. Mike's	OHA Jr.	1	0	1	1	2	...	...	...	...	...
1954-55	Tor. St. Mike's	OHA Jr.	25	12	11	23	18	...	...	...	...	...
1955-56	Tor. St. Mike's	OHA Jr.	30	24	26	50	55	8	5	5	10	24
1956-57	Tor. St. Mike's	OHA Jr.	49	52	36	88	122	4	2	7	9	14
	Toronto	NHL	3	1	0	1	2	...	...	...	...	...
1957-58	Toronto	NHL	67	20	16	36	67	...	...	...	...	...
1958-59	Toronto	NHL	63	22	27	49	94	12	6	5	11	18
1959-60	Toronto	NHL	70	18	21	39	61	10	3	1	4	27
1960-61	Toronto	NHL	70	48	36	84	131	5	1	1	2	6
1961-62	Toronto	NHL	70	33	38	71	87	12	6	6	12	29
1962-63	Toronto	NHL	67	36	37	73	56	9	0	2	2	8
1963-64	Toronto	NHL	70	26	29	55	66	14	4	11	15	20
1964-65	Toronto	NHL	59	23	28	51	76	6	0	3	3	9
1965-66	Toronto	NHL	68	32	24	56	68	4	1	0	1	10
1966-67	Toronto	NHL	63	18	28	46	44	12	3	7	10	8
1967-68	Toronto	NHL	50	19	17	36	30	...	...	...	...	...
	Detroit	NHL	13	7	9	16	2	...	...	...	...	...
1968-69	Detroit	NHL	76	49	29	78	38	...	...	...	...	...
1969-70	Detroit	NHL	74	38	32	70	59	4	0	0	0	2
1970-71	Detroit	NHL	35	14	18	32	30	...	...	...	...	...
	Montreal	NHL	38	17	24	41	11	20	14	13	27	18
1971-72	Montreal	NHL	76	43	53	96	36	6	3	2	5	2
1972-73	Montreal	NHL	78	38	55	93	51	17	9	14	23	6
1973-74	Montreal	NHL	71	31	49	80	47	6	1	2	3	0
1974-75	Tononto	WHA	73	38	44	82	27	6	3	0	3	2
1975-76	Toronto	WHA	75	34	55	89	14	...	...	...	...	...
1976-77	Birmingham	WHA	17	3	20	23	12	...	...	...	...	...
1977-78	Birmingham	WHA	72	14	24	38	22	3	1	1	2	0
	NHL Totals	**18**	**1181**	**533**	**570**	**1103**	**1056**	**137**	**51**	**67**	**118**	**163**

JOE MALONE

Centre. Shoots left. 5'10", 150 lbs., Born, Sillery, Que., February 28, 1890

			Regular Season					Playoffs				
Season	Club	League	GP	G	A	PTS	PIM	GP	G	A	PTS	PIM
1908-09	Quebec	ECHA	12	8	0	8	17	...	...	...	...	...
1909-10	Waterloo	OPHL	11	8	0	8	...	...	...	...	...	...
	Quebec	CHA	2	5	0	5	3	...	...	...	...	...
1910-11	Quebec	NHA	13	9	0	9	3	...	...	...	...	...
1911-12	Quebec	NHA	18	21	0	21	0	2	5	0	5	0
1912-13	Quebec	NHA	20	43	0	43	34	4	9	0	9	0
1913-14	Quebec	NHA	19	24	4	28	20	...	...	...	...	...
1914-15	Quebec	NHA	13	16	5	21	21	...	...	...	...	...
1915-16	Quebec	NHA	24	25	10	35	21	...	...	...	...	...
1916-17	Quebec	NHA	19	41	7	48	12	...	...	...	...	...
1917-18	Montreal	NHL	20	44	0	44	42	2	1	0	1	0
1918-19	Montreal	NHL	8	7	1	8	2	5	6	1	7	0
1919-20	Quebec	NHL	24	39	6	45	12	...	...	...	...	...
1920-21	Hamilton	NHL	20	30	4	34	2	...	...	...	...	...
1921-22	Hamilton	NHL	24	25	7	32	4	...	...	...	...	...
1922-23	Montreal	NHL	20	1	0	1	2	2	0	0	0	0
1923-24	Montreal	NHL	9	0	0	0	0	...	...	...	...	...
	NHL Totals	**7**	**125**	**146**	**21**	**167**	**35**	**9**	**5**	**0**	**5**	**0**

SYLVIO MANTHA

Defence. Shoots right. 5'10", 173 lbs., Born, Montreal, Que., April 14, 1903

			Regular Season					Playoffs				
Season	Club	League	GP	G	A	PTS	PIM	GP	G	A	PTS	PIM
1923-24	Montreal	NHL	24	1	0	1	9	5	0	0	0	10
1924-25	Montreal	NHL	30	2	0	2	16	6	0	1	1	2
1925-26	Montreal	NHL	35	2	1	3	66	...	...	...	...	...
1926-27	Montreal	NHL	43	10	5	15	77	4	1	0	1	0
1927-28	Montreal	NHL	43	4	11	15	61	2	0	0	0	6
1928-29	Montreal	NHL	44	9	4	13	56	3	0	0	0	0
1929-30	Montreal	NHL	44	13	11	24	108	6	2	1	3	18
1930-31	Montreal	NHL	44	4	7	11	75	10	2	1	3	26
1931-32	Montreal	NHL	47	5	5	10	62	4	0	1	1	8
1932-33	Montreal	NHL	48	4	7	11	50	2	0	1	1	2
1933-34	Montreal	NHL	48	4	6	10	24	2	0	0	0	2
1934-35	Montreal	NHL	47	3	11	14	36	2	0	0	0	2
1935-36	Montreal	NHL	42	2	4	6	25	...	...	...	...	...
1936-37	Boston	NHL	5	0	0	0	2	...	...	...	...	...
	NHL Totals	**14**	**542**	**63**	**72**	**135**	**667**	**46**	**5**	**4**	**9**	**66**

JACK MARSHALL

Centre / point. Shoots, 5'9", 160 lbs., Born, St. Vallier, Que., March 14, 1877

			Regular Season					Playoffs				
Season	Club	League	GP	G	A	PTS	PIM	GP	G	A	PTS	PIM
1900-01	Wpg. Victorias	MHL Sr.	2	0	...	...	...	...	...	...	...	...
1901-02	Montreal AAA	CAHL	8	11	...	11	...	3	3	...	3	...
1902-03	Montreal AAA	CAHL	7	8	...	8	...	4	7	...	7	...
1903-04	Mtl. Wanderers	FAHL	4	11	...	11	...	1	1	...	1	...
1904-05	Mtl. Wanderers	FAHL	8	17	...	17	...	...	...	...	...	...
1905-06			Did Not Play									
1906-07	Montagnards	FAHL	3	6	...	6	...	...	...	...	...	...
	Mtl. Wanderers	ECAHA	3	6	...	6	...	2	1	0	1	...
1907-08	Mtl. Shamrocks	ECAHA	9	19	...	19	...	...	...	...	...	...
1908-09	Mtl. Shamrocks	ECHA	12	10	...	10	14	...	...	...	...	...
1909-10	Mtl. Wanderers	NHA	12	2	...	2	8	1	0	0	0	0
1910-11	Mtl. Wanderers	NHA	5	1	...	1	2	...	...	...	...	...
1911-12	Mtl. Wanderers	NHA	3	0	...	0	0	...	...	...	...	...
1912-13	Toronto	NHA	13	3	...	3	8	...	...	...	...	...
1913-14	Toronto	NHA	20	3	3	6	16	2	0	0	0	0
1914-15	Toronto	NHA	4	0	1	1	8	...	...	...	...	...
1915-16	Mtl. Wanderers	NHA	15	1	0	1	2	...	...	...	...	...
1916-17	Mtl. Wanderers	NHA	8	0	0	0	3	...	...	...	...	...

FRED "STEAMER" MAXWELL

Rover. Born, Winnipeg, Man., May 19, 1890

			Regular Season					Playoffs				
Season	Club	League	GP	G	A	PTS	PIM	GP	G	A	PTS	PIM
1914-15	Wpg. Monarchs	MHL Sr.	Not Available			...	...	...	...	...	...	...
1915-16	Wpg. Monarchs	MHL Sr.	Not Available			...	...	...	...	...	...	...
1917-18			Did Not Play									
1918-19	Wpg. Falcons	MHL Sr.	Not Available			...	...	...	...	...	...	...
1919-20	Wpg. Falcons	MHL Sr.	Not Available			...	...	...	...	...	...	...
1920-21	Wpg. Falcons	MHL Sr.	Not Available			...	...	...	...	...	...	...
1921-22	Wpg. Falcons	MHL Sr.	Not Available			...	...	...	...	...	...	...
1922-23	Wpg. Falcons	MHL Sr.	Not Available			...	...	...	...	...	...	...
1923-24	Wpg. Falcons	MHL Sr.	Not Available			...	...	...	...	...	...	...
1924-25	Wpg. Falcons	MHL Sr.	Not Available			...	...	...	...	...	...	...

LANNY McDONALD

Right wing. Shoots right. 6', 194 lbs., Born, Hanna, Alta., February 16, 1953

			Regular Season					Playoffs				
Season	Club	League	GP	G	A	PTS	PIM	GP	G	A	PTS	PIM
1969-70	Lethbridge	AJHL	34	2	9	11	19	...	...	...	...	...
1970-71	Lethbridge	AJHL	45	37	45	82	56	...	...	...	...	...
	Calgary	WCHL	6	0	2	2	6	...	...	...	...	...
1971-72	Medicine Hat	WCHL	68	50	64	114	54	7	2	2	4	6
1972-73	Medicine Hat	WCHL	68	62	77	139	84	17	18	19	37	6
1973-74	Toronto	NHL	70	14	16	30	43	...	...	...	...	...
1974-75	Toronto	NHL	64	17	27	44	86	7	0	0	0	2
1975-76	Toronto	NHL	75	37	56	93	70	10	4	4	8	4
1976-77	Toronto	NHL	80	46	44	90	77	9	10	7	17	6
1977-78	Toronto	NHL	74	47	40	87	54	13	3	4	7	10
1978-79	Toronto	NHL	79	43	42	85	32	6	3	2	5	0
1979-80	Toronto	NHL	35	15	15	30	10	...	...	...	...	...
	Colorado	NHL	46	25	20	45	43	...	...	...	...	...
1980-81	Colorado	NHL	80	35	46	81	56	...	...	...	...	...
1981-82	Colorado	NHL	16	6	9	15	20	...	...	...	...	...
	Calgary	NHL	55	34	33	67	37	3	0	1	1	6
1982-83	Calgary	NHL	80	66	32	98	90	9	3	4	7	19
1983-84	Calgary	NHL	65	33	33	66	64	11	6	7	13	6
1984-85	Calgary	NHL	43	19	18	37	36	1	0	0	0	0
1985-86	Calgary	NHL	80	28	43	71	44	22	11	7	18	30
1986-87	Calgary	NHL	54	14	12	26	54	5	0	0	0	2
1987-88	Calgary	NHL	60	10	13	23	57	9	3	1	4	6
1988-89	Calgary	NHL	51	11	7	18	26	14	1	3	4	29
	NHL Totals	**16**	**1111**	**500**	**506**	**1006**	**899**	**117**	**44**	**40**	**84**	**114**

FRANK McGEE

Rover. Born, Ottawa, Ont., 1880

			Regular Season					Playoffs				
Season	Club	League	GP	G	A	PTS	PIM	GP	G	A	PTS	PIM
1902-03	Ottawa	CAHL	6	14	...	14	...	4	7	...	7	...
1903-04	Ottawa	CAHL	4	12	...	12	...	8	21	...	21	...
1904-05	Ottawa	FAHL	6	17	...	17	...	4	18	...	18	...
1905-06	Ottawa	ECAHA	7	28	...	28	...	6	17	...	17	...

BILLY McGIMSIE

Centre. 5'8", 145 lbs., Born, Woodsville, Ont.., June 7, 1880

			Regular Season					Playoffs				
Season	Club	League	GP	G	A	PTS	PIM	GP	G	A	PTS	PIM
1902-03	Rat Portage	MHL Sr.	...	...	...	...	...	2	3	0	3	...
1903-04	Rat Portage	MHL Sr.	Not Available			...	...	...	...	...	...	...
1904-05	Rat Portage	MHL Sr.	8	30	0	30	...	3	0	0	0	...
1905-06	Kenora	MHL Sr.	9	21	0	21	...	1	2	0	2	...
1906-07	Kenora	MHL Sr.	2	2	0	2	...	2	1	0	1	...

GEORGE McNAMARA

Defence. Shoots left. 6'1", 220 lbs., Born, Penetang, Ont., August 26, 1886

			Regular Season					Playoffs				
Season	Club	League	GP	G	A	PTS	PIM	GP	G	A	PTS	PIM
1906-07	Canadian Soo	IHL	3	0	...	0	8	...	...	...	...	...
1907-08	Mtl. Shamrocks	ECAHA	10	3	...	3	...	...	...	...	...	...
1908-09	Mtl. Shamrocks	ECHA	12	4	...	4	60	...	...	...	...	...
1909-10			Did Not Play									
1910-11	Waterloo	OPHL	16	15	...	15	...	...	...	...	...	...
1911-12	Halifax	MPHL	10	2	...	2	24	...	...	...	...	...
1912-13	Tor. Tecumsehs	NHA	20	4	...	4	23	2	2	0	2	0
1913-14	Toronto	NHA	9	0	1	1	0	...	...	...	...	...
	Toronto	NHA	9	0	1	1	2	...	...	...	...	...
1914-15	Tor. Shamrocks	NHA	18	4	8	12	67	...	...	...	...	...
1915-16	Toronto	NHA	23	5	2	7	74	...	...	...	...	...
1916-17	Tor. 228TH	NHA	11	2	1	3	15	...	...	...	...	...

STAN MIKITA

Centre. Shoots right. 5'9", 169 lbs., Born, Solokce, Czech., May 20, 1940

			Regular Season					Playoffs				
Season	Club	League	GP	G	A	PTS	PIM	GP	G	A	PTS	PIM
1956-57	St. Catharines	OHA Jr.	52	16	31	47	129	14	8	9	17	44
1957-58	St. Catharines	OHA Jr.	52	31	47	78	146	8	4	5	9	46
1958-59	St. Catharines	OHA Jr.	45	38	59	97	197	...	...	...	...	...
	Chicago	NHL	3	0	1	1	4	...	...	...	...	...
1959-60	Chicago	NHL	67	8	18	26	119	3	0	1	1	2
1960-61	Chicago	NHL	66	19	34	53	100	12	6	5	11	21
1961-62	Chicago	NHL	70	25	52	77	97	12	6	15	21	19
1962-63	Chicago	NHL	65	31	45	76	69	6	3	2	5	2
1963-64	Chicago	NHL	70	39	50	89	146	7	3	6	9	8
1964-65	Chicago	NHL	70	28	59	87	154	14	3	7	10	53
1965-66	Chicago	NHL	68	30	48	78	58	6	1	2	3	2
1966-67	Chicago	NHL	70	35	62	97	12	6	2	2	4	2
1967-68	Chicago	NHL	72	40	47	87	14	11	5	7	12	6
1968-69	Chicago	NHL	74	30	67	97	52	...	...	...	...	...
1969-70	Chicago	NHL	76	39	47	86	50	8	4	6	10	2
1970-71	Chicago	NHL	74	24	48	72	85	18	5	13	18	16
1971-72	Chicago	NHL	74	26	39	65	46	8	3	1	4	4
1972-73	Chicago	NHL	57	27	56	83	32	15	7	13	20	8
1973-74	Chicago	NHL	76	30	50	80	46	11	5	6	11	8
1974-75	Chicago	NHL	79	36	50	86	48	8	3	4	7	12
1975-76	Chicago	NHL	48	16	41	57	37	4	0	0	0	4
1976-77	Chicago	NHL	57	19	30	49	20	2	0	1	1	0
1977-78	Chicago	NHL	76	18	41	59	35	4	3	0	3	0
1978-79	Chicago	NHL	65	19	36	55	34	...	...	...	...	...
1979-80	Chicago	NHL	17	2	5	7	12	...	...	...	...	...
	NHL Totals	**22**	**1394**	**541**	**926**	**1467**	**1270**	**155**	**59**	**91**	**150**	**169**

DICKIE MOORE

Right wing. Shoots right. 5'10", 185 lbs., Born, Montreal, Que., January 6, 1931

			Regular Season					Playoffs				
Season	Club	League	GP	G	A	PTS	PIM	GP	G	A	PTS	PIM
1948-49	Montreal	QJHL	22	34	56	71	...	...	...	...	...	...
	Montreal	QSHL	2	0	0	0	0	...	...	...	...	...
1949-50	Montreal	QSHL	...	...	...	...	...	...	...	...	...	...
1950-51	Montreal	QSHL	...	...	...	...	...	...	...	...	...	...
1951-52	Montreal	QSHL	26	15	20	35	32	...	...	...	...	...
	Montreal	NHL	33	18	15	33	44	11	1	1	2	12
1952-53	Buffalo	AHL	6	2	3	5	10	...	...	...	...	...
	Montreal	NHL	18	2	6	8	19	12	3	2	5	13
1953-54	Montreal	QHL	2	0	1	1	4	...	...	...	...	...
	Montreal	NHL	13	1	4	5	12	11	5	8	13	8
1954-55	Montreal	NHL	67	16	20	36	32	12	1	5	6	22
1955-56	Montreal	NHL	70	11	39	50	55	10	3	6	9	12
1956-57	Montreal	NHL	70	29	29	58	56	10	3	7	10	4
1957-58	Montreal	NHL	70	36	48	84	65	10	4	7	11	4
1958-59	Montreal	NHL	70	41	55	96	61	11	5	12	17	8
1959-60	Montreal	NHL	62	22	42	64	54	8	6	4	10	4
1960-61	Montreal	NHL	57	35	34	69	62	6	3	1	4	4
1961-62	Montreal	NHL	57	19	22	41	54	6	4	2	6	8
1962-63	Montreal	NHL	67	24	26	50	61	5	0	1	1	2
1964-65	Toronto	NHL	38	2	4	6	68	5	1	1	2	6
1965-1967			Did Not Play									
1967-68	St. Louis	NHL	27	5	3	8	9	18	7	7	14	15
	NHL Totals	**14**	**719**	**261**	**347**	**608**	**652**	**135**	**46**	**64**	**110**	**122**

PATRICK "PADDY" MORAN

Goaltender. Catches right. 5'11", 180 lbs., Born, Quebec City, Que., Born, March 11, 1877

			Regular Season								Playoffs							
Season	Club	League	GP	MIN	GA	SO	GAA	W	L	T	GP	MIN	GA	SO	GAA	W	L	T
1901-02	Quebec	CAHL	8	480	34	0	4.25	4	4	0	....	....	....	....	....	....	....	....
1902-03	Quebec	CAHL	7	420	46	0	6.57	3	4	0	....	....	....	....	....	....	....	....
1903-04	Quebec	CAHL	6	360	37	0	6.17	5	1	0	....	....	....	....	....	....	....	....
1904-05	Quebec	CAHL	9	540	45	0	5.00	7	2	0	....	....	....	....	....	....	....	....
1905-06	Quebec	ECAHA	10	630	70	0	6.67	3	7	0	....	....	....	....	....	....	....	....
1906-07	Quebec	ECAHA	6	362	58	0	9.61	0	6	0	....	....	....	....	....	....	....	....
1907-08	Quebec	ECAHA	10	603	74	0	7.36	5	5	0	....	....	....	....	....	....	....	....
1908-09	Quebec	ECHA	12	720	106	0	8.83	3	9	4	....	....	....	....	....	....	....	....
1909-10	Haileybury	NHA	11	665	80	0	7.21	3	8	0	....	....	....	....	....	....	....	....
	All-Montreal	CHA	4	240	24	0	6.00	2	2	0	....	....	....	....	....	....	....	....
1910-11	Quebec	NHA	16	983	97	0	5.91	4	12	0	....	....	....	....	....	....	....	....
1911-12	Quebec	NHA	18	1099	78	0	4.26	10	8	0	2	120	3	1	1.50	2	0	....
1912-13	Quebec	NHA	20	1215	75	1	3.70	16	4	0	2	120	5	0	2.50	2	0	....
1913-14	Quebec	NHA	20	1225	73	1	3.58	12	8	6	....	....	....	....	....	....	....	....
1914-15	Quebec	NHA	20	1305	85	0	3.91	11	9	0	....	....	....	....	....	....	....	....
1915-16	Quebec	NHA	22	1391	82	0	3.54	10	10	0	....	....	....	....	....	....	....	....
1916-17	Quebec	NHA	7	307	35	0	6.84	1	5	0	....	....	....	....	....	....	....	....

HOWIE MORENZ

Centre. Shoots left. 5'9", 165 lbs., Born, Mitchell, Ont., June 21, 1902

			Regular Season					Playoffs				
Season	Club	League	GP	G	A	PTS	PIM	GP	G	A	PTS	PIM
1923-24	Montreal	NHL	24	13	3	16	20	6	7	2	9	10
1924-25	Montreal	NHL	30	27	7	34	31	6	7	1	8	10
1925-26	Montreal	NHL	31	23	3	26	39	...	...	...	...	...
1926-27	Montreal	NHL	44	25	7	32	49	4	1	0	1	4
1927-28	Montreal	NHL	43	33	18	51	66	2	0	0	0	12
1928-29	Montreal	NHL	42	17	10	27	47	3	0	0	0	6
1929-30	Montreal	NHL	44	40	10	50	72	6	3	0	3	10
1930-31	Montreal	NHL	39	28	23	51	49	10	1	4	5	10
1931-32	Montreal	NHL	48	24	25	49	46	4	1	0	1	4
1932-33	Montreal	NHL	46	14	21	35	32	2	0	3	3	2
1933-34	Montreal	NHL	39	8	13	21	21	2	1	1	2	0
1934-35	Chicago	NHL	48	8	26	34	21	2	0	0	0	0
1935-36	Chicago	NHL	24	4	11	15	20	...	...	...	...	...
	NY Rangers	NHL	18	2	4	6	6	...	...	...	...	...
1936-37	Montreal	NHL	30	4	16	20	12	...	...	...	...	...
	NHL Totals	**14**	**550**	**270**	**197**	**467**	**563**	**47**	**21**	**11**	**32**	**68**

BILL MOSIENKO

Right wing. Shoots right. 5'8", 160 lbs., Born, Winnipeg, Man., November 2, 1921

			Regular Season					Playoffs				
Season	Club	League	GP	G	A	PTS	PIM	GP	G	A	PTS	PIM
1939-40	Winnipeg	MHL Jr.	24	21	8	29	14	7	8	3	11	2
1940-41	Providence	AHL	36	14	19	33	8	...	...	...	...	...
	Kansas City	AHA	7	2	2	4	0	8	4	1	5	2
1941-42	Kansas City	AHA	33	12	19	31	9	...	...	...	...	...
	Chicago	NHL	12	6	8	14	4	3	2	0	2	0
1942-43	Quebec	QSHL	8	5	3	8	2	4	2	2	4	2
	Chicago	NHL	2	2	0	2	0	...	...	...	...	...
1943-44	Chicago	NHL	50	32	38	70	10	8	2	2	4	6
1944-45	Chicago	NHL	50	28	26	54	0	...	...	...	...	...
1945-46	Chicago	NHL	40	18	30	48	12	4	2	0	2	2
1946-47	Chicago	NHL	59	25	27	52	2	...	...	...	...	...
1947-48	Chicago	NHL	40	16	9	25	0	...	...	...	...	...
1948-49	Chicago	NHL	60	17	25	42	6	...	...	...	...	...
1949-50	Chicago	NHL	69	18	28	46	10	...	...	...	...	...
1950-51	Chicago	NHL	65	21	15	36	18	...	...	...	...	...
1951-52	Chicago	NHL	70	31	22	53	10	...	...	...	...	...
1952-53	Chicago	NHL	65	17	20	37	8	7	4	2	6	7
1953-54	Chicago	NHL	65	15	19	34	17	...	...	...	...	...
1954-55	Chicago	NHL	64	12	15	27	24	...	...	...	...	...
1955-56	Winnipeg	WHL	64	22	23	45	37	14	6	12	18	4
1956-57	Winnipeg	WHL	61	27	26	53	25	...	...	...	...	...
1957-58	Winnipeg	WHL	65	38	36	74	43	7	1	0	1	6
1958-59	Winnipeg	WHL	63	42	46	88	55	7	1	3	4	10
	NHL Totals	**14**	**710**	**258**	**282**	**540**	**121**	**22**	**10**	**4**	**14**	**15**

FRANK NIGHBOR

Centre. Shoots right. 5'9", 160 lbs., Born, Pembroke, Ont., January 26, 1893

			Regular Season					Playoffs				
Season	Club	League	GP	G	A	PTS	PIM	GP	G	A	PTS	PIM
1912-13	Toronto	NHA	19	25	0	25	9	...	...	...	...	...
1913-14	Vancouver	PCHA	11	10	5	15	6	...	...	...	...	...
1914-15	Vancouver	PCHA	17	23	7	30	12	3	4	6	10	6
1915-16	Ottawa	NHA	23	19	5	24	26	...	...	...	...	...
1916-17	Ottawa	NHA	19	41	2	43	18	2	1	6	7	0
1917-18	Ottawa	NHL	10	11	0	11	9	...	...	...	...	...
1918-19	Ottawa	NHL	18	18	4	22	27	2	0	3	3	0
1919-20	Ottawa	NHL	23	26	7	33	18	...	...	...	...	...
1920-21	Ottawa	NHL	24	18	3	21	10	7	1	3	4	2
1921-22	Ottawa	NHL	20	7	9	16	2	2	2	0	2	4
1922-23	Ottawa	NHL	22	11	5	16	16	8	1	2	3	10
1923-24	Ottawa	NHL	20	10	3	13	14	2	0	1	1	2
1924-25	Ottawa	NHL	26	5	2	7	18	...	...	...	...	...
1925-26	Ottawa	NHL	35	12	13	25	40	2	0	0	0	2
1926-27	Ottawa	NHL	38	6	6	12	26	6	1	1	2	0
1927-28	Ottawa	NHL	42	8	5	13	46	2	0	0	0	2
1928-29	Ottawa	NHL	30	1	4	5	22	...	...	...	...	...
1929-30	Ottawa	NHL	19	0	1	1	8	...	...	...	...	...
	Toronto	NHL	22	2	0	2	2	...	...	...	...	...
1931-32	Buffalo	IAHL	1	0	0	0	0	...	...	...	...	...
	NHL Totals	**13**	**348**	**136**	**60**	**196**	**244**	**36**	**11**	**11**	**22**	**25**

REG NOBLE

Centre / defence. Shoots left. 5'8", 180 lbs., Born, Collingwood, Ont., June 23, 1895

			Regular Season					Playoffs				
Season	Club	League	GP	G	A	PTS	PIM	GP	G	A	PTS	PIM
1916-17	Toronto	NHA	14	9	3	12	51	...	...	...	...	...
	Montreal	NHA	6	4	0	4	15	2	0	0	0	3
1917-18	Toronto	NHL	20	28	0	28	43	7	2	1	3	3
1918-19	Toronto	NHL	17	11	3	14	35	...	...	...	...	...
1919-20	Toronto	NHL	24	24	7	31	51	...	...	...	...	...
1920-21	Toronto	NHL	24	20	6	26	54	2	0	0	0	0
1921-22	Toronto	NHL	24	17	8	25	10	7	0	2	2	20
1922-23	Toronto	NHL	24	12	10	22	41	...	...	...	...	...
1923-24	Toronto	NHL	23	12	3	15	23	...	...	...	...	...
1924-25	Toronto	NHL	3	1	0	1	4	...	...	...	...	...
	Mtl Maroons	NHL	27	7	6	13	58	...	...	...	...	...
1925-26	Mtl Maroons	NHL	33	9	9	18	106	8	1	1	2	12
1926-27	Mtl Maroons	NHL	43	3	3	6	112	2	0	0	0	2
1927-28	Detroit	NHL	44	6	8	14	63	...	...	...	...	...
1928-29	Detroit	NHL	43	6	4	10	52	2	0	0	0	2
1929-30	Detroit	NHL	43	6	4	10	72	...	...	...	...	...
1930-31	Detroit	NHL	44	2	5	7	42	...	...	...	...	...
1931-32	Detroit	NHL	48	3	3	6	72	2	0	0	0	0
1932-33	Detroit	NHL	5	0	0	0	6	...	...	...	...	...
	Mtl. Maroons	NHL	20	0	0	0	16	2	0	0	0	0
	NHL Totals	**16**	**509**	**167**	**79**	**246**	**830**	**32**	**4**	**5**	**9**	**33**

BUDDY O'CONNOR

Centre. Shoots left. 5'7", 145 lbs., Born, Montreal, Que., June 21, 1916

			Regular Season					Playoffs				
Season	Club	League	GP	G	A	PTS	PIM	GP	G	A	PTS	PIM
1934-35	Montreal	Jr.	10	15	7	22	4	2	1	1	2	0
	Montreal	Sr.	4	1	0	1	2	...	...	...	...	...
1935-36	Montreal	QSHL	22	14	10	24	6	8	6	5	11	6
1936-37	Montreal	QSHL	19	10	17	27	27	5	0	4	4	2
1937-38	Montreal	QSHL	22	9	14	23	10	1	0	0	0	0
1938-39	Montreal	QSHL	22	13	23	36	28	5	4	5	9	2
1939-40	Montreal	QSHL	29	16	25	44	6	8	8	6	14	2
1940-41	Montreal	QSHL	35	15	38	43	12	8	2	7	9	4
1941-42	Montreal	QSHL	9	1	5	6	4	...	...	...	...	...
	Montreal	NHL	36	9	16	25	4	3	0	1	1	0
1942-43	Montreal	NHL	50	15	43	58	2	5	4	5	9	0
1943-44	Montreal	NHL	44	12	42	54	6	8	1	2	3	2
1944-45	Montreal	NHL	50	21	23	44	2	2	0	0	0	0
1945-46	Montreal	NHL	45	11	11	22	2	9	2	3	5	0
	Montreal	QSHL	2	0	1	1	0	2	2	0	2	0
1946-47	Montreal	NHL	46	10	20	30	6	8	3	4	7	0
1947-48	NY Rangers	NHL	60	24	36	60	8	6	1	4	5	0
1948-49	NY Rangers	NHL	46	11	24	35	0	...	...	...	...	...
1949-50	NY Rangers	NHL	66	11	22	33	4	12	4	2	6	4
1950-51	NY Rangers	NHL	66	16	20	36	0	...	...	...	...	...
1951-52	Cincinnati	AHL	65	11	43	54	4	4	2	3	5	2
1952-53	Cincinnati	IHL	1	0	0	0	0	...	...	...	...	...
	NHL Totals	**10**	**509**	**140**	**257**	**397**	**34**	**53**	**15**	**21**	**36**	**6**

HARRY OLIVER

Centre / right wing. Shoots right. 5'8", 155 lbs., Born, Selkirk, Man., October 26, 1898

			Regular Season					Playoffs				
Season	Club	League	GP	G	A	PTS	PIM	GP	G	A	PTS	PIM
1918-19	Selkirk	MHL Sr.	9	15	9	24	6	...	...	...	...	...
1919-20	Selkirk	MHL Sr.	10	7	6	13	4	...	...	...	...	...
1920-21	Calgary	Big 4	16	14	6	20	11	...	...	...	...	...
1921-22	Calagry	WCHL	20	10	4	14	7	2	1	0	1	...
1922-23	Calagry	WCHL	29	25	7	32	10	...	...	...	...	...
1923-24	Calagry	WCHL	27	22	12	34	14	7	2	2	4	4
1924-25	Calagry	WCHL	24	20	13	33	23	2	0	0	0	0
1925-26	Calagry	WHL	30	13	12	25	14	...	...	...	...	...
1926-27	Boston	NHL	42	18	6	24	17	8	4	1	5	2
1927-28	Boston	NHL	43	13	5	18	20	2	2	0	2	4
1928-29	Boston	NHL	43	17	6	23	24	5	1	1	2	8
1929-30	Boston	NHL	40	16	5	21	12	6	2	1	3	6
1930-31	Boston	NHL	44	16	14	30	18	5	0	0	0	2
1931-32	Boston	NHL	42	13	7	20	22	...	...	...	...	...
1932-33	Boston	NHL	47	11	7	18	10	5	0	0	0	0
1933-34	Boston	NHL	48	5	9	14	6	...	...	...	...	...
1934-35	NY Americans	NHL	47	7	9	16	4	...	...	...	...	...
1935-36	NY Americans	NHL	45	9	16	25	12	5	1	2	3	0
1936-37	NY Americans	NHL	20	2	1	3	7	...	...	...	...	...
	NHL Totals	**11**	**463**	**127**	**85**	**212**	**147**	**35**	**10**	**6**	**16**	**24**

BERT OLMSTEAD

Left wing. Shoots left 6'2", 183 lbs., Born, Scepter, Sask., September 4, 1926

			Regular Season					Playoffs				
Season	Club	League	GP	G	A	PTS	PIM	GP	G	A	PTS	PIM
1944-45	Moose Jaw	SJHL	16	0	3	3	8	4	2	0	2	8
1945-46	Moose Jaw	SJHL	18	24	19	43	32	4	0	1	1	6
1946-47	Kansas City	USHL	60	27	15	42	34	12	2	3	5	4
1947-48	Kansas City	USHL	66	26	26	52	42	7	1	4	5	0
1948-49	Kansas City	USHL	52	33	44	77	54	2	0	1	1	0
	Chicago	NHL	9	0	2	2	4	...	...	...	...	...
1949-50	Chicago	NHL	70	20	29	49	40	...	...	...	...	...
1950-51	Chicago	NHL	15	2	1	3	0	...	...	...	...	...
	Milwaukee	USHL	12	8	7	15	11	...	...	...	...	...
	Montreal	NHL	39	16	22	38	50	11	2	4	6	9
1951-52	Montreal	NHL	69	7	28	35	49	11	0	1	1	4
1952-53	Montreal	NHL	69	17	28	45	83	12	2	2	4	4
1953-54	Montreal	NHL	70	15	37	52	85	11	0	1	1	19
1954-55	Montreal	NHL	70	10	48	58	103	12	0	4	4	21
1955-56	Montreal	NHL	70	14	56	70	94	10	4	10	14	8
1956-57	Montreal	NHL	64	15	33	48	74	10	0	9	9	13
1957-58	Montreal	NHL	57	9	28	37	71	9	0	3	3	0
1958-59	Toronto	NHL	70	10	31	41	74	12	4	2	6	13
1959-60	Toronto	NHL	53	15	21	36	63	10	3	4	7	0
1960-61	Toronto	NHL	67	18	34	52	84	3	1	2	3	10
1961-62	Toronto	NHL	56	13	23	36	10	4	0	1	1	0
	NHL Totals	**14**	**848**	**181**	**421**	**602**	**884**	**115**	**16**	**43**	**59**	**101**

BOBBY ORR

Defence. Shoots left. 6', 199 lbs., Born, Parry Sound, Ont., March 20, 1948

			Regular Season					Playoffs				
Season	Club	League	GP	G	A	PTS	PIM	GP	G	A	PTS	PIM
1962-63	Oshawa	OHA Jr.	34	6	15	21	45	...	...	...	...	...
1963-64	Oshawa	OHA Jr.	56	29	43	72	142	6	0	7	7	21
1964-65	Oshawa	OHA Jr.	56	34	59	93	112	6	0	6	6	10
1965-66	Oshawa	OHA Jr.	47	38	56	94	92	17	9	19	28	14
1966-67	Boston	NHL	61	13	28	41	102	...	...	...	...	...
1967-68	Boston	NHL	46	11	20	31	63	4	0	2	2	2
1968-69	Boston	NHL	67	21	43	64	133	10	1	7	8	10
1969-70	Boston	NHL	76	33	87	120	125	14	9	11	20	14
1970-71	Boston	NHL	78	37	102	139	91	7	5	7	12	25
1971-72	Boston	NHL	76	37	80	117	106	15	5	19	24	19
1972-73	Boston	NHL	63	29	72	101	99	5	1	1	2	7
1973-74	Boston	NHL	74	32	90	122	82	16	4	14	18	28
1974-75	Boston	NHL	80	46	89	135	101	3	1	5	6	2
1975-76	Boston	NHL	10	5	13	18	22	...	...	...	...	...
1976-77	Chicago	NHL	20	4	19	23	25	...	...	...	...	...
1977-78				Did Not Play								
1978-79	Chicago	NHL	6	2	2	4	4	...	...	...	...	...
	NHL Totals	**12**	**657**	**270**	**645**	**915**	**953**	**74**	**26**	**66**	**92**	**107**

BERNIE PARENT

Goaltender. Catches left. 5'10", 180 lbs., Born, Montreal, Que., April 3, 1945

			Regular Season								Playoffs							
Season	Club	League	GP	MIN	GA	SO	GAA	W	L	T	GP	MIN	GA	SO	GAA	W	L	T
1963-64	Niagara Falls	OHA	28	1680	80	4	2.86	....	....	....	4	240	26	0	6.50	0	4	....
1964-65	Niagara Falls	OHA	34	2004	86	2	2.58	....	....	....	8	480	15	1	1.88	6	2	....
1965-66	Oklahoma City	CHL	3	180	11	0	3.67	....	....	....	....	....	....	....	....	....	....	....
	Boston	NHL	39	2083	128	1	3.69	11	20	3	....	....	....	....	....	....	....	....
1966-67	Boston	NHL	18	1022	62	0	3.64	3	11	2	2	....	....	....	....	....	....	....
	Oklahoma City	CHL	14	822	37	4	2.70	....	....	....	....	....	....	....	....	....	....	....
1967-68	Philadelphia	NHL	38	2248	93	4	2.49	16	17	5	5	355	8	0	1.35	2	3	....
1968-69	Philadelphia	NHL	58	3365	151	1	2.69	17	23	16	3	180	12	0	4.00	0	3	....
1969-70	Philadelphia	NHL	62	3680	171	3	2.79	13	29	20	....	....	....	....	....	....	....	....
1970-71	Philadelphia	NHL	30	1586	73	2	2.76	9	12	6	....	....	....	....	....	....	....	....
	Toronto	NHL	18	1040	46	1	2.65	7	7	3	4	235	9	0	2.30	2	2	....
1971-72	Toronto	NHL	47	2715	116	3	2.56	17	18	9	6	243	13	0	3.20	1	3	....
1972-73	Philadelphia	WHA	63	3653	220	2	3.61	33	28	0	1	70	3	0	2.57	0	1	....
1973-74	Philadelphia	NHL	73	4314	136	12	1.89	47	13	12	17	1042	35	2	2.02	12	5	....
1974-75	Philadelphia	NHL	68	4041	137	12	2.03	44	14	10	15	922	29	4	1.89	10	5	....
1975-76	Philadelphia	NHL	11	615	24	0	2.34	6	2	3	8	480	27	0	3.38	4	4	....
1976-77	Philadelphia	NHL	61	3525	159	5	2.71	35	13	12	3	123	8	0	3.90	0	3	....
1977-78	Philadelphia	NHL	49	2923	108	1	2.22	29	6	13	12	772	33	0	2.56	7	5	....
1978-79	Philadelphia	NHL	36	1979	89	4	2.70	16	12	7	....	....	....	....	....	....	....	....
	NHL Totals	**13**	**608**	**35136**	**1493**	**55**	**2.55**	**270**	**197**	**121**	**71**	**4302**	**174**	**6**	**2.43**	**38**	**33**	**....**

BRAD PARK

Defence. Shoots left. 6', 200 lbs., Born, Toronto, Ont., July 6, 1948

Season	Club	League	Regular Season GP	G	A	PTS	PIM	Playoffs GP	G	A	PTS	PIM
1965-66	Tor. Marlboros	OHA Jr.	33	0	14	14	48	14	1	0	1	38
1966-67	Tor. Marlboros	OHA Jr.	28	4	15	19	73	8	4	3	7	17
1967-68	Tor. Marlboros	OHA Jr.	50	10	33	43	120	5	0	6	6	37
	Tor. Marlboros	OHA Sr.	1	0	0	0	0	...	...	...	...	...
1968-69	Buffalo	AHL	17	2	12	14	49	...	...	...	...	...
	NY Rangers	NHL	54	3	23	26	70	4	0	2	2	7
1969-70	NY Rangers	NHL	60	11	26	37	98	5	1	2	3	11
1970-71	NY Rangers	NHL	68	7	37	44	114	13	0	4	4	42
1971-72	NY Rangers	NHL	75	24	49	73	130	16	4	7	11	21
1972-73	NY Rangers	NHL	52	10	43	53	51	10	2	5	7	8
1973-74	NY Rangers	NHL	78	25	57	82	148	13	4	8	12	38
1974-75	NY Rangers	NHL	65	13	44	57	104	3	1	4	5	2
1975-76	NY Rangers	NHL	13	2	4	6	23	...	...	...	...	...
	Boston	NHL	43	16	37	53	95	11	3	8	11	14
1976-77	Boston	NHL	77	12	55	67	67	14	2	10	12	4
1977-78	Boston	NHL	80	22	57	79	79	15	9	11	20	14
1978-79	Boston	NHL	40	7	32	39	10	11	1	4	5	8
1979-80	Boston	NHL	32	5	16	21	27	10	3	6	9	4
1980-81	Boston	NHL	78	14	52	66	111	3	1	3	4	11
1981-82	Boston	NHL	75	14	42	56	82	11	1	4	5	4
1982-83	Boston	NHL	76	10	26	36	82	16	3	9	12	18
1983-84	Detroit	NHL	80	5	53	58	85	3	0	3	3	0
1984-85	Detroit	NHL	67	13	30	43	53	3	0	0	0	11
	NHL Totals	**17**	**1113**	**213**	**683**	**896**	**1429**	**161**	**35**	**90**	**125**	**217**

LESTER PATRICK

Defence / rover. 6'1", 180 lbs., Born, Drummondville, Que., December 31, 1883

Season	Club	League	Regular Season GP	G	A	PTS	PIM	Playoffs GP	G	A	PTS	PIM
1903-04	Brandon	NWHL	2	0	0	0	...	...	...	...	...	...
1904-05	Westmount	CAHL	8	4	0	4	...	...	...	...	...	...
1905-06	Mtl. Wanderers	ECAHA	9	17	0	17	...	2	3	0	3	...
1906-07	Mtl. Wanderers	ECAHA	9	11	0	11	...	6	10	0	10	...
1907-08	Nelson	Sr.	2	1	0	1	...	...	...	...	...	...
1908-09	Edmonton	Sr.	...	...	...	...	...	2	1	...	1	...
	Nelson	Sr.	...	...	...	...	...	...	...	...	...	...
1909-10	Renfrew	NHA	12	23	...	23	25	...	...	...	...	...
1910-11	Nelson	Sr.	...	...	...	...	...	...	...	...	...	...
1911-12	Victoria	PCHA	16	10	0	10	9	...	...	...	...	...
1912-13	Victoria	PCHA	15	14	5	19	12	3	4	0	4	...
1913-14	Victoria	PCHA	9	5	5	10	0	3	2	0	2	...
1914-15	Victoria	PCHA	17	12	5	17	15	...	...	...	...	...
1915-16	Victoria	PCHA	18	13	11	24	27	...	...	...	...	...
1916-17	Spokane	PCHA	23	10	11	21	15	...	...	...	...	...
1917-18	Seattle	PCHA	17	2	8	10	15	2	0	1	1	0
1918-19	Victoria	PCHA	9	2	5	7	0	...	...	...	...	...
1919-20	Victoria	PCHA	11	2	2	4	3	...	...	...	...	...
1920-21	Victoria	PCHA	5	2	3	5	13	...	...	...	...	...
1921-22	Victoria	PCHA	2	0	0	0	0	...	...	...	...	...
1922-1925			Did Not Play									
1925-26	Victoria	WHL	23	5	8	13	20	1	0	0	0	2
1926-27	NY Rangers	NHL	1	0	0	0	2	...	...	...	...	...
	NHL Totals	**1**	**1**	**0**	**0**	**0**	**2**	....	....	....	....	....

LESTER PATRICK

Goaltender. Catches left. 6'1", 180 lbs., Born, Drummondville, Que., December 31, 1883

Season	Club	League	Regular Season GP	MIN	GA	SO	GAA	W	L	T	Playoffs GP	MIN	GA	SO	GAA	W	L	T
1921-22	Victoria	PCHA	2	13	1	0	4.62	0	0	0	....	....	....	....	....	....	....	....
1927-28	NY Rangers	NHL	....	....	....	....	....	....	....	....	1	46	1	0	1.30	1	0	0
	NHL Totals	**1**	....	....	....	....	....	....	....	....	**1**	**46**	**1**	**0**	**1.30**	**1**	**0**	**0**

LYNN PATRICK

Left wing. Shoots left. 6'1", 192 lbs., Born, Victoria, B.C., February 3, 1912

Season	Club	League	Regular Season GP	G	A	PTS	PIM	Playoffs GP	G	A	PTS	PIM
1933-34	Montreal	Sr.	15	5	3	8	4	2	0	0	0	0
1934-35	NY Rangers	NHL	48	9	13	22	17	4	2	2	4	0
1935-36	NY Rangers	NHL	48	11	14	25	29	...	...	...	...	...
1936-37	NY Rangers	NHL	45	8	16	24	23	9	3	0	3	2
1937-38	NY Rangers	NHL	48	15	19	34	24	3	0	1	1	2
1938-39	NY Rangers	NHL	35	8	21	29	25	7	1	1	2	0
1939-40	NY Rangers	NHL	48	12	16	28	34	12	2	2	4	4
1940-41	NY Rangers	NHL	48	20	24	44	12	3	1	0	1	4
1941-42	NY Rangers	NHL	47	32	22	54	18	6	1	0	1	0
1942-43	NY Rangers	NHL	50	22	39	61	28	...	...	...	...	...
1943-45			Military Service									
1945-46	NY Rangers	NHL	38	8	6	14	30	...	...	...	...	...
1946-47	New Haven	AHL	16	2	6	8	16	3	1	0	1	2
	NHL Totals	**10**	**455**	**145**	**190**	**335**	**240**	**44**	**10**	**6**	**16**	**22**

GIL PERREAULT

Centre. Shoots left. 6', 200 lbs., Born, Victoriaville, Que., November 13, 1950

Season	Club	League	Regular Season GP	G	A	PTS	PIM	Playoffs GP	G	A	PTS	PIM
1967-68	Montreal	OHA	47	15	34	49	10	11	8	9	17	5
1968-69	Montreal	OHA	54	37	60	97	29	14	5	10	15	10
1969-70	Montreal	OHA	54	51	70	121	26	...	...	...	...	...
1970-71	Buffalo	NHL	78	38	34	72	19	...	...	...	...	...
1971-72	Buffalo	NHL	76	26	48	74	24	...	...	...	...	...
1972-73	Buffalo	NHL	78	28	60	88	10	6	3	7	10	2
1973-74	Buffalo	NHL	55	18	33	51	10	...	...	...	...	...
1974-75	Buffalo	NHL	68	39	57	96	36	17	6	9	15	10
1975-76	Buffalo	NHL	80	44	69	113	36	9	4	4	8	4
1976-77	Buffalo	NHL	80	39	56	95	30	6	1	8	9	4
1977-78	Buffalo	NHL	79	41	48	89	20	8	3	2	5	0
1978-79	Buffalo	NHL	79	27	58	85	20	3	1	0	1	2
1979-80	Buffalo	NHL	80	40	66	106	57	14	10	11	21	8
1980-81	Buffalo	NHL	56	20	39	59	56	8	2	10	12	2
1981-82	Buffalo	NHL	62	31	42	73	40	4	0	7	7	0
1982-83	Buffalo	NHL	77	30	46	76	34	10	0	7	7	8
1983-84	Buffalo	NHL	73	31	59	90	32	...	...	...	...	...
1984-85	Buffalo	NHL	78	30	53	83	42	5	3	5	8	4
1985-86	Buffalo	NHL	72	21	39	60	28	...	...	...	...	...
1986-87	Buffalo	NHL	20	9	7	16	6	...	...	...	...	...
	NHL Totals	**17**	**1191**	**512**	**814**	**1326**	**500**	**90**	**33**	**70**	**103**	**44**

TOM PHILLIPS

Left wing / right wing. 5'8 ", 168 lbs., Born, Kenora, Ont., May 22, 1883

Season	Club	League	Regular Season GP	G	A	PTS	PIM	Playoffs GP	G	A	PTS	PIM
1902-03	Montreal AAA	CAHL	4	6	0	6	...	4	3	...	3	...
1903-04	Tor. Marlboros	OHA	...	...	...	...	...	2	2	...	2	...
1904-05	Rat Portage	MHL Sr.	8	31	0	31	...	3	8	...	8	...
1905-06	Kenora	MHL Sr.	9	24	0	24	...	...	...	...	...	...
1906-07	Kenora	MHL Sr.	6	18	0	18	...	2	4	...	4	...
1907-08	Ottawa	ECAHA	10	26	0	26	...	...	...	...	...	...
	Edmonton	Sr.	...	...	...	...	...	1	1	0	1	0
1908-09	Edmonton	Sr.	Not Available...			...	...	...	...	...	...	
1909-10	Nelson	Sr.	Not Available...			...	...	...	...	...	...	
1910-11			Did Not Play									
1911-12	Vancouver	PCHA	17	17	0	17	38	...	...	...	...	...

PIERRE PILOTE

Defence. Shoots left. 5'10", 178 lbs., Born, Kenogami, Que., December 11, 1931

Season	Club	League	Regular Season GP	G	A	PTS	PIM	Playoffs GP	G	A	PTS	PIM
1950-51	St. Catharines	OHA Jr.	54	13	13	26	230	9	2	2	4	23
1951-52	St. Catharines	OHA Jr.	52	21	32	53	139	14	3	12	15	50
	Buffalo	AHL	2	0	1	1	4	...	...	...	...	...
1952-53	Buffalo	AHL	61	2	14	16	85	...	...	...	...	...
1953-54	Buffalo	AHL	67	2	28	30	108	3	0	0	0	6
1954-55	Buffalo	AHL	63	10	28	38	120	10	0	4	4	18
1955-56	Chicago	NHL	20	3	5	8	34	...	...	...	...	...
	Buffalo	AHL	43	0	11	11	118	5	0	2	2	4
1956-57	Chicago	NHL	70	3	14	17	117	...	...	...	...	...
1957-58	Chicago	NHL	70	6	24	30	91	...	...	...	...	...
1958-59	Chicago	NHL	70	7	30	37	79	6	0	2	2	10
1959-60	Chicago	NHL	70	7	38	45	100	4	0	1	1	8
1960-61	Chicago	NHL	70	6	29	35	165	12	3	12	15	8
1961-62	Chicago	NHL	59	7	35	42	97	12	0	7	7	8
1962-63	Chicago	NHL	59	8	18	26	57	6	0	8	8	8
1963-64	Chicago	NHL	70	7	46	53	84	7	2	6	8	6
1964-65	Chicago	NHL	68	14	45	59	162	12	0	7	7	22
1965-66	Chicago	NHL	51	2	34	36	60	6	0	2	2	10
1966-67	Chicago	NHL	70	6	46	52	90	6	2	4	6	6
1967-68	Chicago	NHL	74	1	36	37	69	11	1	3	4	12
1968-69	Toronto	NHL	69	3	18	21	46	4	0	1	1	4
	NHL Totals	**14**	**890**	**80**	**418**	**498**	**1251**	**86**	**8**	**53**	**61**	**102**

DIDIER PITRE

Right wing / defence. Shoots right. 185 lbs., Born, Valleyfield, Que., September 1, 1883

Season	Club	League	Regular Season GP	G	A	PTS	PIM	Playoffs GP	G	A	PTS	PIM
1903-04	Mtl. Nationals	FAHL	2	1	0	1	0	...	...	...	...	...
1904-05	Mtl. Nationals	CAHL	2	0	0	0	0	...	...	...	...	...
	American Soo	IHL	13	11	0	11	6	...	...	...	...	...
1905-06	American Soo	IHL	22	41	0	41	29	...	...	...	...	...
1906-07	American Soo	IHL	23	25	11	36	28	...	...	...	...	...
1907-08	Mtl. Shamrocks	ECAHA	10	3	0	3	...	...	...	...	...	...
	Edmonton	Sr.	...	...	...	...	...	2	0	0	0	0
1908-09	Edmonton	Sr.	Not Available...			...	...	...	...	...	...	
	Renfrew	FAHL	Not Available...			...	...	...	...	...	...	
1909-10	Montreal	NHA	12	10	0	10	5	...	...	...	...	...
1910-11	Montreal	NHA	16	19	0	19	22	...	...	...	...	...
1911-12	Montreal	NHA	18	27	0	27	40	...	...	...	...	...
1912-13	Montreal	NHA	17	24	0	24	80	...	...	...	...	...
1913-14	Vancouver	PCHA	15	14	2	16	12	...	...	...	...	...
1914-15	Montreal	NHA	20	30	4	34	15	...	...	...	...	...
1915-16	Montreal	NHA	24	24	15	39	42	5	4	0	4	18
1916-17	Montreal	NHA	20	22	2	24	47	6	7	0	7	...
1917-18	Montreal	NHL	20	17	2	19	17	2	0	0	0	10
1918-19	Montreal	NHL	17	14	4	18	9	10	2	2	4	3
1919-20	Montreal	NHL	22	15	7	22	6	...	...	...	...	...
1920-21	Montreal	NHL	23	15	1	16	23	...	...	...	...	...
1921-22	Montreal	NHL	23	2	3	5	12	...	...	...	...	...
1922-23	Montreal	NHL	23	1	2	3	0	2	0	0	0	0
	NHL Totals	**6**	**127**	**64**	**17**	**81**	**50**	**14**	**2**	**2**	**4**	**0**

JACQUES PLANTE

Goaltender. Catches left. 6', 175 lbs., Born, Shawinigan Falls, Que., January 17, 1929

			Regular Season								Playoffs							
Season	Club	League	GP	MIN	GA	SO	GAA	W	L	T	GP	MIN	GA	SO	GAA	W	L	T
1949-50	Montreal	QSHL	58	3480	180	0	3.10	....	....	....	2	120	7	0	3.50	0	2	....
1950-51	Montreal	QSHL	60	3600	203	0	3.38	....	....	....	7	420	26	1	3.71	2	5	....
1951-52	Montreal	QSHL	60	3350	201	4	3.39	....	....	......	7	420	21	1	3.00	3	4	....
1952-53	Montreal	QSHL	29	1740	61	4	2.10	....	....	....	....	....	....	....	....	....	....	....
	Buffalo	AHL	33	1980	114	2	3.46	....	....	....	....	....	....	....	....	....	....	....
	Montreal	NHL	3	180	4	0	1.33	2	0	1	4	240	7	1	1.75	3	1	....
1953-54	Buffalo	AHL	55	3300	148	3	2.69	....	....	....	....	....	....	....	....	....	....	....
	Montreal	NHL	17	1020	27	5	1.59	7	5	5	8	480	15	2	1.87	5	3	....
1954-55	Montreal	NHL	52	3120	110	5	2.11	31	13	7	12	640	30	0	2.81	6	4	....
1955-56	Montreal	NHL	64	3840	119	7	1.86	42	12	10	10	600	18	2	1.80	8	2	....
1956-57	Montreal	NHL	61	3660	123	9	2.02	31	18	12	10	615	18	1	1.76	8	2	....
1957-58	Montreal	NHL	57	3386	119	9	2.11	34	14	8	10	618	20	1	1.94	8	2	....
1958-59	Montreal	NHL	67	4000	144	9	2.18	38	16	13	11	670	28	0	2.51	8	3	....
1959-60	Montreal	NHL	69	4140	175	3	2.54	40	17	12	8	489	11	3	1.35	8	0	....
1960-61	Montreal	EPHL	8	480	24	0	3.00	....	....	....	....	....	....	....	....	....	...	....
	Montreal	NHL	40	2400	112	2	2.80	22	11	7	6	412	16	0	2.33	2	4	....
1961-62	Montreal	NHL	70	4200	166	4	2.37	42	14	14	6	360	19	0	3.17	2	4	....
1962-63	Montreal	NHL	56	3320	138	5	2.49	22	14	19	5	300	14	0	2.80	1	4	....
1963-64	NY Rangers	NHL	65	3900	220	3	3.38	22	35	8	....	....	....	....	....	....	....	....
1964-65	NY Rangers	NHL	33	1938	109	2	3.37	10	17	5	....	....	....	....	....	....	....	....
	Baltimore	AHL	17	1020	51	1	3.00	....	....	....	5	315	14	1	2.67	2	3	....
1965-1968			Did Not Play															
1968-69	St. Louis	NHL	37	2139	70	5	1.96	18	12	6	10	589	14	3	1.43	8	2	....
1969-70	St. Louis	NHL	32	1839	67	5	2.19	18	9	5	6	324	8	1	1.48	4	1	....
1970-71	Toronto	NHL	40	2329	73	4	1.88	24	11	4	3	134	7	0	3.14	0	2	....
1971-72	Toronto	NHL	34	1965	86	2	2.62	16	13	5	1	60	5	0	5.00	0	1	....
1972-73	Toronto	NHL	32	1717	87	1	3.04	8	14	6	....	....	....	....	....	....	....	....
	Boston	NHL	8	480	16	2	2.00	7	1	0	2	120	10	0	5.00	0	2	....
1973-74			Did Not Play															
1974-75	Edmonton	WHA	40	1592	88	1	3.32	15	14	1	....	....	....	....	....	....	....	....
	NHL Totals	**18**	**837**	**49533**	**1965**	**82**	**2.38**	**434**	**246**	**147**	**112**	**6651**	**112**	**14**	**2.17**	**71**	**37**	**....**

DENIS POTVIN

Defence. Shoots left. 6', 205 lbs., Born, Ottawa, Ont., October 29, 1953

			Regular Season					Playoffs				
Season	Club	League	GP	G	A	PTS	PIM	GP	G	A	PTS	PIM
1968-69	Ottawa	OHA Jr.	46	12	25	37	83	...	...	...	...	...
1969-70	Ottawa	OHA Jr.	42	13	18	31	97	...	...	...	...	...
1970-71	Ottawa	OHA Jr.	57	20	58	78	200	...	...	...	...	...
1971-72	Ottawa	OHA Jr.	48	15	45	60	188	...	...	...	...	...
1972-73	Ottawa	OHA Jr.	61	35	88	123	232	...	...	...	...	...
1973-74	NY Islanders	NHL	77	17	37	54	175	...	...	...	...	...
1974-75	NY Islanders	NHL	79	21	55	76	105	17	5	9	14	30
1975-76	NY Islanders	NHL	78	31	67	98	100	13	5	14	19	32
1976-77	NY Islanders	NHL	80	25	55	80	103	12	6	4	10	20
1977-78	NY Islanders	NHL	80	30	64	94	81	7	2	2	4	6
1978-79	NY Islanders	NHL	73	31	70	101	58	10	4	7	11	8
1979-80	NY Islanders	NHL	31	8	33	41	44	21	6	13	19	24
1980-81	NY Islanders	NHL	74	20	56	76	104	18	8	17	25	16
1981-82	NY Islanders	NHL	60	24	37	61	83	19	5	16	21	30
1982-83	NY Islanders	NHL	69	12	54	66	60	20	8	12	20	22
1983-84	NY Islanders	NHL	78	22	63	85	87	20	1	5	6	28
1984-85	NY Islanders	NHL	77	17	51	68	96	10	3	2	5	10
1985-86	NY Islanders	NHL	74	21	38	59	78	3	0	1	1	0
1986-87	NY Islanders	NHL	58	12	30	42	70	10	2	2	4	21
1987-88	NY Islanders	NHL	72	19	32	51	112	5	1	4	5	6
	NHL Totals	**15**	**1066**	**310**	**742**	**1052**	**1354**	**185**	**56**	**108**	**164**	**253**

WALTER "BABE" PRATT

Defence. Shoots left. 6'3", 210 lbs., Born, Stony Mountain, Man., January 7, 1916

			Regular Season					Playoffs				
Season	Club	League	GP	G	A	PTS	PIM	GP	G	A	PTS	PIM
1933-34	Kenora	MHL Jr.	16	14	7	21	33	9	6	2	8	18
1934-35	Brandon	MHL Sr.	1	0	0	0	0	...	...	...	...	...
	Kenora	MHL Jr.	18	19	23	42	18	2	0	4	4	5
1935-36	Philadelphia	CAHL	28	7	8	15	48	4	0	0	0	2
	NY Rangers	NHL	17	1	1	2	16	...	...	...	...	...
1936-37	NY Rangers	NHL	47	8	7	15	23	9	3	1	4	11
1937-38	NY Rangers	NHL	47	5	14	19	56	2	0	0	0	2
1938-39	NY Rangers	NHL	48	2	19	21	20	7	1	2	3	9
1939-40	NY Rangers	NHL	48	4	13	17	61	12	3	1	4	18
1940-41	NY Rangers	NHL	47	3	17	20	52	3	1	1	2	6
1941-42	NY Rangers	NHL	47	4	24	28	65	6	1	3	4	24
1942-43	NY Rangers	NHL	6	0	2	2	6	...	...	...	...	...
	Toronto	NHL	38	12	25	33	44	6	1	2	3	8
1943-44	Toronto	NHL	50	17	40	57	30	5	0	3	3	4
1944-45	Toronto	NHL	50	18	23	41	39	13	2	4	6	8
1945-46	Toronto	NHL	41	5	20	25	36	...	...	...	...	...
1946-47	Boston	NHL	31	4	4	8	25	...	...	...	...	...
	Hershey	AHL	21	5	10	15	23	11	3	5	8	19
1947-48	Clev / Hershey	AHL	52	3	18	21	47	2	0	0	0	0
1948-49	N. Westminster	PCHL	63	18	48	66	64	12	1	8	9	10
1949-50	N. Westminster	PCHL	59	8	29	37	56	18	2	6	8	22
1950-51	N. Westminster	PCHL	65	8	15	23	54	7	0	0	0	4
1951-52	Tacoma	PCHL	63	7	31	38	20	5	0	1	1	0
	NHL Totals	**12**	**518**	**83**	**209**	**292**	**463**	**63**	**12**	**17**	**29**	**90**

JOE PRIMEAU

Centre. Shoots left. 5'11", 160 lbs., Born, Lindsay, Ont., January 29, 1906

			Regular Season					Playoffs				
Season	Club	League	GP	G	A	PTS	PIM	GP	G	A	PTS	PIM
1925-26	Tor. St. Mary's	OHA Jr.	7	15	2	17	2	...	2	1	3	...
1926-27	Tor. Marlboros	OHA Sr.	10	11	3	14	4	...	...	...	...	...
1927-28	Tor. Ravinas	CPHL	41	26	13	39	36	2	1	0	1	0
	Toronto	NHL	2	0	0	0	0	...	...	...	...	...
1928-29	London	CPHL	35	12	10	22	16	...	...	...	...	...
	Toronto	NHL	6	0	1	1	2	...	...	...	...	...
1929-30	Toronto	NHL	43	5	21	26	22	...	...	...	...	...
1930-31	Toronto	NHL	38	9	32	41	18	2	0	0	0	0
1931-32	Toronto	NHL	46	13	37	50	25	7	0	6	6	2
1932-33	Toronto	NHL	48	11	21	32	4	8	0	1	1	4
1933-34	Toronto	NHL	45	14	32	46	8	5	2	4	6	6
1934-35	Toronto	NHL	37	10	20	30	16	7	0	3	3	0
1935-36	Toronto	NHL	45	4	13	17	10	9	3	4	7	0
	NHL Totals	**9**	**310**	**66**	**177**	**243**	**105**	**38**	**5**	**18**	**23**	**12**

MARCEL PRONOVOST

Defence. Shoots left. 6', 190 lbs., Born, Lac la Tortue, Que., June 15, 1930

			Regular Season					Playoffs				
Season	Club	League	GP	G	A	PTS	PIM	GP	G	A	PTS	PIM
1947-48	Detroit A.C.	IHL	19	5	3	8	53	...	...	...	...	...
	Windsor	OHA Jr.	33	6	18	24	61	12	1	3	4	28
1948-49	Detroit A.C.	IHL	9	4	4	8	24	6	3	1	4	15
	Windsor	OHA Jr.	42	14	23	37	126	4	1	5	6	2
1949-50	Omaha	USHL	69	13	39	52	100	7	4	9	13	9
	Detroit	NHL	...	...	...	...	...	9	0	1	1	10
1950-51	Indianapolis	AHL	34	9	23	32	44	...	...	...	...	...
	Detroit	NHL	37	1	6	7	20	6	0	0	0	0
1951-52	Detroit	NHL	69	7	11	18	50	8	0	1	1	10
1952-53	Detroit	NHL	68	8	19	27	72	6	0	0	0	6
1953-54	Detroit	NHL	57	6	12	18	50	12	2	3	5	12
1954-55	Detroit	NHL	70	9	25	34	90	11	1	2	3	6
1955-56	Detroit	NHL	68	4	13	17	46	10	0	2	2	8
1956-57	Detroit	NHL	70	7	9	16	38	5	0	0	0	6
1957-58	Detroit	NHL	62	2	18	20	52	4	0	1	1	4
1958-59	Detroit	NHL	69	11	21	32	44	...	...	...	...	...
1959-60	Detroit	NHL	69	7	17	24	38	6	1	1	2	2
1960-61	Detroit	NHL	70	6	11	17	44	9	2	3	5	0
1961-62	Detroit	NHL	70	4	14	18	38	...	...	...	...	...
1962-63	Detroit	NHL	69	4	9	13	48	11	1	4	5	8
1963-64	Detroit	NHL	67	3	17	20	42	14	0	2	2	14
1964-65	Detroit	NHL	68	1	15	16	45	7	0	3	3	4
1965-66	Toronto	NHL	54	2	8	10	34	4	0	0	0	6
1966-67	Toronto	NHL	58	2	12	14	28	12	1	0	1	8
1967-68	Toronto	NHL	70	3	17	20	48	...	...	...	...	...
1968-69	Toronto	NHL	34	1	2	3	20	...	...	...	...	...
1969-70	Toronto	NHL	7	0	1	1	4	...	...	...	...	...
	Tulsa	CHL	53	1	16	17	24	2	0	0	0	0
1970-71	Tulsa	CHL	17	0	0	0	4	...	...	...	...	...
	NHL Totals	**21**	**1206**	**88**	**257**	**345**	**851**	**134**	**8**	**23**	**31**	**104**

BOB PULFORD

Centre / left wing. Shoots left. 5'11", 188 lbs., Born, Newton Robinson, Ont., March 31, 1936

			Regular Season					Playoffs				
Season	Club	League	GP	G	A	PTS	PIM	GP	G	A	PTS	PIM
1953-54	Tor. Marlboros	OHA Jr.	17	5	9	14	12	15	4	7	11	12
1954-55	Tor. Marlboros	OHA Jr.	47	24	22	46	43	13	7	10	17	29
1955-56	Tor. Marlboros	OHA Jr.	48	30	25	55	87	11	16	8	24	2
1956-57	Toronto	NHL	65	11	11	22	32	...	...	...	...	...
1957-58	Toronto	NHL	70	14	17	31	48	...	...	...	...	...
1958-59	Toronto	NHL	70	23	14	37	53	12	4	4	8	8
1959-60	Toronto	NHL	70	24	28	52	81	10	4	1	5	10
1960-61	Toronto	NHL	40	11	18	29	41	5	0	0	0	8
1961-62	Toronto	NHL	70	18	21	39	98	12	7	1	8	24
1962-63	Toronto	NHL	70	19	25	44	49	10	2	5	7	14
1963-64	Toronto	NHL	70	18	30	48	73	14	5	3	8	20
1964-65	Toronto	NHL	65	19	20	39	46	6	1	1	2	16
1965-66	Toronto	NHL	70	28	28	56	51	4	1	1	2	12
1966-67	Toronto	NHL	67	17	28	45	28	12	1	10	11	12
1967-68	Toronto	NHL	74	20	30	50	40	...	...	...	...	...
1968-69	Toronto	NHL	72	11	23	34	20	4	0	0	0	2
1969-70	Toronto	NHL	74	18	19	37	31	...	...	...	...	...
1970-71	Los Angeles	NHL	59	17	26	43	53	...	...	...	...	...
1971-72	Los Angeles	NHL	73	13	24	37	48	...	...	...	...	...
	NHL Totals	**16**	**1079**	**281**	**362**	**643**	**792**	**89**	**25**	**26**	**51**	**126**

HARVEY PULFORD

Point. Born, Toronto, Ont., April 22, 1875

			Regular Season					Playoffs				
Season	Club	League	GP	G	A	PTS	PIM	GP	G	A	PTS	PIM
1893-94	Ottawa	AHA	6	0	0	0	...	1	0	0	0	...
1894-95	Ottawa	AHA	7	0	0	0	...	...	...	...	...	...
1895-96	Ottawa	AHA	8	0	0	0	...	...	...	...	...	...
1896-97	Ottawa	AHA	8	0	0	0	...	...	...	...	...	...
1897-98	Ottawa	AHA	7	0	0	0	...	...	...	...	...	...
1898-99	Ottawa	AHA	5	0	0	0	...	...	...	...	...	...
1899-1900	Ottawa	CAHL	6	1	0	1	...	...	...	...	...	...
	Ott. Aberdeens	Sr.	1	0	0	0	...	...	...	...	...	...
1900-01	Ottawa	CAHL	5	0	0	0	...	2	3	0	3	...
1901-02				Not Available		...	...	...	...	...	...	...
1902-03	Ottawa	CAHL	7	0	0	0	...	4	0	0	0	...
1903-04	Ottawa	CAHL	2	0	0	0	...	7	1	0	1	...
1904-05	Ottawa	FAHL	6	1	0	1	...	4	0	0	0	...
1905-06	Ottawa	ECAHA	10	3	0	3	...	6	1	0	1	...
1906-07	Ottawa	ECAHA	10	0	0	0	...	...	...	...	...	...
1907-08	Ottawa	ECAHA	9	1	0	1	...	...	...	...	...	...

BILL QUACKENBUSH

Defence. Shoots left. 5'11", 180 lbs., Born, Toronto, Ont., March 2, 1922

				Regular Season					Playoffs			
Season	Club	League	GP	G	A	PTS	PIM	GP	G	A	PTS	PIM
1940-41	Brantford	OHA Jr.	13	4	9	13	0	...	...	...	...	...
1941-42	Brantford	OHA Jr.	23	5	29	34	16	7	2	4	6	8
1942-43	Indianapolis	AHL	37	6	13	19	10	7	0	1	1	6
	Detroit	NHL	10	1	1	2	4	...	...	...	...	...
1943-44	Indianapolis	AHL	1	1	0	1	0	...	...	...	...	...
	Detroit	NHL	43	4	14	18	6	2	1	0	1	0
1944-45	Detroit	NHL	50	7	14	21	10	14	0	2	2	2
1945-46	Detroit	NHL	48	11	10	21	6	5	0	1	1	0
1946-47	Detroit	NHL	44	5	17	22	26	5	0	0	0	2
1947-48	Detroit	NHL	58	6	16	22	17	10	0	2	2	0
1948-49	Detroit	NHL	60	6	17	23	0	11	1	1	2	0
1949-50	Boston	NHL	70	8	17	25	4	...	...	...	...	...
1950-51	Boston	NHL	70	5	24	29	12	6	0	1	1	0
1951-52	Boston	NHL	69	2	17	19	6	7	0	3	3	0
1952-53	Boston	NHL	69	2	16	18	6	10	0	4	4	4
1953-54	Boston	NHL	45	0	17	17	6	4	0	0	0	0
1954-55	Boston	NHL	68	2	20	22	8	5	0	5	5	0
1955-56	Boston	NHL	70	3	22	25	4	...	...	...	...	...
	NHL Totals	**14**	**774**	**62**	**222**	**284**	**95**	**80**	**2**	**19**	**21**	**8**

FRANK RANKIN

Rover. Born, Stratford, Ont., April 1, 1889

				Regular Season					Playoffs			
Season	Club	League	GP	G	A	PTS	PIM	GP	G	A	PTS	PIM
1906-07	Stratford	OHA Jr.		Not Available...		...	...	...	...	...	...	
1907-08	Stratford	OHA Jr.		Not Available...		...	...	...	...	...	...	
1908-09	Stratford	OHA Jr.		Not Available...		...	...	...	...	...	...	
1909-10	Tor. Eaton's	OHA Sr.		Not Available...		...	...	...	...	...	...	
1910-11	Tor. Eaton's	OHA Sr.		Not Available...		...	...	...	...	...	...	
1911-12	Tor. Eatons	OHA Sr.		Not Available...		...	...	...	...	...	...	
1912-13	Tor. St. Mike's	OHA Sr.		Not Available...		...	...	...	...	...	...	

JEAN RATELLE

Centre. Shoots left. 6'1", 180 lbs., Born, Lac St. Jean, Que., October 3, 1940

				Regular Season					Playoffs			
Season	Club	League	GP	G	A	PTS	PIM	GP	G	A	PTS	PIM
1958-59	Guelph	OHA Jr.	54	20	31	51	11	10	5	4	9	2
1959-60	Guelph	OHA Jr.	48	39	47	86	15	5	3	5	8	4
	Trois-Rivieres	EPHL	3	3	5	8	0	4	0	3	3	0
1960-61	Guelph	OHA Jr.	47	40	61	101	10	14	6	11	17	6
	NY Rangers	NHL	3	2	1	3	0	...	...	...	...	...
1961-62	NY Rangers	NHL	31	4	8	12	4	...	...	...	...	...
	Kitch-Waterloo	EPHL	32	10	29	39	8	7	2	6	8	2
1962-63	NY Rangers	NHL	48	11	9	20	8	...	...	...	...	...
	Baltimore	AHL	20	11	8	19	0	3	0	0	0	0
1963-64	Baltimore	AHL	57	20	26	46	2	...	...	...	...	...
	NY Rangers	NHL	15	0	7	7	6	...	...	...	...	...
1964-65	Baltimore	AHL	8	9	4	13	6	...	...	...	...	...
	NY Rangers	NHL	54	14	21	35	14	...	...	...	...	...
1965-66	NY Rangers	NHL	67	21	30	51	10	...	...	...	...	...
1966-67	NY Rangers	NHL	41	6	5	11	4	4	0	0	0	2
1967-68	NY Rangers	NHL	74	32	46	78	18	6	0	4	4	2
1968-69	NY Rangers	NHL	75	32	46	78	26	4	1	0	1	0
1969-70	NY Rangers	NHL	75	32	42	74	28	6	1	3	4	0
1970-71	NY Rangers	NHL	78	26	46	72	14	13	2	9	11	8
1971-72	NY Rangers	NHL	63	46	63	109	4	6	0	1	1	0
1972-73	NY Rangers	NHL	78	41	53	94	12	10	2	7	9	0
1973-74	NY Rangers	NHL	68	28	39	67	16	13	2	4	6	0
1974-75	NY Rangers	NHL	79	36	55	91	26	3	1	5	6	2
1975-76	NY Rangers	NHL	13	5	10	15	2	...	...	...	...	...
	Boston	NHL	67	31	59	90	16	12	8	8	16	4
1976-77	Boston	NHL	78	33	61	94	22	14	5	12	17	4
1977-78	Boston	NHL	80	25	59	84	10	15	3	7	10	0
1978-79	Boston	NHL	80	27	45	72	12	11	7	6	13	2
1979-80	Boston	NHL	67	28	45	73	8	3	0	0	0	0
1980-81	Boston	NHL	47	11	26	37	16	3	0	0	0	0
	NHL Totals	**21**	**1281**	**491**	**776**	**1267**	**276**	**123**	**32**	**66**	**98**	**24**

CHUCK RAYNER

Goaltender. Catches left. 5'11", 190 lbs., Born, Sutherland, Sask., August 11, 1920

					Regular Season							Playoffs					
Season	Club	League	GP	MIN	GA	SO	GAA	W	L	T	GP	MIN	GA	SO	GAA	W	L	T
1937-38	Kenora	MHL Jr.	22	1320	103	0	4.68	....	....	....	....	....	....	....	....	....	....	....
1938-39	Kenora	MHL Jr.	22	1320	64	0	2.91	....	....	....	....	....	....	....	....	....	....	....
1939-40	Kenora	MHL Jr.	24	1440	66	1	2.75				9	540	18	0	2.00	....	....	....
1940-41	Springfield	AHL	37	2220	89	6	2.41	2	7	3	....	....	....	....	....	....	....	....
	NY Americans	NHL	12	773	44	0	3.66	....	....	....	....	....	....	....	....	....	....	....
1941-42	Springfield	AHL	1	46	3	0	4.00	....	....	....	....	....	....	....	....	....	....	....
	Brooklyn	NHL	36	2230	129	1	3.47	13	21	2	....	....	....	....	....	....	....	....
1942-43	Victoria Navy	PCHL	12	720	39	1	3.25	....	....	....	6	360	26	0	4.33	....	....	....
1943-44	Victoria Navy	PCHL	18	1080	52	1	2.89	....	....	....	....	....	....	....	....	....	....	....
1944-45			Military Service															
1945-46	NY Rangers	NHL	41	2377	150	1	3.79	12	21	7	....	....	....	....	....	....	....	....
1946-47	NY Rangers	NHL	58	3480	177	5	3.05	22	30	6	....	....	....	....	....	....	....	...
1947-48	NY Rangers	NHL	12	691	42	0	3.65	4	8	0	6	360	17	0	2.83	2	4	....
	New Haven	AHL	15	900	40	0	2.67	....	....	....	....	....	....	....	....	....	....	....
1948-49	NY Rangers	NHL	58	3480	168	7	2.90	16	31	11	....	....	....	....	....	....	....	....
1949-50	NY Rangers	NHL	69	4140	181	6	2.62	28	30	11	12	775	29	1	2.25	7	5	....
1950-51	NY Rangers	NHL	66	3940	187	2	2.85	19	28	19	....	....	....	....	....	....	....	....
1951-52	NY Rangers	NHL	53	3180	159	2	3.00	18	25	10	....	....	....	....	....	....	....	....
1952-53	NY Rangers	NHL	20	1200	58	1	2.90	4	8	8	....	....	....	....	....	....	....	....
1953-54	Saskatoon	WHL	68	4080	204	6	3.00	....	....	....	6	360	20	1	3.33	2	4	....
1954-55	Nelson	WIHL	1	120	2	0	2.00	....	....	....	1	120	3	0	3.00	....	....	....
1955-56	Nelson	WIHL	6	360	3	0	3.00	....	....	....	....	....	....	....	....	....	....	.....
	NHL Totals	**10**	**425**	**25438**	**1294**	**25**	**3.05**	**138**	**209**	**77**	**18**	**1135**	**46**	**1**	**2.43**	**9**	**9**	**....**

KEN REARDON

Defence. Shoots left. 5'11", 180 lbs., Born, Winnipeg, Man., April 1, 1921

				Regular Season					Playoffs			
Season	Club	League	GP	G	A	PTS	PIM	GP	G	A	PTS	PIM
1938-39	Edmonton	Jr.	...	0	1	1	8	...	...	...	...	...
1939-40	Edmonton	Jr.	...	...	...	...	...	...	...	...	...	...
1940-41	Montreal	NHL	84	2	8	10	41	3	0	0	0	4
1941-42	Montreal	NHL	41	3	12	15	93	3	0	0	0	4
1942-43	Ottawa	QSHL	26	7	16	23	77	11	0	1	1	25
1943-44	Ottawa	QSHL	1	1	0	1	0	...	...	...	...	...
1944-45				Military Service								
1945-46	Montreal	NHL	43	5	4	9	45	9	1	1	2	4
	Montreal	QSHL	2	0	0	0	4	...	...	...	...	...
1946-47	Montreal	NHL	52	5	17	22	84	7	1	2	3	20
1947-48	Montreal	NHL	58	7	15	22	129	...	...	...	...	...
1948-49	Montreal	NHL	46	3	13	16	103	7	0	0	0	18
1949-50	Montreal	NHL	67	1	27	28	109	2	0	2	2	12
	NHL Totals	**7**	**341**	**26**	**96**	**122**	**604**	**31**	**2**	**5**	**7**	**62**

HENRI RICHARD

Centre. Shoots right. 5'7", 160 lbs., Born, Montreal, Que., February 29, 1936

				Regular Season					Playoffs			
Season	Club	League	GP	G	A	PTS	PIM	GP	G	A	PTS	PIM
1951-52	Montreal	QJHL	49	23	32	55	35	...	...	...	...	...
1952-53	Montreal	QJHL	46	27	36	63	55	7	4	5	9	4
	Montreal	QSHL	1	0	0	0	0	...	...	...	...	...
1953-54	Montreal	QJHL	54	56	53	109	85	7	6	7	13	6
1954-55	Montreal	QJHL	44	33	33	66	65	...	...	...	...	...
1955-56	Montreal	NHL	64	19	21	40	46	10	4	4	8	21
1956-57	Montreal	NHL	63	18	36	54	71	10	2	6	8	10
1957-58	Montreal	NHL	67	28	52	80	56	10	1	7	8	11
1958-59	Montreal	NHL	63	21	30	51	33	11	3	8	11	13
1959-60	Montreal	NHL	70	30	43	73	66	8	3	9	12	9
1960-61	Montreal	NHL	70	24	44	68	91	6	2	4	6	22
1961-62	Montreal	NHL	54	21	29	50	48	...	...	...	...	...
1962-63	Montreal	NHL	67	23	50	73	57	5	1	1	2	2
1963-64	Montreal	NHL	66	14	39	53	73	7	1	1	2	9
1964-65	Montreal	NHL	53	23	29	52	43	13	7	4	11	24
1965-66	Montreal	NHL	62	22	39	61	47	8	1	4	5	2
1966-67	Montreal	NHL	65	21	34	55	28	10	4	6	10	2
1967-68	Montreal	NHL	54	9	19	28	16	13	4	4	8	4
1968-69	Montreal	NHL	64	15	37	52	45	14	2	4	6	8
1969-70	Montreal	NHL	62	16	36	52	61	...	...	...	...	...
1970-71	Montreal	NHL	75	12	37	49	46	20	5	7	12	20
1971-72	Montreal	NHL	75	12	32	44	48	6	0	3	3	4
1972-73	Montreal	NHL	71	8	35	43	21	17	6	4	10	14
1973-74	Montreal	NHL	75	19	36	55	28	6	2	2	4	2
1974-75	Montreal	NHL	16	3	10	13	4	6	1	2	3	4
	NHL Totals	**20**	**1256**	**358**	**688**	**1046**	**928**	**180**	**49**	**80**	**129**	**181**

MAURICE "ROCKET" RICHARD

Right wing. Shoots left. 5'10", 180 lbs., Born, Montreal, Que., August 4, 1921

				Regular Season					Playoffs			
Season	Club	League	GP	G	A	PTS	PIM	GP	G	A	PTS	PIM
1939-40	Verdun	QSHL	1	0	0	0	0	...	...	...	...	...
1940-41	Montreal	QSHL	1	0	1	1	0	...	...	...	...	...
1941-42	Montreal	QSHL	31	8	9	17	27	6	2	1	3	6
1942-43	Montreal	NHL	16	5	6	11	4	...	...	...	...	...
1943-44	Montreal	NHL	46	32	22	54	45	9	12	5	17	10
1944-45	Montreal	NHL	50	50	23	73	46	6	6	2	8	10
1945-46	Montreal	NHL	50	27	21	48	50	9	7	4	11	15
1946-47	Montreal	NHL	60	45	26	71	69	10	6	5	11	44
1947-48	Montreal	NHL	53	28	25	53	89	...	...	...	...	...
1948-49	Montreal	NHL	59	20	18	38	110	7	2	1	3	14
1949-50	Montreal	NHL	70	43	22	65	114	5	1	1	2	6
1950-51	Montreal	NHL	65	42	24	66	97A	11	9	4	13	13
1951-52	Montreal	NHL	48	27	17	44	4	11	4	2	6	6
1952-53	Montreal	NHL	70	28	33	61	112	12	7	1	8	2
1953-54	Montreal	NHL	70	37	30	67	112	11	3	0	3	22
1954-55	Montreal	NHL	67	38	36	74	125	...	...	...	...	...
1955-56	Montreal	NHL	70	38	33	71	89	10	5	9	14	24
1956-57	Montreal	NHL	63	33	29	62	74	10	8	3	11	8
1957-58	Montreal	NHL	28	15	19	34	28	10	11	4	15	10
1958-59	Montreal	NHL	42	17	21	38	27	4	0	0	0	2
1959-60	Montreal	NHL	51	19	16	35	50	8	1	3	4	2
	NHL Totals	**18**	**978**	**544**	**421**	**965**	**1285**	**133**	**82**	**44**	**126**	**188**

GEORGE RICHARDSON

Rover. Born, c.1887

				Regular Season					Playoffs			
Season	Club	League	GP	G	A	PTS	PIM	GP	G	A	PTS	PIM
1906-07	14th Regiment	OHA Sr.		Not Available		...	...	...	...	...	...	...
1907-08	14th Regiment	OHA Sr.		Not Available		...	...	...	...	...	...	...
1908-09	Queen's U.	OHA Sr.		Not Available		...	...	...	...	...	...	...

GORD ROBERTS

Left wing. 5'11", 180 lbs., Born, Ottawa, Ont., September 5, 1891

				Regular Season					Playoffs			
Season	Club	League	GP	G	A	PTS	PIM	GP	G	A	PTS	PIM
1909-10	Ottawa	CHA	1	3	0	3	...	...	...	...	...	...
	Ottawa	NHA	9	13	0	13	34	2	7	0	7	0
1910-11	Mtl. Wanderers	NHA	4	1	0	1	3	...	...	...	...	...
1911-12	Mtl. Wanderers	NHA	18	16	0	16	0	...	...	...	...	...
1912-13	Mtl. Wanderers	NHA	16	16	0	16	22	...	...	...	...	...
1913-14	Mtl. Wanderers	NHA	20	31	13	44	15	...	...	...	...	...
1914-15	Mtl. Wanderers	NHA	19	29	5	34	74	2	0	0	0	15
1915-16	Mtl. Wanderers	NHA	21	18	7	25	64	...	...	...	...	...
1916-17	Vancouver	PCHA	23	43	10	53	42	...	...	...	...	...
1917-18	Seattle	PCHA	18	20	3	23	24	2	0	0	0	3
1918-19				Did Not Play								
1919-20	Vancouver	PCHA	22	16	3	19	13	2	1	0	1	0

LARRY ROBINSON

Defence. Shoots left. 6'4", 225 lbs., Born, Winchester, Ont. June 2, 1951

			Regular Season					Playoffs				
Season	Club	League	GP	G	A	PTS	PIM	GP	G	A	PTS	PIM
1969-70	Brockville	OHA Jr.	40	22	29	51	74	....	....	....	....	....
1970-71	Kitchener	OHA Jr.	61	12	39	51	65	....	....	....	....	....
1971-72	Nova Scotia	AHL	74	10	14	24	54	15	2	10	12	31
1972-73	Montreal	NHL	36	2	4	6	20	11	1	4	5	9
1973-74	Nova Scotia	AHL	38	6	33	39	33	....	....	....	....	....
1974-75	Montreal	NHL	78	6	20	26	66	6	0	1	1	26
1975-76	Montreal	NHL	80	14	47	61	76	11	0	4	4	27
1976-77	Montreal	NHL	80	10	30	40	59	13	3	3	6	10
1977-78	Montreal	NHL	77	19	66	85	45	14	2	10	12	12
1978-79	Montreal	NHL	80	13	52	65	39	15	4	17	21	6
1979-80	Montreal	NHL	67	16	45	61	33	16	6	9	15	8
1980-81	Montreal	NHL	65	12	38	50	37	3	0	1	1	2
1981-82	Montreal	NHL	71	12	47	59	41	5	0	1	1	8
1982-83	Montreal	NHL	71	14	49	63	33	3	0	0	0	2
1983-84	Montreal	NHL	74	9	34	43	39	15	0	5	5	22
1984-85	Montreal	NHL	76	14	33	47	44	12	3	8	11	8
1985-86	Montreal	NHL	78	19	63	82	39	20	0	13	13	22
1986-87	Montreal	NHL	70	13	37	50	44	17	3	17	20	6
1987-88	Montreal	NHL	53	6	34	40	30	11	1	4	5	4
1988-89	Montreal	NHL	74	4	26	30	22	21	2	8	10	12
1989-90	Los Angeles	NHL	64	7	32	39	34	10	2	3	5	10
1990-91	Los Angeles	NHL	62	1	22	23	16	12	1	4	5	15
1991-92	Los Angeles	NHL	56	3	10	13	37	2	0	0	0	0
	NHL Totals	**20**	**1384**	**208**	**750**	**958**	**793**	**227**	**28**	**116**	**144**	**211**

ART ROSS

Defence. Shoots left. 5'11", 190 lbs., Born, Naughton, Ont., January 13, 1886

			Regular Season					Playoffs				
Season	Club	League	GP	G	A	PTS	PIM	GP	G	A	PTS	PIM
1904-05	Mtl. Westmount	CAHL	8	10	...	10	...	...	...	...	...	...
1905-06	Brandon	MHL Sr.	7	6	...	6	...	...	...	...	...	...
1906-07	Kenora	Sr.	...	...	...	....	...	2	0	...	0	0
	Brandon	MHL Sr.	9	5	...	5	...	2	0	...	0	0
1907-08	Mtl. Wanderers	ECAHA	10	8	...	8	...	5	4	...	4	0
	Pembroke	Sr.	1	5	...	5	...	...	...	...	...	...
1908-09	Mtl. Wanderers	ECHA	9	2	...	2	30	2	0	...	0	...
	Mtl. Wanderers	Sr.	2	2	...	2	3	...	...	...	...	...
	Cobalt	Sr.	2	0	...	0	...	...	...	...	...	...
1909-10	Haileybury	NHA	12	6	...	6	31	...	...	...	...	...
	All-Montreal	CHA	4	4	...	4	3	...	...	...	...	...
1910-11	Mtl. Wanderers	NHA	11	4	...	4	24	...	...	...	...	...
1911-12	Mtl. Wanderers	NHA	18	16	...	16	35	...	...	...	...	...
1912-13	Mtl. Wanderers	NHA	19	11	...	11	58	...	...	...	...	...
1913-14	Mtl. Wanderers	NHA	18	4	5	9	74	...	...	...	...	...
1914-15	Ottawa	NHA	16	3	1	4	55	5	2	...	2	...
1915-16	Ottawa	NHA	21	8	8	16	69	...	...	...	...	...
1916-17	Mtl. Wanderers	NHA	16	6	3	9	63	...	...	...	...	...
1917-18	Mtl. Wanderers	NHL	3	1	0	1	12	...	...	...	...	...
	NHL Totals	**1**	**3**	**1**	**0**	**1**	**0**	....	....	....	....	....

BLAIR RUSSEL

Left wing. Born Montreal, Que., September 17, 1890

			Regular Season					Playoffs				
Season	Club	League	GP	G	A	PTS	PIM	GP	G	A	PTS	PIM
1899-1900	Mtl. Victorias	CAHL	7	9	...	9	...	...	...	...	...	...
1900-01	Mtl. Victorias	CAHL	8	8	...	8	...	...	...	...	...	...
1901-02	Mtl. Victorias	CAHL	8	9	...	9	...	...	...	...	...	...
1902-03	Mtl. Victorias	CAHL	8	7	...	7	...	2	0	0	0	...
1903-04	Mtl. Victorias	CAHL	8	17	...	17	...	...	...	...	...	...
1904-05	Mtl. Victorias	CAHL	8	19	...	19	...	...	...	...	...	...
1905-06	Mtl. Victorias	ECAHA	4	7	...	7	...	...	...	...	...	...
1906-07	Mtl. Victorias	ECAHA	10	25	...	25	...	...	...	...	...	...
1907-08	Mtl. Victorias	ECAHA	6	9	...	8	...	...	...	...	...	...

ERNIE RUSSELL

Right wing. Shoots right. 5'6", 160 lbs., Born, Montreal, Que., October 21, 1883

			Regular Season					Playoffs				
Season	Club	League	GP	G	A	PTS	PIM	GP	G	A	PTS	PIM
1904-05	Montreal AAA	CAHL	8	11	...	11	...	...	...	...	...	...
1905-06	Mtl. Wanderers	ECAHA	6	21	...	21	...	2	4	...	4	...
1906-07	Mtl. Wanderers	ECAHA	9	42	...	42	...	5	12	...	12	...
1907-08	Mtl. Wanderers	ECHA	9	21	...	21	...	...	...	...	...	...
1908-09				Did Not Play								
1909-10	Mtl. Wanderers	NHA	13	34	...	34	51	1	4	...	4	3
1910-11	Mtl. Wanderers	NHA	10	18	...	18	56	...	...	...	...	...
1911-12	Mtl. Wanderers	NHA	18	27	...	27	110	...	...	...	...	...
1912-13	Mtl. Wanderers	NHA	15	7	...	7	48	...	...	...	...	...
1913-14	Mtl. Wanderers	NHA	11	2	...	2	21	...	...	...	...	...

JACK RUTTAN

Born, Winnipeg, Man., April 5, 1889

			Regular Season					Playoffs				
Season	Club	League	GP	G	A	PTS	PIM	GP	G	A	PTS	PIM
1905-06	Winnipeg	Jr.		Not Available		...	...	...	...	...	...	...
1906-07	Winnipeg	Jr.		Not Available		...	...	...	...	...	...	...
1907-08	St. John's	College		Not Available		...	...	...	...	...	...	...
1908-09	St. John's	College		Not Available		...	...	...	...	...	...	...
1909-10	Manitoba Varsity	WSHL		Not Available		...	...	...	...	...	...	...
1910-11	Manitoba Varsity	WSHL		Not Available		...	...	...	...	...	...	...
1911-12	Manitoba Varsity	WSHL		Not Available		...	...	...	...	...	...	...
1912-13	Winnipeg	WSHL		Not Available		...	...	...	...	...	...	...

SERGE SAVARD

Defence. Shoots left. 6'2", 210 lbs., Born, Montreal, Que., January 22, 1946

			Regular Season					Playoffs				
Season	Club	League	GP	G	A	PTS	PIM	GP	G	A	PTS	PIM
1963-64	Montreal	OHA Jr.	56	3	31	34	72	17	1	7	8	30
1964-65	Omaha	CHL	2	0	0	0	0	4	0	1	1	4
	Montreal	OHA Jr.	56	14	33	47	81	7	2	3	5	8
1965-66	Montreal	OHA Jr.	20	8	10	18	33	10	1	4	5	20
1966-67	Montreal	NHL	2	0	0	0	0	...	...	...	...	...
	Quebec	AHL	1	0	0	0	2	...	...	...	...	...
	Houston	CHL	68	7	25	32	155	5	1	3	4	17
1967-68	Montreal	NHL	67	2	13	15	34	6	2	0	2	0
1968-69	Montreal	NHL	74	8	23	31	73	14	4	6	10	24
1969-70	Montreal	NHL	64	12	19	31	38	...	...	...	...	...
1970-71	Montreal	NHL	37	5	10	15	30	...	...	...	...	...
1971-72	Montreal	NHL	23	1	8	9	16	6	0	0	0	10
1972-73	Montreal	NHL	74	7	32	39	58	17	3	8	11	22
1973-74	Montreal	NHL	67	4	14	18	49	6	1	1	2	4
1974-75	Montreal	NHL	80	20	40	60	64	11	1	7	8	2
1975-76	Montreal	NHL	71	8	39	47	38	13	3	6	9	6
1976-77	Montreal	NHL	78	9	33	42	35	14	2	7	9	2
1977-78	Montreal	NHL	77	8	34	42	24	15	1	7	8	8
1978-79	Montreal	NHL	80	7	26	33	30	16	2	7	9	6
1979-80	Montreal	NHL	46	5	8	13	18	2	0	0	0	0
1980-81	Montreal	NHL	77	4	13	17	30	3	0	0	0	0
1981-82	Winnipeg	NHL	47	2	5	7	26	4	0	0	0	2
1982-83	Winnipeg	NHL	76	4	16	20	29	3	0	0	0	2
	NHL Totals	**17**	**1040**	**106**	**333**	**439**	**592**	**130**	**19**	**49**	**68**	**88**

TERRY SAWCHUK

Goaltender. Catches left. 5'11", 180 lbs., Born, Winnipeg, Man., December 28, 1929

			Regular Season								Playoffs							
Season	Club	League	GP	MIN	GA	SO	GAA	W	L	T	GP	MIN	GA	SO	GAA	W	L	T
1945-46	Winnipeg	MJHL	10	600	58	0	5.80	...	....	....	2	120	12	0	6.00	0	2	....
1946-47	Galt	OHA Jr.	30	1800	94	4	3.13	...	....	....	2	125	9	0	4.32	0	2	....
1947-48	Windsor Hettche	IHL	3	180	5	0	1.67	...	....	....	...	....	....	...	....	....	...	....
	Windsor	OHA Jr.	4	240	11	0	2.75	...	....	....	...	....	....	...	....	....	...	....
	Omaha	USHL	54	3240	174	4	3.22	...	....	....	3	180	9	0	3.00	1	2	....
1948-49	Indianapolis	AHL	67	4020	205	2	3.06	....	....	....	2	120	9	0	4.50	...	....	....
1949-50	Detroit	NHL	7	420	16	1	2.28	4	3	0	...	....	....	...	....	....	...	....
	Indianapolis	AHL	61	3660	188	3	3.08	....	....	....	8	480	12	0	1.50	8	0	....
1950-51	Detroit	NHL	70	4200	139	11	1.98	44	13	13	6	463	13	1	1.69	2	4	....
1951-52	Detroit	NHL	70	4200	133	12	1.91	44	14	12	8	480	5	4	0.63	8	0	....
1952-53	Detroit	NHL	63	3780	120	9	1.94	32	15	16	6	372	21	1	3.39	2	4	....
1953-54	Detroit	NHL	67	4000	129	12	1.96	35	19	13	12	751	20	2	1.60	8	4	....
1954-55	Detroit	NHL	68	4040	132	12	1.94	40	17	11	11	660	26	1	2.36	8	3	....
1955-56	Boston	NHL	68	4080	181	9	2.66	22	33	13	....	....	....	....	....	....	....	....
1956-57	Boston	NHL	34	2040	81	2	2.38	18	10	6	....	....	....	....	....	....	....	....
1957-58	Detroit	NHL	70	4200	207	3	2.96	29	29	12	4	252	19	0	4.52	0	4	....
1958-59	Detroit	NHL	67	4020	209	5	3.12	23	36	8	....	....	....	....	....	....	....	....
1959-60	Detroit	NHL	58	3480	156	5	2.69	24	20	14	6	405	20	0	2.96	2	4	....
1960-61	Detroit	NHL	37	2080	113	2	3.26	12	16	8	8	465	18	1	2.32	5	2	....
1961-62	Detroit	NHL	43	2580	143	5	3.33	14	21	8	....	....	....	....	....	....	....	....
1962-63	Detroit	NHL	48	2775	119	3	2.57	23	16	7	11	660	36	0	3.27	5	6	....
1963-64	Detroit	NHL	53	3140	138	5	2.64	24	20	7	13	695	31	1	2.66	6	6	....
1964-65	Toronto	NHL	36	2160	92	1	2.56	17	13	6	1	60	3	0	3.00	0	1	....
1965-66	Toronto	NHL	27	1521	80	1	3.16	10	11	4	2	120	6	0	3.00	0	2	....
1966-67	Toronto	NHL	28	1409	66	2	2.81	15	5	4	10	563	25	0	2.66	6	4	....
1967-68	Los Angeles	NHL	33	1936	99	2	3.07	11	14	6	5	280	18	1	3.86	2	3	....
1968-69	Detroit	NHL	11	641	28	0	2.62	3	4	3	....	....	....	....	....	....	....	....
1969-70	NY Rangers	NHL	8	412	20	1	2.91	3	1	2	3	80	6	0	4.50	0	1	....
	NHL Tottals	**21**	**971**	**57205**	**2401**	**103**	**2.52**	**447**	**330**	**173**	**106**	**6306**	**267**	**12**	**2.54**	**54**	**48**	....

FRED SCANLAN

			Regular Season					Playoffs				
Season	Club	League	GP	G	A	PTS	PIM	GP	G	A	PTS	PIM
1897-98	Mtl. Shamrocks	AHA	8	2	0	2	...	...	...	...	...	...
1898-99	Mtl. Shamrocks	CAHL	8	4	0	4	...	1	1	0	1	...
1899-1900	Mtl. Shamrocks	CAHL	7	5	0	5	...	5	2	0	2	...
1900-01	Mtl. Shamrocks	CAHL	8	5	0	5	...	2	0	0	0	...
1901-02	Wpg. Victorias	Sr.	...	...	...	...	...	5	2	0	2	...
1902-03	Wpg. Victorias	Sr.	...	...	...	...	...	4	1	0	1	...

MILT SCHMIDT

Centre. Shoots left. 5'11", 180 lbs., Born, Kitchener, Ont., March 5, 1918

			Regular Season					Playoffs				
Season	Club	League	GP	G	A	PTS	PIM	GP	G	A	PTS	PIM
1933-34	Kitch-Waterloo	OHA Jr.	7	2	4	6	2	4	2	3	5	0
1934-35	Kitch-Waterloo	OHA Jr.	17	20	6	26	14	3	2	2	4	0
1935-36	Kitch-Waterloo	OHA Jr.	5	4	3	7	24	4	4	1	5	11
1936-37	Providence	AHL	23	8	1	9	12	...	...	...	...	...
	Boston	NHL	26	2	8	10	15	3	0	0	0	0
1937-38	Boston	NHL	44	13	14	27	15	3	0	0	0	0
1938-39	Boston	NHL	41	15	17	32	13	12	3	3	6	2
1939-40	Boston	NHL	48	22	30	52	37	6	0	0	0	0
1940-41	Boston	NHL	45	13	25	38	23	11	5	6	11	9
1941-42	Boston	NHL	36	14	21	35	34	...	...	...	...	...
	Ottawa RCAF	Sr.	...	...	...	...	...	6	4	7	11	10
1942-43				Military Service								
1943-44				Military Service								
1944-45				Military Service								
1945-46	Boston	NHL	48	13	18	31	21	10	3	5	8	2
1946-47	Boston	NHL	59	27	35	62	40	5	3	1	4	4
1947-48	Boston	NHL	33	9	17	26	28	5	2	5	7	2
1948-49	Boston	NHL	44	10	22	32	25	4	0	2	2	8
1949-50	Boston	NHL	68	19	22	41	41	...	...	...	...	...
1950-51	Boston	NHL	62	22	39	61	33	6	0	1	1	7
1951-52	Boston	NHL	69	21	29	50	57	7	2	1	3	0
1952-53	Boston	NHL	68	11	23	34	30	10	5	1	6	6
1953-54	Boston	NHL	62	14	18	32	28	4	1	0	1	20
1954-55	Boston	NHL	23	4	8	12	26	...	...	...	...	...
	NHL Totals	**16**	**776**	**229**	**346**	**575**	**466**	**86**	**24**	**25**	**49**	**60**

DAVE "SWEENEY" SCHRINER

Left wing. Shoots left. 5'11", 175 lbs., Born, Saratov, Russia, November 30, 1911

			Regular Season					Playoffs				
Season	Club	League	GP	G	A	PTS	PIM	GP	G	A	PTS	PIM
1930-31	Calagry	AJHL	2	2	0	2	0	...	...	...	...	...
1931-32	Calgary	ASHL	18	19	3	22	32	3	1	2	3	0
1932-33	Calgary	ASHL	15	22	4	26	8	5	3	1	4	6
1933-34	Syracuse	IAHL	44	17	11	28	28	4	0	0	0	0
1934-35	NY Americans	NHL	48	18	22	40	6	...	...	...	...	...
1935-36	NY Americans	NHL	48	19	26	45	8	5	3	1	4	2
1936-37	NY Americans	NHL	48	21	25	46	17	...	...	...	...	...
1937-38	NY Americans	NHL	48	21	17	38	22	6	1	0	1	0
1938-39	NY Americans	NHL	48	13	31	44	20	2	0	0	0	2
1939-40	Toronto	NHL	39	11	15	26	10	10	1	3	4	4
1940-41	Toronto	NHL	48	24	14	38	6	7	2	1	3	4
1941-42	Toronto	NHL	47	20	16	36	21	13	6	3	9	10
1942-43	Toronto	NHL	37	19	17	36	13	4	2	2	4	0
1943-44	Calgary	WCSHL	10	9	9	18	14	3	3	2	5	4
	Vancouver	PCHL	...	...	...	...	...	3	6	3	9	0
1944-45	Toronto	NHL	26	22	15	37	10	13	3	1	4	4
1945-46	Toronto	NHL	47	13	6	19	15	...	...	...	...	...
1947-48	Regina	WCSHL	...	...	...	...	...	...	...	...	...	...
1948-49	Regina	WCSHL	36	26	27	53	30	8	10	2	12	0
	NHL Totals	**11**	**484**	**201**	**204**	**405**	**148**	**59**	**18**	**11**	**29**	**54**

EARL SEIBERT

Defence. Shoots right. 6'2", 210 lbs., Born, Kitchener, Ont., December 7, 1911

			Regular Season					Playoffs				
Season	Club	League	GP	G	A	PTS	PIM	GP	G	A	PTS	PIM
1927-28	Kitchener	OHA Sr.	1	0	0	0	2	...	...	...	...	...
1928-29	Kitchener	OHA Jr.	...	...	...	...	...	...	...	...	...	...
1929-30	Springfield	CAHL	40	4	1	5	84	...	...	...	...	...
1930-31	Springfield	CAHL	38	16	11	27	96	4	2	0	2	16
1931-32	NY Rangers	NHL	44	4	6	10	88	7	1	2	3	12
1932-33	NY Rangers	NHL	45	2	3	5	92	8	1	0	1	14
1933-34	NY Rangers	NHL	48	13	10	23	66	2	0	0	0	4
1934-35	NY Rangers	NHL	48	6	19	25	86	4	0	0	0	6
1935-36	NY Rangers	NHL	17	2	3	5	6	...	...	...	...	...
	Chicago	NHL	24	3	6	9	21	2	2	0	2	0
1936-37	Chicago	NHL	43	9	6	15	46	...	...	...	...	...
1937-38	Chicago	NHL	48	8	13	21	38	10	5	2	7	12
1938-39	Chicago	NHL	48	4	11	15	37	...	...	...	...	...
1939-40	Chicago	NHL	37	3	7	10	35	2	0	1	1	8
1940-41	Chicago	NHL	44	3	17	20	52	5	0	0	0	12
1941-42	Chicago	NHL	45	7	14	21	52	3	0	0	0	0
1942-43	Chicago	NHL	44	5	27	32	38	...	...	...	...	...
1943-44	Chicago	NHL	50	8	23	33	40	9	0	2	2	2
1944-45	Chicago	NHL	22	7	8	15	13	...	...	...	...	...
	Detroit	NHL	25	5	9	14	10	14	2	1	3	4
1945-46	Detroit	NHL	18	0	3	3	18	...	...	...	...	...
	Indianapolis	AHL	24	2	9	11	19	5	0	0	0	0
	NHL Totals	**15**	**645**	**89**	**184**	**273**	**683**	**65**	**9**	**8**	**17**	**76**

OLIVER SEIBERT

Forward. 180 lbs., Born, Berlin, Ont., March 18, 1881

			Regular Season					Playoffs				
Season	Club	League	GP	G	A	PTS	PIM	GP	G	A	PTS	PIM
1900-01	Berlin	WOHA		Not Available		...	...	...	...	...	...	...
1901-02	Berlin	WOHA		Not Available		...	...	...	...	...	...	...
1902-03	Berlin	WOHA		Not Available		...	...	...	...	...	...	...
1903-04	Berlin	WOHA		Not Available		...	...	...	...	...	...	...
1904-05	Canadian Soo	IHL	1	0	0	0	0	...	...	...	...	...
1905-06	Berlin	WOHA		Not Available		...	...	...	...	...	...	...
1906-07	Berlin	WOHA		Not Available		...	...	...	...	...	...	...

EDDIE SHORE

Defence. Shoots right. 5'11", 185 lbs., Born, Ft. Qu'Appelle, Sask., November 25, 1902

			Regular Season					Playoffs				
Season	Club	League	GP	G	A	PTS	PIM	GP	G	A	PTS	PIM
1923-24	Melville	SSHL	2	6	2	8	...	...	...	...	...	...
1924-25	Regina	WCHL	24	6	0	6	75	...	...	...	...	...
1925-26	Edmonton	WHL	30	12	2	14	86	2	0	0	0	6
1926-27	Boston	NHL	40	12	6	18	130	8	1	1	2	40
1927-28	Boston	NHL	43	11	6	17	165	2	0	0	0	8
1928-29	Boston	NHL	39	12	7	19	96	5	1	1	2	28
1929-30	Boston	NHL	42	12	19	31	105	6	1	0	1	26
1930-31	Boston	NHL	44	15	16	31	105	5	2	1	3	24
1931-32	Boston	NHL	45	9	13	22	80	...	...	...	...	...
1932-33	Boston	NHL	48	8	27	35	102	5	0	1	1	14
1933-34	Boston	NHL	30	2	10	12	57	...	...	...	...	...
1934-35	Boston	NHL	48	7	26	33	32	4	0	1	1	2
1935-36	Boston	NHL	45	3	16	19	61	2	1	1	2	12
1936-37	Boston	NHL	20	3	1	4	12	...	...	...	...	...
1937-38	Boston	NHL	48	3	14	17	42	3	0	1	1	6
1938-39	Boston	NHL	44	4	14	18	37	12	0	4	4	19
1939-40	Boston	NHL	4	2	1	3	4	...	...	...	...	...
	NY Americans	NHL	10	2	3	5	9	3	0	2	2	2
	Springfield	AHL	15	1	14	15	18	2	0	1	1	0
1940-41	Springfield	AHL	56	4	13	17	66	3	0	0	0	2
1941-42	Springfield	AHL	35	5	12	17	61	5	0	3	3	6
1943-44	Buffalo	AHL	1	0	0	0	0	...	...	...	...	...
	NHL Totals	**14**	**553**	**105**	**179**	**284**	**1047**	**55**	**6**	**13**	**19**	**179**

STEVE SHUTT

Left wing. Shoots left. 5'11", 185 lbs., Born, Toronto, Ont., July 1, 1952

			Regular Season					Playoffs				
Season	Club	League	GP	G	A	PTS	PIM	GP	G	A	PTS	PIM
1969-70	Tor. Marlboros	OHA Jr.	49	11	14	25	93	...	...	...	...	...
1970-71	Tor. Marlboros	OHA Jr.	62	70	53	123	85	...	...	...	...	...
1971-72	Tor. Marlboros	OHA Jr.	58	63	49	112	60	...	...	...	...	...
1972-73	Nova Scotia	AHL	6	4	1	5	2	...	...	...	...	...
	Montreal	NHL	50	8	8	16	24	1	0	0	0	0
1973-74	Montreal	NHL	70	15	20	35	17	6	5	3	8	9
1974-75	Montreal	NHL	77	30	35	65	40	9	1	6	7	4
1975-76	Montreal	NHL	80	45	34	79	47	13	7	8	15	2
1976-77	Montreal	NHL	80	60	45	105	28	14	8	10	18	2
1977-78	Montreal	NHL	80	49	37	86	24	15	9	8	17	20
1978-79	Montreal	NHL	72	37	40	77	31	11	4	7	11	6
1979-80	Montreal	NHL	77	47	42	89	34	10	6	3	9	6
1980-81	Montreal	NHL	77	35	38	73	51	3	2	1	3	4
1981-82	Montreal	NHL	57	31	24	55	40	...	...	...	...	...
1982-83	Montreal	NHL	78	35	22	57	26	3	1	0	1	0
1983-84	Montreal	NHL	63	14	23	37	29	11	7	2	9	8
1984-85	Montreal	NHL	10	2	0	2	9	...	...	...	...	...
	Los Angeles	NHL	59	16	25	41	10	3	0	0	0	4
	NHL Totals	**13**	**930**	**424**	**393**	**817**	**410**	**99**	**50**	**48**	**98**	**65**

ALBERT "BABE" SIEBERT

Left wing / defence. Shoots left. 5'11", 188 lbs., Born, Plattsville, Ont., January 14, 1904

			Regular Season					Playoffs				
Season	Club	League	GP	G	A	PTS	PIM	GP	G	A	PTS	PIM
1923-24	Kitchener	OHA Jr.	10	9	4	13	...	...	...	...	...	...
1924-25	Niagara Falls	OHA Sr.	20	9	2	11	26	2	2	0	2	3
1925-26	Mtl Maroons	NHL	35	16	8	24	108	8	2	2	4	6
1926-27	Mtl Maroons	NHL	42	5	3	8	116	2	1	0	1	2
1927-28	Mtl Maroons	NHL	39	8	9	17	109	9	2	0	2	26
1928-29	Mtl Maroons	NHL	39	3	5	8	52	...	...	...	...	...
1929-30	Mtl Maroons	NHL	41	14	19	33	94	2	0	0	0	0
1930-31	Mtl Maroons	NHL	42	16	12	28	76	2	0	0	0	6
1931-32	Mtl Maroons	NHL	48	21	18	39	64	4	0	1	1	4
1932-33	NY Rangers	NHL	43	9	10	19	38	8	1	0	1	12
1933-34	NY Rangers	NHL	13	0	1	1	18	...	...	...	...	...
	Boston	NHL	32	5	6	11	31	...	...	...	...	...
1934-35	Boston	NHL	48	6	18	24	80	4	0	0	0	6
1935-36	Boston	NHL	45	12	9	21	66	2	0	1	1	0
1936-37	Montreal	NHL	44	8	20	28	38	5	1	2	3	2
1937-38	Montreal	NHL	37	8	11	19	56	3	1	1	2	0
1938-39	Montreal	NHL	44	9	7	16	26	3	0	0	0	0
	NHL Totals	**14**	**596**	**140**	**156**	**296**	**982**	**53**	**8**	**7**	**15**	**64**

HAROLD "BULLET JOE" SIMPSON

Defence. Shoots right. 5'10", 175 lbs., Born, Selkirk, Man., August 13, 1896

			Regular Season					Playoffs				
Season	Club	League	GP	G	A	PTS	PIM	GP	G	A	PTS	PIM
1914-15	Winnipeg Vics	Sr.	8	8	2	10	16	...	...	...	...	...
1915-16	61st Battalion	MSHL	8	9	2	11	24	2	1	0	1	4
1916-18				Military Service								
1918-19	Selkirk	MSHL	4	0	0	0	0	...	...	...	...	...
1919-20	Selkirk	MSHL	10	19	4	23	6	...	...	...	...	...
1920-21	Edmonton	Big 4	15	2	6	8	21	...	...	...	...	...
1921-22	Edmonton	WCHL	25	21	12	33	15	2	1	...	1	...
1922-23	Edmonton	WCHL	30	15	14	29	6	4	0	1	1	0
1923-24	Edmonton	WCHL	30	10	4	14	6	...	...	...	...	...
1924-25	Edmonton	WCHL	28	11	12	23	16	...	...	...	...	...
1925-26	NY Americans	NHL	32	2	2	4	22	...	...	...	...	...
1926-27	NY Americans	NHL	43	4	2	6	39	...	...	...	...	...
1927-28	NY Americans	NHL	24	2	0	2	32	...	...	...	...	...
1928-29	NY Americans	NHL	43	3	2	5	29	2	0	0	0	0
1929-30	NY Americans	NHL	44	8	13	21	41	...	...	...	...	...
1930-31	NY Americans	NHL	42	2	0	2	13	...	...	...	...	...
1937-38	Minneapolis	AHA	1	0	0	0	0	...	...	...	...	...
	NHL Totals	**6**	**228**	**21**	**19**	**40**	**156**	**2**	**0**	**0**	**0**	**0**

DARRYL SITTLER

Centre. Shoots left. 6', 190 lbs., Born, Kitchener, Ont., September 8, 1950

				Regular Season					Playoffs			
Season	Club	League	GP	G	A	PTS	PIM	GP	G	A	PTS	PIM
1967-68	London	OHA Jr.	54	22	41	63	84	5	5	2	7	6
1968-69	London	OHA Jr.	53	34	65	99	90	6	2	5	7	11
1969-70	London	OHA Jr.	54	42	48	90	126	...	...	...	...	...
1970-71	Toronto	NHL	49	10	8	18	37	6	2	1	3	31
1971-72	Toronto	NHL	74	15	17	32	44	3	0	0	0	2
1972-73	Toronto	NHL	78	29	48	77	69	...	...	...	...	...
1973-74	Toronto	NHL	78	38	46	84	55	4	2	1	3	6
1974-75	Toronto	NHL	72	36	44	80	47	7	2	1	3	15
1975-76	Toronto	NHL	79	41	59	100	90	10	5	7	12	19
1976-77	Toronto	NHL	73	38	52	90	89	9	5	16	21	4
1977-78	Toronto	NHL	80	45	72	117	100	13	8	11	11	12
1978-79	Toronto	NHL	70	36	51	87	69	6	5	4	9	17
1979-80	Toronto	NHL	73	40	57	97	62	3	1	2	3	10
1980-81	Toronto	NHL	80	43	53	96	77	3	0	0	0	4
1981-82	Toronto	NHL	38	18	20	38	24	...	...	...	...	...
	Philadelphia	NHL	35	14	18	32	50	4	3	1	4	6
1982-83	Philadelphia	NHL	80	43	40	83	60	3	1	0	1	4
1983-84	Philadelphia	NHL	76	27	36	63	38	3	0	2	2	7
1984-85	Detroit	NHL	61	11	16	27	37	2	0	2	2	0
	NHL Totals	**15**	**1096**	**484**	**637**	**1121**	**948**	**76**	**29**	**45**	**74**	**137**

ALF SMITH

Right wing. Shoots right. 5'7", 165 lbs., Born, Ottawa, Ont., June 3, 1873

				Regular Season					Playoffs			
Season	Club	League	GP	G	A	PTS	PIM	GP	G	A	PTS	PIM
1894-95	Ottawa	AHA	8	5	0	5	...	...	...	...	...	...
1895-96	Ottawa	AHA	8	7	0	7	...	...	...	...	...	...
1896-97	Ottawa	AHA	8	12	0	12	...	...	...	...	...	...
1897-1903			Did Not Play									
1903-04	Ottawa	CAHL	4	8	0	8	...	7	13	0	13	...
1904-06	Ottawo	FAHL	8	13	0	13	5	...	11	0	11	...
1905-07	Ottawa	ECAHA	10	13	0	13	6	...	10	0	10	...
1906-08	Ottawa	ECAHA	9	18	0	18	...	...	...	...	...	...
	Kenora	MHL Sr.	1	2	0	2	...	2	1	0	1	...
1907-08	Ottawa	ECAHA	9	12	0	12	...	...	...	...	...	...
1908-09	Pittsburgh	WPHL	Not Available			...	...	...	...	...	...	...

BILLY SMITH

Goaltender. Catches left. 5'10", 185 lbs., Born, Perth, Ont., December 12, 1950

					Regular Season								Playoffs				
Season	Club	League	GP	MIN	GA	SO	GAA	W	L	T	GP	MIN	GA	SO	GAA	W	L	T
1970-71	Springfield	AHL	49	2728	160	2	3.51	....	....	....	12	682	29	1	2.56	....	....	....
1971-72	Los Angeles	NHL	5	300	23	0	4.60	1	3	1	....	....	....	....	....	....	....	....
	Springfield	AHL	28	1649	77	4	2.80	....	....	....	4	192	13	0	4.06	....	....	....
1972-73	NY Islanders	NHL	37	2122	147	0	4.16	7	24	3	....	....	....	....	....	....	....	....
1973-74	NY Islanders	NHL	46	2615	134	0	3.07	9	23	12	....	....	....	....	....	....	....	....
1974-75	NY Islanders	NHL	58	3368	156	3	2.78	21	18	17	6	333	23	0	4.14	1	4	....
1975-76	NY Islanders	NHL	39	2254	98	3	2.61	19	10	9	8	437	21	0	2.88	4	3	....
1976-77	NY Islanders	NHL	36	2089	87	2	2.50	21	8	6	10	580	27	0	2.79	7	3	....
1977-78	NY Islanders	NHL	38	2154	95	2	2.65	20	8	8	1	47	1	0	1.28	0	0	....
1978-79	NY Islanders	NHL	40	2261	108	1	2.87	25	8	4	5	315	10	1	1.90	4	1	....
1979-80	NY Islanders	NHL	38	2114	104	2	2.95	15	14	7	20	1198	56	1	2.80	15	4	....
1980-81	NY Islanders	NHL	41	2363	129	2	3.28	22	10	8	17	994	42	0	2.54	14	3	....
1981-82	NY Islanders	NHL	46	2685	133	0	2.97	32	9	4	18	1120	47	1	2.52	15	3	....
1982-83	NY Islanders	NHL	41	2340	112	1	2.87	18	14	7	17	962	43	2	2.68	13	3	....
1983-84	NY Islanders	NHL	42	2279	130	2	3.42	23	13	2	21	1190	54	0	2.72	12	8	....
1984-85	NY Islanders	NHL	37	2090	133	0	3.82	18	14	3	6	342	19	0	3.33	3	3	....
1985-86	NY Islanders	NHL	41	2308	143	1	3.72	20	14	4	1	60	4	0	4.00	0	1	....
1986-87	NY Islanders	NHL	40	2252	132	1	3.52	14	18	5	2	67	1	0	0.90	0	0	....
1987-88	NY Islanders	NHL	38	2107	113	2	3.22	17	14	5	....	....	....	....	....	....	....	....
1988-89	NY Islanders	NHL	17	730	54	0	4.44	3	11	0	....	....	....	....	....	....	....	....
	NHL Totals	**18**	**680**	**38431**	**2031**	**22**	**3.17**	**305**	**233**	**105**	**132**	**7645**	**348**	**5**	**2.73**	**88**	**36**	**....**

CLINT SMITH

Centre. Shoots left. 5'8", 165 lbs., Born, Assiniboia, Sask., December 12, 1913

				Regular Season					Playoffs			
Season	Club	League	GP	G	A	PTS	PIM	GP	G	A	PTS	PIM
1930-31	Saskatoon	SJHL	1	0	0	0	0	...	...	...	...	...
1931-32	Saskatoon	SJHL	4	5	1	6	0	...	...	...	...	...
	Saskatoon	SSHL	18	19	3	22	0	4	6	0	6	4
1932-33	Springfield	CAHL	12	0	0	0	0	...	...	...	...	...
	Saskatoon	SSHL	27	7	6	13	8	...	...	...	...	...
1933-34	Vancouver	NWHL	34	25	14	39	8	7	5	4	9	2
1934-35	Vancouver	NWHL	32	22	22	44	2	8	3	5	8	4
1935-36	Vancouver	NWHL	40	21	32	53	10	7	2	4	6	2
1936-37	NY Rangers	NHL	2	1	0	1	0	...	...	...	...	...
	Philadelphia	AHL	47	25	29	54	15	6	4	3	7	0
1937-38	NY Rangers	NHL	48	14	23	37	0	3	2	0	2	0
1938-39	NY Rangers	NHL	48	21	20	41	2	7	1	2	3	0
1939-40	NY Rangers	NHL	41	8	16	24	2	12	1	3	4	2
1940-41	NY Rangers	NHL	48	14	11	25	0	3	0	0	0	0
1941-42	NY Rangers	NHL	47	10	24	34	4	6	0	0	0	0
1942-43	NY Rangers	NHL	47	12	21	33	4	...	...	...	...	...
1943-44	Chicago	NHL	50	23	49	72	4	9	4	8	12	0
1944-45	Chicago	NHL	50	23	31	54	0	...	...	...	...	...
1945-46	Chicago	NHL	50	26	24	50	2	4	2	1	3	0
1946-47	Chicago	NHL	52	9	17	26	6	...	...	...	...	...
1947-48	Tulsa	USHL	64	38	33	71	10	2	0	1	1	0
1948-49	St. Paul	USHL	2	2	0	2	2	...	...	...	...	...
1949-50	St. Paul	USHL	21	7	15	22	2	2	0	0	0	2
1951-52	Cincinnati	AHL	2	0	0	0	2	...	...	...	...	...
	NHL Totals	**11**	**483**	**161**	**236**	**397**	**24**	**42**	**10**	**14**	**24**	**2**

REGINALD "HOOLEY" SMITH

Centre. Shoots right. 5'10", 165 lbs., Born, Toronto, Ont., January 7, 1903

				Regular Season					Playoffs			
Season	Club	League	GP	G	A	PTS	PIM	GP	G	A	PTS	PIM
1921-22	Toronto	OHA Sr.	5	1	0	1	...	...	...	...	...	...
1922-23	Toronto	OHA Sr.	8	3	0	3	...	2	1	0	1	...
1923-24	Toronto	OHA Sr.	Not Available			...	...	...	...	...	...	...
1924-25	Ottawa	NHL	30	10	3	13	81	...	...	...	...	...
1925-26	Ottawa	NHL	28	16	9	25	53	2	0	0	0	14
1926-27	Ottawa	NHL	43	9	6	15	125	6	1	1	2	19
1927-28	Mtl Maroons	NHL	34	14	5	19	72	9	2	1	3	23
1928-29	Mtl Maroons	NHL	41	10	9	19	120	...	...	...	...	...
1929-30	Mtl Maroons	NHL	42	21	9	30	83	4	1	1	2	14
1930-31	Mtl Maroons	NHL	39	12	14	26	68	...	...	...	...	...
1931-32	Mtl Maroons	NHL	43	11	33	44	49	4	2	1	3	2
1932-33	Mtl Maroons	NHL	48	20	21	41	66	2	2	0	2	2
1933-34	Mtl Maroons	NHL	47	18	19	37	58	4	0	1	1	6
1934-35	Mtl Maroons	NHL	46	5	22	27	41	6	0	0	0	14
1935-36	Mtl Maroons	NHL	47	19	19	38	75	3	0	0	0	2
1936-37	Boston	NHL	47	8	10	18	36	3	0	0	0	0
1937-38	NY Americans	NHL	47	10	10	20	23	6	0	3	3	0
1938-39	NY Americans	NHL	48	8	11	19	18	2	0	0	0	14
1939-40	NY Americans	NHL	47	7	8	15	31	3	3	1	4	2
1940-41	NY Americans	NHL	41	2	7	9	4	...	...	...	...	...
	NHL Totals	**17**	**715**	**200**	**215**	**415**	**1013**	**54**	**11**	**8**	**19**	**109**

TOMMY SMITH

Centre. Shoots left. 5'6" 150 lbs., Born, Ottawa, Ont. Born , September 27, 1886

				Regular Season					Playoffs			
Season	Club	League	GP	G	A	PTS	PIM	GP	G	A	PTS	PIM
1905-06	Ott. Victorias	FAHL	8	12	0	12	...	...	...	...	...	...
	Ottawa	ECAHA	3	6	0	6	...	...	...	...	...	...
1906-07	Pittsburgh	IHL	23	31	13	44	47	...	...	...	...	...
1907-08	Pittsburgh	WPHL	16	33	0	33	...	1	2	0	2	...
1908-09	Pittsburgh	WPHL	6	13	0	13	...	...	...	...	...	...
	Brantford	OPHL	13	33	0	33	...	...	...	...	...	...
1909-10	Brantford	OPHL	1	1	0	1	...	...	...	...	...	...
	Cobalt	NHA	10	24	0	24	...	...	...	...	...	...
1910-11	Galt	OPHL	18	22	0	22	...	1	1	0	1	0
1911-12	Moncton	MPHL	18	53	0	53	48	2	2	0	2	3
1912-13	Quebec	NHA	19	39	0	39	30	2	4	0	4	0
1913-14	Quebec	NHA	20	39	6	45	35	...	...	...	...	...
1914-15	Tor. Ontarios	NHA	10	17	2	19	14	...	...	...	...	...
	Quebec	NHA	9	23	2	25	29	...	...	...	...	...
1915-16	Quebec	NHA	22	16	3	19	30	...	...	...	...	...
1916-17	Montreal	NHA	15	9	3	12	32	6	4	0	4	...
1918-19	Glace Bay	CBHL	Not Available			...	...	...	...	...	...	...
1919-20	Quebec	NHL	10	0	0	0	9	...	...	...	...	...
	NHL Totals	**1**	**10**	**0**	**0**	**0**	**9**	**....**	**....**	**....**	**....**	**....**

ALLAN STANLEY

Defence. Shoots left. Born, Timmins, Ont., March 1, 1926

				Regular Season					Playoffs			
Season	Club	League	GP	G	A	PTS	PIM	GP	G	A	PTS	PIM
1943-44	Boston	EHL	39	9	32	41	...	...	...	...	...	...
1944-45	Boston	EHL	Not Available			...	...	...	...	...	...	...
1945-46	Boston	EHL	30	8	15	23	35	...	...	...	...	...
1946-47	Providence	AHL	54	8	13	21	32	...	...	...	...	...
1947-48	Boston	QSHL	1	0	0	0	0	...	...	...	...	...
	Providence	AHL	68	9	32	41	81	5	0	0	0	4
1948-49	Providence	AHL	23	7	16	23	24	...	...	...	...	...
	NY Rangers	NHL	40	2	8	10	22	...	...	...	...	...
1949-50	NY Rangers	NHL	55	4	4	8	58	12	2	5	7	10
1950-51	NY Rangers	NHL	70	7	14	21	75	...	...	...	...	...
1951-52	NY Rangers	NHL	50	5	14	19	52	...	...	...	...	...
1952-53	NY Rangers	NHL	70	5	12	17	52	...	...	...	...	...
1953-54	Vancouver	WHL	47	6	30	36	43	13	2	5	7	10
	NY Rangers	NHL	10	0	2	2	11	...	...	...	...	...
1954-55	NY Rangers	NHL	12	0	2	2	2	...	...	...	...	...
	Chicago	NHL	52	10	14	24	22	...	...	...	...	...
1955-56	Chicago	NHL	59	4	14	18	70	...	...	...	...	...
1956-57	Boston	NHL	60	6	25	31	45	...	...	...	...	...
1957-58	Boston	NHL	69	6	25	31	37	12	1	3	4	6
1958-59	Toronto	NHL	70	1	22	23	47	12	0	3	3	2
1959-60	Toronto	NHL	64	10	23	33	22	10	2	3	5	2
1960-61	Toronto	NHL	68	9	25	34	42	5	0	3	3	0
1961-62	Toronto	NHL	60	9	26	35	24	12	0	3	3	6
1962-63	Toronto	NHL	61	4	15	19	22	10	1	6	7	8
1963-64	Toronto	NHL	70	6	21	27	60	14	1	6	7	20
1964-65	Toronto	NHL	64	2	15	17	30	6	0	1	1	12
1965-66	Toronto	NHL	59	4	14	18	35	1	0	0	0	0
1966-67	Toronto	NHL	53	1	12	13	20	12	0	2	2	10
1967-68	Toronto	NHL	64	1	13	14	16	...	...	...	...	...
1968-69	Philadelphia	NHL	64	4	13	17	28	3	0	1	1	4
	NHL Totals	**21**	**1244**	**100**	**333**	**433**	**792**	**109**	**7**	**36**	**43**	**80**

BARNEY STANLEY

Right wing. Shoots left. 6', 175 lbs., Born, Paisley, Ont., June 1, 1893

			Regular Season					Playoffs				
Season	Club	League	GP	G	A	PTS	PIM	GP	G	A	PTS	PIM
1914-15	Vancouver	PCHA	5	7	1	8	0	3	6	0	6	0
1915-16	Vancouver	PCHA	14	6	6	12	9	...	...	...	...	...
1916-17	Vancouver	PCHA	23	28	18	46	9	...	...	...	...	...
1917-18	Vancouver	PCHA	18	11	6	17	9	6	3	0	3	9
1918-19	Vancouver	PCHA	20	10	6	16	19	2	0	0	0	0
1919-20	Edmonton	Big 4	12	10	12	22	20	2	0	1	1	5
1920-21	Calagry	Big 4	15	11	10	21	5	...	...	...	...	...
1921-22	Calagry	WCHL	24	26	5	31	17	2	0	0	0	2
1922-23	Regina	WCHL	29	14	7	21	10	2	1	0	1	2
1923-24	Regina	WCHL	30	15	11	26	27	2	1	0	1	2
1924-25	Edmonton	WCHL	25	12	5	17	36	...	...	...	...	...
1925-26	Edmonton	WHL	29	14	8	22	47	2	1	0	1	0
1926-27	Winnipeg	AHA	35	8	8	16	78	3	0	0	0	2
1927-28	Chicago	NHL	2	0	0	0	0	...	...	...	...	...
1928-29	Minneapolis	AHA	40	8	5	13	34	4	1	0	1	2
	NHL Totals	**2**	**2**	**0**	**0**	**0**	**0**	....	....	....	....	....

JOHN "BLACK JACK" STEWART

Defence. Shoots left. 5'11", 185 lbs., Born, Pilot Mound, Man., May 6, 1917

			Regular Season					Playoffs				
Season	Club	League	GP	G	A	PTS	PIM	GP	G	A	PTS	PIM
1935-36	Portage	MHL Jr.	16	0	0	0	6	6	0	1	1	4
1936-37	Portage	MHL Jr.	16	4	1	5	20	4	1	1	2	2
1937-38	Pittsburgh	AHL	48	0	1	1	16	2	0	0	0	0
1938-39	Pittsburgh	AHL	21	0	0	0	20	...	...	...	...	...
	Detroit	NHL	33	0	1	1	18	...	...	...	...	...
1939-40	Detroit	NHL	48	1	0	1	40	5	0	0	0	4
1940-41	Detroit	NHL	47	2	6	8	56	9	1	2	3	8
1941-42	Detroit	NHL	44	4	7	11	93	12	0	1	1	12
1942-43	Detroit	NHL	44	2	9	11	68	10	1	2	3	35
1943-44	Montreal	QSHL	7	3	5	8	18	...	...	...	...	...
1944-45	Winipeg	Sr.	2	0	1	1	2	...	...	...	...	...
1945-46	Detroit	NHL	47	4	11	15	73	5	0	0	0	14
1946-47	Detroit	NHL	55	5	9	14	83	5	0	1	1	12
1947-48	Detroit	NHL	60	5	14	19	91	9	1	3	4	6
1948-49	Detroit	NHL	60	4	11	15	96	11	1	1	2	32
1949-50	Detroit	NHL	66	3	11	14	86	14	1	4	5	20
1950-51	Chicago	NHL	26	0	2	2	49	...	...	...	...	...
1951-52	Chicago	NHL	37	1	3	4	12	...	...	...	...	...
1952-53	Chatham	OHA Sr.	45	2	27	29	134	...	...	...	...	...
1953-54	Chatham	OHA Sr.	21	0	8	8	35	6	0	0	0	8
	NHL Totals	**12**	**565**	**31**	**84**	**115**	**765**	**80**	**5**	**14**	**19**	**143**

NELS "OLD POISON" STEWART

Centre, Shoots left. 6'1", 208 lbs., Born, Montreal, Que., December 20, 1900

			Regular Season					Playoffs				
Season	Club	League	GP	G	A	PTS	PIM	GP	G	A	PTS	PIM
1919-20	Tor. Parkdale	OHA Sr.	8	15	0	15	...	1	1	0	1	...
1920-21	Cleveland	AHA	Not Available			...	...	...	...	...	...	...
1921-22	Cleveland	AHA	Not Available ...			...	...	...	...	...	...	...
1922-23	Cleveland	AHA	20	22	0	22	...	...	...	...	...	...
1923-24	Cleveland	AHA	20	23	0	23	...	8	5	2	7	...
1924-25	Cleveland	AHA	40	21	0	21	...	8	6	3	9	24
1925-26	Mtl. Maroons	NHL	36	34	8	42	119	...	...	...	...	...
1926-27	Mtl. Maroons	NHL	43	17	4	21	133	2	0	0	0	4
1927-28	Mtl. Maroons	NHL	41	27	7	34	104	9	2	2	4	11
1928-29	Mtl. Maroons	NHL	44	21	8	29	74	...	...	...	...	...
1929-30	Mtl. Maroons	NHL	44	39	16	55	81	4	1	1	2	2
1930-31	Mtl. Maroons	NHL	42	25	14	39	75	2	1	0	1	6
1931-32	Mtl. Maroons	NHL	38	22	11	33	61	4	0	1	1	2
1932-33	Boston	NHL	47	18	18	36	62	5	2	0	2	4
1933-34	Boston	NHL	48	22	17	39	68	...	...	...	...	...
1934-35	Boston	NHL	47	21	18	39	45	4	0	1	1	0
1935-36	NY Americans	NHL	48	14	15	29	16	5	1	2	3	4
1936-37	NY Americans	NHL	32	20	10	30	29	...	...	...	...	...
	Boston	NHL	11	3	2	5	6	...	...	...	...	...
1937-38	NY Americans	NHL	48	19	17	36	29	6	2	3	5	2
1938-39	NY Americans	NHL	46	16	19	35	33	2	0	0	0	0
1939-40	NY Americans	NHL	35	6	7	13	6	3	0	0	0	0
	NHL Totals	**15**	**650**	**324**	**191**	**515**	**953**	**54**	**15**	**13**	**28**	**61**

BRUCE STUART

Centre. Shoots left. 6'2", 180 lbs., Born, Ottawa, Ont., 1882

			Regular Season					Playoffs				
Season	Club	League	GP	G	A	PTS	PIM	GP	G	A	PTS	PIM
1898-99	Ottawa	CAHL	1	1	0	1	...	...	...	...	...	...
1899-1900	Ottawa	CAHL	5	11	0	11	...	...	...	...	...	...
1900-01	Quebec	CAHL	6	5	0	5	...	...	...	...	...	...
1901-02	Ottawa	CAHL	8	9	0	9	...	...	...	...	...	...
1902-03	Pittsburgh	WPHL	Not Available			...	...	...	...	...	...	...
1903-04	Portage Lakes	.....	14	44	0	44	6	9	28	0	28	13
1904-05	Portage Lakes	IHL	22	33	0	33	59	...	...	...	...	...
1905-06	Portage Lakes	IHL	20	15	0	15	22	...	...	...	...	...
1906-07	Portage Lakes	IHL	23	20	9	29	81	...	...	...	...	...
1907-08	Mtl. Wanderers	ECAHA	3	3	0	3	...	3	7	0	7	...
1908-09	Ottawa	ECHA	11	22	0	22	30	...	...	...	...	...
1909-10	Ottawa	CHA	2	4	0	4	0	...	...	...	...	...
	Ottawa	NHA	7	14	0	14	17	4	10	0	10	6
1910-11	Ottawa	NHA	3	0	0	0	0	...	...	...	...	...

HOD STUART

Cover point. 6', 190 lbs., Born, Ottawa, Ont., 1879

			Regular Season					Playoffs				
Season	Club	League	GP	G	A	PTS	PIM	GP	G	A	PTS	PIM
1898-99	Ottawa	CAHL	3	1	0	1	...	...	...	...	...	...
1899-1900	Ottawa	CAHL	7	5	0	5	...	...	...	...	...	...
1900-01	Quebec	CAHL	7	2	0	2	...	...	...	...	...	...
1901-02	Quebec	CAHL	8	5	0	5		...	...	...	...	...
1902-03	Pittsburgh	WPHL	4	0	0	0	...	...	...	...	...	...
1903-04	Portage Lakes	.....	14	13	0	13	23	9	4	0	4	12
1904-05	Calumet	IHL	22	18	0	18	19	...	...	...	...	...
1905-06	Pittsburgh	IHL	20	11	0	11	50	...	...	...	...	...
	Calumet	IHL	1	0	0	0	0	...	...	...	...	...
1906-07	Pittsburgh	IHL	4	1	3	4	19	...	...	...	...	...
	Mtl. Wanderers	ECAHA	8	3	0	3	...	4	0	0	0	0

FRED "CYCLONE" TAYLOR

Rover. Shoots left. 5'8", 165 lbs., Born, Tara, Ont., June 24, 1883

			Regular Season					Playoffs				
Season	Club	League	GP	G	A	PTS	PIM	GP	G	A	PTS	PIM
1905-06	Portage	MHL Sr.	4	4	...	4	...	...	...	...	...	...
	Portage Lakes	IHL	6	11	...	11	4	...	...	...	...	...
1906-07	Portage Lakes	IHL	23	18	...	25	31	...	...	...	...	...
1907-08	Ottawa	ECAHA	10	9	...	9	...	...	...	...	...	...
1908-09	Pittsburgh	WPHL	3	0	...	0	0	...	...	...	...	...
	Ottawa	ECHA	11	9	...	9	28	...	...	...	...	...
1909-10	Renfrew	NHA	13	10	...	10	19	...	...	...	...	...
1910-11	Renfrew	NHA	16	12	...	12	21	...	...	...	...	...
1911-12			Did Not Play									
1912-13	Vancouver	PCHA	14	10	8	18	5	...	...	...	...	...
1913-14	Vancouver	PCHA	16	24	15	39	18	...	...	...	...	...
1914-15	Vancouver	PCHA	16	23	22	45	9	3	7	3	10	3
1915-16	Vancouver	PCHA	18	22	13	35	9	...	...	...	...	...
1916-17	Vancouver	PCHA	11	14	15	29	12	...	...	...	...	...
1917-18	Vancouver	PCHA	18	32	11	43	0	7	9	2	11	15
1918-19	Vancouver	PCHA	20	23	13	36	17	2	1	0	1	0
1919-20	Vancouver	PCHA	10	6	6	12	0	1	0	0	0	0
1920-21	Vancouver	PCHA	6	5	1	6	0	3	0	1	1	0
1921-22			Did Not Play									
1922-23	Vancouver	PCHA	1	0	0	0	0	...	...	...	...	...

CECIL "TINY" THOMPSON

Goaltender. Shoots left. 5'10", 180 lbs., Born, Sandon, B.C., May 31, 1903

			Regular Season							Playoffs							
Season	Club	League	GP	MIN	GA	SO	GAA	W	L	T	GP	MIN	GA	SO	GAA	W	L	T
1921-22	Calgary	Jr.	Not Available				....	....	....	....	....	....	....	....	....	....	....	....
1922-23	Pacific Grains	Sr.	Not Available				....	....	....	....	....	....	....	....	....	....	....	....
1923-24	Bellevue	Sr.	Not Available				....	....	....	....	....	....	....	....	....	....	....	....
1924-25	Duluth	AHA Sr.	40	1920	59	11	1.38	17	20	....	....	....	....	....	....	....	....	....
1925-26	Minneapolis	AHA Sr.	36	2160	59	10	1.64	....	....	....	3	180	1	2	0.33	....	....	....
1926-27	Minneapolis	AHA	36	2253	51	9	1.42	17	11	10	6	361	8	1	1.33	3	3	0
1927-28	Minneapolis	AHA	40	2475	51	12	1.23	18	7	5	8	520	3	5	0.38	4	0	4
1928-29	Boston	NHL	44	2710	52	12	1.15	26	13	5	5	300	3	3	0.60	5	0	0
1929-30	Boston	NHL	44	2680	98	3	2.19	38	5	1	6	432	12	0	1.67	3	3	....
1930-31	Boston	NHL	44	2730	90	3	1.98	28	10	6	5	348	13	0	2.24	2	3	....
1931-32	Boston	NHL	43	2698	104	9	2.31	13	19	11	....	....	....	....	....	....	....	....
1932-33	Boston	NHL	48	3000	88	11	1.76	25	15	8	5	429	9	0	1.26	2	3	....
1933-34	Boston	NHL	48	2980	130	5	2.67	18	25	5	....	....	....	....	....	....	....	....
1934-35	Boston	NHL	48	2970	112	8	2.26	26	16	6	4	273	7	1	1.54	1	3	....
1935-36	Boston	NHL	48	2930	83	10	1.70	22	20	6	2	120	8	1	4.00	1	1	....
1936-37	Boston	NHL	48	2970	110	6	2.22	23	18	7	3	180	8	1	2.67	1	2	....
1937-38	Boston	NHL	48	2970	89	7	1.80	30	11	7	3	212	6	0	1.70	0	3	....
1938-39	Boston	NHL	5	310	8	0	1.55	3	1	1	....	....	....	....	....	....	....	....
	Detroit	NHL	39	2386	120	3	2.59	16	17	6	6	374	15	1	2.41	3	3	....
1939-40	Detroit	NHL	46	2830	120	3	2.54	16	24	6	5	300	12	0	2.40	2	3	....
1940-41	Buffalo	AHL	1	60	1	0	1.00	....	....	....	....	....	....	....	....	....	....	....
	NHL Totals	**12**	**553**	**34174**	**1183**	**81**	**2.08**	**284**	**194**	**75**	**44**	**2968**	**93**	**7**	**1.88**	**20**	**24**	**0**

VLADISLAV TRETIAK

Goaltender. Catches left. 6'1", 205 lbs., Born, Dmitrovo, USSR, April 25, 1952

			Regular Season							Playoffs							
Season	Club	League	GP	MIN	GA	SO	GAA	W	L	T	GP	MIN	GA	SO	GAA	W	L	T
1968-69	CSKA	USSR	3	180	2	...	0.67	....	....	....	....	....	....	....	....	....	....	....
1969-70	CSKA	USSR	34	2040	76	...	2.24	....	....	....	....	....	....	....	....	....	....	....
1970-71	CSKA	USSR	40	2400	81	...	2.03	....	....	....	....	....	....	....	....	....	....	....
1971-72	CSKA	USSR	30	1800	78	...	2.60	....	....	....	....	....	....	....	....	....	....	....
1972-73	CSKA	USSR	30	1800	80	...	2.67	....	....	....	....	....	....	....	....	....	....	....
1973-74	CSKA	USSR	27	1620	94	...	3.48	....	....	....	....	....	....	....	....	....	....	....
1974-75	CSKA	USSR	35	2100	104	...	2.97	....	....	....	....	....	....	....	....	....	....	....
1975-76	CSKA	USSR	33	1980	100	...	3.03	....	....	....	....	....	....	....	....	....	....	....
1976-77	CSKA	USSR	35	2100	98	...	2.80	....	....	....	....	....	....	....	....	....	....	....
1977-78	CSKA	USSR	29	1740	72	...	2.48	....	....	....	....	....	....	....	....	....	....	....
1978-79	CSKA	USSR	40	2400	111	...	2.78	....	....	....	....	....	....	....	....	....	....	....
1979-80	CSKA	USSR	36	2160	85	...	2.36	....	....	....	....	....	....	....	....	....	....	....
1980-81	CSKA	USSR	18	1080	32	...	1.78	....	....	....	....	....	....	....	....	....	....	....
1981-82	CSKA	USSR	41	2460	65	...	1.59	....	....	....	....	....	....	....	....	....	....	....
1982-83	CSKA	USSR	29	1740	40	...	1.38	....	....	....	....	....	....	....	....	....	....	....
1983-84	CSKA	USSR	22	1320	40	...	1.82	....	....	....	....	....	....	....	....	....	....	....

HARRY TRIHEY

Centre. Born, Montreal, Que., December 25, 1877

			Regular Season					Playoffs				
Season	Club	League	GP	G	A	PTS	PIM	GP	G	A	PTS	PIM
1896-97	Mtl. Shamrocks	AHA	1	0	0	0	...	...	...	...	...	...
1897-98	Mtl. Shamrocks	CAHL	8	3	0	3	...	...	...	...	...	...
1898-99	Mtl. Shamrocks	CAHL	7	19	0	19	...	1	3	0	3	...
1899-1900	Mtl. Shamrocks	CAHL	7	17	0	17	...	5	12	0	12	...
1900-01	Mtl. Shamrocks	CAHL	7	7	0	7	...	2	1	0	1	...

NORM ULLMAN

Centre. Shoots left. 5'10", 185 lbs., Born, Provost, Alta., December 26, 1935

			Regular Season					Playoffs				
Season	Club	League	GP	G	A	PTS	PIM	GP	G	A	PTS	PIM
1951-52	Edmonton	WCJHL	1	1	0	1	0	1	0	0	0	0
1952-53	Edmonton	WCJHL	36	29	47	76	4	13	4	6	10	0
1953-54	Edmonton	WHL	1	1	0	1	0	...	...	...	...	...
	Edmonton	WCJHL	36	56	45	101	17	10	11	26	37	0
1954-55	Edmonton	WHL	60	25	34	59	23	9	3	1	4	6
1955-56	Detroit	NHL	66	9	9	18	26	10	1	3	4	13
1956-57	Detroit	NHL	64	16	36	52	47	5	1	1	2	6
1957-58	Detroit	NHL	69	23	28	51	38	4	0	2	2	4
1958-59	Detroit	NHL	69	22	36	58	42	...	...	...	...	...
1959-60	Detroit	NHL	70	24	34	58	46	6	2	2	4	0
1960-61	Detroit	NHL	70	28	42	70	34	11	0	4	4	4
1961-62	Detroit	NHL	70	26	38	64	54	...	...	...	...	...
1962-63	Detroit	NHL	70	26	30	56	53	11	4	12	16	14
1963-64	Detroit	NHL	61	21	30	51	55	14	7	10	17	6
1964-65	Detroit	NHL	70	42	41	83	70	7	6	4	10	2
1965-66	Detroit	NHL	70	31	41	72	35	12	6	9	15	12
1966-67	Detroit	NHL	68	26	44	70	26	...	...	...	...	...
1967-68	Detroit	NHL	58	30	25	55	26	...	...	...	...	...
	Toronto	NHL	13	5	12	17	2	...	...	...	...	...
1968-69	Toronto	NHL	75	35	42	77	41	4	1	0	1	0
1969-70	Toronto	NHL	74	18	42	60	37	...	...	...	...	...
1970-71	Toronto	NHL	73	34	51	85	24	6	0	2	2	2
1971-72	Toronto	NHL	77	23	50	73	26	5	1	3	4	2
1972-73	Toronto	NHL	65	20	35	55	10	...	...	...	...	...
1973-74	Toronto	NHL	78	22	47	69	12	4	1	1	2	0
1974-75	Toronto	NHL	80	9	26	35	8	7	0	0	0	2
1975-76	Edmonton	WHA	77	31	56	87	12	4	1	3	4	2
1976-77	Edmonton	WHA	67	16	27	43	28	5	0	3	3	0
	NHL Totals	**20**	**1410**	**490**	**739**	**1229**	**712**	**106**	**30**	**53**	**83**	**67**

GEORGES VEZINA

Goaltender. 5'6", 185 lbs., Born, Chicoutimi, Que., Born January 21, 1887

			Regular Season								Playoffs						
Season	Club	League	GP	MIN	GA	SO	GAA	W	L	T	GP	MIN	GA	SO	GAA	W	L	T
1910-11	Montreal	NHA	16	980	62	0	3.80	8	8	....	....	....	....	....	....	....	....	....
1911-12	Montreal	NHA	18	1109	66	0	3.57	8	10	....	....	....	....	....	....	....	....	....
1912-13	Montreal	NHA	20	1217	81	1	3.99	9	11	....	....	....	....	....	....	....	....	....
1913-14	Montreal	NHA	20	1222	64	1	3.14	13	7	....	2	120	6	1	3.00	1	1	0
1914-15	Montreal	NHA	20	1257	81	0	3.86	6	14	....	....	....	....	....	....	....	....	....
1915-16	Montreal	NHA	24	1482	76	0	3.08	16	7	....	....	....	....	....	....	....	....	....
1916-17	Montreal	NHA	20	1217	80	0	3.94	10	10	0	2	120	6	0	3.00	1	1	0
1917-18	Montreal	NHL	22	1282	84	1	3.93	13	9	0	2	120	10	0	5.00	1	1	0
1918-19	Montreal	NHL	18	1097	78	1	4.27	10	8	0	5	300	18	0	3.60	4	1	0
1919-20	Montreal	NHL	24	1454	113	0	4.66	13	11	0	....	....	....	....	....	....	....	....
1920-21	Montreal	NHL	24	1436	99	1	4.14	13	11	0	....	....	....	....	....	....	....	....
1921-22	Montreal	NHL	24	1468	94	0	3.84	12	11	1	....	....	....	....	....	....	....	....
1922-23	Montreal	NHL	24	1488	61	2	2.46	13	9	2	2	120	3	0	1.50	1	1	0
1923-24	Montreal	NHL	24	1459	48	3	1.97	13	11	0	2	120	2	1	1.00	2	0	0
1924-25	Montreal	NHL	30	1860	56	5	1.81	17	11	2	2	120	2	1	1.00	2	0	0
1925-26	Montreal	NHL	1	20	1	0	3.00	0	1	0	....	....	....	....	....	....	....	....
	NHL Totals	**9**	**191**	**11564**	**633**	**13**	**3.28**	**104**	**82**	**5**	**26**	**1596**	**74**	**4**	**2.78**	**17**	**8**	**1**

JOHN "JACK" WALKER

Rover. Shoots left. 5'8", 150 lbs., Born, Silver Mountain, Ont., November 28, 1888

			Regular Season					Playoffs				
Season	Club	League	GP	G	A	PTS	PIM	GP	G	A	PTS	PIM
1908-09	Port Arthur	NOHA	Not Available			...	...	...	...	...	...	...
1909-10	Port Arthur	NOHA	Not Available			...	...	...	...	...	...	...
1910-11	Port Arthur	NOHA	3	3	0	3	0	...	...	...	...	...
1911-12	Port Arthur	NOHA	11	13	0	13	...	...	...	...	...	...
1912-13	Toronto	NHA	1	0	0	0	0	...	...	...	...	...
	Moncton	MPHL	15	21	0	21	9	...	...	...	...	...
1913-14	Toronto	NHA	20	20	16	36	17	2	3	0	3	2
1914-15	Toronto	NHA	19	12	7	19	11	...	...	...	...	...
1915-16	Seattle	PCHA	18	13	6	19	6	...	...	...	...	...
1916-17	Seattle	PCHA	24	11	15	26	3	4	1	3	4	0
1917-18	Seattle	PCHA	1	0	0	0	0	...	...	...	...	...
1918-19	Seattle	PCHA	20	9	6	15	9	7	3	2	5	12
1919-20	Seattle	PCHA	22	4	8	12	3	7	2	3	5	0
1920-21	Seattle	PCHA	23	6	4	10	6	2	0	0	0	0
1921-22	Seattle	PCHA	20	8	4	12	0	2	0	0	0	0
1922-23	Seattle	PCHA	29	13	10	23	4	...	...	...	...	...
1923-24	Seattle	PCHA	29	18	5	23	0	2	0	0	0	0
1924-25	Victoria	WCHL	28	7	7	14	6	8	8	2	10	0
1925-26	Victoria	WHL	30	9	8	17	16	8	0	0	0	2
1926-27	Detroit	NHL	39	3	4	7	6	...	...	...	...	...
1927-28	Detroit	NHL	39	2	4	6	12	...	...	...	...	...
1928-29	Seattle	NWHL	34	5	8	13	4	5	0	2	2	2
1929-30	Seattle	NWHL	26	6	11	17	2	...	...	...	...	...
1930-31	Seattle	PCHL	34	2	13	15	8	4	0	3	3	0
1931-32	Hollywood	CalHL	...	5	13	18	...	...	...	...	...	...
1932-33	Oakland	CalHL	Not Available			...	...	...	...	...	...	...
	NHL Totals	**2**	**80**	**5**	**8**	**13**	**18**	**....**	**....**	**....**	**....**	**....**

MARTY WALSH

Centre / left wing. Born, Kingston, Ont., October 16, 1883

			Regular Season					Playoffs				
Season	Club	League	GP	G	A	PTS	PIM	GP	G	A	PTS	PIM
1905-06	Queen's U.	OHA Sr.	2	4	0	4	...	...	...	...	...	...
1906-07	Canadian Soo	IHL	7	4	5	9	0	...	...	...	...	...
1907-08	Ottawa	ECAHA	9	28	0	28	...	...	...	...	...	...
1908-09	Ottawa	ECHA	12	42	0	42	41	...	...	...	...	...
1909-10	Ottawa	CHA	2	9	0	9	14	...	...	...	...	...
	Ottawa	NHA	11	19	...	19	44	4	8	0	8	12
	Queen's U.	OHA Sr.	Not Available			...	...	...	...	...	...	...
1910-11	Ottawa	NHA	16	35	0	35	51	2	13	0	13	0
1911-12	Ottawa	NHA	12	9	0	9	0					

HARRY WATSON

Left wing. Shoots left. 6'1", 203 lbs., Born, Saskatoon, Sask., May 6, 1923

			Regular Season					Playoffs				
Season	Club	League	GP	G	A	PTS	PIM	GP	G	A	PTS	PIM
1940-41	Saskatoon	SJHL	6	10	8	18	4	2	3	1	4	0
1941-42	Brooklyn	NHL	47	10	8	18	6	...	...	...	...	...
1942-43	Detroit	NHL	50	13	18	31	10	7	0	0	0	0
1943-44	Montreal	QSHL	7	7	4	11	4	...	...	...	...	...
	Saskatoon	SSHL	2	6	2	8	2	...	...	...	...	...
1944-45	Winnipeg	MHL Sr.	1	2	0	2	0	4	7	0	7	2
1945-46	Detroit	NHL	44	14	10	24	4	5	2	0	2	0
1946-47	Toronto	NHL	44	19	15	34	10	11	3	2	5	6
1947-48	Toronto	NHL	57	21	20	41	16	9	5	2	7	9
1948-49	Toronto	NHL	60	26	19	45	0	9	4	2	6	2
1949-50	Toronto	NHL	60	19	16	35	11	7	0	0	0	2
1950-51	Toronto	NHL	68	18	19	37	18	5	1	2	3	4
1951-52	Toronto	NHL	70	22	17	39	18	4	1	0	1	2
1952-53	Toronto	NHL	63	16	8	24	8	...	...	...	...	...
1953-54	Toronto	NHL	70	21	17	28	30	5	0	1	1	2
1954-55	Toronto	NHL	8	1	1	2	0	...	...	...	...	...
	Chicago	NHL	43	14	16	30	4	...	...	...	...	...
1955-56	Chicago	NHL	55	11	14	25	6	...	...	...	...	...
1956-57	Chicago	NHL	70	11	19	30	9	...	...	...	...	...
1957-58	Buffalo	AHL	52	8	15	23	10	...	...	...	...	...
	NHL Totals	**14**	**809**	**236**	**207**	**443**	**150**	**62**	**16**	**9**	**25**	**27**

HARRY "MOOSE" WATSON

Left wing. Shoots left. 165 lbs., Born, St. John's Nfld., July 14, 1898

			Regular Season					Playoffs				
Season	Club	League	GP	G	A	PTS	PIM	GP	G	A	PTS	PIM
1917-18	Tor. Aura Lees	OHA Jr.	Not Available			...	...	...	...	...	...	...
1918-19	Tor. Dentals	OHA Sr.	Not Available			...	...	...	...	...	...	...
1919-20	Tor. Granites	OHA Sr.	8	14	1	15	...	5	4	1	5	...
1920-21	Tor. Granites	OHA Sr.	9	10	4	14	...	2	2	0	2	...
1921-22	Tor. Granites	OHA Sr.	10	17	3	20	...	2	5	0	5	...
1922-23	Tor. Granites	OHA Sr.	12	21	4	25	...	2	3	0	3	...
1923-24			Not Available			...	...	...	...	...	...	...
1924-25	Tor. Parkdale	OHA Sr.	6	6	2	8	...	...	...	...	...	...
1925-26	Tor. Parkdale	OHA Sr.	1	1	2	...	2	0	0	0	...	...
1926-27	Tor. Parkdale	OHA Sr.	1	2	0	2	...	...	...	...	...	...
1927-28	Tor. Marlboros	OHA Sr.	2	1	1	2	2	...	...	...	...	...
1929-30	Tor. Nationals	OHA Sr.	1	0	0	0	0	...	...	...	...	...
1931-32	Tor. Nationals	OHA Sr.	2	0	0	0	0	...	...	...	...	...

RALPH "COONEY" WEILAND

Centre. Shoots left. 5'7", 150 lbs., Born, Edmondville, Ont., November 5, 1904

			Regular Season					Playoffs				
Season	Club	League	GP	G	A	PTS	PIM	GP	G	A	PTS	PIM
1924-25	Minneapolis	AHA	35	8	0	8	...	...	...	...	...	...
1925-26	Minneapolis	AHA	26	10	4	14	20	3	1	1	2	0
1926-27	Minneapolis	AHA	36	21	2	23	30	6	4	1	5	0
1927-28	Minneapolis	AHA	40	21	5	26	34	8	2	2	4	0
1928-29	Boston	NHL	42	11	7	18	16	5	2	0	2	2
1929-30	Boston	NHL	44	43	30	73	27	6	1	5	6	2
1930-31	Boston	NHL	44	25	13	38	14	5	6	3	9	2
1931-32	Boston	NHL	46	14	12	26	20	...	...	...	...	...
1932-33	Ottawa	NHL	48	16	11	27	4	...	...	...	...	...
1933-34	Ottawa	NHL	7	2	0	2	4	...	...	...	...	...
	Detroit	NHL	39	11	19	30	6	9	2	2	4	4
1934-35	Detroit	NHL	48	13	25	38	10	...	...	...	...	...
1935-36	Boston	NHL	48	14	13	27	15	2	1	0	1	2
1936-37	Boston	NHL	48	6	9	15	6	3	0	0	0	0
1937-38	Boston	NHL	48	11	12	23	16	3	0	0	0	0
1938-39	Boston	NHL	45	7	9	16	9	12	0	0	0	0
	NHL Totals	**11**	**557**	**188**	**179**	**367**	**157**	**54**	**14**	**12**	**26**	**16**

HARRY "RAT" WESTWICK

Rover. Born, Ottawa, Ont., April 23, 1876

			Regular Season					Playoffs				
Season	Club	League	GP	G	A	PTS	PIM	GP	G	A	PTS	PIM
1894-95	Ottawa	AHA	5	1	0	1	...	...	...	...	...	...
1895-96	Ottawa	AHA	8	8	0	8	...	...	...	...	...	...
1896-97	Ottawa	AHA	8	6	0	6	...	...	...	...	...	...
1897-98	Ottawa	AHA	5	1	0	1	...	...	...	...	...	...
1898-99			Not Available			...	...	...	...	...	...	...
1899-1900	Ott. Capitals	OHA Sr.	Not Available			...	...	...	...	...	...	...
1900-01	Ottawa	CAHL	7	6	0	6	...	...	...	...	...	...
1901-02	Ottawa	CAHL	8	11	0	11	...	...	...	...	...	...
1902-03	Ottawa	CAHL	6	6	0	6	...	1	0	0	0	...
1903-04	Ottawa	CAHL	4	5	0	5	...	8	6	0	6	...
1904-05	Ottawa	FAHL	8	15	0	15	...	5	9	0	9	...
1905-06	Ottawa	ECAHA	8	6	0	6	...	6	9	0	9	...
1906-07	Kenora	MHL Sr.	1	0	0	0	...	4	2	0	2	...
	Ottawa	ECAHA	9	14	0	14	...	...	...	...	...	...
1908-09	Ottawa	ECHA	10	8	0	8	...	...	...	...	...	...

FRED WHITCROFT
Rover. Shoots right. 5'10", 158 lbs., Born, Port Perry, Ont., 1883

			Regular Season					Playoffs				
Season	Club	League	GP	G	A	PTS	PIM	GP	G	A	PTS	PIM
1906-07	Peterborough	OHA Sr.	Not Available				...	...	...	...	...	...
	Kenora	MHL Sr.	4	3	0	3	...	2	5	0	5	...
1907-08	Edmonton	Sr.	16	49	0	49	...	2	2	0	2	...
1908-09	Edmonton	Sr.	Not Available				...	...	...	...	...	...
1909-10	Renfrew	NHA	5	3	0	3	13	...	...	...	...	...
	Edmonton	Sr.	2	5	0	5	3	...	...	...	...	...
1910-11	Edmonton	Sr.	Not Available				...	...	...	...	...	...

GORDON "PHAT" WILSON
Defence. Born, Port Arthur, Ont., December 29, 1895

			Regular Season					Playoffs				
Season	Club	League	GP	G	A	PTS	PIM	GP	G	A	PTS	PIM
1919-20	Port Arthur Vets	NOHA	Not Available				...	...	...	...	...	...
1920-21	Iroquois Falls	NOHA	Not Available				...	...	...	...	...	...
1921-22	Iroquois Falls	NOHA	Not Available				...	...	...	...	...	...
1922-23	Port Arthur	MHL Sr.	16	5	6	11	32	2	0	0	0	2
1923-24	Port Arthur	MHL Sr.	15	6	5	11	19	2	1	1	2	4
1924-25	Port Arthur	MHL Sr.	19	7	1	8	...	10	9	3	12	24
1925-26	Port Arthur	TBHL	19	8	5	13	22	3	0	0	0	10
1926-27	Port Arthur	TBHL	20	11	5	16	24	2	0	0	0	4
1927-28	Port Arthur	MHL Sr.	17	7	6	13	19	...	...	...	...	...
1928-29	Port Arthur	MHL Sr.	20	12	9	21	25	2	0	0	0	6
1929-30	Port Arthur	TBHL	19	9	8	17	22	2	1	0	1	4
1930-31	Port Arthur	TBHL	21	9	8	17	32	2	0	0	0	2
1931-32	Port Arthur	TBHL	15	5	2	7	26	2	1	1	2	10

LORNE "GUMP" WORSLEY
Goaltender. Catches left 5'7", 180 lbs., Born, Montreal. Que., May 14, 1929

			Regular Season								Playoffs						
Season	Club	League	GP	MIN	GA	SO	GAA	W	L	T	GP	MIN	GA	SO	GAA	W	L	T
1948-49	St. Francis	QJHL	7	310	16	0	3.10	2	3	0	...	...	...	...	...	...	...	...
	NY Rovers	QSHL	2	120	5	0	2.50	...	...	...	...	...	...	...	...	...	...	...
1949-50	NY Rovers	EHL	47	2830	133	7	2.83	25	17	5	12	720	27	1	2.25	8	2	2
	New Haven	AHL	2	120	4	0	2.00	...	...	...	...	...	...	...	...	...	...	...
1950-51	St. Paul	USHL	64	3840	184	3	2.86	33	26	5	4	240	9	0	2.25	1	3	0
1951-52	Saskatoon	PCHL	66	3960	206	5	3.12	...	...	...	13	818	33	1	2.42	10	3	0
1952-53	Saskatoon	WHL	13	780	50	0	3.85	...	...	...	...	...	...	...	...	...	...	...
	NY Rangers	NHL	50	3000	153	2	3.06	13	29	8	...	...	...	...	...	...	...	...
1953-54	Vancouver	WHL	70	4200	168	4	2.40	39	24	7	12	720	29	0	2.41	7	5	...
1954-55	NY Rangers	NHL	65	3900	197	4	3.03	15	33	17	...	...	...	...	...	...	...	...
1955-56	NY Rangers	NHL	70	4200	203	4	2.90	32	28	10	3	180	15	0	5.00	0	3	...
1956-57	NY Rangers	NHL	68	4080	220	3	3.24	26	28	13	5	315	22	0	4.19	1	4	...
1957-58	Providence	AHL	25	1500	83	0	3.32	...	...	...	...	...	...	...	...	...	...	...
	NY Rangers	NHL	37	2220	86	2	2.32	21	10	6	6	365	28	0	4.60	2	4	...
1958-59	NY Rangers	NHL	67	4011	205	2	3.07	26	29	12	...	...	...	...	...	...	...	...
1959-60	Springfield	AHL	15	900	33	3	2.20	...	...	...	...	...	...	...	...	...	...	...
	NY Rangers	NHL	39	2300	137	0	3.57	8	25	8	12	...	...	...	...	...	...	...
1960-61	NY Rangers	NHL	59	3493	193	1	3.32	19	28	9	10	...	...	...	...	...	...	...
1961-62	NY Rangers	NHL	60	3520	174	2	2.97	22	27	9	6	384	22	0	3.44	7	4	...
1962-63	NY Rangers	NHL	67	3980	219	2	3.30	22	34	9	14	...	...	...	...	...	...	...
1963-64	Montreal	NHL	8	444	22	1	2.97	3	2	2	...	...	...	...	...	...	...	...
	Quebec	AHL	47	2870	128	5	2.72	...	...	...	9	546	29	0	3.19	4	5	...
1964-65	Quebec	AHL	37	2220	101	2	2.73	...	...	...	...	...	...	...	...	...	...	...
	Montreal	NHL	18	1020	50	1	2.94	10	7	1	8	501	14	2	1.68	6	2	...
1965-66	Montreal	NHL	51	2899	114	2	2.36	29	14	6	10	602	20	1	1.99	8	2	...
1966-67	Montreal	NHL	18	888	47	1	3.18	9	6	2	2	80	2	0	1.50	0	1	...
1967-68	Montreal	NHL	40	2213	73	6	1.98	19	9	8	12	669	21	1	1.88	11	0	...
1968-69	Montreal	NHL	30	1703	64	5	2.26	19	6	4	7	370	14	0	2.27	5	1	...
1969-70	Montreal	NHL	6	360	14	0	2.33	3	1	2	...	...	...	...	...	...	...	...
	Minnesota	NHL	8	453	20	1	2.65	5	1	1	3	180	14	0	4.67	1	2	...
1970-71	Minnesota	NHL	24	1369	57	0	2.49	4	10	8	4	240	13	0	3.25	3	1	...
1971-72	Minnesota	NHL	34	1923	68	2	2.12	16	10	7	4	194	7	1	2.17	2	1	...
1972-73	Minnesota	NHL	12	624	30	0	2.88	6	2	3	...	...	...	...	...	...	...	...
1973-74	Minnesota	NHL	29	1601	86	0	3.22	8	14	5	...	...	...	...	...	...	...	...
	NHL Totals		**21**	**860**	**50232**	**2432**	**43**	**2.91**	**335**	**353**	**151**	**70**	**4080**	**192**	**5**	**2.82**	**41**	**25**

ROY "SHRIMP" WORTERS
Goaltender. Catches left. 5'3", 135 lbs., Born, Toronto, Ont., October 19, 1900

			Regular Season								Playoffs						
Season	Club	League	GP	MIN	GA	SO	GAA	W	L	T	GP	MIN	GA	SO	GAA	W	L	T
1922-23	Toronto	OHA Sr.	10	558	37	0	3.98	...	...	...	...	...	...	...	...	...	...	...
1923-24	Pittsburgh	AHA	20	1225	25	7	1.23	15	5	0	8	540	4	4	0.44	5	2	1
1924-25	Pittsburgh	AHA	39	1895	34	17	0.81	25	10	4	4	240	3	1	0.75	3	1	0
1925-26	Pittsburgh	NHL	35	2145	68	7	1.90	18	16	1	2	120	6	0	3.00	0	1	1
1926-27	Pittsburgh	NHL	44	2711	108	4	2.39	15	26	3	...	...	...	...	...	...	...	...
1927-28	Pittsburgh	NHL	44	2740	76	10	1.66	19	17	8	2	120	6	0	3.00	1	1	0
1928-29	NY Americans	NHL	38	2390	46	13	1.15	16	13	9	2	150	1	1	0.40	0	1	1
1929-30	NY Americans	NHL	36	2270	135	2	3.57	11	24	1	...	...	...	...	...	...	...	...
	Montreal	NHL	1	60	2	0	2.00	1	0	0	...	...	...	...	...	...	...	...
1930-31	NY Americans	NHL	44	2760	74	8	1.61	18	16	0	...	...	...	...	...	...	...	...
1931-32	NY Americans	NHL	45	2459	119	5	2.90	12	20	7	...	...	...	...	...	...	...	...
1932-33	NY Americans	NHL	47	2970	116	5	2.34	15	22	10	...	...	...	...	...	...	...	...
	Quebec	CAHL	1	60	3	0	3.00	0	1	0	...	...	...	...	...	...	...	...
1933-34	NY Americans	NHL	35	2240	75	4	2.01	12	13	10	...	...	...	...	...	...	...	...
1934-35	NY Americans	NHL	48	3000	142	3	2.84	12	27	9	...	...	...	...	...	...	...	...
1935-36	NY Americans	NHL	48	3000	122	3	2.44	16	25	7	5	300	11	2	2.20	2	3	0
1936-37	NY Americans	NHL	23	1430	69	2	2.90	6	14	3	...	...	...	...	...	...	...	...
	NHL Totals		**12**	**484**	**30175**	**1143**	**66**	**2.27**	**171**	**233**	**68**	**11**	**690**	**24**	**3**	**2.09**	**3**	**6**	**2**

PHOTO CREDITS

Boston Public Library, Print Department, 51 right, 52 top right, 73 left;

City of Vancouver Archives, #CVA99-126, 22 left;

City of Vancouver Archives, #CVA99-778, 44 right;

Glenbow Archives, 61 bottom right, 75 bottom right;

McCord Museum of Canadian History, Notman Photographic Archives, 16 right, 58 bottom right;

Hockey Hall of Fame, all remaining photos.

The Hockey Hall of Fame's archives include the following collections:

Hockey Hall of Fame – Graphic Artists Collection
Hockey Hall of Fame – Imperial Oil Turofsky Collection
Hockey Hall of Fame – Miles Nadal Collection
Hockey Hall of Fame – Frank Prazak Collection
Hockey Hall of Fame – file photo.

GUIDE TO LEAGUE NAMES

AHA	American Hockey Association
AHA Sr.	American Hockey Association (Senior)
AHAUS	Amateur Hockey Association of the United States
AHL	American Hockey League
AJHL	Alberta Junior Hockey League
ASHL	Alberta Senior Hockey League
Big 4	Saskatchewan Big 4 Hockey League
CAHA	Canadian Amateur Hockey Association
CAHL	Canadian Amateur Hockey League (1899-1905)
CAHL	Canadian-American Hockey League
CalHL	California Hockey League
CBHL	Cape Breton Hockey League
CHA	Canadian Hockey Association
CHL	Central Hockey League (1964-1985)
CPHL	Canadian Professional Hockey League (1926-1929)
CSKA	Central Red Army Sports Club
ECAHA	Eastern Canada Amateur Hockey Association (1906-1908)
ECHA	Eastern Canada Hockey Association (1909)
ECSHL	Eastern Canada Senior Hockey League
EJHL	Edmonton Junior Hockey League
EHL	Eastern Hockey League
EOHL	Eastern Ontario Hockey League
EPHL	Eastern Professional Hockey League
FAHL	Federal Amateur Hockey League (1904-1907)
IAHL	International-American Hockey League
IHL	International Hockey League (1904-1908)
IHL	International Hockey League (1945 to date)
IIHF	International Ice Hockey Federation
Int.	Intermediate
Jr.	Junior
MHL	Manitoba Hockey League
MHL Jr.	Manitoba Hockey League (Junior)
MHL Sr.	Manitoba Hockey League (Senior)
MIHL	Maritime Intermediate Hockey League
MJHL	Maritime Junior Hockey League
MJHL	Manitoba Junior Hockey League
MPHL	Manitoba Professional Hockey League
MMHL	Maritime Major Hockey League
MSHL	Maritime Senior Hockey League
NBIHL	New Brunswick Intermediate Hockey League
NHA	National Hockey Association

NHL	National Hockey League
NOHA	Northern Ontario Hockey Association
NWHL	North West Hockey League
ODHL Jr.	Ottawa District Hockey League (Junior)
ODHL Sr.	Ottawa District Hockey League (Senior)
OHA	Ontario Hockey Association
OHA Sr.	Ontario Hockey Association (Senior)
OHA Jr.	Ontario Hockey Association (Junior)
OHL	Ontario Hockey League
OMJHL	Ontario Major Junior Hockey League
PCHA	Pacific Coast Hockey Association
PCHL	Pacific Coast Hockey League
PHL	Prairie Hockey League
PCL	Pacific Coast League
QHL	Quebec Hockey League
QJHL	Quebec Junior Hockey League
QMJHL	Quebec Major Junior Hockey League
OPHL	Ontario Professional Hockey League
QSHL	Quebec Senior Hockey League
OVHL	Ottawa Valley Hockey League
SJHL	Saskatchewan Junior Hockey League
SPHL	Saskatchewan Professional Hockey League
Sr.	Senior
SJHL	Saskatchewan Junior Hockey League
SSHL	Saskatchewan Senior Hockey League
TBJHL	Thunder Bay Junior Hockey League
TBSHL	Thunder Bay Senior Hockey League
TDHL	Toronto District Hockey League
USHL	United States Hockey League
USAHA	United States Amateur Hockey Association
WCJHL	Western Canada Junior Hockey League
WCSHL	Western Canada Senior Hockey League
WCHA	Western Collegiate Hockey Association
WCHL	Western Canada Hockey League
WHA	World Hockey Association
WHL	Western Hockey League
WIHL	Western International Hockey League
WOHA	Western Ontario Hockey Association
WPHL	Western Pennsylvania Hockey League
WSHL	Winnipeg Senior Hockey League